REVISED EDITION

ILLUSTRATED BIBLE SURVEY

AN INTRODUCTION

ED HINDSON and ELMER L. TOWNS

B&H
ACADEMIC
Nashville, Tennessee

Illustrated Bible Survey
Copyright © 2013, 2017 by Ed Hindson and Knowing Jesus Ministries
All rights reserved.
ISBN: 978-1-4336-5112-0
Published by B&H Academic
Nashville, Tennessee
Dewey Decimal Classification: 200.07
Subject Heading: BIBLE—STUDY AND TEACHING

Printed in the United States of America

1 2 3 4 5 6 7 8 9 10 VP 23 22 21 20 19 18 17

DEDICATION

To the more than 100,000 students
we have been privileged to teach
at Liberty University
over the past forty years.

May God use you to change the
world in your generation.

CONTENTS

LIST OF MAPS

LIST OF ABBREVIATIONS

AUSS	*Andrews University Seminary Studies*
BCOT	Baker Commentary on the Old Testament
BECNT	Baker Exegetical Commentary on the New Testament
BKC	*Bible Knowledge Commentary*
BKCNT	*Bible Knowledge Commentary: New Testament*
BKCOT	*Bible Knowledge Commentary: Old Testament*
CBC	Cambridge Bible Commentary
DSB	The Daily Study Bible
EBC	*The Expositor's Bible Commentary*
GNC	Good News Commentary
HNTC	Holman New Testament Commentary
ICC	International Critical Commentary
ITC	International Theological Commentary
IVP	InterVarsity Press
IVPNTC	*InterVarsity Press New Testament Commentary*
JSOTSup	Journal for the Study of the Old Testament: Supplement Series
KJBC	*King James Bible Commentary*
LXX	Septuagint
MNTC	MacArthur New Testament Commentary
NAC	New American Commentary
NIBC	New International Biblical Commentary
NICNT	New International Commentary on the New Testament
NICOT	New International Commentary on the Old Testament
NIGTC	New International Greek Testament Commentary
NIVAC	New International Version Application Commentary
NT	New Testament
NTC	New Testament Commentary (Baker Academic)
OT	Old Testament
PNTC	Pelican New Testament Commentaries
TFCBC	Twenty-First Century Biblical Commentary
TNTC	Tyndale New Testament Commentary
TOTC	Tyndale Old Testament Commentary
VT	*Vetus Testamentum*
WBC	Word Biblical Commentary
ZECNT	Zondervan Exegetical Commentary on the New Testament
ZIBBC	Zondervan Illustrated Bible Backgrounds Commentary

CONTRIBUTORS

Authors

Edward E. Hindson (ThD, Trinity Graduate School; DMin, Westminster Theological Seminary; DLitt et Phil., University of South Africa; FIBA, Cambridge University) is the dean of the School of Divinity and distinguished professor of religion and biblical studies at Liberty University.

Elmer L. Towns (ThM, Dallas Theological Seminary; DMin, Fuller Theological Seminary) is the distinguished professor of systematic theology and vice president of Liberty University.

Associate Editors

John Cartwright (MDiv, Liberty Baptist Theological Seminary; EdD, The Southern Baptist Theological Seminary) is associate dean of the School of Divinity at Liberty University.

Gabriel Etzel (DMin, Liberty Baptist Theological Seminary, PhD, The Southern Baptist Theological Seminary) is administrative dean of the School of Divinity at Liberty University.

Ben Gutierrez (PhD, Regent University) is professor of religion and vice provost for academic administration at Liberty University.

Wayne Patton (MDiv, Liberty Baptist Theological Seminary; DMin, Liberty Baptist Theological Seminary) is associate dean, College of General Studies at Liberty University.

Editorial Advisors

James A. Borland (ThD, Grace Theological Seminary)
    Professor of New Testament and Theology
Wayne A. Brindle (ThD, Dallas Theological Seminary)
    Professor of Biblical Studies and Greek
Alan Fuhr Jr. (PhD, Southeastern Baptist Theological Seminary)
    Associate Professor of Biblical Studies
Harvey Hartman (ThD, Grace Theological Seminary)
    Professor of Biblical Studies

Gaylen P. Leverett (PhD, Southeastern Baptist Theological Seminary)
  Associate Professor of Theology
Donald R. Love (PhD, Southeastern Baptist Theological Seminary)
  Associate Professor of Biblical Studies
Randall Price (PhD, University of Texas at Austin)
  Distinguished Research Professor of Biblical and Judaic Studies
R. N. Small (PhD, Southeastern Baptist Theological Seminary)
  Associate Professor of Biblical Studies
Michael J. Smith (PhD, Dallas Theological Seminary)
  Associate Professor of Biblical Studies
Gary Yates (PhD, Dallas Theological Seminary)
  Associate Professor of Old Testament and Hebrew

PREFACE

T he Bible is the most important book ever written. It contains sixty-six individual books from Genesis to Revelation. These were collected over 1,500 years into one grand volume that we call the Word of God. Christians accept the Bible as uniquely inspired of God and, therefore, authoritative for our beliefs and practices. The Bible itself proclaims that its authors were "carried along by the Holy Spirit" so that "men spoke from God" (2 Pet 1:21).

We have taught Bible survey courses for a combined total of nearly one hundred years at various institutions but mostly at Liberty University where we have been privileged to serve together for over 30 years. We have taught thousands of students from every walk of life, majoring in everything from accounting to zoology—business, history, journalism, philosophy, psychology, nursing, premed, prelaw, religion, you name it. Our goal has always been to challenge them academically, inspire them spiritually, and motivate them effectively to discover and apply the great truths and practical wisdom of the Bible in providing them with a biblical basis for the Christian worldview.

Introducing the basic content of the books of the Bible generally includes the examination of their authorship, background, message, and application. Our purpose is to provide a college-level textbook that is accessible to students and laymen alike. Therefore, we have left the more technical discussions of authorship and genre to seminary- and graduate-level introductions such as B&H's *The World and the Word* by Merrill, Rooker, and Grisanti and also *The Cradle, the Cross, and the Crown* by Köstenberger, Kellum, and Quarles, which we highly recommend.

For us the Bible is not merely a combination of ancient documents, historical details, and religious information. It is the *living* Word of God that still speaks to the minds, hearts, and souls of men and women today. It confronts our sin, exposes our selfishness, examines our motives, challenges our presuppositions, calls us to repentance, asks us to believe its incredible claims, stretches our faith, heals our hurts, blesses our hearts, and soothes our souls.

Jesus spoke often of His confidence in the Bible with such phrases as "the Scripture must be fulfilled" (John 13:18); "the Scripture cannot be broken" (John 10:35); "you will know the truth, and the truth will set you free" (John 8:32); "I did not come to abolish [the Law or the Prophets] but to fulfill" (Matt 5:17); "man must not live on bread alone but on every word that comes from the mouth of God" (Matt 4:4); "today . . . this Scripture has been fulfilled" (Luke 4:21). Jesus read and quoted the Old Testament Hebrew Scriptures with assurance that they were the Word of God. He also promised His disciples that the Holy Spirit of truth will "guide you into all truth" and "declare to you what is to come" (John 16:13). This promise was realized when the Holy Spirit came upon the apostles enabling them to remember all that Jesus said and taught (John 14:26).

Teaching the Bible is one of the great privileges and blessings of the Christian life. We believe it is our greatest calling to proclaim, clarify, and explain the biblical message. It is not our story; it is God's story. It is the story of His love and grace that has pursued human beings down through the tunnel of time, through the halls of history and into the vast canyon of eternity. The Bible is a story of an infinite yet personal Being who loves us with an inexhaustible love that is expressed in His amazing grace, which reaches out to us time and time again.

We want to thank the editorial team of biblical scholars from Liberty University and the Liberty Baptist Theological Seminary for their advice, assistance, and encouragement in this endeavor. We also want to thank Dr. Gary Smith, who served as the external editor for B&H, and Michael Herbert, MDiv, of Liberty University, who served as the managing editor of the electronic file. It is our prayer that this survey of the Bible will enlighten your mind and open your soul to the One who dared to say, "Everything written about Me . . . must be fulfilled. Then He opened their minds to understand the Scriptures" (Luke 24:44–45).

Ed Hindson and Elmer L. Towns
Liberty University in Virginia

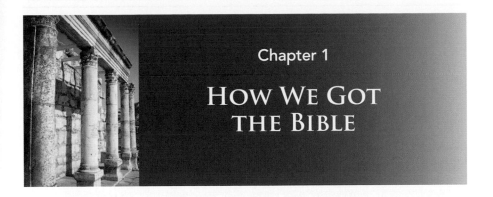

Chapter 1

HOW WE GOT THE BIBLE

T he Bible is a collection of sixty-six books that are recognized by the Christian church as divinely inspired. They are divided into the Old Testament (39 books) and the New Testament (27 books). Collectively these books included law, history, poetry, wisdom, prophecy, narratives, biographies, personal letters, and apocalyptic visions. They introduce us to some of the most amazing people who have ever lived: shepherds, farmers, patriarchs, kings, queens, prophets, priests, evangelists, disciples, teachers, and most of all—the most unique person who ever lived—Jesus of Nazareth.

How We Got the Old Testament

God revealed His Word to ancient Israel over a thousand-year period (c. 1400–400 BC), and then scribes copied the biblical scrolls and manuscripts for more than a millennium after that. The process by which the Old Testament books came to be recognized as the Word of God, and the history of how these books were preserved and handed down through the generations, enhances our confidence in the credibility of the Old Testament as inspired Scripture (2 Tim 3:16).[1]

What Books Belong in the Old Testament?

The canon of Scripture refers to the list of books recognized as divinely inspired and authoritative for faith and practice. Our word *canon* is derived from the Hebrew *qaneh* and the Greek *kanon*, meaning a "reed" or a "measuring stick." The term came to mean the standard by which a written work was measured for inclusion in a certain body of literature. The books of the Bible are not inspired because humans gave them canonical status. Rather, the books were recognized as canonical by humans because they were inspired by God. As Wegner explains, the books of the Old Testament "did not receive their authority because they were placed in the canon; rather they were recognized by the nation of Israel as having divine authority and were therefore included in the canon."[2]

The order and arrangement of the Hebrew canon is different from that of our English Bibles. The Hebrew canon consists of three major sections, the Law (*Torah*), the Prophets (*Nevi'im*), and the Writings (*Kethuvim*). Collectively they are referred to as the Tanak (an acronym built on the first letters of these three divisions—TNK).

The Hebrew Canon			
Law	Prophets		Writings
	Former Prophets	Latter Prophets	
Genesis	Joshua	Isaiah	Psalms
Exodus	Judges	Jeremiah	Job
Leviticus	1 and 2 Samuel	Ezekiel	Proverbs
Numbers	1 and 2 Kings	Minor Prophets	Ruth
Deuteronomy		(Book of the 12)	Song of Songs
			Ecclesiastes
			Lamentations
			Esther
			Daniel
			Ezra
			Nehemiah
			Chronicles

The Septuagint (LXX), the Greek translation of the Old Testament, first employed the fourfold division of the Old Testament into Pentateuch, Historical Books, Poetical Books, and Prophetic Books that is used in the English Bible. The inclusion of historical books within the prophetic section of the Hebrew canon reflects their authorship by the prophets. Daniel appears in the Writings rather than the Prophets because Daniel was not called to the office of prophet even though he functioned as a prophet from time to time. Chronicles at the end of the canon provides a summary

Jewish rabbi copying Hebrew Scripture.

of the entire Old Testament story from Adam to Israel's return from exile though it was written from a priestly perspective.[3]

How Were the Old Testament Books Selected?

When Moses came down from Mount Sinai with the Commandments God gave him, the people of Israel immediately recognized their divine authority and promised to obey them as the words of the Lord (Exod 24:3–8). The writings of Moses were stored at the central sanctuary because of their special status as inspired Scripture (Exod 25:16, 21; Deut 10:1–2; 31:24–26). In Deut 18:15–22, the Lord promised to raise up a prophet "like Moses" to speak His word for subsequent generations. Thus, pronouncements of these messengers of God would also be recognized as possessing divine authority.

When Was the Process Completed?

Jewish tradition affirmed that prophecy ceased in Israel about 400 BC after the ministry of Malachi. First Maccabees 9:27 states, "So there was great distress in Israel, such as had not been since the time that the prophets ceased to appear among them." Baruch 85:3 makes a similar claim, and the Jewish Talmud states that the Holy Spirit departed from Israel after the prophets Haggai, Zechariah, and Malachi in the early postexilic period. Some questions remained regarding some of the "writings" that were already included in Scripture (e.g., Esther) even at the Council of Jamnia in AD 90.[4] However, the evidence suggests that the Hebrew canon was essentially completed and fixed by 300 BC. All of the canonical books of the Old Testament, except for Esther, appear among the copies of the Dead Sea Scrolls (250 BC–AD 70).[5]

A Torah scroll being held in its wooden case at a celebration in Jerusalem.

How Does the New Testament View the Old Testament?

Jesus and the apostles accepted the inspiration of the Old Testament Scriptures and often referred to or quoted them as authoritative. According to Jesus, the words written by the human authors of Scripture were the "command of God" and "God's word" (Mark 7:8–13; cf. Matt 19:4–5). As

God's Word every part of the Old Testament would be accomplished and fulfilled (Matt 5:17–18; 26:54, 56; Luke 24:27, 44; John 7:38), and nothing it predicted could be voided or annulled (Luke 16:17; John 10:35). Jesus described the Old Testament canon as extending from Genesis to Chronicles when speaking of the murders of Abel and the prophet Zechariah in Matthew 23:34–35 and Luke 11:49–51 (cf. Gen 4:8 and 2 Chr 24:20–22).

How Reliable Are the Old Testament Documents?

Though the earliest parts of the Old Testament were written about 1400 BC, the earliest existing Hebrew manuscripts for the Old Testament are the more than 200 biblical manuscripts found at Qumran among the Dead Sea Scrolls, dating from roughly 250 BC to AD 70. Prior to the discovery of the Dead Sea Scrolls in 1947, the earliest extant Hebrew manuscripts of the Old Testament dated 800–1000 years after the time of Christ. The earliest complete copy of the Old Testament is Codex Leningrad, dating to near AD 1000.

Despite these significant chronological gaps between the original manuscripts and the earliest documents, one can have confidence that the original message of the Hebrew Bible was faithfully preserved throughout its long and complicated transmission process.

Scribal practices in the ancient Near East demonstrate the care and precision taken by members of that craft in copying important political and religious texts. Israelite scribes who had a special reverence for the Scriptures as the Word of God were careful when copying the biblical manuscripts.

As the earliest existing Hebrew manuscripts, the Dead Sea Scrolls are an important witness to the textual integrity of the OT. Many of the biblical scrolls found at Qumran reflect a text that closely resembles the later Masoretic Text (MT), the textual tradition represented in the Hebrew Bible today. The close similarity of the Isaiah Scroll (1QIsaᵇ) found at Qumran to later Masoretic manuscripts

A fragment from the Dead Sea Scrolls.

of Isaiah reflects how carefully the scribes copied the text.

After the close of the OT canon (c. 300 BC) and the standardization of the Hebrew text (first century AD), meticulous and careful scribal practices ensured that the received text of the OT was handed down unchanged. A special group of scribes called the Masoretes (AD 500–1000) played a vital role in the transmission and preservation of the OT text. The Masoretes also meticulously counted the letters, words, and verses in the text. For example, the final Masorah at the end of Deuteronomy notes that there are 400,945 letters and 97,856 words in the Torah and that the middle word in the Torah is found in Leviticus 10:16.

The Hebrew text on this collapsed stone from the trumpeting place in Jerusalem reads, "to the place of trumpeting to . . . ." This stone probably marked the place where a trumpeter announced the beginning and end of the Sabbath every week.

The Gezer Calendar is believed to be one of the oldest Hebrew inscriptions found to date. The inscription is on a limestone tablet and dates from 925 BC.

The study of textual criticism is the science that enables scholars to determine and establish the most plausible wording of the original text. The number of textual variants due to handwritten mistakes that affect the meaning of the text are relatively few, and none of these variants change any major OT teaching or Christian doctrine.[6] Rather than undermining a person's confidence in the Scriptures, the textual criticism and transmission history of the Bible enables everyone to see how accurately the Bible today reflects what God originally communicated to His people in His Word. By contrast, no other documents from the ancient world were as accurately copied, preserved, and transmitted as the Old Testament Scriptures.

How We Got the New Testament

Which Books Belong in the New Testament?

The New Testament consists of twenty-seven books that were written from about AD 45 to approximately AD 100. Some authors penned their books, while other authors dictated the contents of a letter or narrative to an assistant (i.e., a scribe). This assistant wrote down what was spoken, and the author checked the document for accuracy. Apparently, Paul handwrote some of his first letters (Gal 6:11), but his later letters, which were dictated, ended with his handwritten salutation to authenticate them (2 Thess 3:17; Col 4:18; also see 1 Pet 4:12). The books of the New Testament were written on leather scrolls and papyrus sheets. These books included the four Gospels, the Acts of the Apostles, Paul's Letters, the General Epistles, and the Revelation (or Apocalypse).

These books were circulated independently at first, not as a collection. Itinerant preachers such as the apostle Matthew may have stayed in the homes of rich believers who had libraries and servants to be their personal scribes. Matthew may have allowed a scribe to copy his Gospel. Hence, the Gospel of Matthew was circulated widely as he traveled from church to church. Paul instructed that some of his letters be circulated (Col 4:16). We do not know if the actual letter (called an "autograph") was circulated to various churches or if copies were made by scribes to be circulated. Regardless, copies were eventually gathered into collections (apparently, there were collections of Paul's letters; see 2 Pet 3:16). They were copied into codices, which are similar to modern-day books, with the pages sewn together on one side to form a binding. In this form the

Greek papyrus.

documents were easier to read. Leather scrolls were harder to use because the entire book had to be unrolled to find a passage. Also, papyrus sheets cracked if rolled into a scroll; hence, the flat papyrus pages were sewn into a book. The codex collection was called in Latin *Ta Bibla*, the words we use to designate our Bible.

The Greek Language

The New Testament books were written in Greek that was different from the classical Greek of the philosophers. Archaeological excavations have uncovered thousands of parchments of "common language Greek," verifying that God chose the language of common people (*Koine* Greek) to communicate His revelation. God chose an expressive language to communicate the minute colors and interpretations of His doctrine. Still others feel God prepared Greeks with their intricate language, allowed them to conquer the world, used them to institute their tongue as the universal "trade language," then inspired men of God to write the New Testament in common Greek for the common people who attended the newly formed churches. This made the Word of God immediately accessible to everyone.

The Manuscript Evidence

The original manuscripts, called "autographs," of the books of the Bible, were lost, mostly during the persecution of the early church. Roman emperors felt that if they could destroy the church's literature, they could eliminate Christianity. Others were lost due to wear and tear. The fact that some early churches did not keep these autographs but made copies and used them demonstrates that they were more concerned with the message than the vehicle of the message. God in His wisdom allowed the autographs to vanish. Like the relics from the Holy Land, they could have been venerated and worshipped. Surely bibliolatry (worship of the Bible) would have replaced worship of God if that were the case.

This is the oldest complete Coptic Psalter, representing one of the most important ancient biblical texts. It dates to the fourth or fifth century and was found buried in a cemetery.

While some may have difficulty with the idea of not having an original manuscript, scholars who work with the nonbiblical documents of antiquities likewise do not have access to those originals. When considering the manuscript evidence, it should be remembered there are close to 5,880 Greek manuscripts (including fragments) and an additional 13,000 manuscript copies of portions of the New Testament. This does not include 8,000 copies of the Latin Vulgate and more than 1,000 copies of other early versions of the Bible. These figures take on even more significance when compared to statistics of other early writings.[7]

THE NEW TESTAMENT CANON

Some writers have supposed that Christians didn't discuss a canon for New Testament books until a few centuries after the life of Jesus. However, because of the presence of the heretic Marcion (died c. 160), this is unlikely. Marcion was a bishop in the church who had a negative view about the God presented in the Old Testament. He rejected the Old Testament and had a severely shortened New Testament canon, consisting of only the Gospel of Luke and ten of Paul's letters. However, even these were edited to remove as much Jewish influence as possible. The church excommunicated Marcion and rejected his teachings and canon.

Another heretical movement, Gnosticism, developed in the second century. In general this group believed that salvation was found in attaining "special knowledge." The Gnostics had their own set of writings defending their beliefs and practices. Included in their writings are false Gospels (for example, the Gospel of Thomas). The Gnostics and Marcion raised the question as to which books were genuine and authoritative for Christians.[8] Metzger concludes: "All in all, the role played by Gnostics in the development of the canon was chiefly that of provoking a reaction among members of the Great Church so as to ascertain still more clearly which books and epistles conveyed the true teaching of the Gospels."[9]

It should also be observed that the New Testament Christian community displaced a canonical consciousness in regard to collecting and circulating authoritative books from one generation to another. Various tests of canonicity included apostolicity, antiquity, orthodoxy, and catholicity (universal acceptance). The widespread acceptance and continuous use of the New Testament documents was attributed to the early church's confidence in their divine inspiration.

TESTS OF CANONICITY

The process through which the canon was formed is rather complicated. However, the following three tests for a book to be considered part of the canon: (1) apostolicity; (2) rule of faith; and (3) consensus.

The test of *apostolicity* means that a book must be written by an apostle or one connected to an apostle. When applied to the New Testament, most books automatically meet this requirement (those written by Matthew, John, Paul, and Peter). Mark and Luke were both associates of Paul. James was a half brother of Jesus, and Jude is either an apostle or the half brother of Jesus. The only book that has much difficulty with this criterion is Hebrews. Many in the early church believed Paul wrote Hebrews, but many New Testament scholars today suggest it was written by Luke. If we don't know who wrote it, how can we connect it to the canon? Hebrews 13:23a says, "Be aware that our brother Timothy has been released." Whoever the author of Hebrews was, this reference places him within the Pauline circle.[10]

The *rule of faith* refers to the conformity between the book and orthodoxy. *Orthodoxy* refers to "right doctrine." Therefore, the document had to be consistent with Christian truth as the standard that was recognized throughout Christian churches (e.g., in Corinth, Ephesus, Philippi). If a document supported heretical teachings, then it was rejected.

Finally, *consensus* refers to the widespread and continuous use of a document by the churches.[11] At first there was not complete agreement—not because a particular book was questioned, but not all books were universally known. However, the books that were included had widespread acceptance. Because the Holy Spirit breathed His life into a book by the process of inspiration (2 Tim 3:16), then the Holy Spirit that indwelt individual believers (1 Cor 6:19–20), and the Holy Spirit that indwelt churches (1 Cor 3:16), gave a unified consensus that a book was authoritative from God.

Applying these criteria to the books contained within the New Testament, and those that were left out, shows the consistency of the canon as it was handed down. Some "Gospels" have been found in recent years and have raised quite a stir, for example, the Gospel of Thomas and the Gospel of Judas. Why aren't these "Gospels" considered authoritative for Christians? First, these Gospels cannot be definitively linked to apostles, even though apostles are named in the titles.[12] Second, some heretical teachings in each document contradict the teachings of Scripture. Third, neither of these documents was used either universally or continuously by the church.[13] Therefore, they each fail at all three criteria.

Randall Price notes that the abundance of ancient manuscript copies of the New Testament puts it in a class all by itself. He points out that the number of New Testament manuscripts is overwhelming when compared to other famous and trusted ancient historical writings. To demonstrate this he provides the following chart:[14]

External Evidence for the New Testament Text		
Type of witness	Number of copies extant	Dating of copies
Uncial manuscripts	274	second–eleventh centuries AD
Minuscule manuscripts	2,555	ninth–sixteenth centuries AD
Lectionary manuscripts	2,280	fourth–sixteenth centuries AD
Versions (translations)	10,000	c. mid-second–ninth centuries AD
Latin (Vulgate)	(8,000)	c. mid-second–fifth centuries AD
Syriac (Diatessaron, Peshitta)		c. second–fifth centuries AD
Coptic (Sahidic, Bohairic)		c. third–fifth centuries AD
Gothic fourth (primary, Byzantine text)		c. fourth century AD
Armenian (secondary translation)		c. early fifth century AD
Georgian (tertiary translation)		c. mid-fifth century AD
Ethiopic (primary and secondary translation)		c. fifth–sixth centuries AD
Arabic (multiple versional influence)		c. eighth century AD
Old Slavonic (primary translation, Byzantine text)		c. ninth century AD
Patristic (early church fathers)	1,000,000+	early second–fifth centuries AD

These other famous and trusted ancient writers are generally quoted with confidence that what is written in a handful of manuscript copies of their original works is accurate. By contrast, the multiplicity of biblical manuscripts gives us the ability to compare and contrast their variant readings by the standard rules of textual criticism to help determine the most probable exact wording of the original text. No other writings from the ancient world can make this claim based upon so much extant evidence.

The New Testament that Christians use today has a long, rich history. The original copies were written almost 2,000 years ago and were copied for over 1,000 years by hand. All the books in the New Testament can be connected to an apostle, have content consistent with sound doctrine, and were used widely throughout the church. The New Testament was translated into many languages early in church history. Wycliffe and Tyndale were early translators of the Bible into English, culminating in the King James Version and many contemporary versions that now exist for the edification of the body of Christ.

All together, the Old and New Testament manuscripts, copies, and translations have stood the test of time. The Bible is God's Book, written to reveal Him and His message of salvation. God has preserved His Word over the centuries to speak to our hearts today. As you read the Bible, let Him speak to you. His words will challenge your thinking, stretch your faith, inform your mind, bless your heart, and stir your soul.

For Further Reading

Beckwith, Roger. *The Old Testament Canon of the New Testament Church: And Its Background in Early Judaism*. Grand Rapids: Eerdmans, 1985.

Bruce, F. F. *The Canon of Scripture*. Downers Grove, IL: IVP, 1988.

Geisler, Norman, and W. Nix. *A General Introduction to the Bible*. Chicago: Moody Press, 1986.

Kaiser, Walter C., Jr. *The Old Testament Documents: Are They Reliable and Relevant?* Downers Grove, IL: InterVarsity Press, 2001.

Merrill, Eugene H. "The Canonicity of the Old Testament." *The World and the Word: An Introduction to the Old Testament*. Nashville: B&H, 2011.

Rooker, Mark F. "The Transmission and Textual Criticism of the Bible." *The World and the Word: An Introduction to the Old Testament*. Nashville: B&H, 2011.

Wegner, Paul D. *A Student's Guide to Textual Criticism of the Bible: Its History, Methods and Results*. Downers Grove, IL: InterVarsity Press, 2006.

Study Questions

1. What does the term *canon* mean in relation to biblical books?
2. What is the threefold division of the Hebrew Bible?
3. What is the function and purpose of textual criticism?
4. How reliable are the Old Testament documents?
5. In which language are the books of the New Testament written?
6. How does the relation of the apostles to the New Testament books influence their credibility?

NOTES

1. For details see Walter C. Kaiser Jr., *The Old Testament Documents: Are They Reliable and Relevant?* (Downers Grove, IL: IVP, 2001).

2. Paul D. Wegner, *The Journey from Texts to Translations: The Origin and Development of the Bible* (Grand Rapids: Baker Academic, 1999), 101.

3. The word *Apocrypha* means "hidden books" and was first used with reference to these works by Jerome c. AD 400. The exact meaning of this term when applied to these books is unclear but implies their biblical authority was doubtful. Thus, they are not included in Protestant versions of the Bible.

4. See Jack P. Lewis, "Jamnia Revisited," in L. M. McDonald and J. A. Sanders, eds., *The Canon Debate* (Peabody, MA: Hendrickson, 2002), 146–62.

5. In the twenty-four-book canon, the Minor Prophets are a single book ("The Book of the 12"), and 1–2 Samuel, 1–2 Kings, 1–2 Chronicles, and Ezra-Nehemiah are viewed as one book each. Josephus arrived at a total of twenty-two books by also viewing Judges-Ruth and Jeremiah-Lamentations as single books.

6. Mark. F. Rooker, "The Transmission and Textual Criticism of the Bible," in Eugene H. Merrill, Mark F. Rooker, and Michael A. Grisanti, *The World and the Word: An Introduction to the Old Testament* (Nashville: B&H, 2011), 109.

7. Josh McDowell, *Evidence That Demands a Verdict* (San Bernardino, CA: Campus Crusade for Christ International, 1972), 48.

8. F. F. Bruce, *The Canon of Scripture* (Downers Grove, IL: InterVarsity, 1988), 153.

9. Bruce M. Metzger, *The Canon of the New Testament* (New York: Oxford University Press, 1987), 90.

10. For more on the authorship of Hebrews, see chapter 40.

11. Also referred to as *universality* or *catholicity*.

12. See Andreas J. Köstenberger and Michael J. Kruger, *The Heresy of Orthodoxy: How Contemporary Culture's Fascination with Diversity Has Reshaped Our Understanding of Early Christianity* (Wheaton, IL: Crossway, 2010), esp. 151ff.

13. See Nicholas Perrin, *Thomas: The Other Gospel* (Louisville: Westminster John Knox, 2007).

14. Randall Price, *Searching for the Original Bible* (Eugene, OR: Harvest House, 2007), 113–14. See Price's discussion throughout the book dealing with the external evidence for the texts of both the Old and New Testaments as well as the substantiation of the church fathers in their references to Scripture in the patristic writings.

Chapter 2

HOW TO READ THE BIBLE

T he Bible is the all-time best-selling book ever written. It is read by more people in more places and diverse cultures than anything ever written by anyone at any time. Yet most people who read the Bible for the first time will admit they are sometimes unsure of what it says, what it means, and how to apply its truths to their personal lives. The key is context, context, context! Just as realtors who sell houses and properties will tell you the key to the sale is "location, location, location," so it is with understanding the Bible.

Whenever you read any book of any kind, you should begin by asking who wrote it. Where was the author? To whom did he write? Where were they located? What did the author intend to communicate? The answers to these questions will give the reader immediate insight into the ideology of the book one is reading. The same is true of the Bible.

Step 1. What Did God Say?

As you approach the Word of God, realize that the nature of God is to reveal Himself. The Bible is a revelation of God, which means He has shown Himself in Scripture. In His revelation God speaks in language we can understand. God does not speak in meaningless words or obscure, esoteric truth in the Bible. Yes, God keeps some things secret that only He understands. "The secret *things belong* to the LORD our God, but those *things which are* revealed *belong* to us and to our children forever, that *we* may do all the words of this law" (Deut 29:29 NKJV). God used Hebrew words to speak to Old Testament prophets who spoke to Hebrew people so they could understand what God was saying. Then God guided New Testament writers to use *Koine* Greek, the language of the common people of the day (classical Greek was the language of the Greek philosophers); but God did not choose to impress people with scholarship but spoke His message to common people in common words so they could understand His message and do what He commanded.

Some critics want to throw out the Bible because it was written to an ancient people originally in ancient languages. But the same critics would not throw out the writings of Socrates, Plato, and Aristotle. Their messages can be interpreted, and we can learn from them today. In essence the principles we use to interpret the Greeks who lived 300 years before Christ are the same principles we use to interpret God's Word.

Just because a book is old does not mean it's useless and out of date. Millions read William Shakespeare today and find a deep meaning in his understanding of people, family relationships, and political squabbles. And when we understand the words Shakespeare uses, he enlightens our understanding of life today. The same can be said of Charles Dickens or Victor Hugo. Whether we read *Les Miserables*, *A Tale of Two Cities*, or *David Copperfield*, we discover a depth of truth that enriches our lives.

So when you read the Bible, you gain affinity with the people in Scripture. Your heart aches when you identify with the suffering of Job. You can experience intimacy with God as David did when he wrote the Shepherd's Psalm (Psalm 23). The Bible has lessons for you today because it expresses truth that transcends culture and is truthful from one age to another. Therefore the ancient truths of the Hebrew prophets or the Greek-speaking apostles apply to the city dweller in a metropolitan area today whether that person lives in Beijing (China), New Delhi (India), or Los Angeles (California). And since life is about relationships, the truth of Scripture crosses the varied histories of time and is always relevant. While living in a tent, Abraham sought to know and walk with God. The same truth could be learned by a South American native living in a primitive hut or a multimillionaire living in a penthouse overlooking Singapore Harbor.

Step 2. How Should We Interpret It?

When you read the Bible, interpret every sentence in the Bible the way people interpreted it when they originally heard it. Most contemporary Bible students follow the advice of Cooper's "Golden Rule of Interpretation." "When the plain sense of Scripture makes common sense, seek no other sense; therefore, take every word at its primary, ordinary, usual, literal meaning unless the facts of the immediate context, studied in the light of related passages and axiomatic and fundamental truths context, indicate clearly otherwise."[1] In other words, if the literal sense makes good sense, seek no other sense, lest you end up with nonsense!

So where do we begin? We must interpret every verse in the Bible in light of what is said in the rest of the Bible. This means we let the Bible interpret itself. Approximately 500 years ago wise Presbyterians explained how to interpret the Bible in the *Westminster Confession of Faith*: "The infallible rule of interpretation of Scripture is the Scripture itself: and therefore, when there is a question about the truth and full sense of any Scripture (which is not manifold, but one), it must be searched and known by other places that speak more clearly."[2]

Next we must interpret the Bible in light of the historical, grammatical, literary method. Look at the historical context of the passage, the grammar of the sentences, and the literary method employed by the original author. The Bible itself claims to be the inspired and inerrant Word of God. The apostle Paul wrote: "All Scripture is inspired by God and is profitable for teaching, for rebuking, for correcting, for training in righteousness" (2 Tim 3:16). However, Paul also reminds us to "be diligent . . . correctly teaching the word of truth" (2 Tim 2:15). Eric Bargerhuff warns: "We must resist the temptation to make a passage 'work' how we want it to work or 'make it say' what we want it to say."[3]

1. Interpret the Bible in Light of Its Historical Background

Everyone lives in a time and culture, even those who lived during Bible times, so we should seek to interpret the Bible through the eyes of those who lived when the Bible was written. God spoke to people who lived in a rural or farming context through terminology that was familiar to them. They understood that sheep must be cared for; therefore, people, like sheep, must have spiritual care. They also understood that seeds, when planted, take time to grow; therefore every Christian must grow even though they mature slowly. They also understood that people light a candle to illuminate a room. No one lights a candle to hide it under a basket. Look for the simple truths to come through the use of ordinary, everyday situations in the historical life of the author's audience.

2. Interpret the Bible in Light of the Author's Purpose and Plan

Every book in the Bible was written for a purpose, so when you begin reading a book in the Bible, find out what that purpose is. When you do this, do not read into the text something that is not there. Interpret every verse in light of the author's purpose.

Book	Reference	Objective
John	20:31	To promote faith in Jesus as the Son of God
1 Corinthians	1:10	To correct church problems and promote unity at Corinth
Galatians	1:6–9	To correct doctrinal heresy of "works salvation" in the churches of Galatia
1 Thessalonians	4:13	To correct false views concerning the return of Christ
1 John	5:13	To provide a basis for Christian assurance
Jude	3	To urge Christians not to waiver but to contend for the faith

3. Interpret Bible Verses in Light of Their Context

Seek to follow the author's thought as it runs through a paragraph. Do not grab hold of an idea from a few isolated words. Some Christians have latched onto one phrase, thinking they have the truth, only to be embarrassed later to find the verse doesn't mean what they thought it did. As an illustration: when the Bible says "touch not; taste not; handle not" (Col 2:21 KJV), it does not mean we are to refrain from eating, drinking, or touching things that are prohibited. No! Paul is quoting what the legalizers of the law said to the Christians in Colossae. Another often misunderstood verse is "'For I know the plans I have for you,' declares the Lord, 'plans to prosper you and not to harm you, plans to give you hope and a future'" (Jer 29:11 NIV). The context indicates that the people of Jerusalem were about to be conquered by the Babylonians and deported to Babylon for seventy years. Despite their immediate suffering, God still had a plan for Israel's national future. The verse is often taken out of context to imply that God is going to bless someone with immediate prosperity.

4. Interpret the Meaning of Words

Words are the basic building blocks of communication. We use words to talk with one another, and we interpret the words biblical authors use to find out what they originally meant. Give careful consideration to the meaning of words when studying the Scripture. First of all, you might look up the historical use of a word to find out what it means. This is called the *etymology* of a word. In other words, how did this term originally develop? Second, the *Usus Loquendi* is the ordinary use of the word in the author's time. Therefore, ask how an author uses a word and what the author's meaning is. Finally, watch for idiomatic expressions, which imply a unique meaning used by an author. When someone says, "He flew down the road," they do not mean he had wings like a bird. It means he traveled fast. Notice what Charles Hodge said over a hundred years ago: "The Holy Spirit chooses to use known human languages to convey to us the Word of God. The usage of the words in those languages, then, throws light on their meaning in the Scriptures."[4] For example, the Greek word for "grace" is *charis*, which is based on the word for "joy" (*char*) and expanded to "gifts" (*charisma*). The interconnection of these words helps us understand that it gives God great "joy" to extend to us His "grace" and empower us with spiritual "gifts," which in turn may be used by Him to extend His "grace," "joy," and "gifts" to others.

5. Interpret the Bible According to Grammatical Principles

Language is not a string of meaningless words. Words are tied together by grammar to give meaning to what the author wants to say. Therefore, pay close attention to the rules of grammar when interpreting the Bible. This involves looking carefully at the tense of the verbs. Sometimes a past-tense verb will trip us up when we try to use it in a modern-day setting. Some people will quote "that our old man is crucified" (see Rom 6:6), and then ask, "What have you crucified today?" However, the text is past tense, "Our old self was crucified" (Rom 6:6). This basically means Christ was crucified in the past on the cross. It's not our responsibility to do the crucifying. It means, based on the fact that Christ was already crucified for our sins, that we should live for Him today.

Look at how the words position themselves in the sentence and what the relationships are between words. Since God has inspired every word in Scripture (2 Tim 3:16), then we ought to study every word and know why God put it there. The interpreter of the English Bible must understand English words and grammar first. However, the average person will never study Hebrew or Greek, so find a good reference Bible that will interpret hard to understand words for you. Also, look for good books written by those who understand Greek and Hebrew.

6. Pay Attention to the Genre of the Passage

Genre refers to a type of literature. We encounter different types of literature every day. Simply reading a newspaper involves sorting out basic facts, opinionated editorial, sports information, advertisements, social agendas, and the comics. The Bible is written in a variety of literary genres. The laws of the Pentateuch are expressed differently from the narratives of the lives of the patriarchs. The books of history contain both factual details and spiritual evaluations. The books of poetry express the inner longings and passions of the souls of the poets, who often use figurative language ("trees clapped their hands") to create a mental image in the reader's mind. The Psalms are songs to be sung, while the Proverbs are earthly wisdom to be applied to daily life. The prophets mix both prose and poetry in both preaching and predictions. The Gospels are biographies of Jesus's life. Acts is both a history and a travel diary of the apostles. The Epistles are handwritten letters, and the Apocalypse (Revelation) is a prophetic vision of the future.

Step 3. How Should We Apply It to Our Lives Today?

Jesus promised, "When he, the Spirit of truth, is come, he will guide you into all truth" (John 16:13 KJV). While part of that promise relates primarily to the apostles who recorded Scripture by the inspiration of the Holy Spirit, it also has application to Christians today as the Holy Spirit illuminates the Word of God to the child of God. The Holy Spirit has a present-day ministry in the life of a Christian "that we might know the things that are freely given to us of God" (1 Cor 2:12 KJV).

According to Ursinus, an early (1534–83) Reformation theologian who wrote the *Heidelberg Confession*:

> The most essential "evidence" of the "certainty of Scripture" is the testimony of the Holy Spirit. This testimony is unique, proper only to those reborn by the Spirit of Christ and known only to them. And it has such power that it not only attests and seals abundantly in our souls the truth of the prophetic and apostolic doctrine, but also effectually bends and moves our hearts to embrace and follow it.[5]

A. W. Tozer, a nineteenth-century pastor, summarizes the ministry of the Holy Spirit in helping the believer understand the Scripture. He wrote: "Man by reason cannot know God; he can only *know about God*. . . . When the Spirit illuminates the heart, then a part of the man sees which never saw before; part of him knows which never knew before, . . . His experience of knowing is above reason, immediate, perfectly convincing and inwardly satisfying."[6]

The Holy Spirit helps us understand Scripture, but He doesn't eliminate the need for knowing the rules of grammar, understanding the meaning of words, or studying the historical background of the text. The Holy Spirit does not replace our personal study; He aids and guides our study of the Bible. The Scripture itself admonishes us to "be diligent (KJV, "study") to present yourself to God as one approved, a worker who doesn't need to be ashamed, correctly teaching the word of truth" (2 Tim 2:15).

Step 4. How Does the Bible Shape Our Worldview?

A worldview is how one perceives the meaning of life itself. It is the sum total of our beliefs about the world and frames the "big picture" that informs our decisions and actions. A worldview is our perception of reality based on our presuppositions of what is true, helpful, meaningful, and valuable. It is the unifying perspective from which we organize our understanding of life.

For the Christian who accepts the inspired truths of the Bible, the challenge is to develop a biblical worldview that is consistent with a personal faith. This will include answering life's basic questions: (1) Where did I come from? (2) Why am I here? (3) How should I live? (4) What are my values? (5) How should I make decisions? (6) Where am I going? (7) Is there life after death?

The biblical worldview is not rose-colored glasses or prescription lenses; it is a new set of eyes, as stated by John Calvin.[7] Christ makes all things new (see 2 Cor 5:17), including the way one sees the world. Through the work of Christ on a believer's heart, the individual now sees the world through the context of Scripture and understands that the work of Christ affects all things, not just religious things.

Therefore, a biblical worldview includes: First, knowing that *God is the source of all truth*. Augustine is credited with first articulating the idea that *all truth is God's truth*. Psalm 19 provides a helpful overview of both God's general revelation (as seen in nature), and God's special revelation (as seen in the Word of God and ultimately in the person of Jesus Christ). Second, to live out a biblical worldview, a person must believe that *the Bible is authoritative* as it speaks to every area of life. If the Bible is more than a human invention—if the Bible truly is God's Word—then the message of the Bible has authority over both the life of the individual and humanity in general. Third, to live out a biblical worldview, a person must *seek to understand and then to apply* God's truth. Right belief should determine right practice, not the other way around. Put another way, orthodoxy (right belief) should determine orthopraxy (right practice). Many times Christians are guilty of letting their experiences determine the way they interpret Scripture, and that error leads to many false beliefs and many false practices. Fourth, and finally, to live out a biblical worldview a person must *center his or her life on the gospel*, which is the declaration of the metanarrative of Scripture: *creation, fall, redemption,* and *restoration*. In explaining this big picture, attention is given to the fact that "the Christian message does not begin with 'accept Jesus as your Savior;' it begins with 'in the beginning God created the heavens and the earth.'"[8]

Derek Tidball wrote, "If we are to be the people God intends us to be . . . we must not only take seriously the word he speaks to us in Scripture, but must allow it to permeate every aspect of our lives."[9] Based on this observation, he pointed out the connection between our beliefs, behavior, and worship, noting that each is to be determined by the basic message of the Bible, which is central to the Christian faith.

For believers, our view of God and our understanding of life itself is based upon our biblical beliefs. Still, we are what Tidball calls "people of our time," who are often affected by current ideas and attitudes that can be quickly and uncritically adapted to our understanding of Scripture.[10] In light of this tendency, serious Bible readers must continue to ask themselves if they are letting the Bible speak to their times or if they are reading their own culture back into the Bible.

As we attempt to determine what the biblical writers intended to communicate to their original audience, we can begin to see how the same beliefs, values, and principles that motivated them can apply to us in the twenty-first century.

The Bible speaks to all of these issues and provides a framework for understanding life itself. If we are created in the image of God (see Gen 1:26), then we are more than simply highly complex animals. If God is eternal (Exod 3:14), is it possible for us to experience eternal life ourselves? Beyond the basic theistic questions of God's existence and our relationship to Him are the Christological questions: (1) Who is Jesus Christ? (2) Is He divine? (3) Did He live a sinless life? (4) Did He die for our sins? (5) Did He literally rise from the dead? (6) Is He really coming again? (7) Can He forgive my sins and change my life? As we attempt to answer these questions in light of the Judeo-Christian ethical values stated in the Bible, we must examine our own lives, values, and choices.

As you read the Bible for yourself, you will encounter these same questions, issues, and claims. Examine them and look deep into the stories, histories, poetry, prophecies, biographies, and letters of the biblical text. You will be swept away into another time and distant places to hear ancient voices that have stood the test of time. You will encounter some of the greatest people who have ever lived. Walk with them on their journey of faith, and let their stories inform your mind and bless your heart on your own spiritual journey. In the end may you find the One who alone makes it all worthwhile, of whom it was said: "See—it is written about me in the scroll—I have come" (Heb 10:7).

For Further Reading

Bargerhuff, Eric. *The Most Misused Verses in the Bible*. Minneapolis: Bethany House, 2012.

Duvall, J. Scott, and J. Daniel Hays. *Grasping God's Word*. Grand Rapids: Zondervan, 2001.

Fee, Gordon, and Douglas Stuart. *How to Read the Bible for All Its Worth*. Grand Rapids: Zondervan, 1982.

Köstenberger, Andreas J., and Richard D. Patterson. *Invitation to Biblical Interpretation*. Grand Rapids: Kregel, 2011.

McQuilkin, Robertson. *Understanding and Applying the Bible*. Rev. and exp. ed. Chicago: Moody, 2009.

Ridenour, Fritz. *So What's the Difference? A Look at Twenty Worldviews, Faiths and Religions*. Ventura: Regal, 2001.

Zuck, Roy B. *Basic Bible Interpretation: A Practical Guide to Discovering Biblical Truth*. Colorado Springs: David C. Cook, 1991.

Study Questions

1. Why is it important to discern the context of a biblical passage?
2. What are some basic rules of interpretation we should apply to reading the Bible?
3. How do the biblical authors' purposes influence the style and shape of their writings?
4. How does the Holy Spirit enable us to apply biblical principles to our daily lives?
5. Why is it important to understand the genre (prose, poetry, prophecy, narrative, biography) of a book or passage in the Bible?
6. How does the Bible inform and shape the believer's worldview?
7. How has your understanding of biblical principles influenced your personal worldview?

Notes

1. David L. Cooper, *Messiah: His Historical Appearance* (Los Angeles: Biblical Research Society, 1958), 19.

2. Orthodox Presbyterian Church, *The Confession of Faith and Catechisms of the Orthodox Presbyterian Church* (Willow Grove, PA: Committee on Christian Education, 2007), chap. 1 of the Holy Scriptures.

3. Eric Bargerhuff, *The Most Misused Verses in the Bible* (Minneapolis: Bethany House, 2012), 163. The author points out that even Adolf Hitler misinterpreted, twisted, and misused Jesus's words to vindicate his persecution of the Jews (14–15).

4. Quoted in James Oliver Buswell, *A Systematic Theology of the Christian Religion* (Grand Rapids: Zondervan, 1969), 25.

5. Ursinus, *Loci*, cited by Heinrich Heppe, *Reformed Dogmatics: Set Out and Illustrated from the Sources*, trans. G. T. Thomson (London: George Allen and Uwin, 1950), 24.

6. A. W. Tozer, *The Divine Conquest* (Old Tappan, NJ: Fleming H. Revell, 1950), 77–78.

7. John Calvin, *Institutes of the Christian Religion* 3.2.34. Calvin notes: "Therefore, as we cannot possibly come to Christ unless drawn by the Spirit, so when we are drawn we are both in mind and spirit exalted far above our own understanding. For the soul, when illumined by him, receives as it were a new eye, enabling it to contemplate heavenly mysteries, by the splendor of which it was previously dazzled." See also Timothy Jones, "John Calvin and the Problem of Philosophical Apologetics," *Perspectives on Religious Studies* 23 (1996): 387–403. Jones comments, "For Calvin, humanity does not need spectacles to repair what sight remains: Humanity needs new eyes (*Inst.* 1: v:14)."

8. Nancy Pearcey, *Total Truth (Study Guide Edition / Paperback Edition): Liberating Christianity from Its Cultural Captivity* (Wheaton, IL: Crossway Books, 2008), 45.

9. Derek Tidball, *The Illustrated Survey of the Bible* (Minneapolis: Bethany House, 2001), 9.

10. Ibid.

Chapter 3

OLD TESTAMENT INTRODUCTION

The Old Testament is made up of thirty-nine books and comprises three-fourths of the Bible. It was written by numerous authors from Moses to Malachi over a period of a thousand years and lays the foundation for biblical history, theology, and morality. One cannot understand the New Testament without reading the Old Testament. Terms like *covenant, law, grace, baptism, prophet, priest,* and *king* find their roots in the Old Testament. Concepts like *justice, forgiveness, redemption, salvation,* and *sanctification* were born in the Hebrew mind long before the New Testament.

In the pages of these amazing books, one encounters a plethora of humans—patriarchs, kings, priests, merchants, farmers, warriors, women, children, prostitutes, saints, and sinners. They are all there, each playing a significant role in God's story. Alec Motyer observes they are "larger than life and yet intensely human, belonging to the distant past and yet portrayed with such vividness and relevance" that they come alive, just like people today.[1]

The deeply personal narratives, dramatic national histories, powerfully passionate poetry, and perceptively predictive prophecies combine to weave the literary tapestry of the Old Testament. Jean-Pierre Isbouts notes that the principal thesis of the Hebrew Bible is the story of people who "were led, admonished, and ultimately saved by the power of one God, the creator of the universe, a Being passionately devoted to moral and social justice."[2]

The Hebrew Bible is divided into three sections: Law (*Torah*), Prophets (*Nevi'im*), and Writings (*Ketuvim*). Jesus referred to all three sections and declared their prophecies were all about Him (Luke 24:44). Our English Bibles are divided into five sections: (1) Pentateuch (Genesis–Deuteronomy), (2) History (Joshua–Esther), (3) Poetry (Job–Songs), (4) Major Prophets (Isaiah–Daniel), (5) Minor Prophets (Hosea–Malachi).

The Pentateuch

The first five books of the Bible, known as the Torah ("Law") or the Pentateuch ("five scrolls"), form the first literary unit of the Hebrew Scriptures. They tell the story of God's dealings with both the human race in general and the Hebrew race in particular. In so doing these chapters trace the actions of God in history from the creation of the world until the death of Moses. For both Jews and Christians, these books are the source of theological truth, biblical morality, and ethical behavior that laid the foundation of Western civilization.

These books take the reader back through the tunnel of time to the beginning of human existence and introduce the ultimate questions: Who are we? Where did we come from? Why are we here? They describe the first steps of the human journey to find God.

Samaritan priests with a copy of their Scripture— the Samaritan Pentateuch.

The five books of the Pentateuch are collectively known as the Torah, the Hebrew word for "law" or "teaching." As such they establish the foundation for a biblical theology of the entire canon of Scripture. Without these books people would have little understanding of the rest of the Bible. These books introduce the following concepts:

Genesis:	The Beginning
Exodus:	Exit from Egypt
Leviticus:	Way of Holiness
Numbers:	Wilderness Journey
Deuteronomy:	Covenant Renewal

Each book in turn introduces the one that follows it. Genesis concludes with Israel in Egypt. Exodus describes Israel's liberation from Egypt and the trek to Mount Sinai. Leviticus describes the religious system of worship that was given at Sinai. Numbers picks up the story of the journey from Sinai to Canaan. Finally, Deuteronomy provides instructions for the new generation, born in the wilderness, as they prepare to enter Canaan in fulfillment of God's promises that began in Genesis.

Critics of the Mosaic authorship of the Pentateuch have generally followed the Documentary Hypothesis, which was given its classical articulation by Julius Wellhausen (1876–83). He argued that anonymous editors compiled the Pentateuch long after Moses from four documents: J (Yahwist, 850 BC), E (Elohist, 750 BC), D (Deuteronomist, 621 BC), and P (Priestly Code, 525 BC).[3]

Despite the widespread acceptance of the Documentary Hypothesis, several reasons cause it to be suspect. First, it is contradicted by the traditional view of the Jews and the early church. Second, the Pentateuch itself declares Moses to be the author (Exod 17:14; 24:4, 7; 34:27; Num 33:1–2; Deut 1:8; 31:9). Third, the rest of the Old Testament presupposes Mosaic authorship of the Pentateuch (Josh 1:7–8; 8:32, 34; 22:5; 1 Kgs 2:3; 2 Kgs 13:23; 14:6; 21:8; 1 Chr 1:1; Ezra 6:18; Dan 9:11–13; Mal 4:4). Fourth, the New Testament designates Moses as the author of the Pentateuch (Matt 19:4–8; Mark 7:10; 12:26; Luke 16:29–31; 20:37; 24:27; John 5:46–47; 7:19, 23; Acts 15:1; Rom 10:5, 19). Fifth, the Pentateuch reflects a thematic literary unity that implies a single author. Sixth, the author

A Torah scroll dating from the sixteenth century AD. It was used in a Spanish Jewish synagogue.

writes as an eyewitness to much of the Pentateuch's content, which would be impossible for a writer long after the events (Exod 15:27; Num 2:1–31; 11:7–8). Seventh, the writer demonstrates a familiarity with Egyptian culture and geography, which would be unlikely for a later Judean writer (Gen 13:10; 16:1–3; 33:18; 39:4; 40:9–11; 41:40, 43).

The Documentary Hypothesis is built on unfounded assumptions and speculation. The documents the theory relies on have never been discovered. There is no archaeological evidence or extrabiblical historical proof that such documents (J, E, P, D) ever existed. After careful analysis of the theory, Moses Segal of Hebrew University rejected it because of "the absurd lengths to which it carries the analysis of the text, breaking up homogenous passages, and even single verses, into smaller fragments."[4]

Conservative evangelical scholars recognize that certain small elements of the Pentateuch were probably added later, such as the account of Moses's death and burial (Deuteronomy 34), but they believe Moses was the substantial author of the Pentateuch.

The Historical Books

The Historical Books, from Joshua to Esther, comprise one-third of the Old Testament and serve as the continuation of the story of Israel after the era of the patriarchs and the exodus. The book of Joshua opens with Joshua leading the tribes of Israel to cross the Jordan River and enter the Promised Land. The book of Judges serves as a transition from the success of the conquest to the difficulties of the settlement of the tribes. The books of Samuel, Kings, and Chronicles trace the history of the kings of Israel through the stages of unity, division, and collapse, resulting in the deportation of Israel into Assyrian and Judah into Babylonian captivity.

The story of Israel's survival after the exile is told in the books of Ezra, Nehemiah, and Esther. The first two record the account of the Jews who returned to Jerusalem after the Babylonian deportation. Esther tells the story of the protection and survival of the Jews of the Diaspora, who did not return to their homeland but remained dispersed throughout the Persian Empire.

Critical scholars have raised numerous questions about the historical accuracy of many technical details in these narratives: miraculous events (e.g., the sun standing still, Josh 10:1–15), exaggerated emphases (e.g., Samson's exploits, Judg 15:16), large numbers (e.g., Gideon's foes, Judg 8:10), the accuracy of dates (e.g., 300 years from the conquest to Jephthah, Judg 11:26), and even the general accuracy of the biblical accounts of the conquest, settlement, and the kingships of David and Solomon.[5] They view the final form of these books as a "Deuteronomistic history," designed to reinforce the theology of the book of Deuteronomy as the determining theological ideology in the history of Israel.

Walter Kaiser points out that there is currently no consensus among critical scholars in regard to any plausible reconstruction of the history of Israel. He counters many of their objections by pointing out that miracles in the historical accounts are not arbitrary explanations but a network of divine interventions that determined the course of events. He also argues that lack of documentation does not prove that certain events never occurred. Several people mentioned in the Bible have only recently been attested in nonbiblical sources (e.g., Belshazzar, Jehoiachin).[6]

The Historical Books cover a period of nearly a thousand years from Joshua's conquest of Canaan (c. 1405 BC) until the Persian period in the days of Ezra and Nehemiah (c. 430 BC). The biblical record defines the following periods of Israel's history:

1405–1390 BC	Conquest of Canaan (Joshua)
1390–1050 BC	Settlement of the Tribes (Judges)
1050–1010 BC	Kingship of Saul (1 Samuel)
1010–970 BC	Kingship of David (2 Samuel)
970–931 BC	Kingship of Solomon (1 Kings 1–11)
931–586 BC	Kings of Israel and Judah (Kings and Chronicles)
605–535 BC	Babylonian Captivity (Kings and Chronicles)
486–464 BC	Dispersion of the Jews (Esther)
458–430 BC	Return from Exile (Ezra and Nehemiah)

The themes of the Historical Books revolve around God's activity in calling, choosing, punishing, redeeming, and using the nation of Israel as His covenant people to accomplish His global purposes. These books tell not only the story of the nation and people of Israel but also the greater story of God's redeeming grace for all people (e.g., Rahab the Canaanite, Ruth the Moabite, Naaman the Syrian). In each book the covenant promises of God are expressed in terms of divine blessing, judgment, forgiveness, restoration, and preservation.

Joshua:	The Conquest
Judges:	The Struggle
Ruth:	Ray of Hope
1–2 Samuel:	Kings and Prophets
1–2 Kings:	Kings of Israel and Judah
1–2 Chronicles:	Priestly Perspective
Ezra:	Rebuilding the Temple
Nehemiah:	Rebuilding the Wall
Esther:	Rescuing the People

Written mostly as narrative prose, with a few outbursts of poetic expression (e.g., Song of Deborah and Barak, Judges 5), the Historical Books transport the reader down the corridor of time through nearly a millennium of human encounters with divine providence. The Lord Yahweh Himself intervenes in Israel's national life to preserve the promises and fulfill the prophecies of His covenant with them time and time again.

Poetic Books

Poetry is one of the world's earliest forms of artistic expression. While it is not as common today in the Western world, it was a familiar mode of communication in the Middle East. In ancient cultures entire epics were recorded and preserved in poetry. They usually originated in verbal and musical expressions and were later recorded in written form.

The Hebrews were imaginative people so their poetic and musical expression would naturally be full of metaphors and images closely connected to their domestic and social life. Not only were poetry and music important parts of weddings, harvests festivals, feasts, and funerals, but they also had a central place in the religious life of Israel. While prose may seem sufficient for recording facts, the Hebrews used poetry to express the soul. The poetic portions of the Old Testament therefore portray the emotions and the experiences of God's people.

The English Bible groups five poetic books together: Job, Psalms, Proverbs, Ecclesiastes, and Song of Songs. The prophetic books also rely heavily on the poetic mode of expression to communicate their timeless message, as do a few portions of the Pentateuch and the Historical Books.

Job:	Questions of Suffering
Psalms:	Songs of Praise and Lament
Proverbs:	Words of Wisdom
Ecclesiastes:	Meaning of Life
Song of Songs:	Songs of Love

The Purposes of Hebrew Poetry Were Multifaceted

1. To express emotion—Poetry is intended to appeal to the emotions, to evoke feelings rather than propositional thinking, and to stimulate a response on the part of the reader. While it certainly challenges us to think, it does so by eliciting an emotional response. Poetry is the language of the soul, and thus, the Hebrew poems still speak to us today and resonate with the deepest issues of the human heart.

2. To facilitate worship—Poetry is easy to memorize and put to music and often took on the role of lyrical expression in the psalms. Many of the psalms were sung in relation to specific worship services at the temple, and poetic books were read in connection with specific religious festivals:[7]

Passover:	Song of Songs, Hallel Psalms
Weeks/Pentecost:	Ruth, Hallel Psalms
Feast of Ab:	Lamentations
Hanukah:	Psalm 30
Tabernacles:	Ecclesiastes, Hallel Psalms

3. To instruct in wisdom—Hebrew wisdom literature is a certain kind of poetic literature used to instruct young people in the ways of wisdom. Hebrew wisdom tends to be practical and was meant to be applied to the many aspects of everyday secular life. While wisdom dealt with the practical, it did not leave out the recognition of God in the daily affairs of life. Hebrew wisdom teaches the reader not only how to live a *good* life but also how to live a *godly* life.

Characteristics of Hebrew Poetry

1. Figurative language—Hebrew poetry is rich in its use of figurative language. Common figures of speech include simile, metaphor, metonymy, personification, anthropomorphism, and hyperbole.

2. Parallelism—Parallelism is the practice of balancing one thought or phrase with a corresponding thought or phrase containing approximately the same number of words or a correspondence of ideas. There are three basic types of parallelism:

Synonymous parallelism—The second line expresses the same thought as the first line, though with different but similar words.

Antithetical parallelism—The second line expresses a thought that is in contrast to the first line.

Synthetic parallelism—The second line completes the thought of the first line in some way.

Forms of wisdom poetry expressions include: proverbs, riddles (Judg 14:13–14), parables (Judg 9:7–15), analogies (Prov 27:17), and songs (Pss 34:11; 119:72). Within wisdom literature two distinct types may be found in the Old Testament: (1) *didactic*, the teaching of practical themes for successful living, and (2) *skeptical*, or philosophical inquiry into the meaning of life (Ecclesiastes), the purpose of pain (Job), or the search for true love (Song of Songs).

Major Prophets

The Major Prophets in the English Bible include the books of Isaiah, Jeremiah, Ezekiel, Daniel, and Jeremiah's poetic Lamentations. They are generally designated as "major" because of their length and prominence in the history of God's revelation to Israel and the nations. Isaiah, Jeremiah, and Ezekiel were preaching prophets as well as writing prophets, whereas Daniel was an administrator who received divine revelations from God. He interpreted the dreams of others and recorded his own visions of the future, so it is not surprising that Jesus recognized him as a prophet (Matt 24:15).

The Hebrew prophets spoke for God. They wrote the books of history ("former prophets") and the books of prophecy ("latter prophets") in the Old Testament. The prophetic books of history are followed in the Hebrew Bible by the prophetic books of preaching and prediction. The two categories of prophetic books form a unit in the middle of the Hebrew Scriptures under the common term "prophets" (Hb. *nevi'im*).

The Hebrew term *nabi'* identifies the prophet as a preacher or pro-claimer of God's Word, as does the Greek term *prophetes*. Biblical prophets were both preachers of truth and predictors of the future. Prophecy has its roots in history, but it also extends into the future. In other words, the nature of predictive prophecy arises out of the prophet's historical context as the revelation of God points him toward the future as well as the present. Thus, the prophets speak both to their own generation and to future generations as preachers and predictors.

The Old Testament prophets spoke for God. They believed they were sent by God with a specific message. Whereas the priests represented the people to God, the prophets presented God to the people. Thus, the prophets spoke with divine authority and divine enabling. Prophets were called by God, account-able to God, and empowered by God. The people of Israel acknowledged them as "holy men of God" who spoke the Word of God (2 Pet 1:21 KJV).

City wall and Citadel of Ahab around his palace at Samaria. Omri, Ahab's father, purchased the hill of Samaria and built Israel's capital there.

Isaiah dates his ministry from the reign of King Uzziah (c. 740 BC) into the reign of Hezekiah (c. 680 BC), clearly placing himself in the days of the Assyrian threats against Judah. During his lifetime Samaria, the capital of the northern kingdom, fell to the Assyrians in 722 BC. The northern tribes were scattered and replaced by Assyrian settlements in the hills of Galilee and Samaria. By contrast, Jeremiah, Ezekiel, and Daniel lived during the last days of Judah and witnessed the fall of Jerusalem to the Babylonians in 605 BC (Daniel), 597 BC (Ezekiel), and 586 BC (Jeremiah). Within their lifetimes their beloved Jerusalem was conquered, Solomon's temple was destroyed, the royal line of the "house of David" was removed, and the Jews were deported to Babylon.

The English Bible includes five books of the Major Prophets. Among these Isaiah and Jeremiah are the longest. They emphasize the preaching of these two great prophets of Judah. Ezekiel and Daniel both include apocalyptic visions of Israel's future and provide hope to the Jewish exiles that God is still on the throne.

Isaiah:	God Is with Us
Jeremiah:	The Babylonians Are Coming
Lamentations:	Jerusalem Is Burning
Ezekiel:	The Glory Will Return
Daniel:	The Messiah Will Come

The messages of the Major Prophets remind us that God holds all nations accountable for their behavior and policies. He alone sets up and takes down kings (Dan 4:17). He is the sovereign Lord of the universe before whom the nations are but "a drop in a bucket" (Isa 40:15). But He also gives us hope even in the most difficult times of our lives (Jer 29:11).

Minor Prophets

The Minor Prophets include the books of Hosea to Malachi, and they follow the Major Prophets in the Hebrew Scriptures. These books are twelve separate compositions in our English Bible, but they appear as a single "Book of the Twelve" in the Hebrew Bible. Along with Isaiah, Jeremiah, and Ezekiel, they form the Latter Prophets. The history of these twelve prophets covered a span of more than three centuries. In terms of larger themes, Hosea–Micah focused on the sin of covenant breaking; Nahum–Zephaniah emphasized the approaching judgment of the Day of the Lord; and Haggai– Malachi promised the reversal of judgment and the future glory of Israel. All together the Minor Prophets are a collection of the messages of twelve individual prophets to Israel and Judah that serve both as predictions of judgment and as promises of hope for the future.[8]

Three of the Minor Prophets (twenty-seven chapters in the English Bible) are focused on the northern kingdom of Israel (capital, Samaria):

Hosea:	God's Unquenchable Love
Amos:	God's Ultimate Justice
Jonah:	God's Universal Concern

Six of the Minor Prophets (twenty chapters in the English Bible) are focused on the southern kingdom (capital, Jerusalem):

Joel:	Day of the Lord
Obadiah:	Doom of Edom
Micah:	Divine Lawsuit
Nahum:	Destruction of Nineveh
Habakkuk:	Destruction of Babylon
Zephaniah:	Disaster Is Imminent

The last three Minor Prophets (twenty chapters in the English Bible) are focused on the Jewish exiles who have returned from Babylon to rebuild the temple and reestablish Jerusalem. They form the final link to the messianic prophecies, which are fulfilled in Jesus in the New Testament:

Haggai:	Rebuild the Temple
Zechariah:	Restore the King
Malachi:	Repent of Sin

The messages of the Minor Prophets still speak to us today. They remind us that God holds all people responsible for their behavior, especially those who claim to belong to Him. Thus, the call of the prophets echoes down the canyon of time, calling us to repent, return, and experience God's grace and forgiveness resulting in revival, restoration, and hope for the future.

The Old Testament propels its readers to look beyond its pages for its final answers. It portrays what Philip Yancey calls "a gradual but certain movement toward grace."[9] Without the Old Testament one cannot fully understand the New Testament. Within the laws, history, poetry, and prophecies of the Hebrew Scriptures, one discovers in the Old Testament a God who loves and leads those who will believe, trust, and follow Him. He is a God who establishes principles of social order and justice. He sets up and takes down kings and rulers. He judges human behavior and holds people accountable for their choices. Yet, in the darkest moments of human failure,

God intervenes with grace beyond comprehension. That grace (Hb. *hen*) and unfailing love (Hb. *chesed*) energize the old covenant. God's contract with the people and nation of Israel was never meant to be limited to them alone. The blessings of the Abrahamic, Mosaic, and Davidic covenants were meant ultimately to bless the whole world (Gen 12:2–3), and indeed they have. For all that was promised to the patriarchs and confirmed by the prophets was fulfilled in "Jesus Christ, the Son of David, the Son of Abraham" (Matt 1:1). It is no wonder Jesus said they rejoiced to see His day (John 8:56).

For Further Reading

Arnold, Bill, and Bryan Beyer. *Encountering the Old Testament*. Grand Rapids: Baker, 2008.

Dillard, R., and T. Longman. *An Introduction to the Old Testament*. Grand Rapids: Zondervan, 1994.

Geisler, Norman L. *A Popular Survey of the Old Testament*. Grand Rapids: Baker, 2007.

Hill, A. E., and J. H. Walton. *A Survey of the Old Testament*. Grand Rapids: Zondervan, 2009.

Merrill, E., M. Rooker, and M. Grisanti. *The World and the Word: An Introduction to the Old Testament*. Nashville: B&H, 2011.

Study Questions

1. In what way does the Pentateuch (*Torah*) lay the foundation for Western civilization?
2. What are the weaknesses of the Documentary Hypothesis?
3. What are the basic themes and periods of Old Testament history?
4. How does Hebrew poetry express emotions and spirituality? How does it differ from English poetry?
5. How do the Major and Minor Prophets still speak to us today?
6. Why does the Old Testament ultimately push us toward God's grace?

Notes

1. Alec Motyer, *The Story of the Old Testament* (Grand Rapids: Baker, 2001), 8.

2. Jean-Pierre Isbouts, *The Biblical World: An Illustrated Atlas* (Washington, DC: National Geographic Society, 2007), 48.

3. For a discussion of the historical development of the Documentary Hypothesis, see Bill Arnold and Bryan Beyer, *Encountering the Old Testament: A Christian Survey* (Grand Rapids: Baker, 1999), 68–75.

4. M. H. Segal, *The Pentateuch* (Jerusalem: Magnes Press, 1967), xii. For a classic refutation, see U. Cassuto, *The Documentary Hypothesis* (Jerusalem: Magnes Press, 1961).

5. For examples, see Albrecht Alt, *Essays in Old Testament History and Religion* (New York: Harper & Row, 1966); Martin Noth, *The History of Israel* (New York: Harper & Row, 1960); John Bright, *A History of Israel* (Philadelphia: Westminster, 1981); J. A. Soggin, *A History of Israel* (London: SCM, 1985); John Hayes and J. Maxwell Miller, eds., *Israelite and Judean History* (Philadelphia: Westminster, 1977).

6. Walter Kaiser, *A History of Israel* (Nashville: B&H, 1988), 1–15.

7. See details in Eugene H. Merrill, Mark F. Rooker, and Michael A. Grisanti, *The World and the Word* (Nashville: B&H, 2011), 496.

8. Paul R. House, *Old Testament Theology* (Downers Grove, IL: IVP, 1998), 348.

9. Philip Yancey, *The Bible Jesus Read* (Grand Rapids: Zondervan, 1999), 12.

Chapter 4

GENESIS

The Beginning

Genesis is the book of beginnings. It tells the story of the beginning of the human race in general and the beginning of the Hebrew race in particular. The Hebrew Bible titles the book *bereshith* ("in the beginning"), the first word in the Hebrew text. Genesis introduces the basics of the biblical message that God is an absolute personal being who cares about His creation and the human struggle of the fallen world. He speaks, creates, calls, blesses, promises, and visits His creation to intervene personally in the lives of His people. Genesis uniquely tells the story of the successes and failures of people like Adam and Eve, Cain and Abel, Noah's family, Abraham and Sarah, Isaac and Rebekah, Jacob's wives and his twelve sons. Unlike ancient mythological literature, Genesis shows its heroes as they really were, giving a glimpse of human nature in the ancient world.

KEY FACTS

Author:	Moses
Recipients:	Israelites
Date:	1445 BC
Key Word:	Create (Hb. *bara*)
Key Verse:	"In the beginning God created the heavens and the earth" (1:1).

The book of Genesis is an anonymous work that was traditionally attributed to Moses until the eighteenth century. Proponents of the Documentary Hypothesis argue that Genesis, like the rest of the Pentateuch, is the result of various conflicting documents that were edited, redacted, and conflated into their present form many centuries after Moses. Some biblical critics even deny that there was ever a historical Moses. Conservative scholars still hold to the Mosaic authorship of Genesis.[1] His Egyptian education, as the adopted son of Pharaoh's daughter, would have provided him with the skills to compose such a book. While Moses probably used sources like ancient patriarchal family records (Gen 5:1), he was the ultimate author, compiler, and editor of the Genesis record.

Background and Structure

The book of Genesis involves three basic settings. Genesis 1–11 recounts the ancient history of the world from creation until the birth of Terah (c. 2296 BC) and takes place in the *Fertile Crescent*. Genesis 12–36 unfolds between the birth of Terah and Joseph's arrival in Egypt (1899 BC) and takes place mostly in *Canaan*. Genesis 37–50 elapses between Joseph's arrival in Egypt and the death of Joseph (1806 BC) and takes place mostly in *Egypt*. Conservative scholars generally date the patriarchs as follows:

Patriarch	Date
Abraham	2166–1991 BC
Isaac	2066–1886 BC
Jacob	2006–1859 BC
Joseph	1916–1806 BC

A key structural marker used throughout the book is the ten *toledoth*, "the records of" (Gen 2:4; 5:1; 6:9; 10:1; 11:10; 25:12, 19; 36:1, 9; 37:2). This *toledoth* introduces a section rather than concludes it and usually starts out broadly and then narrows to a person, line, or group of interest to the writer.[2]

Outline[3]

I. Primeval History (1:1–11:9)
   A. Creation (1:1–2:25)
   B. Fall (3:1–5:32)
   C. Flood (6:1–9:29)
   D. Nations (10:1–11:9)

II. Patriarchal History (11:10–50:26)
    A. Abraham (11:10–25:11)
    B. Isaac (25:12–26:35)
    C. Jacob (27:1–36:43)
    D. Joseph (37:1–50:26)

Message

Genesis provided Israel with an explanation of her place in the history of the world. After 400 years of slavery, it is easy to see how such a history could be lost. Thus in Genesis, Moses explains how God's original plan for creation was marred by sin and how Israel was set aside for the special purpose of mediating God's redemptive blessings to the world. As a divine history of the world, Genesis covers more time than any other biblical book. John J. Davis remarks, "It completely transcends the primitive mythology of the ancient world."[4]

Genesis also emphasizes the importance of the Abrahamic covenant, which gave Israel a right to the land (Gen 15:18–21). Because they would soon have to take the land by fighting the Canaanites, Israel needed to understand that it was God's will for the nation to remove and exterminate the Canaanites (Gen 9:25; 15:16). Thus, the book was written so Moses' generation would trust God by better understanding Israel's past heritage, present purpose, and future destiny as they anticipated entrance into the Promised Land.

I. Primeval History (Genesis 1:1–11:9)

The book's prologue (chaps. 1–11) explains God's redemptive program and the messianic lineage from Eden to Abraham. This section explains the terrible progress of sin and the reason God's redemptive program was necessary. Thus, it is the foundation of the biblical worldview.

A. Creation (Genesis 1:1–2:25)

The first two chapters of Genesis describe God's original work of creation. Genesis 1:1 assumes the existence of God (*Elohim*) and the fact of creation. Knowledge of the original creation would help the nation comprehend God's goal of eventually restoring creation to its original state. Knowledge of God's

View of Earth from outer space.

six days of work and one day of rest would help Israel understand the foundation of their workweek (Exod 20:8–11) and Sabbath rest as the sign of the Mosaic covenant.

In chapter 1 the creation of the world is summarized, and in chapter 2 it is scrutinized in greater detail. G. C. Aalders observes that the creation is one of absolute beginning and not a transformation of a preexistent one. He states, "The words 'In the beginning' must be taken in their absolute sense . . . although the alternative interpretation is linguistically possible, it does not reflect common Hebrew usage."[5] The biblical description of creation is *ex nihilo* (from nothing) by the power of God's spoken word ("then God said," 1:3, 6, 9, 11, 14, 20, 24, 26, 29). Thus, the original creation was instantaneous, having an appearance of age and living things (plants and animals) reproducing "according to their kinds" (1:12, 21, 24–25). O. T. Allis comments, "The account of creation is definitely theistic. . . . God is distinct from both man and nature. He is the Creator of both. All things owe their existence to His almighty fiat."[6]

The opening verses of Genesis clearly refute:

Atheism	There is no God.
Pantheism	All is God.
Polytheism	There are many gods.
Materialism	Matter is eternal.
Humanism	Man is the measure.
Naturalism	Nature is ultimate.

The Genesis account of creation contradicts secular evolution, which theorizes that all life, including humans, evolved over billions of years from lower life forms by natural processes. Theories of origins that accommodate evolution (gap theory, day=age theory, revelatory day theory, theistic evolution, etc.) have all proven to be inadequate explanations of the obvious contrast between the biblical account of creation and general evolutionary theory. The results of the naturalistic evolutionary hypothesis have left a spiritual void that "erases all moral and ethical accountability and ultimately abandons all hope for humanity."[7]

B. Fall (Genesis 3:1–5:32)

The major crisis for the newly created world comes in chapter 3 when Adam and Eve sin. This resulted in their expulsion from the garden of Eden because of their sinful rebellion against God. Their descendants followed in the rebellious ways of their parents resulting in the long story of human depravity and its terrible consequences. Spiritual death and human suffering came immediately as the result of their sin and eventually lead to their physical death (3:3, 19). As a result, the apostle Paul observes, "Death reigned" because of Adam's sin (Rom 5:17).

While the immediate consequences of human sin resulted in broken communication with the Creator (Gen 3:7–13), God graciously stepped into their fallen condition asking, "What have you done?" (3:13 NLT). After pronouncing the penalty for their sin, God provided for their redemption by predicting their ultimate salvation by the "seed" of the woman who would "crush" the head of the serpent (3:15 NIV). This promise of the annihilator of the wicked instigator is called the *proto-evangelium* or what Aalders calls "the gospel announced by God Himself to our first parents."[8] This is a ray of hope to enlighten the human predicament.

The genealogy from Adam to Noah traces the line from which the messianic blessing (Gen 3:15) would eventually come (Gen 4:25–5:32). The fact that people still retained the image of God even in their fallen condition (Gen 5:1; 9:6) reveals humanity's dignity and why God sought to redeem them from the curse. Moreover, Enoch's translation (Gen 5:24) as well as Lamech's description of Noah as the "comforter" (Gen 5:29 HCSB) provided hope that the reality of the curse would one day be done away with.[9]

REFLECTION

Biblical Worldview

The early chapters of Genesis lay the foundation for the biblical worldview. The world is pictured as the creation of God and human beings as created in "the image of God" (1:27). Therefore, God is a unique personal Being, who is distinct from His creation, and humans are clearly distinct from animals. Our human self-identity is the result of our capacity to know God personally. However, our fallen sinful nature causes us to run from God rather than running to Him. Therefore, God intervenes in human history to reveal Himself to us so that we might know Him and fulfill His purposes for our lives, our families, and our society.

C. Flood (Genesis 6:1–9:29)

The growing power of sin approached epic proportions as the human race became involved in perpetual wickedness (Gen 6:1–7) and God moved to destroy humanity through the flood. Because Noah was a man who walked with God and was righteous (6:9), God safely preserved him in the ark while the world was flooded. The global extent of the flood is indicated

by the fact that all of the high mountains were covered (7:19), all living things perished (7:21), and the flood lasted 371 days. It is also evident from extrabiblical and New Testament testimony (2 Pet 3:3–7) and the use of unique terms for the deluge (Hb. *mabbul*, and Gk. *kataklusmos*).[10]

God's intent to restore creation is seen in His provision of the Noahic covenant following the flood (Gen 8:20–9:17). The creation of human government with the power of capital punishment would serve as a deterrent preventing humanity from regressing back to the level of violence exhibited in the antediluvian world. However, man's sinful nature continued in the postdiluvian world (Gen 8:21).

Mount Ararat, located in Eastern Turkey near Igdir, as seen in the evening.

D. Nations (Genesis 10:1–11:9)

The subsequent dispersion of the nations at the tower of Babel (Genesis 10; 11:1–9) and the confusion of languages that resulted was not reversed until the day of Pentecost in Acts 2. As the nations turned away from God, He chose Abraham so that God could bring a blessing to the whole world through His descendants.

A reproduction of a tablet from the Gilgamesh Epic, a Babylonian account of a great flood.

II. Patriarchal History (Genesis 11:10–50:26)

The rest of the book of Genesis focuses the reader's attention on patriarchal history. Moses' goal in this section was to give the wilderness generation an incentive to cooperate with God's covenant purposes by accepting the Mosaic covenant. From this point onward Genesis focuses on four great patriarchs: Abraham, Isaac, Jacob, and Joseph.

A. Abraham (Genesis 11:10–25:11)

Abram ("great father") was later called Abraham, the "father of a multitude," including Isaac, the son of promise. In Gen 12:2–3, 7, the messianic promises from Gen 3:15 were transformed and restated in the Abrahamic promises. According to these promises, land, seed, and blessing would be given to Abram's descendants; and through these descendants the entire world would be blessed. The seed aspect of these blessings specifically amplifies the unconditional promise of one who would defeat the forces of evil in Gen 3:15.

Genesis 15 introduced the Abrahamic covenant as a formal covenant relationship with Abram. This took the form of an official treaty between God and Abram. The ritual of cutting the animals in half was symbolic of an official treaty between two individuals. However, the unconditional nature of this treaty was seen in the fact that Abram was asleep while God alone passed through the animal pieces (Gen 15:12, 17). Thus, the fulfillment of the treaty was totally dependent on God. With total faith in God's promises, Abram "believed the LORD," and God credited him with righteousness (Gen 15:6; see Rom 4:3, 9, 22; Gal 3:6; Jas 2:23).

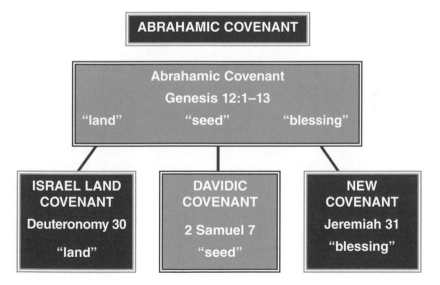

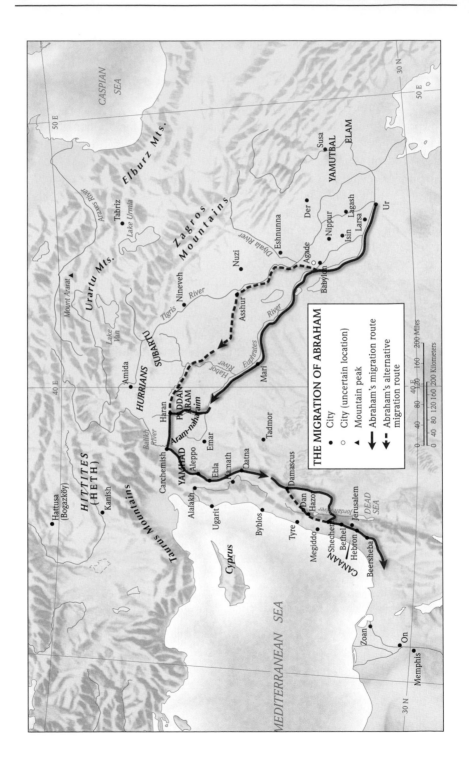

Despite God's promise that Abram would have a son from his "own body" (15:4), Sarai insisted they use Hagar their Egyptian slave as a surrogate mother (16:1–3). As a result, Hagar's son Ishmael ("God hears") became the ancestor of the Arab peoples. God's selection of Isaac by a miraculous birth to Abraham and Sarah in their old age was a deliberate reflection of His divine will (18:9–15). To reflect the great lineage that would come from this line, Abram's name was changed to Abraham ("father of multitudes"), and Sarai's name was changed to Sarah ("princess").

The birth of Isaac ("laughter") caused Sarah to laugh with God instead of laughing at Him (cf. 18:12–15; 21:6–7). Years later God tested Abraham's faith in this promise by asking him to sacrifice Isaac on Mount Moriah (22:1–16). Despite the request Abraham's faith was expressed by telling the servants, "We'll come back to you" (22:5). At the most dramatic moment "the angel of the LORD" called to Abraham to stop (22:11).[11] He had passed the test of faith, and God provided a ram instead. Therefore, Abraham named the place "The LORD Will Provide" (Hb. *yahweh yir'eh*; "Jehovah Jireh," 22:14 KJV).

B. Isaac (Genesis 25:12–26:35)

Genesis 25:12–18 identifies Isaac as God's chosen son of the promise as well as Isaac's youngest son, Jacob (Gen 25:23), rather than his oldest son, Esau. Esau's character weaknesses are seen in the despising of his birthright (Gen 25:27–34) and his rebellious marriages to Hittite women (Gen 26:34–35). The Abrahamic covenant was reconfirmed to Isaac (Gen 26:1–5, 23–25) with God's promises of personal blessing and protection (Gen 26:12–16).

C. Jacob (Genesis 27:1–36:43)

The theme of deception recurs throughout the story of Jacob's life. Despite the fact that Jacob deceived Isaac and cheated Esau out of the blessing of the firstborn (Gen 27:1–40), the Abrahamic covenant was reconfirmed to Jacob in Gen 28:10–17. This illustrates the unconditional nature of the covenant. Jacob went to his mother's ancestral home in Haran (28:10) where he married Leah and Rachel, the daughters of Laban, his mother's brother (29:1–29). En route to Haran, Jacob stopped at Luz, where he encountered God personally in the dream of the angelic stairway. Believing it to be the "gate of heaven," he renamed it Bethel ("house of God"), and vowed that the Lord (*Yahweh*) would be his God (28:16–21). Jacob's marriages to Leah and Rachel produced twelve sons who would become the twelve tribes of Israel (Gen 29–30:24). One of his sons, Judah, would perpetuate the messianic line of Christ (Matt 1:1–2). When God told Jacob to return to Bethel (35:1), he insisted his family "get rid of the foreign gods" they had accumulated (35:2), and he called it "God of Bethel" (v. 7, *el bethel*), indicating his full intention to serve the Lord. As a result, God changed his name from Jacob to Israel (35:10).

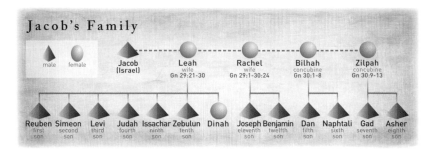

D. Joseph (Genesis 37:1–50:26)

Genesis 37–50 focuses on Joseph as the human instrument God would use to relocate the sons of Jacob to Egypt. God's selection of the younger brother to accomplish His will reveals a pattern (Isaac over Ishmael, Jacob over Esau, Judah and Joseph over Reuben, Ephraim over Manasseh) throughout Genesis, indicating that God is not limited by human preferences for the firstborn. God revealed His purpose for Joseph in a dream, but his brothers became envious and sold him as a slave into Egypt (Genesis 37).

Despite his brother's evil intentions and subsequent deception of their father, Jacob, Genesis 39–41 records how Joseph was promoted to second in command over all of Egypt as a grand vizer to Pharaoh (probably Sesostris III).[12] Joseph's exaltation resulted in all the brothers being reunited (Genesis 45) and bringing their father, Jacob, to Egypt (Genesis 46), where they settled in Goshen in the delta region.

Genesis 48–50 concludes with Jacob's blessing of Joseph's sons (Gen 48:8–22), Jacob's prophetic blessings pronounced on each of the tribes (Gen 49:1–28), Jacob's burial in Canaan (Gen 50:1–14), Joseph's prediction that the nation would return to Canaan (Gen 50:24), and the oath by the sons of Israel that they would bury Joseph's bones in Canaan (Gen 50:25).

Of particular significance is the prediction that the Messiah would come from Judah (Gen 49:10; Matt 1:2, 6).[13] While Judah received the birthright, Joseph was given a double blessing through the adoption of his sons, Ephraim and Manasseh, as "sons of Israel" (50:25), each becoming a future tribe of Israel. Thus, the author sets the stage for the story of the exodus that follows.

Practical Application

Genesis begins with the act of creation and ends with Israel still awaiting her prophetic destiny. In between the author lays the foundation of all biblical theology. Genesis defines human beings as a unique and distinct creation made "in the image of God" (1:27) and given a mandate to rule God's creation (1:28). However, Adam's sin brought death and disorder to the creation, and this resulted in divine judgment (1:24; 6:5–7; 11:8). As the world turned away from God, He turned to one man, calling Abraham to believe and follow Him (Gen 12:1–3), promising to make of his descendants "a great nation" (v. 2) that would bless all peoples. The election of Israel was confirmed by the Abrahamic covenant (15:1–6) and reaffirmed to his descendants Isaac, Jacob, and Jacob's twelve sons—the forefathers of the nation of Israel. Paul House observes, "Genesis acts as a foundational prelude to Israel's greatest defining moment (Sinai) and Israel's immediate future (the conquest of Canaan)."[14] As you read the promises of God in Genesis, remember that they are foundational to all His promises to those who believe in Him today as well.

For Further Reading

Davis, John J. *Paradise to Prison: Studies in Genesis*. Grand Rapids: Baker, 1975.

Hamilton, Victor. *Genesis*, 2 vols. NICOT. Grand Rapids: Eerdmans, 1990.

Matthews, Kenneth. *Genesis 1:1–11:26* and *Genesis 11:27–50:26*. NAC. Nashville: B&H, 1996, 2005.

Morris, Henry M. *The Genesis Record: A Scientific and Devotional Commentary on the Book of Beginnings*. Grand Rapids: Baker, 1976.

Ross, Allen. *Creation and Blessing: A Guide to the Study and Exposition of Genesis*. Grand Rapids: Baker, 1996.

Study Questions

1. In what way are human beings uniquely created by God?
2. How does the fallen nature of humanity affect our relationship to God?
3. How does the biblical description of the flood (Genesis 6–9) indicate its extent?
4. In what way is Abraham's faith an example to us today?
5. What can we learn about the importance of character and personal integrity from the contrasting stories of Jacob and Joseph?

Notes

1. See the extensive discussion and references in Eugene H. Merrill, Mark F. Rooker, and Michael A. Grisanti, *The World and the Word: An Introduction to the Old Testament* (Grand Rapids: Baker Academic, 2011), 136–73. They view Moses as the substantial and predominant author, with minor editorial insertions such as the reference to Dan in Gen 14:14. Others, like William Sanford LaSor, David Alan Hubbard, and Frederic William Bush, *Old Testament Survey*, 2nd ed. (Grand Rapids: Eerdmans, 1996), 8–13, view the book as being shaped by "inspired authors, editors, and tradition bearers of God's chosen people."

2. Allen Ross, *Creation and Blessing: A Guide to the Study and Exposition of Genesis* (Grand Rapids: Baker, 1996), 72–73.

3. The outline follows Bruce Wilkinson and Kenneth Boa, *Talk thru the Bible* (Nashville: B&H, 2002), 5–7.

4. John J. Davis, *Paradise to Prison: Studies in Genesis* (Grand Rapids: Baker, 1975), 26.

5. G. C. Aalders, *Genesis*, BSC (Grand Rapids: Zondervan, 1981), 1:51.

6. O. T. Allis, *God Spake by Moses* (Philadelphia: Presbyterian & Reformed, 1977), 12.

7. John MacArthur, *The Battle for the Beginning* (Nashville: Thomas Nelson, 2001), 15.

8. Aalders, *Genesis*, 1:108.

9. Ross, *Creation & Blessing*, 174.

10. See John Whitcomb and Henry Morris, *The Genesis Flood* (Philadelphia: Presbyterian and Reformed, 1961); Henry Morris, *The Genesis Record* (Grand Rapids: Baker, 1976), 163–244.

11. The Angel of the LORD is a theophany (appearance of God in human form) and is most likely a preincarnate appearance of Christ in the Old Testament (Gen 18:1; 22:11; Josh 5:13–15; Judg 6:11–16; 13:3). See James Borland, *Christ in the Old Testament* (Chicago: Moody Press, 1978).

12. On the conservative view of the chronology, see Davis, *Paradise to Prison*, 266–67.

13. Ross, *Creation & Blessing*, 703. Judah was selected for this honor because Reuben, Simeon, and Levi were disqualified.

14. Paul House, *Old Testament Theology* (Downers Grove, IL: InterVarsity Press, 1998), 58; cf. E. Merrill, "A Theology of the Pentateuch," in *A Biblical Theology of the Old Testament*, ed. Roy Zuck (Chicago: Moody Press, 1991), 30.

Chapter 5

EXODUS

Liberation of Israel

The book of Exodus tells a dramatic story of slavery, emancipation, and liberation. Its images are so powerful they are quoted more than 120 times in the Hebrew Bible. Exodus is the story of the Israelites' exit from bondage in Egypt. The account includes the years of Israel's servitude in Egypt, the call of Moses, the confrontation with Pharaoh, the dramatic events of the exodus, and Israel's arrival at Mount Sinai to receive the law from Jehovah (Yahweh) God.

Exodus is also the story of God's love for His people. Yahweh is not an aloof, inactive, functionless deity. He sees, hears, observes, and cares about the struggles of His people (Exod 3:7). He is an intensely involved, vitally concerned moral being who demands that His creatures reflect His moral attributes. Jewish scholar Nahum Sarna observes, "History, therefore, is the arena of divine activity. . . . The nation is the product of God's providence, conditioned by human response to His demands."[1]

The pyramids at Giza in Egypt. The three great pyramids are on the left. The lesser pyramids are on the right.

KEY FACTS

Author:	Moses
Recipients:	Israelites
Date:	1445 BC
Key Word:	Passover (Hb. *pesach*)
Key Verse:	"God replied to Moses, 'I AM WHO I AM. This is what you are to say to the Israelites: I AM has sent me to you'" (Exod 3:14).

The Mosaic authorship of the book is vigorously debated, but several lines of evidence point to Moses as the book's author. First, the book is interconnected with Genesis, for Exod 1:1–7 picks up where Gen 50:26 leaves off. Furthermore, Jacob's family that came down to Egypt in Exod 1:1–7 bears resemblance to Gen 46:8–27. Second, the book of Exodus itself claims that Moses spoke and recorded some of the book's content (Exod 15:1; 17:14; 24:4, 7, 12; 31:18; 34:27). Third, the rest of the Old Testament claims Moses as the book's author (Josh 8:31; Mal 4:4). Fourth, the New Testament indicates that Moses wrote Exodus (John 1:45; 5:46–47; 7:19, 22–23; Mark 7:10; 12:26; Luke 2:22–23; 20:37; Rom 10:5). Fifth, extrabiblical material, including the Dead Sea Scrolls (CD 5:1–2; 7:6, 8–9; 1 QS 5:15) and the Babylonian Talmud (*Baba Bathra* 14b–15a), indicate that Moses authored the book.

The details of the Exodus account reflect an Egyptian cultural background, which included the enslavement of foreigners as brick makers, the common use of midwives to deliver babies, the use of birth stools, snake charming by priestly magicians, worship of

The Sphinx in front of the Khafre Pyramid at Giza in Egypt.

calf deities such as Apis, the veneration of the Nile River, the reference to the king as Pharaoh ("Great House"), and the occupation of the Egyptian delta by Semites.[2] The covenant structure and pattern of the Israelite legal system reflected in Exodus clearly indicates a firsthand knowledge of scribal methods, international treaties, and legal terminology typical of the mid–second millennium BC. Kitchen argues convincingly that the content of Exodus can hardly reflect the work of a "runaway rabble of brick-making slaves."[3] Rather, he suggests it is the work of a Hebrew leader who was experienced with the life of the Egyptian court and yet had a traditional Semitic social background, just as Moses is described in the book of Exodus.

Date of the Exodus

The date of the book is contingent upon how one dates the exodus event. Hill and Walton correctly observe, "Pinpointing the date of the exodus constitutes one of the major chronological problems of Old Testament study."[4] The significance of the exodus date in turn affects the date of the conquest of Canaan, the length of the Judges period, and the credibility of various chronological references in the Old Testament (1 Kgs 6:1; Judg 11:26). Those holding to the early date (1446 BC) for the exodus identify Thutmose III (1504–1450 BC) as the pharaoh of the oppression and Amenhotep II (1450–1425 BC) as the pharaoh of the exodus. Those preferring the late date (1290 BC) view Ramesses I (1320–1318 BC) and Seti I (1318–1304 BC) as the pharaohs of the oppression and Ramesses II (1304–1237 BC) as the pharaoh of the exodus.

The Merneptah Stele that contains the first mention of Israel.

Arguments for the *early date* (1446 BC) are generally based on the following observations:[5] (1) First Kings 6:1 states the exodus occurred 480 years prior to King Solomon's fourth year (966 BC), dating the exodus in 1446 BC. (2) Jephthah claimed Israel had occupied Canaan for 300 years (Judg 11:26). Adding forty years for the wilderness journey puts the date of the exodus between 1446 and 1400 BC. (3) The Merneptah Stele (c. 1220 BC) refers to "Israel" as an already established people in the land in the record of Ramesses II's son. This hardly allows time for the exodus, wilderness wandering, conquest, and settlement of Canaan by the Israelites. (4) The Amarna Tablets (c. 1400 BC) refer to a period of chaos in Canaan, which would equate with the Israelite conquest. (5) The Dream Stele of Thutmose IV, who followed

Amenhotep II, indicates he was not the firstborn legal heir to the throne, the eldest son having died.

The following arguments support the *late date* of the exodus: (1) The biblical data is reinterpreted as symbolic (480 years = 12 generations) or exaggerated generalizations (Jephthah's 300 years). (2) No extrabiblical references to "Israel" exist prior to the Merneptah Stele (c. 1220 BC). (3) Archaeological evidence seems to be lacking for a fifteenth-century BC conquest at some archaeological sites. (4) The Israelites helped build the cities of Pithom and Rameses (Exod 1:11), which were completed by Ramesses II. (5) Overlapping judgeships may account for tabulating a shorter period of time for the conquest, settlement, and Judges era.

The major weakness of the late-date view is that it totally discards any literal reading of the biblical chronology in favor of highly debatable and inconclusive archaeological data. It is entirely likely that future excavations will continue to clarify this picture. In the meantime minimalist critics discount the entire story of the exodus and conquest as Jewish mythology, making any date for the exodus irrelevant for them. Those who take the biblical account at face value have offered a more than adequate defense of their position.[6] Thus, assuming Mosaic authorship and the early date of the exodus, one could date the writing of the book anytime between the two years after the exodus (1444 BC) and Moses' death (1406 BC). The earlier end of this spectrum seems more appropriate since the events described occurred then.

Statue of Rameses (Ramesses II) and his daughter at the Karnak Temple in Egypt.

Route of the Exodus

Scholars have advanced three theories as possible explanations for the route of the exodus. First, the *northern theory* places Mount Sinai in the northwestern area of the Sinai. However, this is not consistent with the ten-day journey between Kadesh and Mount Sinai (Deut 1:2) and does not acknowledge that God led Israel away from the Philistine fortresses along the coast (Exod 13:17). Second, the *central theory* places Mount Sinai in Arabia (at Jabel-Al Lawz), beyond the gulf of Aqaba, east of the Sinai Peninsula. However, scholars have been reluctant to embrace this view because it is

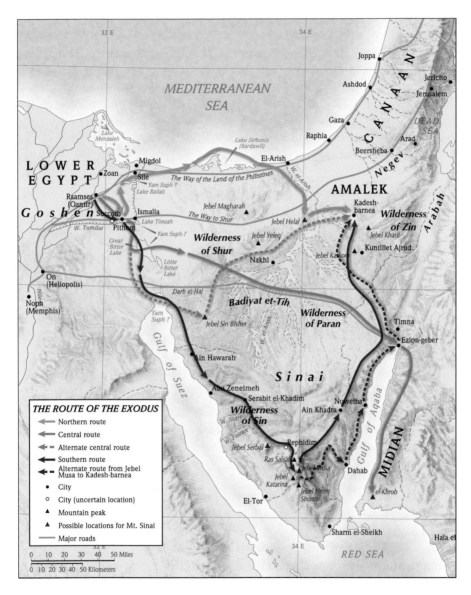

virtually impossible to reach the crossing point into Arabia in eleven days.[7] Third, the *southern theory* places Mount Sinai near the southern tip of the Sinai Peninsula. This theory takes into consideration the general direction of the movement of the nation after leaving Egypt. Whichever of these three views the interpreter holds, dogmatism should be avoided since new archeological discoveries are constantly being made adding new light to the subject.[8]

Message

The book of Exodus focuses on Moses' life, which can be divided into three forty-year time periods. They include the period from his birth to his rearing as a prince of Egypt (Acts 7:13), the time he spent in Midian as a shepherd (Exod 7:7), and the time he spent as leader of the people in the exodus and wilderness journeys (Acts 7:36). The book of Exodus covers the first two of these periods and introduces the third period.

Outline

I. **Exodus from Egyptian Bondage (1:1–18:27)**
   A. Redemption (1:1–12:30)
   B. Liberation (12:31–15:21)
   C. Preservation (15:22–18:27)
II. **Instruction for the Redeemed Nation (19:1–40:38)**
   A. Offer of the Covenant (19:1–25)
   B. Covenant Text (20:1–23:33)
   C. Covenant Ratification Ceremony (24:1–18)
   D. Tabernacle of Worship (25:1–40:38)

I. Exodus from Egyptian Bondage (Exodus 1:1–18:27)

The first half of the book involves God's redemption of his elect nation Israel from Egypt in three phases: redemption (1:1–12:30), liberation (12:31–15:21), and preservation (15:22–18:27). Moses begins by providing information concerning why redemption was necessary (1:1–22).

A. Redemption (1:1–12:30)

After Jacob's descendants migrated into Egypt, they began to experience numerical growth (1:1–7) as promised by the Abrahamic covenant (Gen 13:16).[9] Following Joseph's death, a pharaoh arose who did not know Joseph[10] and subjugated the Jewish people (1:8–14). Another pharaoh attempted to reduce Israel's population through the practice of infanticide (1:15–22), but God multiplied the people.

The next major section (1:8–12:30) focuses on how God used Moses to accomplish Israel's redemption. By divine plan Moses was raised and educated in Pharaoh's household (2:1–10) so that he could be used to deliver Israel from Egypt. However, as Moses grew into adulthood, his spiritual immaturity led to the killing of an Egyptian, so it was necessary for God to train his servant an additional forty years in the wilderness of Midian, the place where he would later lead the Israelites for forty years.

The major turning point came when Moses encountered God at the burning bush (3:1–10). In the process God revealed Himself as "I AM WHO I AM" (3:14) in response to Moses' question, "What is his name?" (3:13). The term "I AM" is the first-person form of the Hebrew verb *hayah*, "to be." The name implies that God is the Self-Existent One. The name was written as YHWH (יהוה) and is generally vocalized as Yahweh ("Jehovah," KJV).

Exodus 5:1–12:30 describes how God redeemed Israel by demonstrating His sovereignty over the Egyptian pantheon that was holding the nation in bondage. Yahweh's request to release His firstborn son, Israel, eventually

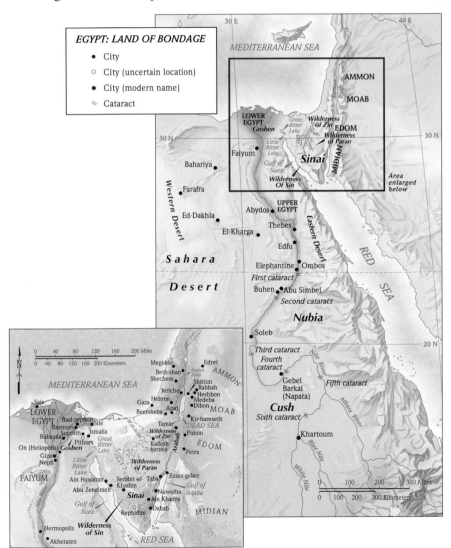

resulted in the death of the firstborn Egyptians in the tenth plague. Given the context of the story, it is obvious the ten plagues were intended to show Yahweh's superiority over the gods of Egypt and Pharaoh himself (Exod 12:12).

The climax to the account was the tenth plague, the Passover (12:1–4) when the "death angel" passed over Egypt, claiming the lives of the firstborn, including Pharaoh's son. To escape this plague, the Israelites sacrificed an unblemished lamb, spread its blood on their doorposts, roasted the lamb, and ate it along with unleavened bread and bitter herbs. This sacrificial meal (*pesach*) was the prelude to the exodus. Their faith became the basis of the nation's redemption. Thus, God mandated that Israel celebrate the Passover Feast and Feast of Unleavened Bread (*matsah*) throughout the generations to commemorate the speed with which redeemed Israel left Egypt (12:15–20). Jesus shed His blood for our redemption at the time of Passover (John 19:14), fulfilling John the Baptist's statement: "Behold, the lamb of God who takes away the sin of the world!" (John 1:29 NASB).[11]

B. Liberation (Exodus 12:31–15:21)

After Pharaoh finally gave Israel permission to leave Egypt (12:31–36), the redeemed nation journeyed from Rameses to Succoth (12:37–42). This was the first major move of the nation after 430 years of bondage in Egypt (12:40). Although the nation was delivered from slavery, her liberation was tested by Pharaoh's pursuing army (14:3–14). However, God accomplished the nation's complete liberation from Egypt by allowing Israel miraculously to pass through the Red Sea (14:15–22) and by drowning the pursuing Egyptian army (14:23–31). The nation then celebrated its liberation by singing the famous Song of the Sea (15:1–21).

C. Preservation (15:22–18:27)

Israel's liberation from Egypt (12:31–15:21) did not end its problems, for now it needed God's preservation in the barren wilderness (15:22–18:27). God's miraculous provisions included guidance to the oasis at Elim (15:22–27) and the provision of manna (Hb. *man hu*, "what is it?") to feed the people. Despite these provisions (15:22–18:27), the people routinely grumbled, did not believe God, and were disobedient. Although they were elect (4:22–23) and redeemed (12:21–30), they still needed further guidance regarding how to live the sanctified life. That guidance would be provided in the Mosaic covenant (chaps. 19–40).

II. Instruction for the Redeemed Nation (Exodus 19:1–40:38)

Although God sovereignly guided and provided for the nation, it was unclear how this newly redeemed nation was to conduct itself toward God, toward one another, and toward the rest of the world. These issues were resolved through the provision of the Mosaic covenant (chaps. 19–40), which taught them how redeemed people are to live in this world.

A. Offer of the Covenant (Exodus 19:1–25)

After Israel traveled to the foot of Mount Sinai (19:1–2), God explained that Israel would become a holy nation and a kingdom of priests if they accepted the covenant and adhered to its terms (19:3–6). Thus, the Mosaic covenant offered the nation the opportunity to be the vessel through which God would transmit His redemptive purposes to the rest of mankind. After Israel accepted God's offer of the covenant (19:7–8), the nation then

Jebel Musa, the traditional site of Mount Sinai, in the southern Sinai Peninsula.

consecrated itself to God (19:9–15) as God manifested Himself to Moses on Mount Sinai (19:16–25) in preparation for giving the covenant text (chaps. 20–23).

B. Covenant Text (Exodus 20:1–23:33)

The covenant text (chaps. 20–23) spells out the obligations Israel must meet in order to allow the suzerain (God) to bless the vassal (Israel). The covenant text consists of the Decalogue, the Ten Commandments, (20:1–21) and the book of the covenant (20:22–23:33). The Decalogue is the foundational covenant text while the book of the covenant spells out how the Decalogue is to be applied in the everyday life of the nation. The first four of the Ten Commandments pertain to the individual's relationship to God while the remaining six pertain to how members of the community are to relate to one another.

Ten Commandments
Exodus 20:1–17

RESPONSIBILITIES TO GOD

1. "No other gods" vs. polytheism
2. "Do not make an idol" vs. idolatry
3. "Do not misuse the name" vs. profanity
4. "Remember the Sabbath" vs. secularism

RESPONSIBILITIES TO PEOPLE

5. "Honor your father and mother" vs. rebellion
6. "Do not murder" vs. murder
7. "Do not commit adultery" vs. adultery
8. "Do not steal" vs. theft
9. "False testimony" vs. lying
10. "Do not covet" vs. materialism

C. Covenant Ratification Ceremony (Exodus 24:1–18)

The duplicate copies of the covenant text (24:3–4, 12), the vassal's verbal commitment to follow the terms of the covenant (24:3), the sprinkling of the altar with blood (24:4–8), and the meal between the covenant parties (24:9–11) are all germane to ancient Near East covenant ratification ceremonies.[12]

D. Tabernacle of Worship (Exodus 25:1–40:38)

The construction of the tabernacle (*mishkan*) or "tent of meeting" represented how God was to dwell among His people and how the nation would fellowship with God. The tabernacle was to be created according to exact divine specifications since it represented the place where God would dwell among His people (25:8). The ark of the covenant and mercy seat represented His presence (25:1–22), the table of bread represented His provision (25:23–30), and the lamp stand represented His guidance (25:31–40; 27:20–21; 30:22–33).

Of paramount significance was the existence of the veil separating the holy place from the most holy place (26:31–35). This veil represented the barrier between holy God and sinful man (Matt 27:51). The bronze altar where the animal sacrifices were to be offered (27:1–8) illustrated that people could only come to a holy God through the atoning work of a sacrifice

A cutaway illustration of the tabernacle from Randall Price, Rose Guide to the Temple (Torrance, CA: Rose Publishing, Inc, 2012). Used by permission.

rather than through their own meritorious works. The single doorway indicated there was only one way into God's presence, not many ways. The description of the priesthood (chaps. 28–29) explained how certain elements were necessary before any person could approach God. The existence of the laver (30:17–21) communicated that a person must be cleansed both physically and spiritually before approaching God, and the altar of incense signified the importance of worship and prayer (30:1–10, 34–38).

Ark of the covenant replica.

The instructions for building the tabernacle (35:1–39:31) and inspecting it (39:32–43) were given to Moses, and then it was erected (40:1–33) and indwelt by God (40:34–38). The presence of God's glory (*kabod*) represented His personal presence with His people. The tabernacle instructions and construction (chaps. 25–40) explained to the redeemed nation how they were to worship God, who now lived among them.

REFLECTION

Drawing Nearer

When Jesus died on the cross, the veil of the temple was rent from top to bottom, exposing the holy of holies (Matt 27:51). He became the ultimate sacrifice for our sins, and through His blood we have access to the presence of God (Heb 4:15–16; 10:19–22). Therefore, we are encouraged to "draw near" to God. As you grow in your faith, be encouraged to seek His presence. He wants you to come closer and really get to know Him. Are you ready? It is never too late to get started on your spiritual journey.

Practical Application

The book of Exodus is foundational to both Jewish and Christian theology. Arnold and Beyer state, "The exodus as salvation event was the formative beginning of the nation of Israel historically and theologically."[13] It illustrates how God is the Redeemer from injustice, sin, and oppression and, thus, serves as a paradigm for all future redemption. As the great Liberator, Yahweh sets His people free to worship and serve Him. He is also the source of the Judeo-Christian ethical system, which is summarized in the Ten Commandments. As you read this book, ask God to reveal the importance of obeying His laws and living by His standards.

For Further Reading

Cassuto, Umberto. *A Commentary on the Book of Exodus*. Jerusalem: Magnes Press, 1967.
Davis, John J. *Moses and the Gods of Egypt*. Grand Rapids: Baker, 1998.
Hannah, John D. "Exodus." *BKC*. Colorado Springs, CO: Chariot Victor, 1983, 103–62.
Kaiser, Walter. "Exodus." *EBC*. Grand Rapids: Zondervan, 2008, 1:333–561.
Motyer, Alec. *The Message of Exodus*. Downers Grove, IL: InterVarsity Press, 2005.
Sarna, Nahum. *Exploring Exodus*. New York: Schocken Books, 1986.

Study Questions

1. How did God use Moses' background to prepare him to confront the pharaoh of Egypt?
2. What is the significance of the divine name: I AM?
3. How does the Passover prefigure Christ's death for us?
4. How do the Ten Commandments form the basis of the Judeo-Christian ethic?
5. How does the tabernacle symbolically picture our relationship to God?
6. What is God teaching you about the importance of worship?

Notes

1. Nahum Sarna, *Exploring Exodus* (New York: Schocken Books, 1986), 1.
2. Randall Price, *The Stones Cry Out* (Eugene, OR: Harvest House, 1997), 125–40; K. A. Kitchen, *On the Reliability of the Old Testament* (Grand Rapids: Eerdmans, 2003), 241–312.
3. Kitchen, *On the Reliability of the Old Testament*, 295.
4. Andrew E. Hill and John H. Walton, *A Survey of the Old Testament*, 3rd ed. (Grand Rapids: Zondervan, 2009), 105.
5. Ibid. See charts 106–7.
6. See detailed discussions in J. Maxwell Miller and J. H. Hayes, *A History of Ancient Israel and Judah* (Philadelphia: Westminster Press, 1986); contra Bryant Wood, "Did the Israelites Conquer Jericho?" *Biblical Archaeology Review* (September/October 1990): 45–69; William Dever, "How to Tell an Israelite from a Canaanite," *Recent Archaeology in the Land of Israel*, ed. H. Shanks (Washington, DC: Biblical Archaeology Society, 1985), 35–41.
7. Gordon Franz, "Is Mount Sinai in Saudi Arabia?" *Bible and Spade* 13(4):101–13.
8. For example, see Lennart Möller, *The Exodus Case* (Copenhagen: Scandinavia, 2002).
9. Genesis 46:26 says that sixty-six people entered Egypt while Exodus 1:5 places the number at seventy. However, the Genesis text omits Joseph, Joseph's two sons Ephraim and Manasseh, and Jacob (see Gen 46:27). While the LXX, Acts 7:14, and a Qumran document list the number at seventy-five, this number probably includes Joseph's three grandsons and two great grandsons that are mentioned in Numbers 26 (See Gen 46:26 in the LXX where these names are added); Gleason Archer, *A Survey of Old Testament Introduction* (Chicago: Moody, 1985), 238.
10. Joseph died at the end of the Twelfth Dynasty. The decline of the Twelfth Dynasty led to the chaotic reign of the Asiatic Hyksos. Later native Egyptians overthrew the Hyksos. These events ushered in the Eighteenth Dynasty of the New Kingdom period. This was the regime that oppressed Israel. Its founder, Ahmose I (1570–1546), oppressed the chosen people since he viewed them as pro-Hyksos agents. Charles Dyer and Gene Merrill, *The Old Testament Explorer: Discovering the Essence, Background, and Meaning of Every Book in the Old Testament* (Nashville: Thomas Nelson, 2001), 43–44.
11. See Brant Pitre, *Jesus and the Jewish Roots of the Eucharist* (Garden City, NY: Doubleday, 2011).
12. For a comparison of the six elements of the contemporary Hittite suzerain-vassal treaty structure with the Mosaic covenant, see M. Kline, *Treaty of the Great King* (Grand Rapids: Eerdmans, 1963).
13. Bill Arnold and Bryan Beyer, *Encountering the Old Testament* (Grand Rapids: Baker, 1999), 111.

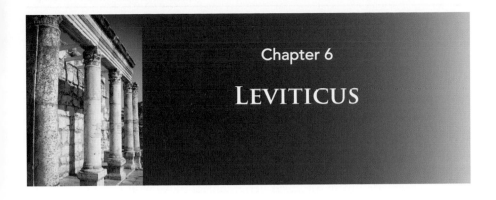

Chapter 6

LEVITICUS

Way of Holiness

Holiness and ceremonial cleanness are the major themes of the book of Leviticus, which is the worship guide for both priests and laymen in Israel. It describes the way laymen needed to approach the Holy One, how priests were to assist this process, and how all the people were to live in personal holiness. Gordon Wenham states: "Holiness characterizes God himself and all that belongs to him. . . . Holiness is intrinsic to God's character."[1] Thus, He commands, "Be holy, for I am holy" (Lev 11:44–45; 19:2; 20:26, author's translation).

KEY FACTS

Author:	Moses
Recipients:	Israel at Sinai
Date:	1445 BC
Key Word:	Holiness (Hb. *qodesh*)
Key Verse:	"He is to lay his hand on the head of the burnt offering so it can be accepted on his behalf to make atonement for him" (Lev 1:4).

The purpose of the book of Leviticus was to teach Israel how they were to walk in practical holiness with God, which was necessary because of Israel's status as God's elect (Exod 4:22–23), redeemed (Exodus 12), and regenerated (Exod 14:31) nation. A people of such exalted spiritual status needed to know how their daily behavior should conform to their status as holy people.

Background

The book of Leviticus picks up where Exodus left off. God revealed the contents of Leviticus to Moses after the renewal of the Mosaic covenant (Exodus 32–34) and His indwelling of the tabernacle (Exod 40:34–38). Because the events of the book transpired after their arrival at Sinai but before the nation departed from Sinai, no geographical movement is represented in the book of Leviticus. All of the allotted events took place while the nation was encamped at Sinai.

The Jews entitled this book "The Law of the Priests" and "The Law of the Offerings" after its subject matter.[2] The LXX entitled it *Leuitikon*, which means "that which pertains to the Levites," and so the English title comes from the Greek. Leviticus is a book about the priestly offerings and the religious festivals of the Jewish people.

Author

Although the book of Leviticus is an anonymous work, several lines of evidence point to Moses as the book's author. First, the book repeatedly reiterates how God imparted the law to Moses (1:1; 27:34). This concept appears fifty-six times in Leviticus's twenty-seven chapters. Second, Leviticus is the sequel to Exodus. Harrison notes the connection between the two books when he says, "Leviticus enlarges upon matters involving the ordering of worship at the divine sanctuary that are mentioned only briefly in Exodus."[3]

Outline

I. Way to the Holy One: Sacrifice (1:1–10:20)
    A. Laws of Sacrifice (1:1–7:38)
    B. Laws of Priesthood (8:1–10:20)
II. Way of Holiness: Sanctification (11:1–27:34)
    A. Laws of Purity (11:1–15:33)
    B. Day of Atonement (16:1–34)
    C. Holiness Code (17:1–27:34)

Message

The message of Leviticus is that the nation could achieve progressive sanctification and thus become distinct from the surrounding nations through daily access to God via the sacrifices (chaps. 1–10) and through obedience (chaps. 11–27). Thus, the book places great emphasis on holiness (Hb. *qodesh*) which is used eighty-seven times in the book.

I. Way to the Holy One: Sacrifice (Leviticus 1:1–10:20)

In the first major section of the book (chaps. 1–10), Moses explains that sacrifices are essential for the Israelites to maintain access to God and thereby experience practical sanctification. Because God graciously accepts an innocent animal substitute as a payment for the penalty of sin, the nation can continue to experience daily fellowship with God in spite of their sin.

A. Laws of Sacrifices (Leviticus 1:1–7:38)

Moses outlines the five sacrifices that guarantee the Jew ongoing fellowship with God (chaps. 1–7). The first three sacrifices were voluntary (1:1–3:17) and were a sweet savor to the Lord (1:9, 13, 17; 2:9; 3:5, 16). The first sacrifice, the *burnt offering*, was given for the purpose of making atonement for sins in general and as a sign of a person's dedication (1:1–17). The second sacrifice was the meal or the *grain offering*, and it was offered as thanksgiving for the harvest (2:1–16). The third sacrifice was the fellowship or *peace offering*, which expressed thanksgiving and celebration regarding the reconciliation between the worshipper and God that was procured by the burnt offering (3:1–17).

Sacrificial System			
Name	**Reference**	**Elements**	**Significance**
Burnt Offering	Leviticus 1; 6:8–13	Bull, ram, male goat, male dove, or young pigeon without blemish. (Always male animals, but species of animal varied according to individual's economic status.)	Voluntary. Signifies propitiation for sin and complete surrender, devotion, and commitment to God.
Grain Offering. Also called Meal or Tribute Offering	Leviticus 2; 6:14–23	Grain, flour, or bread (always unleavened) made with olive oil and salt; or incense.	Voluntary. Signifies thanksgiving for firstfruits.

Sacrificial System (continued)			
Name	**Reference**	**Elements**	**Significance**
Fellowship Offering. Also called Peace Offering, which includes: (1) Thank Offering, (2) Vow Offering, and (3) Freewill Offering	Leviticus 3; 7:11–36; 22:17–30; 27	Any animal without blemish. (Species of animal varied according to individual's economic status.) Can be grain offering.	Voluntary. Symbolizes fellowship with God. (1) Signifies thankfulness for a specific blessing; (2) offers a ritual expression of a vow; and (3) symbolizes general thankfulness (to be brought to one of three required religious services).
Sin Offering	Leviticus 4:1–5:13; 6:24–30; 12:6–8	Male or female animal without blemish—as follows: bull for high priest or congregation; male goat for king; female goat or lamb for common person; dove or pigeon for slightly poor; tenth of an ephah of flour for the very poor.	Mandatory. Made by one who had sinned unintentionally or was unclean in order to attain purification.
Guilt Offering	Leviticus 5:14–6:7; 7:1–6; 14:12–18	Ram or lamb without blemish.	Mandatory. Made by a person who had either deprived another of his rights or had desecrated something holy. Made by lepers for purification.

The final two sacrifices (4:1–6:7) were compulsory and were issued for the purpose of restoring broken fellowship between the sinner and God. People brought a *sin offering* (4:1–5:13) for the purpose of making atonement for specific sins. The other offering, known as the trespass or *guilt offering* (5:4–6:7), was designed to atone for sin as well as make restitution for particular sins. Atonement involved offering a ram without defect. Restitution occurred with a monetary payment for the sin. This offering not only forgave the offender for specific sins, but it also reminded them that sin has ongoing temporal consequences even after God has forgiven it.[4]

B. Laws of Priesthood (Leviticus 8:1–10:20)

Because of the priests' importance in leading the nation into practical sanctification and fellowship with God through the proper administration of the sacrifices, the next three chapters (chaps. 8–10) are devoted to the priesthood. Specifically, these chapters cover the priests' consecration (chap. 8), commencement (chap. 9), and condemnation (chap. 10). While Exodus 28–29 explained how the priests were to be selected, anointed, and outfitted for their ministry, Leviticus 8–9 essentially provides the fulfillment of these instructions.

Plate of pure gold with inscription: "HOLY TO THE LORD." Ex 28:36

Turban or mitre Ex 28:36-38

The shoulder straps for the breastplate capped with two onyx stones bearing the names of Israel's twelve sons, six on each, in order of their birth Ex 28:9-10

Twelve gemstones, each bearing a name of one of the twelve tribes Ex 28:17-21

Sash Ex 28:4,39,40

Ephod, woven and reflecting the colors of the sanctuary Ex 28:5-15,31

Fringe composed of alternating pomegranates and gold bells; the pomegranates are woven from blue, purple, and scarlet yarn Ex 28:33-35

Artist's rendition of the high priest's garments (Exod 28:1–38).

II. Way of Holiness: Sanctification (Leviticus 11:1–27:34)

The laws of sanctification were intended to mark Israel as a unique people who were "separated" from the practices of their pagan neighbors. Thus, the laws of Leviticus designate everything as either "holy" or "common," and common things, in turn, were considered either "clean" or "unclean." Wenham notes that clean things became "holy" when they were sanctified and "holy" things, when defiled, could become either common or polluted. Thus, the laws of purity were related to the entire concept of sanctification.

A. Laws of Purity (Leviticus 11:1–15:33)

Moses continues with the theme of Israel's progressive sanctification through fellowship with God by commanding the nation to embrace the clean and to reject the unclean (chaps. 11–15). Although many of these distinctions seem related to hygienic concerns, their overriding purpose was to distinguish Israel from the pagan practices of her Canaanite neighbors. The basic principles of holiness and cleanness were related to wholeness and completeness; thus everything presented at the tabernacle had to be physically perfect and without blemish.[5] Even priests and worshippers were required to "wash" in a *mikveh* in the days of the temple (Lev 14:8).

B. Day of Atonement (Leviticus 16:1–34)

The Day of Atonement (*yom kippur*) was the holiest day on the Hebrew calendar. It occurred ten days after the Feast of Trumpets, following the "days of awe."[6] In Leviticus 16 it represents the high point in the unit dealing with the sacrifices (chaps. 1–16). On this special day the properly attired high priest (Aaron) would enter into the holy place. First, a bull was slaughtered for Aaron's sins. Then two goats were selected to be used for the differ-ent purposes of propi-

A mikveh from the Second Temple period located just below the southern steps in Jerusalem.

tiation and expiation. The first goat was killed and its blood was sprinkled on the mercy seat on the ark of the covenant in the most holy place. This event represented the only time during the year when Aaron could enter the most holy place. After the sins of the nation were symbolically transferred to the second goat (the "scapegoat"), it was then released into the wilderness.

C. Holiness Code (Leviticus 17:1–27:34)

Moses continues to exhort national sanctification and distinctiveness through obedient (chaps. 17–27) adherence to God's instruction. Next Moses focuses on how Israel should exhibit holy behavior toward God and man (chap. 19). He points out that a proper understanding of God's holy character furnishes a natural incentive for obeying both the horizontal (man to man) and vertical (man to God) aspects of the Decalogue (19:1–4). The principles of moral and social behavior in this section form the foundation for Judeo-Christian ethics.

The nation could also experience sanctified obedience by appearing before the Lord regularly to worship and celebrate various aspects of their covenant relationship with Him. Thus, Moses laid down requirements for national worship (chaps. 23–24) by enumerating Israel's seven religious feasts. They include Passover and Unleavened Bread (23:4–8), Firstfruits (23:9–14), Pentecost (23:15–22), Trumpets (23:23–25), Atonement (23:26–32), and Booths or Tabernacles (23:33–35).

The first four feasts took place in the *spring*. Passover (*pesach*) remembered the nation's redemption from Egypt. Unleavened Bread (*matsot*) commemorated the nation's separation from Egypt. Firstfruits (*bikkurim*) praised God for the firstfruits of the harvest in expectation for the full harvest. Pentecost (*shavu'oth*) involved the marking of the wheat harvest as well as thankfulness for the harvest. Uniquely, these spring feasts were fulfilled with the death, burial, and resurrection of Christ and the baptism of the Holy Spirit on the day of Pentecost (Acts 2).

The *fall* feasts began with Trumpets (*rosh hashanah*) celebrating the beginning of the New Year. Atonement (*yom kippur*) dealt with annual covering of national sin. Tabernacles (*succoth*) remembered God's provision throughout the wilderness wanderings from Egypt to Canaan.

Israel was expected to continue to practice sanctified obedience after arriving in Canaan (chaps. 25–26). Israel could honor God in the land by honoring His Sabbath-rest principle by resting on the weekly Sabbath (23:1–3) as well as the Sabbath (25:1–7) every seventh year. They were also to honor it on a forty-nine-year basis by allowing the fiftieth year or the Jubilee Year to be a year of rest (25:8–55).

Jewish Feasts and Festivals				
Name	**Month**	**Date**	**Reference**	**Significance**
Passover	Nisan	(Mar./Apr.): 14–21	Exod 12:2–20; Lev 23:5	Commemorates God's deliverance of Israel out of Egypt.
Festival of Unleavened Bread	Nisan	(Mar./Apr.): 15–21	Lev 23:6–8	Commemorates God's deliverance of Israel out of Egypt. Includes a Day of Firstfruits for the barley harvest.
Festival of Harvest, or Weeks (Pentecost)	Sivan	(May/June): 6 (seven weeks after Passover)	Exod 23:16; 34:22; Lev 23:15–21	Commemorates the giving of the law at Mount Sinai. Includes a Day of Firstfruits for the wheat harvest.
Festival of Trumpets (Rosh Hashanah)	Tishri	(Sept./Oct.): 1	Lev 23:23–25; Num 29:1–6	Day of the blowing of the trumpets to signal the beginning of the civil new year.
Day of Atonement (Yom Kippur)	Tishri	(Sept./Oct.): 10	Exod 30:10; Lev 23:26–33;	On this day the high priest makes atonement for the nation's sin. Also a day of fasting.
Festival of Booths, or Tabernacles (Sukkot)	Tishri	(Sept./Oct.): 15–21	Lev 23:33–43; Num 29:12–39; Deut 16:13	Commemorates the forty years of wilderness wandering.
Festival of Dedication, or Festival of Lights (Hanukkah)	Kislev and Tebeth	(Nov./Dec.): 25–30; and Tebeth (Dec./Jan.): 1–2	John 10:22	Commemorates the purification of the temple by Judas Maccabaeus in 164 BC.
Feast of Purim, or Esther	Adar	(Feb./Mar.): 14	Esther 9	Commemorates the deliverance of the Jewish people in the days of Esther.

In order to provide an incentive for sanctification through obedience once inside the land, Moses explained the law of covenant blessings and curses (chap. 26). He told the Israelites that obedience was the condition for blessing by enumerating the physical, material, and national blessings that would come when Israel obeyed the terms of the covenant (26:4–13; Deut 28:1–14). Moses then summarized the physical, material, and national curses for disobedience (26:14–39; Deut 28:15–68).

In the final section of the book (chaps. 17–27), Moses has assembled a wide variety of material explaining how Israel could experience sanctification by conforming their daily lives to God's revealed will. While the book of Exodus explained how Israel received its calling to be a kingdom of priests (Exod 19:5–6), the book of Leviticus explains how Israel is to live out this priestly calling.

Practical Application

The holiness of God is the dominant theological theme of Leviticus. God is pictured as an ever-present, personal, holy God who demands holiness from those who want to have a covenant relationship with Him. The New Testament writer Peter draws on the theme of holiness when he quotes the Levitical injunction, "But as the One who called you is holy, you also are to be holy in all your conduct; for it is written, Be holy because I am holy" (1 Pet 1:15–16). Paul adds, "I urge you to present your bodies as a living sacrifice, holy and pleasing to God" (Rom 12:1). Only the sacrificial atonement of the sinless Son of God is sufficient to cleanse us from sin and unrighteousness (1 John 1:7).

For Further Reading

Gane, Roy. *Leviticus, Numbers*. NIVAC. Grand Rapids: Zondervan, 2004.

Harrison, R. K. *Leviticus: An Introduction and Commentary*. TOTC. Downers Grove, IL: InterVarsity, 1980.

Lindsey, Duane F. "Leviticus." *BKC*. Colorado Springs: Chariot Victor, 1983.

Rooker, Mark F. *Leviticus*. NAC. Nashville: B&H, 2000.

Ross, Allen. *Holiness to the Lord: A Guide to Leviticus*. Grand Rapids: Baker, 2002.

Wenham, Gordon J. *The Book of Leviticus*. NICOT. Grand Rapids: Eerdmans, 1979.

Study Questions

1. How does Leviticus serve as a worship guide for the Jewish people?
2. Why is holiness important, and how does it distinguish God's character and His people?
3. How do the blood sacrifices prefigure the death of Christ?
4. How does the "Holiness Code" form the basis of the Judeo-Christian ethical system?
5. To what degree is personal holiness important to Christian believers today, and how can it be attained and maintained?

Notes

1. Gordon J. Wenham, *The Book of Leviticus*, NICOT (Grand Rapids: Eerdmans, 1979), 22.

2. R. K. Harrison, *Leviticus*, TOTC (Downers Grove, IL: InterVarsity, 1980), 13.

3. Ibid., 13–14.

4. For some of the more specific and nuanced differences between these sacrifices, see J. Barton Payne, *Encyclopedia of Biblical Prophecy: The Complete Guide to Scriptural Predictions and Their Fulfillment* (New York: Harper & Row, 1973), 193; Andrew E. Hill and John H. Walton, *A Survey of the Old Testament*, 3rd ed. (Grand Rapids: Zondervan, 2009), 125; *Nelson's Complete Book of Charts and Maps* (Nashville: Thomas Nelson, 1996), 44–45.

5. Later revelation makes clear that these laws are no longer binding upon the church (Ps 147:19–20; Mark 7:19; Acts 10:11–16).

6. For details see K. Howard and M. Rosenthal, *The Feasts of the Lord* (Orlando: Zion's Hope, 1991), 119–33.

Chapter 7

NUMBERS

Wilderness Journey

The book of Numbers tells the story of the wilderness journey. It serves as a travel diary of the Israelites after the exodus. The Hebrew title of the book is *bemidbar*, "in the wilderness." The English title is taken from the LXX *arithmoi* ("numbers") after the two censuses (chaps. 1, 26). After the giving of the law, the Lord instructed Moses to number the army of Israel, which included every male twenty years and older. Then God surrounded His dwelling place, the tabernacle, with an inner circle of priests and their assistants, the Levites, to safeguard it from ritual impurity. The rest of the Israelites encircled the Levites, camping under the banner of their respective tribes.[1] The census was designed to reorganize Israel into a military camp in preparation for the conquest of the Promised Land.

The Kadesh-barnea region south of Canaan.

KEY FACTS

Author:	Moses
Recipients:	Israel in the wilderness
Date:	1444–1406 BC
Key Word:	Number (Hb. *paqad*)
Key Verse:	"Your corpses will fall in this wilderness—all of you who were registered in the census, the entire number of you twenty years old or more—because you have complained about me" (14:29).

The story of the wilderness journey began with celebration and preparation at Mount Sinai. But it quickly turned to disappointment and failure as the people turned back at Kadesh-barnea and wandered in the desert for nearly forty years until the disobedient generation of adults perished in the wilderness. By the end of the story, the new generation, born in the wilderness, remobilized and proceeded to Moab in preparation to enter the Promised Land.

Author and Background

Numerous lines of evidence point to Moses as the author of the book of Numbers. First, the opening words of the book are "The Lord spoke to Moses" (1:1). This phrase occurs more than eighty times throughout the book. The book refers to itself as the statutes God gave to Moses (36:13). The book also refers to Moses' writing activity in relation to the book (33:1–2). Numbers appears in the middle of the Pentateuch and therefore provides the transition from Exodus-Leviticus to Deuteronomy, books that contain self-claims of Mosaic authorship (Exod 17:14; 19:7; 24:4; Deut 1:1; 31:24). This belief is reaffirmed by the New Testament, which assumes Mosaic authorship over the entire Pentateuch (Matt 8:4; 19:8; Luke 24:44; John 1:45; 5:46–47; Rom 10:5).[2]

The events recorded in Numbers took place over a period of thirty-eight years and nine months (Num 1:1; Deut 1:3), presumably between 1444 BC and 1406 BC. The book describes the first generation's pilgrimage to Canaan and failure to obtain the benefits of God's promises due to unbelief. In a

practical sense Numbers speaks to us today about the importance of obedience in our spiritual journey as well.

Message

Numbers tells the story of the initial success and ultimate failure of
the exodus generation. The Israelite males who experienced the miraculous deliverance of the exodus from Egypt succumbed to doubt, fear, and
unbelief. Having left the bondage of Egypt, they turned back in unbelief
at Kadesh-barnea and wandered in the Sinai wilderness thirty-eight more
years. By contrast the generation of Israelites who were born in the wilderness made the commitment to trust the Lord and moved on by faith.

The structure of the book comes from chapters 1 and 26, which represent the different censuses for the first and second generations respectively.
Chapters 13 and 14 mark a transition away from the prominence of the first
generation and refocus on the second generation. The first *faithless* generation failed to follow God in the wilderness (1:1–25:18), but the second *faithful* generation willingly followed God into the Promised Land (26:1–36:13).
The primary genre of the book is narrative. However, Dyer and Merrill note
the many subgenres displayed in the book, including census lists, travel
procedures, regulations for the priests and the Levites, sacrifice and ritual
instructions, inheritance rights, prophetic oracles, and poetry.[3]

Outline

I. First Generation (1:1–25:18)
    A. Preparation of the First Generation at Sinai (1:1–10:36)
    B. Failure of the First Generation (11:1–25:18)
II. Second Generation (26:1–36:13)
    A. Reorganization of Israel on the Plains of Moab (26:1–30:16)
    B. Preparation for Conquest of the Land (31:1–36:13)

I. First Generation (Numbers 1:1–25:18)

A. Preparation of the First Generation at Sinai (Numbers 1:1–10:36)

In the first major section of the book, Moses remembers the numerous
blessings God gave to the first generation (chaps. 1–10). These blessings are
divided into those pertaining to the organization of Israel (chaps. 1–4) and
those related to the nation's sanctification (chaps. 5–10). The section dealing
with the ordering of the tribes begins with a census of the tribes (1:1–45)

for the purpose of military organization and their arrangement around the tabernacle (2:1–34).

The next section (chaps. 3–4) records a census of the Levites so they could be organized into various clans. Not only were these clans arranged in different locations around the tabernacle (3:1–39), but they also were given various responsibilities over the tabernacle (4:1–33). While all priests were Levites, not all Levites were priests. A priest had not only to be a Levite, but he also had to be a descendant of Aaron. Only the priests had the privilege of administering the sacrifices while the nonpriest Levites were considered the priests' helpers.

Not only does Numbers describe the external order of the first generation (chaps. 1–4); it also describes its internal order through sanctification (chaps. 5–10). Four areas of spiritual blessing are emphasized. First, the people were to be sanctified by separation from those who were physically unclean (5:1–4). Second, the people were sanctified through the *Nazirite vow*, allowing them to devote themselves to God for a season (6:1–21). People could also be sanctified through the *Aaronic blessing* assuring them of God's continued grace upon them (6:22–27).[4] Third, they were sanctified through worship (7:1–9:14) at the tabernacle (7:1–89). Ultimately, the Israelites were sanctified through divine guidance by the cloud above the tabernacle (9:15–10:36). Today Jewish congregations sing Num 10:35 ("arise Adonai") as the scrolls are lifted in the Torah processional.[5]

Upon departing for the Wilderness of Paran (10:11–13), the Israelites were given divine guidance in the pillar of cloud by day and the pillar of fire by night (10:33–36). In sum the nation was sanctified through separation (5:1–4), vows (6:1–21), worship (7:1–9:14), and guidance (9:15–10:36). They had everything they needed to conquer Canaan. Furthermore, their journey from Sinai to Kadesh-barnea was a mere eleven days (Deut 1:2).

Silver amulet containing the blessing Moses gave to Aaron and his sons to use in blessing Israel.

B. Failure of the First Generation (Numbers 11:1–25:18)

Unfortunately, unbelief resulted in the first generation's disqualification from the blessings of Canaan. Chapters 11–12 foreshadow the climactic

This area northeast of Jebel Musa (Mount Sinai) is probably the Wilderness of Paran.

failure that transpired at Kadesh-barnea (13:1–14:45). Their unbelief and disobedience were so pervasive that Moses' own family challenged his divinely given authority (12:1–16). Disgruntled over Moses' marriage and ministerial supremacy, Moses' brother, Aaron, and sister, Miriam, rose up against him at Hazeroth. The divine judgment upon Miriam came in the form of leprosy, though Moses' gracious intercession led to her healing. After encamping in the wilderness of Paran (12:16), the nation finally arrived at Kadesh-barnea where the rebellion now reached its apex (13:1–14:45).

Racial Prejudice

Miriam and Aaron's objection was motivated by jealousy and prejudice. Moses' "Cushite wife" ("Ethiopian," KJV) may possibly refer to Zipporah (cf. Hab 3:7, which uses "Midianite" and "Cushite" interchangeably) or a second wife of African descent (the normal Hebrew usage of "Cushite") assuming Zipporah had died. However one interprets this text, it is clear that God defended Moses in this decision. Miriam's leprosy (extreme whiteness) was the opposite of the complexion of Moses' wife. While God called the Israelites into a unique covenant with Him, He did not exclude others from the opportunity of His blessings. Isaac married Rebekah, an Aramean; Jacob married Rachel and Leah, Aramean sisters; Judah fathered twins by Tamar, a Canaanite; and Joseph married Asenath, an Egyptian. All of these women later became mothers of the various tribes of Israelites. A thorough reading of the Pentateuch makes clear that the Abrahamic covenant was spiritual rather than racial.

Moses selected twelve men, one from each ancestral tribe, to scout out the land of Canaan in advance. After the spies returned with a negative report (13:26–33), Israel lapsed into unbelief and rebelled against God's command to take Canaan (14:1–10). Their desire to return to Egypt and to kill Moses and Aaron showed both a rejection of what God accomplished for them and a rejection of God's divinely chosen leaders. Although Moses' gracious intercession once again spared the first generation from immediate extinction (14:11–19), God permanently disinherited them from the land's blessings (14:20–38). Only Joshua and Caleb, the two faithful spies, plus all those who were under twenty years of age were exempt from responsibility. The determination of the age of twenty and above as the basis of God's judgment was based on the age of accountability and responsibility for military service (Num 1:3).

This is the turning point of the wilderness journey. What began so well ended in total failure as the majority of the Israelites turned back in unbelief. At this point the fate of the first generation was sealed. The exodus generation would not be the conquest generation. What originally was an eleven-day journey into Canaan (Deut 1:2) now became a forty-year sojourn of continual wandering in the wilderness (15:1–20:13).

Numbers 20:1 represents a key chronological marker in the book. It is the first month of the fortieth year after the exodus event (20:1). At this point Israel had wandered in the wilderness for thirty-eight years three months and ten days. But the book of Numbers reports almost nothing about these thirty-eight years that intervened between their first departure from Kadesh-barnea (14:25) and their second (20:22). However, the story of Moses' own failure (20:1–13), the nation's rebellion against Moses (20:2–5) at Meribah, and Aaron's death at Mount Hor (20:22–29) conveys the same lesson. All of these accounts provide a realistic picture of the consequences of unbelief. It seems highly unlikely that a later generation of Israelites would have simply mythologized these stories in such a negative manner.[6]

The Israelites' brief success against the king of Arad (21:1–3) was followed by failure when the people rebelled against Moses as they traveled along Edom's eastern border. God responded by sending serpents to destroy the people. Moses' intercession and God's grace through the provision of the bronze serpent prevented the entire generation from being destroyed (21:4–9). The Gospel of John refers to the lifting up of the bronze serpent in the wilderness as something comparable to the lifting up of the Son of Man (John 3:14).

Israel then traveled around Edom's eastern border and entered the territory of Moab east of Jericho (21:10–20). This area is still known today as Wadi Musa (Arabic for the "Valley of Moses"). The nation then experienced two victories over the Amorite king Sihon (21:21–32) and Og, the king of Bashan (21:33–35). The arrival at Moab introduces the Balaam oracles (22:1–24:25). Balaam was a *Baru* or sorcerer who specialized in manipulating and receiving information from various ancient Near East deities through incantation and divination. Although hired by Balak ("the Destroyer") the Moabite king to curse Israel, Balaam could only bless the covenanted nation and curse her adversaries through seven oracles (chaps. 23–24), which emphasize God's blessing on Israel.[7]

II. Second Generation (Numbers 26:1–36:13)

The second half of the book of Numbers shifts the reader's attention to the second generation's hopes for a better future. The story line in Numbers clearly indicates that God will bypass one generation if necessary and move on to the next generation.

A. Reorganization of Israel on the Plains of Moab (Numbers 26:1–30:16)

The second generation's blessings included Israel's political blessings (26:1–27:22). These involved another census for purposes of military conquest and inheritance rights (26:1–51), the divine decree that daughters with no surviving brothers had a right to inherit land from their fathers (27:1–11), the selection of Joshua as the new leader (27:12–23), and various blessings that would follow if the nation kept the covenant (chaps. 28–30).

B. Preparation for Conquest of the Land (Numbers 31:1–36:13)

A second set of blessings pertains to preparation for the conquest of Canaan. This section includes exhortations for covenant faithfulness and begins with the defeat of the Midianites (31:1–12). This section also mentions the settlement of Gad, Reuben, and half of Manasseh in the Transjordan (32:1–42). Fortunately, these eastern tribes pledged to help the other tribes conquer the land of Canaan. This section also explains the selection of leaders responsible for apportioning the land (34:13–39) as well as the establishment of Levitical cities (35:1–8) and cities of refuge (35:9–34) in Canaan. The Levitical cities allowed the Levites to live among the people throughout the land. The cities of refuge allowed justice to be exacted against murderers and also prevented innocent blood from being spilled due to vigilantism, thereby keeping the land free from spiritual pollution (35:33–34).

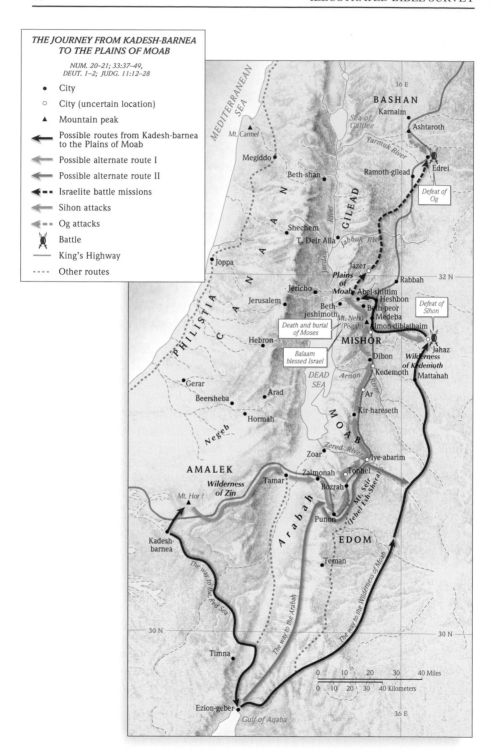

**THE JOURNEY FROM KADESH-BARNEA
TO THE PLAINS OF MOAB**

NUM. 20–21; 33:37–49,
DEUT. 1–2; JUDG. 11:12–28

- • City
- ○ City (uncertain location)
- ▲ Mountain peak
- ← Possible routes from Kadesh-barnea to the Plains of Moab
- ← Possible alternate route I
- ← Possible alternate route II
- ◄- - Israelite battle missions
- ← Sihon attacks
- ◄- - Og attacks
- ⚔ Battle
- — King's Highway
- - - - - Other routes

In conclusion, Moses emphasized the need for faith and obedience by the second generation by reminding them that the first generation was blessed (chaps. 1–10) yet disinherited solely due to disobedience (chaps. 11–25). The second generation was challenged to remain faithful to the Lord so they could receive their inheritance in the Promised Land (chaps. 26–36). Thus, the new generation, born in the wilderness, would accomplish what the exodus generation failed to do. The apostle Paul used these stories as "examples" for his readers as well (1 Cor 10:1–13).

Practical Application

Numbers is replete with many rich theological themes. They include God's holiness, man's sinfulness, the necessity of covenant obedience, and the consequences of disobedience. The book of Numbers also provides a practical insight into the depravity of human nature and the necessity of divine intervention in a fallen world. The wilderness journey reminds us that we too are on a spiritual pilgrimage in a fallen world. Just as the Israelites had to learn the lessons of obedience, so do we need to walk by faith in God's Word and obedience to His commands.

For Further Reading

Allen, Ronald B. "Numbers." *EBC*. Grand Rapids: Zondervan, 1990.
Cole, R. Dennis. *Numbers*. NAC. Nashville: B&H, 2000.
Feinberg, Jeffrey. *Walk Numbers!* Baltimore: Lederer Books, 2002.
Merrill, Eugene H. "Numbers." *BKC*. Colorado Springs, CO: Chariot Victor, 1983.
Wenham, Gordon J. *Numbers*. TOTC. Downers Grove, IL: InterVarsity, 1981.

Study Questions

1. In what way does the book of Numbers function as a travel diary?
2. What was the significance of age twenty as an age of accountability for Israelite men?
3. What lessons about racial discrimination can be learned from the incident involving Moses' wife?
4. Why was the failure of the Israelites at Kadesh-barnea so decisive?
5. How did the establishment of cities of refuge ensure social justice in Israel?
6. What does the book of Numbers teach us about our walk with God?

Notes

1. For a messianic Jewish perspective, see J. E. Feinberg, *Walk Numbers!* (Baltimore: Lederer Books, 2002), 13ff.

2. Cf. Raymond B. Dillard and Tremper Longman III, *An Introduction to the Old Testament* (Grand Rapids: Zondervan, 1994), 83; Merrill, "Numbers," in *BKC* (Colorado Springs, CO: Chariot Victor, 1983), 215; Gordon J. Wenham, *Numbers*, TOTC (Downers Grove, IL: InterVarsity, 1981), 4:15–16; R. K. Harrison, *Introduction to the Old Testament* (Peabody, MA: Hendrickson, 2004), 615–16.

3. Charles Dyer and Gene Merrill, *The Old Testament Explorer: Discovering the Essence, Background, and Meaning of Every Book in the Old Testament* (Nashville: Thomas Nelson, 2001), 96.

4. A partial copy of the Aaronic blessing written in paleo-Hebrew was discovered in 1979 in the Hinnom Valley in Jerusalem inscribed on two silver scrolls. These are the oldest copies of a biblical text ever found to date. Their existence clearly indicates the antiquity of the text of Numbers. See details in Eugene H. Merrill, Mark Rooker, and Michael A. Grisanti, *The World and the Word: An Introduction to the Old Testament* (Grand Rapids: Baker Academic, 2011), 232–34.

5. See details in Feinberg, *Walk Numbers!* 57.

6. Liberal scholars persist in segmenting the book into various unrelated documents, which they believe were edited to produce the current form of the book as late as the fourth century BC. Contra this approach, see Brevard Childs, *Introduction to the Old Testament as Scripture* (Philadelphia: Fortress Press, 1979), 199ff. James Hoffmeier, *Ancient Israel in Sinai: The Evidence for the Authenticity of the Wilderness Tradition* (New York: Oxford University Press, 2005), 153–59.

7. The beginning of each oracle is discernible through the repetition of the formula "he took up his discourse and he said" (23:7, 18; 24:3, 15, 20, 21, 23). Balaam is routinely held up in Scripture in a negative light and as an object of universal condemnation (Num 31:7–8, 15–16; Deut 23:3–6; Josh 13:22; 24:9–10; Neh 13:1–3; Mic 6:5; 2 Pet 2:15–16; Jude 11; Rev 2:14). The Deir Alla inscription found in Jordan in 1967, dating from 800 BC, also refers to Balaam as a divine seer.

Chapter 8

DEUTERONOMY

Covenant Renewal

The book of Deuteronomy completes the Torah scrolls as the final book of the Law. It contains Moses' three speeches to the new generation of Israelites who were about to enter the Promised Land. The book ends with the Song of Moses (32:1–43), the blessing of Moses (33:1–29), and the transition of leadership to Joshua (34:1–12). The book begins in Hebrew with the title *'elleh haddebarim*, "these are the words." Although the LXX title, *Deuteronomion* (sometimes translated as "second law") is the source of the English title Deuteronomy, this is not actually a "second law" but an expansion of the original law given at Mount Sinai.

KEY FACTS

Author:	Moses
Recipients:	New generation of Israelites
Date:	1406 BC
Key Word:	Listen (Hb. *shema*)
Key Verses:	"Listen, Israel: The LORD our God, the LORD is one. Love the LORD your God with all your heart, with all your soul, and with all your strength" (6:4–5).

Various lines of evidence point to Moses as the primary author of the book. Deuteronomy contains roughly forty references indicating Moses is the author who spoke the words and recorded them in this book (Deut 1:5,

9; 4:44; 5:1; 27:1; 29:1–2; 31:1, 9, 22, 24; 30; 33:1, 36). The rest of the Old Testament frequently claims Moses as the book's author (Josh 1:7–8; Judg 1:20; 3:4; 1 Kgs 2:3; 2 Kgs 14:6; 18:6; 2 Chr 25:4; Ezra 3:2; Neh 1:7; Ps 103:7; Dan 9:11; Mal 4:4). Christ specifically referred to Moses as the author of Deuteronomy (Matt 19:7; Mark 7:10; 10:3–5), and New Testament figures and writers routinely referred to Moses as the book's author (Matt 22:24; Mark 12:19; Luke 20:28; Acts 3:22–23; 7:37–38; Rom 10:19; 1 Cor 9:9; Heb 10:28). Therefore, Jewish and Christian tradition presumed Mosaic authorship until the eighteenth century when W. M. L. de Wette, following B. Spinoza, theorized that Deuteronomy was written much later than Moses and suggested it was actually the lost "Book of the Law," which was conveniently "discovered" in the days of Josiah in 622 BC (2 Chr 34:14–33).[1]

The preamble (1:1–5), the record of Moses' death (34:1–12), and various other sections (2:10–12, 20–23; 3:13b–14) were probably written by someone other than Moses. However, these additions notwithstanding, Moses still was responsible for composing the bulk of the book. It has been observed: "No ancient texts have been found" and "no contemporary corroboration unearthed" to substantiate the critical view.[2]

View of the southern Jordan Valley from atop Mount Nebo looking northwest toward Jericho. This view toward Canaan would have been the first sighting the Israelites had of the Promised Land.

Background

The book was probably written around 1405 BC, at the end of the wilderness wanderings and on the eve of the conquest of Canaan (4:44–49; 34:1–4). These events transpired at least forty years after the exodus from Egypt (Num 14:33–34; Deut 2:7, 14; Josh 5:6). The book was written just before Moses' death and covers the seventy-day period between the first day of the eleventh month of the fortieth year after the Exodus from Egypt (Deut 1:3) and the crossing of the Jordan, which transpired on the tenth day of the first month of the forty-first year after the exodus from Egypt (Josh 4:19). The events of the entire book occurred as the nation was encamped on the plains of Moab prior to entering Canaan (Deut 1:1, 5; 29:1; Josh 1:2). The audience consisted of the second generation that emerged from the wilderness wanderings as they awaited the Canaan conquest.

Outline

I. Past: Review of Israel's History (1:1–4:49)
II. Present: Record of Israel's Laws (5:1–26:19)
    A. Principles of the Covenant (5:1–11:32)
    B. Priorities of the Covenant (12:1–25:19)
    C. Practice of the Covenant (26:1–19)
III. Future: Revelation of Israel's Destiny (27:1–34:12)
    A. Ratification of the Covenant (27:1–30:20)
    B. Preparation of the Community (31:1–34:12)

Message

Deuteronomy was written to invoke covenant renewal on the part of the second generation so they could enter Canaan, conquer the Canaanites, and experience prosperity and peace in the land. To accomplish this goal, Moses reviewed God's past acts on Israel's behalf (1:1–4:40), instructed the second generation to honor the Mosaic covenant (4:41–26:19), and explained what God would do for Israel (27:1–34:12). In this third category Moses promised that God would bless or curse Israel based on their obedience and disobedience (27:1–28:68), ultimately restore Israel (29:1–30:20), and would provide the nation with a new leader (31:1–34:12). Moses persuasively argued that his audience must "'hear' (50 times) and 'do,' 'keep,' 'observe' (177 times) God's commands out of a heart of 'love' (21 times)."[3]

Deuteronomy is sermonic and follows a threefold division. The first sermon, found in chapters 1–4, is retrospective and historical. It seeks to encourage Israel to remember what God did for her by reciting God's saving acts on her behalf. The second sermon, found in chapters 5–26, is introspective, emotional, and legal. It calls for Israel to love God with all her heart, to reverence Him, and to serve Him. Moses explains what God expects Israel to do through the exposition of the principles of His covenant Law. The third sermon, found in chapters 27–34, is prospective and prophetic. It invokes hope by explaining what God will do for Israel and by providing a final summation of the covenant demands.

Although the book contains some narrative material, it also includes legal material. However, the book is largely a sermonic and persuasive exposition of the law (1:5). The entire structure of the book can be compared to a suzerain vassal treaty since it contains the six parts found in a fifteenth–thirteenth century BC Hittite treaty. These six divisions are: *preamble* (1:1–5), *historical prologue* surveying "the past relationship between the parties" (1:6–4:40), *stipulations* or covenant obligations (4:41–26:19), "storage and public reading *instructions*" (27:2–3; 31:9, 24, 26), covenant deity *witnesses* (31–32; 32:1), and *curses and blessings* showing how the suzerain will respond to the vassal's compliance with the treaty terms (chaps. 27–30).[4] Various subgenres represented in the book include travel itineraries, exhortations, hymns, and poetry.[5]

Deuteronomy contains several unique features. First, the book contains almost 200 references to the land as the Israelites prepare to conquer and pos-

The tablet containing the Kadesh treaty between the Hittites and the Egyptians (1269 BC) in the Istanbul Archaeological Museum. Photograph by Giovanni Dall'Orto.

sess the Promised Land. Second, the book is frequently quoted throughout Scripture: 356 times in the Old Testament and about eighty times in the New Testament. Deuteronomy is used extensively by Christ not only to validate His messiahship and summarize the law but also to rebut Satan (Matt 4:4, 7, 10, quoting Deut 6:16, 13; 8:3). Finally, it serves as Moses' farewell address to the nation. Thus, Deuteronomy represents his last will and testament.

I. Past: Review of Israel's History (Deuteronomy 1:1–4:49)

In Moses' first sermon (1:1–4:41), he seeks to invoke covenant renewal on the part of the second generation, who were born in the wilderness, by reminding them of what God did for Israel. He reminds them of the discipline that was imposed on the first generation with the hope that the second generation will not repeat the same mistakes but will instead honor God's covenant. Moses then traces Israel's journey from Sinai to Kadesh (1:6–18) and then from Kadesh to Moab (2:1–23). Included in this section are God's commands for Israel not to disturb the Edomites (2:1–7), Moabites (2:8–15), and Ammonites (2:16–23) since he gave a land inheritance to each of these groups. Moses completes this historical review by reminding the second generation of his own disinheritance (3:21–29) as a warning to future generations (4:1–40).

II. Present: Record of Israel's Laws (Deuteronomy 5:1–26:19)

Moses now transitions away from what God did for Israel and instead moves toward Israel's obligations to God in the covenant relationship. Moses accomplishes this goal by expounding on how the Decalogue is applicable to daily life in Canaan.

A. Principles of the Covenant (Deuteronomy 5:1–11:32)

In the first major section of his second sermon (chaps. 5–26), Moses articulates the covenant law (5:1–21) as well as its essence (6:1–8) and application (7:1–11:32) in view of the impending Canaan conquest. He unfolds the essence of the covenant in the form of the *Shema* (6:4–5). This principle involves loving God with all one's heart and the totality of one's being and teaching the covenant to one's children (6:6–9). This statement of faith and

Contemporary Jewish man praying at the Western Wall in Jerusalem. He is wearing a traditional phylactery tied to his forehead.

practice is the core of Judaism to this day. It emphasizes that the religion of the Old Testament was a matter of the heart. It was not merely a series of rituals and regulations but a matter of spiritual devotion to the one true God. As a result of their devotion, God promised to give the Israelites the land of Canaan as a gift of His grace (9:1–6).

REFLECTION

Loving God

True spirituality involves loving God with all one's heart. Jesus reiterated this Old Testament truth when he quoted Deut 6:4–5 in answer to the question about the greatest commandment (Matt 22:36–38). Both the Old and New Testaments remind us that we can only love others when we truly love God. Examine your own heart and ask yourself, "Do I really love God the way I ought to, and does my behavior toward others reflect that love?"

B. Priorities of the Covenant (Deuteronomy 12:1–25:19)

In the second major section of Moses' second sermon (4:41–26:19), Moses applies each of the Ten Commandments to a variety of specific situations. This section is developed in the form of case laws applied to a variety of scenarios the second generation will likely encounter in daily life in Canaan.[6] Thus, Moses explains the intent of the Ten Commandments as an inward motivation toward godly behavior in the civil, social, and ceremonial life of Israel.

Moses begins by explaining the laws arising from the first four commandments, prohibitions against having other gods besides Yahweh (chap. 12). Here Moses explains the necessity of destroying the Canaanite places of worship (12:1–4), worshipping Yahweh only in a centralized location (12:5–14), not imitating pagan religious practices (12:29–32), not following false prophets or those making graven images (chap. 13), not profaning God's name with unclean food (chap. 14), not abusing the poor and enslaved (chap. 15), and not forgetting to celebrate the three main feasts (16:1–17).

Moses explains how these laws protect the innocent by forbidding revenge murder (19:1–22:4), adultery (22:5–23:18), theft (23:19–24:7), lying (24:8–25:4), and coveting (25:5–19).

C. Practice of the Covenant (Deuteronomy 26:1–19)

In the third section of his second major sermon, Moses exhorts his audience to remember the covenant. As the nation offers its first fruits (26:1–11) and the third-year tithe to the Lord (26:12–15), the people will be able to remember how God has blessed them through the covenant. Israel will also be prepared to honor the covenant when the people understand that their blessings are attached to their adherence to the covenant terms (26:16–19).

III. Future: Revelation of Israel's Destiny (Deuteronomy 27:1–34:12)

In the third major sermon Moses continues with his theme of covenant renewal by forecasting Israel's destiny, calling the new generation to ratify the covenant (27:1–28:68) and receive life and the promises of the land covenant (29:1–30:20). He concludes the final sermon with a statement about the transition of leadership to the next generation.

Mount Ebal, a mountain in Samaria located on the north side of the ancient city of Shechem. Mount Gerizim was to the south of Shechem on the opposite site of the valley.

A. Ratification of the Covenant (Deuteronomy 27:1–30:20)

Moses begins this part of the sermon by discussing the covenant renewal ceremony that is to take place in Shechem after the second generation enters Canaan. Half of the tribes are to go up to Mount Gerizim to represent the covenant blessings for obedience. The other half of the tribes are to journey to Mount Ebal to represent the covenant curses for disobedience (27:11–13).

Moses then outlines the blessings (28:1–14) and curses (28:15–68) the nation would experience for obedience and disobedience. These curses seem to grow in intensity until they culminate in deportation. When taken as a whole, they spell out the history of the nation in advance.

B. Preparation of the Community (Deuteronomy 31:1–34:12)

Moses concludes his third sermon with transitional information explaining that the new leadership under Joshua will guide the second generation in its conquest of Canaan. Moses also predicts the apostasy that Israel's future generations will exhibit (31:14–22), insisting that the covenant text should be stored in the ark of the covenant (31:24–29). The events surrounding the death of Moses (32:48–34:12) were probably written by Joshua. They serve as a final reminder to the second generation to honor God's covenant and follow this new leader. Moses died (32:48–52; 34:5–8) having only seen Canaan from a distance (34:1–4). His burial by God was in an unmarked grave on Mount Nebo.

Mount Nebo and the Jordan Valley. Mount Nebo is where Moses was buried.

Practical Application

The theology of Deuteronomy emphasizes the giving of the law as an act of God's grace to enable Israel to establish a covenant community of spiritual righteousness and social justice. In the process the book portrays history as theology. It is "God in action," as Hill and Walton so aptly express it.[7] The most direct Christological reference in the book is the prediction that God would one day raise up a prophet like Moses (Deut 18:15–18). This prediction of the coming prophet provoked people to ask John the Baptist, "Are you Elijah?" (John 1:21). "I am not," he replied. "He is the one coming after me" (John 1:27), pointing to Jesus as the Lamb of God (John 1:21, 29). Thus, Jesus fulfilled the law as the ultimate prophet and sacrifice for our sins. He forgave our sins and erased the curse of the law, "nailing it to the cross" (Col 2:14).

For Further Reading

Craigie, Peter. *The Book of Deuteronomy*. NICOT. Grand Rapids: Eerdmans, 1976.
Deere, Jack S. "Deuteronomy." In *BKC*. Colorado Springs, CO: Chariot Victor, 1983.
Kline, Meredith. *Treaty of the Great King*. Grand Rapids: Eerdmans, 1963.
Merrill, Eugene H. *Deuteronomy*. NAC. Nashville: B&H, 1994.
Thompson, J. A. *Deuteronomy: An Introduction and Commentary*. TOTC. Downers Grove, IL: InterVarsity, 1974.

Study Questions

1. Why was it important for Moses to review the law for the new generation of Israelites?
2. How does Deuteronomy parallel suzerain vassal treaties of the ancient Near East?
3. In what way does Deuteronomy read like a series of case laws?
4. Why are the blessings and curses included?
5. What is the significance of the prediction of the coming prophet?

Notes

1. See Eugene H. Merrill, Mark Rooker, and Michael A. Grisanti, *The World and the Word: An Introduction to the Old Testament* (Grand Rapids: Baker Academic, 2011), 252–57. Cf. M. Noth, *The Deuteronomistic History* (Sheffield: JSOT Press, 1981) and A. F. Campbell and M. A. O'Brien, *Unfolding the Deuteronomistic History* (Minneapolis: Fortress Press, 2000).

2. Merrill, Rooker, and Gristanti, *The World and the Word*, 255.

3. Bruce Wilkinson and Kenneth Boa, *Talk Thru the Bible* (Nashville: Thomas Nelson, 2002), 38.

4. John H. Walton, *Chronological and Background Charts of the Old Testament*, rev. and exp. ed. (Grand Rapids: Zondervan, 1994), 86.

5. Charles Dyer and Gene Merrill, *The Old Testament Explorer: Discovering the Essence, Background, and Meaning of Every Book in the Old Testament* (Nashville: Thomas Nelson, 2001), 129.

6. Adapted from Gordon H. Johnston, "Relationship Between the Decalogue and the Case-Laws of Deuteronomy" (unpublished class notes in OT 104A Principles of Hebrew Exegesis, Dallas Theological Seminary, Summer 2001), 1–5.

7. Andrew E. Hill and John H. Walton, *A Survey of the Old Testament*, 3rd ed. (Grand Rapids: Zondervan, 2009), 176.

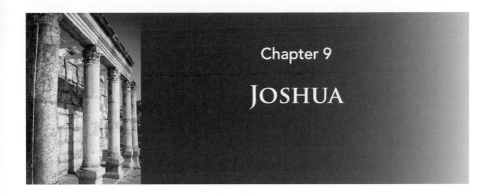

Chapter 9

JOSHUA

The Conquest

The book of Joshua tells the story of the conquest and settlement of the Promised Land under the leadership of Joshua (*yehoshua'*, "the Lord is salvation"). The title of the book in the Septuagint (the Greek translation of the Old Testament) is rendered *Iēsous*, which is also the Greek spelling of the name *Jesus* (savior). Thus, Joshua is depicted as a savior or deliverer of the Israelites. He is the representative of Yahweh and the human instrument of the fulfillment of God's promises of a land to the children of Israel (Gen 15:12–15).

While the book of Joshua opens the section of the Historical Books in the English Bible, it was the first book of the Former Prophets in the section of the Prophets (*nevi'im*) in the Hebrew Bible. Marten Woudstra explains: "The intent of the Former Prophets is to present an interpretive (prophetical) history of God's dealings with his covenant people Israel."[1]

KEY FACTS	
Author:	Joshua
Recipients:	Israel in the Promised Land
Date:	Circa 1380–1370 BC
Key Word:	Meditate or Recite (Hb. *hagah*)
Key Verse:	"Do not let this Book of the Law depart from your mouth; meditate on it day and night, so that you may be careful to do everything written in it. Then you will be prosperous and successful" (1:8 NIV 1984).

Author

Like the other historical books, Joshua is an anonymous work, but several lines of evidence point to Joshua as the author. The Babylonian Talmud (*Baba Bathra* 14b) names Joshua as the author. Plus the book itself portrays Joshua's involvement in various writing projects (8:32; 18:8–9; 24:26). The events spoken of in the book are narrated from the perspective of an eyewitness. Moreover, the writer sometimes uses the first-person plural pronouns "we" (5:1) and "us" (5:6) when describing the events of the book. Other indications of a fifteenth-thirteenth-century BC composition include the employment of ancient names of Canaanite peoples, deities, and cities (3:10; 13:4–6; 15:9, 13–14) and the fact that the covenant renewal ceremony (chap. 24) reflects Hittite suzerain vassal treaty structures from that era.[2]

Background and Date

Because the events of the book are narrated from the perspective of an eyewitness, how one dates the book is contingent upon how one dates the exodus and the conquest of Canaan. While many date the exodus in 1290 BC and the conquest in 1250 BC, it seems better to date the exodus in 1446 BC and the conquest in 1406 BC. According to 1 Kgs 6:1, the exodus happened 480 years before Solomon began building the temple (966 BC) in the fourth

View to the northwest of the western edge of the Jordan Valley as seen from atop the tel of Old Testament Jericho.

year of his reign. Thus, the exodus took place in 1445/1446 BC. Because of the existence of an additional forty-year period in between the exodus and the entrance into Canaan (Exod 16:35; Num 14:34–35), the beginning of the conquest took place in 1406 BC.

All things considered, the conquest probably began in 1405 BC and was completed around 1399 BC. Joshua 1–14 depicts the conquest that transpired from 1405 BC to 1399 BC, while Joshua 15–24 took place between 1399 and 1374 BC.

Furthermore, archaeological evidence supports the early date for the conquest. The excavations of Jericho, Ai, and Hazor have led to a vigorous debate about the date of the destruction of these Canaanite cities during Israel's conquest of Canaan.[3] Both Jericho and Hazor clearly show evidence of being burned in the fifteenth century BC, which fits with the early date for the exodus. References to Joshua's death (24:24) and the elders that outlived him (24:31) indicate that these final notations were added by another inspired writer, perhaps Phinehas (24:33).

The structure of the book of Joshua contains three major sections: the conquest of Canaan in Joshua 1–12, the division of Canaan in 13–21, and the conditions necessary for remaining and prospering in Canaan in 22–24.

Outline

I. **Conquest of Canaan (1:1–12:24)**
   A. Preparation of the People (1:1–5:15)
   B. Progression of the Conquest (6:1–12:24)
      1. Central Campaign (6:1–9:27)
      2. Southern Campaign (10:1–43)
      3. Northern Campaign (11:1–12:24)
II. **Division of Canaan (13:1–21:45)**
   A. Unconquered Land (13:1–7)
   B. East Bank Tribes (13:8–33)
   C. West Bank Tribes (14:1–19:51)
   D. Designated Cities (20:1–21:45)
III. **Conclusion of Joshua's Ministry (22:1–24:33)**
   A. Dispute About the Altar (22:1–34)
   B. Covenant Renewal and Death of Joshua (23:1–24:33)

Message

I. Conquest of Canaan (Joshua 1:1–12:24)

The first major section of the book describes Israel's conquest of Canaan. This section can be divided into the following two parts: preparations for the conquest in chapters 1–5 and the conquest itself in chapters 6–12.

The Jordan River flows south from Mount Hermon through Israel, finally emptying into the Dead Sea.

A. Preparation of the People (Joshua 1:1–5:15)

The opening chapters of Joshua emphasize the importance of spiritual preparation for the people of Israel. Before the author deals with the actual account of the conquest, he introduces several key elements that will be essential for Israel's military success against such overwhelming odds. These preparations will include meditating on the Word of God and reciting its principles (1:7–9); challenging the people to total obedience (1:16–18); sending out two spies to identify their options (2:1–24); miraculously crossing the Jordan River on dry ground (3:1–17); setting up the memorial stones as a testimony to future generations (4:1–24); establishing the battle camp at Gilgal (4:20); circumcising the men who were not circumcised in the wilderness (5:2–9); and celebrating the Passover (5:11–12).

While Joshua prepared to attack Jericho, the major Canaanite fortress city in the Jordan Valley, he encountered the theophanic "commander of the LORD's army" (5:12–15). The divine nature of this person is evident in His command to Joshua to remove his shoes because he is standing on holy ground. Just as Moses met God at the burning bush (Exod 3:1–6) and removed his shoes, so now Joshua has a similar experience confirming that God was calling him to lead the Israelites to victory, just as Moses led them in the exodus. Both men had a divine encounter and experienced a miraculous water crossing that affirmed their leadership to the people of Israel.

Standing stones at Gezer dating to about 1500 BC and reminiscent of the twelve stones Israel set up on the west bank of the Jordan.

B. Progression of the Conquest (Joshua 6:1–12:24)

1. Central Campaign (Joshua 6:1–9:27). The central campaign was built on a divide-and-conquer theory that drove a wedge between northern and southern Canaan, thus inhibiting these two entities from forming an alliance. This strategy allowed Israel to defeat each of them separately. Jericho was the first Canaanite city Israel conquered in her central geographic thrust. The fall of Jericho resulted from Joshua's obedience to follow the plan of the "commander of the Lord's

Defense walls of Old Testament Jericho (may date to 3000 BC).

army." The walls of Jericho fell as a result of Israel's faith and God's enormous power. Joshua also records how Rahab and her household were saved from genocide that was imposed on all of the inhabitants of Jericho (6:22–23, 25). Joshua includes this story as an example of God's grace, showing his readers how they too could experience divine protection if they honored God's covenant.

The nation's subsequent defeat at Ai (7:1–26) is included to show how individual covenant disobedience (6:19; 7:1, 11, 15) damages the success of the entire community. Things quickly turned around for Israel when she did away with Achan, the covenant transgressor (8:1–29) and finally experienced victory at Ai.[4] The covenant renewal ceremony at Shechem (8:30–35) reinforced the nation's need for continual obedience to the covenant (Exod 20:25; Deuteronomy 27; Josh 8:35).

2. Southern Campaign (Joshua 10:1–43). In the southern campaign the king of Jerusalem became fearful of Israel due to the nation's resounding victories at Jericho and Ai. Thus, he persuaded the southern coalition (Hebron, Jarmuth, Lachish, and Eglon) to attack the Gibeonites, thereby drawing Israel into open conflict (10:1–5). However, God's blessing was upon Israel, evidenced by His confounding of the enemy, by the hailstorm He sent to defeat Israel's enemies, and by the miraculous extension of the day that allowed Israel time to rout the enemy.[5] Joshua eventually captured the five fleeing kings, publicly executed them, and conquered the southern territory (10:16–43).

3. Northern Campaign (Joshua 11:1–12:24). After some time Joshua advanced against the gathering northern Canaanite coalition to fight them at Merom (11:1–5) and handily defeated them with a surprise attack, routing their forces and destroying Hazor, the major Canaanite fortress city in the north (11:6–11). The summary of Israel's conquests in chapter 12 lists Israel's conquests of thirty-one individual city-states in Transjordan (12:1–6) and Canaan (12:7–24).

II. Division of Canaan (Joshua 13:1–21:45)

A. Unconquered Land (Joshua 13:1–7)

At this point the author inserts a list of unconquered regions that still remained independent of Israelite control (vv. 1–6). These included pockets of Philistines, Geshurites, Canaanites, Amorites, and Phoenicians (Sidonians of Lebanon). These will be left for future generations to deal with, as is described in Judg 1:1–3:6. These areas were not completely absorbed until the time of David and Solomon many years later.

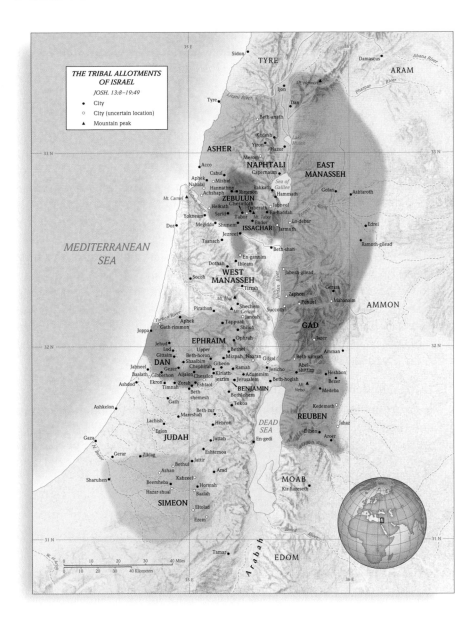

THE TRIBAL ALLOTMENTS
OF ISRAEL
JOSH. 13:8–19:49
• City
○ City (uncertain location)
▲ Mountain peak

B. East Bank Tribes (Joshua 13:8–33)

Now that the Transjordan tribes fulfilled their obligations in helping liberate Canaan, the soldiers from these tribes were released from military obligation and allowed to return home. These tribes included Reuben (vv. 15–23), Gad (vv. 24–28), and half of Manasseh (vv. 29–31). Much of this area was later known as Gilead (Josh 22:9; Judg 10:8). However, the author later records the crisis that occurred when the eastern tribes erected a large altar on the frontier at the Jordan River (Josh 22:9–12).

C. West Bank Tribes (Joshua 14:1–19:51)

The decision to divide the land by lot (14:1–5) shows that Israel's gains came about through compliance with the covenant since Moses originally mandated division by lot as the method to be used when apportioning the land among the tribes (Num 26:55; 33:54; 34:13). Caleb's proclamation of God's faithfulness in finally awarding him what was originally promised is included to show God's faithfulness to His faithful servant Caleb. Caleb's desire to drive out the Canaanites is also included as a positive example for Joshua's readers to follow. However, Judah's failure to drive the Jebusites from Jerusalem (15:63) left the city under Jebusite control until the time of David (2 Samuel 5). In the meantime Shiloh would serve as the nation's religious headquarters for the next 300 years. The tribe of Levi was to serve as the nation's priests and was given no territorial allotment. Joshua 15 describes the borders of Judah, and 16–17 explain where the tribes of Ephraim and Manasseh would settle, while the inheritance of the rest of the tribes are given in Joshua 19.

D. Designated Cities (Joshua 20:1–21:45)

More examples of God's faithfulness to His covenant promises are given through the establishment of the promised cities of refuge (20:1–9) and the Levitical cities (21:1–42). The distribution of Levites among the people and the establishment of cities of refuge were to help ensure spiritual, social, and civil justice in the future.

III. Conclusion of Joshua's Ministry (Joshua 22:1–24:33)

Now that Joshua has described the conquest in Joshua 1–12 and the division of Canaan in chapters 13–21, he transitions into the third and final section of his book where he assembles material showing the second generation how they can remain in the land as well as experience prosperity in the land (chaps. 22–24).

A. Dispute About the Altar (Joshua 22:1–34)

Joshua begins this final section by recounting how the soldiers from the Transjordan tribes, after being given permission to return home, built an altar in the Jordan Valley, potentially rivaling Shiloh as the central sanctuary (22:1–34). Although there was an initial threat of war between the tribes, the situation was resolved amicably. Thus, the altar was called *Ed*, which means "witness." In other words, the altar was a witness to the unity between the eastern and western tribes, which were united in their devotion to the Lord.

B. Covenant Renewal and Death of Joshua (Joshua 23:1–24:33)

Joshua's farewell address to the nation's leaders attributes the nation's past blessings to its covenant fidelity (23:1–12). He also explains that they will remain in Canaan and prosper in the land only when they comply with the Mosaic covenant. Joshua concludes the book by recording the second covenant renewal ceremony at Shechem. Joshua summarized the history of Israel from her election to the conquest (24:2–13), reviewed the covenant terms (24:14–24), and encouraged the covenant's preservation (24:25–28).[6] The book of Joshua contains two covenant renewal ceremonies (8:30–35; 24:14–28); one of these ceremonies took place toward the beginning of the conquest, and the last of these ceremonies took place after the land was conquered and divided. This section includes Joshua's affirmation: "As for me and my family, we will worship the LORD" (24:15 NLT).

Not only does this section record the deaths of Joshua (24:29–30) and Eleazar the high priest (24:33), but it also records information regarding the burial of Joseph's bones in Shechem (24:32). This detail is included to emphasize Israel's faithfulness to Joseph's request to bury his mummified remains in the Promised Land (Gen 50:29).

Practical Application

For many people life is an ongoing battle: a conflict of values, a struggle of wills, a war of nerves, a battle of beliefs. God never promised this life would be easy. But He does promise to go with us through every conflict. Total surrender to Him is the first step to complete and total victory.

The book of Joshua also teaches the importance of faith and obedience as keys to God's blessings. The reader is drawn to focus on key spiritual disciplines that are essential for spiritual formation—prayer, meditation, faith, and courage are highlighted as keys to Joshua's success. The underlying theology of the book reminds the reader that spiritual discipline is the key to victorious living. Vigilance must be consistent so that today's success might not turn into tomorrow's defeat.

There is nothing more satisfying than looking back over a job well done. Before Joshua died, he gathered the tribes of Israel together for his farewell address and reminded them of all that God had done for them; from the call of Abraham, to that of Moses. From the patriarchs to the exodus, God had kept His covenant promises to the people of Israel. Now, with the conquest, they stood on the edge of the fulfillment of those promises.

As Joshua recounted their history, each lesson was intended to reinforce their faith in God, who had kept His promises alive all those years. "Now fear the LORD and serve Him with all faithfulness," he urged them (24:14 NIV). Thus he challenged them to throw away the idols of the Amorites and Canaanites, whose land they had just conquered.

This may sound like a strange request, but Joshua knew they would be tempted by their new surroundings. Relying on past victories, they would be vulnerable to fall away from God, who had so incredibly blessed them. Sometimes, when everything is going well is when we fall farthest away from God. Our need for Him is not as great, so our prayers are not as fervent.

Somehow Joshua knew these challenges would face them in the future. "But as for me and my household," he declared, "we will serve the LORD" (v. 15 NIV). It was a high and holy day. A new nation was established in the Promised Land, the covenant with God was renewed (v. 25), and the people of that generation kept their promises to God, even the elders who outlived Joshua (v. 31).

For Joshua's generation, there was total victory. They had seen the tragic results of halfhearted commitments in the desert and refused to go back. Realizing they only had one real choice, they marched ahead to victory. The story of Joshua reminds us to do the same. We really can't go back to Egypt, and we dare not continue wandering in a spiritual wilderness. It is time to face the challenges of our generation and march ahead by faith, one step at a time.

For Further Reading

Campbell, Donald K. "Joshua." In *BKC*. Colorado Springs, CO: Chariot Victor, 1983.

Constable, Thomas L. "A Theology of Joshua, Judges, and Ruth." In *A Biblical Theology of the Old Testament*. Ed. Roy B. Zuck and Eugene H. Merrill. Chicago: Moody, 1991.

Hess, Richard. *Joshua: An Introduction and Commentary*. TOTC. Downers Grove, IL: InterVarsity, 1996.

Howard, David M. *Joshua*. NAC. Nashville: B&H, 2002.

Madvig, Donald H. "Joshua." In EBC. Grand Rapids: Zondervan, 1992, 239–371.

Woudstra, Martin. *The Book of Joshua*. NICOT. Grand Rapids: Eerdmans, 1981.

Study Questions

1. What spiritual preparations were made by the Israelites before they attempted to conquer the cities of Canaan?
2. How do we know the "commander of the Lord's army" was a divine being?
3. Why was Achan's sin a transgression punishable by death?
4. How did Joshua divide the land of Canaan in order to conquer it?
5. How did the conquest fulfill God's covenant promises to Abraham's descendants?
6. What principles for victorious living can we learn from Joshua's example?

Notes

1. Marten Woudstra, *The Book of Joshua*, NICOT (Grand Rapids: Eerdmans, 1981), 3.

2. Richard Hess, *Joshua: An Introduction and Commentary*, TOTC (Downers Grove, IL: InterVarsity Press, 1996), 26–31.

3. Cf. details in E. M. Blaiklock and R. K. Harrison, *New International Dictionary of Biblical Archaeology* (Grand Rapids: Zondervan, 1983), 258–61; J. J. Bimson, *Redating the Exodus and Conquest* (Sheffield: University of Sheffield, 1978), 115–45.

4. The actual site of Ai has been disputed by archaeologists. Bryant Wood has suggested Ai be identified with Khirbet el-Maqatir (which shows a burn layer about 1400 BC) rather than the previously suggested Khirbet et-Tell. Bryant Wood, "Kh. el-Maqatir, 1999 Dig Report," *Bible and Spade* 12, no. 4 (Fall 1999): 109–14.

5. For a discussion of the various interpretations of Joshua's long day, see J. Carl Laney, *Answers to Tough Questions: A Survey of Problem Passages and Issues from Every Book of the Bible* (Grand Rapids: Kregel, 1997), 60–61.

6. The structure of this covenant renewal ceremony contains the relevant sections of a fifteenth–thirteenth-century BC suzerain-vassal Hittite treaty. See John H. Walton, *Chronological and Background Charts of the Old Testament*, rev. and exp. ed. (Grand Rapids: Zondervan, 1994), 86.

Chapter 10

JUDGES AND RUTH

Heartache and Hope

JUDGES

The Struggle

The book of Judges introduces us to the long years of Israel's struggle to maintain control of the Promised Land and serves as the transition from the conquest to the kingdom. It deals with events following Joshua's death (c. 1380 BC). The book of Judges was written from a prophetic viewpoint following the days of the judges (cf. 17:6; 18:1; 19:1; 21:25, "In those days there was no king in Israel"). Many believe the books of Judges and Ruth originally formed one document in the Hebrew Bible.

After Joshua's death, a loose tribal confederacy emerged with various military heroes empowered by the Spirit of God to bring deliverance from their common enemies. The main body of the story revolves around six cycles of apostasy, repentance, and deliverance. God intervenes time and again to rescue the struggling Israelites from military oppression, spiritual depression, and ethnic annihilation.

KEY FACTS

Author:	Anonymous (possibly Samuel)
Recipients:	Israelites
Date:	1050–1000 BC
Key Word:	Judges (Hb. *shophetim*)
Key Verse:	"The LORD raised up judges, who saved them from the power of their marauders" (2:16).

The book of Judges derives its title from the Latin *Liber Judicum*, but the Hebrew title is *shophetim*. The verbal form ("to judge") describes the activity of the various deliverers whom God used despite their personal challenges, oddities, or inadequacies. The real key to their success was the empowerment of the Spirit of God (3:10; 6:34; 11:29; 13:6, 25; 15:14) who enabled them to accomplish great feats.

Author and Date

While the author is not indicated by the text, Jewish tradition has ascribed authorship to Samuel the prophet since he was the major spiritual figure at the time of the judges. The critical view, which would attribute the authorship of this book to a Deuteronomistic recension based on mythological hero sagas, must be rejected in light of the many historical details that may only be attributed to the time of the judges themselves.[1]

If Samuel the prophet was the author or editor of Judges, its composition would date from circa 1050–1000 BC. The chronological material in the book has been subject to a great deal of discussion and widely variant dating based on one's view of the date of the exodus and conquest. However, a simple adding of numbers of years assigned to each judge may not be the key to the chronology of this period, for there probably were overlapping judgeships functioning at the same time but in different locations. Jephthah's reference (11:26) to 300 years from Joshua (1405 BC) to himself (1105 BC) coincides with the statement in 1 Kings 6:1 regarding 480 years from the exodus (1446 BC) to the fourth year of Solomon's reign (966 BC).

Background

The events recorded in the book of Judges occurred during one of the most turbulent and transitional times in the history of the ancient Near East. In Egypt the confusion of the Amarna period allowed Joshua a free hand in the conquest and settlement of Canaan. Assuming the early date for the Exodus, the first judges were contemporary with the powerful pharaohs of the nineteenth dynasty while the later judges were contemporary with the period of confusion that followed. Meanwhile, to the north, the kingdom of Mitanni fell to the Hittites about 1370 BC. Further west, the great Minaon and Mycenean empires collapsed, and a period of mass migrations (people movements) followed, ultimately bringing the Bronze Age culture to an end and introducing the Iron Age. The Israelite disadvantage of not having iron weapons and chariots is mentioned several times throughout the book of Judges.

Outline

I. Reason for the Judges (1:1–2:23)
II. Rule of the Judges (3:1–16:31)
    A. First Cycle: Othniel Versus Cushan (3:1–11)
    B. Second Cycle: Ehud Versus Eglon (3:12–31)
    C. Third Cycle: Deborah and Barak Versus the Canaanites (4:1–5:31)
    D. Fourth Cycle: Gideon Versus the Midianites (6:1–10:5)
    E. Fifth Cycle: Jephthah Versus the Ammonites (10:6–12:15)
    F. Sixth Cycle: Samson Versus the Philistines (13:1–16:31)
III. Ruin of the Judges (17:1–21:25)
    A. Idolatry (17:1–18:31)
    B. Immortality (19:1–21:25)

Message

Most of the biblical judges were heroes or deliverers more than legal arbiters. They were raised up by God and empowered to execute the judgment of God upon Israel's enemies. The sovereignty of God over His people is seen in these accounts as God, the ultimate Judge (11:27), judges Israel for her sins, brings oppressors against her, and raises up human judges to deliver her from oppression when she repents.

The Valley of Jezreel as viewed from the top of the Megiddo tel.

Location of the judges throughout Israel.

I. Reason for the Judges (Judges 1:1–2:23)

The period of the judges followed the death of Joshua (1:1) when Israel was left with no central ruler. While the book of Joshua represents the apex of victory for the Israelite tribes, the book of Judges tells the story of their heartache and struggle to maintain control of the land. While the conquest of the land was relatively quick and decisive, the settlement of the tribal territories was slow and cumbersome. Many pockets of resistance remained (1:27–36), and the Israelites eventually settled on a policy of coexistence rather than conquest.

The author concludes this section noting the cycles of apostasy, oppression, repentance, and deliverance that would follow because they would continue to sin and God would continue to "raise up judges" to deliver them (2:11–16).

II. Rule of the Judges (Judges 3:1–16:31)

The six cycles of the judges include years of oppression, deliverance, and rest, punctuated by interludes that discuss minor judges and the usurper Abimelech (9:1–57). Each cycle portrays a downward spiral that includes Barak's reluctance, Deborah's insistence, Gideon's cowardice, Jephthah's foolish vow, and Samson's immoral relationship with foreign women. The recurring theme in these chapters is Israel's apostasy, displayed in her covenant violations of idolatry and immorality. This resulted in moral and spiritual weakness so lying, stealing, adultery, and murder were often condoned.

A. First Cycle: Othniel Versus Cushan (Judges 3:1–11)

The author introduces this section by listing those nations that continued to harass Israel, culminating in the invasion of Cushan-rishathaim ("Cushan the doubly wicked") from Aram-naharaim ("Mesopotamia" KJV), the area of northeastern Syria. After an eight-year oppression the Lord raised up Othniel of the tribe of Judah to defeat him because the "Spirit of the LORD" came upon him. The description of the Spirit-empowered judges is repeated seven times emphasizing the real source of their power (3:10; 6:34; 11:29; 13:25; 14:6, 19; 15:14). Othniel's victory was followed by forty years of peaceful rest (3:11).

B. Second Cycle: Ehud Versus Eglon (Judges 3:12–31)

The second recorded invasion was led by Eglon the king of Moab and a confederacy of Moabites, Ammonites, and Amalekites (3:13). They recaptured a rebuilt Jericho, the "City of Palms," and used it as a base against Israel for eighteen years (3:14). Eventually, God "raised up" Ehud, a left-handed Benjamite, who assassinated Eglon with a dagger hidden on his right hip, and this led to an attack that drove the Moabites back across the Jordan River (3:26–30). The chapter ends with a brief reference to Shamgar, son of Anath, who slew 600 Philistines (probably a lifetime total) with an ox goad (3:31).

C. Third Cycle: Deborah and Barak Versus the Canaanites (Judges 4:1–5:31)

By the third cycle of the judges, Israel lost control of the northern region to the Canaanites at Hazor. Sisera was the commander of a Canaanite army that included 900 iron chariots, and he used them to oppress the Israelites in that area for twenty years.[2] God spoke to Deborah, who was serving as a judge at that time, to summon Barak to challenge the northern tribes to confront the Canaanites at Wadi Kishon in the Jezreel Valley. When Barak refused to go unless Deborah accompanied him, she told him the credit for the victory would go to a woman (4:9).

Barak's troops took the high ground at Mount Tabor and attacked the Canaanites in the valley below. Deborah and Barak's victory song indicates the "river Kishon swept them away" (5:21), implying a flash flood that bogged the chariots in the swampy ground and caused Sisera to abandon his chariot and flee to the tent of a woman named Jael. She killed

Mount Tabor, from which Barak attacked Sisera.

the unsuspecting commander with a tent peg and a mallet (4:21), thus fulfilling Deborah's earlier prediction. The entire account emphasizes the lack of male leadership in Israel at that time.

D. Fourth Cycle: Gideon Versus the Midianites (Judges 6:1–10:5)

The story of Israel's leadership crisis continued with the raiding attack of the Midianites and their Arab Bedouin allies. Things were so bad the Israelites hid in the mountain clefts while swarms of armed desert bandits pillaged the land for seven years. At that time the angel of the Lord called Gideon from the tribe of Manasseh to lead a resistance. Fearful and reluctant, Gideon went from hiding in a winepress to making excuses and putting out fleeces. The spiritual weakness of Israel was indicated by the fact that Gideon's own father had a Baal altar on the family farm, which Gideon finally tore down. After this the Spirit of the Lord came upon Gideon, so he blew a trumpet (shofar) and rallied 32,000 men to go against the Midianite and Amalekite raiders.

Fearful himself, Gideon was told to let all those who were afraid to go home, and two-thirds of his "army" of volunteers left. When God thinned his numbers down to only 300 men at the spring of Harod ("trembling"), Gideon had to be reassured of success by overhearing the dream of the barley cake (7:9–15). During the night he equipped his men with trumpets, pitchers, and torches and surprised the unsuspecting raiders. The enemy was thrown into confusion so the Israelites won an incredible victory by daybreak (7:16–23).[3]

The Harod Spring at Ainharaod at the foot of the Gilboa mountain range. This is where Gideon gathered his men before fighting the Midianites.

E. Fifth Cycle: Jephthah Versus the Ammonites (Judges 10:6–12:15)

When the Ammonites in Transjordan attacked the Israelites in Gilead, the elders in desperation called the outcast Jephthah from the land of Tob (11:3) to lead Israel in battle. When Jephthah's negotiations with the Ammonites failed, he made a vow to the Lord Yahweh that "whatever" came out of his house to greet him upon his return from battle "will belong to the LORD, and I will offer it as a burnt offering" (11:31). When his daughter, not an animal,

The hills of Gilead.

came out first, he was devastated. Scholars have long debated whether he actually sacrificed his own daughter or dedicated her to a lifetime of virginity, never to marry and carry on his family line (11:34–40).[4] Either way she bewailed her "virginity," and he grieved that he would have no descendants.

F. Sixth Cycle Samson Versus the Philistines (Judges 13:1–16:31)

The final cycle involved Samson from the tribe of Dan. By this time the tribe of Dan had already abandoned their God-given territory in the land of the Philistines, leaving Samson's family and a few others in a displaced persons "camp" (13:25). The uniqueness of Samson was the Nazirite vow that was imposed on him from birth (13:5; cf. Num 6:2–12). Tragically, Samson ultimately violated all three stipulations of the vow, touching the "unclean" dead lion (14:8–9), participating in a "drinking feast" (Hb. *mishteh*, 14:10), and finally having his head shaved (16:19). Even his initial victory over 1,000 Philistines was accomplished with an "unclean" jawbone of a dead animal (15:15).

Philistine coffin displayed at the Hecht Museum, Israel.

Samson's life story revolved around three women, presumably all Philistines: (1) the woman of Timnah, whom he attempted to marry (14:1–15:6); (2) the prostitute at Gaza (16:1–3); and (3) Delilah of the Valley of Sorek (16:4–20). Despite his gift of physical strength given by the power of the Spirit, Samson's inability to conquer his own passions ultimately led to his demise. Thus, the final cycle of the judges ends with Samson crushed beneath the rubble of a destroyed Philistine temple and Israel still without a leader.[5]

III. Ruin of the Judges (Judges 17:1–21:25)

The final chapters of Judges emphasize just how bad things really were in Israel at that time. Religious compromise led to moral corruption that ultimately resulted in a civil war. These closing chapters reveal that morality was "upside down" during the era of the judges. Throughout this section the author emphasizes "there was no king in Israel," and chaos reigned because "everyone did whatever seemed right to him" (17:6; 18:1; 19:1; 21:25).

A. Idolatry (Judges 17:1–18:31)

Micah was an Israelite from Ephraim who maintained a shrine of various "household idols" (17:5) so he bribed a Levite from Bethlehem to be his own personal priest (17:13). In the meantime as the tribe of Dan was migrating north, they happened upon Micah's house, stole his idols, and talked the Levite into going with them. The apostate tribe of Dan not only abandoned its God-given inheritance but forsook the Lord as well.[6] The Danites attacked the city of Laish and renamed it Dan (18:28–31), making it Israel's most northern city but also a place infamous for its pagan practices (1 Kgs 11:29).

B. Immorality (Judges 19:1–21:25)

The closing chapters of Judges tell the sad story of immorality, moral confusion, and a civil war between the tribes of Israel and the tribe of Benjamin. The end result was a brutal civil war that annihilated all but 600 men of Benjamin. Had the tribe of Benjamin been exterminated, there never would have been a King Saul, an Esther, a Mordecai, or the apostle Paul. The book of Judges ends leaving the reader realizing again that "there was no king in Israel" (21:25). Thus, the stage of divine revelation was set for the books that follow. Despite the dark days of the judges, a ray of hope was about to shine.

RUTH

Ray of Hope

The book of Ruth is one of the great love stories of all time. It is a romantic drama of a destitute young Moabite widow who marries a wealthy and compassionate Israelite named Boaz. Like the book of Esther, it is named for the woman who is the main character. Historically, Ruth is the "lynchpin of the covenant" and provides an essential key to the transition from the judges to the kings of Israel.[7] Theologically, the story of Ruth and Boaz illustrates the biblical concept of redemption.

In spite of her humble origin, Ruth plays an important role in the history of the Old Testament as the great grandmother of King David (Ruth 4:18) and an ancestress in the line of Jesus of Nazareth. Set in the dark days of the judges (1:1), Ruth is a ray of light and hope for Israel's future. As a Gentile who marries a Hebrew from Bethlehem, she pictures the love of God for both Hebrews and Gentiles. God's promise to Abraham that He would bless all nations begins to come to fruition through Boaz and Ruth, and it will eventually result in the birth of the Messiah. Indeed, the Christmas story has its beginning in Ruth's journey to Bethlehem where her personal and spiritual destiny was fulfilled.

KEY FACTS	
Author:	Anonymous (possibly Nathan)
Recipients:	Israelites
Date:	1020–1000 BC
Key Word:	Redeemer (Hb. go'el)
Key Verse:	"May you be powerful in Ephrathah and your name well known in Bethlehem" (4:11b).

Background

The reader must grasp at least four elements in order to understand fully the message of the book of Ruth. First, the Moabites were the descendants of Lot (Gen 19:30–38) and engaged in numerous battles with Israel throughout biblical history (Judg 3:12–30; 1 Sam 14:47; 2 Sam 8:11–12; 2 Kgs 3:4–27) so the relationship was not friendly. Second, the right of redemption (Lev 25:25–28) gave the next of kin (Hb. go'el) the responsibility of buying back foreclosed property that was taken because of poverty. Third, under the principle of Levirate marriage (Deut 25:5–10), the next of kin of a deceased man was to marry his widow and produce an offspring in order to prevent the deceased man's lineage and name from dying out.[8] Fourth, according to Deut 23:3, a Moabite male, or any of his descendants up to the tenth generation, could not gain entrance into Israel's public assembly. What is evident in the ten-generation genealogy is the affirmation of David's right to rule as king as a descendant of the illegitimate birth of Perez ten generations earlier (cf. Deut 23:2; Gen 38:1–30), which explains the list of names at the end of the book.

Outline[9]

   I. Love's Resolve: Ruth's Determination (1:1–22)
  II. Love's Response: Ruth's Devotion (2:1–23)
 III. Love's Request: Boaz's Decision (3:1–18)
 IV. Love's Reward: Family's Destiny (4:1–22)

Message

In times of national infidelity, God sovereignly used the faithfulness of an unlikely woman named Ruth to change the course of history. Although Ruth was a female, Gentile, pagan, poverty stricken, widowed, and a Moabitess, Ruth broke with her own pagan background (Gen 19:30–38; Deut 23:3–6) to embrace the people of Israel and their God. But in spite of her background, God used her to perpetuate the Davidic and messianic lineage. As a result of God's covenant promise to bless obedience (Deut 28:1–14) as well as bless all who bless Israel (Gen 12:3), God blessed Ruth by giving her a new husband, a son, and a privileged genealogical position.

I. Love's Resolve: Ruth's Determination (Ruth 1:1–22)

As the curtain rises on the drama, the first chapter describes the journey of Elimelech's family to Moab. It explains how Naomi became an impoverished widow and how Ruth attached herself to Naomi. However, against this negative backdrop of covenant infidelity (1:1–5) and Naomi's dire circumstances (1:6–14), the writer inserts a note of optimism and hope. He records Ruth's positive example of not wanting to leave Naomi's side (1:15–18) and her profession of commitment to the people of Israel and their God.

Fields of Boaz near Bethlehem.

II. Love's Response: Ruth's Devotion (Ruth 2:1–23)

The second chapter records how Ruth providentially met her future husband and kinsman redeemer Boaz ("in him is strength"). Ruth's commitment to Naomi is seen in her desire to glean from among the grain (Lev 19:9–10) on behalf of her mother-in-law (2:1–7). "Gleaning" meant picking up the scraps as one followed the "reapers" in the harvest. The sovereign guidance of God directed Ruth to the field of Boaz though from her point of view "she happened to come to the portion of the field belonging to Boaz" (2:3 NASB). There Ruth met her redeemer (Hb. *go'el*), Boaz, the wealthy Israelite from Bethlehem.

III. Love's Request: Boaz's Decision (Ruth 3:1–18)

Chapter 3 records the steps leading to the eventual marital union between Boaz and Ruth. Naomi recognized that while she was too poor to buy back her Bethlehem property and too old to have children to perpetuate her family's name, Boaz as the kinsman redeemer could rectify both of these situations by marrying her daughter-in-law Ruth. Because Boaz took no further steps in this regard, Naomi hatched a plan whereby Ruth would propose marriage.

IV. Love's Reward: Family's Destiny (Ruth 4:1–22)

The marriage between Boaz and Ruth is finalized in the book's fourth chapter as Boaz fulfills the position of the redeemer. Obed's birth reversed Naomi's prior emptiness and bitterness. Through Ruth and Boaz Elimelech's lineage was perpetuated. According to 4:17, Obed's birth also preserved the line that led to David. Since Boaz was not only the kinsman redeemer but also the one carrying the Davidic lineage, Ruth's marriage to Boaz permanently enshrined her in both David's and the Messiah's genealogy (Matt 1:5). God's grace was extended to a Gentile woman, indicating his desire to bring the blessing of Abraham to all people—Hebrews and Gentiles alike.

Practical Application

The books of Judges and Ruth paint a contrast between God's justice and His grace. Israel's constant disobedience resulted in God's temporary judgments that were meant to bring His people to repentance. Each cycle of judgment-repentance-redemption saw Israel fall farther from God until all hope seemed lost. Thus, the story of Ruth stands in stark contrast as a ray of hope in the dark days of the judges. When everything appeared to be going wrong, God was going right—fulfilling His promises, even through the most unlikely candidates. Judges–Ruth teaches us that we too can be used of God to shine His light in the darkness of our times because we too are objects of His love and grace.

For Further Reading

Block, Daniel I. *Judges, Ruth*. NAC. Nashville, B&H, 1999.

Cundall, A. E., and Leon Morris, *Judges and Ruth*. TOTC. Downers Grove, IL: InterVarsity Press, 1968.

Hindson, Edward E. "Judges." In *King James Bible Commentary*. Nashville: Thomas Nelson, 1999.

Hubbard, R. L. *The Book of Ruth*. NICOT. Grand Rapids: Eerdmans, 1988.

Lindsey, Duane F. "Judges." In *BKC*. Colorado Springs, CO: Chariot Victor, 1983.

Wood, Leon. *The Distressing Days of the Judges*. Grand Rapids: Zondervan, 1975.

Younger, K. Lawson. *Judges, Ruth*. NIVAC. Grand Rapids: Zondervan, 2002.

Study Questions

1. What was Israel's major struggle for survival during the era of the judges?
2. In what way does God function as the ultimate Judge?
3. How did God use Israel's enemies to get their attention to spiritual matters?
4. What were some of the unusual characteristics of the judges that God overcame in using them?
5. How did the process of religious compromise lead to moral corruption and civil catastrophe in Judges?
6. How does God's providential provision for Ruth encourage you to trust God with your future?

Notes

1. For a detailed discussion of the authorship questions related to the book of Judges, see R. K. Harrison, *Introduction to the Old Testament* (Grand Rapids: Eerdmans, 1969), 680–94.

2. Sisera served under "Jabin . . . who reigned in Hazor" (4:2), probably a dynastic title of the ruler of a rebuilt Hazor (cf. Josh 11:1–11), although K. A. Kitchen, *Ancient Orient and Old Testament* (Downers Grove, IL: InterVarsity, 1975), 68, suggests otherwise. Cf. Y. Yadin, *Hazor* (Jerusalem: Steinmatzky, 1970).

3. See Chaim Herzog and M. Gichon, *Battles of the Bible* (New York: Random House, 1978), 54–62.

4. Those favoring the view that he actually sacrificed his daughter point to the general spiritual confusion at the time, noting that the sinful Israelites did occasionally make such sacrifices (2 Chr 28:3). They also note that this was the oldest known view among Jewish commentators. Those favoring the view that she was not actually sacrificed point to the fact that human sacrifice violated Mosaic law (Lev 18:21; 20:2–5) and that Jephthah was filled with the Spirit when he made the vow (11:29). They also point out the use of the *waw* ("and") in 11:31 is indefinite and can be translated "or," implying that he had a choice of either making a sacrifice "or" a dedicated offering.

5. For details, see E. Hindson, "Judges," *King James Bible Commentary* (Nashville: Thomas Nelson, 1999), 263–71.

6. The apostasy of Dan may be the reason it is the only tribe of Israel not named in the book of Revelation (cf. Rev 7:4–8).

7. Andrew E. Hill and John H. Walton, *A Survey of the Old Testament*, 3rd ed. (Grand Rapids: Zondervan, 2009), 250.

8. See detailed discussion in Donald Leggett, *The Levirate and Goel Institutions in the Old Testament with Special Attention to the Book of Ruth* (Cherry Hill, NJ: Mack Publishing, 1974).

9. Based on Norman L. Geisler, *A Popular Survey of the Old Testament* (Grand Rapids: Baker, 1996), 108.

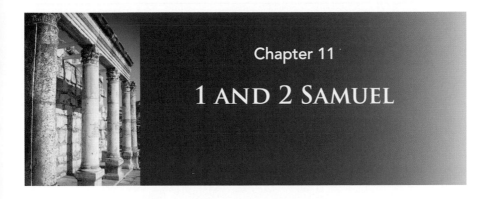

Chapter 11

1 AND 2 SAMUEL

Kings and Prophets

The books of 1 and 2 Samuel form the transition from the era of the judges to that of the kings. They introduce a series of contrasts between good and evil judges, plus faithful and unfaithful kings. As 1 Samuel opens, the era of the judges is still in the forefront, but it is fading fast. The leadership of Israel rests on the undisciplined and elderly Eli, the high priest of the tabernacle at Shiloh and one of the last of the minor judges (1 Sam 4:18). Throughout the early chapters of 1 Samuel, the author draws a sharp contrast between Eli and his ungodly sons and the godly prophet Samuel. By the middle of the book (1 Samuel 15–16), the same kind of contrast is drawn between Saul and David.

In 2 Samuel the narrative shifts to the reign of David as he rises above Saul's son Ish-bosheth to become the king, first of Judah and then of all the tribes of Israel (5:1–4). The book records David's wars of conquest including the capture of Jerusalem and the relocation of the ark of the covenant to the City of David (6:1–19). But the author also records David's failures: his adultery with Bathsheba (11:1–26), Absalom's rebellion (15:1–18:30), Sheba's revolt (20:1–26), and the disastrous census (24:1–25). Like all the prophetic writers, the author presents a portrait of his historical figures from the perspective of their faithfulness to God's covenant.

Author and Date

First Chronicles 29:29 states that "the acts of David" (KJV) were written in the books of Samuel the seer, Nathan the prophet, and Gad the seer. This could indicate that Samuel may have written some of the earlier material in the first book. However, the books of 1 and 2 Kings and 1 and 2 Samuel are probably the products of multiple authors.

KEY FACTS

Author:	Anonymous (Samuel, Nathan, or Gad?)
Date:	Circa 960 BC
Recipients:	United Kingdom of Israel
Key Word:	Anointed (Hb. *mashiach*)
Key Verse:	"So Samuel took the horn of oil, anointed him . . . and the Spirit of the LORD took control of David from that day forward. Then Samuel set out and went to Ramah" (1 Sam 16:13).

The name *Samuel* means "the name of God," "his name is God," or "asked of God." The Masoretes originally considered both 1 and 2 Samuel as one book. The Greek Septuagint calls 1–2 Samuel and 1–2 Kings "First, Second, Third, and Fourth Kingdoms." The content of each of the books is generally the same as 1–2 Samuel and 1–2 Kings. Each of these books was included in the section of the "Former Prophets" in the Hebrew Bible because it was believed that they were written by prophets, whereas 1–2 Chronicles was placed in the "writings" (*Kethuvim*) because they were written by priests.

The books of 1–2 Samuel are anonymous but named in honor of Samuel who authored other works (1 Sam 10:25; 1 Chr 29:29) and was the head of a group of prophets (1 Sam 10:5; 19:20). However, Samuel could not be the author of all of the books' contents since they record his death (1 Sam 25:1) and events after his death (2 Sam 1–24). *Baba Bathra* 15a asserts that the prophets Nathan and Gad wrote the rest of the material (cf. 1 Chr 29:29). These books were probably written circa 960 BC after the death of David in 971 BC and during the reign of Solomon (cf. 2 Chr 9:29).[1]

Outline

First and 2 Samuel follow a fourfold structure. In the first section the house of Samuel is exalted while the house of priest-judge Eli is abased (1 Samuel 1–7). The second part is about conflicts between Samuel and Saul (1 Samuel 8–15) while the third records the struggles between David and Saul (1 Samuel 16–31). The concluding section (2 Samuel) is about the reign of David.

Outline

I. Transition from Eli to Samuel (1 Samuel 1:1–7:17)
II. Reign of Saul (1 Samuel 8:1–31:13)
  A. Saul's Selection (1 Samuel 8:1–11:15)
  B. Samuel's Warning (1 Samuel 12:1–25)
  C. Saul's Rejection (1 Samuel 13:1–17:58)
  D. Saul's Failures (1 Samuel 18:1–31:13)
III. Reign of David (2 Samuel 1:1–24:25)
  A. David's Faith (2 Samuel 1:1–10:19)
  B. David's Faults (2 Samuel 11:1–12:31)
  C. David's Foes (2 Samuel 13:1–20:26)
  D. David's Fame (2 Samuel 21:1–24:25)

Message

By showing the deficiencies of the final phase of the judges' era (chaps. 1–7), 1 Samuel is an apologetic for the new monarchy, which God graciously establishes for His people in spite of their sin. The book also highlights the inferiority of Saul in comparison to David (chaps. 13–31) whose rule was yet to be inaugurated. The promises to David anticipate the coming of David's greater son who will rule in perfect obedience to God's covenant (Gen 49:10; Deut 17:14–20; 2 Sam 7:12–16; Ps 89:36–37; 132:11–17; Isa 7:14; 9:6–7). Therefore, 1 Samuel is the first biblical book in the English Bible to use the term "anointed one" or *messiah* (2:10).

The message of 1–2 Samuel also highlights the role of the prophets in relation to the kings. Samuel and Nathan confront the sins of Saul and David and call them to repentance (1 Samuel 13; 15; 2 Samuel 12). Whereas Saul makes excuses for his mistakes, David genuinely repents saying, "I have sinned." These stories set the stage for future accounts of prophets (e.g., Elijah, Elisha, Isaiah, Jeremiah) confronting the errant kings of Israel and Judah.

I. Transition from Eli to Samuel (1 Samuel 1:1–7:17)

God used Samuel to anoint Israel's first two kings, thereby transitioning the nation away from the judges' era and into the monarchy. Thus, the writer shows the preeminence of Samuel over the existing regime as represented by the household of judge-priest Eli at Shiloh. The spirituality of Samuel's lineage is seen in Hannah's prayer for a child and her vow to dedicate her child to the Lord (1:9–18). Chapter 2 focuses on the wickedness of Eli's sons, Hophni and Phinehas, emphasizing the spiritual failure of this judge and his sons. The third chapter begins by mentioning the rarity of visions in those days (3:1) presumably due to the wickedness of Eli's household. Consequently, God discloses His plans to the boy Samuel. The tender picture of God standing at the foot of his bed and calling the child by name shows the compassion of God for one person and His rejection of another. The message to Samuel is that God will bypass a disobedient generation and call a new generation to follow Him. God reveals that He will destroy Eli's household (3:12–14) and confirms Samuel as His divine spokesperson (3:17–21).

Excavated area of Tel Shiloh in Israel. The tabernacle was set up here by Joshua after the conquest of Canaan, and it remained here for 400 years.

Under Eli's weak leadership Israel lost the ark in a war with the Philistines (4:1–22), but before long the ark was returned (6:1–18). Samuel challenged the nation to repent so God helped Israel defeat the Philistines (7:2–17).

II. Reign of Saul (1 Samuel 8:1–31:13)

The failure of the judges demonstrates the need for the coming monarchy. The failures of Samuel's sons show the inadequacy of divine rule through this family (8:1–5). However, 1 Samuel is not simply an apology for the monarchy. It is more specifically an apology for the kingship of David and his dynastic successors by showing that God will only rule through an elect, obedient king.

A. Saul's Selection (1 Samuel 8:1–11:15)

As Samuel aged, the people of Israel insisted that they should select a king "like all the other nations" (8:5, author's translation). The events surrounding the selection of Saul as king (9:1–10:16) demonstrate that he was the people's choice. The people seemed to focus on Saul's outward appearance (9:2) rather than his heart (16:7). Even the events of Saul's coronation (10:17–27) reveal God's displeasure. Samuel indicated that the people had rejected God (10:19) in requesting such a king.

B. Samuel's Warning (1 Samuel 12:1–25)

Samuel's subsequent warning against national covenant unfaithfulness (12:13–25) demonstrated that God's vision for Israel's king was vastly different from the vision the people espoused. Samuel's warning accompanied by thunder and rain caused great fear so the people cried out: "We have added to all our sins the evil of requesting a king for ourselves" (12:19). Thus, the author skillfully shows that Israel's request for a king was ill motivated and ill timed. Saul was from the tribe of Benjamin, not Judah, the promised messianic tribe (Gen 49:10). God's timing was also awaiting a descendant from the tenth generation of Judah's son Perez (cf. Ruth 4:18–22), but the people did not yet understand this.

C. Saul's Rejection (1 Samuel 13:1–17:58)

Saul's poor choices caused his kingdom to deteriorate rapidly (1 Samuel 13) because he usurped the priestly functions while waiting for Samuel to offer the sacrifices at Gilgal. This caused God to vow that he would remove the kingdom from Saul (13:14; 16:7). Saul's disobedience (15:1–29) of the divine command to exterminate the Amalekites (Exod 17:8–16) caused Yahweh to reject him as king (15:23). Samuel's confrontation with Saul over his sin in chapters 13 and 15 emphasizes the ministry of the prophet as a covenant enforcer. Samuel's anointing of David (chap. 16) and David's resounding victory over Goliath in the valley of Elah (chap. 17) clearly introduce David as God's choice to lead the nation of Israel (chap. 17). David won a dramatic victory over the Philistines because he separated himself from Saul's ways, depended on God alone, and believed that "the battle is the LORD's" (17:47).

View looking eastward from Brook Elah, where David killed Goliath.

D. Saul's Failures (1 Samuel 18:1–31:13)

Saul's final years were filled with constant acts of jealousy and animosity toward David. Saul failed to kill David and wasted several years of time and energy pursuing David in the Judean wilderness. The theme of preservation is evident as David continues to escape Saul's pursuit in the wilderness of Judah near the Dead Sea caves (22:1–2; 24:1–3). David's character is also highlighted as he refuses to kill Saul, showing his respect for the office of king and the significance of God's anointing. This is especially seen in the incident at the cave of En Gedi when David humiliates Saul but refuses to kill him. As a consequence Saul

En Gedi Waterfall. Along the western coast of the Dead Sea is the oasis called En Gedi. This was one of the places settled by the tribe of Judah.

acknowledges that one day David will be king (24:20). Saul's life ends in a tragic battle with the Philistines on Mount Gilboa when Saul commits suicide (31:1–13).

III. Reign of David (2 Samuel 1:1–24:25)

The book of 2 Samuel follows a fourfold division. The first section exemplifies David's triumphs (chaps. 1–10) while the second emphasizes David's transgression (chaps. 11–12). The third section highlights David's troubles (chaps. 13–20), and the fourth represents six nonchronological appendices dealing with the greatness of the Davidic covenant and kingdom (chaps. 21–24).

A. David's Faith (2 Samuel 1:1–10:19)

These chapters describe how David, the elect king, consolidates and unifies the entire nation under his authority. The high point for David is the reception of the Davidic covenant (7:11–16). The covenant's unconditional nature and conditional blessing (7:14) sets the tone for the remainder of the book. Further evidences of David's political ascent include his capture of Jerusalem from the Jebusites (5:7–10; cf. Judg 1:8, 21), his alliance with Hiram, king of Tyre (5:11–12), his many children which were a sign of covenant blessing (5:13–16), his defeat of the Philistines (5:17–25), and his decision to move the ark of the covenant to Jerusalem (6:1–19). In faith David won many military victories over his enemies because the Lord helped him by defeating his foes (8:6,14). Thus, David extended Israel's borders from Egypt to the Euphrates in partial fulfillment of what God originally promised Abraham (Gen 15:18).

B. David's Faults (2 Samuel 11:1–12:31)

David's covenant violations take place in the book's pivotal eleventh chapter. They involve adultery (11:1–3) and murder (11:14–27) as well as a host of deceptive acts committed in an attempt to cover up these sins. Having been attracted by Bathsheba's beauty, David sent for her, slept with her, and she became pregnant. Attempting to cover this up, David made arrangements for her husband's death and then married her. However, God sent the prophet Nathan to confront David's sin with the judicial parable about the rich man who stole a poor man's sheep (12:1–4). Infuriated by the story, David pronounced judgment upon himself and his household. God forgave David, but David suffered severe consequences: the death of the baby (12:15–22) plus the ruin of his family in the following chapters.

C. David's Foes (2 Samuel 13:1–20:26)

The outworking of the curses that Nathan predicted would come upon David impacted both David's immediate family (chaps. 13–18) and the nation (chaps. 19–20). Tamar's rape by her half brother Amnon and his execution by her brother Absalom eventually led to Absalom's ill-fated rebellion and death. David's restoration to power finally came after the failed revolts of Absalom (chaps. 16–18) and Sheba (chap. 20).

D. David's Fame (2 Samuel 21:1–24:25)

The author concludes with six nonchronological appendixes extolling the preeminence of the Davidic covenant. Each appendix brings out a different facet of David's covenant obedience. He vindicated the Gibeonites against whom Saul had sinned (21:1–9), properly buried the bones of Saul and Jonathan (21:10–14), defeated the Philistines (21:19–22), sang a song of thanksgiving (22:1–51), and gave his farewell words expressing his confidence in the "permanent covenant" (23:1–7). The author concludes with a list of David's warriors (23:8–39) and an account of the military census and resulting plague, which stopped at the threshing floor of Araunah in Jerusalem (24:1–17). David obeyed God in purchasing the threshing floor to build "an altar to the LORD," and on this site Solomon would later build the temple (24:18–25). Thus, the book ends with Israel strategically positioned to build the temple during Solomon's reign.

Practical Application

The books of 1 and 2 Samuel explain the offices of both the prophet and the king and their interconnection with each other. The prophet rises above judges, priests, and kings as the spokesman for God. The "seer" (*roeh*) becomes the "prophet" (*nabi'*) who sees what is in the mind of God (1 Sam 9:9) and announces it to the people of God, calling them to repentance and faith. These books give us a model of the proper relationship between religion and politics. God's plan is for the spiritual sphere to inform the political leaders by calling them to administer righteousness and justice based on the truth of God's Word.

Samuel himself is a model of piety, patriotism, and perseverance. He is the only person in the Old Testament to hold all the offices of prophet, priest, and judge. Wise and courageous, he boldly rebuked kings, elders, and people, challenging them to be faithful to God and His covenant.[2] From his childhood encounter with the Lord through his final days of ministry, he was the epitome of the "man of God." He stood like a beacon of hope in some of Israel's darkest days. Hebrews 11:32 lists him as one of the heroes of the faith.

The books of 1 and 2 Samuel also focus on the life and character of David, Israel's greatest king. While he was far from perfect, the Bible calls him a "man after God's own heart" (1 Sam 13:14 NIV). David became a great leader because he knew God personally. He overcame incredible obstacles. He fled from Saul's jealousy and Absalom's animosity. But he eventually secured the borders, extended the kingdom, wrote the Psalms, and led Israel in worship.

David was unique. He knew God personally and it showed. He spoke of God's activity in his life with total confidence that God would deliver him from his enemies. He showed every essential quality of leadership. He was confident, courageous, and kind. He admitted his failures, repented of his sins, and sought the Lord with all his heart.

As you consider these two giants of the faith, Samuel and David, notice they stand in contrast to two great failures: Eli and Saul. One cannot read their stories without asking which path he or she will choose. Both Eli and Saul had position, authority, and influence, but character weaknesses destroyed them. It has often been said that ability and personality may gain you position, but only character will enable you to keep it.

For Further Reading

Arnold, Bill. *1 and 2 Samuel*. NIVAC. Grand Rapids: Zondervan, 2003.
Bergen, Robert. *1, 2 Samuel*. NAC. Nashville: B&H, 1996.
Gordon, Robert. *I and II Samuel: A Commentary*. Grand Rapids: Zondervan, 1986.
Merrill, Eugene H. "1 and 2 Samuel." In *BKC*. Colorado Springs, CO: Chariot Victor, 1983. 431–82.
Vannoy, J. Robert. *1–2 Samuel*. CBC. Carol Stream, IL: Tyndale House, 2009.
Youngblood, Ronald F. "1, 2 Samuel." In *EBC*. Grand Rapids: Zondervan, 1992.

Study Questions

1. In what way did Samuel represent the transition from the judges to the kings?
2. Why was Israel's initial request for a king wrongly motivated?
3. What are some of the obvious contrasts between Saul and David?
4. How does the Davidic covenant point to its ultimate fulfillment in Jesus Christ?
5. What lessons can we learn from 1–2 Samuel about the importance of obedience to God's Word?

Notes

1. Cf. Ronald F. Youngblood, "1, 2 Samuel," in *EBC* (Grand Rapids: Zondervan, 1992), 3:554; Eugene H. Merrill, "1 and 2 Samuel," in *BKC* (Colorado Springs, CO: Chariot Victor, 1983), 431.

2. Walter A. Elwell, ed., *Baker Encyclopedia of the Bible*, s.v. "Samuel" (Grand Rapids: Baker, 1988), 2:1891.

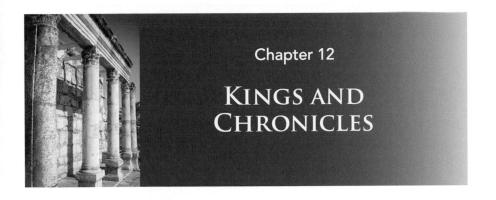

Chapter 12

KINGS AND CHRONICLES

The Rise and Fall of Israel and Judah

1–2 KINGS

Kings of Israel and Judah

The books of 1 and 2 Kings tell the story of the kings of Israel (northern kingdom) and Judah (southern kingdom) from the death of David until the Babylonian captivity almost 400 years later. Written from the perspective of the prophets, the book of Kings (Hb. *melakim*) was undoubtedly one book in its original form. Patterson and Austel observe:

> Thematically the continuity of the Elijah narrative (1 Kings 17–2 Kings 2), itself part of the prophetic section dominating 1 Kings 16:29–2 Kings 9:37, and the recurring phrase "to this day" (1 Kings 8:8; 9:13; 10:12; 2 Kings 2:22; 10:27; 14:7; 16:6; 17:23, 34, 41; 21:15) clearly indicate that the two books of Kings form a single literary unit.[1]

KEY FACTS

Author:	Anonymous (Jeremiah?)
Date:	560 BC
Recipients:	Jews of the captivity and dispersion
Key Word:	King (Hb. *melek*)
Key Verse:	"My lord, you swore to your servant by the LORD your God, 'Your son Solomon is to become king after me'" (1 Kgs 1:17).

Author

The author/compiler of the books of Kings refers to three additional sources: (1) Acts of Solomon (1 Kgs 11:41); (2) Chronicles of the Kings of Israel (17 references); and (3) Chronicles of the Kings of Judah (15 references). In addition, the account of the reign of Hezekiah (2 Kgs 18:13–20:19) is nearly a verbatim citation of Isaiah 36:1–39:8, indicating this material originally came from Isaiah or a common source used in both.

Although 1–2 Kings is an anonymous work, several pieces of evidence point to Jeremiah as a possible author or final editor. First, Jewish tradition (*Baba Bathra* 15a) cites Jeremiah as the author. Second, similarities of style can be detected between the books of Jeremiah and Kings (Jeremiah 40–44; 52; 2 Kgs 24:18–25:30). Third, both describe God's righteous judgment on apostasy, idolatry, and immorality. Fourth, because the phrase "to this day" is used repeatedly throughout the book (1 Kgs 8:8; 9:13; 10:12; 12:19; 2 Kgs 2:22; 10:27; 14:7; 16:6; 17:23, 34, 41; 21:15), most of 1–2 Kings was written prior to the Babylonian exile and therefore would fit the general time period of Jeremiah's ministry. The only clear evidence of a later date is the reference to the release of Jehoiachin (2 Kgs 25:27–30), which was probably added in 560 BC after Jeremiah's death.

Background

If Jeremiah wrote his book throughout his ministry, then the intended recipients would be the people of Judah before the exile in 586 BC and afterwards. Since the final form was completed after 560 BC, Jeremiah's prophecy (see Dan 9:1–3) and 1–2 Kings were written for the benefit of the Jews of the Babylonian captivity and the dispersion. The books begin with the end of David's reign and the beginning of Solomon's reign (971 BC) and end with the three deportations to Babylon (605, 597, 586 BC) and the release of Jehoiachin (560 BC).

Kings of Israel[2]					
King	**Lineage**	**Scripture**	**Years of reign**	**Dates of reign** (Thiele)[2]	**Prophet**
Jeroboam I	Son of Nebat	1 Kgs 11:26–14:20	22	931–910	Ahijah, man of God from Judah, old prophet at Bethel, Iddo
Nadab	Son of Jeroboam I	1 Kgs 15:25–28	2	910–909	
Baasha	Son of Ahijah	1 Kgs 15:27–16:7	24	909–886	Jehu
Elah	Son of Baasha	1 Kgs 16:6–14	2	886–885	
Zimri	Chariot commander under Elah	1 Kgs 6:9–20	7 days	885	
Omri	Army commander under Elah	1 Kgs 6:15–28	12	885–874	
Ahab	Son of Omri	1 Kgs 16:28–22:40	22	874–853	Elijah, Elisha, Micaiah, unnamed prophets
Ahaziah	Son of Ahab	1 Kgs 22:40–2 Kgs 1:18	2	853–852	Elijah, Elisha
Joram	Son of Ahab	2 Kgs 1:17–9:26	12	852–841	Elisha
Jehu	Son of Nimishi, army commander under Ahab	2 Kgs 9:1–10:36	28	841–814	Elisha
Jehoahaz	Son of Jehu	2 Kgs 13:1–9	17	814–798	Elisha
Jehoash	Son of Jehoahaz	2 Kgs 13:10–14:16	16	798–782	Elisha

Kings of Israel (continued)					
King	**Lineage**	**Scripture**	**Years of reign**	**Dates of reign** (Thiele)[2]	**Prophet**
Jeroboam II	Son of Jehoash	2 Kgs 14:23–29	41	793–753	Jonah, Amos, Hosea
Zechariah	Son of Jeroboam II	2 Kgs 14:29–15:12	6 months	753–752	Hosea
Shallum	Son of Jabesh	2 Kgs 15:10–15	1 month	752	Hosea
Menahem	Son of Gadi	2 Kgs 15:14–22	10	752–742	Hosea
Pekahiah	Son of Menahem	2 Kgs 15:22–26	2	742–740	Hosea
Pekah	Son of Remaliah	2 Kgs 15:25–31	20	752–732	Hosea, Obed
Hoshea	Son of Elah	2 Kgs 15:30–17:6	9	732–722	Hosea

Adapted from a chart by Andrew Woods. Used by permission.

Details of the black obelisk of Shalmaneser III that records his campaign into the southern Levant in 841 BC. Jehu, the Israelite king, is depicted bowing down.

Kings of Judah					
King	Lineage	Scripture	Years of reign	Dates of reign (Thiele)	Prophet
Rehoboam	Son of Solomon	1 Kgs 11:42–14:31	17	931–913	Shemiah, Iddo
Abijam	Son of Rehoboam	1 Kgs 14:31–15:8	3	913–911	Iddo
Asa	Son of Abijam	1 Kgs 15:8–24	41	911–870	Azariah, Obed, Hanani
Jehoshaphat	Son of Asa	1 Kgs 22:41–50	25	870–848	Jehu, Jahaziel, Eliezer
Jehoram	Son of Jehoshaphat	2 Kgs 8:16–24	8	848–841	Obadiah
Ahaziah	Son of Jehoram	2 Kgs 8:24–9:29	1	841	
Athaliah	Daughter of Ahab	2 Kgs 11:1–20	6	841–835	
Joash	Son of Ahaziah	2 Kgs 11:1–12:21	40	835–796	Joel
Amaziah	Son of Joash	2 Kgs 14:1–20	29	796–767	Unnamed prophets
Uzziah/ Azariah	Son of Amaziah	2 Kgs 15:1–7	52	767–740	Isaiah
Jotham	Son of Uzziah	2 Kgs 15:32–38	16	740–732	Isaiah, Micah
Ahaz	Son of Jotham	2 Kgs 16:1–20	16	732–716	Isaiah, Micah
Hezekiah	Son of Ahaz	2 Kgs 18:1–20:21	29	716–687	Isaiah, Micah
Manasseh	Son of Hezekiah	2 Kgs 21:1–18	55	687–642	Nahum, unnamed prophets
Amon	Son of Manasseh	2 Kgs 21:19–26	2	642–640	

Kings of Judah (continued)					
King	Lineage	Scripture	Years of reign	Dates of reign (Thiele)	Prophet
Josiah	Son of Amon	2 Kgs 21:26–23:30	31	640–608	Jeremiah, Zephaniah, Huldah
Jehoahaz	Son of Josiah	2 Kgs 23:30–33	3 months	608	Jeremiah
Jehoiakim	Son of Josiah	2 Kgs 23:34–24:5	11	608–597	Jeremiah, Habakkuk, Daniel, Uriah
Jehoiachin	Son of Jehoiakim	2 Kgs 24:6–16; 25:27–30	3 months	597	Jeremiah, Daniel
Zedekiah	Son of Josiah	2 Kgs 24:17–25:7	11	597–586	Jeremiah, Daniel, Ezekiel

Adapted from a chart by Andrew Woods. Used by permission.

Problems remain concerning how to fit all of the kings of the divided era into the time frame (931–586 BC) and how to synchronize the reigns of the kings of Judah and the kings of Israel. Edwin Thiele has proposed resolving these problems by acknowledging various methods used by the northern and southern kingdoms to calculate accession years and co-regencies for the various kings.[3]

Outline

I. United Kingdom Under Solomon (1 Kings 1:1–11:43)
II. The Divided Kingdom Through the Assyrian Invasion (1 Kings 12:1–2 Kings 17:41)
III. The Southern Kingdom Through the Babylonian Captivity (2 Kings 18:1–25:30)

The tripartite building at Megiddo, a building dating from the period of King Solomon, 970–930 BC.

Message

The kings, as the nation's representatives, are evaluated from a covenant perspective by the prophetic author. Thus, the books trace the glory of the united kingdom under Solomon, its eventual division, and how the kings of the divided kingdoms led the people into increasing apostasy and idolatry culminating in the Assyrian and Babylonian captivities.

The books of 1 and 2 Kings represent the outworking of both covenant discipline and God's unconditional covenant promises to Judah. The books mention several prophets, thereby explaining how the ministry of the prophets began to develop in the era of the kings. The books also show how the kings functioned as the people's representatives. Thus, their covenant rebellion negatively impacted the entire nation and was consistently confronted by God's true prophets.

Each king is identified with a consistent formula that includes an introduction (name, age at accession, and patriarchal or matriarchal reference), accession, covenant evaluation, historical record, capital city (Jerusalem or Samaria), and concluding reference (death, burial, duration of reign, and successor). By contrast, the prophets generally appear on the scene without formal introduction in times of national crises.

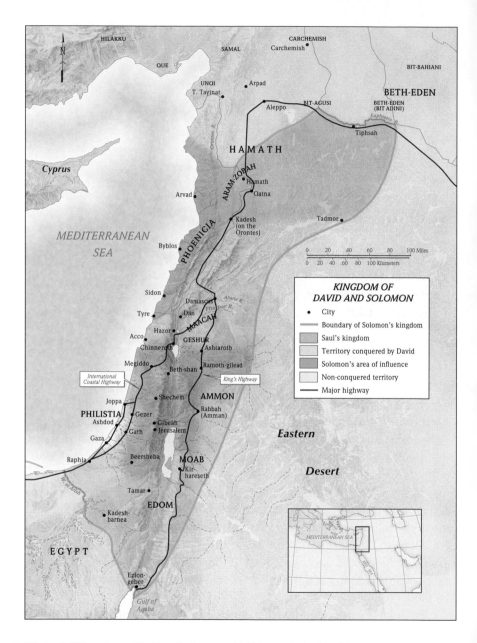

I. United Kingdom Under Solomon (1 Kings 1:1–11:43)

In the books of Kings, the various kings of the nation are evaluated by the Mosaic (Deuteronomy 28) and Davidic (2 Sam 7:14–16) covenants so the exiles will learn from this history and be deterred from future covenant disobedience. The first major section (1 Kings 1–11) puts Solomon under covenant inspection and begins by explaining the transfer of the kingdom from David to Solomon (1:1–2:12).

Solomon's covenant obedience led to his successful consolidation of the nation, "So the kingdom was established in Solomon's hand" (2:46b). So prosperous was Solomon that God expanded Israel's borders to the degree originally promised in the Abrahamic covenant (4:21; cf. Gen 15:18–21) and reaffirmed to Joshua (Josh 1:3–4). Because the temple represented the presence of God among His people, the pinnacle of Solomon's career was His construction and dedication of the temple (1 Kings 5–8). Solomon prepared to build the temple by contracting with Hiram, the king of Tyre, for building materials (5:1–12), workers, and administrators needed to accomplish this all-important task (5:13–18). Following these preparations, Solomon oversaw the construction (6:1–7:51) and dedication (8:1–66) of the temple from the fourth to the eleventh years of his reign. The connection between Solomon's covenant obedience and the presence of God is brought out clearly in the dedication of the temple (8:1–66). God's glory residing on the ark of the covenant in the most holy place assured the people of Israel that God was with them. Unfortunately, Solomon lost most of God's blessings due to covenant disobedience (11:1–13), for his proliferation of wives (11:1–8) turned him away from wholeheartedly following the Lord.

II. The Divided Kingdom Through the Assyrian Invasion (1 Kings 12:1–2 Kings 17:41)

This section begins with the division of the kingdom (1 Kgs 12:1–24). Rehoboam listened to the inexperienced advice of the younger men, rather than the older men, concerning Jeroboam's request for tax relief. This rash decision alienated Jeroboam and the ten northern tribes, thereby causing them to secede from Judah, rejecting the Holy City, the temple, and the Davidic line. The writer mentions the reigns of a series of wicked northern rulers (1 Kgs 15:25–16:28) leading up to Ahab and his Phoenician wife Jezebel (1 Kgs 16:1–22:40). The writer skillfully uses each of these reigns to solidify, in the minds of the exiled readers, the connection between covenant disobedience and covenant curses.

The inclusion of the Elijah narratives (1 Kings 17–2 Kgs 2:11) is designed to express the courage of the prophets and expose the evil of the northern kings. These chapters demonstrate just how evil the kings of the north were. They show the callousness of the nation since Elijah's miraculous ministry did not return the nation to covenant faithfulness. They also serve as a polemic revealing the supremacy of Yahweh over Baal in the

confrontation between Elijah, the lone prophet of God, and the 450 prophets of Baal on Mount Carmel (chap. 18).[4]

The book of 1 Kings records the call of Elisha to succeed Elijah as Israel's next great prophet (19:16–21). In the closing chapters the young prophet is trained to take over the spiritual leadership of Israel at a time when the kings no longer follow the Lord. The book of 2 Kings transitions away from the Elijah narratives (1 Kgs 17:1–2 Kgs 1:18) and into the Elisha narratives (2 Kgs 2:1–8:15) when Elijah gives Elisha a double portion of the Spirit just before Elijah's rapture into heaven in a chariot of fire (2 Kgs 2:1–18). The inauguration of Elisha's ministry (2 Kgs 2:19–25) continued to show Yahweh's supremacy over Baal. Though less spectacular by some standards than Elijah's miracles, Elisha's miraculous deeds were effective in demonstrating Yahweh's supremacy over life, death, and agricultural productivity (2 Kgs 4:1–6:7). The miraculous healing of leprous Naaman of Aram (Syria) demonstrates Yahweh's supremacy and grace to all people, even those outside the covenant community.

A potential bright spot emerges in the north through the reign of Jehu. After he is anointed as king by Elisha (2 Kgs 9:1–10), Jehu eradicates many of Israel's Baal worshippers (2 Kgs 10:18–28). However, these improvements only represented partial reforms since Jehu permitted some false religion in the land of Israel (2 Kgs 10:29–31).

To help his readers understand the fate of the northern kingdom, the writer provides three reasons for the north's downfall (2 Kgs 17:7–17): (1) They followed other gods (17:7–12). (2) They rejected the ministries of the prophets who sought to enforce the covenant (17:13–14). (3) They rejected the covenant itself (17:15–17). The end result was the Assyrian captivity (17:18). Sadly, Judah failed to learn from the consequences suffered by the northern kingdom since she too would experience captivity at the hands of the Babylonians in 586 BC (17:19–23).

III. The Southern Kingdom Through the Babylonian Captivity (2 Kings 18:1–25:30)

The third and final major section depicts Judah's final days as the remaining Hebrew kingdom. This section shows the exiles how Judah's rebellion led to her captivity. It also encourages the exiles by reminding them of God's grace since the southern kingdom lasted 140 years beyond the northern kingdom's destruction.

The reforms of Hezekiah (18:1–12) categorize him as one of Judah's best kings. When Assyria under Sennacherib invaded Judah (18:13–37), God miraculously spared Judah on the basis of Hezekiah's prayer (19:14–28) and what God had promised in the Davidic covenant (19:34). This victory was a major turning point in Judah's survival. While the northern kingdom had fallen to Assyria in 722 BC, Judah survived the Assyrian threat in 701 BC and enjoyed nearly a century of divine protection until the Babylonian invasion in 605 BC.

Unfortunately, Manasseh's reign (21:1–18) was so wicked and violent that he sealed Judah's fate of divine destruction. Josiah, the last godly king of Judah (1 Kings 22–23), began his reign with an extensive temple renovation (22:1–7), which allowed him to discover a copy of the neglected law of Moses (22:8–20). The fact that the law was not readily accessible prior to Josiah's day reveals how neglectful Judah was during the reign of Manasseh. The rediscovery of the covenant law caused Josiah to lead the nation in covenant renewal (23:1–3) and reform (23:4–25). However, the history of the southern kingdom concludes with the reigns of Josiah's sons, who illustrate that covenant rebellion brings unavoidable covenant discipline. As a result, Judah became a vassal of Babylon resulting in the first deportation in 605 BC. Because of Jehoiachin's covenant violations (24:8–16), the second deportation to Babylon in 597 BC transpired (24:10). Finally, Zedekiah (24:17–25:7) rebelled against Babylon and rejected the warnings of the prophet Jeremiah. When Babylon launched its final siege against Jerusalem, Zedekiah was captured, deported, imprisoned, and blinded after trying to escape from King Nebuchadnezzar of Babylon. The closing verses record the destruction of Jerusalem in 586 BC (25:8–17) and the third deportation (25:18–21).

Theological Significance

The history of Israel's kings is recorded and explained from the prophetic perspective. The author continually notes the interaction between the prophets and the kings. When the kings listen to the message of God's servants the prophets, they make the right decisions and experience the blessings of God. When the leaders reject the prophets' inspired message, the entire nation suffers. Thus, everything ultimately rises or falls spiritually, socially, militarily, and politically because of the decisions of leadership. As God's anointed leaders, the kings are held accountable to maintain the standards of God's covenant. Failure to do so ultimately brought the curses of the covenant on both Israel and Judah (Deut 28:15–68).

1–2 CHRONICLES

Priestly Perspective

The books of 1–2 Chronicles tell the story of Israel's history in a parallel account to the books of 1–2 Samuel and 1–2 Kings from a priestly perspective. While many of the details are similar, the chronicler includes specific items that were especially of interest to the priestly community. Some of his major focuses are the temple, its worship leaders, and religious services.

KEY FACTS

Author:	Anonymous (Ezra?)
Date:	445 BC
Recipients:	Jews returned to Judah
Key Word:	Temple/holy place (Hb. *miqdash*)
Key Verse:	"Then he summoned his son Solomon and charged him to build a house for the LORD God of Israel" (1 Chr 22:6).

Because Chronicles is an anonymous work, most scholars refer to the author as "the Chronicler." Most also agree that both books were written by the same author on account of tradition as well as commonality in style, flavor, viewpoint, themes, and literary patterns. Tradition supports the notion that Ezra and Nehemiah were the authors. The writer displays the style and interest of a Levitical scribe. The writer consistently acknowledges his sources, focuses on the temple priesthood, and traces the line of David through Judah. Such a description fits Ezra, who was a Levitical scribe (Ezra 7:1–6), with the possibility that Nehemiah added some final thoughts.[5]

Background

Chronicles covers the history of the world from a Jewish perspective. It was written after 538 BC since it concludes with Cyrus's first year and his first decree after conquering Babylon (2 Chr 36:22–23). If Ezra is the primary author, then it probably was not written much after 445 BC since that is the date of the last recorded event of his life (Neh 8:1–12). If tradition is accurate and Nehemiah is a contributing author, then the books were not written after 425 BC since this is the date of the last recorded event of his life (Neh 13:6). However, Zerubbabel's genealogy pushes the date even later since it records individuals who must have lived well into postexilic times (1 Chr 3:17–24); therefore, the final version may date as late as 400 BC.[6]

The recipients were without a Davidic king and currently under Persian domination. Questions in their minds would no doubt have been whether God was going to fulfill the Davidic covenant and if they still were connected to this covenant. Furthermore, these beleaguered returnees saw their own rebuilt temple as paltry in comparison to the former grandeur of Solomon's temple (Ezra 3:12; Hag 2:3). Thus, they were in desperate need of encouragement after the seventy years of captivity had expired.[7]

Outline

I.   Genealogies: From Adam to Zerubbabel (I Chronicles I:1–9:44)
II. David's Reign: Preparation for the Temple (I Chronicles 10:1–29:30)
III. Solomon's Reign: Building the Temple (2 Chronicles 1:1–9:31)
IV. Judah's Kings: Faith, Apostasy, and Decline (2 Chronicles 10:1–36:23)

Message

In order to exhort the Jewish returnees to unite and resume temple worship, the writer reminds them of their genealogical connection with God's past purposes in general and with the Davidic covenant in particular (1 Chronicles 1–9). To this end the writer also features David's priority of pursuing temple worship (1 Chronicles 10–29), Solomon's priority of building the temple (2 Chronicles 1–9), and the revivals and reforms of those southern kings who pursued true worship of God as well as the apostasy of those southern kings who did not (2 Chronicles 10–36). Rather than continuing the history begun in Samuel and Kings, the author of Chronicles writes a parallel history to reveal the primacy of national worship. The distinctive purposes behind Samuel and Kings in comparison to the purposes behind Chronicles are captured on the following chart.[8]

Samuel and Kings	Chronicles
Divided kingdom	Southern kingdom only
Political history	Religious history
Prophetic authorship	Priestly authorship
Prophetic perspective	Levitical perspective
Moral concerns	Spiritual concerns
Written soon after the events	Written long after the events
Negative	Positive
Covenant rebellion and judgment	Hope
Man's failings	God's faithfulness
Kings and prophets	Temple and priests
Throne	Temple
Inclusion of kings' sins	Omission of kings' sins
Disobedience	Revival and reform
Wars	Fewer wars
National history	Davidic line
Classified with the former prophets	Classified with the writings
Excludes genealogies	Includes genealogies

I. Genealogies: From Adam to Zerubbabel
(1 Chronicles 1:1–9:44)

In the first major section the writer establishes the genealogical ancestry of the returnees to stimulate them toward resuming faithful worship in the rebuilt temple. He shows the returnees their genealogical connection to God's redemptive purposes in general and the Davidic covenant in particular. Knowledge of their Davidic lineage would have encouraged the returnees since they may have questioned their relationship to the Davidic covenant because they had no present reigning Davidic king.

The writer begins this section by tracing the genealogical connection between Adam and Israel (1:1–2:2). The author next shows how Jacob is connected to David (2:1–13) and how David through Solomon is connected to Zerubbabel's descendants (3:9–19). Then he records all of the tribes in order to show the solidarity of the nation (4:1–8:40). Levi also warrants special attention because the author wanted to explain the roles the priests and the Levites played in temple worship.

II. David's Reign: Preparation for the Temple
(1 Chronicles 10:1–29:30)

The book's second major section traces David's prosperous reign and his priority of pursuing genuine worship. The author records these events so that his audience will learn from his positive example and resume temple worship. Thus, many of the sinful and negative events surrounding David's life in the books of Samuel are omitted. The writer deems these as inconsistent with his primary purpose of promoting a resumption of temple worship among the returnees. The writer notes how "all" the nation gathered as "all" the elders came to anoint David as king at Hebron (11:1–3). This material concludes with a unified description of David's inauguration as king (12:38–40).

Then extensive treatment is given to explaining David's high priority for worship when he brings the ark to Jerusalem accompanied by sacrifices and worship (16:1–6) and the rehearsal of various psalms (16:7–36; Pss 105:1–15; 96:1–13; 106:1, 47–48).

Reconstruction of David's Jerusalem.

The writer also includes information about the Davidic covenant (17:1–15) since it reveals David's heart for worship. He sought to build a house for God so that he could worship Him; therefore, the returnees should follow David's lead and continue temple worship.

The writer includes the events surrounding David's census sin because the conclusion of these events is David's purchase of the temple site from Ornan the Jebusite (21:1–22:1). This purchase happened because God told David to erect an altar at this threshing floor in order to stop the plague of pestilence that resulted from his numbering of the troops. David could not go to sacrifice at Gibeon where the tabernacle and altar of burnt offering were located because of the presence of a destroying angel, so God encouraged David to build an altar at this place. Later Solomon would erect the temple on this plot of real estate where David built this altar.

III. Solomon's Reign: Building the Temple
(2 Chronicles 1:1–9:31)

Solomon's construction of the temple fits into the writer's argument in three important ways. First, this section reveals Solomon's commitment to faithful worship that the writer hopes his audience will imitate. Second, this section shows how Israel became the greatest nation on the face of the earth as Solomon made worship in the temple his top priority. Because the writer seeks to emphasize the greatness of Solomon's reign, many of his sins are omitted, such as his idolatry, pagan wives, and effort to kill Jeroboam. Third, this section emphasizes God's sovereignty in bringing to pass many of the promises in the Davidic covenant. The writer notes that Solomon became the wisest man that ever lived since God was pleased to grant his request for wisdom (1:6–13). This connects wisdom with a desire to worship.

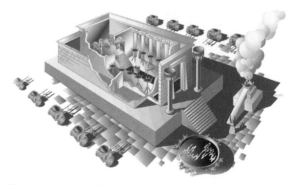

Reconstruction of Solomon's temple (957–597 BC) in Jerusalem. Shown is the temple (center) flanked on the north and south by ten lavers (five on each side of the temple), the molten sea (lower center), and the altar of burnt offerings (right).

Second Chronicles devotes six chapters to Solomon's construction and dedication of the temple on Mount Moriah (chaps. 2–7). Solomon's heart for worship is seen in the elaborate preparations he made for the temple (2:1–18). Solomon's desire for worship is evidenced in how he did not allow his previous prosperity to quench his appetite for achieving his primary goal, which was the temple's construction. No expense was spared as Solomon hired Hiram, the king of Tyre to provide materials and manpower for the project. Solomon's heart for worship is also seen in his transfer of the ark from David's tabernacle at Zion to the interior of the temple (5:1–14). The ark represented God's presence among His people.

IV. Judah's Kings: Faith, Apostasy, and Decline (2 Chronicles 10:1–36:23)

The final section contrasts the blessings on those reforming kings who prioritized worship with the withdrawal of divine blessings from those kings that apostatized from godly temple worship. In faith the reforming kings, including Asa (chaps. 14–16), Jehoshaphat (chaps. 17–20), Joash (chap. 24), Hezekiah (chaps. 29–32), and Josiah (chaps. 34–36), trusted God and were blessed. In fact, "about 70 percent of chapters 10–36 deals with eight good kings, leaving only 30 percent to cover the twelve evil rulers."[9] This disproportionate treatment shows that the writer sought to encourage the returnees toward resuming temple worship by pointing to the positive example of the good reforming kings.

The author reinforces the lesson that temple defilement results in a forfeiture of blessings through the reigns of Manasseh (33:1–20) and Amon (33:21–25). After defiling the temple with pagan images, Manasseh was

Assyrian siege ramp at Lachish.

deported to Babylon by the king of Assyria (Esarhaddon in 681–669 BC or Ashurbanipal in 668–627 BC). However, after he humbled himself and repented, he was able to return to Jerusalem where he pursued orthodox worship. The Chronicler includes Manasseh's captivity, conversion, and return despite the fact that these events are omitted from 2 Kings. The Chronicler devotes two chapters to the religious reforms that took place during Josiah's reign (1 Chronicles 34–35). Josiah's reforms took on even greater dimensions when the law (Deuteronomy 28) was discovered (34:14–33).

The writer concludes his survey of Judah's kings by surveying the four remaining wicked kings of the southern kingdom, whose reigns resulted in the Babylonian captivity (2 Chr 36:1–14). This closes the treatment of Judah's kings by associating covenant rebellion with temple defilement, which finally resulted in the deportation to Babylon and the destruction of Solomon's temple (36:15–21).

The book ends on the optimistic note of Cyrus's decree to rebuild the temple (36:22–23). God's call for proper worship continues from the Babylonian era into the Persian era. Thus, the people in Jerusalem should recognize that their calling to worship is part of God's sovereign design as they resume worshipping the Lord in the rebuilt postexilic temple. English Bible readers should note that these verses conclude the Hebrew canon with the words: "let him go up" (Hb. *ya'al*). This is still the desire of religious Jews today to make *aliya* and "go up" to Jerusalem.

Practical Application

The major theological theme of 1–2 Chronicles is the importance of true worship. This emphasis explains why the word "heart" is found thirty-two times. Therefore, the books focus on those institutions of Judaism that have worship as their focus. These institutions include the priesthood, Levites, the ark, and the temple. The temple is of particular interest to the writer. "As a chronicle of the temple, the book surveys its conception (David), construction and consecration (Solomon), corruption and cleansing (the kings of Judah), and conflagration (Nebuchadnezzar)."[10] As we read the books of Kings and Chronicles, we are challenged to evaluate our own personal spiritual lives as well as our corporate worship. Ask yourself, "Am I really serious about my walk with God and my expressions of worship as an offering to Him?"

For Further Reading

Constable, Thomas L. "1 Kings" and "2 Kings." In *BKC*. Colorado Springs, CO: Chariot Victor, 1983.

Hill, Andrew E. *1 and 2 Chronicles*. NIVAC. Grand Rapids: Zondervan, 2003.

House, Paul, R. *1, 2 Kings*. NAC. Nashville: B&H, 1995.

Patterson, R. D., and Hermann J. Austel. "1 & 2 Kings." In *EBC*. Grand Rapids: Zondervan, 1988.

Thiele, Edwin R. *Chronology of the Hebrew Kings*. Grand Rapids: Zondervan, 1977.

Wiseman, Donald J. *First and Second Kings*. TOTC. Downers Grove, IL: InterVarsity Press, 1993.

Wood, Leon. *Israel's United Monarchy*. Grand Rapids: Baker, 1979.

Study Questions

1. How do 1 and 2 Kings express the perspective of the prophets in dealing with the kings of Israel and Judah?
2. What was King Solomon's crowning achievement?
3. How did God use Elijah and Elisha in the lives of the kings?
4. Why did God allow Assyria and Babylon to conquer Israel and Judah?
5. What lessons can we learn about the use and abuse of power and authority from these stories?
6. How does Chronicles differ from the books of Samuel and Kings?
7. What lessons can we learn from these books about the importance of worship in our own lives?

Notes

1. R. D. Patterson and Hermann J. Austel, "1 & 2 Kings," in *EBC*, ed. F. E. Gaebelein (Grand Rapids: Zondervan, 1988), 4:4. The Latin Vulgate title, "Third and Fourth Kings," is followed in most Roman Catholic versions.

2. Edwin R. Thiele, *Chronology of the Hebrew Kings* (Grand Rapids: Zondervan, 1977).

3. Edwin R. Thiele, "Chronology of the Last Kings of Judah," *Journal of Near Eastern Studies* 3 (1944): 137–286; idem, *Chronology of the Hebrew Kings*.

4. See Leah Bonner, *The Stories of Elijah and Elisha as Polemics Against Baal Worship* (Leiden: E. J. Brill, 1968).

5. Other positions on the authorship of Chronicles and Ezra-Nehemiah are possible. H. G. M. Williamson, *Ezra, Nehemiah*, WBC (Waco: Word, 1977), xxii; *Israel in the Book of Chronicles* (Cambridge: Cambridge University Press, 1977), 5–70; S. Japhet, "The Supposed Common Authorship of Chronicles and Ezra-Nehemiah Investigated Anew," *VT* 18 (1968): 332–72; R. L. Braun, *1 Chronicles*, WBC (Waco: Word, 1979), 52–54; and J. A. Thompson, *1, 2 Chronicles*, NAC (Nashville: B&H, 1994), 29, all argue that the author of Ezra-Nehemiah is not the Chronicler.

6. R. K. Harrison, *Introduction to the Old Testament* (Grand Rapids, MI: Eerdmans, 1969), 1153.

7. The seventy years of discipline transpired either between 605 BC (first deportation) and 535 BC (the people arrived back in the land) or 586 BC (third deportation) and 515 BC (the rebuilding of the temple). Whichever scheme one follows, Kings (550 BC) was written during this time of discipline while Chronicles (400 BC) was written afterward.

8. Adapted from Bruce H. Wilkinson and Kenneth Boa, *Talk Thru the Bible* (Nashville: Thomas Nelson, 2005), 102; *Nelson's Complete Book of Charts and Maps* (Nashville: Thomas Nelson, 1996), 144.

9. Wilkinson and Boa, *Talk Thru the Bible*, 111–12.

10. Ibid., 111.

Chapter 13

EZRA AND NEHEMIAH

Rebuilding Jerusalem

EZRA
Rebuilding the Temple

T he book of Ezra describes the resettlement of the Jewish people after their seventy-year exile in Babylon. The book is named for Ezra, the priest who led a second contingent of Jews back to the Promised Land. Shortly after the Persian king Cyrus II began to rule over Babylon (539 BC), he recorded an account of his conquest on a clay cylinder. It was written in Babylonian cuneiform and is popularly referred to as the Cyrus Cylinder. It declares that he began a campaign to restore various people groups held captive in Babylon by allowing displaced people to return to their homelands. This decree fulfilled the prophecy of Isa 44:28–45:7 almost 150 years earlier when God called Cyrus by name and told what He would do for His people. Furthermore, the timing was also predicted by Jeremiah, who foretold the captivity in Babylon would last for seventy years (Jer 25:11).

KEY FACTS

Author:	Ezra: Scribe and Priest
Date:	446–444 BC
Recipients:	Postexilic Jews in Jerusalem (Judah)
Key Word:	Go up (Hb. *'olah*)
Key Verse:	"Anyone of his people among you—may his God be with him, and let him go up to Jerusalem in Judah and build the temple of the LORD, the God of Israel" (1:3 NIV 1984).

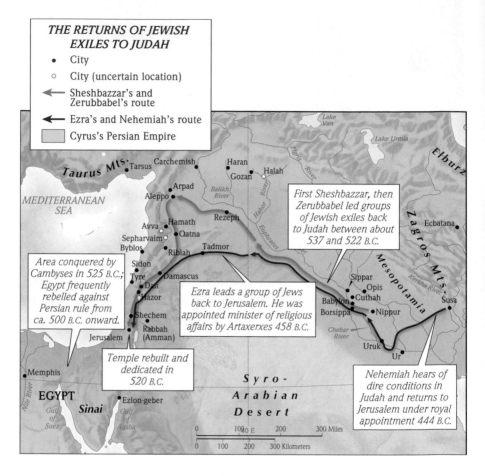

THE RETURNS OF JEWISH EXILES TO JUDAH

- City
- City (uncertain location)
- Sheshbazzar's and Zerubbabel's route
- Ezra's and Nehemiah's route
- Cyrus's Persian Empire

First Sheshbazzar, then Zerubbabel led groups of Jewish exiles back to Judah between about 537 and 522 B.C.

Area conquered by Cambyses in 525 B.C.; Egypt frequently rebelled against Persian rule from ca. 500 B.C. onward.

Ezra leads a group of Jews back to Jerusalem. He was appointed minister of religious affairs by Artaxerxes 458 B.C.

Temple rebuilt and dedicated in 520 B.C.

Nehemiah hears of dire conditions in Judah and returns to Jerusalem under royal appointment 444 B.C.

Author

If Ezra wrote the books of Chronicles,[1] then he likely also wrote the book of Ezra since the latter seems to pick up where the former left off (2 Chr 36:22–23; Ezra 1:1). Furthermore, they both exhibit a priestly emphasis, common themes or concepts (lists, prominence of the Levites and the temple servants, and descriptions of religious holidays), and many common words and phrases ("singer," "gate keeper," "temple servants," "house of God," "heads of families").[2] While critical scholars attempt to date the book much later, some conservative scholars have identified the similarities of the Hebrew in Ezra to that of Haggai, and the Aramaic sections (4:7–6:18; 7:12–26) with fifth-century BC royal Aramaic.[3]

Background and Date

Following Israel's seventy-year captivity, there were three postexilic returns of Jews from Persia to Jerusalem. The first contingent returned under the leadership of Sheshbazzar and Zerubbabel in about 538 BC, and a second group followed Ezra eighty years later in 458 BC.

The book of Ezra centers on the first two returns. The book's first section (chaps. 1–6) concerns the return under Sheshbazzar and Zerubbabel to rebuild the temple between 538 and 515 BC. The book's second section (chaps. 7–10) concerns the return under Ezra to adorn the temple and to reform the people by rebuilding them spiritually. Sandwiched in between these two sections is nearly a six-decade period during which the book of Esther transpired (482–473 BC). This entire picture is captured on the following chart.

Return of the Jewish Exiles				
Return	**First**	**Intermediate**	**Second**	**Third**
Date	538–515 BC	482–473 BC	458–457 BC	444–424 BC
Jewish Leader	Zerubbabel/ Sheshbazzar	Esther	Ezra	Nehemiah
Persian Leader	Cyrus	Xerxes I	Artaxerxes I	Artaxerxes I
Biblical Reference	Ezra 1–6	Esther	Ezra 7–10	Nehemiah

Ezra probably finished the Ezra part of Ezra-Nehemiah between 458 BC, when he arrived in Jerusalem, and a few years after 444 BC, when Nehemiah arrived in Jerusalem.[4] Ezra probably did not write the book after Nehemiah's return to Jerusalem (13:6) since he does not mention this return. While some have challenged this early date for the composition of Ezra, the late date theory seems unlikely since Ezra was a contemporary of Nehemiah. Kidner notes that proponents of later dates claim nothing more than probability for their suggested reconstructions.[5]

Outline

Message

In order to preserve the nation from assimilating into the surrounding Gentile cultures and in order for it to fulfill God's messianic purposes, God sovereignly worked among the Persian leaders, as well as among His people, to preserve Judah's religious and worship identity. Preservation was also accomplished through the community's commitment to put away their foreign wives so syncretism could be avoided and covenant standards and distinctives could be maintained (chaps. 7–10).

A unique characteristic of the book is that some of its sections were recorded in Aramaic (4:8–6:18; 7:12–26), which was the *lingua franca* of the Persian period. Sixty-seven of the book's 280 verses are in Aramaic, making up almost one-fourth of the book. Fifty-two of these verses are official records or letters Ezra apparently copied and inserted into his work. The rest of the book is composed in late Hebrew.

I. Restoration of the Temple (Ezra 1:1–6:22)

Ezra seeks to show how God acted sovereignly in history to preserve the religious culture of the nation of Israel so that she could fulfill her covenant destiny. In the book's first major section, Ezra reveals how God providentially acted so that His people could return to their land and rebuild their temple.

A. Return Under Zerubbabel (Ezra 1:1–2:70)

This section begins with a discussion of the first return under Sheshbazzar and Zerubbabel. God's sovereign work on His nation's behalf is evident when God moves the heart of the pagan Persian king Cyrus II to issue a decree allowing the Jews to return to their land (1:1–4). This work was consistent with what God had earlier promised through the prophet Jeremiah regarding the termination of the seventy-year captivity (Jer 25:11; 29:10).

Contemporary Court of the Men at the Western (or Wailing) Wall at Jerusalem. Contemporary Jews revere this remnant of Herod's temple and make pilgrimages from around the world to pray at the wall and conduct religious ceremonies there.

B. Rebuilding the Temple Under Zerubbabel and Jeshua (Ezra 3:1–6:22)

For the Jewish culture to be preserved, God had to revitalize the nation's worship identity. Thus, he sovereignly raised up two leaders named Jeshua and Zerubbabel to erect the altar (3:1–2), reestablish the sacrificial system (3:3–6), and lay the temple foundation (3:7–9). However, God's work never occurs without opposition. Opponents of the Jews won a temporary victory by procuring an injunction halting the rebuilding of the temple and the walls of Jerusalem (4:1–23). These formidable challenges were met by God's raising up of two prophets, Haggai and Zechariah, to exhort the people to resume building the temple (5:1–2). In spite of efforts by local authorities, God caused Darius I to find Cyrus's initial decree in the royal archives (5:3–17) and moved him to authorize the building to continue (6:1–12). As a result, the temple was completed on March 12, 515 BC (6:13–15).

II. Reformation of the People (Ezra 7:1–10:44)

God's sovereign purpose for Judah included confronting the nation regarding her syncretistic tendencies. The pressure of living under Persian rule in the midst of people with vastly different religious beliefs caused some of the Jews to compromise their religious beliefs and spiritual standards. By taking foreign wives, the Jews were inclined to merge pagan beliefs and practices with the principles of the covenant.

A. Ezra Leads the Second Return from Persia to Jerusalem (Ezra 7:1–8:36)

The genealogy of Ezra is given in 7:1–5 indicating he was of the priestly line of Aaron. Like many of the Jews of his time, Ezra had political connections with the Persian government because "the king had granted him everything he requested" (7:6). Also, the fact that "the hand of Yahweh his God was on him" introduces Ezra as a godly man and spiritual leader among the Jews.

Ezra was a serious scholar who "determined in his heart to study the law of the LORD, obey it, and teach its statutes" (7:10). His example set a standard for Jewish scribes who took seriously their charge to copy and preserve the Word of God for future generations. Unfortunately, many of the scribes of Jesus's time degenerated into arguing about prescriptions of the law and failed to live by its principles (Matt 23:1–36).

Jewish scribe on Mount Zion near David's tomb.

B. Ezra Leads Reformation Among the People (Ezra 9:1–10:44)

Judah's sin of intermarriage with the pagans was reported to Ezra (9:1–2). Consequently, he led the people through moral reformation and covenant renewal. This reformation began with Ezra's prayer of confession regarding the returnees' sin (9:5–15). The returnees expressed remorse (10:1) and pledged to put away their foreign wives (10:2–5). Throughout these events God was preserving the nation from assimilating into the surrounding Gentile cultures so that her messianic purposes could be accomplished. As a result, Israel's unique identity was preserved, orthodox Judaism was defined, and according to Talmudic tradition, the Hebrew canon was established.

The Second Temple

The *first temple* is called *Solomon's temple* because it was built by King Solomon (2 Kings 5–8) around 966 BC (1 Kgs 6:1). This temple was plundered (2 Chr 36:7) and eventually destroyed by the Babylonians when the Jews were taken into captivity in 586 BC (2 Kgs 25:9). The *second temple* is sometimes referred to as *Zerubbabel's temple* because it was rebuilt under the leadership of Zerubbabel (515 BC) when the Jews returned from the seventy years of Babylonian captivity (Ezra 6:13–15). The ministries of the postexilic prophets Haggai and Zechariah were largely dedicated to motivating the returnees to rebuild this second temple (Ezra 5:1–2; Hag 1:1–15). This temple was later desecrated by the Seleucid king Antiochus IV Epiphanes during the intertestamental period (169–167 BC). The desecration and eventual liberation of the temple from Seleucid rule was predicted 400 years in advance by the sixth-century exilic prophet Daniel (Dan 8:9–14; 11:31–32). This intertestamental liberation also forms the background for the holiday in Judaism known as the Feast of Lights or Hanukkah, which means "dedication" (John 10:22).

NEHEMIAH

Rebuilding the Wall

The book of Nehemiah is the second in the historical sequence that describes the Jewish return after the Babylonian captivity to repopulate the land, reestablish temple worship, and rebuild the walls around Jerusalem. The books of Ezra and Nehemiah are one book in the Hebrew Masoretic text and tell a continuous narrative of the Jewish return to the Holy Land.[6] The title of Nehemiah ("comfort of Yahweh") is derived from the central character and the phrase "the words of Nehemiah" (1:1). He was a Jew living in Persia in the fifth century BC. The fact that he was the king's cupbearer indicates that he was a man of character and integrity.

In 445 BC in the twentieth year of King Artaxerxes I Longimanus, Nehemiah learned of the terrible conditions of the people who had returned to Jerusalem (1:2–3). The walls were still destroyed, and the burned-out gates were not repaired. Nehemiah mourned in prayer and fasting (1:5–11) and appealed to King Artaxerxes to allow him to return to Jerusalem to rebuild its walls. The king gave Nehemiah permission to restore the walls, resources to do the job, and even appointed Nehemiah as governor over Jerusalem and Judah. Although there was some opposition, they built the walls in fifty-two days.

KEY FACTS

Authors:	Ezra and Nehemiah
Date:	444–425 BC
Recipients:	Postexilic Jews in Jerusalem
Key Word:	Amen (Hb. 'amēn)
Key Verse:	"So we rebuilt the wall … for the people worked with all their heart" (4:6 NIV 1984).

Background and Date

The book of Nehemiah was written in the Hebrew language and was connected to the book of Ezra, forming one unbroken history. It was probably written by Ezra, with Nehemiah contributing his narrative written in first person (1:1–7:73; 11:1–13:31). Ezra could have included these passages from Nehemiah's personal diary. Chapters 8–10 were written in third person by Ezra because he mentioned himself by name numerous times. Ezra included information from official documents: (1) a list of Jerusalem residents (11:3–24); (2) a list of residents of farming communities (11:25–36); and (3) a list of priests and Levites (12:1–26). The events of the book cover a nineteen-year period from Nehemiah's first return in 444 BC to his second return around 425 BC.

Nehemiah is identified as the son of Hacaliah (1:1), and he had a brother named Hanani (1:2; 7:2). Some have suggested he might also be a priest because his name "the governor Nehemiah" (10:1) is mentioned in a paragraph that ends with, "These were the priests" (10:8). This view is supported by the *Syrian Version* that reads, "Nehemiah the elder, the son of Hacaliah, the chief of the priests." The *Latin Vulgate* also called him "Nehemiah the priest," and 2 Macabees 1:8 said, "Nehemiah offered sacrifices."[7]

Outline

The book of Nehemiah consists of two main units joined by the hinge of chapter 7. The first major unit (chaps. 1–6) involves the reconstruction of the wall and concludes with a census or registration of the new inhabitants of Jerusalem that returned with Zerubbabel (7:1–73), which serves as a bridge to the final section. The second major unit (chaps. 8–13) involves the restoration of the people. Unlike the first major unit, this section is religious rather than political and includes the people's revival and covenant renewal (8:1–10:39) and further registration of Jerusalem's inhabitants accompanied by Nehemiah's later reforms (11:1–13:30).

Nehemiah's Jerusalem.

Outline

I. Rebuilding the Wall (1:1–7:73)
   A. Nehemiah's Concern (1:1–11)
   B. Nehemiah's Commission (2:1–20)
   C. Nehemiah's Construction and Confrontation (3:1–6:19)
   D. Nehemiah's City (7:1–73)
II. Renewing the People (8:1–13:31)
   A. Revival of the Citizens (8:1–10:39)
   B. Reforming the Society (11:1–13:31)

Message

The story of Nehemiah shows the necessity of courageous leadership if God's people are to experience God's protection and guidance in accomplishing God's will. Against overwhelming odds Nehemiah was able to motivate the people to "rise up and build" (2:18 NKJV). The rapid completion of the walls was a testimony to the success of his godly, courageous leadership. Nehemiah's story also reveals the importance of prayer by the godly worker to complete any project for God. In the middle of writing his diary, Nehemiah includes the prayer that crossed his lips while doing the work of God, "Remember me" (1:8; 4:14; 5:19; 6:14; 13:14, 22, 29, 31) and "Think upon me my God" (5:19; 6:14, author's translation). He constantly realized "the gracious hand of God upon me" (2:8, 18, author's translation).

I. Rebuilding the Wall (Nehemiah 1:1–7:73)

The first major section of the book of Nehemiah records how God sovereignly worked through Nehemiah to restore the nation politically. He did so through the rebuilding of Jerusalem's walls so that his covenanted nation could be preserved from assimilation into the surrounding Gentile nations in preparation for the coming Messiah.

A. Nehemiah's Concern (Nehemiah 1:1–11)

The book begins with a recounting of Nehemiah's concern with the vulnerability of Jerusalem. After receiving the report from Hanani concerning Jerusalem's vulnerable condition (1:1–3), Nehemiah not only expressed grief (1:4) but also directed a prayer to God regarding Jerusalem's vulnerable condition (1:5–11). In this prayer Nehemiah acknowledged the sins of the nation (1:6–7) and reminded God of His covenant promises of national restoration (1:8–10). Thus, the stage was now set for God sovereignly to act through his servant Nehemiah to rebuild Jerusalem's walls so that these covenantal promises to Israel could be fulfilled.

B. Nehemiah's Commission (Nehemiah 2:1–20)

The sovereignty of God in preserving the political and cultural distinction of Israel is evident in the book's second chapter. God strategically placed Nehemiah into the position of cupbearer in Artaxerxes's court so that he in turn could influence Artaxerxes to do something about the vulnerable condition of Jerusalem. The Persian king was the son of Xerxes. Esther would have been his stepmother and may have influenced his appreciation for Nehemiah's concerns. Nehemiah returned to Jerusalem around 445 BC and surveyed the condition of the walls, then gathered the leaders of the city to share his vision.[8] "I told them how the gracious hand of my

Tomb of Xerxes in modern-day Iran.

God had been on me, and what the king had said to me. They said, 'Let's start rebuilding,' and they were strengthened to do this good work" (2:18).

C. Nehemiah's Construction and Confrontation (Nehemiah 3:1–6:19)

The next chapter records how various Jewish families began to build the sections of the wall that Nehemiah assigned them (chap. 3). Nehemiah's administrative genius is seen in his ability to delegate responsibilities and check on their progress through accountability. However, God's work is never accomplished without opposition. First, the writer describes external threats Nehemiah and his team faced. Ridicule from Sanballat the governor of Samaria, Tobiah the Ammonite, and Geshem the Arabian was answered through Nehemiah's imprecatory prayer (4:1–6). The opponents mocked, threatened, spread rumors, and used political intrigue to put fear in the hearts of those working on the wall. In response to these threats, Nehemiah armed the workers with swords and spears to ensure the success of the project (4:16–18).

Second, Nehemiah had to deal with internal threats. He had to overcome the threat of the builders' discouragement and the threat of dissention and discouragement due to a financial crisis and covenant violations by the workers (5:1–13).

This section concludes by noting the completion of the wall in record time despite the ongoing subversive efforts of Tobiah (6:15–19). The sovereign hand of God is discernible in all of these events. The wall was rebuilt in a mere fifty-two days despite the fact that it was in ruin for ninety-four years following the nation's first return under Zerubbabel. Even Nehemiah's enemies recognized the rapid reconstruction of the wall was nothing less than the sovereign work of God (6:16). In the process Nehemiah's efforts fulfilled Daniel's prophecy that the walls of Jerusalem would be rebuilt "in difficult times" (Dan 9:25).

The broad wall built during Hezekiah's time (late eighth century BC). The unusual thickness of the wall suggests that this might be the "Broad Wall" mentioned in Nehemiah 3:8 and 12:38.

D. Nehemiah's City (Nehemiah 7:1–73)

The book's first major section on rebuilding the wall concludes with a transitional record of guarding the city (7:1–3) and a record of the Jews who came back in the first return under Zerubbabel (7:4–73). The nation was spiritually revived forty years earlier through the restoration of its religious system as recorded in the book of Ezra and politically revived through Nehemiah's rebuilding of the Jerusalem wall. Thus, the nation could now protect itself from Gentile attacks and the dangers of assimilation if they maintained their faithfulness to God's Word. Such distinctiveness would place her in a position to fulfill her future covenant purpose by bringing forth the Jewish Messiah.

II. Renewing the People (Nehemiah 8:1–13:31)

A. Revival and Covenant Renewal (Nehemiah 8:1–10:39)

Unfortunately the Jewish people did not consistently follow Ezra's original teachings, so Ezra reread portions of the law (8:1–4). This was followed by the people's repentant and reverential reactions to what they heard (8:5–16) and the observance of the Feast of Tabernacles (8:17–18). Ezra's reading and the people's response to the law was necessary for the nation to become culturally and religiously distinct and thus prepared to fulfill her future covenant destiny. Ezra's reading of the law produced its intended effect as the nation repented of its sins (9:1–38) and renewed its commitment to the Mosaic covenant (10:1–39). Such covenant renewal translated into Israel's marital (10:30), commercial (10:31), and religious (10:39) distinction among the nations.

The story of Ezra's preaching illustrates some changes in the process of religious instruction after the return from the Babylonian exile. Ezra stands up on a wooden pulpit to read the Scriptures and then interprets them in order to explain their meaning to a mixed audience of men, women, and older children ("those who could understand," 8:3). This interpretation was necessary because Ezra read the Torah in Hebrew, but the people needed it interpreted and explained in Aramaic, the common language of the people at that time. As Ezra preached, the audience responded by lifting up their hands and saying, "Amen" (8:6).

B. Reforming the Society (Nehemiah 11:1–13:31)

With the wall now rebuilt, the nation was free to begin to repopulate the city. Thus, the writer is careful to record the leaders and the people chosen by lot to reside in the city of Jerusalem (11:1–2). The writer also preserves a record of the heads of the families residing in Jerusalem (11:3–24) as well as the villages occupied by the Jews living outside Jerusalem (11:25–36).

Unfortunately, during the time Nehemiah was away from Jerusalem in Persia (13:6), some of the people wandered away from their covenant commitments. In God's providence Nehemiah returned to Jerusalem in order to hold the nation accountable for adhering to its prior covenant commitments. Nehemiah's covenant enforcement took the form of excluding foreigners from the assembly (13:1–3), removing Tobiah from the temple (13:4–9), restoring the Levitical tithes (13:10–14), stopping Sabbath breaking (13:15–22), and disciplining those who had intermarried with pagans (13:23–29). Nehemiah was a man of prayer, vision, determination, and administrative skill. The result of his efforts set the stage for the foundation of Orthodox Judaism in the years that followed.

Practical Application

The books of Ezra and Nehemiah demonstrate how God uses dedicated people to accomplish His purposes. The rebuilding of both the temple and the walls of Jerusalem came about as the result of men who were determined to get the job done despite the opposition they faced. Both books remind us that serving God is never an easy task. There will always be external opposition to the plans and purposes of God, but these can be overcome by His sovereign power working through our human efforts as we surrender ourselves completely to Him. Ask yourself anew, "What does God want to accomplish through my life today?"

Ezra and Nehemiah had a vision of a better future for Jerusalem and the people of Israel. The revival under their leadership set the stage for the next four hundred years. Their reforms brought security, stability, and spiritual revival. Their vision for the future kept them focused on their goals with specific plans of action for their people.

Jerusalem once again became a viable city with a hope and future (Jer 29:11). The promises of God were kept alive by Zerubbabel. who led the Jews to return and rebuild the temple seventy-five years before Nehemiah arrived to rebuild the walls (Ezra 5:2; Hag 2:23). In the person of Zerubbabel, the messianic seed returned to the Promised Land (Matt 1:12). The stage was set for the coming of the Messiah. It was only a matter of time.

Their legacy had been secured and their future assured. We too will leave a legacy one day. What will it be: one of faith and action, or of doubt and hesitation? The choices we make today will determine our destiny tomorrow.

For Further Reading

Breneman, M. *Ezra, Nehemiah, Esther*. NAC. Nashville: B&H, 1993.

Fensham, F. C. *The Books of Ezra and Nehemiah*. NICOT. Grand Rapids: Eerdmans, 1983.

Kidner, Derek. *Ezra and Nehemiah*. TOTC. Downers Grove, IL: InterVarsity Press, 1979.

Smith, Gary V. *Ezra-Nehemiah, Esther*. CBC. Carol Stream, IL: Tyndale House, 2010.

Williamson, H. G. *Ezra, Nehemiah*. WBC 16. Waco, TX: Word, 1985.

Yamauchi, Edwin M. "Ezra-Nehemiah." In *EBC*. Grand Rapids: Zondervan, 1988.

Study Questions

1. How did Ezra's love for the Word of God influence his life and ministry?
2. Why was the building of the second temple so important for the Jewish people and religion?
3. How do we see God's providence at work in the events described in the book of Ezra?
4. How did Ezra's reforms set the standards for Orthodox Judaism?
5. How can we keep a proper balance between spiritual devotion and external legalism?
6. What is God challenging you to do to make a difference in your world today?

Notes

1. Not all agree with this conclusion. H. G. M. Williamson (*Israel in the Book of Chronicles* [Cambridge: Cambridge University Press, 1977], 1–86) weighs the evidence and comes to the conclusion that Ezra and Nehemiah were not written by the author who wrote Chronicles.

2. For a list of words and constructions showing similarities between Chronicles, Ezra, and Nehemiah, see S. R. Driver, *An Introduction to the Literature of the Old Testament*, 12th ed. (New York: Scribner's Sons, 1906), 535–40.

3. Cf. John Whitcomb, "Ezra, Nehemiah, and Esther," in *Wycliffe Bible Commentary* (Chicago: Moody, 1962), 423; Edwin Yamauchi, *The Stones and the Scriptures* (Grand Rapids: Baker, 1981), 81–91; Stephen Miller, *Daniel*, NAC 18 (Nashville: B&H, 1994), 30–32.

4. See detailed discussion in M. Breneman, *Ezra, Nehemiah, Esther*, NAC (Nashville: B&H, 1993), 15–48; and J. S. Wright, *The Date of Ezra's Coming to Jerusalem* (London: Tyndale Press, 1958).

5. D. Kidner, *Ezra and Nehemiah*, TOTC (Downers Grove, IL: InterVarsity Press, 1979), 146–58.

6. Cf. Talmud (*Baba Bathra* 15a), Josephus (*Contra Apion* 1.8) and Melito of Sardis (Eusebius, *Ecclesiastical History*, 4.26). See R. K. Harrison, *Introduction to the Old Testament* (Grand Rapids: Eerdmans, 1969), 1,135.

7. Edwin M. Yamauchi, "Ezra-Nehemiah," in *EBC*, ed. F. E. Gaebelein (Grand Rapids: Zondervan, 1988), 4:572.

8. The likely year of Artaxerxes's accession was 464 BC, making 445 BC his nineteenth year. Cf. Harold Hoehner, *Chronological Aspects of the Life of Christ* (Grand Rapids: Zondervan, 1977), 127–28.

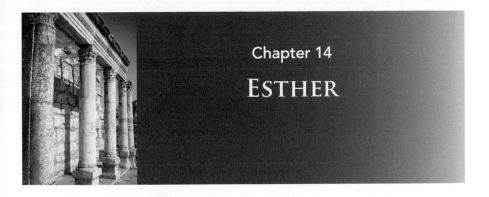

Chapter 14

ESTHER

Rescuing the People

The story of Esther is filled with palace intrigue, personal adventure, and anti-Semitic drama. Hill and Walton write, "It would be difficult to find a more riveting, dramatic, and suspenseful plot in the pre-Hellenistic world than the book of Esther."[1] The cast of characters alone would make it a best seller in today's world: the powerful king, the defiant queen, the diabolical villain, and the courageous Esther. The anti-Judaic thread of Gentile animosity runs through nearly every chapter as does the providential hand of the unnamed God of the Jews.

Despite the book's popularity, critics have questioned, criticized, debated, and sometimes excluded Esther as an inspired canonical book.[2] It is the only Old Testament book missing among the documents and fragments of the Dead Sea Scrolls. Esther is also the only Old Testament book in which the name of God does not appear.[3] Yet the religious practice of fasting by Esther, Mordecai, and the Jews certainly indicates a dependence on God's divine intervention (4:16). Despite these challenges Esther has remained a message of hope over the centuries for Jewish and Christian readers alike.

KEY FACTS

Author:	Anonymous Persian Jew (Mordecai?)
Date:	Circa 450–400 BC
Recipients:	Jews of the Diaspora
Key Word:	Fast(ing) (Hb. *tsôm*)
Key Verse:	"Go and assemble all the Jews … and fast for me. … After that, I will go to the king. … If I perish, I perish" (4:16).

Title

The title of the book is derived from its central character, an obscure Jewish girl who became one of the queens of Persia. Esther's Hebrew name, *Hadassah* (2:7), means "myrtle," but it was changed to the pagan name *Ester* derived from the Persian word for "star" (*stara*). Esther's name was a form of the name of the Babylonian goddess *Ishtar* or *Ashtar*. The book of Esther is one of the five books the Jews called the *Megilloth* or "Rolls." The other four books are Song of Songs, Ruth, Lamentations, and Ecclesiastes. These books were read at Israel's various feasts. The book of Esther was read at the Feast of *Purim*, celebrating the deliverance and preservation of the Jews during the Persian period.

The Persian king Darius I seated on his throne.

Author

The book of Esther is an anonymous work by a Jewish writer living in Persia (ancient Iran). His familiarity with Persian culture is frequently revealed, indicating the book did not come from the Hellenistic period. The author knew about the seven royal advisers who "saw the king's face" (1:14 KJV), the well-organized postal system (1:22; 3:13; 8:10; 9:20, 30), the practices of showing respect for high officials (3:2), the recording and rewarding of the king's benefactors (2:23; 6:8), the king's signet ring (3:10; 8:8), Persia's irrevocable royal decrees (1:19), the observance of "lucky" days (3:7), the king's horse with a royal crown (6:8), the practice of eating while reclining on couches (7:8), and the fact that Persian kings did everything on a grand scale (six-month banquets, displaying wealth).[4] Therefore many believe Mordecai was probably the original author.

Background

The events in the book of Esther cover a period of ten years, from 483 to 473 BC. The story begins in the third year of Xerxes (Greek name), called *Achashverosh* in Hebrew and *Khshayarsh* in Persian. Xerxes ruled the Persian Empire from India to Africa (1:1) from 486 to 464 BC. Thus, the events recorded in the book happened after Zerubbabel's return to Jerusalem

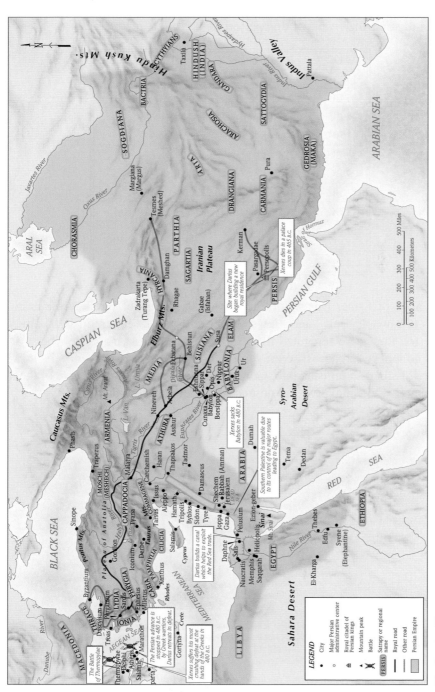

The Persian Empire.

in 538 BC and before Nehemiah's return in 444 BC. Conservative scholars generally date the events of this period as the following:[5]

538 BC	Return Under Zerubbabel
515 BC	Dedication of Second Temple
483 BC	Xerxes's Military Planning at Susa
482 BC	Deposition of Queen Vashti
481 BC	Xerxes's Invasion of Greece
480 BC	Esther's Arrival in Susa
479 BC	Esther's Coronation in Susa
474 BC	Decree to Exterminate the Jews
473 BC	Esther's Banquets and Feast of Purim
464 BC	Death of Xerxes and Ascension of Artaxerxes
444 BC	Nehemiah Dispatched by Artaxerxes

The book of Esther was written to Jews living outside Israel. While many Jews (the words "Jew" and "Jews" are used fifty-one times) in Persia may have felt they were separated from God's protective care and love because they no longer had access to the temple or lived in the Holy Land, the message of Esther is unmistakable: God loves His people and takes care of them no matter where they live and no matter what their circumstances.

Xerxes's throne hall or second audience hall at Persepolis.

Outline

The book has two main parts. First it records the threat or the risk to the Jews (chaps. 1–5). This section can be further divided into Esther's ascension to the throne (1:1–2:20) and Haman's plot to destroy the Jews (2:21–5:14). This section features Xerxes's four banquets (1:3, 5–8, 9; 2:18). In the second main part the book records the deliverance or rescue of the Jews (chaps. 6–10). This section can be further divided into Mordecai's triumph over Haman (6:1–8:3) and Israel's triumph over her enemies (8:4–10:3). This section features Esther's second banquet (7:1–10) and the Feast of Purim (9:20–32).

Outline

I. Danger to the Jews (1:1–5:14)
   A. Demotion of Vashti (1:1–22)
   B. Destiny of Esther (2:1–23)
   C. Decree Against the Jews (3:1–15)
   D. Decision of Esther (4:1–5:14)
II. Deliverance of the Jews (6:1–10:3)
   A. Valor of Mordecai Rewarded (6:1–14)
   B. Venture of Esther (7:1–10)
   C. Victory of the Jews (8:1–9:32)
   D. Vindication of Mordecai (10:1–3)

Message

The book of Esther is a continuous story that contains six banquets and seven decrees. It begins with a crisis when Queen Vashti refused to appear for her husband King Ahasuerus (Xerxes) and embarrassed him before his government leaders. The story tells of Vashti's banishment and how a young Jewish girl was chosen to be queen in her place. A subplot reveals Prime Minister Haman's hatred of the Jews primarily because Mordecai would not bow to him. Haman persuaded King Xerxes to order the execution of the Jews, but Esther's wisdom and intercession thwarted Haman's evil intent. In celebration of their victory, the Jews instituted a celebration of the annual Feast of Purim ("lots").

I. Danger to the Jews (Esther 1:1–5:14)

The book of Esther describes how God sovereignly worked on behalf of the Jewish people in Persia to spare them from eradication so the nation could fulfill her future covenantal and messianic purposes. The first major section of the book describes the threat that developed against the Jews and how God orchestrated events behind the scenes.

A. Demotion of Queen Vashti (Esther 1:1–22)

The story begins by describing how God providentially arranged for Vashti's dismissal as Xerxes's queen so that Esther, who would be the divine instrument of Jewish deliverance, could be elevated to the position of queen in Vashti's place. The author notes the extent of Xerxes's Persian Empire, from India to Africa (1:1), and his elaborate banquet, which many scholars believe was held for the purpose of planning his invasion of Greece.

B. Destiny of Esther (Esther 2:1–23)

After an extensive search, Esther was elevated to the role of queen in the place of Vashti. However, her decision to hide her Jewish identity and take a pagan name was typical of many Jews living in the *diaspora* ("dispersion") outside of Israel. The author also notes that Esther was far from perfect by Jewish standards. Mordecai, a Benjamite, was Esther's guardian. His work brought him into contact with Persian government officials, and eventually he became the target of anti-Judaic prejudice.

This chapter ends with Mordecai preventing a plot to kill the king, but for some mysterious reason Mordecai was not rewarded for his heroic efforts.

C. Decree Against the Jews (Esther 3:1–15)

Despite Mordecai's intervention to

Dating from the sixth century BC, this glazed brick frieze shows the Persian Royal Guard. The relief was found at the Palace of Darius at Susa.

foil an assassination plot against Xerxes (2:21–23), Haman, the king's advisor, hatched a plot to eradicate the Jews. After Xerxes's promotion of Haman (3:1), Mordecai refused to bow down to Haman (3:2–4). Consequently, Haman flew into a rage culminating in his ambition to exterminate all of the Jews (3:5–6). Had this ethnic cleansing succeeded, it would have exterminated the line of Christ because his ancestors were then living in Judah under the Persian administration (Matt 1:12–13; Luke 3:26).

The Source of Anti-Semitism

God promised to bless the world through the Jews (Gen 12:3; Isa 42:6; 49:6). Thus, the three greatest blessings God could ever give the world will come through the Jews. These blessings include the Scripture (Rom 3:2), the Savior (Matt 1:1–17; John 4:22; Rom 9:5), and the future kingdom (Isa 2:2–3; Zech 14:16–18). Because of this divine pattern, Satan has a special animosity toward the Jew. His ambition has always been to stop this flow of blessings by prematurely eradicating Israel. Therefore, Satan is the ultimate source of anti-Semitism. Even today Satan works through fallen people to eradicate the Jew in an attempt to thwart God's promise that the Messiah will ultimately reign over all the earth (Isa 66:15–20; Zech 14:4–11; Rev 5:10; 20:4).

D. Decision of Esther (Esther 4:1–5:14)

As the drama unfolds, the Jews are mourning, fasting, weeping, and lamenting (4:3) because of this threat. While God's name is not mentioned specifically, it is obvious to Jewish readers that they are calling on God to help them. Mordecai used his influence with Esther to convince her that she was the instrument God had chosen and strategically placed in a position of power to deliver the Jews during this dark hour. At this point Esther made her courageous decision to risk her life to appeal to the king saying, "If I perish, I perish," and asked the Jews to fast and pray for God's protection (4:15–16).

Esther's poise, grace, and wisdom are shown in a series of clever choices she made to present her case to Xerxes. It was unlawful for her, or anyone else, to enter the king's presence without being invited. First, she appeared in her royal robes in the courtyard opposite the throne room. Impressed, Xerxes extended the golden scepter of approval and asked what she wanted. When offered "half the kingdom" (5:3), Esther cleverly responded that she merely wanted to invite him and Haman to a banquet (5:5). At the banquet she extended another invitation to do it again the next day.

II. Deliverance of the Jews (Esther 6:1–10:3)

The book's second major section describes how the Jews were ultimately delivered by Esther's courageous and clever intervention.

A. Valor of Mordecai Rewarded (Esther 6:1–14)

Upon discovering in the king's chronicles that Mordecai's previous good deed on his behalf had gone unrewarded, Xerxes decided to reward Mordecai. Inadvertently, Haman was instructed to honor Mordecai in a manner he would have preferred for himself. Humiliated, the angry and frustrated Haman expressed his exasperation to his wife and friends, who warned him that he would not prevail against Mordecai because Haman's downfall was certain (6:13).

B. Venture of Esther (Esther 7:1–10)

The triumph of the Jews over Haman reaches its climax at Esther's second banquet. When Xerxes asks Esther to state her request (7:1–2), she reveals Haman's plot to eradicate the Jews and asks the king to spare her life and the lives of her people (7:3–6). The end result was the hanging of Haman on the gallows he had prepared for Mordecai (7:9–10).

C. Victory of the Jews (Esther 8:1–9:32)

Because of the immutability of Persian law, Esther influenced Xerxes to issue yet another decree allowing the Jews to defend themselves against those who might try to attack them. Because the second decree represents God's providential work to spare His people from extinction, many have noted how Xerxes's second decree parallels his first decree.

The great audience hall at Persepolis begun by Darius I (Darius the Great) and completed by Xerxes.

Xerxes's First Decree (Esther 3)	Xerxes's Second Decree (Esther 8)
Haman requests the decree (3:8–9).	Esther requests the decree (8:3–6).
Xerxes authorizes the decree (3:10–11).	Xerxes authorizes the decree (8:7–8).
Scribes compose the decree (3:12).	Scribes compose the decree (8:9).
Decree disseminated (3:13–15).	Decree disseminated (8:10–14).
Susa confused (3:15).	Susa rejoices (8:15).
Jews mourn (4:1–3).	Jews rejoice (8:16–17).

Chapter 9 explains the significance of the Festival of Purim ("lots"). Since Haman cast lots to determine when he would execute the Jews, they celebrated their victory over this procedure with feasting, rejoicing, and sending gifts (9:18–19). To this day the Jews celebrate "Esther's Banquet" at the Feast of Purim on the fifteenth of Adar (February–March) in remembrance of God's blessing and protection.

D. Mordecai's Vindication (Esther 10:1–3)

The book concludes with a reminder of the blessings or curses individuals experience when they bless or curse God's covenant people. While Haman was hung on his own gallows due to his ambition to destroy the Jews, Mordecai was elevated to second in command (10:3) in the Persian Empire so he enjoyed the enduring respect of the Jews (10:3b) on account of his work on their behalf. Esther's courageous intervention and Mordecai's elevation secured the messianic promise by securing the future of the Jewish people who would give birth to their ultimate Deliverer.

Practical Application

The providence of God is obvious throughout the book of Esther. While God's name is not specifically mentioned, His providential intervention to rescue His people is unmistakable. The timing of God is seen time and time again in the details of the story. These are not accidents of timing but divine appointments by which the reader easily discerns the presence of Israel's unseen and unspoken God. We too must learn to trust God even when He seems silent. In reality, He is always at work on our behalf.

For Further Reading

Baldwin, Joyce. *Esther*. TOTC. Downers Grove, IL: InterVarsity Press, 1984.
Breneman, M. *Ezra, Nehemiah, Esther*. NAC. Nashville: B&H, 1993.
Jobes, Karen. *Esther*. NIVAC. Grand Rapids: Zondervan, 1999.
Tomasino, A. "Esther" 1 & 2 Kings, 1 & 2 Chronicles, Ezra, Nehemiah, Esther. In *ZIBBC*, ed. J. Walton. 3:468–502, Grand Rapids: Zondervan, 2009.
Whitcomb, John C. *Esther: Triumph of God's Sovereignty*. Everyman's Bible Commentary. Chicago: Moody, 1979.

Study Questions

1. How is God's presence revealed in the book of Esther?
2. What lessons can be learned about pride and humility in the book of Esther?
3. How can we trace God's hand in our lives even when we can't see His face or hear His name?
4. What does Esther's experience tell us about God's working in our own lives?
5. How did God use Esther to protect the messianic line of Christ?

Notes

1. A. Hill and J. Walton, *A Survey of the Old Testament* (Grand Rapids: Zondervan, 2009), 348.

2. See details in R. Beckwith, *The Old Testament Canon of the New Testament Church* (Grand Rapids: Eerdmans, 1985), 283–91.

3. E. W. Bullinger, *The Companion Bible* (Grand Rapids: Kregel, 1999), appendix 60, 85 suggests the name Yahweh (Jehovah) is hidden in four acrostics (1:20; 5:4; 5:13; 7:7), which Hebrew readers would easily recognize.

4. E. Yamauchi, *Persia and the Bible* (Grand Rapids: Baker, 1990). The linguistic differences between Esther and Ezra-Nehemiah demand a different author who was living in Persia, was an eyewitness of these events, and had access to official court records.

5. Cf. John Whitcomb, *Esther: Triumph of God's Sovereignty* (Chicago: Moody Press, 1979), 12–28; C. Dyer and E. Merrill, *Old Testament Explorer* (Nashville: Word, 2001), 360–65; J. Stafford Wright, "The Historicity of the Book of Esther," in *New Perspectives on the Old Testament*, ed. J. Barton Payne (Waco: Word, 1970), 37–47.

Chapter 15

JOB

Questions of Suffering

W hy do bad things happen to good people? This is a question for the ages, which every person on earth will face sooner or later. Those who have not had their own experiences in suffering know someone who has. So when calamity strikes, many are inclined to ask, "Why me, Lord?"

KEY FACTS

Author:	Anonymous
Date:	Uncertain
Recipients:	Suffering believers
Key Word:	Reject or Take back (Hb. *mâ'as*)
Key Verses:	"I had heard reports about you, but now my eyes have seen you. Therefore I reject my words and am sorry for them; I am dust and ashes" (42:5–6).

Suffering draws out the deepest human emotions, which are best communicated through the literary form of poetry. God has provided the story of a man who suffered more than anyone can even imagine. Through the avenue of poetic expression, the reader is drawn into the heart of Job to feel his frustration and pain. Furthermore, as wisdom literature, the book of Job deals with some of life's most important philosophical questions. How can an all-powerful God allow the righteous to suffer?

Ultimately, God's sense of justice is called into question, and the book of Job provides a wisdom-based response to these most pressing and relevant issues. The book of Job addresses these questions of human suffering from five perspectives to help the reader grapple with these issues. Norman Geisler summarizes these by the following:

1. Author: Suffering is pernicious (satanic).
2. Job: Suffering is a puzzle (serious).
3. Friends: Suffering is penal (sinful).
4. Elihu: Suffering purifies (shortcomings).
5. God: Suffering is providential (sovereignty).

Geisler adds: "There is some truth in all these views of suffering. But as applied to Job's situation, the friends were wrong. Job was not suffering because of his sins."[1] God's providential purposes were being accomplished by His sovereign permission to allow Job to suffer so that he, his friends, and all who read this amazing story may benefit from it.

Author and Date

The authorship and date of composition for Job are shrouded in mystery. Significant clues in the book provide evidence of an early setting for the events surrounding the narrative of Job. Some believe Job lived during the time of the patriarchs because of the total lack of Mosaic references within the book. Job was a priest to his family; his age was that of the patriarchs; and there are no references to the tabernacle, temple, feasts, or sacrifices that accompanied the Mosaic law.[2] Additionally, the various places and names within the book reflect a setting prior to the conquest of Canaan.[3] Therefore, the internal evidence supports an early setting for the narrative of Job, but the actual time of the writing remains uncertain.

Structure and Style

The book of Job is a literary masterpiece with an unusual structure of poetic dialogue set within a narrative framework. While many Bible readers are familiar with the narrative story line of Job, this only provides the background for the dialogue itself, a dramatic roller coaster of rich lament, forceful accusation, and biting sarcasm. The

Modern Arab man wearing typical head cloth (called kaffiyeh) worn by Middle Easterners for millennia.

literary genius of Job is characterized by the unique mixture and wide variety of literary forms employed, including the narrative prologue and epilogue (1:1–2:13; 42:7–17), Job's initial speech of lament (3:1–26), and a self-contained poem expressing the virtues of wisdom (28:1–28). The poetic dialogue between Job and his three friends contains three cycles of speeches, each using rich examples of metaphor, hyperbole, sarcasm, irony, and a host of word pictures. The "God speech" (38:1–41:34) contains more than seventy rhetorical questions aimed at expressing in no uncertain terms God's unfathomable wisdom.[4]

Outline

The changes in genre and style reveal a number of clear structural breaks within the book that are indicated by introductory references to a new speaker. Based on these indicators, the following outline may be helpful in discerning the flow of the book of Job:[5]

I. Prologue: Opening Narrative (1:1–2:13)
II. Dialogue: Job and His Friends (3:1–27:23)
   A. Job's Lament (3:1–26)
   B. First Cycle of Speeches (4:1–14:22)
   C. Second Cycle of Speeches (15:1–21:34)
   D. Third Cycle of Speeches (22:22–27:23)
III. Interlude: Poem on Wisdom (28:1–28)
IV. Monologues: Job, Elihu, and God (29:1–42:6)
   A. Job's Closing Oration (29:1–31:40)
   B. Elihu's Speeches (32:1–37:24)
   C. God's Response to Job (38:1–41:34)
   D. Job's Reply to God (42:1–6)
V. Epilogue: Closing Narrative (42:7–17)

Message

I. Prologue: Opening Narrative (Job 1:1–2:13)

The narrator introduces the reader to Job, a man whose righteous character is affirmed three times in the first two chapters of the book (1:1, 8; 2:3). Job is also described as a wealthy man from a distant land, "the greatest man among all the people of the east" (1:3). Taking the reader into the realm of supernatural conflict, the narrator sets the stage with the first test as the Lord presents his servant Job as a model of righteousness before Satan. Satan replies with the accusatory challenge, "Does Job fear God for nothing?"

(1:9). God then allows Satan to take from Job everything he has but sets limits by not allowing Satan to take his health (1:12).

Next the author takes the reader into a second cosmic test, with Satan charging that Job will indeed curse God if his health is taken. The Lord in turn allows Satan to take his health, but he must preserve his life (2:4–6). In the midst of his physical affliction, the response remains the same; Job does not curse God (2:10) even though Job's wife says, "Why don't you curse God and die?" (2:9 GNT). This is not necessarily a statement of unbelief but the realistic agony of a woman who has lost all her children and is about to lose her husband. The opening narrative concludes with the introduction of Job's three friends: Eliphaz, Bildad, and Zophar. While these friends came to sympathize with and comfort Job, they would later become adversarial as they accuse Job of heinous sins in the dialogue that follows.

II. Dialogue: Job and His Friends (Job 3:1–27:23)

Job's lament breaks the silence between Job and his three friends and introduces the dialogue that follows. Job curses the day of his birth (3:1–10) and questions why God would allow him to be born if His only plan was to bring him to a place of such intense suffering (3:11–26). While still not accusing God of injustice, Job indicates that he wishes he had died at birth.

Camels are still used by bedouins and others as a mode of travel in the Middle East.

Structured around three cycles of speeches, the poetic dialogue in chapters 4–27 is a literary masterpiece that communicates the full range of emotions experienced by the afflicted. Additionally, the dialogue calls into question widely accepted assumptions regarding the reason people suffer, namely, the retribution of a just God against the sinner. Job's friends assume he must have done something terribly wrong, unjust, or unwise to experience such an incredible tragedy.[6]

REFLECTION

Why Me?

Life's deepest suffering causes us to ask life's toughest questions. Why me? Why this? Why now? The agony of suffering rips away our self-sufficiency. When the bottom falls out of our lives, we tend to curse God, question God, or pray to God. You may have already suffered deep emotional anxiety, physical pain, or spiritual despair, but for most of us, the worst is yet to come. We have no guarantees of avoiding pain and suffering in a fallen world, but we can prepare our minds and hearts for the inevitable. When suffering comes, what will you do? Run away from God or run to him? Question His wisdom or cling to His sovereignty?

Throughout their speeches Eliphaz, Bildad, and Zophar mount various arguments in support of their theological positions, ranging from a vision to experience and tradition, or reason and speculation; but in the end they are unable to mount any evidence to prove that Job is suffering because he is a sinner. As Job responds to each of his friend's speeches, he maintains his innocence in the midst of many accusations to the contrary (9:21; 16:17;

Four Arabic men conversing near their camels.

23:10). Instead of confessing to a sin he did not commit, Job calls into question the justice of God, which only heightens the ire of the three friends.

Apparently Job is not aware of the heavenly test in which he is a participant although a slight hint of this comes in the vision in 4:17–21 when God indicates He cannot trust some of His angels because they do evil things. In keeping with his desire to know what charges God has against him, Job desires an opportunity to have his day in court with God (9:32; 13:6–19; 31:35–37). Job is convinced that if he could only have the opportunity to present his case to God, then God would realize He is judging the wrong man, and Job would be proclaimed innocent (13:3–27). However, God is not immanently present, and Job's frustration mounts as he longs for an encounter with God but finds no way to confront the Almighty (23:1–17). Nevertheless, Job holds on to his faith, hoping that one day he will be vindicated as he stands before his God (9:33–35; 16:18–22; 19:25–27). In this context Job states his faith in the resurrection when he says: "I know that my redeemer lives. . . . And after my skin has been destroyed, yet in my flesh I will see God" (19:25–26 NIV).

III. Interlude: Poem on Wisdom (Job 28:1–28)

The book deals with one of wisdom's most pressing questions: the apparent inequity of divine justice and retribution. Understanding the issue of divine justice as the driving theological question in the book, it is only fitting that a poem praising the virtues of wisdom is included. Comparing the search for wisdom with the difficult endeavor of mining for precious metals and gems under the surface of the earth, the poem suggests that the value of wisdom far exceeds that of riches, and its gain is far more elusive. Nevertheless, in keeping with Proverbs, the poem concludes that wisdom ultimately rests in the fear of the Lord (28:28), even when man is unable to comprehend the activity of God (Eccl 3:14).

IV. Monologues: Job, Elihu, and God (Job 29:1–42:6)

A. Job's Closing Oration (Job 29:1–31:40)

Job concludes his speeches by reflecting on his life prior to his suffering (29:1–25) and by contrasting that with the plague of despair that now accompanies his every hour (30:1–19). With one last affirmation of his innocence, Job challenges God to judge him honestly, even suggesting appropriate punishments for various sins; and yet in all of this, Job affirms that he is innocent of all such iniquities (31:1–40).

B. Elihu's Speeches (Job 32:1–37:24)

Elihu's speeches begin with a short narrative commentary introducing the young man Elihu, who up until this point has remained silent. Elihu was angry at Job for "justifying himself rather than God" and was upset with the three friends "because they had found no way to refute Job, and yet had condemned him" (32:2–3 NIV). His entrance into the dialogue remains somewhat of a mystery, and as quickly as he enters the scene, he exits without further reference in the epilogue. The justice of God is clearly affirmed in Elihu's speech (37:23), and God's ways are deemed "beyond our understanding" (36:26; 37:5 NIV). Furthermore, within his speech Elihu introduces a "middle ground" in understanding the purposes of God in suffering, suggesting that God may use suffering as a means to keep men from sin (33:29–30), to chastise (33:19), and to maintain a healthy degree of reverence before the Almighty (37:24). In other words, God may permit suffering to mature and grow our faith.

C. God's Response to Job (Job 38:1–41:34)

At long last the Lord replies to Job and brings clarity concerning the misconstrued theology of the three friends and, more particularly, the misconceived accusations of injustice mounted against God by the suffering Job. Although Job looked forward to a day when he would question God and God would answer him, God now questions Job. Through the use of more than seventy rhetorical questions, God appeals to creation as a demonstration of his unfathomable wisdom. The main point expressed through God's speech is captured by Job 41:11 (NIV), "Who has a claim against me that I must pay? Everything in heaven belongs to me." God does not explain the rationale or the reason behind Job's suffering, and He reveals no compulsion to justify His actions before Job. God reminds us, as He did Job, that He is God and we are not.

D. Job's Reply to God (Job 42:1–6)

In response to God, Job repents of his wrongheaded thinking and the fact that he "spoke of . . . things too wonderful for me to know" (42:3 NIV). There is no indication in Job's response of any awareness regarding why he suffered. Rather, Job simply responds in faith knowing it is enough that God is in control. As a true believer Job submits to God's sovereign will and stops questioning His intentions. In so doing, Job remains a powerful example to all of us who struggle with the seemingly insurmountable questions of life, only to fall in faith, exasperated, into the arms of God.

A view of Orion Nebula, the constellation bearing the name of a giant Greek hunter who, according to the myth, was bound and placed in the heavens. Job 38:31 may allude to this myth. God is consistently portrayed as the creator of the Orion constellation (9:9; Amos 5:8). The plural of the Hebrew term for Orion is rendered "constellations" in Isa 13:10.

V. Epilogue: Closing Narrative (Job 42:7–17)

In the narrative epilogue to the book, Job is vindicated, and his health is restored to him. The three friends are condemned for their false accusations and misguided theology, and Job is called upon to serve as a priest and pray on their behalf (42:7–9). As for Job's restoration, God prospers him once again and blesses him with twice the wealth he had prior to Satan's challenge (42:10, 12).

Practical Application

The epilogue of Job makes clear that the strict retribution theology of the three friends was wrong in Job's case, and this certainly holds true in many cases of suffering experienced throughout history. Their wrong perspective reminds us not to judge others too quickly else we fall into the same hypocritical trap. Elihu's suggestion that suffering can be used as a preventative measure against sin is certainly valid. Scripture clearly affirms that suffering *can* be chastisement for sin (Heb 12:7–11). But it can also be permitted by a loving God as the apostle Paul attests in 2 Cor 12:7–9 when he affirms God's promise that His grace is sufficient for our every need. In the end the main point in the book of Job is that God is just, even when people do not understand their difficult circumstances. Thus we are called to trust God in spite of our circumstances.

For Further Reading

Alden, R. I. *Job*. NAC. Nashville: B&H, 1993.

Anderson, Francis. *Job*. TOTC. Downers Grove, IL: InterVarsity Press, 1976.

Ellison, H. L. *Job: From Tragedy to Triumph*. Grand Rapids: Eerdmans, 1977.

Hartley, John. *The Book of Job*. NICOT. Grand Rapids: Eerdmans, 1988.

Smick, Elmer, and Tremper Longman. "Job." In *EBC*. Grand Rapids: Zondervan, 2010.

Zuck, Roy. "Job." *BKC OT*. Colorado Springs: Victor, 2000.

Study Questions

1. Describe the enormity of Job's losses. Why did God allow this to happen to him?
2. How did these tragedies impact Job's wife?
3. What was wrong with the advice of Job's three friends?
4. How was Elihu's perspective different and unique?
5. Is God really the final answer to the problem of suffering? How do you know?
6. What is the most serious challenge you have faced with the issue of personal suffering? How are you handling it?

Notes

1. Norman Geisler, *A Popular Survey of the Old Testament* (Grand Rapids: Baker, 2007), 192.

2. Arguing from a lack of evidence is somewhat precarious, for every writer is selective and may choose not to mention people, places, or things, yet that does not mean they do not exist at that time. Although the prophet Amos does not mention the giant Goliath, this lack of evidence cannot be used to prove that Amos prophesied before David fought Goliath. Nevertheless, when a large amount of evidence is not mentioned that one might expect to fit into the story, then one can hypothesize evidence for dating a book.

3. Additionally, the geographical location of "Uz" (Job 1:1) reflects a setting outside the region of Canaan, perhaps in Edom or Midian. See Robert L. Alden, *Job*, NAC (Nashville: B&H, 1993), 29.

4. Note the implied irony in these questions. Throughout the dialogue Job envisions a day when he will stand in court and question God regarding the circumstances of his suffering, but he is frustrated by God's silence and inapproachable standing. However, in spite of Job's intentions, when God does speak, God questions Job.

5. The main points of the outline are taken from E. H. Merrill, M. Rooker, and M. Grisanti, *The Word and the World* (Nashville: B&H, 2011), 502–3.

6. Grisanti distinguishes the arguments of the three friends as follows: "Eliphaz, an empiricist, based his counsel on experience. Bildad, a traditionalist, grounded his advice on the orthodoxy of the past. Zophar was a rationalist who carefully avoided any minimizing of Job's sin." See E. H. Merrill, M. Rooker, and M. Grisanti, *The World and the Word*, 504.

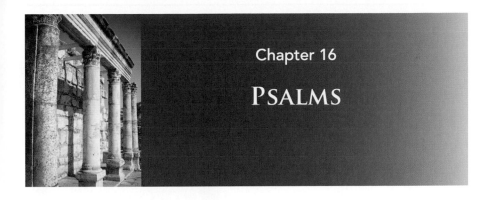

Chapter 16

PSALMS

Songs of Praise

The Psalms are songs of prayer and praise. Many were written to be sung as expressions of faith and worship. The Psalms reflect the passion of the true worshipper and express the full range of human emotions as we enter into God's presence and seek His help for daily living. Vernon Whaley observes: "Throughout the Bible's pages, saints of God used music to express both their joy and their sorrow. We read anthems of gladness—and grievance. Ballads were sung to inspire prophets, enthrone kings, celebrate marriages, and lament deaths."[1]

KEY FACTS

Authors:	David, Moses, Asaph, and others
Dates:	1450–450 BC
Recipients:	People of Israel
Key Word:	Praise (Hb. *tehilim*)
Key Verse:	"May the words of my mouth and the meditation of my heart be acceptable to you, LORD, my rock and my Redeemer" (19:14).

Background and Authors

The title Psalms comes from the name of the book in the Greek Septuagint (*Psalmoi*). The term *psalmos* in Greek refers to a song sung to the accompaniment of a harp. The New Testament also uses the designation "psalms" or the "book of Psalms" (Luke 20:42, 44; Acts 1:20). The Hebrew title for the book, *Tehilim*, means "praise" or "songs of praise." This word is derived from the root *halal* ("to praise"), the basis for the English word "hallelujah." Psalms opens the third division of the Hebrew Bible known as the Writings (*kethuvim*) and is grouped with the poetic books in English Bibles.

The individual psalms were composed by many different individuals. Titles (or superscriptions) with various types of information are found in 116 of the 150 psalms. Of these 116 titles, 103 of them connect the psalm to a specific individual:

David	73 psalms
Asaph	12 psalms
Sons of Korah	10 psalms
Jeduthun	3 psalms
Solomon	2 psalms
Ethan the Ezrahite, Heman the Ezrahite, and Moses	1 psalm each

The titles of thirteen psalms (Psalms 3; 7; 18; 34; 51; 52; 54; 56; 57; 59; 60; 63; 142) contain historical notations linking them to specific events in David's life. Some psalm superscriptions include information regarding the literary genre, liturgical function, or musical performance of the psalms.

Terracotta stamped relief of a harpist. It is from Mesopotamia in the first half of the second millenium BC.

Formation of the Psalter

The psalms are divided into five books. The first four books conclude with a doxology or word of praise (Pss 41:13; 72:18–19; 89:52; 106:48), and the praise song in Psalm 150 provides a conclusion for the fifth book and Psalms as a whole. The reason for this fivefold division of Psalms is unclear, though rabbinic sources suggest this arrangement may reflect an attempt to parallel the five books of the Torah.

Book I   Psalms 1–41: Psalms of Man and Creation (Genesis)
Book II   Psalms 42–72: Psalms of Israel's Redemption (Exodus)
Book III   Psalms 73–89: Psalms of Temple Worship (Leviticus)
Book IV   Psalms 90–106: Psalms of Our Earthly Journey (Numbers)
Book V   Psalms 107–150: Psalms of Praise for Worship of God
            (Deuteronomy)

Literary Forms of the Psalms

The individual songs in the Psalter can be classified into eight or nine basic literary types or genres. The German scholar Hermann Gunkel was a pioneer of modern study of Psalms in his work identifying the major literary forms in Psalms.[2] Other scholars have refined Gunkel's approach and the ways the psalms are classified.[3] Studying the psalm genres provides understanding into the shared literary forms, elements, and themes of the different types of psalms. Modern scholarship has greatly enhanced the understanding of the connection between the psalms and various temple services and rituals (e.g., songs sung at thanksgiving meals, national feasts, enthronement festivals). Ugaritic studies have provided new insights into the nature of Semitic poetry in general.[4]

A rabbi prepares to read directly from the open Torah in front of the Western Wall in Jerusalem.

Hymns

Hymns are songs of praise that focus on the Lord's eternal attributes and His great acts in creation and history. Worship begins with response to the person of God and the desire to honor God for who He is. Reflection on the Lord's incomparable power, holiness, love, mercy, and faithfulness led the people of Israel to celebrative praise as they gathered at the temple. The two basic features of a hymn are the call to praise and the reason for praise. The reason explains why the Lord is worthy of worship.

REFLECTION

Music in Your Heart

Singing has always been an expression of worship. The angels sang together at creation (Job 38:4–7); Moses and Miriam led Israel in singing praise for their deliverance from Egypt (Exod 15:1–21); Deborah and Barak sang praises to God for their victory over the Canaanites (Judg 5:1–31); Jesus and the disciples sang a hymn at the Passover meal (Matt 26:30). The apostle Paul urged believers to be "filled by the Spirit: speaking to one another in psalms, hymns, and spiritual songs, singing and making music from your heart to the Lord" (Eph 5:18–19). Whether you can sing audibly or not, ask yourself if there is music in your heart. If not, why not? If not now, when? Maybe it is time to start singing by letting God fill your heart with joy, peace, purpose, and passion.

Laments

Laments are prayers offered in times of trouble, pleading for God's help, intervention, and deliverance. They are offered by individuals facing personal distress or by the entire community when experiencing national calamity. Laments comprise nearly one-third of the Psalter, making them the largest category of psalms. True worship is not only celebration but also involves approaching God with pain and hurt. The key elements of a lament include: (1) address and introductory petition, (2) lament, (3) confession of trust, (4) petition, (5) praise or vow of praise.

A special type of lament is the penitential psalm, in which the psalmist confesses his sin and prays for the Lord's forgiveness and restoration. The intensity of emotion expressed in these psalms reflects the seriousness of sin and its consequences. In Psalm 38, the psalmist acknowledges that he is deserving of the physical and emotional anguish he has received as punishment for his sin, but he prays that God would show mercy and turn from His anger. Psalm 51 is David's prayer of confession after he committed adultery with Bathsheba and tried to cover his sin by having her husband Uriah killed in battle (2 Samuel 11–12). David not only prayed for the blotting out of his sin but also for God to purify his heart so that he would no longer be inclined to sin. In response to his forgiveness, David vowed that he would teach sinners the Lord's ways.

Thanksgiving Psalms

Thanksgiving psalms are prayers expressing thanks to God for specific answers to prayer or for deliverance from danger. The lament is offered before the deliverance, and the thanksgiving is offered after. The three basic elements of a thanksgiving song are: (1) the proclamation or resolve to praise ("I will praise . . ."); (2) the report of the deliverance ("You have healed me"); (3) concluding praise or instruction for other worshippers ("give thanks"). The thanksgiving psalms represent the fulfillment of the vow of praise expressed in the lament when the psalmist was petitioning the Lord for help and deliverance in the midst of adversity (Ps 66:13–15).

Psalms of Confidence

The psalms of confidence are expressions of trust in the Lord and praise to the Lord for the security He provides to those who trust in Him. Psalms 23; 46; 62; 91; and 125 are representative examples of the songs of confidence,

Shepherd with sheep along the desert highway between Amman and Aqaba near Qatrana.

and metaphors of God's protection and security are especially prominent in these psalms. Psalm 23 presents the Lord as the Shepherd-King who provides for His people, leads them through life, and delivers them from danger. The psalmist rejoices that he is an honored guest in the house of the Lord.

Psalms of Ascent

Psalms 120–134 are songs of praise the people sang as they made pilgrimage to Jerusalem. These are sometimes called *hallel* psalms. The one who trusts in the Lord is as secure as Zion because the Lord surrounds His people like the mountains that surround Jerusalem. The righteous are confident that the Lord will not allow the wicked to prevail over them forever. These psalms express step-like parallelism emphasizing the verb *'aliah*, "go up" in these fifteen songs of Zion.

Royal Psalms

The royal psalms are prayers that celebrate the special relationship between the Lord and the house of the Davidic king. The Lord chose Israel as His royal-priestly people through whom He would mediate His presence and blessing to all peoples (Exod 19:5–6), and He chose the house of David to rule over Israel. The Lord unconditionally promised that He would

Overview of the city of Jerusalem.

establish the throne of David "forever" (2 Samuel 7; Ps 89:28–29, 33–37), with the condition that the Lord would bless or punish each Davidic king based on his obedience to the law of God (Ps 89:30–32).

Kingship (or Enthronement) Psalms

While the focus of the royal psalms is the human Davidic king, the theme of the kingship (or enthronement) psalms is the Lord's kingdom rule over His creation. These psalms include Psalms 47; 93; and 95–99. The expression, "The LORD reigns!" (or "God reigns" in 47:8) appears in 93:1; 96:10; 97:1; and 99:1; and Ps 95:3 declares that "the LORD is a great God, a great King above all gods." The Lord's sovereignty is supreme and absolute because He is the Creator of all things (Ps 93:3–5).

Wisdom Psalms

Like Proverbs the wisdom psalms often teach practical lessons about everyday living. The wisdom psalms teach the value of living a godly life by focusing on the central importance of the law of God (Psalm 119) and the contrasting ways of the righteous and the wicked. Psalm 1 is representative of the wisdom psalms and, as the introductory psalm, provides a wisdom orientation for the entire Psalter. The wise individual avoids the influence of the wicked by delighting in the law of the Lord.

Imprecatory Psalms

The imprecatory psalms are prayers of extreme emotion and anger calling on God to bring severe judgment on the enemies of God and of the psalmist. Psalms belonging to this category include Psalms 35; 55; 58; 59; 69; 79; 109; and 137. David prays in Psalm 58 for his enemies to vanish like stillborn children who never see the light of day. These psalms were certainly honest expressions of what was on the psalmist's heart, but more than that, they were also righteous prayers calling for God to execute justice against the wicked for their abuse and persecution of His people.

Practical Application

Claus Westermann noted that the words for praise are most often found in the imperative.[5] Therefore, the vocabulary of the Psalms exhorts us to praise God with our words and voices. Hymns of praise are addressed to God alone as we praise Him for who He is. Songs of thanksgiving are expressions of appreciation for specific blessings that we have received from God.

Psalms portrays the person and nature of God through the use of metaphor and imagery. The Lord is a Warrior, Shepherd, Redeemer, Rock, Refuge, and Shield for His people; but the prevailing metaphor and unifying theological concept in Psalms is that the Lord is King over all creation. The Lord's kingship is eternal and absolute (Pss 135:6; 145:13), and He is worthy of worship and praise because He is the "great King over the whole earth" (Ps 47:2). The Lord's kingship demands a response of praise and worship from His subjects (Psalms 100; 105:1–3; 150). The angels of heaven, all of humanity, and even the creation itself declares God's glory and greatness (Pss 19:1–6; 148:4). The practical value of the Psalms is evident in their universal expressions of human passion, prayer, and praise. As we read them and sing them, we experience true worship from our hearts to the heart of God.

Messianic Psalms

The book of Psalms is the most frequently quoted Old Testament book in the New Testament Scriptures. At least twenty-five of the 116 quotations from Psalms predictively refer to Christ, the anointed messianic King. After His resurrection Jesus told His disciples that "all things must be fulfilled, which were written in the law of Moses, and in the prophets, and in the psalms, concerning me" (Luke 24:44 KJV). The entire Old Testament was a picture, prophecy, type, and prediction of Christ's life, ministry, death, and resurrection. For the apostles and the early Christians, the life of Christ became a lens through which they read the Old Testament in general and Psalms in particular. Their Christological perspective gave a clear understanding to the pictures of the Messiah in the Psalms.[6] These include:

Ps 2:7	God's Son	Matt 3:17
Ps 8:4–5	Made lower than angels	Heb 2:5–9
Ps 16:8–11	Raised from the dead	Acts 2:25–32
Ps 22:1	Forsaken by God	Matt 27:46
Ps 22:16	Pierced hands and feet	John 19:37
Ps 22:18	Casting lots for clothing	Matt 27:35
Ps 40:6–8	Came to do God's will	Heb 10:5–9
Ps 41:9	Betrayed by a friend	John 13:18
Ps 68:18	Ascended to heaven	Eph 4:7–11
Ps 110:1	His Deity	Matt 22:41–45
Ps 110:4	His priestly ministry	Heb 6:20

The Psalms have given voice to the praise, prayer, and worship of God's people for more than 3,000 years. No matter what tune they are set to, they help us address the Almighty with words of love, devotion, and concern. They are the poetic cry of the human soul set to music as we call out to our heavenly Father. Take time to read them. Meditate on their thoughts. Concentrate on their expressions until they inflame your soul with songs of worship, praise, and gratitude.

For Further Reading

Allen, Leslie. *Psalms 101–150*. WBC. Waco, TX: Word, 1983.
Bullock, Hassell. *Encountering the Book of Psalms*. Grand Rapids: Baker, 2001.
Craigie, Peter. *Psalms 1–50*. WBC. Waco, TX: Word, 1983.
Kidner, Derek. *Psalms 1–72*. TOTC. Downers Grove, IL: InterVarsity, 1973.
_____. *Psalms 73–150*. TOTC. Downers Grove, IL: InterVarsity, 1975.
Longman, Tremper. *How to Read the Psalms*. Downers Grove, IL: InterVarsity, 1988.
Westermann, Claus. *The Praise of God in the Psalms*. Richmond, VA: John Knox, 1965.
Wilson, Gerald. *Psalms*, vol. 1. Grand Rapids: Zondervan, 2002.

Study Questions

1. What is the major purpose of Psalms in regard to worship?
2. How do the psalms express the heart of God's people?
3. Why do some of the psalms seem angry, depressed, or even vindictive?
4. What are the messianic psalms, and how are they interpreted in the New Testament?
5. How should the poetic language of the psalms be understood?
6. Which is your favorite psalm and why?

Notes

1. Vernon Whaley, *Called to Worship* (Nashville: Thomas Nelson, 2009), 149. See his insights on "Worship in the Psalms," 149–79.

2. Hermann Gunkel, *The Psalms: A Form Critical Introduction* (Philadelphia: Fortress Press, 1967).

3. Cf. Claus Westermann, *The Praise of God in the Psalms* (Richmond, VA: John Knox Press, 1965), and S. Mowinckel, *The Psalms in Israel's Worship* (Nashville: Abingdon Press, 1967).

4. See Peter Craigie, *Psalms 1–50*, WBC (Waco: Word, 1983), 48–56.

5. Westermann, 15.

6. See Walter C. Kaiser, *The Messiah in the Old Testament* (Grand Rapids: Zondervan, 1995), 92–135.

Chapter 17

PROVERBS

Words of Wisdom

The Proverbs are wise sayings that express deep truths in capsule form. They tell us how to live life successfully. Their focus is earthly rather than heavenly. Their form is similar to that of the wisdom literature of the ancient Near East. However, the Jewish sages infused their literature with an understanding that all wisdom, even things related to everyday practical matters, begins with the fear of the Lord (1:7). Therefore, Hebrew wisdom literature taught people not only how to make good choices in life but also how to make godly choices.[1]

KEY FACTS

Author:	Solomon and others
Date:	950–700 BC
Recipients:	Jewish students of all ages
Key Word:	Wisdom (Hb. *chokmah*)
Key Verse:	"The fear of the LORD is the beginning of wisdom, and the knowledge of the Holy One is understanding" (9:10).

Form and Function

A proverb (Hb. *māshāl*) is a short poetic sentence conveying wisdom in a concise and memorable form. Proverbs are typically based on experience and observation and are written in such a simple way that they produce reflection within the mind of the reader. Most proverbs take the form of a two-line unit, with the second line corresponding to the first line through some form of parallelism. Indeed, the key literary characteristic within the individual proverb is parallelism.[2]

Various types of parallelism may be seen in the following examples:

Synonymous
Pride comes before destruction,
and an arrogant spirit before a fall. (16:18)

Antithetical
Genuine righteousness leads to life,
But pursuing evil leads to death. (11:19)

Synthetic
The one who conceals hatred has lying lips,
And whoever spreads slander is a fool. (10:18)

Comparative
Good news from a distant land
is like cold water to a parched throat. (25:25)

Overview and first pylon of the first temple at Luxor, which was built by Rameses (Rameses II).

In a general sense the proverbs can be grouped into two major forms: instructive discourses (1–9; 22:17–24:22; 31:1–9) and pithy sayings (10:1–22:16; 24:23–34; 25–29). Additionally, the book of Proverbs concludes with appendices of the sayings of Agur (30:1–33), Lemuel (31:1–9), and the poem concerning the ideal wife (31:10–31).

The sayings tend to be concise in form, lack an extended structural arrangement, and are noted for their extensive use of figurative language. If one were to categorize the sayings, it may be sufficient to recognize the examples listed above as well as the prolific use of antithetical parallelism used to contrast wisdom and folly. For example:

> A wise son brings joy to his father,
> but a foolish man despises his mother. (15:20)
>
> A wise person is cautious and turns from evil,
> but a fool is easily angered and is careless. (14:16)

Within Proverbs certain distinct subgenres reflect variety among the sayings. For instance, among the sayings of Agur (30:1–33), one finds an extensive use of numerical formula, where Proverbs contains a numerical introduction followed by a list of coordinated items. Also scattered among the proverbs are "better than" sayings, where one thing is esteemed as "better than" another. For example:

> Better a little with the fear of the LORD
> than great treasure with turmoil. (15:16)
>
> Better a meal of vegetables where there is love
> than a fatten ox with hatred. (15:17)

Repeated warnings (19:13–14; 21:9, 19; 27:15–16) are directed at marrying or provoking a contentious spouse ("Better to live on the corner of a roof than to share a house with a nagging wife," 21:9; 25:24). Additional subgenres within Proverbs include "comparative sayings," where the use of simile (translated with "like" or "as") heightens the impact of the point (see Proverbs 25 for an extensive use of comparative sayings) and "abomination sayings," which contrast what the Lord "detests" with what pleases Him (15:26, see also 11:1; 15:8–9; 16:5; 20:23). Finally, it is worth noting the use of acrostic in the final poem extolling the characteristics of the virtuous wife (31:10–31).[3]

Authorship

Most of these proverbs are attributed to King Solomon. Solomon's name appears at three different parts of the book (1:1; 10:1; 25:1), and according to the biblical account, Solomon's wisdom was divinely granted and surpassed that of all other sages (1 Kgs 4:29–34). More specifically Solomon "spoke 3,000 proverbs" (1 Kgs 4:32); and while the book of Proverbs contains only 915 individual proverbs, it is clear that Solomonic origin for the majority of Proverbs is consistent with the biblical account of Solomon's reign. Jesus accepted the historicity of the biblical account of Solomon's wisdom (Matt 12:42), and thus there is little reason from Scripture to question Solomon as the author/originator of the proverbs attributed to him. It is also important to recognize that the text itself indicates that the final compilation of the book of Proverbs did not occur until the time of Hezekiah (25:1).

Outline

The book of Proverbs is unique within Scripture in that it is a collection of collections; that is, individual discourses and sayings were compiled into collections. Then these collections were compiled into the book of Proverbs. Within the text itself the collections are easily recognized by their headings:

I. Discourses of Solomon (1:1–9:18)
II. Proverbs of Solomon (10:1–22:16)
III. Sayings of the Wise (22:17–24:34)
IV. Proverbs of Solomon, Copied by the Men of Hezekiah (25:1–29:27)
V. Appendices (30:1–31:31)
   A. Sayings of Agur (30:1–33)
   B. Sayings of Lemuel (31:1–9)
   C. Poem of the Ideal Wife (31:10–31)

Interpretation

Wisdom is meant to be applied, not just studied or memorized. Correct application, however, always depends on accurate interpretation. As with other unique literary forms in Scripture, certain guidelines prove helpful when applied to the reading of Proverbs. Perhaps most importantly, one must recognize that in regard to form, the proverbs are poetry, not prose. Thus one must think in terms of parallel lines as the primary means by which thoughts relate to one another. Additionally, with the rich use of figurative language in Hebrew poetry, it is always necessary to contemplate carefully the point of comparison, substitution, sarcasm, or exaggeration in the figures of speech employed within a proverb.

In terms of function, proverbs are wisdom literature, and thus certain guidelines prove helpful beyond the mere discernment of poetic features. First, Proverbs concentrates primarily on practical issues rather than focusing on theological issues. The bulk of content in Proverbs has a decidedly practical orientation and, as such, is meant to be applied to daily life. While the proverbs do not specifically tell the reader how to get to heaven, they do give instructions on how to live in the meantime. Finally, proverbs are general truths, not specific promises or guarantees from God. When applied, the general point taught in a proverb is likely to hold true, but in a fallen world exceptions will confound even the wisest individuals. Thus, in the classic example of Prov 22:6 NKJV, "Train up a child in the way he should go, and when he is old he will not depart from it," the general rule is that parental discipline and instruction will typically result in a positive outcome. However, this is not a guarantee. The wisdom of Prov 22:6 holds true as a general rule, not an absolute promise.

Message

Most of Proverbs is a collection of individual proverbs and unrelated truths. In other words, after Proverbs 1–9, the proverbs are not arranged in topical order. As one searches through these wisdom sayings, it is possible to find topical themes that express overall concepts of Hebrew wisdom on specific subjects.

The following list is merely representative of popular topics. Other topical arrangements are certainly possible although the general teaching of what entails wisdom and folly is consistently clear throughout.[4]

Marriage and Sexuality

One of the most important choices people can make concerns their potential marriage partner. A spouse can be the greatest asset or the worst liability to one's life and general happiness. The book of Proverbs contains timely advice regarding the value of marriage, its moral responsibility, traits of a good partner, and the quality of true love. The proverbs were originally addressed to young men, but the precepts are easily adapted to both men and women of every age.

- Marital faithfulness comes with wisdom, and the benefits of sexuality are a blessing within marriage (5:15–19).
- The folly of infidelity contains many pitfalls and temptations that can lead to the destruction of one's marriage, health, and life (5:20–23; 6:20–35; 7:6–27; 23:26–28).

- Great caution ought to accompany one's choice of a spouse as a protection against living unhappily with a contentious person (14:1; 19:13–14; 21:9, 19; 27:15–16).
- It is better to choose a spouse based on character than on outward appearance (31:10–31).

Wealth and Poverty

Proverbs contains a balanced view of wealth and poverty. Some people are poor due to misfortune while others are poor due to their own laziness. Some are rich because of greed and corruption while others are blessed by God and their own diligence.

- Lazy behavior results in poverty while diligence results in wealth (10:4; 20:13). However, poverty may also result from corruption and injustice (13:23).
- A degree of practical security comes with wealth while poverty results in numerous pitfalls (10:15). However, the security wealth provides is limited (11:4, 28). Furthermore, wealth may even become a liability (13:8).
- In a world where injustice is common, favoritism often benefits the rich (14:20; 19:4).
- Profit comes not only as a result of hard work but also from wise planning. Meanwhile, haste leads to poverty (21:5).
- Great wealth without the peace of God has little benefit (15:16; 28:6).

A modern Middle Eastern potter fashioning pottery in the same manner used in biblical times.

Power of the Tongue

The tongue can be a powerful instrument for good or evil. As with other topics, one finds that Proverbs presents a balanced and realistic perspective on the power and use of the spoken word:

- Spoken words have tremendous power to encourage and discourage (12:18, 25; 15:4, 23; 16:24; 18:21; 25:11). However, even encouragement needs to be measured (25:20).
- Spoken words have power to lessen and to heighten tension and strife (15:1).
- The ability to refrain from speaking is a mark of wisdom, while hasty speech may result in ruin (10:19; 13:3; 15:28; 17:27–28; 18:13). Furthermore, it is better to listen with discernment than speak with haste (10:14).
- The Lord abhors lying, slander (6:16–19), and gossip (11:9, 12–13; 16:28).

Principles on Child-Rearing

The book of Proverbs is especially helpful in providing advice on raising a family. In Proverbs child-rearing is a family affair, and discipline begins in the home. The responsibility of raising children is as great today as at any time in history, and Proverbs provides God-given wisdom on a topic relevant to many today.

- Discipline is an act of love (13:24), whether from God or from a parent (3:11–12).
- Children are a heritage to their parents, and thus a wise son or daughter brings joy while a foolish one brings grief (10:1; 15:20; 17:21).
- Discipline will bring success in life while a lack of discipline results in a child's demise and disgrace to his parents (23:13–14; 29:15).

Personal Discipline

The book of Proverbs consistently presents the sluggard as a fool and the diligent person as wise. Various traits of the diligent and the lazy are explored, as are the rewards of diligence and the consequences of lazy behavior.

- A diligent person, like the ant, does not need a taskmaster to find motivation (6:6–8), while the sluggard cannot find enough motivation to rise out of bed (26:14).
- Poverty is quick to overcome the sluggard, while diligence produces wealth (6:9–11; 10:4; 24:30–34).
- The diligent man prizes what he has earned while the lazy man neglects what is given to him (12:27).
- The procrastination of the sluggard results in missed opportunity and a lack of accomplishment (20:4).

Friendship

The book of Proverbs places a high value on friendship and relationships between neighbors. Knowing how necessary it is to have a good friend by your side in the time of trouble, one may learn from the book of Proverbs how to gain friends and how to be a good friend to others.

- Due to the influence of one's friends, it is important to choose friends wisely (12:26; 22:24–25).
- It is better to have few friends who are dependable and loyal than many friends who are not (18:24).
- A good friend is dependable during times of adversity, while poor friends are quick to distance themselves when needed most (17:17; 27:10).

Proverbs is filled with practical advice regarding principles of success (10:4–5), honesty (11:1), humility (11:2), and generosity (11:24). The book also includes warnings against adultery (5:1–23), drunkenness (23:29), and excessive appetite (23:2). In many ways Proverbs serves as a teacher's manual for teaching biblical principles of success, prosperity, and godly living.

Practical Application

The book of Proverbs emphasizes the fear of the Lord as the key to wisdom and knowledge. While Proverbs focuses on matters of earthly living, it reminds us that God is the ultimate source of truth (2:5–6). His storehouse of wisdom is available to those who trust Him and keep His commandments (2:7–10). Hill and Walton note that the theological focus of the Proverbs keeps us balanced between this life and the next. It prevents us from "oversimplifying the complexities of life and offering pat answers to hard questions."[5]

REFLECTION

As you examine your own life, what are the tough questions for which you need real answers? The Bible reminds us, "Now if any of you lacks wisdom, he should ask God—who gives to all generously" (Jas 1:5). So why are you waiting? Ask Him by faith and see what happens!

The purpose of a proverb is to clarify truth in such a way that it can be easily remembered. The biblical proverbs are experiences of divinely inspired wisdom. They teach us moral values, principles of practical living, and warn us against the destructiveness of wrong choices. While knowledge involves the accumulation of information, wisdom involves the practical application of that information. Never be content to merely learn the facts, but rather be determined to live the truth.

For Further Reading

Atkinson, David. *The Message of Proverbs*. Downers Grove, IL: InterVarsity, 1996.
Garrett, Duane. *Proverbs, Ecclesiastes, Song of Songs*. NAC. Nashville: B&H, 1993.
Kidner, Derek. *The Proverbs: An Introduction and Commentary*. TOTC. London: Tyndale, 1964.
Koptak, Paul. *Proverbs*. NIVAC. Grand Rapids: Zondervan, 2003.
Longman, Tremper. *How to Read Proverbs*. Downers Grove, IL: InterVarsity, 2002.
Ross, Allen. "Proverbs." *EBC*. Grand Rapids: Zondervan, 1991.
Waltke, Bruce. *The Book of Proverbs*. NICOT. Grand Rapids: Eerdmans, 2004.

Study Questions

1. In what way does Proverbs exhibit the wisdom of God?
2. Describe the various types of proverbs, with biblical examples.
3. What factors are important in interpreting the book of Proverbs?
4. What practical matters are addressed in the book of Proverbs?
5. Why are there so many warnings against wrong choices and wrong behavior in Proverbs?

Notes

1. Gordon D. Fee and Douglas Stuart, *How to Read the Bible for All Its Worth*, 3rd ed. (Grand Rapids: Zondervan, 2003), 225–32.

2. For a brief introduction to the various kinds of parallelism, see the introduction to Hebrew poetry in the introduction to this volume.

3. See Ted A. Hildebrandt, "Proverb" in D. Brent Sandy and Ronald L. Giese Jr., ed., *Cracking Old Testament Codes: A Guide to Interpreting the Literary Genres of the Old Testament* (Nashville: B&H, 1995), 233–54.

4. For an alternate topical survey, see Daniel Estes, *Handbook on the Wisdom Books and Psalms* (Grand Rapids: Baker, 2005), 221–61. Estes comments on the content of Proverbs by analyzing the following themes: cheerfulness, contentment, decisions, diligence, friendship, generosity, humility, kindness, parenting, purity, righteousness, and truthfulness.

5. A. Hill and J. Walton, *A Survey of the Old Testament* (Grand Rapids: Zondervan, 2009), 447.

Chapter 18

ECCLESIASTES AND SONG OF SONGS

Life and Love

The books of Ecclesiastes and the Song of Songs explore the basic issues of the meaning of life and the expressions of human love. The poetry of the one is philosophical, pragmatic, and inquisitive. The other is sensual, romantic, and emotional. Together they speak to issues that are of vital importance to young people: Why am I here, and does anybody really care?

ECCLESIASTES

Meaning of Life

Ecclesiastes is written like a postmodern sermon. It begins with the shocking statement: "Everything is meaningless" (1:2 NIV) or "futile." The author was frustrated by injustice and the inability of man to straighten what is crooked (1:15). He was also frustrated by the transitory nature of life and the inability of wisdom to provide any sense of guarantee over what tomorrow might bring. He observed oppression and corruption and noted that life does not always play out the way one might expect. Although many things have changed in the past 3,000 years, these same basic observations hold true today regarding life "under the sun."

KEY FACTS	
Author:	Solomon
Date:	970–950 BC
Recipients:	Young people of Judah
Key Word:	Futility (Hb. *hevel*)
Key Verse:	"The sayings of the wise are like cattle prods . . . given by one Shepherd" (12:11).

Author and Title

While the wise sage of Ecclesiastes has traditionally been identified as King Solomon, the name of Solomon is never explicitly referenced within the book. This, however, does not rule out Solomonic authorship. Allusions to Solomon's wisdom and lifestyle are clear in chapter 2, and the writer identifies himself by way of introduction as "son of David, king in Jerusalem" (1:1).

The author identifies himself only as *"Qohelet,"* a term meaning "one who gathers or assembles." Most English Bibles translate "Qohelet" as either "Teacher" or "Preacher," based on an understanding that the wise sage Qohelet is speaking to an assembly of people. Ecclesiastes takes its name from the Greek and Latin titles for "preacher" (Gk. *ekklesia*). The Hebrew title Qohelet indicates a teacher of wisdom, but the text conjures up images of Solomonic grandeur, wisdom, and authority. However, the authorship of the book is technically anonymous, and it is reasonable to refer to the main character of the book simply as "Qohelet."[1]

Modern orthodox Jews pray in old Jerusalem in a manner similar to the Hebrews of the OT.

Outline

Key words and themes consistently reappear throughout the book, and the overarching observation that all is *hevel* ("futility") introduces and concludes the main body of material through a literary technique that "bookends" the contents (1:2; 12:8).[2] The reader will also recognize the repetition of an "enjoy life" refrain found seven times throughout the book (2:24–25; 3:12–13; 3:22; 5:18–20; 8:15; 9:7–10; 11:9), and the occurrence of familiar phrases such as "chasing after the wind," "under the sun," and "this too is *hevel*." The book is guided by programmatic questions directing the initial quest to find a solution through wisdom for the fallen condition (1:3; 3:9).[3]

Outline

I. Prologue (1:1–18)
II. Pleasures of Life (2:1–26)
III. Plan of God (3:1–5:20)
IV. Problems of Life (6:1–8:17)
V. Process of Living (9:1–12:8)
VI. Postscript (12:9–4)

The wisdom and message of Ecclesiastes are expressed through a wide range of literary forms and techniques, including autobiographical narrative (1:12–2:11), example story (9:13–16), allegory (12:1–7), reflection speeches (2:12–16; 9:1–6), and poem (3:2–8). Throughout the book one finds a wide variety of proverbs and sayings, most notably in chapters 7; 10; and 11. Included among the proverbs is a high concentration of "better than" sayings (4:3, 6, 9, 13; 6:3, 9; 7:1–3, 5, 8; 9:4, 16, 18), along with numerous aphorisms and admonitions. To suggest that Ecclesiastes is anything short of a literary masterpiece is a gross understatement.

Message

The key to unraveling the mysteries of Ecclesiastes is to recognize the recurring themes or motifs found throughout the book and come to an informed understanding of how those themes relate to one another. The following seven themes represent the content of Ecclesiastes:

1. The Vanity of Life

"Vanity of vanities, saith the Preacher, vanity of vanities; all is vanity" (Eccl 1:2 KJV). Qohelet uses the word translated "vanity," "futility," "meaningless," or "worthless" thirty-eight times in the book. It is the Hebrew word *hevel*, literally meaning "vapor" or "mist." The metaphor of "futility" (*hevel*) is used throughout Ecclesiastes to describe various aspects of life experienced in a fallen world.[4] These include the "fleeting," sometimes "senseless," even "absurd" aspects of our earthly existence. The dilemma facing Qohelet is that there seems to be no solution to the fallen condition. And so he searches to find through wisdom a solution to the dilemma of *hevel*, seeking *yitron*, a Hebrew word variously translated as "surplus," "gain," or "profit" (1:3; 3:9). The pursuit of *yitron* drives Qohelet's quest in the book of Ecclesiastes. Indeed, this wise sage seeks to find if wisdom can provide any solution to the dilemma of the futility of life.

2. Life "Under the Sun"

The expression "under the sun" is used twenty-nine times to refer to the activities of man as observed and experienced from a human perspective (1:3, 13). Qohelet is not overly pessimistic in his assessment of the fallen world. He is simply realistic in observing life from a human perspective, in other words, life without God. This perspective reveals the random emptiness of human existence.

3. The Value of Wisdom

Ecclesiastes is written from a wisdom perspective. Although Qohelet acknowledges the lim-

Arab farmer plowing his field with a simple double-yoked plow and team of two donkeys.

its of wisdom to provide any lasting solution to the fallen condition, he nevertheless upholds the value of wisdom (2:13–14). In finding what is good for a man in the "*hevel*" days of his life (6:12), Qohelet affirms the application of probabilistic wisdom to a wide variety of affairs, which suggests ways in which a person might make the most of every opportunity given by God (7:1–29; 10:1–20; 11:1–8).

4. The Sovereignty of God

Throughout the book Qohelet recognizes that a sovereign God rules over the affairs of mankind and that mortal man has little power over his own fate. Qohelet recognizes man's inability to fathom the ways of God yet realizes that God "has made everything beautiful in its time" (3:11 NIV). Qohelet acknowledges that God has purposed to keep man from ever fully grasping the mysteries of His sovereign ways, knowing that God "works so that people will be in awe of him" (3:14). In the end Qohelet notes that wisdom can only plan for contingencies but cannot guarantee the future (7:13–14; 9:11–12; 11:1–6).

5. The Inevitability of Death

As Qohelet observes life "under the sun," he cannot escape the reality that death is coming (3:18–21; 12:1–7). The inevitability of death highlights the transitory nature of mortal life so this adds a somewhat depressing tone to Ecclesiastes. However, the recognition of life's brevity and a day of reckoning provides the impetus for Qohelet's conclusion to make the most of every opportunity (9:1–10).

6. The Enjoyment of Life

Seven times Qohelet concludes that life should be enjoyed to its fullest. Altogether, he uses the word "joy" (*simchah*) seventeen times, so the enjoyment of life is not a minor aspect to Qohelet's wisdom. Rather, it is a conclusion revealed through structured refrains spaced throughout the book (2:24–26; 3:12–13; 3:22; 5:18–20; 8:15; 9:7–10; 11:9–10). Furthermore, one can observe a degree of escalation throughout these refrains, moving from observation (2:24–26; 3:12–13; 3:22; 5:18–20) to commendation (8:15) and then to imperative command (9:7–10; 11:9–10).[5] In light of the brevity of life, man should enjoy the simple things in life while he has the opportunity.

7. Remembering God

Although Qohelet realizes that wisdom does not have the capacity to explain fully the ways of God, he clearly understands that wisdom demands reverence for God (5:1–7). Life is brief; death and judgment are surely coming (3:17–19; 12:14), so the wise person will acknowledge his Creator all of the days of his life. Only a fool would live his few short years without remembering God (12:1, 13). In one of the author's strongest appeals, he urges: "Remember your Creator in the days of your youth" before you are too old to appreciate what God has given you (12:1).

Jewish men dancing during a private ceremony in the Court of the Men at the Wailing Wall in Jerusalem.

Practical Application

Walter Kaiser observes: "Qoheleth was working on the problem of man's attempt to find meaning in all aspects of God's world without coming to know the world's Creator, Sustainer, and Judge."[6] The concerns raised in Ecclesiastes can also be found in the other Wisdom Books: Job, Proverbs, and the Song of Songs, as well as in some of the Psalms.

Philip Yancey provides an excellent perspective on the brilliance of Ecclesiastes to foresee the quandary of the postmodern world: flat emotions, radical indifference, a sense of drifting, and a resigned acceptance of a world gone mad. He views the author as the "first existentialist" and observes that the "bleak despair" of Ecclesiastes rises from the "golden age" of Israel's prosperity, not deprivation. He adds: "Existential despair did not germinate in the hell holes of Auschwitz or Siberia but rather in the cafes of Paris, the coffee shops of Copenhagen, and the luxury palaces of Beverly Hills."[7] Thus, it is the burden of excess that humans cannot handle. All that life offers eludes any sense of meaning and purpose without God.

SONG OF SONGS

Songs of Love

KEY FACTS

Author:	Solomon
Date:	970–950 BC
Recipients:	Young people of Judah
Key Word:	Love (Hb. *ahavah*)
Key Verse:	"Young woman of Jerusalem . . . do not stir up or awaken love until the appropriate time" (2:7).

Many people are surprised to find such explicit and openly erotic lyrics in the Bible. The lovers show no embarrassment in enjoying each other's love. However, though sensuous, the lyrics are never distasteful. The Song of Songs teaches that love, romance, sex, and marriage were created by God to be enjoyed within marriage between a man and a woman. In this sense the Song of Songs serves as a model for marital relationships for all of God's people.

Perhaps the greatest benefit the believer can gain by studying the Song of Songs is the reminder that love is a gift from God and should be enjoyed as a gift. What God has created and declared as good (Gen 1:31) should be enjoyed in the context of marriage. The positive presentation of the love relationship in the Song of Songs provides a necessary balance to the prohibitions against illicit sexual expression found throughout the rest of Scripture. This song affirms the strength of true love that is essential to every marriage.

Author

The title of the book, "Solomon's Song of Songs" (1:1 NIV), seems to identify King Solomon as the author of the Song.[8] The title can literally be translated from the Hebrew "The Greatest Song of Solomon." However, the phrase "of Solomon" does call into question whether this was a song "by Solomon," "about Solomon," or "for Solomon."[9] In support of Solomonic authorship is the fact that 1 Kgs 4:32 credits the king with at least 1,005 songs, so the fact that Solomon was a writer of songs is without question. Therefore, the clear implication in the title is that this is the greatest of Solomon's many songs. Mark Rooker notes that Solomon's name appears seven times in the book (1:1, 5; 3:7, 9, 11; 8:11–12). He also observes that twenty-one varieties of plant life and fifteen species of animals harmonize with Solomon's knowledge of such matters (1 Kgs 4:33). The reference to place-names throughout Israel (from Jerusalem to Carmel and Hermon to Engedi) indicate the geography of the united monarchy. Altogether forty-nine unique terms use the imagery of nature in a premodern world to describe the intricacies of human love.[10]

Interpretation

Historically, the most common method used in interpreting the Song was to treat the Song as an *allegory* of God's love for Israel. Many church fathers viewed the book typologically as a picture of Christ's love for His bride, the church, and this agrees with the New Testament description of Christ's relationship to the bride, the church.

Enclosed garden, used as a description in Song 4:12.

Others interpret the book *literally*. It is only natural that the Bible would contain an expression of one of life's strongest human emotions, that is, marital love. While the topic of love between a man and a woman may seem too secular for the inspired canon, God "created them male and female" (Gen 1:27) so it would seem fitting for Him to inspire a song that deals with the power of love between the sexes.

Imagery and Drama

Assuming an approach that embraces a "literal" understanding of the Song as an inspired love song, one is still faced with interpretive challenges. Modern-day love songs with their vivid figurative imagery and idiomatic expressions can be difficult to understand. How much more a song that was written nearly 3,000 years ago! Three major issues challenge today's reader.

First, the poetic imagery of the ancient Near Eastern culture seems strange to modern-day readers. The lovers speak of spices and perfumes and compare each other to agricultural elements that seem less than flattering to the modern ear but nevertheless communicated a level of attraction and a range of emotions that demonstrate the full force and potential of erotic love. Second, the story line and changeover between speakers within the Song makes it sometimes difficult to follow. The Song appears to move from romantic courtship to marriage and subsequent intimacy. As the lovers sing to each other (as in a romantic duet), they tell a story of unfolding love that expresses how the lovers feel about each other. The third problem pertains to the drama that seems to underlie the lyrics of the Song. The standard approach is to see the Song as depicting the love between Solomon and his beloved while a less popular approach details a dramatic plot involving a woman, her shepherd lover, and Solomon as a villain who has come to take the woman into his harem. The "three-character" plot, called the "Shepherd Hypothesis," seems unlikely since that means Solomon wrote or accepted a Song where he is depicted as a villainous monarch seeking to steal a bride from the embrace of her true love.

Norman Geisler suggests a possible plot for the drama of the Song.[11] He views it as an antiphonal love song sung by the bride and groom at their wedding. In a kind of Jewish "Cinderella story," the virgin was sent to the vineyard by her brothers after the death of their parents. While working there, she meets and falls in love with a shepherd who promises to return to her one day. In his absence she dreams of him only to awake and he is not there. Finally, when he returns for her, he is none other than King Solomon, and his royal coach takes her to the palace where they will be married. Later they return to her village where her brothers praise her (she is a "wall" of virtue).

Outline

Although some have argued that the Song is an anthology of shorter love lyrics, the progression of the lovers' relationship provides a discernible movement that unifies the Song from beginning to end. Furthermore, a literary consistency in language and motif suggests a single author rather than a collection. However, it is difficult to outline the book according to a detailed plot or linear progression of events. As a song, the individual units function like snapshots in a photo album that provide lyrical glimpses into the progression of the lovers' relationship from courtship through marriage and into maturation. These cycles of love lyrics are broken only by the interruption of short choruses by the "friends" of the lovers and the threefold repetition of a refrain ("do not stir up or awaken love until the appropriate time") within the song (2:7; 3:5; 8:4).

I. Romantic Courtship (1:1–3:5)
II. Ravashing Intimacy (3:6–5:1)
III. Royal Marriage (5:2–8:4)
IV. Epilogue (8:5–14)

I. Romantic Courtship (Song of Songs 1:1–3:5)

Following a superscription (1:1), the song immediately begins with the female voice expressing her strong desire for romantic affection, "Let him kiss me with the kisses of his mouth" (1:2 NIV), thus setting the tone of lyrical love language that escalates throughout the book. However, while desire for intimacy is clearly communicated throughout this "courtship" section (1:4, 16; 2:3–6, 10–13; 3:4), the lovers show restraint until the wedding night in fulfilling their physical desires (4:16–5:1). The word pictures they express about each other's appearance are like mental imprints in an age before photography. They memorize every feature of the other person to enhance their longing while they are apart.

II. Ravishing Intimacy (Song of Songs 3:6–5:1)

The shift from courtship to marriage is indicated by the picture of a great wedding processional accompanied by all the extravagance of royalty (3:6–11). In this processional account Solomon is identified by name (3:7, 9, 11), and the indication that this is a wedding processional is clear (3:11). Solomon praises the beauty of his beloved on their wedding night (4:1–7) and expresses the depth of his love for her (4:8–11). The consummation of the marriage is expressed in delicate metaphor so as to celebrate its sensuous beauty with taste and elegance. There is no hesitation in the invitation of the beloved (4:16) now that the wedding has taken place, and the fulfillment of sexual intimacy is unrestrained and celebrated as a gift from the Creator (5:1).[12]

III. Royal Marriage (Song of Songs 5:2–8:4)

The third segment of the Song opens with another dream sequence (as with 3:1–4) where the beloved is separated from her lover (5:2–8). However, she regrets this separation (5:8) and affirms her love for him through renewed praise over his appearance (5:10–16). Through the prompting of the friends (5:9; 6:1), the lovers are reconciled, and the growth of their commitment is reaffirmed in full: "I am my love's and my love is mine" (6:3).

IV. Epilogue (Song of Songs 8:5–14)

Although the poem expressing the power and value of love functions as the climatic conclusion to the Song (8:6b–7), the Song continues beyond this climax through a flashback affirming the purity of the beloved prior to her relationship with Solomon (8:8–12) and a restatement of the lovers' desire to be possessed by each other in the coming years of their marriage (8:13–14).

Practical Application

As lyrical love poetry the Song of Songs exalts the virtues of love and evokes the emotions that run deep in the attraction God created between the sexes. As wisdom literature the Song of Songs teaches God's people how to express their love to the one to whom they commit their hearts

"Listen! My love is approaching. Look! Here he comes, leaping over the mountains, bounding over the hills. My love is like a gazelle or a young stag" (2:8–9).

and bodies in marriage. While allegorical interpretations of the Song of Songs are not based on careful exegesis of the text, the overall *typological picture* of marital love certainly illustrates God's love for His people. Thus, both Old and New Testament writers use marital themes to describe the relationship of God to Israel (Isa 62:4–5; Jer 3:1–11; Hos 2:19–20), and Christ to the church (Eph 5:21–33; Rev 19:7–9; 20:9–11). In fact, husbands are told to love their wives like Christ loved the church and gave Himself for her (Eph 5:25).

For Further Reading

Carr, G. Lloyd. *The Song of Solomon*. TOTC. Downers Grove, IL: InterVarsity, 1984.

Garrett, Duane. *Proverbs, Ecclesiastes, Song of Songs*. NAC. Nashville: B&H, 1993.

Hess, Richard. *Song of Songs*. BCOT. Grand Rapids: Baker, 2005.

Kaiser, Walter. *Ecclesiastes: Total Life*. Chicago: Moody Press, 1979.

Keel, Othmar. *The Song of Songs*. Trans. F. J. Gaiser. Minneapolis: Fortress Press, 1994.

Longman, Tremper. *Book of Ecclesiastes*. NICOT. Grand Rapids: Eerdmans, 1998.

———. *Song of Songs*. NICOT. Grand Rapids: Eerdmans, 2001.

Provan, Ivan. *Ecclesiastes / Song of Songs*. NIVAC. Grand Rapids: Zondervan, 2001.

Study Questions

1. What is unique about the author's approach in writing Ecclesiastes?
2. What indications does the text give that the writer is Solomon?
3. How is the Hebrew term *hevel* ("meaningless," "vapor," or "futility") used throughout the book?
4. Is there any real purpose to life without God?
5. How do the "goads" and "nails" of wisdom help us find the meaning of life?
6. What does the Song of Songs teach us about human love?
7. How does the Song of Songs caution the reader?

Notes

1. Walter Kaiser, *Ecclesiastes: Total Life* (Chicago: Moody, 1979), 7–42.

2. The technical term for this literary technique is *inclusio*.

3. Kathleen A. Farmer, *Who Knows What Is Good?* ITC (Grand Rapids: Eerdmans, 1991).

4. While a wide variety of commentators have opined concerning the use of *hevel* in Ecclesiastes, perhaps the most comprehensive work espousing a multivalent approach is Douglas B. Miller, *Symbol and Rhetoric in Ecclesiastes* (Atlanta: Society of Biblical Literature, 2002).

5. R. N. Whybray, "Qohelet, Preacher of Joy," *Journal for the Study of the Old Testament* 23 (1982): 87–98.

6. Kaiser, *Ecclesiastes: Total Life*, 16.

7. Philip Yancey, *The Bible Jesus Read* (Grand Rapids: Zondervan, 199), 143–67.

8. The Latin title is "Canticles," from the Vulgate, *canticum canticorum*.

9. The Hebrew syntax is not as clear as the English. The English reader may not see such flexibility in this phrase, but the Hebrew does allow for a variety of uses.

10. Mark Rooker, "The Book of the Song of Songs," in Eugene Merrill, Mark Rooker, and Michael Gristanti, *The World and the Word* (Nashville: B&H, 2011), 547.

11. Norman Geisler, *A Popular Survey of the Old Testament* (Grand Rapids: Baker, 2007), 225–27.

12. Although Bible translations often attribute the final portion of 5:1 to the "friends" of the bride ("Eat, O friends, and drink; drink your fill, O lovers," Song 5:1 NIV 1984), some have argued that the speaker was God Himself, celebrating the consummation of the marriage and approving of it as "good." See Daniel J. Estes, *Handbook on the Wisdom Books and Psalms* (Grand Rapids: Baker, 2005), 421.

Chapter 19

ISAIAH

God Is with Us

I saiah was the greatest literary genius of the Hebrew prophets. His amazing book of prophecy includes Isaiah's unique prophecies about Immanuel (Isaiah 7–12) and the suffering servant (Isaiah 42; 49–53). The book is set in the tumultuous days of the Assyrian and Babylonian threats to Judah's future and the survival of the messianic line of the "house of David." It combines elements of sublime poetry with preached sermons and prose narratives. It includes extended doublets, arch trajectories, and unique palindromes (sentences beginning and ending with the same words), chiastic parables, and cross alliteration.[1] Thus, Isaiah has often been called the "Shakespeare of Israel" and the "Prince of the Prophets."

KEY FACTS	
Author:	Isaiah
Date:	740–680 BC
Recipients:	Israel and Judah
Key Word:	Believe (Hb. *'âman*)
Key Verse:	"For a child will be born for us.... He will be named Wonderful Counselor, Mighty God, Eternal Father, Prince of Peace" (9:6).

Isaiah (*yesha'yahu*, "Yahweh is salvation"), the son of Amoz, was a prominent citizen in Jerusalem in the eighth century BC. He had access to the royal court and gave advice on personal matters and foreign affairs to the kings of Judah (Isa 7:3–4; 37:5–7; 38:1–8; cf. 2 Kings 19–20). Isaiah was married to a prophetess (Isa 8:1) and had at least two children, Shear-Jashub ("A remnant shall return") and Maher-Shalal-Hash-Baz ("Swift to the plunder, swift to the spoil"). The names of these two sons served as prophetic "signs" illustrating and confirming Isaiah's message (Isa 8:18).

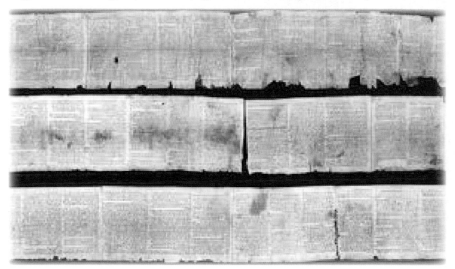

The Great Isaiah Scroll, discovered among the Dead Sea Scrolls at Qumran in 1947.

Background and Date

Isaiah ministered in Judah circa 740–686 BC during a time of great national crisis. The Lord commissioned Isaiah as a prophet in the year of King Uzziah's death after a long and effective reign that brought prosperity and stability to Judah. Isaiah subsequently served during the reigns of four kings in Judah—Jotham (740–735 BC), Ahaz (735–715 BC), Hezekiah (715–686 BC), and Manasseh (686–642 BC). Assyria became a major threat to Israel and Judah as they expanded their empire westward under the vigorous leadership of Tiglath-pileser III (745–727 BC). The Assyrians eventually established an empire that extended across the Fertile Crescent from present-day Iran in the east to Egypt in the west.

The Assyrians destroyed Damascus and decimated northern Israel around 722 BC (2 Kings 17). The Assyrians took the people into exile and

Relief from 730–727 BC showing King Tiglath-pileser III (of Assyria) capturing the city of Astartu. This relief was found in the palace at Nimrud.

turned the land of Israel into an Assyrian province. Judah became an Assyrian vassal during the reign of Ahaz, but Hezekiah rejected his father's pro-Assyrian policies and rebelled against Assyria. The Assyrian response was severe, as Sennacherib invaded in 701 BC and captured forty-six cities in Judah. Jerusalem was spared when the Lord destroyed the Assyrian army surrounding the city in response to the faith of Hezekiah, who prayed for the Lord to deliver the city (2 Kings 18–19; Isaiah 36–37). Having avoided disaster from Assyria, Isaiah next warned Judah of a more fearful invasion in the future from the Babylonians.

Authorship

The book of Isaiah presents itself as the "vision" of the eighth-century prophet by that name (Isa 1:1; cf. 2:1; 13:1; 20:2 for specific oracles also attributed to Isaiah), and the traditional view is that Isaiah composed the book about 700 BC. Critical scholarship has argued for multiple authorship of the book and has viewed chapters 40–66 as coming after the time of Isaiah. They propose an unnamed exilic writer called Second Isaiah (Deutero-Isaiah) as the author of chapters 40–55, and a postexilic writer referred to as Third Isaiah (Trito-Isaiah) who composed chapters 56–66. More contemporary critical scholarship has moved beyond the three-author view but continues to view the composition of the book as occurring over several centuries from the eighth through the fifth centuries BC. Critical scholarship argues for a later date for Isaiah 40–66 because of the shift to a more poetic,

theoretical, and conciliatory tone plus an exilic perspective reflected in these chapters. Conservative scholars have pointed out several unifying factors in the whole of Isaiah. The use of the title "Holy One of Israel" appears equally in both "halves" of the book. Jesus quoted from both "halves" attributing both to Isaiah the prophet (John 12:38–40; Luke 4:17–21). Several scholars have pointed out that references to vegetation (plants and trees) and geography (locations and topography) in chapters 40–66 reflect a Judean, not Babylonian, Jewish author. The reference to enemies at war with Israel in 41:10–13 argues against an exilic setting because Israel experienced no wars while they were in exile. Smith comments on several *linguistic connections* between chapter 1 and chapters 65–66.[2] Some of these include:

The foundations of the Broad Wall in Jerusalem attributed to the building activities of Hezekiah as he prepared his city for revolt against the Assyrians.

Heaven and Earth	1:2	65:17; 66:1, 22
I Have No Pleasure	1:11	66:4
Seek	1:12	65:1
Hear the Word of the Lord	1:11	66:5
The Woman Zion	1:21, 26	66:7–13
You Have Chosen	1:29	66:4
Fire Not Quenched	1:31	66:24

Motyer argues for a single author who both spoke and wrote his words and then edited them to pass them on to his disciples.[3] He argues: "There is, however, no external, manuscriptal authority for the separate existence at any time of any of the three supposed divisions of Isaiah."[4] He concludes: "The whole book is a huge mosaic in which totally pre-exilic material is made to serve pre-exilic, exilic, post-exilic and eschatological purposes."[5] In other words, one prophet, Isaiah himself, spoke of events that would happen in the immediate future (deliverance from Assyria), the distant future (Babylonian captivity), the messianic era (the Anointed One), and the eschatological future (new heavens and new earth).[6]

The canonical witness of the New Testament confirms Isaiah's authorship of all parts of the book. Relevant New Testament references include Matt 3:3 (quoting Isa 40:3); Matt 4:4 (quoting Isa 9:1–2); Luke 4:17 (introducing a quote of Isa 61:1–3); John 12:39 (introducing a quote of Isa 53:1); Acts 8:28–35 (quoting Isa 53:7–8); and Rom 10:20 (quoting Isa 65:1). These New Testament texts attribute Isaianic authorship to passages critical scholars attribute to Second and Third Isaiah. No ancient manuscript evidence supports the division of Isaiah 1–39 and 40–66 as separate works. The oldest complete Hebrew text, the Great Isaiah Scroll from Qumran (1QIsaᵃ) contains no break in the text between chapters 39 and 40.

Outline

I. Prophecies Against Judah (1:1–6:13)
   A. Coming Judgment and Blessing (1:1–5:30)
   B. Call of the Prophet (6:1–13)
II. Promise of Immanuel (7:1–12:6)
III. Prophecies Against the Nations (13:1–23:18)
IV. Predictions of Judgment and Blessing (24:1–27:13)
V. Perilous Woes (28:1–33:24)
VI. Promise of Destruction and Triumph (34:1–35:10)
VII. Prayers for Deliverance (36:1–39:8)
VIII. Prophetic Consolation (40:1–66:24)
   A. The Promise of Peace (40:1–48:22)
   B. Provision of Peace (49:1–57:21)
   C. Program of Peace (58:1–66:24)

Message

I. Prophecies Against Judah (Isaiah 1:1–6:13)

The book of Isaiah opens with five sermons that serve as a thematic introduction to the book. The opening chapters present in abbreviated form the message of Isaiah as a whole—the Lord will send a purging judgment against His sinful people, producing a righteous remnant that will enjoy the future blessings of salvation and restoration.

A. Coming Judgment and Blessing (Isaiah 1:1–5:30)

The opening message in Isaiah 1 is both a covenant lawsuit establishing Israel's guilt and a call to repentance that exhorts the people to change their sinful ways. As an unfaithful covenant partner, the Lord's people were like a rebellious child deserving judgment (1:3–4; cf. Deut 21:18–21). Consequently the covenant curse of an invading enemy army left Judah bloody and battered (1:5–6). Even Judah's religious rituals become an offense to God. Yet, if they would repent and become both willing and obedient, they could be forgiven. "Though your sins are scarlet, they will be as white as snow" (1:18). The people had a choice either to obey God and "eat" ('akal) the best of the land or to persist in their rebellion and be "devoured" ('akal) by the sword in judgment (1:19–20). Next Isaiah foresees the eschatological coming of God to Zion and the establishment of His kingdom of peace (2:1–4; 4:2–6) and the judgment of the proud both now in his time (3:1–4:1) as well as in the future (2:5–22).

B. Call of the Prophet (Isaiah 6:1–13)

In Isaiah 6, Isaiah recounts his call to the prophetic ministry undoubtedly many years prior to this writing, although his use of imperfect verbs indicates that he is describing the scene as it happened. He dates his call from the year King Uzziah died (740 BC). Since Isaiah introduces himself as prophesying during the reign of Uzziah, some view this as a recommissioning to prepare him for a difficult ministry

The reinternment funerary inscription discovered in the nineteenth century of the Jewish King Uzziah. Its Aramaic writing translates, "Hither were brought the bones of Uzziah, King of Judah. Do not open."

in the reign of Ahaz. The death of King Uzziah left Isaiah concerned about the future of the kingdom, so the vision of Yahweh seated on the throne of heaven reassured him that God was still in control of the destiny of his people. Isaiah's confrontation with God (vv. 1–4) led to his confession: "Woe is me" (v. 5) and his consecration (vv. 6–7). The vision of God radically changed Isaiah, so when the Lord asked: "Who will go for us?" Isaiah replied, "Here I am. Send me" (v. 8). Newly cleansed and commissioned, Isaiah launched on his prophetic ministry even though his audience in the time of Ahaz would close their ears to the messages he would deliver (6:9–10).

II. Promise of Immanuel (Isaiah 7:1–12:6)

The identity of the promised child in 7:14 is a source of major controversy. While some have suggested it refers to the birth of a child into the family of Isaiah or Ahaz, the extended prophecy points beyond the immediate context to a divine child who is identified in 9:6 as the "Mighty God" (*'el gibbor*). The ultimate fulfillment of the Immanuel prophecy was the virgin birth of Jesus Christ, who was literally God incarnate and who would preserve the line of David forever (Matt 1:21–23).[7] Smith notes: "This ruler was not Ahaz's son or Isaiah's son, but an unknown future king specifically identified in 9:1–7 in clear messianic terms."[8]

The invasion of foreign armies on the immediate horizon would fail, Isaiah promised, "For God is with us" (8:10). The prophet goes on to predict that "a great light" will shine in Galilee (9:2), a verse quoted in Matt 4:16 and Luke 1:79 in relation to Jesus's Galilean ministry. Then he announces that a son will be born, given by God Himself (9:6). The fourfold title makes clear that this is not a typical human child. He is described as "Wonderful Counselor" (*pele' yo'ets*), "Mighty God" (*'el gibbor*), "Everlasting Father" (*'abi'ad*), "Prince of Peace" (*shar shalom*). His government is also described in a fourfold manner: (1) peace without end, (2) throne of David, (3) justice and righteousness, (4) reign forever. Again Smith notes these messianic promises, descriptive parameters, titles, and time frames rule out any possible human rulers.[9] God Himself will come in the future to rule the world.

Unlike the arrogant Assyrian rulers who are depicted as lofty trees, Messiah would emerge as a tiny Branch from the stump of the felled Davidic dynasty (11:1–2). From this humble origin, His kingdom would extend over the nations and bring peace and harmony to the earth, reversing even the effects of the fall and the curse upon humanity and the creation (11:6–11). "In that day" (in the future) the Lord's people will sing for joy because of the blessings of his reign over them (12:1–6). This hymn of thanksgiving ends with the assurance that "the Holy One of Israel is among you" (12:6), again emphasizing the Immanuel ("God is with us") connection throughout these chapters.

Pictures of Christ in Isaiah	
1. Virgin Birth (7:14)	11. Angel of the Lord (37:36)
2. Light in Galilee (9:1–2)	12. A Forerunner Prepares His Way (40:3)
3. Divine Child (9:6)	13. Incarnate God (40:9)
4. Mighty God (9:6)	14. Servant of the Lord (42:1–4)
5. Wonderful Counselor (9:6)	15. Redeemer of Israel (44:6)
6. Prince of Peace (9:6)	16. Light of the Gentiles (49:6)
7. Branch of Jesse (11:1)	17. Suffering Servant (52:13–53:12)
8. Anointed King (11:2)	18. Resurrected Lord (53:10)
9. Banner of the Nations (11:10)	19. Anointed Messiah (61:1–3)
10. Holy One of Israel (12:6)	20. Coming Conqueror (66:15–16)

III. Prophecies Against the Nations (Isaiah 13:1–23:18)

The Lord's judgment would extend beyond Israel and Judah to include all of the nations and people surrounding them. Isaiah's oracles against the nations include messages directed against Babylon (13:1–14:23; 21:1–10), Assyria (14:24–27), Philistia (14:28–32), Moab (15:1– 16:14), Syria and Israel (17:1–14), Cush and Egypt (18:1–20:6), Dumah (21:11–12), Arabia (21:13–17), Jerusalem (22:1–25), and Tyre (23:1–18).

The Lord would judge both the great superpowers and the smaller nation-states that were struggling for survival. These oracles focused primarily on other nations (*goyim*, "Gentiles") but were delivered for the benefit of God's people so that God's people would not be tempted to depend on alliances with any of these nations. These messages served to assert the Lord's sovereignty over the nations. Yahweh was not just a nationalistic deity but the ruler and judge of all peoples. The promise of God's judgment of Israel's enemies offered hope for the future and provided assurance that the Lord had not abandoned His people, even though they would also be judged (17:1–11; 22:1–14).

IV. Predictions of Judgment and Blessing (Isaiah 24:1–27:13)

Some scholars have called this section "The Little Apocalypse" because of its similarities to the book of Revelation. The previous chapters focus on the historical judgment of the nations surrounding Judah that were involved in the international conflicts and political intrigues of Isaiah's day, but this portion of Isaiah's message looks forward to the final judgment of all nations and the coming of God's eschatological kingdom to earth on the day of the

Lord. The recurring phrase "on that day" (24:21; 25:9; 26:1; 27:1) refers to a future day and reflects the eschatological perspective of this section. At that time God will "swallow up death" (25:7–8 NIV), invite the righteous to his royal banquet on Mount Zion (25:1–13), and cause the dead to live again (26:19).

V. Perilous Woes (Isaiah 28:1–33:24)

A series of five woe oracles (28:1; 29:1, 15; 30:1; 31:1) announce the coming destruction of Israel and Judah, and then a final woe (33:1) announces the doom of Assyria. Israel's leaders are drunkards lacking moral and spiritual sense (28:1–13). Since they have dismissed the prophetic calls to trust in God as simplistic baby talk in contrast to their wise military strategies, the Lord will speak to them through the foreign language of the invading Assyrian army that will sweep through their land. The Lord Himself will wage warfare against the city of Jerusalem (29:1–3) to purge the city of its sin. The final woe against Assyria in 33:1–24 offered Hezekiah hope against the foreign invaders, for God promised that He would destroy the "destroyer," Assyria.

VI. Promise of Destruction and Triumph (Isaiah 34:1–35:10)

These two prophecies are apocalyptic in nature. God will judge all the nations with cataclysmic catastrophes. The mountains will melt, and the heavens will dissolve in the Lord's "day of vengeance" (34:1–10). The "birds of prey" will be gathered by the Lord to the great day of battle (34:15). The language is similar to the description of the battle of Armageddon in Rev 16:14–16. After the "day of vengeance," the desert will "blossom like a wildflower," and God's people "will see the glory of the LORD" (35:1–2). The redeemed will walk on the highway of holiness and "come to Zion with singing" (35:8–10). Thus, this section ends with the promise of triumph in the future.

VII. Prayers for Deliverance (Isaiah 36:1–39:8)

These narratives dealing with the reign of Hezekiah, his passionate prayers, and the deliverance of Jerusalem from the Assyrian army in 701 BC function as a hinge for the two halves of the book of Isaiah. The story of Hezekiah's faith and the deliverance of Jerusalem in 36–37 provide closure to the first half of the book as the Lord brings the *Assyrian* crisis to an end. The story of Hezekiah's healing and the visit of the Babylonian envoys to

Jerusalem in 38–39 introduce the threat of *Babylonian* invasion and exile that will be taken up in the second half of the book (Isaiah 40–66).

Chronologically, the events in 38–39 occurred before the deliverance of Jerusalem narrated in 36–37, but these events were placed at the end of the first half of the book to lead into the promise of the return from Babylon in 40–66. This arrangement also reveals that Hezekiah's prayer for healing strengthened his faith to pray for help in light of the greater crisis of the invasion of Jerusalem by Sennacherib in 701 BC.

VIII. Prophetic Consolation (Isaiah 40:1–66:24)

Isaiah 40 to 66 forms the "Book of Consolation," which is predominantly a message of salvation and hope written in exquisite poetry. In the first half of the book, the future Messiah is portrayed more as triumphant King, while in the second half of the book, he assumes the role of Suffering Servant before becoming an anointed Conqueror. While the future rebuilding of Jerusalem and the temple is in view in some of these chapters (44:20–45:13), the prophet's audience is preexilic, and several references in these chapters predate the exile.[10]

A. The Promise of Peace (Isaiah 40:1–48:22)

In these chapters the prophet and the future inhabitants of Jerusalem receive a renewed call to share the eschatological news of comfort because their mighty

The Taylor Prism lists the campaigns of Sennacherib, King of Assyria, who invaded Judah in 701 BC. It dates to 691 BC and was found in Nineveh.

God will come to gather His people and rule the earth like a shepherd takes care of his sheep (40:1–11). The prophet's message was that Israel's days of warfare would be complete, its sins would be forgiven, and the Lord would come to reward His people. Isaiah described this eschatological gathering in terms similar to the exodus (43:16–21; 51:9–11; 52:10–12; 55:12–13). Ultimately, the Lord would gather His people out of many nations (43:5–7), and all nations would observe the Lord's power to save (52:10–12). Israel would not need to leave the land of bondage in haste as they did from Egypt

(52:12), and the wilderness would be transformed into a paradise as the Hebrew people make their way home (41:8–20; 43:19–21).

Isaiah announced that two figures would play a key role in Israel's restoration and renewal. The Lord would raise up the Persian ruler Cyrus as his "anointed one" to defeat many nations and rebuild Jerusalem (44:28–45:7). Cyrus made this possible by issuing the decree that would allow the Jews to return to their homeland (fulfilled in Ezra 1:1–5). Beyond Israel's military subjugation to Babylon, the larger issue impeding their restoration was the problem of Israel's sin and separation from the Lord. Rather than a conquering king, a Suffering Servant would accomplish Israel's ultimate restoration by giving his own life as a sin offering for the people. The role and mission of this figure are highlighted in a series of four Servant Songs (42:1–7; 49:1–6; 50:4–9; 52:13–53:12).

B. Provision of Peace (Isaiah 49:1–57:21)

The identity of the Servant of the Lord in Isaiah 40–55 is a major source of discussion and controversy because some view the Servant as the nation of Israel; others point to the prophet Isaiah; and a few think he is Cyrus; but the New Testament claims the Servant is Jesus. The Servant idea in Isaiah has corporate or national significance in some passages and individual features in other verses. In some places the Servant is identified as the nation of Israel (41:8; 42:18–19; 43:10; 44:1, 21; 45:4). As the Lord's national Servant, Israel was commissioned with the task of reflecting the Lord's greatness to the nations, but Israel failed in its mission by not obeying the Lord (42:18–22). Because of Israel's disobedience, the Lord would commission an individual Servant to restore His people. The individual features of the Servant are especially prominent in the four Servant Songs. The most detailed and well-known of the Servant Songs in Isaiah 52:13–53:12 prophesies more extensively and specifically concerning the sacrificial atonement of the Servant and points ahead to the death and resurrection of Jesus.

The progress of revelation from the Old Testament to the New clearly identifies Jesus Christ as the Isaianic Servant. In Acts 8, Philip explains to the Ethiopian eunuch that the innocent lamb led to slaughter in Isaiah 53 refers to Jesus (Acts 8:32–34). In several other passages the New Testament quotes from the Servant Songs and applies these passages to the person and work of Jesus:

1.   Matthew 8:17 quotes from Isa 53:4 ("He took up our infirmities and carried our diseases" NIV).

2. Luke 22:37 quotes from Isa 53:12 ("And he was numbered with the transgressors" NIV).
3. John 12:38 quotes from Isa 53:1 ("Lord, who has believed our message and to whom has the arm of the Lord been revealed?" NIV).
4. First Peter 2:21–25 cites and quotes from Isa 53:4–5, 9, 11–12 ("He committed no sin, and no deceit was found in his mouth," and "by his wounds you have been healed" NIV).

Numerous other allusions and references apply Isaiah's Servant Songs to Jesus in the New Testament. The declaration of Jesus that he came to serve others and "give his life as a ransom for many" in Mark 10:45 (NIV) likely alludes back to Isa 53:11–12. The description of Jesus as "the Lamb of God, who takes away the sin of the world" in John 1:29 likely recalls Isa 53:7. Paul's description of Jesus as a "servant" who experiences death so that he might be ultimately exalted and recognized as Lord over all in Phil 2:6–11 (NIV) also reflects how Jesus fulfills the role of Isaiah's Suffering Servant. Isaiah 40–57 promises Israel's return, but the full restoration of Israel would only occur when the people truly repented of their sinful ways and returned to the Lord (55:1–13).

"Like a lamb led to the slaughter . . . He did not open His mouth" (Isa 53:7).

C. Program of Peace (Isaiah 58:1–66:24)

Isaiah saw the sinful patterns of the present (unacceptable fasting in 58) carrying over into the time when the people would return to the land. Consequently, Israel's restoration and complete salvation would await the future time when God's kingdom would come to earth and the Lord would deliver His people from their sins once for all.

The focus of Isaiah 60–62 is the future glory of Zion as the center of the Lord's earthly kingdom. The nations will be drawn to Jerusalem and to the light of God's salvation. The nations will bring tribute to Zion in honor of the Lord. The inclusion of the Gentiles in the blessings of the future kingdom is a prominent theme in Isaiah. Premillennialists believe these passages describe the future millennial (1,000-year) reign of Christ (Rev 20:1–6).

Portions of Isaiah 63–66 reveal that a tribulation and judgment will precede the coming of the Lord's earthly kingdom. This judgment will separate sinners from the righteous and purge the earth of its wickedness. The Lord will march out as the Anointed Warrior to exact His vengeance on the Edomites (who represent all God's enemies in 63:1–6) and return from battle with the blood of his enemies spattered on his garments. This same imagery appears in Rev 19:11–16, describing the triumphal return of Jesus Christ as the Divine Warrior from heaven who comes to rule as the King of kings.

The book of Isaiah ends much as it began, with a message of both impending doom ("The LORD will come with fire," 66:15) and deliverance ("all mankind will come to worship me," 66:23). The one recurring theme is that "God is with us." Jesus Christ (*yeshu'a ha meshiach*) is the virgin's Son, Immanuel, the Branch of the Lord, the Mighty God, the Prince of peace, the coming Messiah, the Suffering Servant, the Anointed Warrior, the Glorious King! "All the prophets testify about him" (Acts 10:43).

Practical Application

The message of Isaiah has significantly impacted the New Testament presentation of the person and work of Jesus Christ. Next to Psalms, Isaiah is the most referenced Old Testament book in the New Testament, with approximately 100 citations and 500 allusions. Some estimate that one out of every seventeen verses in the New Testament contains material taken from Isaiah. The New Testament announces that the blessings of the eschatological kingdom prophesied by Isaiah are fulfilled in the person of Jesus. The eschatological kingdom of God is inaugurated at the first coming of Jesus and will be consummated at His second coming.

Isaiah reminds us time and again that the God of heaven sovereignly rules over the entire world. He blesses those who seek Him and judges those who reject Him. He raises up and takes down kings and nations. He saves the lost and cares for the hurting. As we read the prophet's messages, we are confronted with a series of choices to stand firm in our faith (7:9), to cry out to God (12:6), to praise His name (25:1), and to repent and rejoice (44:22–23).

In fact, the book of Isaiah ends with a serious warning about the consequences of sin and the reality of judgment. There is a real hell to be avoided and a real heaven to be gained. Before each of us there lies a choice between the way of life and the way of death (66:22–24). In the end, we must decide which we will choose.

As we read Isaiah's amazing prophecies of the Lord's ultimate triumph over sin, evil, and death, we are encouraged to trust Him to help us face the challenges we struggle with in our lives. The same God who answered Hezekiah's prayers is ready to answer our prayers, meet our needs, and deliver us from evil as well. What obstacles and challenges are you facing right now? Turn to God; He will help you!

For Further Reading

Beyer, Bryan. *Encountering the Book of Isaiah*. Grand Rapids: Baker, 2007.
Delitzsch, Franz. *Biblical Commentary on Isaiah*. 2 Vols. Grand Rapids: Eerdmans, 1965. Reprint.
Hindson, Edward E. "Isaiah." In *KJBC*. Nashville: Thomas Nelson, 1999.
Motyer, J. A. *The Prophecy of Isaiah: An Introduction and Commentary*. Downers Grove, IL: InterVarsity, 1993.
Oswalt, John. *The Book of Isaiah: Chapters 1–39*. NICOT. Grand Rapids: Eerdmans, 1986.
————. *The Book of Isaiah: Chapters 40–66*. NICOT. Grand Rapids: Eerdmans, 1997.
Smith, Gary V. *Isaiah 1–39*. NAC. Nashville: B&H, 2007.
————. *Isaiah 40–66*. NAC. Nashville: B&H, 2009.

Study Questions

1. What is the major difference between Isaiah 1–39 and 40–66?
2. How would you defend the unity of the authorship of both sections?
3. How does the Immanuel Prophecy (Isaiah 7–12) emphasize the deity of Christ?
4. What does God's judgment of the nations indicate about His sovereignty over the whole world?
5. What lessons in prayer did Hezekiah learn, and how did they affect his life and the city of Jerusalem?
6. How did God use Cyrus the Great to accomplish his sovereign purposes?
7. How did the Suffering Servant prophecy (Isaiah 52–53) predict the death and resurrection of Christ?

Notes

1. See the extended discussion and examples cited by J. A. Motyer, *The Prophecy of Isaiah: An Introduction and Commentary* (Downers Grove, IL: InterVarsity, 1993), 13–25.

2. Gary Smith, *Isaiah 40–66*, NAC (Nashville: B&H, 2009), 95–97.

3. J. A. Motyer, *The Prophecy of Isaiah: An Introduction and Commentary* (Downers Grove, IL: InterVarsity, 1993), 13–34.

4. Ibid., 27.

5. Ibid., 31.

6. See the excellent article by G. K. Beale, "A Specific Problem Confronting the Authority of the Bible," in L. Tipton and J. Waddington, eds., *Resurrection and Eschatology* (Phillipsburg, NJ: Presbyterian & Reformed, 2008), 135–76.

7. For an extended discussion see E. Hindson, *Isaiah's Immanuel* (Philadelphia: Presbyterian and Reformed, 1978).

8. Smith, *Isaiah 40–66*, 219.

9. Ibid., 242.

10. See Smith, *Isaiah 40–66*, 26–51. He argues for an Assyrian crisis setting for chapters 40–66 with an early destruction of Babylon (chaps. 46–47) by Sennacherib in 689 BC.

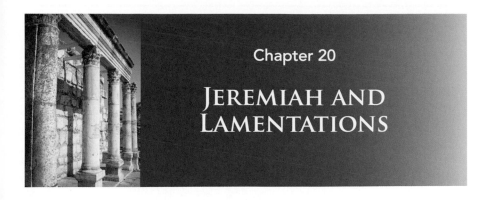

Chapter 20

JEREMIAH AND LAMENTATIONS

The Weeping Prophet

JEREMIAH

The Babylonians Are Coming

J eremiah ("Yahweh lifts up") was one of Judah's greatest prophets. His ministry spanned half a century in the darkest days of Judah's history. In spite of his numerous warnings to the people and kings of Judah, the "weeping prophet" lived to see his beloved Jerusalem destroyed by the Babylonians. In the early days of his ministry, Jeremiah called the people of Judah to repent of their sinful ways and return to the Lord. His early ministry coincided with that of Zephaniah and Habakkuk and the priestly ministry of Hilkiah, all of which culminated in the great revival of 622 BC under King Josiah.[1]

KEY FACTS

Author:	Jeremiah
Date:	626–562 BC
Recipients:	People of Judah and Jerusalem
Key Word:	Covenant (Hb. *berith*)
Key Verses:	"The days are coming . . . when I will make a new covenant with the house of Israel . . . and write it on their hearts" (31:31, 33).

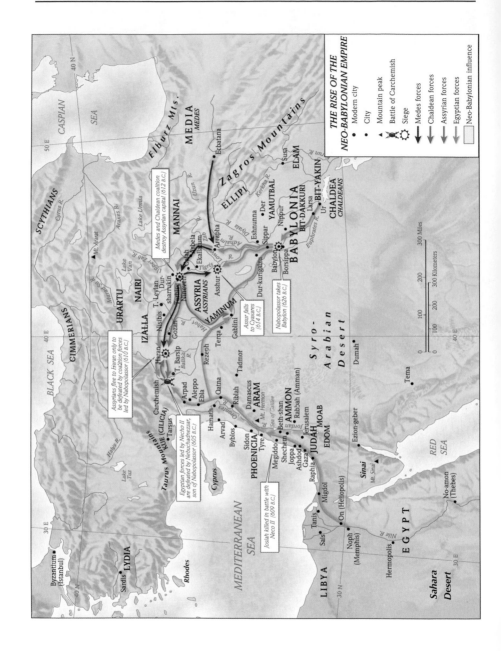

THE RISE OF THE NEO-BABYLONIAN EMPIRE

- Modern city
- City
- ▲ Mountain peak
- ⚔ Battle of Carchemish
- ☼ Siege
- Medes forces
- Chaldean forces
- Assyrian forces
- Egyptian forces
- Neo-Babylonian influence

Medes and Chaldean coalition destroy Assyrian capital (612 B.C.)

Assyrians flee to Haran only to be defeated by coalition forces led by Nabopolassor (610 B.C.)

Assur falls to Cyaxares (614 B.C.)

Nabopolassor takes Babylon (626 B.C.)

Egyptian forces led by Necho II are defeated by Nebuchadnezzar, son of Nabopolassor (605 B.C.)

Josiah killed in battle with Neco II (609 B.C.)

Background

Jeremiah began his prophetic ministry in 626 BC and prophesied until Judah's last days as a nation, warning of the coming Babylonian exile as the Lord's punishment for Judah's sins. Jeremiah prophesied during the reign of Judah's last five kings: *Josiah* (640–609 BC), *Jehoahaz* (609 BC), *Jehoiakim* (609–597 BC), *Jehoiachin* (597 BC), and *Zedekiah* (597–586 BC). The moral failure of Judah's leadership was largely responsible for the spiritual corruption of the nation. The covenant between the Lord and David promised an eternal dynasty to David, but it also warned that the Lord would punish David's sons if they were disobedient (2 Sam 7:14–16). During the ministry of Jeremiah, the Lord brought the Davidic dynasty to a temporary end, but Jeremiah promised that the Lord would raise up an ideal Davidic ruler (the Messiah) in the future (cf. Jer 23:5–6; 30:8–9, 21; 33:15–17).

Jeremiah warned that the Lord was sending the Babylonians to punish Judah. In 605 BC, Nebuchadnezzar led the Babylonian army to victory over the Egyptians at Carchemish, establishing his control over Syria and northern Israel. Next, Nebuchadnezzar marched south to Jerusalem and took away the first wave of exiles, including Daniel. Jehoiakim became a vassal to Babylon but rebelled in 602 BC and again in 597 BC. Nebuchadnezzar captured Jerusalem in 597 BC and deported King Jehoiachin and thousands of exiles, including Ezekiel. The third stage of the exile occurred when Nebuchadnezzar responded to Zedekiah's rebellion with a siege on Jerusalem that lasted eighteen months in 588–586 BC. Jerusalem and the temple were destroyed, and Judah came to an end as a nation. Zedekiah and most of the people in Judah were deported to Babylon in August 586 BC.

The Babylonians allowed Jeremiah to remain in the land of Judah (39:11–40:6), and he ministered there until he and his scribe Baruch were kidnapped by a faction of Jews and taken away as hostages to Egypt (43:1–7). Jeremiah likely continued his prophetic ministry to the Jewish community in Egypt until his death.

Authorship

The book of Jeremiah appears to have a long and complex compositional history. Jeremiah and his scribe Baruch (cf. 36:4–21; 43:1–7; 45:1–5) were largely responsible for the contents of the book. The Lord commissioned Jeremiah and Baruch to compose a scroll of Jeremiah's prophecies in 605 BC, more than twenty years after the prophet began his ministry (36:1–2). This original scroll likely contained only the oracles and messages found in Jeremiah 1–25. When King Jehoiakim destroyed this scroll, Jeremiah and

Baruch composed an expanded version (36:27–32). Baruch likely continued to collect messages and narratives of Jeremiah throughout his ministry,
including the reference to the release of Jehoiachin in 562 BC in 52:31–34.

The seal of Baruch.

Outline[2]

I.   Call of the Prophet: Fire Within (1:1–19)
II. Concern of the Prophet: Doom of Judah (2:1–25:38)
III. Rejection of the Prophet: Personal Illustrations (26:1–45:5)
IV. Oracles Against the Nations: Judgment of the Lord (46:1–51:64)
V.   Epilogue: The Fall of Jerusalem (52:1–34)

Message

I. Call of the Prophet: Fire Within (Jeremiah 1:1–19)

The Lord called Jeremiah in Judah's last days to warn of the impending Babylonian exile and to provide one final opportunity for the people to
repent and avoid national destruction. Jeremiah objected that he was too
young and did not know what to speak, but the Lord promised to put His
words in the prophet's mouth. The call of Jeremiah reflects the same basic
elements found in other Old Testament call passages (see chart on p. 235).

Despite the enormity of the task, the Lord promised that He would enable
Jeremiah to fulfill his commission despite his feelings of personal inade-
quacy. The source of strength for the ministry would be the Lord Himself.
The verbs "uproot," "tear down," "destroy," "overthrow," and "build up"

appear as summary statements of the dual nature of the prophet's message throughout the book (1:10; 24:6; 31:4–5; 42:10; 45:5).

	Jeremiah	Moses	Gideon	Isaiah	Ezekiel
Vision of God	"The word of the Lord came to me."	Burning Bush	Angel of the Lord Appears	Sees the Lord Seated on His Throne	Vision of God on the Chariot Throne
Voice of God **Commission to Task**	"I appointed you as a prophet to the nations."	"I am sending you to Pharaoh."	"Go and save Israel out of Midian's hand."	"Go and tell this people."	"Son of man, I am sending you to the Israelites."
Objection of Unworthiness	"I do not know how to speak; I am only a child."	"Who am I?"	"How can I save Israel?"	"Woe is me! I am undone. For I am a man of unclean lips, and I live among a people of unclean lips."	"When I saw it [the glory of God], I fell facedown." "I sat among them for seven days over-whelmed."
Promises of God's Protection and Enablement	"Do not be afraid of them, for I am with you and will rescue you."	"I will be with you."	"The Lord is with you, mighty warrior."	"Your guilt is taken away and your sin is atoned for."	"Do not be afraid, though briers and thorns are all around you and you live among scorpions."

II. Concern of the Prophet: Doom of Judah (Jeremiah 2:1–25:38)

This first major section of the book focuses on Jeremiah's message of judgment against Judah. The Lord will judge His people for their failure to turn from their sinful ways. Along with Jeremiah's poetic oracles, and laments, a series of prose sermons provides order and arrangement for this section by serving as reflective summaries on the prophet's message of judgment. These prose sermons particularly focus on Judah's defective understanding of their covenant with the Lord (11:1–13). They believed the Lord would protect them as His covenant people regardless of their behavior. So the purpose of these sermons was to undermine the people's false confidence in their status as the Lord's chosen people and their misplaced trust in the temple (7:1–15).

The indictment in Jeremiah 2 takes the form of a covenant lawsuit or legal dispute. Like a prosecuting attorney Jeremiah presented the Lord's case against His unfaithful people. Though a devoted bride in her early days, Israel had become like an unfaithful wife, prostituting herself by following other gods. Judah also prostituted itself by making foreign alliances with Egypt and Assyria, so the Lord warned that they would be disappointed by these alliances. Their decision to trust in man rather than God was doomed to failure. Despite his message of impending judgment, Jeremiah wept and mourned over Judah (4:19–21).

Jeremiah's temple sermon (7:1–15) was one of the defining and critical moments in his ministry. This sermon was delivered "early in the reign of Jehoiakim" (26:1 NIV) (c. 609 BC) at a time when Judah could avoid the disaster of the Babylonian invasion if its leaders and people would turn from their sinful ways (7:3–7; cf. 26:3–6). Jeremiah courageously announced that the Lord was prepared to destroy Jerusalem and His temple because the people substituted empty ritual for true obedience. Judah also would be destroyed because the people chose to believe in the empty promises of the false prophets instead of Jeremiah's warnings of coming judgment (8:1–9:26).

Painting of Jeremiah as the weeping prophet.

One of the "Lachish Letters" found in the ruins of the city of Lachish destroyed by Nebuchadnezzar. The letter contains a report of a junior military officer to his superior indicating his compliance with orders received by means of a fire signal. The text reads: "Know that we are watching for the signals of Lachish according to all the indications that my lord has given, for we cannot see the signal of Azekah."

Archaeology and the Book of Jeremiah

The archeological evidence for the historical accuracy of Jeremiah is astounding. Several discoveries verify the people and events mentioned in this book. The most prominent discoveries include the *Lachish* and *Arad Ostraca* (ink-inscribed pottery shards) that date from the years just prior to the destruction of Jerusalem. The Lachish Letters are from one of the last cities in Judah still standing as the Babylonians were attacking. They refer to requesting reinforcements from Egypt and a warning from a prophet. The name is illegible but ends in *yahu* and may refer to Jeremiah (*Yirmeyahu*) himself. The Arad Letters (200 ostraca) written in Hebrew and Aramaic mention the name Pashur (Jer 20:1) and refer to the temple as "the house of Yahweh."

Additional personal names from the book of Jeremiah have been confirmed as well. Two seal impressions have been found bearing the name of Jeremiah's scribe Baruch: "Berekyahu, son of Neriyahu, the scribe." One contains the fingerprint of Baruch himself. Another clay seal reads: "Belonging to *Gemariah* (son of) Shaphan" (Jer 36:12). Another bulla (seal) was found at Lachish referring to *Gedaliah* "overseer of the royal house" (Jer 36:12). Yet another seal reads: "Belonging to *Seriah* son of Neriah," Baruch's brother (Jer 51:59). And still another seal reads: "Belonging to *Jehucal*, son of Shelemiah" (Jer 37:3), one of the court officials serving King Zedekiah. A jar handle was found at Ramat Rahel between Jerusalem and Bethlehem which reads: "Belonging to *Eliakim*, steward of Jehoiachin" (Jer 22:24).

A clay prism dated about 570 BC found in Babylon during the excavations of Nebuchadnezzar's palace refers to Nebuzaradan as "the chancellor," an appointment received after his military career (Jer 39:9). The account of the Babylonian conquest of Jerusalem refers to their military commanders sitting in the Middle Gate of Jerusalem. The remains of this gate were excavated by Nahman Avigad and can be seen today in Jerusalem's Jewish Quarter. Even the most critical scholars have admitted the historical accuracy of the details of Jeremiah's account of the last days of Judah.

Jeremiah expresses a series of laments, complaints, and confessions (11:18–23; 12:1–6; 15:10–21; 18:19–23; 20:7–18) that are reflections of some of the laments in Psalms. They provide an autobiographical insight into the soul of the prophet and remind us that preaching is a difficult business. The prophet was hated by kings, priests, and people alike for his strong preaching. But time revealed that Jeremiah was right and they were wrong. Jeremiah's two visits to the potter in 18:1–19:15 were prophetic sign acts that visualized how the covenantal relationship between the Lord and His people had reached a breaking point. When the prophet called the people to turn from their sinful ways, they stubbornly refused in open defiance of the Lord (18:12–13). In light of this response, there was nothing left but for the Lord to bring destruction upon Judah, which was dramatically portrayed by Jeremiah's smashing a clay jar in front of the people.

Lachish, Israel, was the last fortress to fall before Jerusalem fell to the Babylonians in 587 BC. Seen here are ruins on the tel of the ancient city of Lachish, which included a citadel, a palace, and a Persian temple.

The Lord's judgment would especially target Judah's kings and prophets because their failed leadership was largely responsible for Judah's spiritual corruption. Jehoahaz (609 BC) would die in Egyptian exile (22:10–12). Jehoiakim (609–597 BC) would die and not even be given the honor of a proper burial (22:15–19). Jehoiachin (597 BC) would never return from his exile in Babylon, and none of his sons would rule on the throne (22:24–30). As the final king of Judah, Zedekiah (597–586 BC) would be taken away in exile to Babylon as the Lord Himself fought on the side of the Babylonian army (21:1–10; 34:1–5). Chapters 22–25 include Jeremiah's prophecy of the Davidic king or "Righteous Branch" (23:5–6) who would restore the Davidic kingdom in the future and the prophecy of a seventy-year Babylonian captivity that was coming in the immediate future (25:11).

III. Rejection of the Prophet: Personal Illustrations (Jeremiah 26:1–45:5)

Jeremiah 26–45 is a narrative story of Jeremiah's ministry, documenting Judah's rejection of the prophet's message and recounting the fall of Jerusalem to the Babylonians. Jeremiah encountered various forms of persecution and opposition because he preached an unpopular message. Even after the fall of

Jerusalem in 586 BC, the people persisted in their disobedience, and Jeremiah was eventually kidnapped and taken away to Egypt (43:1–6). However, judgment was not God's final word for His people. The Lord promised to bring the exiles back to the land after seventy years (29:10), and 30:1–33:26 contains Jeremiah's Book of Consolation, which promises the ultimate restoration of Israel. At that time the Lord will establish a new covenant with His people so they will obey Him and consequently enjoy His blessings forever.

Jeremiah's message of hope for Israel's future contrasted with the empty promises of the false prophets. Even in his message of judgment, a message of hope and restoration for Israel stands at a prominent position in the center of the book. Thus, God's promise in this section was: "For I know the plans I have for you . . . to give you a future and a hope" (29:11). The Lord would restore Israel because He loved His people with an eternal love (31:2–6). The return from exile would be like a second exodus as the Lord redeemed His people from bondage in a foreign land. The second exodus will surpass the first because the Lord will establish a new covenant that will be better than the one enacted at Mount Sinai (31:31–34). The New Testament reveals that believers today currently enjoy the blessings of the new covenant through the death of Jesus and the giving of the Spirit (Matt 11:28; 1 Cor 11:25; Heb 8:7–10; 10:15–18), but the complete fulfillment of this new covenant made originally with the house of Israel and Judah awaits the future time of restoration when "all Israel will be saved" (Rom 11:26–27).

Jeremiah warned that Judah would not be able to resist the Babylonians (37:6–10) and that submission to Babylon was the only way Jerusalem would be spared from destruction (38:2–3, 17–18, 20–23). But Zedekiah refused to listen because he feared the royal and military officials who wished to continue their resistance against Babylon.

Ebed-melech the Cushite

One of the most touching stories in the narrative section is that of Jeremiah's rescue by an African court official named Ebed-melech ("servant of the king"). Under pressure from his own court officials, King Zedekiah permitted them to imprison Jeremiah in a cistern in the guard's courtyard (38:1–6). Sinking into the mud and his own refuse, Jeremiah was left to die. But a "court official" of African descent, a Cushite from Ethiopia, came to the prophet's rescue. Ebed-melech risked his own life, insisting that Jeremiah be released and treated more humanely (38:7–10).

In this story the Ethiopian came to the prophet's rescue and was later himself saved by the prophet's intervention (39:13–18). In a contrasting story in Acts 8:26–39, the prophet/evangelist Philip comes to the aid of the Ethiopian official on the road to Gaza. Philip heard him reading from the text of Isaiah 53 and pointed him to faith in Jesus as the promised Messiah.

The Babylonians captured Jerusalem in 586 BC, after a siege lasting for a year and a half, in fulfillment of Jeremiah's prophecies of judgment. Zedekiah attempted to flee but was captured by the Babylonian army near Jericho. Nebuchadnezzar executed Zedekiah's sons and then blinded the king before taking him away as a prisoner to Babylon (39:1–7). The walls of Jerusalem were torn down, and most of the people in the land were taken away as exiles to Babylon. In the meantime Jeremiah was set free from prison by the Babylonians and was later forcibly taken to Egypt by Jewish rebels (42:1–43:7).

The promise of salvation at the conclusion to this section is extended to two lone individuals, the Ethiopian Ebed-melech (39:15–18) and Jeremiah's scribe Baruch (45:1–5). The promise to Baruch parallels the earlier promise to Ebed-melech, who had acted to save Jeremiah's life when he was thrown into the cistern. Obedience to the Lord was a matter of life and death, and only those who followed the Lord would enjoy the blessings of His salvation.

IV. Oracles Against the Nations: Judgments of the Lord (Jeremiah 46:1–51:64)

Israel's restoration would also include the *judgment of its enemies*, so the book of Jeremiah concludes with a series of oracles against nine foreign nations: Egypt (46:1–28), Philistia (47:1–7), Moab (48:1–47), Ammon (49:1–6), Edom (49:7–22), Damascus (49:23–27), Kedar and Hazor (49:28–33), Elam (49:34–39), and Babylon (50:1–51:64). Jeremiah's primary focus is on the judgment of Babylon. The Lord used Babylon as his "hammer" of judgment against Judah and the nations (50:23; 51:20–23), but he would also hold Babylon accountable for its crimes and violence. The Lord would judge the false gods of Babylon (50:2–3), and He would also execute vengeance against Babylon for the violence it inflicted upon Judah (50:11–14, 28–35; 51:5, 10–11, 24, 34–37, 49–53). The Lord would reverse the fortunes of Judah and Babylon by restoring His people at the same time He was bringing an enemy army to destroy Babylon.

Babylon in Scripture is also representative of human opposition to God and His people. Babylon was the site of the rebellion that led to the confusion of human language and the division of the nations (Gen 11:1–9). Revelation 17–18 depicts the destruction of the future empire of Antichrist as the fall of Babylon. This reference to Babylon in Revelation appears symbolic rather than geographic. Just like the Babylon of the past, the future empire of Antichrist would oppose God and persecute God's people in an even greater way.

V. Epilogue: The Fall of Jerusalem (Jeremiah 52:1–34)

The final verse of Jeremiah 51 states, "The words of Jeremiah end here," and the narrative of the fall of Jerusalem in chapter 52 serves as an appendix to the book that was likely added by a later editor. This account closely parallels 2 Kings 25 and serves canonically to connect the book of Jeremiah with the story of the covenant failure of Israel and Judah in the books of Kings. The record of Jerusalem's fall in Jeremiah 39 focuses more on the fate of King Zedekiah and the prophet Jeremiah, while this chapter emphasizes more the destruction of the temple and the removal of the temple articles to Babylon. King Jehoiachin was deported to Babylon in 597 BC, and his release from prison in Babylon is the last recorded event in the book of Jeremiah (52:27–30), providing a glimmer of hope for the restoration of Israel and the Davidic monarchy.

LAMENTATIONS

Jerusalem Is Burning

The book of Lamentations is a series of five separate laments over the fall of Jerusalem to the Babylonians in 586 BC. The intensely emotional nature of the book indicates that the writer experienced these events firsthand. Lamentations was most likely composed shortly after 586 BC. Commemoration of the destruction of Jerusalem is attested at an early time in the Old Testament (Jer 41:5; Zech 7:3–5; 8:19), and the reading of Lamentations later became part of the ceremonies marking the fall of Jerusalem on the ninth of Ab. Lamentations is part of five books in the Hebrew canon known as the *Megilloth* (also including Ecclesiastes, Esther, Ruth, and Song of Solomon) that were associated with specific Hebrew festivals.

KEY FACTS

Author:	Jeremiah
Date:	586 BC
Recipients:	Jewish refugees
Key Word:	Faithful love (Hb. *chêsêd*)
Key Verse:	"Because of the LORD's faithful love we do not perish, for his mercies never end. They are new every morning; great is your faithfulness!" (3:22–23).

Background

The poems in the book most closely resemble the communal laments in the Psalms. These laments expressed the people's sorrow following military defeats (Pss 44; 60; 74; 79; 80). Lamentations 1, 2, and 4 are introduced by the exclamation "how" (*'ek/'ekah*), and David used similar terminology in the funeral dirges that lament the deaths of Saul and Jonathan (2 Sam 1:19–27). Lamentations 1–4 are acrostic poems. The poems in 1:1–22 and 2:1–22 have three lines in each verse, with each new verse beginning with successive letters of the Hebrew alphabet. Chapter 4 is the same but with each verse having two lines. The acrostic in 3:1–66 is the most elaborate, with twenty-two stanzas of three verses each. Chapter 5 is not an acrostic but has twenty-two verses corresponding to the number of letters in the Hebrew alphabet. The length and positioning of 3:1–66 make this poem the key chapter in the book. In the midst of this disaster, the writer encourages people to trust in the covenant faithfulness (*chesed*) of the Lord as their source of hope for the future (3:21–36).

Author

The book of Lamentations is an anonymous composition that appears in the Hebrew Bible in the Writings section of the canon, but early tradition identifies Jeremiah as the author of the book. The first verse of Lamentations in the Greek Septuagint (LXX) attributes the book to Jeremiah, and the Septuagint also placed Lamentations after the book of Jeremiah as does the English Bible. Second Chronicles 25:35 states that Jeremiah composed laments at the death of Josiah, and the book of Jeremiah often portrays the prophet as weeping over the destruction of his people (Jer 9:1–2; 14:17–22).

Outline

I. Mourning Widow (1:1–22)
II. Weeping Daughter (2:1–22)
III. Afflicted Man (3:1–66)
IV. Tarnished Gold (4:1–22)
V. Fatherless Child (5:1–22)

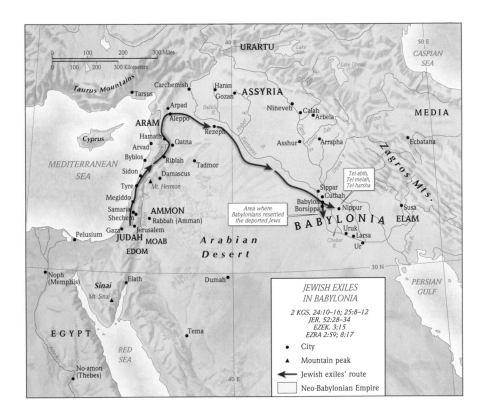

Message

I. Mourning Widow (Lamentations 1:1–22)

This poem portrays Jerusalem as a grieving widow mourning her destruction. Jerusalem's lovers and friends refer to the nations she depended on through alliances. She trusted in them rather than trusting in the Lord for protection, but suddenly they abandoned her so she was reduced to slavery. The recurring refrain that "there is no one to comfort" Jerusalem reflected the city's hopeless condition (1:2, 9, 16–17, 21).

II. Weeping Daughter (Lamentations 2:1–22)

This lament faces the harsh reality that the Lord Himself brought about the destruction of the daughter of Jerusalem. As the Divine Warrior, the Lord poured out His anger on the city and even abandoned His own sanctuary. The poet wept over the suffering and death all around him and encouraged the people to give full expression of their grief to the Lord. There was hope that their cries would turn away the Lord's anger.

III. Afflicted Man (Lamentations 3:1–66)

This first-person lament describes intense suffering with vivid emotion and metaphors that were representative of the community. The Lord relentlessly attacked him by ravaging his body, confining him in a dark dungeon, mangling him like a wild animal, and shooting him with arrows. The Lord gave him bitter food and drink, broke his teeth, and then trampled him underfoot. The piling up of metaphors reflected the intensity of his afflictions. This beleaguered individual probably is the personified city of Jerusalem.

Despite this suffering, the Lord's covenant faithfulness (*chesed*) offers hope for the future because the Lord's mercy, compassion, and love for His people is greater than His anger over their disobedience. The poet's faith is such that he speaks as if God has answered his prayer even as he speaks it.

IV. Tarnished Gold (Lamentations 4:1–22)

This poem contrasts Zion's glorious past with its deplorable present. Jerusalem was "the perfection of beauty" and "the joy of the whole earth" (2:15; Ps 48:2), but the city was ravaged by war because of the Lord's judgment. Jerusalem's fate was worse than that of Sodom. The Babylonian siege of Jerusalem was brutal because it lasted for a year and a half (2 Kgs 25:1–3), so some of the residents of Jerusalem were reduced to cannibalism.

Beggar at the Damascus gate in Jerusalem.

V. Fatherless Child (Lamentations 5:1–22)

The poet called for the Lord to remember those that survived the fall of Jerusalem and to intervene on their behalf. Judah forfeited the land given to them as an "inheritance" from the Lord (Exod 32:13; Deut 12:9–10; 15:4), but the lamenter petitions the Lord to restore His people. While acknowledging God's sovereignty, it appeared that the Lord abandoned His people. The time of the fall of Jerusalem and Babylonian exile was a national calamity (Psalm 137) and constituted the greatest theological crisis faced by ancient Israel. The Lord appears to have abandoned His covenant promises. The survivors were left to wonder if the Lord was willing to restore them. Lamentations gives voice to the suffering of these survivors and offers theological reflection to help them through this crisis. God's dealings with Israel serve as a serious reminder to us today. If God allowed Israel to come under judgment for her sins, we dare not believe that we will escape if we take His warnings lightly.

Practical Application

In the midst of this hopelessness and despair, Jeremiah offered hope and the promise of a new beginning for Israel as the people of God. Jeremiah prophesied that the Lord will bring the Jews back to their homeland, restore the Davidic dynasty, and establish a new covenant that would erase the failures of the past and guarantee Israel's obedience and blessing. Judgment would not be the final word because the Lord's love for His people was everlasting. His great faithfulness is "new every morning" (Lam 3:23). No matter what seems to go wrong in our lives, we have the assurance that God is in control and His love will sustain us.

For Further Reading

Dearman, J. A. *Jeremiah, Lamentations*. NIVAC. Grand Rapids: Zondervan, 2002.

Feinberg, Charles. *Jeremiah: A Commentary*. Grand Rapids: Zondervan, 1982.

Harrison, R. K. *Jeremiah and Lamentations*. TOTC. Downers Grove, IL: InterVarsity Press, 1973.

Huey, F. B. *Jeremiah, Lamentations*. NAC. Nashville: B&H, 1993.

Ryken, Philip. *Jeremiah and Lamentations*. Wheaton, IL: Crossway, 2001.

Thompson, J. A. *The Book of Jeremiah*. NICOT. Grand Rapids: Eerdmans, 1980.

Study Questions

1. What nation threatened Judah in the days of Jeremiah, and what advice did he give them?
2. How did Jeremiah describe his call to the ministry?
3. What words of hope did the prophet give to the people of Jerusalem?
4. What was the ultimate fulfillment of the prophecy of the new covenant?
5. What is a "lament," and how does it help us express our deepest feelings?

Notes

1. "Jeremiah," in Walter Elwell, ed. *Baker Encyclopedia of the Bible* (Grand Rapids: Baker, 1988), 2:1, 110–13.

2. Outline follows N. Geisler, *A Popular Survey of the Old Testament* (Grand Rapids: Baker, 2006), 275.

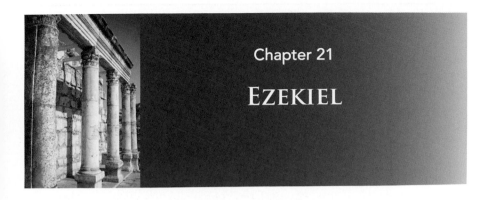

Chapter 21

EZEKIEL

The Glory Will Return

The book of Ezekiel is structured around three visions of the Lord. In the first vision (chaps. 1–3), the Lord appeared to Ezekiel and commissioned him to be a prophet to his fellow exiles in Babylon. In the second vision (chaps. 8–11), Ezekiel saw the glory of the Lord depart from Jerusalem and saw him remove his protective presence because the people defiled the temple with their idolatry and their wickedness. In the final vision (chaps. 40–48), Ezekiel saw the glory of the Lord return to Jerusalem (43:1–9; cf. 37:27) after the rebuilding of the temple and the restoration of Israel in the last days.

KEY FACTS

Author:	Ezekiel
Date:	593–571 BC
Recipients:	Jewish exiles in Babylon
Key Word:	Glory (Hb. *kābōd*)
Key Verse:	"I saw the glory of the God of Israel there, like the vision I had seen in the plain" (8:4).

Author and Background

Ezekiel ("God has strengthened") was transported into exile with Jehoiachin and other leading citizens of Judah (2 Kgs 24:10–16) as part of the second Babylonian deportation in 597 BC. He received his call as a prophet in July 593 BC, on his thirtieth birthday (1:1–3), and ministered among his fellow exiles while living at Tel Abib in Southern Mesopotamia near Nippur. Chronological notations in the book indicate that Ezekiel's ministry extended until at least 571 BC. The prophet came from a priestly family, which helps explain his emphasis on sin as uncleanness and defilement (5:11; 7:20; 20:43; 22:4; 36:29; 43:8) and his interest in the rebuilding of the future temple (chaps. 40–48).

Ezekiel settled with a group of Jewish exiles near the city of Nippur by the Chebar River. Shown here are ruins of a temple in Nafur, Iraq (ancient Nippur).

Outline

I. The Judgment of Judah and Jerusalem (1:1–24:27)
II. The Judgment of the Nations (25:1–32:32)
III. The Future Restoration of Israel (33:1–48:35)

Message

I. The Judgment of Judah and Jerusalem (Ezekiel 1:1–24:27)

Ezekiel 1–3 narrates the details of Ezekiel's prophetic call. This account contrasts the awesome power of the Lord with the frailty of Ezekiel as a human being (a "son of man," used ninety-three times). Ezekiel needed to know that his strength for ministry came from the Lord and not from himself. The four living creatures that helped propel the chariot of the Lord with their wings are identified as *cherubim* in Ezek 10:20. The Lord appeared seated on a throne above a crystal expanse that looked like the sky. The sovereign Lord of heaven asserted His sovereignty in the land of Babylon, and no human ruler or army would be able to oppose Him. His voice was like the roar of mighty rivers. The flashes of lightning, flames of fire, glowing metals, and shining jewels reflected the Lord's radiance and majesty. When seeing the greatness of God's glory, Ezekiel fell on his face in awe and worship (1:28).

Ezekiel's role as a prophet is compared to the work of a "watchman" who stood on the city wall and warned the people of approaching attacks from an enemy army (3:17–21). If Ezekiel warned the people of the coming judgment and they refused to believe, then the people were responsible for their own destruction; but if the prophet failed to warn them, then their blood would be on his hands. Ezekiel was only responsible for proclaiming the message, not for

Winged lamassu (face of a man, body of a bull, wings of a bird).

how the people responded. To make sure the people recognized that Ezekiel's message was coming from God, the prophet was only able to speak when enabled by the Lord.

Ezekiel portrayed the siege of Jerusalem through a series of *four sign acts* in order to show the exiles that the fall of Jerusalem was near (chaps. 4–5). The prophet built a model of Jerusalem and raised siege works against it. He lay on his side for 430 days to symbolize the accumulated sin of Israel and Judah. The Lord made the prophet eat bread from an odd assortment of grains cooked over dung and to drink small portions of water in order to illustrate the future famine conditions in the besieged city of Jerusalem. Ezekiel shaved his head and beard and then burned one-third of his hair, cut up another third with a sword, and the last third he scattered into the wind. The small portion the prophet tucked inside his belt represented the tiny remnant that would survive the fall of Jerusalem.

In Ezekiel's *second vision* of the Lord, the glory of the Lord departed from the Jerusalem temple in response to the people's idolatry (chaps. 8–11). Ezekiel saw the people worshipping idols, an "abomination" that defiled the sanctuary where the Lord lived among His people. The people engraved images of gods in the form of animals on its walls, some women practiced the mourning rites associated with the fertility god Tammuz, and some men were worshipping the sun god on the temple steps. The Lord would not share His glory with these false gods, and He would not tolerate the demeaning of His holiness.

Thus the glory of the Lord moves to the door of the temple (9:3; 10:4), then to the east gate of the temple (10:18–19), and then out of the city of Jerusalem completely (11:23–33). The departure of the Lord's presence from the Mount of Olives meant the removal of the Lord's protection when the Babylonian army invaded; His earlier protection of Jerusalem was over (Pss 46:5–9; 48:4–8; 76:3).

Relief figure of an auroch (bull) from the facade of the Ishtar Gate in Babylon.

Along with his symbolic acts, Ezekiel told *three parables* to portray the sinfulness of Judah and the certainty of coming judgment (chaps. 15–17). The first parable compared Jerusalem to a charred vine that was worthless for producing fruit; the second portrayed Jerusalem as an unfaithful bride (16:1–52); and the third illustrated Judah's political situation with a parable about two eagles, a cedar tree, and a vine (17:1–24).

II. The Judgment of the Nations (Ezekiel 25:1–32:32)

Like Isaiah 13–23 and Jeremiah 46–51, Ezekiel has a series of oracles against foreign nations. The Lord's sovereignty extended beyond Israel and Judah and included all nations. Judah would receive comfort in knowing that the Lord would ultimately punish the nations that mistreated them. These oracles would also serve as a warning against forming alliances with other nations, for they too would become the objects of God's judgments. In line with the overall message of the book, the purpose of these judgments was to cause all peoples to know that the Lord was the true God.

In 587 BC, Ezekiel delivered an extensive message of *judgment against Tyre*, the capital of Phoenicia and a prosperous commercial trading center. Soon the Lord would bring an enemy army against Tyre that would reduce the city to a bare rock and a place to cast fishing nets. Nebuchadnezzar besieged Tyre for thirteen years (585–572 BC), destroying many of its buildings; but many of its citizens escaped to an island fortress. Alexander the Great was finally able to reduce Tyre's island fortress to rubble in 332 BC, literally casting its remains into the sea (26:19).

The *lament over Tyre* in Ezekiel 27 appropriately portrays the city as a stately ship made from the products of its many trading partners. People from Tyre sailed the seas and accumulated great wealth by exchanging many goods and engaging in slave trade, but a powerful wind would eventually shatter the ship of Tyre in the heart of the seas (27:35–36). The peoples of the earth would react with shock and horror over the downfall of Tyre and its vast financial empire.

View of columned roadway at Tyre leading west to the sea, showing the underground area.

Ezekiel also delivered a series of *oracles against Egypt* (29:1–32:31). During the Assyrian and Babylonian crises, Judah often trusted in political and military alliances with Egypt rather than the Lord as their source of security (Isa 30:1–3; 31:1–3; Jer 37:4–10; Ezek 17:15–17). Nevertheless, Egypt's promises of help often did not materialize. At best help provided only temporary relief from some pressing threat. Trusting in Egypt was like using a reed stalk for a walking stick because that stick would splinter as soon as Judah leaned on it for support (29:6–7; Isa 36:6).

Ezekiel employed powerful imagery to portray the downfall of the proud and arrogant Egyptians. Addressing the pharaoh as a "monster" from the sea

(29:2–3; 32:2), the prophet depicts the king as a fearsome crocodile in the Nile River. Though the pharaoh boasted of his great strength, the Lord would catch him in his net and cast him into an open field to be consumed by the birds of the air (29:1–5; 32:1–3). The Lord's judgment would ultimately fall not only on evil human rulers but also on the evil powers that stood behind them.

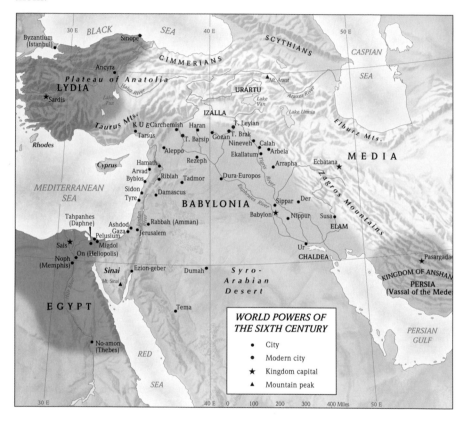

III. The Future Restoration of Israel (Ezekiel 33:1–48:35)

The final section of Ezekiel's prophecy turns to the hope of Israel's future restoration. The Lord would restore His people in spite of their flagrant disobedience for the sake of His own reputation. He will do this so that all peoples from all nations would know that He is the Lord. The Lord would also bring about Israel's spiritual and national restoration so they might enjoy His presence and the rich blessings of the Promised Land forever. Ezekiel's final messages entail prophecies of hope for the regathering, regeneration, and restoration of the people of Israel.

Israel in Bible Prophecy

Ezekiel 36 provides the theological ground for the restoration of future Israel to fulfill God's promises and restore His glory. Ezekiel 37 gives the mechanics of the restoration through the vision of the valley of dry bones (36:1–14). The whole "house of Israel" will be regathered to the Promised Land prior to their spiritual rebirth. Thus, a two-stage return is promised in the "last days." Stage one is physical and portrays the political revival of national Israel (the bones coming together), and stage two is spiritual and portrays the regeneration of the nation (breath entering into them). The word "forever" is used five times in 37:25–28, repeatedly affirming the eternality of God's restoration, and requires an eschatological fulfillment. Ezekiel's prophecies predict Israel's victory over Gog and Magog (chaps. 38–39), the conversion of Israel (39:22–29), and the erecting of the restoration temple and the return of the Shekinah glory (chaps. 40–48).

When the Lord restores Israel, he will cause the land to be fruitful and productive. Israel will rebuild their ruined cities and will enjoy the blessings of the Promised Land they forfeited because of their disobedience. The Lord will save them to regain His own reputation that was profaned by Israel's exile and bring about the spiritual transformation of His people so they will never again need to be punished. The Lord will cleanse them from their past wickedness and will give them a new heart and spirit to follow Him (36:22–36). Ezekiel's prophecy parallels Jeremiah's promise of a new covenant and of God's writing the law on the heart of His people (Jer 31:31–34).

A view from Megiddo of the Valley of Jezreel with the town of Nazareth in the distance.

Ezekiel's *vision of the dry bones* (37:1–14) confirmed the Lord's promise to restore and spiritually renew the people of Israel. The valley is pictured as a battlefield littered with the bones of dead soldiers. The Lord commanded Ezekiel to prophesy to the bones, and then the Lord put flesh on the bones and breathed life into them. Humanly speaking, there was no hope for the future. But God's "breath" (*ruach*) would bring the dry bones to life, and God's "Spirit" (*ruach*) would bring renewal to Israel as a nation. Israel's restoration would be like a resurrection from the grave.

Ezekiel's object lesson involving the two sticks provided a second confirmation of the Lord's promise to restore Israel. Ezekiel wrote the names "Judah" and "Joseph" on the two sticks and then joined the sticks together so they became one. This sign act symbolized the reunification of the northern and southern kingdoms as one nation. The Davidic Messiah would reign over the reunified nation and would lead the people to follow the Lord. The stages of Israel's regathering are progressive and sequential, with 37:21–22 describing Israel's physical regathering from the nations, and 37:23–25, describing the spiritual rebirth of Israel at the time of Christ's second coming when He will reign as the Davidic Messiah.[1] The Lord would establish a "covenant of peace" with Israel guaranteeing that He would dwell among His people forever.

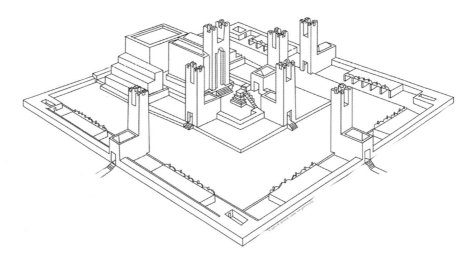

Artist's Rendering of Ezekiel's Temple. Taken from: *The Popular Bible Prophecy Commentary* Copyright © 2006 by Pre-Trib Research Center, Tim LaHaye, and Ed Hindson. Published by Harvest House Publishers, Eugene, Oregon 97402, www.harvesthousepublishers.com. Used by permission.

The Gog and Magog Invasion	
Ancient Name	**Modern Nation**
Rosh (ancient Scythians–known as Rashu, Rasapu, Ros, and Rus	Russia
Magog (ancient Scythians)	Central Asia (Islamic southern republics of the former Soviet Union with a population of sixty million Muslims. This territory could include modern Afghanistan.)
Meshech (ancient Muschki and Musku in Cilicia and Cappadocia)	Turkey (also southern Russia and Iran)
Tubal (ancient Tubalu in Cappadocia)	Turkey (also southern Russia and Iran)
Persia	Iran (name changed to Iran in 1935)
Ethiopia (ancient Cush, south of Egypt)	Sudan
Libya (ancient Put, west of Egypt)	Libya
Gomer (ancient Cimmerians—from seventh century BC in central/western Anatolia)	Turkey
Beth-togarmah (Tilgarimmu—between ancient Carchemish and Haran)	Turkey
Taken from *The Popular Encyclopedia of Bible Prophecy,* copyright © 2004 by Tim LaHaye and Ed Hindson. Published by Harvest House Publishers, Eugene, Oregon 97402, www.harvesthousepublishers.com. Used by permission.	

The vision of *Gog and Magog* in Ezekiel 38–39 concerns an end-time invasion when Israel is securely back in the land. A powerful and arrogant ruler named Gog would form a coalition of seven nations to invade Israel, but the Lord Himself would destroy these enemies by pouring down torrential rains, hailstones, and burning sulfur, which would cause such confusion they will turn against one another. No such victory over an enemy invasion of this sort has ever occurred, indicating that this battle is still in the future. The total destruction of this enemy army would cause the nations to recognize the glory of the Lord. The Lord would pour out His Spirit on them so they never again need to be punished for their disobedience.[2]

The prophecy of Ezekiel concludes with an extended vision of the *eschatological temple* and the return of God's glory on the future temple.[3] Scholars have offered several different interpretations of this vision of the new temple. Some have interpreted the vision symbolically to represent the restoration of the relationship between God and Israel. Others view the passage as an idealized prophecy concerning the rebuilding of the temple in the postexilic period under Zerubbabel, but that temple fell far short of what Ezekiel envisions. Another interpretation is that the passage is fulfilled figuratively in Jesus Christ as the replacement of the temple and in the church as God's spiritual temple. However, the detailed measurements and specifications concerning the layout and design of this temple strongly suggest that a real physical sanctuary will exist in Jerusalem during the earthly millennial kingdom (see Rev 20:1–10). Other Old Testament prophets also anticipated the restoration of Jerusalem and the temple in the future kingdom (see Isa 2:2–4; 60:7, 13; 62:9; Mic 4:1–3; Zech 14:16–19).

The most important feature of Ezekiel's vision is the promise that the Lord would return to His temple to dwell among His people in Jerusalem (43:1–12). The Lord will again establish His throne in Jerusalem, and the people will be purged of their sins so they can live in God's presence (43:6–9). The name of Jerusalem would become "the LORD is there" (48:35 NIV).

The detailed layout for the temple gates, courts, and rooms in Ezek 40:1–43:12 describes the structure that will be rebuilt. The most significant feature of the description of the future temple is its enormous size of 500 cubits (or 1,500 yards) on a side (42:16–20), which is three times larger than the temple in Jesus's day. The size of the temple suggests its prominence and importance in the future messianic kingdom.

Ezekiel also devotes significant attention to the priests, the Levites, and the services at the temple (43:13–46:14). The priests would offer the regular daily sacrifices, including sin offerings that made atonement for the sins of the people and the leaders (45:17, 22). The use of animal sacrifices in the future temple appears to present a problem in light of the fact that Jesus offered the perfect and final sacrifice for sin (Heb 10:10–14). Some interpreters have resolved this tension by arguing that these sacrifices will serve as a memorial of Christ's death in the millennium or that they will be required to remove physical impurity so sinners can enter into the presence of a holy God.[4]

Ezekiel describes a river flowing out from the temple that begins as a tiny stream but eventually becomes a mighty river (47:1–12; cf. Zech 14:8). The river brings fertility to the land and even causes the Dead Sea to come to life so fishermen will cast their nets there. This river recalls the one flowing from the garden of Eden (Gen 2:10). The millennial kingdom of Christ will bring about a reversal of the curse and the return of the earth to Eden-like conditions. John's vision of the eternal kingdom also envisions the new Jerusalem as a new Eden, with its river flowing from the city and the tree of life providing food and healing for the nations (Rev 22:1–2).

Practical Application

The Lord's judgment and salvation of Israel would cause all peoples to know that He is the true God (5:13; 12:20; 20:42; 37:13, 28; 39:28). The expression "know that I am the LORD" appears seventy-two times in the book of Ezekiel. Israel's restoration would also involve spiritual transformation, not just a return to the land following exile. The Lord would give the people a "new heart" by pouring out His Spirit upon them so they would be obedient to His commandments and never again have to face His judgment (11:18–20; 36:26–28). Ezekiel's warnings and promises to Israel remind us to take God's message seriously or we too may face His judgment and lose His blessings.

For Further Reading

Allen, Leslie C. *Ezekiel*. 2 vols. WBC. Dallas: Word, 1990, 1994.
Block, Daniel I. *Ezekiel*. 2 vols. NICOT. Grand Rapids: Eerdmans, 1997, 1998.
Cooper, Lamar E. *Ezekiel*. NAC. Nashville: B&H, 1994.
Craigie, Peter C. *Ezekiel*. DSB. Philadelphia: Westminster, 1995.
Duguid, Iain M. *Ezekiel*. NIVAC. Grand Rapids: Zondervan, 1999.
Feinberg, Charles L. *The Prophecy of Ezekiel*. Chicago: Moody, 1969.

Study Questions

1. Describe the circumstances of Ezekiel's ministry during the Babylonian captivity.
2. What term was applied to Ezekiel to emphasize his human limitations?
3. How does Ezekiel describe the glory of God departing from the temple? What is the significance of this departure?
4. What did the vision of the dry bones signify?
5. What will be the result of the invasion of Israel by Gog and Magog?
6. Why should we be concerned about the glory of God in our lives?

Notes

1. See comments in Tim LaHaye and Ed Hindson, *The Popular Bible Prophecy Commentary* (Eugene, OR: Harvest House, 2006), 179–89.

2. Ibid., 189–95. It is interesting to note that Babylon is not named in this prophecy, even though Ezekiel was living there as a captive Jew at that time.

3. Cf. detailed discussion in Randall Price, *The Temple in Bible Prophecy* (Eugene, OR: Harvest House, 2005).

4. See Charles Feinberg, "Millennial Offering and Sacrifices," *The Prophecy of Ezekiel* (Chicago: Moody Press, 1969), 263–70.

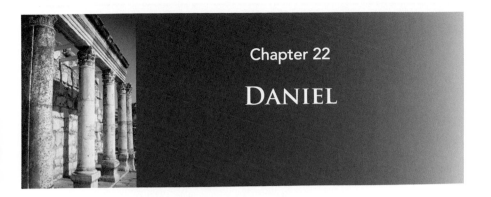

Chapter 22

DANIEL

The Messiah Will Come

The book of Daniel, written in both Hebrew (1:1–2:4a; 8:1–12:13) and Aramaic (2:4b–7:28), combines the personal histories and prophecies of Daniel during the Babylonian captivity and the first few years of the Persian era (605–535 BC). It also includes detailed prophecies of the fate of the Jewish people under Gentile rule in "the time of the end" (Dan 8:19) or what Jesus called the "times of the Gentiles" (Luke 21:24). Daniel foretells the rise and fall of four Gentile empires (2:1–49; 7:1–28), the coming of the Messiah (7:13–14; 9:25–26), the rise of the Antichrist (8:21–25; 9:26–27; 11:36–45), the time of tribulation (12:1–7), the triumph of the kingdom of God (2:44), and the final resurrection (12:13).

KEY FACTS	
Author:	Daniel
Date:	605–535 BC
Recipients:	Jews and Gentiles
Key Word:	Interpretation (Aramaic *peshar*)
Key Verses:	"Daniel, I've come now to give you understanding ... for you are treasured by God" (9:22–23).

Background

Daniel ("God is my Judge"), a contemporary of Jeremiah and Ezekiel, went into captivity to Babylon in 605 BC. His book records events and visions dating up to 535 BC (10:1), indicating that he lived through the entire seventy years of the Babylonian captivity. Nebuchadnezzar, the Babylonian prince, attacked the city of Jerusalem in August 605 BC and removed Jehoiakim, the king of Judah, sometime after he defeated the Egyptians at the Battle of Carchemish in May–June 605 BC.

An artist's reconstruction of Babylon as it would have appeared in the sixth century BC (courtesy of the University of Chicago).

The Babylonian setting of the book is indicated by the constant references to the language, culture, and history of the Neo-Babylonian Empire. The author identifies Babylonian cultural concepts (e.g., trial by ordeal), deities (Bel, Nebo, Marduk), architectural details (plaster walls in the palace), and long-forgotten historical information (the co-regency of Belshazzar and Nabonidus). The Persian sections of the book also reflect Persian loan words ("satraps"). Even critical scholars have admitted, "We have here true reminiscence of the elaborate organization and civil service of Persia."[1]

Date and Authorship

Since the eighteenth century critical scholars have criticized the book of Daniel and have called it a pseudonymous forgery of the Maccabean period (170–160 BC). The detailed and accurate prophecies in the book of Daniel are the target of criticism by those who reject the concept that prophecy predicts events beyond the immediate setting of the prophet. Many deny that Daniel could predict what would happen in the distant future, so they assert that these "prophetic" statements were made *post-eventu* (after the fact). They suggest that a second-century Jew was actually writing about the persecution of Antiochus Epiphanes some four centuries later, using the fictitious name "Daniel" of Babylon as an example to the Jews of his own time.

Was Daniel a Prophet?

Contemporary critics are quick to point out that Daniel was listed in the section of the "Writings" (*kethuvim*) in the Hebrew Bible and not among the "Prophets" (*nevi'im*). Thus, they assert that Daniel was not considered a prophetic book and in some cases even suggest it is apocryphal. However, several key factors weigh against this analysis. First, Daniel served as an administrator in a foreign court. He was not a preaching prophet to the nation of Israel. Second, he claimed to receive visions from God that were clearly prophetic in nature. Thus, Daniel's book was placed among the prophets in Greek and English translations because he clearly demonstrated the gift of prophecy, even if he didn't hold the office of prophet. Jesus specifically called him "the prophet Daniel" (Matt 24:15). Third, the second-century BC Septuagint (LXX) lists Daniel among the "prophets" as did Josephus (first century AD), Melito (second century AD), and Origen (third century AD). Finally, several fragments in the Dead Sea Scrolls refer to words that were "written in the book of Daniel the prophet," indicating a pre-Christian acceptance of Daniel as a prophetic book.

The book of Daniel specifically dates its proceedings and prophecies according to the regal years of various Babylonian and Persian monarchs (1:1, 21; 2:1; 5:31; 7:1; 8:1; 9:1; 10:1; 11:1). Daniel dates himself repeatedly by describing himself as a Judean exile (1:1–6; 2:25; 5:13; 6:13). Additional confirmation for dating the book in this era comes from historical figures associated with Daniel, such as Nebuchadnezzar (1:18), Belshazzar (5:29), and Cyrus (6:28). Literary and archaeological sources confirming the existence of these kings support a literal historical setting for the book of Daniel, and the accuracy of the details within the book argues for a date of composition in the sixth century BC, around 535 BC.

The language of the book argues for a date much earlier than the second century. Linguistic evidence from the Dead Sea Scrolls, which furnish authentic samples of second-century Hebrew and Aramaic, demonstrate that the Hebrew and Aramaic chapters of Daniel were composed many centuries earlier.[2] The few Persian and Greek terms appearing in the book refer to government officials (6:1–2) or musical instruments (3:1–5) and do not provide ample evidence of a late date for the composition.[3]

The argument that prophecies cannot predict details in advance is contrary to the evidence, for several of Daniel's prophecies were fulfilled long after the Persian and Maccabean era: the rise of the Roman Empire (2:33; 7:7), the coming of "Messiah the Prince" 483 years after the command to "restore and rebuild Jerusalem" (9:25), the death of the Messiah (9:26), and the destruction of Jerusalem and the second temple (9:26). These cannot easily be explained away as lucky guesses. Objective evidence, therefore, appears to exclude the late date hypothesis and indicates sufficient reason to affirm Daniel's authorship in the sixth century BC. The fact that Jesus Himself (Matt 24:15) referred to "Daniel the prophet" is ample testimony to the Savior's belief that Daniel was the author of the book.

Outline

I. Daniel's Personal History (1:1–6:28)
   A. Four Hebrews (1:1–21)
   B. Four Empires (2:1–49)
   C. Furnace of Fire (3:1–30)
   D. Fate of Nebuchadnezzar (4:1–37)
   E. Fall of Babylon (5:1–30)
   F. Fearless Prayer (6:1–28)
II. Daniel's Prophetic Visions (7:1–12:13)
   A. Four Beasts (7:1–28)
   B. Ram and Goat (8:1–27)
   C. Seventy Sevens (9:1–27)
   D. Israel's Future (10:1–12:13)

Message

The overall theme of Daniel is God's sovereignty over the people of Israel and the nations of the world. Despite the threats of Gentile powers, "the Most High God is ruler over human kingdoms" (5:21). He alone sets up and takes down human authorities who rule by His divine permission (2:21). The book is made up primarily of historical narrative (chaps. 1–6) and apocalyptic prophetic visions (chaps. 7–12). The latter may be defined as symbolic, visionary prophecies that are mainly eschatological in nature. Often composed during oppressive conditions, apocalyptic literature is written to provide encouragement to the people of God by providing a clear revelation of the future.

I. Daniel's Personal History (Daniel 1:1–6:28)

A. Four Hebrews (Daniel 1:1–21)

The book of Daniel begins with Daniel and his three friends, Hananiah, Mishael, and Azariah (1:6), being taken captive to Babylon as intellectual hostages by Nebuchadnezzar in August 605 BC. The four Hebrews were placed in a three-year training program to learn the language (Akkadian), literature (written in cuneiform script), and the sciences of the Babylonians. Every attempt was made to accommodate them to Babylonian life and culture to prepare them for government service to the Babylonian Empire. Accordingly, their Hebrew names were changed to Babylonian names (Belteshazzar, Shadrach, Meshach, Abednego); and they were allotted

Relief figure of a dragon from the façade of the Ishtar Gate at Babylon.

a portion of the king's diet. Immediately these young men asked to be exempt from eating the king's food, probably based on a kosher dietary principle, because they determined in their hearts not to defile themselves (1:8). Ultimately they won the favor of their guards and with God's blessing proved themselves to be "ten times better" than all the other captives (1:20).

B. Four Empires (Daniel 2:1–49)

The second chapter involves Nebuchadnezzar's fantastic dream of a great metallic statue and his insistence that the wise men and magicians of Babylon reproduce his dream and interpret it. At this point the text of Daniel switches to Aramaic. While the wise men failed to reproduce and interpret the dream, "the mystery was then revealed to Daniel" after much prayer (2:19). Daniel pointed out that God revealed to the king what would happen "in the last days" (2:28) and identified the elements of the metallic statue. The head of gold symbolized Nebuchadnezzar and the kingdom of Babylon (2:38), and it would be followed by kingdoms of silver, brass, and iron (2:32–33). Finally, the feet of "iron mixed with clay" indicated the instability of the entire statue (2:41–42). Later prophecies in Daniel 7–8 identify the second kingdom as Media-Persia (arms of silver) and the third as Greece (belly of brass). The fourth kingdom is unnamed in Daniel, but most commentators identify it with Rome.

Daniel then explained that in the days of the ten toes of iron and clay, the God of heaven would destroy the earlier kingdoms, symbolized by the stone falling on the toes of the statue, and then He would replace them with the kingdom of God (2:44). While commentators differ on how this should be interpreted, premillennialists identify the stone with the second coming of Christ because only then will human governments literally be replaced by the kingdom of God on earth.

C. Furnace of Fire (Daniel 3:1–30)

Nebuchadnezzar required Shadrach, Meshach, and Abednego and all of his government officials to worship a golden statue when certain music played. The musical instruments mentioned included Greek terms for lyre (*kitharis*), harp (*psalterion*), and pipes (*sumphonia*) expressed in Aramaic. Such terms were well-known in the Middle East by the sixth century.[4] Daniel's absence in this account is explained in 2:49, for Daniel gave up his role as a provincial official in order to remain at the king's court in Babylon, serving as chief of the wise men. His political responsibilities were given to Daniel's three friends who were serving in the province (3:1); thus they were required to attend the event described in chapter 3.

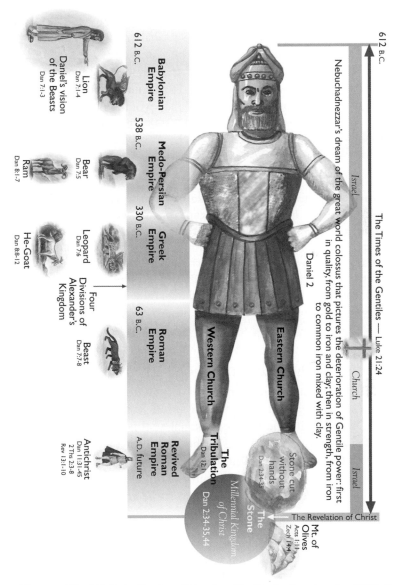

Diagram of Daniel's Statue Prophecy. Taken from The Popular Encyclopedia of Bible Prophecy, *copyright © 2004 by Tim LaHaye and Ed Hindson. Published by Harvest House Publishers, Eugene, Oregon 97402, www.harvesthousepublishers.com. Used by permission.*

The names of Daniel's three friends, along with Nebuzaradan (Jer 39:9–13) and Neriglissar (Jer 39:3, 13), were found in a Babylonian text from the time of Nebuchadnezzar.[5] The furnace was probably a brick kiln used to fire bricks. The fact that the Hebrews did not burn and were released (3:25–26) follows the Babylonian legal concept of trial by ordeal, innocence being validated by surviving one's punishment. Their faith in God was clear; "He can rescue us . . . but even if he does not," they would not bow (3:17–18).

REFLECTION

Politically Incorrect

Daniel understood what it was like to live in a hostile environment. He and his friends had been taken captive and were now serving the Babylonians. They were under pressure to behave with the utmost political correctness. Their choices to stand with God meant walking out of step with the Babylonian world. Spiritual correctness often means being willing to suffer the consequences of being politically incorrect. What would you have done if you had been in their situation?

D. Fate of Nebuchadnezzar (Daniel 4:1–37)

The Babylonian monarch dreamed of a great tree being cut down, leaving only the stump wet with the dew "for seven periods of time" (4:14–16). The chapter begins with the king's personal testimony of God's power for his "miracles and wonders" (4:1–2). The king heard angels ("holy ones") say, "the Most High is ruler over human kingdoms" (4:17); and after a period of temporary insanity (possibly lycanthropy) afflicted him with animal-like behavior (4:33), the king's sanity returned so he praised God, the king of heaven (4:37).

E. Fall of Babylon (Daniel 5:1–30)

Belshazzar served as co-regent with his father, Nabonidus, from 553 to 539 BC when Babylon fell to the Medes and Persians on October 12, 539 BC. The biblical account skips over several monarchs who apparently had little or no contact with Daniel: Amel Marduk (562–560 BC), Neriglissar (560–556 BC), and Labashi Marduk (556 BC).

Belshazzar's appearance in this chapter was explained as a myth by biblical critics until the discovery of the Nabonidus Chronicle, which clarified that Belshazzar, whose name was missing from the ancient Babylonian king list, ruled as co-regent with his father for fourteen years while Nabonidus resided in Tema (Arabia). Thirty-seven archival texts now attest to the historicity of Belshazzar as the second ruler in Babylon, thus explaining his offer to make whoever could read the handwriting on the wall the "third ruler" in the kingdom.[6]

During an extravagant banquet, in which Belshazzar desecrated the temple vessels taken from Jerusalem, a divine handwritten message appeared on the plaster wall of the palace, reading:

MENE	numbered
MENE	numbered
TEKEL	weighed
PERES	divided

When the king could find no one to explain it, the queen (probably Amytis, the queen mother and widow of Nebuchadnezzar) suggested they call for Daniel, now an old man probably in his eighties. Daniel read the writing and told Belshazzar that God had numbered his kingdom, weighed it on the scales of justice, found it

Likely from Babylon, the Stela of Nabonidus shows King Nabonidus holding the standard used during a religious ceremony. He is wearing traditional dress. To his right are the symbols of the gods Sin, Venus, and Shamash.

lacking, and would divide it and give it to the Medes and Persians. That very night Babylon fell without a battle to Cyrus the Great, and Belshazzar was executed (5:30).

F. Fearless Prayer (Daniel 6:1–28)

The sixth chapter refers to Darius the Mede as ruling Babylon on behalf of the Median-Persian coalition, possibly under the authority of Cyrus. As was the case of Belshazzar prior to the twentieth century, there are no extra-biblical references to Darius the Mede. Some have suggested this may be another designation for Cyrus, but others argue that this is unlikely since Cyrus was a Persian. Whitcomb made a strong case for identifying Darius as Gubaru the governor of Babylon, who ruled the city on behalf of the Medes and Persians.[7] When the ruler succumbed to pressure to pass a law against prayer, Daniel, now in his eighties, refused to comply and continued praying with his windows open (6:10). Despite the attempts of Darius to release him,

Daniel was thrown into the lions' den overnight but survived because of his innocence and protection by an angel (6:22).

Median soldiers in the royal Persian guard as shown on a relief made of glazed bricks found at Susa.

II. Daniel's Prophetic Visions (Daniel 7:1–12:13)

A. Four Beasts (Daniel 7:1–28)

The second half of the book records four prophetic visions of future events that will affect the Jewish people in the years ahead. In the vision Daniel saw four huge beasts, animals that were comparable to the four elements in the metallic statue in chapter 2. The winged lion was a well-known symbol of ancient Babylon. The bear represented the Medes and Persians; the four-headed leopard symbolized Greece and the four divisions of the Hellenistic Empire. The monster with iron teeth represented the Roman Empire.

Daniel's vision went beyond that of Nebuchadnezzar's dream in focusing on the ten horns of the fourth beast and a little horn that came up afterwards (7:8) and eventually "made war with the saints" (7:21 KJV) for three and one-half "times" (7:25). The book of Revelation calls this individual the beast (Rev 13:1–11) although he is generally designated as the Antichrist. God the Father is pictured as the "Ancient of Days" who judges the little horn and presents the kingdom to Christ, designated as "a son of man" (7:11–14).

He, in turn, shares the greatness of the kingdom with the saints of God, who are pictured as true believers (7:27).

B. Ram and Goat (Daniel 8:1–27)

This vision pictures the coming clash between Persia and Greece. The ram with two horns symbolizes the Medes and Persians coming from the East, moving westward (8:3–4). The goat with one horn represents Alexander the Great of Greece, coming from the West, moving eastward. In this prophecy Daniel predicted the triumph of Greece over Persia 200 years in advance. Alexander defeated the Persians at Issus in 333 BC and Arbela in 331 BC, within three years of his ascension to the throne at age twenty. But Alexander died in Babylon in 323 BC at the age of only thirty-two, thus the "great horn" of the goat was "broken" and his kingdom was divided into four sections. One of these four territories (Syria) produced a "little horn" of Greek origin, Antiochus IV Epiphanes (a type of Antichrist), who persecuted the Jews and desecrated the temple for "2,300 days" (170–164 BC).

Alexander the Great fighting Darius III at the Battle of Issus in 333 BC. The scene comes from a first-century mosaic found in Pompeii.

C. Seventy Sevens (Daniel 9:1–27)

After reading Jeremiah's prophecy of the seventy years' captivity (Jer 25:11; 29:10) during the first years of Darius the Mede (c. 538 BC), Daniel realized the time for his people to return to Jerusalem was near. Knowing they were not spiritually ready to return, Daniel poured his heart out in prayer, confessing his sins and the sins of his people, acknowledging that the curse of their covenant law was still upon them (9:3–19).

In response to Daniel's prayer, the angel Gabriel revealed the prophecy of the seventy "sevens" (Hb. *Shavu'ah*)—seventy sevens ("weeks") of years—decreed about "your people" (the Jews) and "your holy city" (Jerusalem). The seventy times seven (490 years) would culminate in sealing up "vision and prophecy" and "anoint the most holy place" (9:24). But after seven sevens and sixty-two sevens (69 x 7 = 483 years), the Messiah would be "cut off" (killed) and the city (Jerusalem) and the sanctuary (temple) would be destroyed (v. 26). During the final "seven" years (the seventieth seven), "the prince that shall come" (KJV) (Antichrist) will break his covenant with the Jews and bring about the "abomination of desolation" (9:27). Jesus clearly indicated that the "abomination" was still a future event, indicating that this prophecy was not fulfilled by Antiochus Epiphanes (Matt 24:15).

The prophecy indicates that the first sixty-nine sevens (483 years) will begin with the decree to rebuild the city, presumably Artaxerxes's decree to Nehemiah to rebuild the walls of Jerusalem in 444 BC. It will culminate 483 years later (based on a lunar sabbatical calendar) with the death of the Messiah in AD 32. While many evangelicals agree with this interpretation, some debate the fulfillment of the final seventieth seven. Most premillennialists view this as the seven years of tribulation yet to come in the future, which will result in the eschatological restoration indicated by the prophetic goals to "seal up vision and prophecy" and "anoint the most holy place" (9:24).

D. Israel's Future (Daniel 10:1–12:13)

The final vision is dated in the "third year of Cyrus" (536/535 BC) at the end of the seventy years of the Babylonian captivity. By that time Zerubbabel and nearly 50,000 Jewish captives were returning to Jerusalem. Daniel received his final vision for the Jewish people "in the last days" (10:14). The prophecy focuses on the Hellenistic kingdoms of the intertestamental period (331–160 BC) after the division of Alexander's empire (11:3–4). The prophecy traces the future conflicts of the "king of the South" (Egypt) with the "king of the North" (Hellenistic Syria under the Seleucids), culminating in a detailed prophecy about a "vile person" (KJV) (Antiochus IV Epiphanes) who will rule by "intrigue" (11:21–35).

Daniel 11:36–45 is often regarded as a reference to the Antichrist. Miller states (305–6), "Exegetical necessity requires that 11:36–45 be applied to someone other than Antiochus IV." He adds, "He is none other than the 'little horn' of Daniel 7 and the 'ruler who will come' of Daniel 9:26."[8] This section ends with a description of the wars of Antichrist and his final defeat at the "time of the end" (11:40–45).

Chapter 12 closes the prophecy with the promise of the final triumph of God's people in the future messianic era.[9] A "time of distress" (tribulation) will come in the future, but those whose names are "written in the book" (i.e., Book of Life) will "escape" (12:1). Then Daniel is told to seal the prophecy "until the time of the end" (12:9) because he will "rest" (die), then later "stand to receive your allotted inheritance at the end of the days" (12:13). Thus, the book ends with the promise of a literal bodily resurrection in anticipation of our participation in God's eternal kingdom. Daniel predicts the whole future of Israel: return from captivity, rebuilding the temple, conflicts of the future, coming of Messiah, Messiah's death, the destruction of Jerusalem and the second temple, the rise of Antichrist, the time of tribulation, the triumphal return, the resurrection of the Jewish saints, and the future messianic kingdom.

Chapter 2 Nebuchadnezzar's Dream of the Image		History	Chapter 7 Daniel's Vision of the Four Beasts	
Prophecy		*Fulfillment*	*Prophecy*	
Dream 2:31–35	Interpretation 2:36–45	World Empire	Interpretation 7:15–28	Dream 7:1–14
2:32 Head (gold)	2:38 You– Nebuchadnezzar	Babylonian 612–539 BC	7:17 King	7:4 Lion with wings of an eagle
2:32 Breasts and arms (silver)	2:39 Inferior kingdom	Medo-Persian 539–331 BC	7:17 King	7:5 Bear raised up on one side
2:32 Belly and thighs (bronze)	2:39 Third kingdom	Grecian 331–63 BC	7:17 King	7:6 Leopard with four heads and four wings its back
2:33 Legs (iron) Feet (iron and clay)	2:40 Fourth kingdom	ROME — Ancient Rome 63 BC–AD 476	7:23 Fourth kingdom	7:7, 19 Fourth beast with iron teeth and claws of bronze
		ROME — Revived Roman Empire	7:24 Ten kings	7:7–8 Ten horns
			7:24 Different king	7:8 Little horn utter- ing great boasts
2:35 Great mountain	2:44 Kingdom which will never be destroyed	Messianic kingdom	7:27 Everlasting kingdom	7:9 Thrones were set up

Taken from H. Wayne House and Randall Price, *Charts of Bible Prophecy*, 63. Copyright © 2003 by H. Wayne House and World of the Bible Ministries, Inc. Used by permission of Zondervan (www.zondervan.com).

Practical Application

Daniel emphasizes the sovereignty of God over the nations of the world in general and over the nation of Israel in particular. The book also underscores the importance of faith, hope, character, and endurance. Daniel and his friends are pictured as determined to obey God rather than men, even at the risk of their own lives (chaps. 1; 3; 7). This amazing book of personal narrative and prophetic pronouncement reveals the heart of God for His people and their confidence in Him for their future hope. We too must often determine in our hearts to obey God and resist temptation. The pressures of the world will ultimately expose our true character, just as it did with Daniel and his friends. When the pressure comes (and it will), be prepared to deal with it by having your heart focused on God.

Daniel lived all the way through the seventy years of the Babylonian captivity. His courage as a young man could still be seen in his later years. The teenager who refused the king's food and wine (1:8) eventually won over the distraught monarch (4:37). He risked his very life to tell the truth to Belshazzar (5:30) and to call out to God when prayer had been outlawed by Darius the Mede (6:10).

Daniel was so beloved of God that the Lord unveiled the future to him through his many dreams and visions of the end times. He saw the Son of Man coming in the clouds of heaven to receive a kingdom from God the Father. By faith he embraced the hope of the resurrection, and so should we.

The incredible life of this amazing man challenges us to live lives of faith, integrity, and perseverance as well. Whatever challenges, threats, or problems come our way, we too can endure to the end by the grace of God, the power of His Spirit, and the truth of His Word. In every obstacle life throws at us, God is greater, His grace is sufficient, and His love never fails. Trust Him, walk by faith, and live expecting great things from God.

For Further Reading

Archer, Gleason. "Daniel." *EBC*. Grand Rapids: Zondervan, 1985.
Culver, Robert D. *Daniel and the Latter Days*. Chicago: Moody Press, 1977.
Miller, Stephen R. *Daniel*. NAC. Nashville: B&H, 1994.
Walvoord, John F. *Daniel: The Key to Prophetic Revelation*. Chicago: Moody Press, 1971.
Whitcomb, John C. *Daniel*. Chicago: Moody Press, 1985.
Wood, Leon. *A Commentary on Daniel*. Grand Rapids: Zondervan, 1973.
Young, Edward J. *The Prophecy of Daniel: A Commentary*. Grand Rapids: Eerdmans, 1977.

Study Questions

1. Why did God elevate Daniel and his friends among the Jewish captives in chapter 1?
2. How do the details of the interpretation of the metallic statue (chap. 2) and the four beasts (chap. 7) explain the historical fulfillment of biblical prophecy?
3. What character qualities enabled Daniel (chaps. 1; 6) and his friends (chap. 3) to stand for God against the pressure to compromise their convictions?
4. What was the significance of the handwriting on the wall in 5:5?
5. To what does the prophecy of the seventy "sevens" (chap. 9) refer?
6. Why should we have confidence in biblical prophecies?
7. What is the final promise and prophecy of Daniel 12?

Notes

1. J. A. Montgomery, *A Critical and Exegetical Commentary on the Book of Daniel*, ICC (Edinburgh: T&T Clark, 1964), 269.

2. K. Kitchen, "The Aramaic of Daniel," in *Notes on Some Problems in the Book of Daniel*, ed. D. J. Wiseman (London: Tyndale Press, 1965), 31–79. Gleason Archer, "The Hebrew of Daniel Compared with Qumran Sectarian Documents," in *The Law and the Prophets*, ed. J. H. Skilton (Nutley, NJ: Presbyterian & Reformed, 1974), 470–81.

3. E. Yamauchi, *Persia and the Bible* (Grand Rapids: Baker, 1990), 380–82.

4. T. C. Mitchell and R. Joyce, "The Musical Instruments in Nebuchadnezzar's Orchestra," in Wiseman, *Notes on Some Problems in the Book of Daniel*, 19–27.

5. W. H. Shea, "Daniel 3: Extra-Biblical Texts and the Convocation on the Plain of Dura," *AUSS* 20 (1982): 37–50.

6. P. A. Beaulieu, *The Reign of Nabonidus, King of Babylon 556–539 BC* (New Haven: Yale University Press, 1989), 156–57.

7. John C. Whitcomb, *Darius the Mede* (Philadelphia: Presbyterian and Reformed, 1963).

8. Stephen R. Miller, *Daniel* NAC (Nashville: B&H, 1994), 305. Church fathers such as Chrysostom, Jerome, and Theodorat clearly identify this king as the future Antichrist. See Gleason Archer, trans., *Jerome's Commentary on Daniel* (Grand Rapids: Baker, 1977).

9. J. J. Slotki, *Daniel-Ezra-Nehemiah* (London: Socino Press, 1978), 100–101.

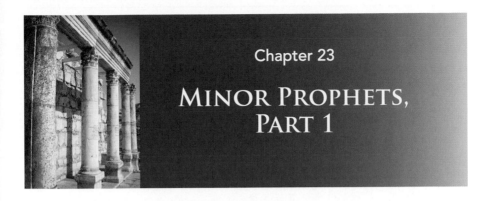

Chapter 23

MINOR PROPHETS, PART 1

Wrath and Mercy

The Minor Prophets, including the books from Hosea to Malachi, form the final section of the Old Testament canon in the English Bible. They cover a period of 300 years from the eighth to the fifth centuries BC. This time began with an era of great prosperity for both Israel (northern kingdom) and Judah (southern kingdom) but ended with disaster for both kingdoms. The earlier Minor Prophets predicted the fall of both Samaria and Jerusalem to the Assyrians and Babylonians. Then, in turn, they predicted the fall of Assyria and Babylon and the final restoration of Judah. The three postexilic prophets (Haggai, Zechariah, and Malachi) preached to the Jews who returned to Jerusalem after the Babylonian captivity. The twelve Minor Prophets were each written separately but collected on one scroll, known as "The Twelve" in the Hebrew Bible. Together with Isaiah, Jeremiah, and Ezekiel they were considered the "Latter Prophets."

HOSEA

God's Unquenchable Love

Hosea ("salvation") prophesied from the reign of Jeroboam II (791–750 BC) to the reign of Hezekiah (715–687 BC), and his ministry likely covered a time span of thirty-five to forty years. Most of Hosea's recorded messages focus on the coming judgment of Israel and thus occurred before the fall of Samaria in 722 BC. Hosea prophesied concerning Judah as well as Israel (cf. Hos 1:7, 11; 4:15; 5:5, 12–14; 6:4, 11; 8:14; 10:11; 11:12; 12:2).

KEY FACTS

Author:	Hosea
Date:	755–720 BC
Recipients:	Israel and Judah
Key Word:	Repent (Hb. *shuv*)
Key Verse:	"Afterward, the people of Israel will return and seek the LORD their God and David their king ... in the last days" (3:5).

View of an Israelite street paved with basalt flagstones as it approaches the south gate of the ancient city-fortress of Dan, the most northern city of ancient Israel. It dates to the period of the divided kingdom and was probably constructed during the reign of Jeroboam (849–842 BC) over an earlier pavement.

Background

Hosea's ministry began at a time of great economic prosperity for Israel, but that rapidly disintegrated into one of national catastrophe by the end of his ministry. Both Israel and Judah prospered under the lengthy and effective reigns of Jeroboam II and Uzziah. Israel's political size and economic stability, however, were not indicators of spiritual vitality. Israel turned away from the Lord, worshipped Baal, and engaged in the perverse rites and practices that accompanied such worship. Israel wrongly credited Baal, rather than Yahweh, as the provider of the wealth and economic blessing they enjoyed. The veneration of the golden-calf gods in the sanctuaries at Dan and Bethel and various forms of religious syncretism corrupted their worship of the Lord and blurred important distinctions between Yahweh and the pagan gods.

Outline

I. Personal and National Problem: Unfaithfulness (1:1–3:5)
II. Prospect of Judgment and Salvation (4:1–14:9)
    A. Judgment for Israel's Rebellion (4:1–6:3)
    B. Judgment Results in Israel's Ruin (6:4–11:11)
    C. Judgment Turns to Restoration (11:12–14:9)

Message

I. Personal and National Problem: Unfaithfulness (Hosea 1:1–3:5)

God commanded Hosea to marry a promiscuous and *unfaithful wife*, who subsequently gave birth to three children with symbolic names. Both the woman and the children were metaphors of Israel's covenant unfaithfulness toward the Lord. Israel had prostituted itself by turning away from the Lord and following other gods. Scholars have interpreted the marriage of Hosea and Gomer in several different ways. Some have viewed the marriage as an allegory or parable rather than an actual union. Others have argued that Gomer was a cult prostitute or that she was guilty of spiritual infidelity. Still others have suggested that she became promiscuous only after they were actually married.

II. Prospects of Judgment and Salvation (Hosea 4:1–14:9)

The marriage of Hosea and Gomer was a powerful object lesson of Israel's unfaithfulness toward the Lord and the Lord's unfailing commitment to His people. Moving beyond the issue of Gomer's infidelity, Hosea 4–14 presents a detailed explanation of Israel's covenant infidelity. Like a prosecuting attorney presenting the Lord's case against Israel, Hosea charged Israel with three separate indictments:

"The LORD has a charge to bring against you who live in the land."
(4:1 NIV)

"They have broken the covenant; they were unfaithful to me there."
(6:7 NIV)

"The LORD has a charge to bring against Judah; he will punish Jacob
according to his ways and repay him according to his deeds."
(12:2 NIV)

Chapters 4–14 consist of three cycles of alternating messages of judgment and salvation:

Cycle 1	Cycle 2	Cycle 3
Judgment (4:1–5:15a)	Judgment (6:4–11:7)	Judgment (11:12–13:16)
Salvation (5:15b–6:3)	Salvation (11:8–11)	Salvation (14:1–9)

This structure reflects that though the Lord would punish Israel severely
for its many sins, He would not reject His people forever and would ultimately restore and bless them. The Lord's purging judgment would turn
Israel away from its worship of false gods and would cause them to recognize Him alone as their source of security and blessing.

A. Judgment for Israel's Rebellion (Hosea 4:1–6:3)

The prophet charged that Israel was guilty of disobedience to Yahweh's
covenant commands, specifically calling attention to their violation of six
of the Ten Commandments (4:2). Ultimate fault lay with Israel's priests and
prophets who had failed to teach the word of the Lord (4:4–5). Consequently
the people were perishing for their lack of knowledge. Israel's spiritual leaders were greedy and selfish, and the priests loved to feed themselves on the

*Canaanite high place and altar at Tel Dan. The structure dates to the time of Jeroboam II,
son of Joash (eighth century BC), and replaced an ealier structure constructed by
Jeroboam, son of Nebat, in the tenth century.*

sacrifices and offerings the people presented to the Lord. Selfish priests had produced a pleasure-seeking people who turned to the worship of false gods and the practice of abhorrent Canaanite fertility rites as a means of satisfying their sinful lusts. Nevertheless, some will return to God, and He will heal them (5:15–6:3).

B. Judgment Results in Israel's Ruin (Hosea 6:4–11:11)

In the second phase of his covenant lawsuit against Israel, Hosea delivered two extended indictments of Israel's sins against the Lord (6:4–7:16 and 10:1–15) and between them a detailed description of how the Lord intended to punish them for their crimes (8:1–9:17). Injustice and violence characterized Israelite society because the people did not think the Lord saw their actions. The people defrauded one another in their business dealings, and drunken princes conspired against one another and engaged in bloody conflict for control of the throne. Four of Israel's last six kings came to the throne by murdering their predecessor.

Hosea employed a series of four extended metaphors that contrasted the Lord's faithfulness to Israel with Israel's unfaithfulness to Him. Israel was compared to spoiled grapes, a wild vine, a

"They will follow the LORD; he will roar like a lion. When he roars, his children will come trembling from the west" (Hos 11:10).

trained heifer, and a rebellious son. Even in judgment, however, Yahweh's fatherly love would trump His anger, and He would not completely destroy His people (11:8–11). The Lord would preserve a remnant and restore them to their homeland. His roaring as a lion in judgment would cause the survivors of the exile to come trembling before Him in repentance.

C. Judgment Turns to Restoration (Hosea 11:12–14:9)

The final message in the book of Hosea is one of hope and promise. The consistent message of the prophets was that Israel's salvation and restoration would follow its time of judgment. Hosea called the people to return to the Lord with a confession of their sin and repudiation of their trust in military alliances and false gods. When Israel "returned" (*shuv*) to the Lord (14:1), then the Lord would "turn" (*shuv*) from his anger and would freely love them again (14:4).

Practical Application

Hosea presented the covenant relationship between the Lord and Israel as a marriage. The marriage metaphor communicated the depth of the Lord's love for Israel and the intimacy of their relationship. The portrayal of the covenant between Yahweh and Israel as a marriage also highlighted the treachery and betrayal behind Israel's sin. Israel was to give exclusive love and worship to the Lord as her husband, but committed spiritual adultery against Him by following after false gods. Israel did not simply break God's laws; they broke His heart.

The marriage metaphor carried over into the New Testament as a picture of Christ's love for the church. Christ bought the church through His death on the cross so that she could be His pure and holy bride, and husbands are to follow His example of sacrifice in loving their wives (Eph 5:25–27). Paul ministered on behalf of the church so he could present her as a pure virgin to Christ at the time of the Second Coming (2 Cor 11:2), and the second coming of Christ to earth will be the time for the eschatological banquet and the marriage supper of the Lamb when Christ is finally joined to His bride to live with her for all eternity (cf. Matt 22:1–14; Rev 19:6–10).

REFLECTION

Tough Love

Counselors often recommend "tough love" when dealing with the rebellious and the wayward. We are urged not to be "enablers" of their addictions or codependent in their emotions. But tough love often leads to tough forgiveness. How do you respond when someone deeply hurts you? If they repent, are you willing to forgive? God is—in fact, He already has.

JOEL
Day of the Lord

The book of Joel derives its name from its central character. His Hebrew name, *Yo'el*, combines the names Yahweh and Elohim, meaning "Yahweh is God." Nothing is known today of the prophet Joel except that he was the son of Pethuel. The temple references found throughout the book (1:8–10, 13–14; 2:17) have caused some to speculate that he was born into a priestly family. The book's multiple references to Zion and the house of the Lord (1:9–14; 2:15–17; 3:1–6, 16–21) indicate that he may have lived in or near Jerusalem.

KEY FACTS

Author:	Joel
Date:	835–825 BC
Recipients:	Judah
Key Words:	Day of the Lord (Hb. *yom yahweh*)
Key Verse:	"Everyone who calls on the name of the LORD will be saved" (2:32 NIV).

Background and Date

No chronological data is disclosed in the book. Therefore biblical scholars have to depend on internal factors to date this prophecy. Three completely different dates have been suggested for the original composition: (1) early preexilic (835–830 BC); (2) late preexilic (609–585 BC); and (3) postexilic (515–350 BC). The latter view is argued on the basis of the reference to Greeks (3:6) and the assumption that the temple refers to the rebuilt second temple. Conservative scholars have generally preferred either of the preexilic dates arguing that the reference to the Valley of Jehoshaphat (3:12) fits with preexilic times since Jehoshaphat (872–848 BC) was the last godly king of Judah prior to Joash. Also, the prophet lists Judah's preexilic enemies as Tyre, Sidon, Philistia, Egypt, Edom, and the Sabeans (Joel 3:2–19) while failing to mention Assyria, Babylon, and Persia from exilic and postexilic times.

View to the northeast of the Kidron Valley toward the Mount of Olives. The mount dominates the north edge of the village of Silwan (ancient Siloam).

Outline

I.   The Locust Plague and a Call to Repent (1:1–20)
II. The Imminent Day of the Lord and a Call to Repent (2:1–17)
III. The Ultimate Day of the Lord (2:18–32)
IV. The Future Judgment of the Nations (3:1–21)

I. The Locust Plague and a Call to Repent (Joel 1:1–20)

In the aftermath of an unusually severe locust plague, the prophet Joel called the people of Israel to repentance. Locust invasions are still common in the Middle East and were one of the covenant curses Moses had warned would occur if Israel was disobedient to Yahweh's commands (see Deut 28:38, 42). The Lord had sent locusts as one of the plagues against the Egyptians in the exodus (Exod 10:4–19), but now He had punished His own people with the destructive insects (cf. Amos 4:9). Like an invading army, wave after wave of the locusts decimated the land. This crisis called for the people to repent. They were to call a public fast and a solemn assembly in which they would confess their sins and pray for the Lord's forgiveness and mercy. Joel warned that failure to repent would bring more judgment. The "Day of the Lord" was near, and the Lord was about to bring even greater destruction upon Israel.

What Is the "Day of the Lord"?

The "Day of the Lord" is a prominent motif in the Old Testament prophets and refers to a day of battle when Yahweh would dramatically intervene on earth to accomplish His work of both judgment and salvation. The prophets employed "Day of the Lord" terminology to refer both to the near events of their own day and to Yahweh's work of judgment and salvation in the eschatological last days. Thus, the prophets could warn that the Day of the Lord was "near" as enemy armies prepared to attack Israel and Judah (cf. Joel 1:15; Zeph 1:7), but they also anticipated a final Day of the Lord that would involve all nations (cf. Isa 2:7–22; Zech 14:1–21). In continuity with the prophets, the writers of the New Testament employ "Day of the Lord" terminology for the judgments and salvation of the last days associated with the second coming of Christ (cf. Matt 24:42; 1 Cor 5:5; 1 Thess 5:2–5; 2 Thess 2:2–3; 2 Pet 3:10–12).

II. The Imminent Day of the Lord and a Call to Repent (Joel 2:1–17)

The prophet called for the sounding of an alarm and warned of a second locust invasion that would attack the land. The locusts in chapter 2 more likely represent the human army of an enemy nation that would sweep through the land. The Assyrian annals and other ancient Near Eastern literature compared human armies to locusts, and the numbers, movements, and sounds of a locust swarm resembled that of an invading army.[1] After this warning Joel once again called the people to repent, for God is a gracious and forgiving God (2:12–17). Although the text does not state it explicitly, between 2:17 and 18 there appears to be a rare example of obedience to prophetic preaching in the Old Testament. The priests took Joel's warnings of judgment seriously and called the sacred assembly as the prophet had instructed. With contrite hearts the priests and people prayed that the Lord would spare them from the coming judgment.

III. The Ultimate Day of the Lord (Joel 2:18–32)

Joel anticipated a great future restoration when the Lord would remove their enemies, bring great fertility back to the land, and pour out His Spirit on all peoples. In past times the Lord had primarily given His Spirit to select leaders, but at this future time He would give His Spirit to all kinds of people—young and old, male and female. The prophets Isaiah (Isa 59:21) and Ezekiel (Ezek 36:26–27) had also promised that this age of future blessing would involve the defeat of their enemies, great fertility, and the pouring out of God's Spirit in new and fresh ways. This outpouring of the Spirit would occur at a time when cataclysmic signs in the heavens and on the earth warned of the impending arrival of God's final judgment. Even in this terrible time of judgment, those who genuinely called upon the Lord would be saved.

The apostle Peter announced that Joel's prophecy was fulfilled typologically and analogically with the outpouring of the Holy Spirit on the day of Pentecost (Acts 2:15–21). It would appear that Pentecost and the giving of the Spirit to believers today is the initial fulfillment of Joel's prophecy, but the ultimate fulfillment of this prophecy awaits the catastrophic events of the end times (Rev 6:12–17) and the full restoration of Israel at the time of Christ's earthly kingdom (cf. Acts 3:19–21; Rom 11:26–27). Joel's original prophecy focused on the giving of the Spirit to all Jews, but the fuller revelation expands the prophecy to include Gentiles as well (Acts 10:44–48; 11:15–18; 15:8–9).

IV. The Future Judgment of the Nations (Joel 3:1–21)

The future restoration of Israel would also involve the judgment of the nations. Like other prophets Joel prophesied a final assault on Israel by the armies of the nations (Ezekiel 38; Zeph 3:6–8; Zechariah 12; 14; cf. Rev 19:11–21), and the Lord would gather these nations to destroy them in retribution for their mistreatment of Israel. The book of Joel begins with the "Day of the Lord" as a time of judgment upon Israel (1:15) and concludes with this day as judgment for the nations. Joel's command for Israel to beat their plowshares into swords and their pruning hooks into spears (3:10) reversed the prophecies of peace and the end of warfare in Isa 2:2–4 and Mic 4:1–4. The warriors of Israel would reap a great harvest when they defeated their enemies and would then enjoy a time of unending peace and prosperity in the future.

Practical Application

Joel's prophecy concerning the outpouring of the Spirit was initially fulfilled with the giving of the Spirit at Pentecost, demonstrating that the last days prophesied by the prophets were inaugurated with the first coming of Christ and that the church presently enjoys a foretaste of the eschatological blessings promised by God in anticipation of Israel's full and final restoration. The message of both judgment and hope in the prophets reminds us that we too will be judged for our disobedience and blessed with hope when we truly call upon the Lord.

AMOS
God's Ultimate Justice

Amos ("burden bearer") prophesied during the reigns of Uzziah (792–740 BC) of Judah and Jeroboam II (793–753 BC) of Israel. The reign of Jeroboam II was a time of unprecedented prosperity in the northern kingdom, and Israel expanded its territories back to the borders of the Davidic-Solomonic Empire (2 Kgs 14:23–29). Unfortunately, this economic prosperity also brought spiritual apathy and moral decline. The northern kingdom began to worship calf idols shortly after breaking away from Judah and the Jerusalem temple (1 Kings 12). Another main area of disobedience took the form of social injustice, as the rich and powerful exploited the poor and needy. Wealth, possessions, and pleasure took priority over their relationship with God.

KEY FACTS

Author:	Amos
Date:	760 BC
Recipients:	Judah and Israel
Key Word:	Rebellion (Hb. *pasha'*)
Key Verse:	"For the LORD says to the house of Israel: Seek me and live!" (5:4).

Background and Date

Amos was from the small village of Tekoa in Judah (2 Sam 14:2; 2 Chr 11:6), which was just a few miles south of Bethlehem, but God called him to travel north to Israel. He delivered a scathing message that denounced the sins of the northern kingdom and warned of the judgment God was preparing to send. Amos prophesied around 760 BC when the Lord sent him to warn northern Israel that their time of unprecedented prosperity was about to come to an abrupt halt. It would be replaced by a time of national calamity as the Lord judged the people for their sins. Two years after Amos preached in Israel, the Lord sent an earthquake to demonstrate His displeasure (1:1). Archaeological evidence from Hazor and several other ancient Israelite cities appears to confirm this event. This quake was of such a magnitude that it was remembered by the prophet Zechariah some 200 years later (Zech 14:5).

Ruins of a Byzantine chapel at Tekoa over what was probably the tomb of Amos, a prophet whose hometown was Tekoa.

Outline

   I.   Eight Oracles of Judgment Against the Nations (1:1–2:16)
  II.   Three Sermons of the Coming Judgment of Israel (3:1–6:14)
 III.   Five Visions of Israel's Coming Judgment (7:1–9:10)
 IV.   Five Promises of Israel's Restoration (9:11–15)

Message

I. Eight Oracles of Judgment Against the Nations
(Amos 1:1–2:16)

Amos opened his book of prophecies with the startling image of God as a roaring lion.[2] The Israelites who believed that God was obligated to protect them were being presumptuous, assuming His grace would always be available. They needed to realize that God could not be taken lightly. Rather than protecting them, Yahweh would roar out in judgment against them. The Lord's powerful voice would melt and wither the land. This judgment would include an earthquake that occurred in Israel two years after Amos's preaching and would culminate with northern Israel's military defeat and exile at the hands of the Assyrian army.

This section describes the sins and coming judgment of eight nations, six foreign nations as well as Judah and Israel. Each oracle begins with the formula, "For three sins . . . , even for four, I will not turn back my wrath" (NIV 1984), a poetic way of saying that the sins of these people were many and that God was calling them to account. God's sense of universal justice meant He held all these nations accountable not only for how they treated Israel but also for how they acted toward one another. Amos characterized their sins as "transgressions/rebellion" (*pesha⁽*), indicating that these nations like Judah and Israel were guilty of covenant unfaithfulness toward Yahweh.

II. Three Sermons of the Coming Judgment of Israel (Amos 3:1–6:14)

With incredible bravery Amos left the security of Judah to travel north to the capital city of Samaria to call the northern kingdom to repentance. His first three messages are introduced by the call to "hear this word" in 3:1; 4:1; and 5:1 (NIV) and the last two with the announcement of "woe" upon Israel (5:18; 6:1). The prophecies of judgment demanded a response because they were not absolute predictions of what must happen in the future as much as they were warnings of what would happen if Israel did not repent and change its ways. By seeking the Lord and practicing true justice, Israel could avert disaster and experience blessing instead of judgment.

These human-faced monumental shedu *from Assyria date from the time of Ashurnasirpal II (ninth century BC).*

If the people of Samaria did not repent, judgment would be severe, and the invasion of a foreign army would leave Israel like a lamb torn out of the mouth of a lion. Ironically, the winged lion (*shedu*) was the national symbol of Assyria, which God would bring against the northern kingdom. God would destroy their temple in Bethel and all their opulent homes if they did not repent (3:14–15).

The theme of warning carries over into chapter 4. With biting sarcasm Amos compared the wealthy women of Samaria to well-fed cattle in that they oppressed the poor and were consumed with their own selfish pleasures. While they presently lived in pleasure, a time was coming when they would be led away as captives with hooks in their noses. They were to prepare to meet God, not as their Savior but as their Judge (4:12).

The recurring laments (5:1–17) and "woes" (5:18–27; 6:1–4) carry forward the message of doom and destruction. Amos contrasted the present luxury of the people of both Judah and Israel with the deprivation they would experience when they were taken away into exile. The people had become spiritually and morally desensitized as they lounged on their ivory-inlaid couches and pampered themselves with meats, music, and wine. The term for "feasting" (*marzeach*) in 6:7 was used outside the Bible to refer to pagan religious banquets that included drunken revelry and sexual immorality.[3] Life had become one big party, but those who partied the most would be among the first taken away in exile.

III. Five Visions of Israel's Coming Judgment (Amos 7:1–9:10)

Amos received five visions at the temple in Bethel that initially portray God's grace in delaying the judgment against Israel, but in the end they

Ruins of Bethel, which was located at the intersection of major crossroads. This region was thus heavily traveled for much of the Old Testament era.

display His resolve to judge and destroy if the people refuse to repent. In the midst of these visions, the priest at Bethel confronted Amos, reflecting how the prophet's message was ultimately rejected by Israel's corrupt religious leaders in the north (7:10–17). In the first two visions Amos witnessed two natural disasters befalling Israel—a locust plague and a fire sweeping through the land. In his third vision Amos saw the Lord measuring a wall with a plumb line. The point of the vision was that Israel did not measure up to God's standards of righteousness, so the nation would collapse just like an unstable wall. Amos saw a basket of summer fruit in his fourth vision, emphasizing that Israel was ripe for judgment.

In the fifth vision Amos saw Yahweh ordering the destruction of Israel's idolatrous sanctuary at Bethel (9:1–4). The people of Israel viewed their religious rituals as their protection against calamity, but instead of providing protection, the collapsing walls of the sanctuary would fall on those gathered there for worship. To this very day the ancient ruins of Bethel stand as a witness to the fulfillment of Amos's prophecy.

IV. Five Promises of Israel's Restoration (Amos 9:11–15)

Amos concluded his prophecies of unrelenting judgment with a message of hope concerning Israel's future restoration. God promised: (1) to restore the Davidic dynasty, (2) to make Israel victorious over her enemies, (3) agricultural productivity, (4) future prosperity, and (5) permanent settlement in the land. Though the northern kingdom had broken away from the house of David, Amos promised that God would reunite Israel under Davidic rule. Yahweh would restore the fallen tent of the Davidic dynasty, and the future Davidic ruler, the Messiah, would lead Israel. Amos 9:9 foresees the day when Israel will be regathered and securely planted in the land a second time never to be removed again.

Practical Application

Amos is an example of a courageous layman who dared to speak out against the evils of society. He even risked his life to cross the border of northern Israel and venture into the heart of apostasy to tell the truth to those who really didn't want to hear it. He reminds us of the courage of the early Christian apostles, evangelists, and missionaries who risked (and often gave) their lives to spread the gospel in foreign lands and hostile environments. Amos, like all of them, reminds us to get out of our comfort zones and go where no one else has gone to proclaim God's truth.

OBADIAH
Doom of Edom

Obadiah ("servant of Yahweh") is the shortest book in the Old Testament. The short heading of the book of Obadiah provides no details about the prophet or the time of his ministry. Some scholars have placed the book in the time of Edom's revolt against Judah in the early part of the ninth century BC (2 Kgs 8:20–22; 2 Chron 21:8–20), but others have suggested Obadiah prophesied in the aftermath of the Babylonian conquest of Judah in 586 BC. Obadiah announced that God would judge Edom (also called Seir) because of its participation with Judah's enemies in the plundering of Jerusalem.

KEY FACTS

Author:	Obadiah
Date:	840–830 BC
Recipients:	Judah and Edom
Key Word:	Pride (Hb. *zâdôn*)
Key Verse:	"The day of the LORD is near for all nations. As you have done, it will be done to you" (v. 15 NIV).

The treasury building in the ancient Nabatean (Edomite) city of Petra.

Background

The Edomites were descendants of Esau and had a stormy relationship with Israel throughout their history. This mirrored the original rivalry between the brothers Jacob and Esau (Genesis 25–27). During Israel's wilderness wanderings, Edom denied Israel safe passage through their territories (Num 20:14–21). David later conquered Edom and brought it into his empire (2 Sam 8:13–14), and Edom remained under the control of the house of David until its successful revolt during the reign of Jehoram two centuries later (2 Kgs 8:20–22). Over the next 150 years, Judah and Edom had frequent skirmishes over territories and trade routes, and the bitter rivalry culminated with Edom's involvement in the Babylonian destruction of Jerusalem. However, the Babylonians annexed Edom in 553 BC and brought the Edomite kingdom to an end. In the fourth century BC, the Nabatean Arabs took control of Edom and established Petra as their capital.

Outline

I. Doom of Edom (1–16)
II. Deliverance of Judah (17–21)

Message

I. Doom of Edom (Obadiah 1–16)

Edom was lifted up because of excessive pride. They trusted in their political and military advisors for their security, and they believed their mountain fortresses made them invulnerable to enemy attack. The narrow canyon leading into Petra insulated them from invasion. However, even though they nested like eagles in a lofty place in the mountains, the rocks and crags would not protect them from the army the Lord was bringing against them. Even their allies would turn against them and plunder their treasures (vv. 1–9). Edom would also be judged for the way they mistreated Judah and rejoiced after the defeat of Jerusalem (vv. 10–14).

II. Deliverance of Judah (Obadiah 17–21)

While the doom of Edom was permanent, judgment was not God's final word for Judah. The Lord would *restore* His people and cause them to triumph over their enemies. Reversing what had happened with the fall of Jerusalem, Judah's exiles would subjugate Edom and rule over their territories. With this restoration of Israel, the kingdom of God would be fully established on earth, indicating an eschatological context for the ultimate fulfillment of Obadiah's prophecies. Ultimately, Mount Zion will eclipse Mount Seir, and Isa 63:1 predicts the Messiah will march through Edom in judgment on His way to establish the kingdom of God on earth.

Practical Application

The judgment of the Edomites is a reminder that God stands opposed to all forms of human arrogance and pride. The Edomites are representative of all of God's enemies, and oracles against Edom appear in eschatological contexts in the Old Testament prophets pointing to the judgment of the last days (Isaiah 34; 63). While judging Edom, God would also restore His people Israel, and the restoration of Israel would be essential to the establishment of God's eschatological kingdom. In light of Obadiah's indictment of Edom, we too are reminded not to gloat over God's judgment of others, lest His judgment fall on us as well.

JONAH

God's Universal Concern

Jonah ("dove" in Hb.) was a prophet in Israel from the town of Gath-hepher near Nazareth, who prophesied to northern Israel during the reign of Jeroboam II (793–753 BC). First, Jonah prophesied Jeroboam's military successes in expanding Israel's borders (2 Kgs 14:25). However, shortly after this God sent Jonah from northern Israel to preach impending doom to the Assyrians in the city of Nineveh. He wasn't afraid of the Assyrians; he was afraid God would forgive them.

The book clearly has a didactic purpose to teach about God's redemptive concern for the Assyrian people, but no literary clues within the book itself suggest that the book of Jonah should be read as anything other than a straightforward historical narrative. The supernatural elements are explained by God's involvement in Jonah's life, and similar miraculous events appear in the historical narratives of the lives of Elijah and Elisha (1–2 Kings). Jesus affirmed the historicity of the Jonah narrative on two separate occasions: when He compared His coming burial to Jonah being in the fish for three days and when He spoke of the judgment of Nineveh in connection with the cities of Israel in His own day (Matt 12:39–41; Luke 11:29–30).

KEY FACTS

Author:	Jonah
Date:	770–750 BC
Recipients:	Northern Israel
Key Word:	Prepare or Appoint (Hb. *mânâh*)
Key Verse:	"I knew that you are a gracious and compassionate God" (4:2).

Background

Nineveh was a prominent Mesopotamian city located on the Tigris River (modern Iraq). The city was an important ancient center for the worship of the goddess Ishtar, and its strategic location enabled the city to control important trade routes by land and river. The narrator portrays Nineveh as a "great city" (1:2; 3:2) and a "very important city" (3:3 NIV 1984). The statement that "a visit required three days" in 3:3 (NIV 1984) does not refer to how long it took to walk around the city walls. More likely it refers to how long it would take Jonah to communicate his message at the various city gates and public squares. The statement in Jonah 4:11 that Nineveh had a population of 120,000 likely refers to the entire administrative district of Nineveh rather than to just the city proper.

In the early seventh-century BC, the Assyrian king Sennacherib made Nineveh his capital. Sennacherib expanded the city so that it covered some 1,800 acres, and he built an impressive palace there. Sennacherib's Nineveh was surrounded by a protective double wall nearly sixty feet thick. The library built by Ashurbanipal (669–627 BC) was one of Nineveh's most important buildings and a significant archaeological discovery from this period.

Outline

I. Jonah Flees from His Prophetic Calling (1:1–2:10)
    A. Jonah's Disobedience and Its Consequences (1:1–17)
    B. Jonah's Deliverance and Thanksgiving (2:1–10)
II. Jonah Fulfills His Prophetic Calling (3:1–4:11)
    A. Jonah's Obedience and Nineveh's Repentance (3:1–10)
    B. Jonah's Displeasure at the Lord's Salvation (4:1–11)

Restored gate at the site of the ancient city of Nineveh, located on the left bank of the Tigris River (in Iraq today).

The book of Jonah is a two-part story. The first part of the book is about God's mercy to His disobedient prophet. The Lord spared Jonah even when the prophet disobeyed the command to go and preach to Nineveh. The second part of the book is about God's mercy to the wicked people of Nineveh. The Lord spared the city because of their repentant response when Jonah warned of their coming destruction.

Three Great Acts of Salvation in the Book of Jonah

1. God spares the sailors, and the sailors *worship* (Jon 1:16).
2. God spares Jonah, and Jonah *worships* (Jon 2:1–9).
3. God spares Nineveh, and Jonah *complains* (Jon 4:1–8).

Message

I. Jonah Flees from His Prophetic Calling (Jonah 1:1–2:10)

A. Jonah's Disobedience and Its Consequences (Jonah 1:1–17)

Jonah's disobedience to the word of the Lord led the prophet in a dangerous direction. Jonah "went down" to Joppa on the Mediterranean coast and boarded a ship for Tarshish (west) in the opposite direction of Nineveh (east), believing he could flee from the presence of the Lord. Jonah was in fact embarking on a downward path of destruction. The sailors eventually threw Jonah down into the sea, and the prophet "went down" (2:6 KJV) toward a watery grave until the Lord rescued him from drowning.

B. Jonah's Deliverance and Thanksgiving (Jonah 2:1–10)

Jonah's prayer is his response of thanksgiving to the Lord for saving him from death. The prayer closely follows the form of songs of thanksgiving in the Psalms where the worshipper expresses thanks to God for some specific act of deliverance. These songs of thanksgiving accompanied the offering of sacrifices and the payment of vows the petitioner made to the Lord when praying for deliverance. From the belly of the fish, Jonah recalled how he cried out to the Lord as he was drowning at sea. Jonah portrayed himself as descending to the underworld (Sheol) because he was as good as dead. He said: "You raised my life from the Pit" (2:6). Therefore, Jesus referred to His own resurrection as "the sign of . . . Jonah" (Matt 12:39–41; 16:4).

Joppa (modern Jaffa at Tel Aviv) was the seaport for Jerusalem. Joppa was destroyed by Vespasian in the late first or early second century AD.

II. Jonah Fulfills His Prophetic Calling (Jonah 3:1–4:11)

A. Jonah's Obedience and Nineveh's Repentance (Jonah 3:1–10)

The story turns from the salvation of Jonah to the salvation of the Ninevites. Jonah obeyed the second time the Lord commanded him to go to Nineveh, and once there he began to announce that the city would be destroyed in forty days. The king and people of Nineveh took the warning of destruction seriously and expressed their repentance by fasting from food and drink, wearing sackcloth, crying out to God, and turning from their violent behavior. The Assyrians repented and God relented. When the prophet announced judgment, even in an unqualified and unconditional way, the pronouncement included the possibility that true repentance would lead to the avoidance of the disaster that was threatened (cf. Jer 18:7–10; Joel 2:12–14; Zeph 2:3).

B. Jonah's Displeasure at the Lord's Salvation (Jonah 4:1–11)

Rather than rejoicing in his successful preaching mission and the salvation of the Ninevites, Jonah was angered that the Lord spared the city. The possibility that the Lord might show mercy to the Assyrians was why Jonah refused to go to the city in the first place. Jonah's statement about the Lord's grace and compassion appears elsewhere in the Old Testament with reference to the Lord's treatment of Israel (Exod 34:6–7; Num 14:18–19; Joel 2:13), but Jonah is scandalized that the Lord would show the same grace to the people of Nineveh. The Lord then used a vine, a worm, and a scorching east wind to show the prophet Jonah his misplaced priorities. If Jonah was absorbed in his own comfort and concerned about an insignificant plant that provided shade from the heat, should not the Lord be concerned about the welfare of the 120,000 inhabitants of Nineveh?

The real problem in the story is Jonah's prejudice against the Assyrians. Jonah's unresolved anger and the Lord's unanswered question, "Should I not be concerned about that great city?" (4:11 NIV 1984), at the end of the book reflect the difference between the Lord's heart and the prophet's. The Lord has a redemptive concern for all peoples, while Jonah believed the Lord's mercy and grace were only for Israel because of its special status as the chosen people of God. The lack of resolution as the book closes invites the reader to examine if his or her heart is more in line with the angry prophet or the merciful God.

Practical Application

The story of Jonah is a reminder that the Lord's plan of salvation extends beyond Israel to include all the nations, even those who were Israel's greatest enemies. The Lord promised Abraham that he would become a blessing to all peoples (Gen 12:3), and foreigners like Rahab, Ruth, and the queen of Sheba came to know the Lord as the true God. God even demonstrated His grace to the hated Assyrians. Jesus expressed this same compassion when He told His disciples to "love your enemies and pray for those who persecute you" (Matt 5:44). However, as we see with Jonah, this is easier said than done. Who does God want you to love in spite of how they have treated you?

MICAH

Divine Lawsuit

Micah was a prophet in Judah during the reigns of Jotham, Ahaz, and Hezekiah (740–687 BC). Therefore he was a contemporary of the prophet Isaiah. He prophesied concerning both the northern and southern kingdoms at the height of the Assyrian crisis. Micah and Isaiah shared a common belief that the Lord would restore Zion as the center of His worldwide kingdom of peace and righteousness (Isa 2:1–5; Mic 4:1–5). Micah's name means "Who is like Yahweh?" After the Lord revealed His plans of judgment and then salvation for Israel, the prophet himself exclaimed, "Who is a God like you?" (Mic 7:18).

KEY FACTS

Author:	Micah
Date:	740–689 BC
Recipients:	Judah
Key Word:	Remnant (Hb. *she'êrîth*)
Key Verse:	"Bethlehem Ephrathah, ... one will come from you to be ruler over Israel. ... His origin is ... from antiquity" (5:2).

Background

During Micah's ministry Samaria fell to the Assyrians in 722 BC, and Judah became an Assyrian vassal. The Assyrian king Sennacherib invaded Judah and captured forty-six cities. Jerusalem was spared in 701 BC when the angel of the Lord destroyed the Assyrian army that surrounded the city in response to Hezekiah's faith and prayer for the Lord's help (Isaiah 36–37). Micah was from the village of Moresheth (Mic 1:1) and even had the courage to announce the impending judgment of his own hometown (Mic 1:14). Micah and Isaiah made an interesting tandem since Micah was an outsider from a small village and Isaiah was from Jerusalem.

Outline

   I. Message of Judgment: "Hear All People" (1:1–2:13)
  II. Message of Hope: "Hear, Heads of Jacob" (3:1–5:15)
 III. Message of Pardon: "Hear, O Mountains" (6:1–7:20)

The command to "hear" (*shema'*) introduces the three major sections of the book (1:2; 3:1; 6:1), and each section contains a message of judgment and salvation. The call to "hear" or "listen" would remind Micah's Jewish audience of Deut 6:4 ("Hear O Israel: The LORD our God, the LORD is One," NIV). This basic statement of the Jewish faith is known as the *Shema'* and would have immediately come to their minds as a call from God Himself.

Message

The extended message of salvation at the center of the book, as well as the emphasis on salvation at the end of each section, reflects Micah's focus on the hope of Israel's future salvation. In each section the message of hope directly reverses the preceding message of judgment. In the first section Micah warned that Judah would go into exile (1:16; 2:4, 10), and then God promised that a remnant would return from exile (2:12–13).

I. Message of Judgment: "Hear All People" (Micah 1:1–2:13)

Micah portrayed the Lord marching out from His holy temple as a warrior and the earth crumbling and melting at His presence. The object of the Lord's anger was Israel and Judah, His own people. The Lord would first judge Samaria for its idolatry, and then the same fate awaited Jerusalem. Seeing the destiny that awaited his homeland, Micah composed a lament for the towns in Judah that would lie in the path of the invading Assyrian army (1:8–16).

These basalt relief orthostats, which show the various classes of the Assyrian army, belong to a doorway. They are from the period of Tiglath-pileser III (744–727 BC).

The Lord was angry that social injustice had become common in Israel and Judah. Through various legal and illegal means, the wealthy and the powerful conspired to steal the land of needy families (2:1–11). In ancient Israel the land belonged to the Lord, but He gave this land to His people as a special gift. God gave every tribe, clan, and family their property as an allotment from the Lord (Joshua 14). For this reason property in Israel was not permanently to change hands. Land sold because of debt was to be redeemed by the individual or family, and all land reverted to its original owners in the Year of Jubilee, every fiftieth year (Leviticus 25). To steal family property, as Ahab and Jezebel did with Naboth's vineyard, was to steal the family's inheritance from the Lord, and that was considered a serious crime (1 Kings 21). Because this practice was common, Micah announced that a foreign army would take possession of the land as Israel went away into exile. Because the rich had deprived the poor of their land, the Lord would now do the same to them.

The Problem of Social Injustice

"Perhaps, after the fall of Samaria, the social injustices of elite classes are exacerbated by a flood of refugees into Jerusalem from the North. The swollen numbers of refugees into Jerusalem increase the demand for food and lower the price of labor. Moreover, in times of drought or other misfortunes, the rich, contrary to the Law, loaned money to the poor at exorbitant interest, leading to foreclosures on the property, thereby forcing the free landholder into indentured slavery (cf. 2 Kings 4:1; Neh. 5:1–5; Amos 2:6). In other words, by adding field to field the rich cannibalized the poor (Mic. 3:1–5; cf. Ezek. 34:2–3; Pss. 14:4; 53:5; Hab. 3:14)."[4]

II. Message of Hope: "Hear, Heads of Jacob" (Micah 3:1–5:15)

Micah laid the blame for the spiritual and moral corruption of Israel and Judah with their sinful leaders. With their greed and disregard for the poor, their rulers had become like cannibals who chopped the people up and made them into stew (3:1–4). The prophets misled the people with their empty promises of "peace" for their own financial gain when the people needed to hear of the Lord's coming judgment (3:5–8). When judgment fell, the Lord would not respond to these corrupt leaders. When they cried out to Him, the Lord would give no answer to those who had failed to show mercy to others, and there would be no revelation from God to guide them through their darkest hour (3:9–12).

View overlooking Bethlehem, birthplace of King David and Jesus, Son of David.

An extended promise of Israel's future salvation stands at the center of the book of Micah in 4:1–5:15. This section includes Micah's famous prophecy of the future birth of the Messiah at Bethlehem (5:2). God promised to raise up another "ruler over Israel" who would come from Bethlehem, David's hometown. Matthew 2:3–6 quotes this passage on the lips of the chief priests and scribes in response to Herod's question about where the Messiah would be born. Matthew, in turn, sees the fulfillment of Micah's prediction of a future Davidic king whose "origin is . . . from antiquity" in the birth of Jesus at Bethlehem.

III. Message of Pardon: "Hear, O Mountains" (Micah 6:1–7:20)

In the final judgment section of the book, Micah called the people into the courtroom as the Lord brought a lawsuit against His people. The mountains and heavens were called as witnesses to hear the Lord's indictment against Israel because they witnessed the formal sealing of the covenant between the Lord and Israel in the days of Moses (Deut 4:26; 30:19; 31:18). In His indictment the Lord contrasted His past faithfulness to Israel's unfaithfulness and

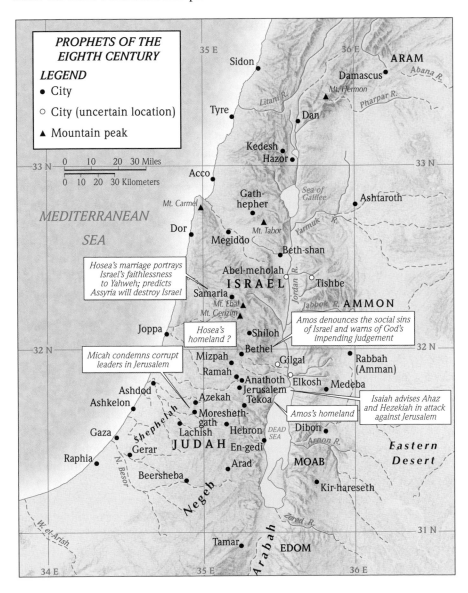

reminded the people of what He expected from them as His covenant partner. The Lord was not primarily interested in Israel's sacrifices and offerings, no matter how extravagant they might be, but rather in their humble obedience to Him reflected in a lifestyle of mercy and justice toward others (6:1–8).

After a brief lament (7:1–6) the concluding word of hope in Micah is a song of praise to the Lord for His promised deliverance (7:18–20). The righteous would endure the time of God's discipline for Israel, knowing deliverance and vindication were on the other side of judgment. Israel would enjoy a second exodus when the Lord brought them home from their exile and rebuilt the walls of Jerusalem.

Practical Application

Micah announced that the Lord's plans for Israel and Judah involved judgment and salvation. Israel and Judah were deserving of judgment because they worshipped idols and abandoned the practice of social justice. Following the judgment, the Lord would preserve a remnant and would restore Israel. The future Messiah would come from the line of David, would be born in Bethlehem, and would reign over a kingdom of peace and righteousness. There is no indication of a time gap between these events or between the first and second comings of Christ (5:1–5). The first coming of Christ and the additional revelation of the New Testament clarified the working out of God's prophetic timetable and His plans for the church and Israel. Like the Old Testament prophets Jesus also warned that the judgment of Jerusalem would take place in the near future and that there would be a future renewal and restoration at His second coming (Matthew 24).

The first six Minor Prophets express God's love for sinful people: Hosea's unfaithful wife, apostate northern Israel, sinful southern Judah, and ungodly Assyria. The prophets were God's spokesmen to cry out against idolatry, self-indulgence, and social injustice. They called for repentance, brokenness, and personal and social transformation.

The prophets also proclaimed God's promise of a second chance. Just as Hosea forgave Gomer, so God was willing to forgive Israel and Judah. Jonah's cry for mercy led to a second opportunity to deliver God's message. Micah was convinced that Israel's current rebellion had not eliminated the possibility of her future salvation.

When you are struggling with your own failures, remember the promise of the prophets. Everyone who calls on the name of the LORD will be saved (Joel 2:32). Seek the LORD and you will live (Amos 5:4). "Who is a God like you, forgiving iniquity . . . because he delights in faithful love. He will again have compassion on us . . . [and] cast all our sins into the depths of the sea"

(Mic 7:18–19). Run to Him; feel the embrace of His love. He will not reject a broken heart.

For Further Reading

Chisholm, Robert B. *Interpreting the Minor Prophets*. Grand Rapids: Zondervan, 1990.

Feinberg, Charles. *The Minor Prophets*. Chicago: Moody, 1976.

Hays, J. Daniel. *The Message of the Prophets*. Grand Rapids: Zondervan, 2010.

McComiskey, Thomas E., ed. *The Minor Prophets: An Exegetical and Expository Commentary*. Grand Rapids: Baker, 2009.

Smith, Gary V. *Hosea, Amos, Micah*. NIVAC. Grand Rapids: Zondervan, 2001.

———. *The Prophets as Preachers: An Introduction to the Hebrew Prophets*. Nashville: B&H, 1994.

Waltke, Bruce K. *A Commentary on Micah*. Grand Rapids: Zondervan, 2007.

Study Questions

1. How did God use Hosea's personal problems to speak to the people of Israel?
2. How did Peter use Joel's prophecy in his sermon on the day of Pentecost?
3. How do acts of social justice demonstrate our faith in God?
4. What does Jonah teach us about loving our enemies?
5. Why is the issue of social injustice important to God?

Notes

1. Mark W. Chavalas, "Joel," in *ZIBBC*, ed. John H. Walton (Grand Rapids: Zondervan, 2009), 5:45.

2. J. A. Motyer, *The Day of the Lion: The Message of Amos* (London: InterVarsity Press, 1974), 28. Motyer notes that the prophet reverses the normal Hebrew order of words (verb-subject) and places the name of Yahweh first to emphasize the Lord's emphatic displeasure.

3. See Philip J. King and Lawrence E. Stager, *Life in Biblical Israel* (Louisville: Westminster John Know, 2001), 355–57.

4. Bruce K. Waltke, *An Old Testament Theology* (Grand Rapids: Zondervan, 2007), 830.

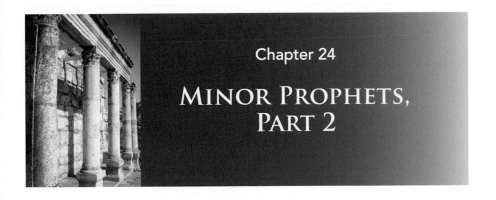

Chapter 24

MINOR PROPHETS, PART 2

Wrath and Mercy

NAHUM

Destruction of Nineveh

N ahum ("comfort") is the counterpart to the book of Jonah. We know nothing about Nahum beyond his name and that his hometown was Elkosh. In the previous century the Lord spared Nineveh from threatened judgment because of their repentant response to the preaching of Jonah. However, a generation later the Assyrians were again brutalizing Judah and the surrounding nations in the Middle East, so God decided to destroy this violent nation. Both Jonah and Nahum end with a question, and both reference the Mosaic confession that the Lord was both gracious and slow to anger as well as just and unwilling to excuse the guilty (Exod 34:6–7; Jonah 4:2; Nah 1:3). The Lord in His compassion delayed the judgment of Nineveh, but His justice also demanded that the Assyrians be held accountable for their violence and atrocities.

KEY FACTS

Author:	Nahum
Date:	650–620 BC
Recipients:	Judah
Key Word:	Vengeance (Hb. *nâqam*)
Key Verse:	"The LORD is good, a stronghold in a day of distress; he cares for those who take refuge in him" (1:7).

Background

Nahum delivered his message against Nineveh and the Assyrians sometime between 663 and 612 BC. The fall of the Egyptian city Thebes (No-amon in 3:8) occurred in 663 BC, and Nineveh fell to the Babylonians in 612 BC. The fall of Nineveh appears imminent (2:1; 3:14, 19), and so it seems likely that Nahum delivered his messages during the reign of Josiah around the same time Jeremiah commenced his prophetic ministry (c. 627 BC). The Medes captured the Assyrian capital of Ashur in 614 BC so the Assyrians transferred their capital to Nineveh. Nineveh was a magnificent city of impressive architecture with temples and palaces. The Medes and Babylonians joined together in the capture and destruction of Nineveh in 612 BC. The Babylonian Chronicles provided an account of the fall of Nineveh, which still remains in ruins today.

Outline

   I. Destruction of Nineveh Decreed (1:1–15)
  II. Destruction of Nineveh Described (2:1–13)
 III. Destruction of Nineveh Defended (3:1–19)

Message

I. Destruction of Nineveh Decreed (Nahum 1:1–15)

Nahum began his prophecy with a portrayal of Yahweh as the Divine Warrior. As a holy God who is rightly jealous for His honor and reputation, the Lord exacted vengeance on His enemies. At His approach the earth trembled, the sea and rivers dried up, and the mountains melted. The Lord's attributes combined absolute power with perfect righteousness so He was both a refuge for those who humbly trusted in Him and the destroyer of those who arrogantly opposed Him.

A colossal stylized bull with human face from the time of Sargon II of Assyria.

II. Destruction of Nineveh Described (Nahum 2:1–13)

Nahum's second oracle turned more directly to the destruction of Nineveh. Assyria had perfected the brutal techniques of siege warfare but would now become the victims of an invading army led by the Lord Himself. The prophet dramatically portrayed the chaos that would engulf the city of Nineveh in the present tense as if these events were occurring before his eyes, enabling the reader to sense the terror of the residents of Nineveh. The shields and uniforms of the enemy soldiers are scarlet because they are covered in blood. Their chariots dart through the city like torches and flashing lightning.

III. Destruction of Nineveh Defended (Nahum 3:1–19)

Nahum's woe oracle pronounced a death sentence on Nineveh and explained more fully the reasons for the Lord's judgment of the city. God's justice demanded the Assyrians experience the suffering and degradation they inflicted on others. Assyrian armies had slaughtered their enemies, but now the corpses of the dead Assyrians would be piled high in Nineveh. Like a prostitute Nineveh had seduced other nations into alliances and then had betrayed them because of her greed and lust for wealth. As punishment for her prostitution, the Lord would expose her nakedness and pelt her with filth.

The Cruelty of Assyria

Assyrian artwork reflects how much the Assyrians glamorized the violence of warfare and used such violence to intimidate other peoples into submission. Assyrian depictions of their conquests include the flaying of enemy soldiers, victims impaled on wooden poles, dismembered bodies, and severed heads stacked in front of city walls. The inscriptions of Assyrian kings also detail their brutal treatment of conquered foes:

"Like fat steers . . . I speedily cut them down and defeated them. I cut their throats like lambs. I cut off their lives as one cuts a string." *Sennacherib*

"I flayed as many nobles as had rebelled against me [and draped] their skins over the pile [of corpses]; some I spread out within the pile, some I erected on statues upon the pile. . . . I flayed many right through my land [and] draped their skins over the walls." *Ashurbanipal*

"Their dismembered bodies I fed to the dogs, swine, wolves, and eagles, to the birds of the heaven and the fish in the deep." *Ashurbanipal*

Practical Application

The Lord's judgment of Assyria in history is a preview of his final eschatological judgment of all nations and peoples. As with Assyria in the past, all peoples will be judged according to the Noahic covenant and its prohibition of violence and the shedding of blood (Gen 9:5–6; Isa 24:1–5; Amos 1:3–2:3). The Noahic covenant was the basis for judgment of Nazi Germany and the Soviet Empire as much as it was for ancient Assyria, and the Lord will judge America and all other nations in the future on the basis of this covenant as well. In the New Testament, Christ will come to earth as the Divine Warrior and strike the nations that oppose Him with the sword of His mouth (Rev 19:11–21). As with Nineveh in the book of Nahum, the final Babylon of the end times is also portrayed as a prostitute because of its materialism, idolatry, and evil influence on other peoples (Revelation 18).

HABAKKUK

Destruction of Babylon

Habakkuk ("embrace") prophesied in Judah prior to the Babylonian invasion and warned that the Lord would send the Babylonians to punish the people in Jerusalem (1:6). Habakkuk was a contemporary of Jeremiah and Zephaniah as well as Daniel and Ezekiel. Even in this time of national judgment, the Lord would not leave His people without a prophetic voice, and even in its final days as a nation, Judah could have turned to the Lord in repentance. Habakkuk's message is a personal one in which the prophet laments and dialogues with the Lord over the justice of His ways in using the Babylonians to punish Judah's sins.

KEY FACTS

Author:	Habakkuk
Date:	620–605 BC
Recipients:	Judah
Key Word:	Faith (Hb. 'ĕmûnâh)
Key Verse:	"But the righteous one will live by his faith" (2:4).

Background

At the end of the seventh century BC, the Babylonians replaced the Assyrians as the dominant power in the ancient Near East. The Babylonians under Nabopolassar declared their independence from Assyria in 626 BC. The Medes and Babylonians captured the cities of Ashur in 614 BC and Nineveh in 612 BC and then finished off what was left of the Assyrian army at Haran in 609 BC. This left Judah under Egyptian control with Jehoiakim as Judah's puppet king (2 Kgs 23:31–24:16) until the battle at Carchemish in 605 BC. After his victory over Egypt at Carchemish, Nebuchadnezzar marched south and took the first wave of exiles (including Daniel) from Judah in 605 BC. Habakkuk appears to have prophesied just prior to the first Babylonian invasion in 605 BC when Egypt was controlling Judah.

Outline

I.   Faith Tested (1:1–17)
II. Faith Taught (2:1–20)
III. Faith Triumphant (3:1–19)

I. Faith Tested (Habakkuk 1:1–17)

Habakkuk's first question was, Why does the Lord not punish injustice in Judah? (See 1:1–4.)

Habakkuk complained that the Lord had not answered his prayers to judge violence and injustice in the land. The Lord often delays judgment in order to show mercy, but the prophet believed the Lord's inactivity only made the problem of injustice worse. The law of Moses no longer had any impact on people's lives, and the wicked outnumbered and took advantage of the righteous. How can a person continue to have faith in God when He does nothing to stop these evil people? The Lord explained that He was not ignoring Habakkuk's prayer or the violence in Judah but was in fact answering his prayer in a manner that was even beyond the prophet's understanding. The Lord was raising up the Babylonians (Chaldeans) to punish the wicked people in Judah for their sin.

II. Faith Taught (Habakkuk 2:1–20)

Habakkuk's second question was, How can God use the Babylonians to punish Judah?

Habakkuk did not understand how a holy God, too pure even to look on evil, could use the Babylonians to punish Judah when the Babylonians were even more wicked and violent than Judah. It appeared to the prophet as if the

Lord was promoting injustice in the world by failing to punish the wicked. The Lord's response was that His sovereign purposes were beyond human understanding and could not be reduced to Habakkuk's simplistic formulas regarding who was most deserving of judgment. The Lord would ultimately punish sinners but in His time and His way. He would first judge Judah and then would judge Babylon.

The promise in 2:4 that "the righteous one will live by his faith" is quoted in the New Testament by Paul, who applied Hab 2:4 to argue that justification (a right standing with God) was "by faith" in Christ alone rather than by the works of righteousness (Rom 1:17; Gal 3:11). Both the original context of Hab 2:4 and Paul's later use of the verse stress the importance of trust in God's promise. The writer of Hebrews also quoted Hab 2:4 to encourage faithfulness to the Lord in the midst of the difficult circumstances his readers were encountering (Heb 10:38).

Though the Lord delayed His judgment, the five woe oracles in 2:6–20 guaranteed the final destruction of the Babylonian Empire. The Babylonians would now experience the violence they inflicted upon others as fitting retribution for their crimes.

III. Faith Triumphant (Habakkuk 3:1–19)

Habakkuk's third question was, Will the Lord have mercy?

Ancient Babylon as seen along the Euphrates River.

After hearing the Lord's responses to his complaints, Habakkuk concluded with a prayer for deliverance and a confession of trust in the Lord to do what was right in the midst of Judah's national crisis. This prayer was a hymn to be sung to the accompaniment of stringed instruments. Habakkuk heard of the Lord's great works in the past and prayed for the Lord to act once again in a powerful way on behalf of His people and to temper His anger against Judah with mercy. Habakkuk longed for the Lord's deliverance even as he feared what the day of the Lord's anger would mean for Judah. In one of the greatest confessions of faith in all of Scripture (3:16–19), the prophet affirmed that he would rejoice in the Lord and would wait for His deliverance even in the darkest hour of judgment when Judah was deprived of crops and food. Habakkuk was confident that judgment would turn to salvation.

Practical Application

Habakkuk's interaction with God is a reminder that the life of faith often involves lament, complaint, and the pouring out of one's honest emotions and feelings to God. Questioning God and His ways, when done with the right attitude, can lead to a deeper faith and a greater understanding of God's ways. The Lord does not rebuke or turn away the person that comes to Him with honest questions. True prayer is a dialogue with God and involves waiting on God and listening for Him to speak. God is more than a cosmic force and the dispenser of divine blessings, so vibrant prayer is personal communication with God that involves our intellect, will, and emotions. True faith leads to boldness before God but also humbly submits to God's sovereignty even when His ways are not fully understood.

ZEPHANIAH

Disaster Is Imminent

Zephaniah ("hidden") was of royal descent, the great-great grandson of Hezekiah (1:1), who ruled in Judah from 715 to 686 BC. Zephaniah's ancestor is not specifically identified as the king, but this connection provides the best explanation for the extended listing of four generations of the prophet's genealogy. The superscription indicates that Zephaniah prophesied during the reign of the godly king Josiah (640–609 BC). The evil reigns of Manasseh and Amon had plunged Judah into apostasy, but Josiah carried out a series of reforms in response to the discovery of the Book of the Law in the eighteenth year of his reign. Then he sought to purge the land of idolatry and to bring the people back to the Lord (2 Kings 22–23). Zephaniah's preaching led to a revival in the days of Josiah, Judah's last godly king.

KEY FACTS

Author:	Zephaniah
Date:	630–625 BC
Recipients:	Judah
Key Word:	Seek (Hb. *bâqash*)
Key Verse:	"Seek the LORD, all you humble of the earth.... Seek righteousness, seek humility" (2:3).

Background

Zephaniah's condemnation of Judah's idolatry in his opening message (1:4–6) indicates that he began his ministry prior to Josiah's major reform. Zephaniah's preaching thus helped influence perhaps the greatest revival in Judah's history. Zephaniah began his ministry at approximately the same time as Jeremiah, who began to prophesy in Josiah's thirteenth year (627 BC). Zephaniah ministered during an important transition time as the Neo-Assyrian Empire was coming to an end and the Babylonians were rising to power in the Middle East.

Outline

I. Judgment of Judah (1:1–2:3)
II. Judgment of the Nations (2:4–15)
III. Justification of the Remnant (3:1–20)

Message

I. Judgment of Judah (Zephaniah 1:1–2:3)

The Day of the Lord is the central theme of the book of Zephaniah. The prophet warned that the Day of the Lord was "near" (1:7, 14) and made repeated references to the "day" of God's wrath. The Lord's judgment would fall on the entire earth. Reversing his work of creation, the Lord would destroy all living things. After warning of this worldwide catastrophe, Zephaniah focused his message on Yahweh's impending judgment of Judah. The people presumptuously believed no harm would come to them because they were the Lord's chosen people, but the Lord would in fact search the city of Jerusalem with a lamp to make sure every evildoer and idol worshipper was punished.

II. Judgment of the Nations (Zephaniah 2:4–15)

The Lord is sovereign over all peoples and would also judge the nations for their wickedness and evil. Zephaniah referenced nations from all points of the compass—Philistia to the west, Moab and Ammon to the east, Cush to the south, and Assyria to the north—to demonstrate the encompassing nature of God's judgment.[1] Although the surrounding nations will arrogantly taunt the people of Judah, the remnant of Judah will possess these nations when the Lord restores His people. Judgment would fall not only on the smaller nations surrounding Judah but also on the imperial power of Assyria. Despite their military prowess, they would not be able to stand against the Lord. The Lord would destroy Assyria and turn the great city of Nineveh into a barren wasteland.

This wall relief from Nineveh's North Palace shows the Assyrian king inspecting prisoners while surrounded by his attendants. It dates to around 645–635 BC.

III. Justification of the Remnant (Zephaniah 3:1–20)

Zephaniah warned that the day of the Lord's judgment was coming against Judah and the nations (3:1–5), but the prophet also viewed these near events as providing a pattern for the Lord's work of judgment and salvation in the eschatological Day of the Lord. Judgment, however, was not the final word for Judah or the nations. In the last days the Lord would purify the speech of all peoples so they might worship and serve Him (3:9–10). He would purge evildoers from His own people and form a pure and holy remnant that would no longer practice injustice and deceit. Zephaniah stressed that the Lord's blessings were for the "humble" who put their trust in Him (3:11–12; cf. 2:3). The Lord would dwell among His people, and those who trusted in the Lord could rest in the promise that He would deliver the afflicted and the oppressed.

Practical Application

Zephaniah's preaching led to a revival in Judah in the days of King Josiah. His ministry reminds us of the importance of preaching that confronts evil, calls for repentance, and leads to revival. We cannot expect to see revival in our own time without preaching that challenges sin and confronts evil. Real revival is not the result of emotional hype but true humility. It will only come when we seek the Lord with all our heart.

HAGGAI

Rebuild the Temple

The name *Haggai* means "festal" and perhaps indicates that he was born during one of Israel's feasts. Haggai in tandem with Zechariah challenged the postexilic community to resume the work of rebuilding the temple so he delivered four messages in a fifteen-week period from August to December 520 BC in the second year of Darius king of Persia.

First Message (1:1–15)	Sixth month, first day (August 29)
Second Message (2:1–9)	Seventh month, twenty-first day (October 17)
Third Message (2:10–19)	Ninth month, twenty-fourth day (December 18)
Fourth Message (2:20–23)	Ninth month, twenty-fourth day (December 18)

KEY FACTS

Author:	Haggai
Date:	520 BC
Recipients:	Returned exiles in Jerusalem
Key Word:	Signet (Hb. *chôthâm*)
Key Verse:	"On that day ... I will take you ... and make you like my signet ring, for I have chosen you" (2:23).

Background

Cyrus's decree in 538 BC granted both permission and resources for rebuilding the temple (Ezra 3:7; 5:13–15) so the returnees and their leaders began the project with urgency and enthusiasm (Ezra 3:8–13; 5:16). The prophets Haggai and Zechariah returned to Jerusalem with a 50,000-member Jewish remnant in the first return under Sheshbazzar and Zerubbabel (Ezra 2:64–65). Once they arrived, they built an altar and reinstated the Levitical sacrifices; then they began to lay the foundation for the temple in 536 BC (Ezra 3:1–13). However, the enormity of the rebuilding process, economic hardships, and opposition from the surrounding peoples stalled the project for sixteen years. Haggai challenged the nation to build the temple because the people were discouraged, disillusioned, and had given up on finishing the Lord's house.

Outline

   I. First Message: Rebuking (1:1–15)
  II. Second Message: Recharging (2:1–9)
 III. Third Message: Ruling (2:10–19)
 IV. Fourth Message: Reigning (2:20–33)

Message

I. First Message: Rebuking (Haggai 1:1–15)

The people believed they were too poor and that it was not time to rebuild the temple, but Haggai countered that they were in poverty because of their failure to rebuild it. In their misplaced priorities the people had devoted themselves to building their own homes rather than the Lord's house.

Stonework showing examples of carpenters with their tools.

Haggai challenged the people to "think carefully" (KJV, lit. "set your heart on") their ways and the consequences of their selfishness and greed (1:5, 7). The Lord used the preaching of Haggai to "rouse" (v. 14) the hearts of His people to rebuild the temple in the same way He prompted Cyrus to issue the initial decree for its rebuilding (2 Chron 36:22–23). The Lord initiated this project, but the people's choice to obey the Lord was a necessary part of the process. There is a perfect balance here between divine sovereignty and human responsibility. In response to the people's obedience, the Lord promised that His empowering presence would enable them to complete their task.

II. Second Message: Recharging (Haggai 2:1–9)

The three oracles in Haggai 2 focus on the blessings the Lord had in store for His people as they resumed the work of temple reconstruction in Jerusalem. The postexilic community was a poor and struggling people with limited economic resources, so it was naturally discouraging to compare the modest structure they were building with the glories of Solomon's first temple. Some of the older people still remembered the glorious first temple, so they felt like giving up when they considered the inferiority of the new temple. The Lord recharged the people with the challenge to be strong, to rejoice, and to remember His presence among them. The enablement of the Spirit would help them complete their task. Ezra 6:8 indicates that shortly after this prophecy God fulfilled this promise by causing the Persian king Darius to order his officials to pay for the full cost of the temple out of the royal treasury. The Lord even promised that the glory of the new temple would surpass that of the first built by Solomon. Many years later King Herod the Great remodeled and expanded the second temple, which stood in Jesus's time.

III. Third Message: Ruling (Haggai 2:10–19)

Echoing the original message delivered in 1:5, 7, Haggai's threefold encouragement was for the people to "give careful thought" (2:15, 18 NIV) to their ways, to realize they and their offerings were unclean, and to observe closely how their punishment would soon turn into a blessing after they repent. Until this time the postexilic community had experienced poor harvests and economic deprivation, but from this day forward the Lord promised that He would provide abundant harvests. The people would now experience the blessings of the Mosaic covenant rather than the curses if they continued to seek the Lord.

IV. Fourth Message: Reigning (Haggai 2:20–33)

In Haggai's final message the Lord promised to bless Zerubbabel, the weak governor of Judah. Zerubbabel was a member of the house of David and the grandson of Jehoiachin, the king of Judah taken away to Babylon in 597 BC (2 Chron 36:8–10). The Lord's promise to make Zerubbabel "like a signet ring" reversed the curse the prophet Jeremiah had announced against Jehoiachin as the representative of the house of David (Jer 22:24–25). The signet ring was a visible symbol of the king's authority. The Lord had temporarily rejected the line of David, but He would once again restore the Davidic king as His human vice-regent and earthly representative of His heavenly rule. Zerubbabel in fact merely anticipated the ideal Davidic ruler of the future who would reign over the nations. Zerubbabel's role as governor over Judah was confirmation that the Lord was not finished with the house of David. His present rule pointed to the future reign of his descendant Jesus Christ (see Matt 1:12; Luke 3:27) who ultimately will fulfill the magnitude of this prophecy in His millennial reign.

Practical Application

Haggai's insistence that the Jews rebuild the temple reminds us of the importance of corporate worship. The temple was merely the symbol of God's presence among His people. Eventually, the tabernacle and both temples were destroyed by the Philistines, Babylonians, and Romans. God made clear that He is not the curator of religious museums. While places of worship ought to be treated with respect, they do not replace the heart and soul of the worshipper. Therefore, in the New Testament believers are assured that their bodies are the temple of God (1 Cor 6:19; 2 Cor 6:16). If it was important for the Jews to treat God's temple with respect, it is much more important that we allow His glory to be seen in us.

ZECHARIAH

Restore the King

Zechariah ("the Lord remembers") was a postexilic prophet who foretold the coming of Israel's true and final King. He reminded the people of Jerusalem that God would remember them and come to their rescue when they called upon the Lord in the last days. His book outlines God's future prophetic program for Israel from the first coming through the second coming of the Messiah.

KEY FACTS

Author:	Zechariah
Date:	520–500 BC
Recipients:	Postexilic Judah
Key Word:	Grace (Hb. *chên*)
Key Verse:	"Then I will pour out the spirit of grace and prayer on the house of David and the residents of Jerusalem, and they will look at me whom they pierced" (12:10).

Background and Date

The first part of the book of Zechariah covers the period of the prophet's ministry in Jerusalem from 520 BC until the completion of the second temple in 515 BC. Some conservative scholars date portions toward the end of the book as late as 500–470 BC at the end of Zechariah's life. His immediate focus in the early chapters is one of encouragement to the postexilic community to build the temple, restore the priesthood, and cleanse the city. His ultimate purpose in the closing chapters focuses on the promise of the coming Messiah and His reign over Jerusalem as both King and Priest.

Outline

I.   Call to Repentance (1:1–6)
II. Eight Night Visions (1:7–6:15)
III. Four Messages (7:1–8:23)
IV. Two Burdens (9:1–14:21)
     A.   First Burden: False Shepherds (9:1–11:17)
     B.   Second Burden: The King Is Coming (12:1–14:21)

Message

I. Call to Repentance (Zechariah 1:1–6)

Less than two months after Haggai had successfully challenged the postexilic community to resume building the temple in Jerusalem, Zechariah called the people to repent and return to the Lord in October–November 520 BC. Without true spiritual renewal on the people's part, rebuilding the temple was useless. The Lord promised that He would "return" (*shuv*) to His people if they would return to Him (1:3). The people's obedient response set in motion the Lord's promise to bless them and to bring about Jerusalem's restoration.

II. Eight Night Visions (Zechariah 1:7–6:15)

Zechariah delivered his next message on February 15, 519 BC. Zechariah received a series of eight visions with an angelic interpretation of each. These visions reflect the Lord's gracious response to the people's repentance in 1:6. The blessings of the community in the immediate future also foreshadowed the final restoration of Israel and Zion that would occur in the more distant future.

In his *first vision* Zechariah saw four horsemen on colored horses. The "man" on the red horse was the angel of the Lord, and the other horsemen were angelic messengers. After patrolling the whole earth, the messengers reported that they found the whole world at peace and asked God to be merciful to Jerusalem. In the *second vision* Zechariah saw four horns crushed. These horns represented the powerful nations that had destroyed Israel and Judah and taken them away into exile (1:18–21). In the *third vision* Zechariah

Sunset over the Judean hills.

saw a man with a measuring rod surveying Jerusalem in preparation for the rebuilding of its walls. Zechariah's *fourth vision* refers to the restoration of the high priest Joshua for service at the temple (3:1–10). In his *fifth vision* Zechariah saw two olive trees and a lampstand with seven lamps (4:1–14). The golden lampstand (menorah) was one of the articles in the holy place of the tabernacle and temple, and the seven lamps on the lampstand in this vision represent the presence of the Lord at the rebuilt temple. The two olive trees provided oil for the lamps and appear to represent Joshua the high priest and Zerubbabel the governor. The book of Revelation uses these same symbols to represent the two witnesses (11:1–12) and the seven churches (1:20). In the *sixth vision* Zechariah saw a flying scroll that measured thirty feet by fifteen feet and was covered with written curses against those who had broken God's commandments (5:1–4). Zechariah's *seventh vision* included a woman in a measuring basket who was taken to another land (5:5–11). The woman represented wickedness in the land, and a female figure was likely used because the Hebrew word for "wickedness" (*rish`ah*) is feminine. The *eighth vision* of the four horse-drawn chariots resembles and resolves the opening vision of the four horsemen in 1:7–17. The riders in the first vision asked the Lord to deliver Jerusalem from its enemies, and this vision brings the answer to that request as the Lord goes out to establish justice in all the earth.

Olive trees in the garden of Gethsemane in Jerusalem.

The night visions concluded with a symbolic act confirming the Lord's promise to bless Joshua the high priest and Zerubbabel the governor as they led the rebuilding of the temple (6:9–15). The Lord commanded Zechariah to place a crown on the head of Joshua, reflecting how Joshua would be both a priest and a ruler over the people, and this anticipates how the offices of priest and king would be fulfilled in the person of Jesus Christ. The cooperation between Joshua as high priest and Zerubbabel as representative of the house of David also foreshadowed Jesus's fulfillment of both royal and priestly roles. Jesus was the Son of David, but He also offered the perfect sacrifice for sin and intercedes for believers as their high priest (Heb 4:14–16; 7:24–28; 9:11–14).

III. Four Messages (Zechariah 7:1–8:23)

Zechariah delivered his next message in 518 BC in response to questions from a delegation from Bethel regarding whether they should continue fasting and mourning over the fall of Jerusalem since they were no longer in exile. Zechariah responded that the Lord was more concerned with their practice of justice than their observance of ritual fasts. After looking backward to the lessons learned from the exile, Zechariah pointed forward to the future hope for Jerusalem. The Lord promised to dwell among His people and to bring all of the exiles back to the land. Jerusalem would once again become a great city, and their rituals of mourning would become festive celebrations.

IV. Two Burdens (Zechariah 9:1–14:21)

Zechariah 9–14 has a more eschatological focus and portrays the coming of the Messiah, the final restoration of Israel, and the future kingdom of God.

A. First Burden: False Shepherds (Zechariah 9:1–11:17)

In Israel's future restoration the Lord promised that He would march out as the heavenly warrior and defeat Israel's enemies in Syria, Phoenicia, and Philistia. Most surprisingly, after this judgment the Lord would preserve a remnant from the Philistines to worship Him and to be like one of the tribes in Israel. In connection with Israel's great victory, Israel's future king (Messiah) would come as a humble man of peace, riding on a donkey instead of a horse or war chariot. Jesus fulfilled this prophecy with His triumphal entry into Jerusalem on Palm Sunday (Matt 21:1–11; Mark 11:1–10; Luke 19:28–38; John 12:12–15); but the Jews rejected Jesus as their king and conspired with the Romans to have Him crucified. The complete and final fulfillment of this prophecy will occur only when Jesus returns at His Second Coming.

Zechariah's Messianic Prophecies

Zechariah predicted both the first coming and the second coming of the Messiah. He pictures Israel's future King as both rejected and yet ruling. His prophecies ultimately focus on the future triumph of the coming King when God Himself in the person of Jesus Christ fulfills these incredible prophecies. The Messiah will be:

1. The Branch that sprouts from the Davidic line of kings (3:8; 6:12)

2. The King-Priest who combines both offices in one person (6:13)

3. The Lowly King who rides into Jerusalem on a donkey (9:9)

4. One who is betrayed for thirty pieces of silver (11:12–13)

5. One who is pierced in crucifixion (12:10)

6. The Good Shepherd who is smitten (13:7–9)

7. One who opens a fountain of cleansing for the house of David and the inhabitants of Jerusalem (13:1)

8. One who is Yahweh Himself (13:9)

9. God who comes to split the Mount of Olives and defend Jerusalem (14:1–4)

10. The King who rules the Holy City of Jerusalem (14:16)

B. Second Burden: The King Is Coming (Zechariah 12:1–14:21)

This second oracle also promised the future restoration of Israel but warned that this salvation would come only after the Lord had once again cleansed and purged His people through judgment. In his final message Zechariah portrays Israel's eschatological future from the time of the nation's recognition of her true Messiah

An olive press.

until the establishment of the future messianic kingdom. The last chapter of Zechariah portrays the final assault on Jerusalem to occur in the last days when the Lord will come down to fight on behalf of His people. The Lord's arrival will split the Mount of Olives in two, destroy the enemy forces, and provide a way of escape for His people. With this victory the Lord's kingdom will come to earth as a time of unprecedented blessing and peace. Revelation 19–20 adds to this portrayal of the future kingdom by revealing that Christ Himself will return as the conquering warrior to defeat His enemies. Then He will rule from Jerusalem as King over all the earth.

Practical Application

Zechariah presents a theology of holiness. He was concerned that the postexilic Jewish community should properly prepare their hearts for the Lord's blessing. They could do this by establishing a holy worship, holy priesthood, holy temple, and holy city. But in the end he recognized that these ideals would only be realized when God Himself came to rescue Jerusalem and rule the world in the person of the Messiah. Only a Holy God could bring true holiness from heaven to an earthly kingdom. In light of this, we are reminded that while God can use us to make a difference on earth, the ultimate promise of world peace will only be realized when Christ Himself returns.

MALACHI
Repent of Sin

The ancient versions are divided on whether Malachi ("my messenger") is a personal name or a title. The use of personal names in the headings for other prophetic books would suggest the same here. Malachi's name is a reminder of his role as God's prophet and connects his ministry to a future prophet ("my messenger") the Lord promised to send in preparation for the future day of the Lord (3:1).

KEY FACTS

Author:	Malachi
Date:	435–430 BC
Recipients:	Postexilic Judah
Key Word:	Curse (Hb. *chêrem*)
Key Verse:	"Look, I am going to send the prophet Elijah before the great and terrible Day of the LORD comes" (4:5).

Background

The heading of the book contains no specific details concerning the date of Malachi's ministry. He prophesied in the postexilic period after the rebuilding of the temple and the reinstitution of the sacrifices and rituals associated with the temple. The term "governor" in 1:8 fits with the Persian period. Malachi was most likely a contemporary of Ezra and Nehemiah. Like Ezra and Nehemiah, Malachi dealt with the problems of intermarriage, corrupt priests, failure to pay tithes, and social injustice. Malachi's ministry can be dated about 430 BC. He represents the last of the classical prophets, and his message closes the Old Testament with a final call to repentance.

Outline

I. God's Love Announced (1:1–5)
II. God's People Denounced (1:6–4:3)
   A. Question of Worship (1:6–2:9)
   B. Question of Divorce (2:10–16)
   C. Question of Justice (2:17–3:5)

    D. Question of Tithing (3:6–12)

    E. Question of Rewards (3:13–4:3)

III. God's Messenger Pronounced (4:4–6)

    The book of Malachi is structured around disputations in which the Lord dialogues with His people in a series of questions and answers. Altogether the book raises twenty-three questions, following the pattern of: (1) accusation, (2) interrogation, (3) refutation, and (4) conclusion. This literary form is effective in that it reflects the people's spiritual condition. The recurring expression "but you say" on the part of the people reflects how they have responded to God in an argumentative and disrespectful manner.

A view of the Edomite territory near Petra.

Message

I. God's Love Announced (Malachi 1:1–5)

    In the opening disputation the people questioned the Lord's love for them. Their struggles as an impoverished remnant living under foreign oppression led them to doubt God's care for them (cf. Isa 40:27; 49:14). The Lord reminded them of His election of Jacob over Esau. "Love" and "hate" were covenantal terms in the ancient Near East, and the Lord made a covenant with Jacob (Gen 28:12–17) but not with Esau. The Lord chose Jacob and his descendants to be the objects of His favor and to have a key role in salvation history as the instrument of divine blessing to the whole world.

II. God's People Denounced (Malachi 1:6–4:3)

A. Question of Worship (Malachi 1:6–2:9)

The Lord demanded that Israel honor Him with worship that was worthy of His name, but the corrupt priests allowed the people to offer defective sacrifices that were blind, lame, and sick. These animals were not appropriate for sacrifice (Lev 9:2–3; Deut 15:21). The people would vow unblemished animals to the Lord and then offer cheap substitutes that would be unacceptable to God. In addition, the priests did not fear God, so God will reject them (2:1–9).

B. Question of Divorce (Malachi 2:10–16)

The Lord instituted marriage as a sacred covenant relationship, but the men in the community dishonored the Lord in their marriages in two specific ways. First, they intermarried with foreign women who worshipped other gods. Second, divorce had become a common occurrence in the community. The Lord's intent from the beginning was for marriage to be a lifelong commitment between one man and one woman (Gen 2:21–25). Mosaic law allowed for divorce, but it was regulated and restricted in Israel (Deut 24:1–4). Jesus confirmed in His teaching that marriage was for a lifetime, although the New Testament appears to allow for divorce in cases of adultery or when an unbeliever abandons a believing spouse (Matt 5:31–32; 19:3–9; 1 Corinthians 7).

C. The Question of Justice (Malachi 2:17–3:5)

The people wearied the Lord by questioning His justice and whether He was committed to punishing wickedness and rewarding righteousness. The Lord would send a "messenger" to prepare the way for His coming, and the fact that Malachi's name means "my messenger" indicates that his ministry prefigures the role of this future spokesman for God. The New Testament identifies this messenger as John the Baptist, who as the messianic forerunner, prepared the people for the coming of Jesus (Matt 11:10; Mark 1:2; Luke 7:27).

D. Question of Tithing (Malachi 3:6–12)

The Lord charged that the people were robbing Him by failing to give their tithes as set forth in Mosaic law. Tithing was a reminder to the people that everything they owned came from the Lord and belonged to Him. Their tithes provided for the Levites who served at the temple (Num 18:21–32), for the poor and needy (Deut 14:28–29; 22:21–29; 26:12–13), and even for their own festive celebrations before the Lord (Deut 14:22–26). The Lord invited the people to test Him and see how He would bless them and provide for their needs if they were faithful in giving their tithes.

E. Question of Rewards (Malachi 3:13–4:3)

The people again challenged the Lord's justice by asking if there was any reward or benefit in serving Him. It appeared to them as if the wicked prospered and got away with their sins. The Lord responded that two fates await the righteous and the wicked. The Lord knew the righteous and had recorded their names in His "scroll of remembrance." They would be spared on the future day of judgment while the wicked would be burned up like useless chaff thrown into the furnace.

III. God's Messenger Pronounced (Malachi 4:4–6)

The Lord promised that He would send the prophet Elijah prior to the future Day of the Lord to restore His people, and this promise clarifies and expands on the earlier prophecy that the Lord would send His "messenger" to prepare for His coming (3:1). Elijah would call the people to repentance as he had done at an earlier time of national apostasy. The New Testament explains that John the Baptist is the fulfillment of this prophecy. John the

The Chapel of Elijah on Mount Horeb, commemorating the traditional site to which Elijah fled after his confrontation with the prophets of Baal on Mount Carmel. Malachi prophesied that Elijah would precede the Day of the Lord.

Baptist resembled Elijah in his appearance and diet (cf. Matt 3:4 and 2 Kgs 1:8) and ministered in the spirit of Elijah by calling the people of his day to repent of their sinful ways (Matt 11:10–14). Ironically, the last book of the Old Testament ends with both a call to repentance and a threat of a curse, following the prophetic pattern of the Hebrew prophets.

The book of Malachi forms an important bridge between the Old and New Testaments. The final prophetic word in the Old Testament canon anticipates the ministry of John the Baptist as the prophetic forerunner to Jesus Christ. The Lord is the "sun of righteousness" (4:2) as the source of salvation, and Jesus would come as "the light of the world" to make that salvation possible (John 8:12).

Practical Application

The final six Minor Prophets ministered in times of incredible transition in the ancient world. The empires of Assyria (Nahum) and Babylon (Habakkuk) were about to fall. Judah would go into captivity (Zephaniah), but return to rebuild the Temple (Haggai) and await the coming of the King (Zechariah and Malachi). But without true repentance and real faith, Israel's life would remain little more than religious rituals.

Without Jesus the Old Testament remains silent and unfulfilled like the dull thud of Joseph's coffin lid at the end of Genesis (50:26). While the Hebrew canon closes with the admonition to "go up" to Jerusalem and start all over again (2 Chron 36:23), the Christian canon of the Old Testament closes with a call to restoration and repentance: "Otherwise, I will come and strike the land with a curse" (Mal 4:6). Without Jesus the promises of God remain unfulfilled. Without the Messiah these predictions are but silent echoes of a long-forgotten past, quickly dismissed by critical scholars as nothing more than the wishful thinking of Jewish mythology. But for the Christian believer, they are "very great and precious promises" based on "the prophetic word strongly confirmed" from men who "spoke from God as they were carried along by the Holy Spirit" (2 Pet 1:4, 19, 21).

For Further Reading

Chisholm, Robert B. *Interpreting the Minor Prophets*. Grand Rapids: Zondervan, 1990.

Hays, J. Daniel. *The Message of the Prophets*. Grand Rapids: Zondervan, 2010.

Kaiser, Walter C. *Malachi: God's Unchanging Love*. Chicago: Moody, 1984.

McComiskey, Thomas E., ed. *The Minor Prophets: An Exegetical and Expository Commentary*. Grand Rapids: Baker, 2009.

Merrill, E. H. *An Exegetical Commentary: Haggai, Zechariah, Malachi*. Richardson, TX: Biblical Studies Press, 2003.

Verhof, P. A. *The Books of Haggai and Malachi*. Grand Rapids: Baker, 1984.

Study Questions

1. What city in Assyria was the focus of Nahum's prophecy?
2. What city was the focus of Habakkuk's prophecy?
3. How did Zephaniah's preaching lead to revival?
4. Why was the temple so important to the Jews?
5. How did the prophecy of the signet ring apply to Jesus Christ?
6. List Zechariah's prophecies that were fulfilled by Jesus.
7. Why does Malachi end with the threat of a curse?

Note

1. J. Daniel Hays, *The Message of the Prophets: A Survey of the Prophetic and Apocalyptic Books of the Old Testament* (Grand Rapids: Zondervan, 2010), 337.

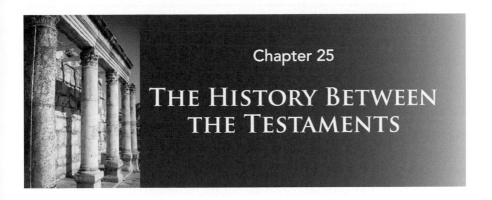

Chapter 25

THE HISTORY BETWEEN THE TESTAMENTS

The Intertestamental Period

The history of the Jewish people between the Old and New Testaments covers a period of approximately 400 years. This period is sometimes called the "silent years" because as Josephus the historian remarked, "the succession of prophets" was interrupted.[1] The Old Testament ended with Malachi, and there was no sure word from heaven after that. God seemed silent, but that did not mean God was not at work in the world. He was preparing the world for the coming of Christ.

Many of the things that happened in this period did not go well for the Jews. Their troubles had begun even when the prophets Jeremiah, Ezekiel, and Daniel were still speaking. The political oppression of the Jewish people extending from the biblical period through the "silent years" can be divided into four eras when the Babylonians, Medo-Persians, Greeks, and Romans ruled over them. In between the Grecian and the Roman eras, the Jews won for themselves nearly a century of self-rule under a family of Jewish priests called the Hasmoneans. In each of these periods, God was at work preparing the Jews for the coming Messiah.

The Babylonian Captivity (605–538 BC)[2]

After a series of attacks, Jerusalem finally fell to Nebuchadnezzar's forces in 586 BC. The temple was destroyed, and the Jews were taken captive to Babylon. There the Jews learned to preserve their identity without a temple by gathering around their religious teachers. Most scholars believe Jews developed the habit of regularly meeting for prayer and study at this time. Eventually the study and prayer groups were called "synagogues" (literally, "gatherings"). This development in Jewish culture helped pave the way for Christians to form similar groups. The New Testament word *ekklēsia* (translated "church" in most English Bibles today) literally means "congregation" or "assembly."

The Medo-Persian Period (539–331 BC)

The Medo-Persian domination of Jerusalem began when Cyrus defeated the Babylonians in 539 BC. Almost immediately Cyrus reversed the grievous Babylonian policy that displaced subjugated peoples from their ancestral homes. Cyrus believed his conquered peoples would be more manageable and more profitably taxed if they were happily returned to their temples and cities to prosper in their native lands.

The providential hand of God was seen in Cyrus's proclamation, for this meant the Jews could return to their homeland. Zerubbabel the political leader and Joshua the high priest led the first band of captives back to Jerusalem (Ezra 2:2), bringing back the temple furniture with them (Ezra 5:14–15; 520 BC). Immediately they set up an altar for burnt offerings, kept the

The Cyrus Cylinder, inscribed with the famous Edict of Cyrus the Great in 538 BC.

Feast of Tabernacles, and took steps to rebuild the temple (Ezra 3:2–8). The temple was finished in 516 BC with the encouragement and motivation of the prophets Haggai and Zechariah.

In 458 BC, Ezra led a group of captives back from Persia to Jerusalem who instituted moral reforms among the people. Nehemiah was appointed governor of Jerusalem and Judea in 445 BC and received a decree from King Artaxerxes I to rebuild the walls. This was accomplished in fifty-two days (Neh 6:15), and dedication ensued (Neh 12:27). Ezra led the people in a solemn assembly of fasting, confession of sin, and recommitment to the nation's covenant with God. Old Testament law was made central to Jewish life. Sabbath worship was stressed; non-Israelites, including Samaritans, were expelled; and the priesthood was carefully regulated.

During this time Aramaic increasingly replaced Hebrew as the common language of the region. Ezra began the habit of first reading the Scripture in Hebrew and then giving an understandable translation in Aramaic (Neh 8:8). This practice was repeated so broadly by later generations that the Aramaic translations became more or less standardized. These translations were called

"Targums." The Targums characteristically avoided descriptions of God as if He had body parts. Phrases like "the hand of the Lord" or "the eyes of the Lord" were replaced by references to the Lord's "work" or "knowledge." God was seen as Spirit, Creator, Provider, and Sustainer. The teaching of the synagogues during New Testament times can in part be traced in these Targums.

The Grecian Period (331–164 BC)

The Grecian period of domination began when Alexander the Great expanded his empire and its culture across the land of Israel beginning around 331 BC. Alexander conquered the Persian Empire and forever changed the cultural face of the Middle East. This shift toward Greek culture is called "Hellenization." Upon Alexander's death in 323, his vast empire was divided among his four generals. Ptolemy I (323–285 BC) inherited Egypt and soon gained control of Israel. For over a century the descendants of Ptolemy in Egypt ruled the Jewish lands with a measure of respect for the Jewish faith.

The Jewish community in and around Jerusalem faced a new threat with the coming of Alexander and Greek culture. Egypt became Hellenized, so it is not surprising that its great port city of Alexandria became a cultural center of Hellenization. The threat to Jews at this time did not come from armies but through culture's influence on Israel's way of life and religion. In response many Jews retreated into their synagogues and remained isolated from the world.

At this time the Hebrew Bible began to be translated into Greek even though there was much controversy over this move. Some Jews thought it was a transgression to translate the pure Word of God written in the Hebrew language, the language of God, into a pagan language. But Jews

Carved around 330 BC, this head of Alexander the Great features him as a youth with wavy locks that adorn his forehead like the mane of a lion (the characteristic "anastole" of all portraits of Alexander).

scattered over the Mediterranean world couldn't speak or read Hebrew so the new translation was greeted with pragmatic enthusiasm. The oldest translations of the books of the Hebrew Bible into Greek are collectively known as the Septuagint (c. 250 BC).[3] About 80 percent of the New

Testament's quotations of the Old Testament come from the old Greek translation called the Septuagint.

For generations the Ptolemies of Egypt were challenged for their right to govern Israel by the Syrian fragment of Alexander's empire to Israel's north. This Syrian branch of the empire was led by the descendants of Seleucus I, one of Alexander's generals. In 198 BC, the Seleucids won the upper hand when Antiochus III defeated Ptolemy V at the headwaters of the Jordan River. The Syrians tried to force the Jews to adopt Hellenistic culture and religion. Soon circumcision was outlawed, along with Sabbath observance, Jewish festivals, Jewish Scripture, and the Jewish diet. It literally became a capital offence to practice the Jewish religion.

Fragment of an Exodus passage from the Septuagint, the Greek translation of the Hebrew Scriptures.

At this time Jewish culture began to divide among those who were compliant and those who resisted. Spiritual opponents of Hellenism were called the "Hasidim" ("pious ones"). Those politically opposed to Hellenism were called "zealots." The turmoil came to a head when Antiochus IV Epiphanes stormed Jerusalem, murdered many of its citizens, offered a sow on the temple's altar, and erected an idol to the Olympian Zeus. Then the Jews were ordered to offer sacrifices to the Grecian gods, but many Jews resisted unto death.

The Maccabean Revolt and Jewish Independence (164–63 BC)

Coin bearing the image of Antiochus IV Epiphanes.

A few months after Antiochus Epiphanes desecrated the temple, an agent was sent to Modein, a small village northwest of Jerusalem, to force its citizens to offer a pagan sacrifice. An aged man named Mattathias from the priestly Hasmonean family refused. When a bystander volunteered to offer the sacrifice, Mattathias killed the turncoat as well as the Seleucid agent. For a year Mattathias led his five sons and as many as would join them in military actions against the Seleucids and compromising Jews. Hiding by day, attacking by night, they tore down pagan altars, forcibly circumcised children, and promoted the Jewish religion among the people. Upon Mattathias's death, his third son, Judas, nicknamed Maccabeus (the "Hammer"), took over leadership of the rebellion. This family of priests and warriors became known as the Maccabees. By 164 BC, Judas Maccabeus gained control of the temple. The ceremony by which the Jews rededicated the temple is still celebrated by Jews today as Hanukkah ("Dedication"). Political freedom took longer for the Jews, but it eventually came.

Judas's brother Jonathan was given the office of high priest. Because the Hasmoneans were not descendants of the line of Zadok, religious opposition to the family began to grow. At this time the Essenes separated from the temple,[4] and the Pharisees and Sadducees also became distinct religious groups. The *Pharisees* became the largest and most influential religious group within Judaism. They attempted to strictly adhere to both the entire Hebrew canon and the oral law (traditions). The Sadducees, mainly came from among the priestly supporters of the Hasmoneans. They gave preference to the Torah and tended to be anti-supernaturalists, denying a future resurrection. The Herodians favored political cooperation with the Romans and supported the Herodian dynasty. The Zealots were revolutionaries who were intent on overthrowing foreign occupying powers. The Essenes retreated from Jerusalem and lived in a communal setting near the Dead Sea and are credited with copying the Dead Sea Scrolls.

In the meantime, Jonathan's brother Simon eventually gained full release from paying Syrian taxes in 142 BC. This fully established the Hasmonean-Maccabean period of Jewish self-rule (142–63 BC).[5] Simon's son John Hyrcanus (134–104 BC) expanded Israel's territory into Samaria to the north and Idumea to the south. Hyrcanus forced both circumcision and the Jewish law upon the Idumeans. In 108 BC, Hyrcanus destroyed the Samaritan temple. At this time some discontent with the Hasmoneans began to grow among the Jews. A Pharisee's challenge against Hyrcanus's right to be high priest led Hyrcanus to shift his allegiance from the Pharisees to the Sadducees. Opposition from the Pharisees intensified as the Hasmonean priests began to adopt Hellenistic attitudes. The civil war between Aristobulus II and Hyrcanus II weakened Israel to such an extent that the Roman general Pompey had little trouble when he invaded Israel and added it to Rome's expanding empire in 63 BC.

The Roman Period (63 BC–AD 134)

When Pompey captured Jerusalem in 63 BC, he appointed Hyrcanus II as high priest. A wealthy Idumean named Antipater, whose support Pompey enjoyed during the hostilities, was appointed governor over Judea. Soon Antipater's two sons also became regional rulers: Phasael over Judea and Herod over Galilee. When the Parthians invaded Syria and stormed Jerusalem in 40 BC, Phasael was killed, but Herod escaped to Rome. There the Roman Senate declared Herod "king of the Jews." With the troops Rome supplied, Herod conquered Jerusalem to become "Herod the Great," king of the Jews (37–4 BC). This is the Herod responsible for the great landscaping and architectural project that transformed the Jewish temple into a marvel of the ancient world. For this reason the temple that stood in Jesus's day is sometimes called "Herod's temple." Thus, Rome, under Augustus Caesar, ruled over Israel as the New Testament opened in the time of Christ. Other Roman officials appear throughout the pages of the New Testament, including Pontius Pilate, Sergius Paulus, Gallio, Felix, and Festus, as well as later Caesars and the various Herods who ruled on behalf of Rome.

Political Oppression Created a Longing for the Messiah

The restrictive policies of foreign domination and the disappointing outcome of Jewish self-government worked together to increase among the Jews a general longing for perfect justice and the coming of their promised Messiah. The developing economies of a succession of empires lured Jews to foreign markets or otherwise displaced them as refugees away from their homeland. The synagogues these Jews established abroad took the Scriptures far beyond the borders of ancient Israel. Eventually these synagogues became the launching pads for churches as Paul preached Christ in them "first to the Jew, and also to the Greek" (Rom 1:16). In God's time, according to Paul, "when the time came to

This veiled (symbolizing a sacred nature) bust represents Augustus, who ruled from 27 BC to AD 14, at a mature age as Pontifex Maximus.

completion, God sent his Son" (Gal 4:4) into the world that was already prepared for Him.

The Dead Sea Scrolls

The most famous of the intertestamental texts are the Dead Sea Scrolls. These appear to be from the library of a sect of Jews called the Essenes, who rebelled against the Jerusalem temple and the Maccabean leadership. During the time of Jesus, these sectarians lived as monks near the Dead Sea. This all-male community followed a "Teacher of Righteousness" who they believed was inspired to interpret Old Testament texts. The discovery of the Dead Sea Scrolls helped verify the accuracy and authenticity of the text of the Old Testament Scriptures.

A fragment from the Dead Sea Scrolls.

For Further Reading

Bruce, F. F. *New Testament History*. New York: Doubleday, 1969.

Jeffers, J. S. *The Greco-Roman World of the New Testament Era*. Downers Grove, IL: InterVarsity, 1999.

Metzger, Bruce M. *The New Testament: Its Background, Growth, and Content*. 3rd ed. Rev. and enl. Nashville: Abingdon, 2003.

Price, Randall. *Secrets of the Dead Sea Scrolls*. Eugene, OR: Harvest House, 1996.

Richardson, Peter. *Herod: King of the Jews and Friend of the Romans*. Columbia: University of South Carolina Press, 1996.

Russell, D. S. *Between the Testaments*. London: SCM Press, 1960.

Scott, J. Julius, Jr. *Jewish Backgrounds of the New Testament*. Grand Rapids: Baker, 1995.

Tenney, Merrill. *New Testament Times*. Grand Rapids: Eerdmans, 1995.

Vanderkam, J. C. *The Dead Sea Scrolls Today*. Grand Rapids: Eerdmans, 1994

Notes

1. Josephus, *Against Apion*, 1.8.

2. Though Jerusalem fell to Babylon in 586 BC, deportations from Jerusalem to Babylon began as early as 605. This makes the captivity of Israel in Babylon roughly compatible to Jeremiah's round prediction of seventy years, shortened a little because of God's mercy (Jer 29:10; cf. 2 Chr 36:15–23).

3. The oldest traditions say that seventy-two scribes originally worked to translate the "divine law" into Greek. The Latin word for "seventy" is *septuaginta*. Eventually the entire Old Testament in Greek was called the Septuagint. The oldest accounts of the translation are in the Letter of Aristeas and the Fragments of Aristobulus. A masterful review of the current state of scholarly opinion can be found in Jennifer M. Dines, *The Septuagint* (London: T&T Clark, 2005).

4. See sidebar "The Dead Sea Scrolls," page 337. The Essenes eventually settled in a community near the Dead Sea. The Dead Sea Scrolls are believed to be part of their library.

5. For ease of reference, historians often separate the military process of winning Jewish independence from the period of Jewish self-rule under the Hasmonean priests. The struggle for independence is called the Maccabean period (167–142 BC). The period of self-rule is called the Hasmonean period (142–63 BC).

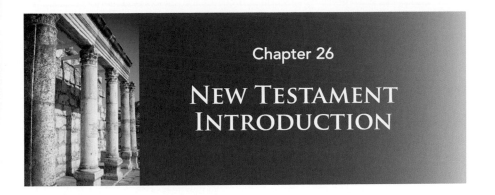

Chapter 26

NEW TESTAMENT INTRODUCTION

T he New Testament is the story of Jesus Christ and the church He established. It begins with His birth and moves through the details of His life and ministry, climaxing with His death and resurrection. From the opening pages of the Gospels, Jesus is depicted as the greatest person who has ever lived. History records many great men and women whose lives have made a deep impact on others; however, the greatest of them does not hold a candle to the blazing brilliance of Jesus.

As the opening pages of the New Testament unfold before us, we walk with Him on the grassy hillsides of Galilee. We sail with Him across the lake and travel with His disciples as they traverse the hills and valleys of Judea. We listen as He teaches, and we watch as He dies for the sins of the world. Then, with amazing wonder, we see Him rise from the dead and commission His disciples to go into all the world proclaiming the "good news." We read on with heartfelt anticipation as the church is born and the message of salvation is spread throughout the Roman Empire. We see the triumph and troubles of the early Christians and read the inspired words of the apostles that carry us to the final promise of Christ's return.

From Jesus's first coming as a baby in a manger to His triumphal return at His Second Coming, the New Testament is all about Him. Jesus is deity on foot! He walks among men, but He lives above men. He looks like a man, but He talks like God. He is fully human and yet totally divine. He is the window through which we see the nature and character of God. And He is the mirror through which we see ourselves in relation to God. Oxford theologian Alister McGrath states, "Jesus is God—that is the basic meaning of the incarnation."[1] While God is infinite, immortal, and invisible, He is revealed personally in Jesus Christ in the pages of the New Testament.

The Manuscripts

The New Testament consists of twenty-seven books that were written in *Koine* Greek, or common Greek. All the authors were Jews, with the possible exception of Luke. Some authors penned their books themselves, while others dictated the contents to an assistant or scribe.[2] The original manuscripts, or "autographs," no longer exist. However, about 5,000 copies do exist as well as 13,000 portions of New Testament manuscripts. By comparing these, biblical scholars can determine the original text of the New Testament with incredible accuracy. In fact, the New Testament is the most validated and authoritative document of the ancient world. By contrast, other ancient works, such as Plato (7 copies), Pliny (7 copies), Thucydides (8 copies), Herodotus (8 copies), Aristotle (49 copies), and Julius Caesar (10 copies), have minimal ancient manuscript support compared to the New Testament.[3]

Folio from Papyrus 46 (c. 200 AD), containing 2 Cor 11:33–12:9.

The Canon

The various books of the New Testament were originally written between AD 45 and AD 95. At first they circulated independently but were eventually copied and collected to be circulated among the churches. Written in common Greek, they could be read easily by the ordinary people of the Roman Empire. The New Testament contains twenty-seven different books by nine different authors written over a span of only half a century. As questions arose about which books should be accepted as inspired and authoritative, the rules of canonicity began to develop with a major emphasis on apostolic authorship and consistent Christian orthodoxy.[4]

Merrill Tenney observed, "A survey of this literature will show that in the last third of the first century the church was rapidly consolidating into a recognized institution."[5] As those years passed, the churches began to acquire a doctrinal solidarity based on apostolic authority that led to the eventual recognition of the twenty-seven books of the New Testament canon. J. Gresham

Machen noted, "From the very beginning Christianity was a religion with a Book."[6] For the original Christians the authority of Jesus was continued by the authority of the apostles and reaffirmed by the subsequent generations of orthodox believers.

The Divisions

The books of the New Testament are generally organized into four divisions: the Gospels, the Acts of the Apostles, the Letters, and the Revelation.

Gospels:	Matthew, Mark, Luke, and John
Acts of the Apostles:	From Pentecost to Paul's imprisonment
Letters:	Paul's letters to the churches and Timothy, Titus, and Philemon; the general letters of James, Peter, John, Jude, and the letter to the Hebrews
Revelation:	Prophecies of Christ's return and the church's glorious future

The Gospels

The word *gospel* (Gk. *Euangelion*) was used by Christians to refer to the message of Jesus Christ contained in the four Gospels in the New Testament. The word *gospel*, that is, "good news," was used to describe the announcement of important events. It literally means "God announcement." English translators chose to represent this word with the Old English term *godspell*, which literally meant "God's story" or "good story." Today the term is most popularly explained as the "good news." The Gospels tell us about the life, deeds, teaching, death, and current position of Jesus and what this can mean for us today, tomorrow, and into eternity. The Gospels are declarations of what is true—specifically, the truth about Jesus as well as the truth Jesus told.

The four Gospels present four portraits of Jesus, each in its own characteristic manner. I. Howard Marshall commented: "The greatness of this person could not have been captured in one picture. So we have four portraits, each bringing out its own distinctive facets of the character of Jesus."[7] Matthew, the Hebrew tax collector, writes for the Hebrew mind. Mark, the travel companion of Paul and Peter, writes for the Roman mind. Luke, Paul's physician-missionary, writes with the Greek mentality in view. John's Gospel is different by nature from the other three. It is an interpretation of the facts of Jesus's life with an emphasis on His deity.

Four Portraits of Christ	
Matthew	King of the Jews
Mark	Servant of the Lord
Luke	Son of Man
John	Son of God

With the exception of scant references by ancient secular writers, our entire knowledge of the life of Jesus comes from these Gospel accounts.[8] Most likely the early accounts were passed on verbally and then recorded in the Greek manuscripts between AD 60 and AD 90. All four Gospels build on genuine historical tradition and preserve different aspects of it so that we might see the Savior in the fullness of His person. The basic purpose of the Gospels is to present the good news of the Redeemer-Savior. They present Jesus as the Messiah of Israel, the Son of God, and the Savior of the world. The Gospels were written so that their readers would come to believe in Christ and receive eternal life (cf. John 20:31).

Because Matthew, Mark, and Luke have more stories in common with one another, these three Gospels are called the "Synoptic Gospels." Their story lines are similar but not identical. By contrast, the Gospel of John focuses more on the seven lengthy discourses of Christ. If John wrote after the other three Gospels were written, his major purpose was to emphasize things he remembered that Jesus said and did that were not recorded in the other Gospels (e.g., the resurrection of Lazarus). Scholars have proposed various theories of dependence or interdependence of the original composition of the three Synoptic Gospels with

A page from the Book of Kells, a manuscript containing the four Gospels (c. AD 800). The Gospels were often represented in illustrations with different creatures (traditionally, a man, a lion, an ox, and an eagle) symbolizing the different perspectives of Jesus that each presented.

some scholars favoring Matthew and others Mark as the first Gospel written. Still others have proposed an original source document called Q (German, *Quell*, "source") that was used as a source of information by Matthew and Luke.[9] However, no one has ever discovered manuscript evidence for such a document.

Acts of the Apostles

The book of Acts is the biographical account of the earliest Christians and the historical record of their evangelistic endeavors. It represents the historic transition from Judaism to Christianity. The early church's initial setting was thoroughly Jewish and involved the temple, the synagogues, feast days, and issues of circumcision and kosher diets. But as the story develops, so does the outreach of Christianity into the Gentile world of the Roman Empire in the first century AD. Steve Ger writes, "In a series of vignettes, or 'postcards,' some historical, some biographical, still others theological, Acts reveals the successes and defeats, conquests and tragedies . . . and the ultimate triumph of these pioneers of the Jesus movement."[10]

The book of Acts begins with the ascension of Christ and His commission to the apostles to take the gospel message from Jerusalem to the rest of the world (Acts 1:8). The story of the early church begins with the outpouring of the Holy Spirit on the day of Pentecost (chap. 2) and focuses initially on the ministry of Peter (chaps. 2–10). Then the story shifts to the ministry of Paul (chaps. 11–28), with Luke, the author, often providing an eyewitness account (e.g., references to "we" in 16:10–17; 20:5–15; 21:1–18; 27:1–28:16). This section includes Paul's three missionary journeys, his arrest in Jerusalem, internment in Caesarea, and imprisonment in Rome.

The book ends with a final "update" as Paul awaits his trial before Caesar and the gospel message continues spreading as the church continues to grow. Ger writes: "The book of Acts grants readers a unique and fascinating glimpse into the world of the early church. We peer through two millennia and still see the vivid foundations of our own faith."[11] The book of Acts shows us the gospel in action. As the earliest Christians spread out across the Roman Empire, the "good news" of salvation in Jesus Christ goes with them. Despite the obstacles of rejection, persecution, and even martyrdom, the life-changing message of Christ resonates in the minds of the lost and reverberates in the hearts of the redeemed.

Timetable for Early Period of the Church		
Beginning Date	Pentecost, May AD 30	Acts 2:5
Gospel advances to Jews	AD 30	Acts 2–7
Gospel advances to Samaritans	AD 31	Acts 8
Conversion of the apostle Paul	AD 32	Acts 9
Paul's first visit to Jerusalem	AD 35	Acts 9
Gospel advances to Gentiles	c. AD 37–38	Acts 10–11
Herod Agrippa dies	AD 44	Acts 12
First missionary journey	AD 46–48	Acts 13–14
Jerusalem Council	AD 49	Acts 15
Second missionary journey	AD 50–52	Acts 16–18
Third missionary journey	AD 53–57	Acts 19–21
Paul's journey to Jerusalem	Pentecost, May AD 57	Acts 20:16

The Letters

The New Testament Epistles are personal letters written to churches and individuals. While they follow the typical form of first-century letters in the Roman world, they uniquely express Christian truth. Even Paul's greetings of "grace and peace" are unparalleled in the ancient world. F. F. Bruce said, "Paul's letters are our primary source for his life and work [and] . . . our knowledge of the beginnings of Christianity, for they are the earliest datable Christian documents . . . [many] . . . of them having been written between eighteen and thirty years after the death of Christ."[12]

The content of the New Testament Letters is doctrinal and personal. The apostolic authors wrote to express the great truths of the Christian life: love, forgiveness, grace, faith, salvation, and sanctification. They also wrote to answer questions, solve problems, resolve conflicts, and give personal advice. The authors believed they were the recipients of God's grace through Jesus Christ and committed their lives to spread the message of that grace to the world. Roland Allen notes, "In a little more than ten years St. Paul established the Church in four provinces of the empire: Galatia, Macedonia, Achaia, and Asia."[13] From there the message went in all directions by the end of the first century.

As the early Christian leaders spread out across the Roman Empire, they used letters to communicate with one another. The typical letters of the Greco-Roman period included an address, a greeting, a body, and a conclusion. Just like their Greco-Roman counterparts, the New Testament Letters written in common (*koine*) Greek range from rhetorical masterpieces designed for public dissemination (e.g., Romans, Hebrews) to short personal notes (e.g., Philemon, 2 and 3 John).[14] Many of the biblical letters indicate the use of scribes (amanuenses) who wrote what the human authors dictated. For example, Tertius identifies himself as writing the letter to the Romans (16:12) on behalf of Paul, but in other cases only the body of the letter was written down by an assistant (cf. 2 Thess 3:17; Gal 6:11).

The Epistles are arranged in the New Testament as those written by the apostle Paul and signed by him (13 letters) and those written by James, Peter, John, and Jude (7 letters) with Hebrews recognized by some as Pauline and by others as anonymous, and thus it is positioned in the canon between the Pauline and the General Epistles.

The Pauline Epistles include Romans, 1 Corinthians, 2 Corinthians, Galatians, Ephesians, Philippians, Colossians, 1 Thessalonians, 2 Thessalonians, 1 Timothy, 2 Timothy, Titus, and Philemon.

A manuscript from the Dead Sea Scrolls as currently preserved at the Citadel in Amman, Jordan.

The Writings of the Apostle Paul[15]	
When	**What**
Written after his first missionary journey	Galatians
Written during his second missionary journey	1 Thessalonians 2 Thessalonians
Written during his third missionary journey	Romans 1 Corinthians 2 Corinthians
Written during his first Roman imprisonment	Ephesians Philippians Colossians Philemon
Written after his release from prison	1 Timothy Titus
Written during his second Roman imprisonment	2 Timothy

General Epistles

The General Epistles include Hebrews, James, 1 Peter, 2 Peter, 1 John, 2 John, 3 John, and Jude. The early church historian Eusebius (AD 265–340) designated the books from James through Jude as "catholic" (or universal) epistles because they are generally addressed to all the churches. The letter to the Hebrews has no epistolary greeting, although the final verses (13:22–25) close with a reference to Timothy and a final greeting, causing most medieval scholars to ascribe the book to Paul, although Tertullian (c. AD 200) ascribed it to Barnabas. Since the Reformation most biblical scholars have preferred to leave the identity of the author anonymous.

The Apocalypse

The final book of the New Testament is the Revelation (Gk. *apocalypsis*). It was written by John on the island of Patmos in the Agean Sea, off the cost of Asia Minor. John was exiled there by the Roman authorities and claimed to receive his prophetic vision of the future from the risen, glorified Christ Himself (Rev 1:1–20). Written in apocalyptic symbolism, the book makes use of numbers, animals, and colors as graphic symbols of prophetic realties. The Revelation (or Apocalypse) uses "and" (Gk. *kai*) more than 1,200 times. The constant use of this conjunction creates a sense of fast-passed movement in the book from one event to the next. The reader is swept away into the dramatic events of the eschatological future, culminating in the triumphal return of Jesus Christ as "King of kings and Lord of lords" (Rev 19:16).

Thus the New Testament begins with the first coming of Christ and ends with the promise of His Second Coming. It begins with Jesus and ends with Jesus, reminding us that these twenty-seven books are really all about Him! They tell the story of Jesus's birth, life, ministry, death, resurrection, and ascension. They record His commission to His disciples to evangelize the world with His "good news" as well as their commitment to do just that, even at the risk of their own lives. They include the personal letters of the apostles detailing the basic doctrines of the Christian church and their instructions for practical Christian living. Throughout those letters the authors write continually of their expectation of the Savior's return, which finds its final expression in the Revelation.

Practical Application

The New Testament introduces us to the person of Jesus Christ. It connects His claims to the Old Testament messianic prophecies and presents

Him as the promised Messiah (Gk. *christos*). As you study these books, you will come face-to-face with those claims and the beliefs and practices of those who first accepted them. As you read, remember that these books were not only written to their original readers, but they continue to speak to us today as well. Let your reading challenge your mind, stretch your faith, and stir your soul. Examine each book for yourself, and let the Spirit of God speak to your heart. Examine the claims of Christ, the life He lived, and the death He died. Ask yourself, how does that one unique and solitary life affect your life? Listen to the words of Jesus as He says, "Follow Me." Remember the words of the apostle who wrote, "These are written so that you may believe that Jesus is the Messiah, the son of God, and that by believing you may have life in his name" (John 20:31).

For Further Reading

Carson, D. A., D. J. Moo, and L. Morris. *An Introduction to the New Testament.* Grand Rapids: Zondervan, 1992.

Gundry, Robert H. *A Survey of the New Testament,* 4th ed. Grand Rapids: Zondervan, 2003.

Guthrie, Donald. *New Testament Introduction.* Downers Grove, IL: IVP, 1990.

Johnson, Luke T. *The Writings of the New Testament.* Philadelphia: Fortress, 1986.

Köstenberger, A. J., L. S. Kellum, and C. L. Quarles. *The Cradle, the Cross, and the Crown: An Introduction to the New Testament.* Nashville: B&H, 2011.

Machen, J. Gresham. *New Testament: An Introduction to Its History and Literature.* Edinburgh: Banner of Truth, 1976.

Tenney, Merrill C. *New Testament Survey.* Grand Rapids: Eerdmans, 1961.

Study Questions

1. Who is the major person and theme of the books of the New Testament?
2. Why have the four Gospels often been called four portraits, and what is the major focus of each one?
3. What is the major story line of the book of Acts?
4. In what way were the New Testament letters similar to other Greco-Roman letters of the first century, and in what way were they unique?
5. Why did the apostles use letters to communicate with Christian churches and individual believers?
6. Why was the Apocalypse (Revelation) placed at the end of the New Testament?

Notes

1. Alister McGrath, *Understanding Jesus* (Grand Rapids: Zondervan, 1990), 107.

2. For example, Paul handwrote some of his earlier letters (Gal 6:11) and dictated his later ones, adding a handwritten salutation to authenticate them (Col 4:18; 2 Thess 3:17).

3. Cf. F. F. Bruce, *The Canon of Scripture* (Downers Grove, IL: InterVarsity Press, 1988), 153; Bruce Metzger, *The Canon of the New Testament* (New York: Oxford University Press, 1987), 90; Josh McDowell, *Evidence That Demands a Verdict* (San Bernardino: Campus Crusade, 1972), 48.

4. For example, the Gnostic "Gospels" of Thomas and Judas fail all the basic standards of canonicity. See Andreas Köstenberger, Michael Kruger, and I. Howard Marshall, *The Heresy of Orthodoxy* (Wheaton: Crossway, 2010), 151ff.

5. Merrill Tenney, *New Testament Survey* (Grand Rapids: Eerdmans, 1993), 127.

6. J. Gresham Machen, *New Testament: An Introduction to Its History and Literature* (Edinburgh: Banner of Truth, 1976), 13.

7. I. Howard Marshall, "The Gospels and Jesus Christ," *Eerdmans Handbook to the Bible* (Grand Rapids: Eerdmans, 1987), 470.

8. See F. F. Bruce, *Jesus and Christian Origins Outside the New Testament* (Grand Rapids: Eerdmans, 1974); and Gary Habermas, *The Historical Jesus: Ancient Evidence for the Life of Christ* (Joplin, MO: College Press, 1996).

9. Cf. David Alan Black, *Why Four Gospels? The Historical Origins of the Gospels* (Grand Rapids: Kregel, 2001); and R. H. Stein, *The Synoptic Problem: An Introduction* (Grand Rapids: Baker, 1987).

10. Steven Ger, *Acts: Witness to the World* (Chattanooga: AMG Publishers, 2004), xi.

11. Ibid., 1.

12. F. F. Bruce, *Paul: An Apostle of the Heart Set Free* (Grand Rapids: Eerdmans, 1977), 16. Bruce adds, "Paul's transparent honesty was incompatible with any such artificiality . . . [because] he wears his heart on his sleeve."

13. Roland Allen, *Missionary Methods: St. Paul's or Ours?* (Eastford, CT: Martino, 2011), 3.

14. See detailed discussion in D. A. Carson, D. J. Moo, and L. Morris, *An Introduction to the New Testament* (Grand Rapids: Zondervan, 1992), 231–35.

15. Bill Jones, *Putting Together the Puzzle of the New Testament* (Colorado Springs: Authentic, 2009), 181.

Chapter 27

MATTHEW

The King of the Jews

M atthew's Gospel serves as the introduction to the entire New Testament. Thus it is saturated with 130 references to the Hebrew Scriptures, emphasizing that Jesus is the fulfillment of the messianic prophecies and types of the Old Testament.[1] The Gospel of Matthew is the most Jewish of all the Gospels. In its inspired pages Jesus of Nazareth is presented as the "King of the Jews" so it is a bridge from the Old to the New Testament. From the opening genealogy to the Great Commission, Jesus is at center stage in this masterful biography of the Messiah. It gives a glimpse of the Savior through Jewish eyes as He challenges His own people to know and love God with all their hearts, souls, and minds.

KEY FACTS

Author:	Matthew (also called Levi)
Recipients:	Written initially for Jewish Christians
Written Where:	Unknown
Date:	AD 60–65
Key Word:	Kingdom (Gk. *basileia*)
Key Verse:	"Where is he who has been born King of the Jews? For we saw his star at its rising and have come to worship him" (2:2).

Author

The titles in every ancient manuscript of this book describe it as the Gospel "according to Matthew." Matthew (or "Levi," as he is called in Mark and Luke) was collecting taxes near Capernaum in the territory of Herod Antipas when he answered Jesus's call, "Follow Me!" (Matt 9:9–13; Mark 2:13–17; Luke 5:27–31). Matthew immediately began to follow Jesus, so Jesus had supper with Matthew, other tax collectors, and sinners that same evening. He was an educated man who could read and write, plus he had to be conversant in Aramaic, Latin, and Greek in order to fulfill his obligations.

Sea of Galilee with a view of the boat landing at Capernaum.

The author shows unusual familiarity with money and coins, which one would expect from a former tax collector. In the dispute over paying taxes, Mark and Luke use the common term *dēnarion*. Matthew alone uses the more precise term *nomisma* (state coin). Matthew also uses three terms for money that occur nowhere else in the New Testament: "tribute" (*didrachmon*), "money" (*statēr*), and "talent" (*talanton*). He also uses "gold" (*chrusos*), "silver" (*arguros*), and "brass" (*chalkos*), which are used elsewhere in the New Testament but do not appear in any other Gospels. In addition, Matthew refers to the "penny" (*dēnarion*), "silver-piece" (*argurion*), and "tribute" (*kēnsos*), which are used in the other Gospels.[2]

Matthew alone records the two parables of the "talents" (large amounts of money of the highest value). He also includes references to "debt," "reckoning," and "money changers," which do not occur elsewhere in other Gospels but which would be familiar to a tax collector (KJV, "publican").

Recipients

Matthew's Gospel names no audience for its message other than that which is implied in its Great Commission. Its message was ultimately intended to go to "all nations" (28:19). Matthew originally crafted this Gospel for a group of Christians who were already familiar with the Old Testament. Both church tradition (external evidence) and the contents of the Gospel itself (internal evidence) suggest that this Gospel was originally written for Jewish Christians who were given the responsibility to share its message with the world.

Irenaeus, Origen, and Eusebius explicitly state that Matthew first wrote in the Hebrew language (or in Aramaic, another Semitic language often referred to as Hebrew) for Hebrew Christians he was serving.[3] Some of the earliest quotations and allusions to Matthew's Gospel come from Syria, a region rich in Jewish culture that also became the hub of early Christian missionary work (Acts 11:19–26; 13:1–3). References to Matthew in the *Didache* (first or early second century) suggest an early Syrian readership for Matthew. Ignatius, a church leader in Antioch of Syria, also shows a familiarity with Matthew's Gospel. These facts suggest that Matthew could have written his Gospel in Syria.

The Herodium, a fortress-palace built by Herod the Great about four miles southeast of Bethlehem, 7.5 miles south of Jerusalem. Herod was buried there. In 40 BC Herod retreated to Masada after the Parthians took Syria. On this location near Bethlehem, he clashed with and defeated the Parthians. To commemorate his victory, Herod built a fortress on the site of the battle and named it for himself. Herod plays an important role in Matthew's account of Jesus's birth and early childhood (Matt 2:1–23).

Internal evidence also suggests that the Gospel was written for Jewish converts to Christianity. Only Matthew's Gospel explicitly restricts the early mission of Jesus and the twelve apostles "to the lost sheep of the house of Israel" (10:6; 15:24). Although Matthew's Gospel hints at a future time when Gentiles would be gathered into the kingdom of heaven with Abraham, Isaac, and Jacob (8:11–12) and records Jesus's Great Commission to make disciples of "all nations" (28:19), the emphasis in Matthew's Gospel is that Jesus's initial ministry was primarily to the Jews.

As would be expected for a Jewish audience, Matthew refers to Jewish practices without taking time to explain them as other Gospel writers do (Mark 7:3; John 19:40). He more often describes Jesus as "Son of David" (1:1; 9:27; 12:23; 15:22; 20:30–31; 21:9, 15; 22:45). He often reverently avoids using God's name in his unique phrase "kingdom of heaven" (33 times) where the other Gospels prefer to use "kingdom of God."

Occasion and Date

Irenaeus (late second century) and Eusebius (fourth century) cite Papias (early second century) as a source for their dating of Matthew. Irenaeus tells us *when* Matthew wrote, and Eusebius tells us *why*. However, both of them described only that Matthew wrote "in Hebrew" (which could mean Aramaic). If the New Testament's Greek Gospel according to Matthew is based on this Semitic text, the comments of Irenaeus and Eusebius suggest a date as early as AD 60–65.

According to Irenaeus, Matthew wrote while Peter and Paul were preaching in Rome and before any of the other Gospels were written. If Irenaeus's report is accurate, Matthew's Gospel—or at least its Semitic basis—was written before the deaths of Paul and Peter in the early to mid-60s AD. Eusebius reports that both apostles died under Nero, who himself was dead by AD 68. This would mean that Matthew's original Semitic Gospel was written prior to his Greek version and probably served as the basis for it.

Genre and Structure

Matthew, the tax collector turned disciple, writes to Jewish believers to emphasize the legitimacy of Jesus as the long-awaited Jewish Messiah. For the unbelievers he portrays the One who is the Savior of all people everywhere. His arguments are cogent, his style is vibrant, and his portrayal of Christ is magnificent.

Matthew provides some of Jesus's most prominent sermons, parables, and miracles, plus a record of important messages such as the Sermon on the Mount (chaps. 5–7), the parables of the kingdom (chap. 13), and the Olivet Discourse (chaps. 24–25). He also provides an eyewitness account of such significant events as the transfiguration, the triumphal entry, the crucifixion, and the resurrection. He explains the character and nature of the ministry of John the Baptist as the last of the prophets. He takes us to Caesarea Philippi, a Gentile area, where Jesus announces that He will build His church, and then he lets us listen as the risen Savior challenges His disciples to "go . . . and make disciples of all nations" (Matt 28:19).

Matthew also gives special attention to the rejection of Jesus by the Jewish leaders. He exposes the religious blindness of his fellow countrymen, and he demonstrates Jesus's superior understanding of the person of God, the intent of the law, and the proper application of biblical truth. The evangelist is especially critical of the scribes and Pharisees while pointing out that the common people gladly listened to the Savior. Throughout Matthew's Gospel he draws our attention to the One who is the rightful king of Israel. Jesus is portrayed as being born as a King, living and dying as a King, and coming again as the ultimate King of kings.

Matthew uses 115 words found nowhere else in the New Testament. Matthew recorded specific details of Jesus's teaching/sermons and preserved them in his Gospel. Whether these were originally recorded in the "sayings" (*logia*) in Aramaic, as Papias suggests, is now difficult to determine. This Gospel records the unique message of Jesus in natural-flowing Greek prose rather than clumsy translated Greek from an Aramaic original.

The most unique term in Matthew's Gospel is the "kingdom of heaven" (Greek *he basileia tōn ouranōn*), which occurs thirty-two times. It appears only in Mathew and nowhere else in the New Testament. By contrast, "the kingdom of God" occurs fifteen times in Mark, thirty-three times in Luke, and only five times in Matthew (6:33; 12:28; 19:24; 21:31, 43).

Outline

I. Person of the King (1:1–4:25)
II. Proclamation of the King (5:1–7:29)
III. Power of the King (8:1–12:50)
IV. Parables of the Kingdom (13:1–13:53)
V. Presentation of the King (13:54–23:39)
VI. Prophecies of the King (24:1–25:46)
VII. Passion and Triumph of the King (26:1–28:20)

Message

I. Person of the King (Matthew 1:1–4:25)

Matthew's Gospel opens with the genealogy of Jesus traced all the way back through King David to Abraham, the forefather of the Jewish people. This emphasizes Jesus's Jewish identity and position as the royal "Son of David." This kingly emphasis is sustained throughout the book.

In Matthew, Jesus Is King
King's Name—Emmanuel (1:23)
King's Authority—Will come a leader (2:6)
King's Coming—Prepare the way (3:3)
King's Proclamation—Repent because the kingdom of heaven has come near (4:17)
King's Loyalty—Seek first His kingdom (6:33)
King's Opposition—Suffer many things (16:21)
King's Sacrifice—Give His life (20:28)
King's Task—The King of the Jews (27:37)
King's Triumph—He is risen (28:6)
King's Dominion—All power (28:19)
King's Command—Go . . . make disciples (28:19)

Jesus was born to the virgin Mary (1:18–23). John the Baptist prepared the way for His coming (3:1–17). He resisted temptation (4:1–11) and began His ministry by calling twelve disciples in Galilee (4:12–25).

II. Proclamation of the King (Matthew 5:1–7:29)

Most commentators recognize that Matthew arranged Jesus's sermons so readers could better follow what Jesus said about specific subjects. Matthew's Gospel describes five extended teaching sessions, which are arranged in five major discourses.

Chapter	Discourse	Theme
5–7	Sermon on the Mount	The Righteousness of the Kingdom of Heaven
9:36–10:42	Sending of the Twelve	Announcing to Israel the Kingdom of Heaven
13	Parables of the Kingdom	Principles of the Kingdom of Heaven
17:22–18:35	Kingdom and the Church	Applying Kingdom Principles to the Church
23–25	Sermon on Eschatology	God's Judgment When His Kingdom Comes

The Sermon on the Mount. The Sermon on the Mount contrasts the righteousness of the kingdom of heaven with the righteousness of the scribes and Pharisees. According to Jesus, true righteousness cannot be defined by following lists of things to do or not do (5:20). A follower of Christ must not only avoid murder, adultery, and breaking oaths but also avoid the causes of these sins: hatred, lust, and the desire to manipulate the truth (5:21–26, 28–30, 33–37). Since God designed marriage to be permanent, no one should seek legal loopholes for divorce (5:31–32; cf. 19:8–12). True righteousness is not merely a matter of external deeds but the attitudes and intentions of the heart.

View of the Sea of Galilee from near the Church of the Beatitudes in Israel.

III. Power of the King (Matthew 8:1–12:50)

The Sending of the Twelve. Jesus's instructions to the twelve apostles helped them speak to Israel, but many of their principles are still applicable today. Jesus instructed all His disciples to pray that God would send more laborers into the harvest (9:38). Faithful preaching will encounter persecution (10:16–23), even from family members (10:34–36). Cooperation with missionaries is like cooperating with Jesus (10:42).

Miracles. Matthew reports no fewer than twenty-one miracles, though summary statements like 8:16 show that Jesus performed far more miracles than the ones Matthew described. Five of the healing miracles Matthew described included the casting out of demons (8:32; 9:32; 12:22; 15:28; 17:18), while others mentioned specific diseases (8:14; 9:2; 9:20, 27; 12:10; 20:30). Jesus also miraculously fed thousands of people with a few loaves and fish—not once but twice (14:13; 15:32). He calmed a raging storm at sea (8:26), raised the dead (9:25), walked on water (14:25), and miraculously directed Peter to find money in a fish's mouth so they could pay the temple tax (17:27). The power of Jesus in Matthew's Gospel extends far beyond that of ordinary kings. Jesus is shown to have power over all demons, disease, death, hunger, the weather, and even over the basic elements of the earth.

Miracles of Jesus			
Miracle	**Bible Passage**		
Water Turned to Wine				John 2:1
Many Healings	Matt 4:23	Mark 1:32		
Healing of a Leper	Matt 8:1	Mark 1:40	Luke 5:12	
Healing of a Roman Centurion's Servant	Matt 8:5		Luke 7:1	
Healing of Peter's Mother-in-law	Matt 8:14	Mark 1:29	Luke 4:38	
Calming of the Storm at Sea	Matt 8:23	Mark 4:35	Luke 8:22	
Healing of the Wild Men of Gadara	Matt 8:28	Mark 5:1	Luke 8:26	
Healing of a Lame Man	Matt 9:1	Mark 2:1	Luke 5:18	
Healing of a Woman with a Hemorrhage	Matt 9:20	Mark 5:25	Luke 8:43	
Raising of Jairus's Daughter	Matt 9:23	Mark 5:22	Luke 8:41	
Healing of Two Blind Men	Matt 9:27			
Healing of a Demon-Possessed Man	Matt 9:32			
Healing of Man with a Withered Hand	Matt 12:10	Mark 3:1	Luke 6:6	
Feeding of 5,000 People	Matt 14:15	Mark 6:35	Luke 9:12	John 6:1
Walking on the Sea	Matt 14:22	Mark 6:47		John 6:16
Healing of the Syrophoenician's Daughter	Matt 15:21	Mark 7:24		
Feeding of 4,000 People	Matt 15:32	Mark 8:1		
Healing of an Epileptic Boy	Matt 17:14	Mark 9:14	Luke 9:37	
Healing of Two Blind Men at Jericho	Matt 20:30			
Healing of a Man with an Unclean Spirit		Mark 1:23		

Miracles of Jesus (continued)				
Miracle		**Bible Passage**		
Healing of a Deaf, Speechless Man		Mark 7:31		
Healing of a Blind Man at Bethesda		Mark 8:22		
Healing of Blind Bartimaeus		Mark 10:46	Luke 18:35	
A Miraculous Catch of Fish			Luke 5:4	John 21:1
Raising of a Widow's Son			Luke 7:11	
Healing of a Stooped Woman			Luke 13:11	
Healing of a Man with Dropsy			Luke 14:1	
Healing of Ten Lepers			Luke 17:11	
Healing of Malchus's Ear			Luke 22:50	
Healing of a Royal Official's Son				John 4:46
Healing of a Lame Man at Bethesda				John 5:1
Healing of a Blind Man				John 9:1
Raising Lazarus				John 11:38

IV. Parables of the Kingdom (Matthew 13:1–53)

The parables of the kingdom relay many important principles. The Sower teaches that certain differences between people will produce different responses when the gospel is preached (13:1–9, 18–23). The Wheat and Tares and the Net show that some people will be included and some rejected when the kingdom comes. The Hidden Treasure and the Pearl show that the kingdom is more valuable than all other possessions (13:44–46).

V. Presentation of the King (Matthew 13:54–23:39)

Matthew's Gospel reaches a climax at this point when Jesus presents Himself at the synagogue in His hometown of Nazareth and is rejected (13:54–58). Next, John the Baptist is beheaded (14:1–12). While still more miracles follow, the tension with the Jewish leaders continues to grow. At a crucial point Jesus withdraws and takes the disciples north to Caesarea Philippi, a Gentile city, where He announces a new assembly ("church," Gk. *ekklesia*) which He will build upon the foundation of the apostles and their confession: "You are the Messiah, the Son of the living God." (16:16). This is immediately followed by the transfiguration of Christ in all His glory before Peter, James, and John (17:1–9).

Mount Hermon, where some scholars believe Jesus's transfiguration occurred.

Afterward, Jesus predicted His betrayal and death (17:22–23). He dealt with the rich young ruler who turned away "because he had many possessions" (19:22). By contrast to wealth and position, Jesus announced, "The last will be first, and the first last" (20:16). The triumphal entry follows as Jesus officially presents Himself as the promised Messiah (21:1–11). Shouts of "hosanna to the son of David" clearly indicated the common people accepted His claim, but chapter 22 makes equally clear that the leaders (Herodians, Sadducees, and Pharisees) did not. Having brilliantly answered these opponents' questions, Jesus denounced them as religious hypocrites (23:1–36) and wept over Jerusalem because of their continued rejection.

VI. Prophecies of the King (Matthew 24:1–25:46)

Having visited the temple one last time, Jesus predicted the temple would be destroyed stone by stone (24:1–2). His prophecy (called the Olivet Discourse) was literally fulfilled forty years later when the Romans destroyed the temple in AD 70. However, Jesus also predicted a time of tribulation that would come in the end times and be followed by His triumphal return in the clouds of heaven (24:30–31). Afterwards He announced He would judge the nations to determine who could enter His kingdom (25:34).[4]

VII. Passion and Triumph of the King (Matthew 26:1–28:20)

Soon after Peter confessed that Jesus is "the Messiah, the Son of the living God" (16:16), "Jesus began to point out to His disciples that He must go to Jerusalem and suffer many things from the elders, chief priests, and scribes, be killed, and be raised the third day" (16:21; cf. 20:18–19). On the way to Jerusalem, Jesus explained that His death would be a "ransom"—a payment so others could be free (20:28). When Jesus established the Lord's Supper, He taught that His blood would be "shed for many for the forgiveness of sins" (26:28). After His death and resurrection Jesus appeared to His disciples to announce His royal authority, "All authority has been given to Me in heaven and on earth" (28:18). He also promised to be with the disciples until "the end of the age" as they go to "make disciples of all nations, baptizing them in the name of the Father and of the Son and of the Holy Spirit" (28:19–20).

Practical Application

Matthew's message is about King Jesus and the kingdom of heaven. This Gospel describes the powerful and victorious role of King Jesus as well as the standards, blessings, and ultimate triumph of the kingdom of God. Matthew tells that Jesus bought us with the sacrifice of His own life and His victory over death. Now Jesus expects His followers to proclaim the gospel to the end of the age. Jesus taught His followers to pray, "Your kingdom come. Your will be done on earth as it is in heaven" (6:10), showing that one day He will establish His kingdom.

Jesus's promise, "I am with you always" (28:20) guarantees the success of the church's mission because it is really His mission carried out by His disciples. The closing promise, though given to the apostles, is transmitted to every generation of believers (cf. John 17:20). The phrase "to the end of the age" means that Christ's empowerment to evangelize the world is available in every age, even to the end of the church age. There is no excuse, then, for failing to exercise that power in our day. Jesus followed His great prediction "I will build my church" (Matt 16:18) with his Great Commission "Go, therefore, and make disciples of all nations" (28:19). Therefore, we must conclude that He intends for all of us who believe in Him to continually take the promise of His gospel and the claims of His lordship to the entire world in our generation.

For Further Reading

Blomberg, Craig. *Matthew*. NAC. Nashville: B&H, 1992.
Hindson, Ed, and James Borland, *Matthew: The King Is Coming*. Chattanooga: AMG, 2006.
Keener, Craig S. *A Commentary on the Gospel of Matthew*. Grand Rapids: Eerdmans, 1999.
MacArthur, John. *Matthew*. MNTC, 4 Vols. Chicago: Moody, 1987–1989.
Osborne, Grant R. *Matthew*. ZECNT. Grand Rapids: Zondervan, 2010.
Turner, David L. *Matthew*. BECNT. Grand Rapids: Baker, 2008.
Walvoord, John F. *Matthew: Thy Kingdom Come*. Chicago: Moody, 1974.

Study Questions

1. What evidence in the Gospel itself and in the testimony of ancient Christians demonstrates that Matthew the tax collector is the author of this Gospel?
2. For whom was this Gospel initially written, and why do we think so?
3. Why is Matthew's Gospel so naturally divided into more than one outline?
4. What is the major theme in Matthew's Gospel, and how is that theme presented?
5. What evidence do we have that the message of Matthew's Gospel was ultimately intended for the whole world?

Notes

1. See list in W. Graham Scroggie, *A Guide to the Gospels* (Grand Rapids: Kregel, 1985), 267–72. Scroggie's detailed analysis remains a classic even today. Cf. also G. R. Osborne, *Matthew*, ZECNT (Grand Rapids: Zondervan, 2010), 21–24.

2. See Donald Guthrie, *New Testament Introduction* (Downers Grove, IL: InterVarsity, 1990), 52.

3. Cf. Stanley D. Toussaint, *Behold the King: A Study of Matthew* (Portland, OR: Multnomah, 1980), 19. Also, John F. Walvoord, *Matthew: Thy Kingdom Come* (Chicago: Moody, 1974), 13.

4. Matthew uses a lesson on the judgment of the world to conclude each of the five major "sermons" in his Gospel (7:21–27; 10:32–42; 13:47–50; 18:23–35; 25:31–46). For a detailed study of the Olivet Discourse, see John MacArthur and Richard Mayhue, *Christ's Prophetic Plans* (Chicago: Moody, 2012).

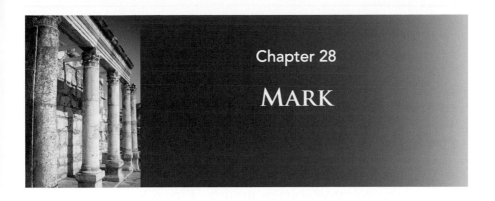

Chapter 28

MARK

The Divine Servant

The Gospel of Mark presents Jesus as "the Son of God" and the perfect slave/servant of God. A slave's birth was unimportant, so Mark does not include the birth of Christ. A slave is expected to rush from task to task and to do any job immediately so a key word in Mark is "immediately" (Gk. *eutheos*). The narrative is action packed so Jesus's acts of service are relived and His words and works are rehearsed. Jesus, the servant, used His supernatural powers to heal the sick and raise the dead because He was actually the Savior-King. Jewish officials felt threatened by Him and plotted His death; but after three days in the tomb, He supernaturally rose from the dead, appeared to many eyewitnesses, and then ascended to heaven. His final commission was that His disciples should be servants and "go into all the world and preach the gospel to all creation. Whoever believes and is baptized will be saved, but whoever does not believe will be condemned" (Mark 16:15–16).

KEY FACTS	
Author:	John Mark
Recipients:	Christian believers in Roman culture
Date:	AD 65
Key Word:	Immediately (Gk. *eutheos*)
Key Verse:	"For even the Son of Man did not come to be served, but to serve, and to give his life as a ransom for many" (10:45).

361

Author

The testimony to Mark's authorship of the Gospel was early and undisputed. In the early second century Papias and Justin Martyr both say the second Gospel was written by Mark based on information from Peter.[1] The Greek title *Kata Markon*, "according to Mark," appears on the earliest manuscripts. It is hard to believe that anyone would ascribe this Gospel to such a minor character as John Mark if he were not the actual author. John was his Jewish name while Mark was his Roman name.

Mark lived in Jerusalem during the time of Jesus, and it is thought that the upper room was in his mother, Mary's, house. The early church often met there so Mark was well acquainted with the apostles. Mark was probably at the house in AD 44 when an angel released Peter from the deadly grasp of Herod Agrippa I (Acts 12:12). Mark was also a cousin of Barnabas (Col 4:10) and assisted Paul and Barnabas on their first missionary journey until he left them midway and returned to Jerusalem (Acts 13:5, 13).

Paul refused to allow Mark on the next journey, so Barnabas took Mark with him to Cyprus in about AD 50. Ten years later, however, Mark was with Paul in Rome as a "coworker" (Col 4:10; Phlm 24) so his initial failure was not final. Mark also served alongside Peter in Babylon for a while. Even as Timothy was Paul's son in the faith, in the same way Peter called Mark his son (1 Pet 5:13). In his final epistle Paul asked for Mark to join him in Rome, noting that Mark was "useful to me in the ministry" (2 Tim 4:11).

Recipients

There are several indications that Mark wrote his Gospel with a Gentile Roman audience in mind. First, Mark is the only Gospel writer to mention that Simon the Cyrenian, the man who carried Jesus's cross, was the father of Alexander and Rufus (15:21). But why include the names of the sons of this little-known character? In Rom 16:13, Paul greeted a Roman Christian named Rufus. It is hard to imagine any other reason for Mark to include this reference unless he was writing to believers in Rome who knew this man.

Second, Mark uses Latinisms twelve times in his Gospel, though none of the other Gospels do this. Mark's Gospel was written in Greek, but Mark takes certain Latin words and turns them into Greek. Examples are *spekoulatora* for executioner (6:27), *kenson* for taxes (12:14), *quadrans* for the value of the widow's two coins (12:42), *praetorium* for the governor's residence (15:16), and *centurion* for a leader of 100 (15:39).

Third, Mark translates any Semitic words he uses such as *Boanerges* (3:17), *talitha koum* (5:41), *corban* (7:11), *Ephphatha* (7:34), *Bartimaeus*

(10:46), *Abba* (14:36), *Golgotha* (15:22), and Jesus's words on the cross *Eloi, Eloi, lemá sabachtháni*, "My God, my God, why have you abandoned me?" (15:34).

Fourth, there is only one quote from the Old Testament (1:2–3) and a marked absence of references to the law of Moses. This shows that Mark does not presume his readers have much of a biblical background. Also, Mark regularly explains Jewish customs and geography for his Gentile readers. Mark explains that the Jews will not eat unless they first wash their hands (7:2–4), that the Mount of Olives is "across from the temple complex" (13:3), and that the Jews sacrifice the Passover lamb "on the first day of Unleavened Bread" (14:12).

Ancient marketplace in Rome, Italy.

Occasion and Date

According to early church tradition, Mark was a close disciple of Peter so he heard Peter tell and retell the stories about Jesus everywhere they went. After relating the story of the transfiguration, Peter expressed a desire for believers to "be able to recall these things at any time" (2 Pet 1:15). These words may indicate Peter's desire to leave behind a written record of Jesus's words and deeds before his martyrdom in AD 64–65.

Irenaeus, an early church father around AD 180, says that after Peter's departure, Mark, the disciple and interpreter of Peter, handed down in writing what Peter had preached.[2] This would date Mark's Gospel sometime after AD 65 and before the Jewish temple was destroyed in AD 70. Others conservatively dated this Gospel about AD 60, before the concluding events recorded in the book of Acts (AD 62).

Some scholars insist that Mark was the first Gospel written because Matthew and Luke share large literary connections with Mark including his story order and word selection.[3] Others, however, favor Matthew as the first written Gospel. Still others view both as reflecting early oral traditions. Perhaps a better way forward is to note that Mark follows the outline of Peter's typical preaching as seen, for example, in his message to Cornelius and his household (Acts 10:34–43). Long before any Gospel accounts were written down, there was a spoken presentation of the message. This oral tradition included a set format that was repeated, though with some variation, over and over again. It is possible that the three Synoptic Gospels—Matthew, Mark, and Luke—view Christ in a similar manner and have many verbal correspondences not because they copied one another but because this was the way Christ's life was regularly told in the early church.

Mark's theological purpose was to explain the most significant life in all of human history. Who was Jesus? He was the Son of God (Mark 1:1, 11; 14:61; 15:39); Son of Man (2:10; 8:31; 13:26); Messiah (8:29); and Lord (1:3; 7:28). With Peter and the other apostles passing off the scene, it was imperative to have an authentic written record of the good news found in Jesus Christ.

Genre and Structure

The Gospel genre is unique because the Gospels are not just biographies that recount a person's background, family history, and career. A Gospel is a unique blend of narrative, poetry, and proverb. It is filled with figures of speech and paints life situations that one can relive as though he were there. Mark's King is a Savior-King who conquered demons, disease, and death.

In a brief prologue of just thirteen verses, Mark introduces Jesus Christ, the main character, to his audience. Mark weaves in both expectation, "Prepare the way for the Lord" (1:3), and conflict as Christ is immediately "tempted by Satan" (1:13). This is followed by a large section (1:14–8:30) that serves to complicate the plot as in a Greek tragedy. There was success but also hostility, opposition, and conflict. Withdrawal from public sight was sometimes required. This culminated in a crisis moment when Peter and the disciples recognized Jesus as the Messiah (8:29–30).

Mark's drama follows (8:31–15:47) when Christ announces His coming death on three separate occasions (8:31; 9:31; and 10:33) and prepares His disciples for His death and departure. But in the epilogue (16:1–20) Christ rises from the dead, making possible the Gospel of Mark—the good news about Jesus Christ.

Outline

I. Prologue: The Servant's Identity (1:1–13)
II. The Servant's Words and Works (1:14–8:30)
III. The Servant's Journey to the Cross (8:31–10:52)
IV. The Servant's Ministry and Death in Jerusalem (11:1–15:47)
V. Epilogue: The Servant's Ultimate Victory (16:1–20)

Message

Mark's goal was to present Jesus as the Servant Son of God. He dispenses with any mention of Jesus's birth and childhood and rushes immediately to Jesus's miraculous works. Though Mark includes many teachings and several sermons of Christ, he specializes in what makes Jesus unique. Mark only includes four parables Jesus told but recounts nearly twenty miracles. All of Jesus's activity in Mark focuses on His Galilean ministry until the final week in Jerusalem. About 93 percent of Mark's account, which represents the basic oral preaching of the Gospel story, is also included in parts of Matthew and Luke. By contrast, John, writing later than the three Synoptics, presents different material not seen elsewhere in 92 percent of his Gospel.

Mark's first chapter portrays Jesus's long Sabbath day ministry in Capernaum, His adopted hometown on the northern edge of the Sea of Galilee. First, Jesus came "preaching" (1:14), for He was first and foremost a preacher of the good news. Second, Jesus called four disciples to accompany Him in full-time ministry (1:16–20). John's account reveals that Andrew, Peter, James, and John were following

The synagogue at Capernaum. Jesus was confronted by a demoniac while teaching here (Mark 1:21–27).

Christ for about six months prior to John the Baptist's imprisonment but on an itinerant basis.[4] Their lives would radically change from this moment as they became fishers of men. Third, Jesus cast a demon from a man in the synagogue in the middle of His sermon (1:23–26). Fourth, Jesus healed Peter's mother-in-law (1:29–31). Finally, way into the night Jesus continued to heal all who came to the door of Peter's home (1:32–34).

The next paragraph is a significant commentary on Jesus's prayer life, for the next day, "very early in the morning, while it was still dark, He got up, went out, and made His way to a deserted place. And He was praying" (1:35). Jesus's prayer life was successful because He got up early enough, went far enough away, and stayed long enough. The phrase "was praying" is in a verb tense that portrays continued action in past time. Jesus's prayer life was planned, private, and prolonged.

Some call Mark a passion story with a long introduction. Christ's passion includes His entrance into Jerusalem, His cleansing of the temple, His answering the questions of His opponents, the last supper, His agony in the garden, His arrest, trial, and crucifixion, His burial and resurrection, His postresurrection appearances, and His ascension. Mark 11–16 make up the passion narrative. Mark 1–10 lead up to Christ's passion and point to it. Mark 8:31 says, "Then he began to teach them that it was necessary for the Son of Man to suffer many things and be rejected by the elders, chief priests, and

Sea of Galilee at Nof Ginnosar looking across the Sea to the hills of Galilee.

scribes, be killed, and rise after three days." Jesus repeated this dire prediction in Mark 9:31 and 10:33. Six chapters (11–16) are devoted to that last fateful week in the Savior's life. Just before Mark tells the passion story, he pens his key verse in 10:45. Jesus came to serve and to give His life a ransom for many.

Action-Packed Emphasis

Throughout his Gospel, Mark presents more works of Jesus and fewer of His words. Mark's writing is action packed, forceful, fresh, vivid, dramatic, realistic, graphic, simple, direct, swift, rough, brief, and to the point. Mark used the historical present tense more than 150 times in 673 verses and was fond of using the imperfect tense, which describes continuous action in the past. The historical present is like saying, "Here He comes; He is looking at the blind man; He touches him; the blind man sees; he bows before Jesus and thanks Him." It records the events as occurring before our eyes. It has the eyewitness quality of an on-the-spot reporter. The reader can relive the stories through Peter's eyes and Mark's vivid retelling.

Attention to Detail

Another characteristic of Mark is his attention to detail. This can be seen in his treatment of the demoniac in Mark 5:1–20. Mark uses twenty verses to recount this story while Matthew writes only seven. Similarly, the story of the woman who touched Jesus's garment occupies just three verses in Matthew but ten in Mark.

Yet Mark's Gospel is still the most concise, containing only 673 verses, compared to Matthew's 1,068 and Luke's 1,147. Why is this so? Mark's emphasis is different. Sixty percent of the words in Matthew are Jesus's words, 51 percent of Luke, but for Mark it is just under 42 percent. Mark's emphasis is on Jesus's mighty works.

As one might expect, Peter figures more prominently in Mark's account than he does in either Matthew or Luke. Three notable places where this occurs are in 1:36 where Peter leads the contingency looking for Jesus, only to find Him in private prayer; 11:21 where Peter remarks about the withered fig tree; and 13:3 where Peter heads the list of the four fishermen disciples who ask Jesus about His predicted destruction of the Jewish temple.

Jesus's mighty works in Mark include at least eighteen separate miracles, as well as places where it says He healed the multitudes (Mark 1:32–34; 3:10–12; 6:53–56). Two of Jesus's miracles are recorded in Mark and nowhere else. One is the restoring of speech and hearing to a deaf and dumb man in the Decapolis (7:32–35); the other is the healing of a blind man at Bethsaida (8:22–26). Mark told about these miracles to show that Jesus was indeed the Son of God.

Fishing boats in the Middle East.

Mark includes more personal details about Jesus than any other Gospel. Mark is the only writer to mention that Jesus was a carpenter (6:3) during His early adulthood. Mark shows Jesus's full humanity as well as His deity. Jesus got tired and hungry, just as every person does (4:38; 6:31; 11:12). He experienced great heaviness of heart and sorrow as He prayed in the garden of Gethsemane the night before His crucifixion (14:33–36). Mark notes Jesus's anger and sorrow at the hardness of people's hearts in a synagogue (3:5) and how He rebuked His disciples for turning little children away from Him (10:14). Jesus was also compassionate toward a leprous man (1:41) and toward a huge crowd who were like sheep without a shepherd (6:34).

The Last Twelve Verses of Mark

The authenticity of the ending of Mark 16:9–20 is disputed among scholars. The vast majority of Greek manuscripts of Mark include these last twelve verses. However, in two prominent early manuscripts of the fourth century these verses are missing. The problem then carries over into Bible translation. While the verses are included in the KJV, modern translations usually use footnotes (NKJV) or a combination of footnotes and brackets (NASB, ESV, CSB, NIV) to indicate that some manuscripts lack the verses.

Practical Application

Mark's Gospel has a special appeal to those who are marginalized by society. His emphasis on Jesus as God's "slave/servant" was especially appealing to the thousands of slaves in the Roman Empire. While Jesus was an incredible miracle worker, He was also a common man (a carpenter) who appealed to common people to believe in Him. As we read Mark's account today, how can it help us understand the concepts of ordinary people? When we share our faith in Christ, how can we present Him in such a way that today's postmodern society can receive Him by faith as well?

For Further Reading

Black, David Alan, ed. *Perspectives on the Ending of Mark: 4 Views*. Nashville: B&H, 2008.

Brooks, James A. *Mark*. NAC. Nashville: B&H, 1991.

Evans, Craig A. *Mark 8:27–16:20*. WBC. Nashville: Thomas Nelson, 2001.

France, R. T. *The Gospel of Mark: A Commentary on the Greek Text*. NIGTC. Grand Rapids: Eerdmans, 2002.

Study Questions

1. Who was John Mark, and how did he come to be the author of this Gospel? Explain Mark's relationship to Peter and how that may have influenced what he wrote.
2. What is the key verse of Mark's Gospel, and what does it tell us of the message Mark tries to get across to his readers?
3. Were Roman Christians the original recipients of Mark's Gospel? What are some indications this might be the case?
4. What are some of the unique features found in the Gospel of Mark?
5. What are some of the issues discussed regarding the dating of Mark's Gospel and the Synoptic Problem? How does the concept of an oft-repeated oral tradition enter into this equation?

Notes

1. Eusebius, *Ecclesiastical History*, III.xxxix, cites Papias; Justin Martyr, *Dialogue with Trypho*, chap. 56.

2. Irenaeus, *Against Heresies*, 3.1.1.

3. Robert H. Stein, *Luke*, NAC, vol. 24, ed. David S. Dockery (Nashville: B&H, 1992), 27–30; R. T. France, *The Gospel of Mark: A Commentary on the Greek Text* (Grand Rapids: Eerdmans, 2002), 35–45.

4. Compare Mark 1:14 with John 3:24. All the material in John up to that point occurred *before* John was placed in prison. Jesus had at least six of the twelve disciples before John was arrested by Herod Antipas. This calling in Mark 1:14 was a second calling to a permanent, full-time following and took place "after John was arrested."

Chapter 29

LUKE

The Son of Man

L uke was a medical doctor, a missionary, an evangelist, a historian, a researcher, and the writer of the third Gospel. His account of Jesus's life and ministry emphasizes that He is the perfect Son of God and the Savior of all mankind. Luke countenances no parochialism so his Gospel shows that Jesus loves all, mingles with all, died for all, and calls all to be saved. Luke is the longest book in the New Testament and gives a full picture of the life of Christ. Luke begins by explaining how Jesus's coming was predicted by the angel Gabriel's message to Mary, and he concludes with a glimpse of Jesus ascending back to heaven after His resurrection from the dead.

KEY FACTS

Author:	Luke
Recipient:	Theophilus
Where:	Caesarea
Date:	AD 60
Key Word:	People (Gk. *laos*)
Key Verse:	"For the Son of Man has come to seek and to save the lost" (19:10).

Author

Luke, the author of the Gospel that bears his name, is only mentioned by name three times in the New Testament (Col 4:14; 2 Tim 4:11; Phlm 24). He wrote in polished Greek, and tradition says Luke was from Syrian

Antioch and was a brother of Titus.[1] Both external and internal evidence strongly suggest that Luke was the author. The external evidence consists of comments made around AD 200 when Irenaeus, Clement of Alexandria, Tertullian, and the Muratorian Canon unequivocally name Luke as the author of this Gospel.[2]

The internal evidence begins with the fact that Luke and Acts have a common author.[3] Most modern scholars assume this. Both are addressed to Theophilus (Luke 1:3; Acts 1:1), and Acts 1:1 refers back to the "first narrative" the author wrote. The second key piece of internal evidence is that three passages in Acts repeatedly use the first-person plural "we" when describing the action (Acts 16:10–17; 20:5–21:18; and 27:1–28:16). That means the author was a participant in those sections, all of which were on Paul's missionary journeys. The author would not have been Paul or any of his named companions in Acts. Since the author is present during Paul's Roman imprisonment at the end of Acts, Paul may have mentioned him in one of his letters written during this imprisonment (the Prison Epistles are Ephesians, Philippians, Colossians, and Philemon). Through process of elimination, Luke stands out as the most likely candidate[4]—a conclusion confirmed by the external evidence cited above. If Luke authored Acts, he was also the author of the Gospel traditionally attributed to him.

Paul calls Luke "the dearly loved physician" (Col 4:14), and there seems to be an interest in sickness and healing in the third Gospel. Mark says Peter's mother-in-law had a fever (1:30), but Luke notes it was "a high fever" (Gk. *megalo*, 4:38). Mark says a man had "a serious skin disease" (1:40), but Luke adds that this disease was "all over him" (5:12). Mark tells of a man with "a paralyzed hand" (3:1), but Luke observes that his right hand was paralyzed (6:6). Mark reports that Peter cut off a man's ear (14:47), but only Luke adds that Jesus touched his ear and healed him (22:51). Luke has five healings in his account that neither Matthew nor Mark mention.[5] While none of this proves that a doctor wrote the third Gospel, a focus on sickness and healing is certainly consistent with the assertion that Luke, a physician, is the author.

Recipient

The recipient of the Gospel of Luke was "most honorable Theophilus" (Luke 1:3). The term "most honorable/excellent" is found three other times when Paul addresses the Roman officials Felix and Festus (Acts 23:26; 24:2; 26:25). This suggests that Theophilus may have been a Roman official or a nobleman who recently became a Christian.

Luke explains Jewish customs such as the Passover and Unleavened Bread to his readers (22:1, 7). The genealogy of Jesus in Luke 3:23–38 extends back to the first man, Adam, whereas Matthew traces it only to Abraham, the progenitor of the Hebrew nation (1:1–16). Luke's readers are seemingly unfamiliar with Palestinian geography because he describes Nazareth (1:26), and later Capernaum (4:31), as "a town in Galilee." The conclusion is that Luke's primary recipient (Theophilus), and others beyond him, were Gentiles with largely Greek backgrounds.

Synagogue at Capernaum dating from the fourth century AD.

Occasion and Date

The occasion calling for Luke to write his Gospel was that Theophilus, and other new believers like him, needed a clear account of the life and ministry of Jesus as an aid to confirm their faith. However, the precise dating of Luke's writing is difficult to determine. Some conservative evangelicals argue for a date around AD 60, and others posit a date in the mid-60s or even after AD 70.[6]

Two issues are involved. First, did Luke use Mark as a primary source for writing his Gospel? If so, then Luke could not be written before Mark. Many hold that Mark was penned around AD 65 or a little later, although Robert Gundry argues that "no compelling reasons exist to deny an early date in the period A.D. 45–70 . . . and—if Luke's gospel reflects Mark—Mark [was] still earlier in the fifties or late forties."[7] The idea of "Markan priority"—that Mark's Gospel was written first and that Matthew and Luke used it in composing their own accounts—is a complicated issue. Most critical scholars and some evangelicals are convinced of this thesis. However, it is unnecessary to make Matthew and Luke subservient and indebted to a written form of Mark. The oral preaching of the Jesus story had already taken on a set form of expression for several decades as seen in the sermon outlines of Peter and Paul in Acts 2; 10; and 13. The fact that Matthew, Mark, and Luke each tell of Jesus's great Galilean ministry in a particular order and use some of the same vocabulary can easily be attributed to the widespread existence of the oral communication of the gospel.

Second, does Paul remain in prison at the end of Acts because Luke did not know the outcome of this first Roman trial when Acts was published? This seems possible. If that is the case, and Paul's martyrdom at the hands of emperor Nero (mid- to late 60s) has not yet happened at the time of writing, then Acts was likely written in the early to mid-60s. When would Luke have been able to write his Gospel? Paul's detention in Caesarea from AD 58 to 60 gave Luke the opportunity to research and interview early eyewitnesses, even some of the apostles, deacons, and other early Christians in Israel. He had access to the people he needed to receive firsthand information. Additionally, Luke was with Paul during his two-year house arrest in Rome. That was an ideal time to compose the book of Acts. Since Acts was the sequel to Luke, it makes sense to date Luke prior to Acts—around AD 60.

Genre and Structure

Luke pens a formal literary introduction noting his purpose in writing, his methodology, and the attempts others had made in such writing. Luke's purpose is to give "an orderly sequence" of the events about Christ's birth, life, and sacrificial death followed by His resurrection and ascension back to heaven. He wants Theophilus and other readers to "know the certainty of the things about which you have been instructed" (1:3–4). First, in order to do this well, Luke gathered his information from competent, reliable, firsthand sources—"the original eyewitnesses and servants of the word" (1:2). Luke knew the facts both as an inquirer and as an observer. Second, he recorded his message accurately. Third, the length of his search took him back to the beginning of things, so only Luke gives the account of the angel Gabriel speaking to Zachariah and Mary. His material is primarily chronological but always planned and logical. Fourth, Luke's use of *anothen* (literally "from above"), suggests he probably was aware of divine inspiration. Luke's Greek style is often considered "the most refined in the New Testament."[8]

Outline

I. Prologue (1:1–4)
II. Christ's Presentation, Baptism, and Temptation (1:5–4:13)
III. Christ's Preaching and Miracles (4:14–9:50)
IV. Christ's Perean Ministry and Parables (9:51–19:27)
V. Christ's Passion, Resurrection, and Ascension (19:28–24:53)

Message

The Comprehensive Gospel

The Gospel of Luke is the most comprehensive of the four Gospels. It records events prior to Matthew's story of Mary and Joseph, reaching back to Gabriel's announcements to Zechariah and Mary. Its conclusion also extends beyond the other Gospels to the ascension of Christ and the disciples' worship in the temple after that.[9]

A model of the temple built by Herod the Great with the surrounding courts.

Universal Appeal

Luke's is also the most universal Gospel because the good news about Jesus is for the whole world, not for the Jews only. Jesus's lineage is traced back not just to Abraham but to Adam (3:23–38). The salvation he brings is "a light for revelation to the Gentiles" (2:32). Quoting from Isaiah, Luke reminds us of God's promise that "everyone will see the salvation of God" (3:6). Jesus reminds His hearers of God's compassion to Gentiles in the Old Testament (4:24–27). He rebukes James and John for wanting to call fire down on the Samaritans (9:54); the "good Samaritan" outclassed the Jewish priest and Levite (10:33); and the only leper out of ten who returned to give Jesus thanks was a Samaritan (17:6).

Historical Details

Luke references more historical events in the Roman Empire during the life of Jesus than the other Gospels. "Caesar Augustus" issued the census proclamation "while Quirinius was governing Syria" (2:1–2); Jesus began ministry in the fifteenth year of Tiberius Caesar's reign when Pontius Pilate governed Judea (3:1); Annas and Caiaphas were high priests at the time (3:2); Pilate slaughtered some Galileans along with their sacrifices (13:1). Luke even records that Jesus referred to Herod Antipas as "that fox" (13:32). Luke's account is not "once upon a time"; it is historically grounded.

Individual Focus

Another Lukan emphasis is on the individual person. Whereas Matthew's parables are about the kingdom, Luke's nineteen peculiar parables are about individuals. The lost sheep and the lost shekel, the good Samaritan, the prodigal son, the Pharisee and the tax collector in the temple, the dishonest manager, and the ten servants who received some money to invest each portray individuals for whom Christ came. Luke's narratives also include individuals like Zechariah and Elizabeth, Anna and Simeon, Mary and Martha, Cleopas and his friend, as well as Zacchaeus, Mary

Statue of Augustus, Roman emperor from 27 BC to AD 14.

Magdalene, Simon the Cyrenian, Joseph of Arimathea, the widow of Nain, the three hesitant disciples, the women who helped Jesus financially, and a host of others. Luke sees supreme value in each person's soul before God.

The Parables of Jesus	
Parable	Reference
1. The Speck and the Log	Matt 7:1–6; Luke 6:37–43
2. The Two Houses	Matt 7:24–27; Luke 6:47–49
3. Children in the Marketplace	Matt 11:16–19; Luke 7:32
4. The Two Debtors	Luke 7:42
5. The Unclean Spirit	Matt 12:43–45; Luke 11:24–26
6. The Rich Man's Meditation	Luke 12:16–21
7. The Barren Fig Tree	Luke 13:6–9
8. The Sower	Matt 13:3–8; Mark 4:3–8; Luke 8:5–8
9. The Tares	Matt 13:24–30
10. The Seed	Mark 4:20
11. The Grain of Mustard Seed	Matt 13:31–32; Mark 4:31–32; Luke 13:19
12. The Leaven	Matt 13:33; Luke 13:21
13. The Lamp	Matt 5:15; Mark 4:21; Luke 8:16; 11:33
14. The Dragnet	Matt 13:47–48
15. The Hidden Treasure	Matt 13:44
16. The Pearl of Great Value	Matt 13:45–46
17. The Householder	Matt 13:52
18. The Marriage	Matt 9:15; Mark 2:19–20; Luke 5:34–35
19. The Patched Garment	Matt 9:16; Mark 2:21; Luke 5:36
20. The Wine Bottles	Matt 9:17; Mark 2:22; Luke 5:37
21. The Harvest	Matt 9:37; Luke 10:2
22. The Opponent	Matt 5:25; Luke 12:58
23. Two Insolvent Debtors	Matt 18:23–35
24. The Good Samaritan	Luke 10:30–37
25. The Three Loaves	Luke 11:5–8
26. The Good Shepherd	John 10:1–16
27. The Narrow Gate	Matt 7:14; Luke 13:24
28. The Guests	Luke 14:7–11
29. The Marriage Supper	Matt 22:2–9; Luke 14:16–23

The Parables of Jesus (continued)	
Parable	**Reference**
30. The Wedding Clothes	Matt 22:10–14
31. The Tower	Luke 14:28–30
32. The King Going to War	Luke 14:31
33. The Lost Sheep	Matt 18:12–13; Luke 15:4–7
34. The Lost Coin	Luke 15:8–9
35. The Prodigal Son	Luke 15:11–32
36. The Unjust Steward	Luke 16:1–9
37. The Rich Man and Lazarus	Luke 16:19–31
38. The Slave's Duty	Luke 17:7–10
39. Laborers in the Vineyard	Matt 20:1–16
40. The Talents	Matt 25:14–30; Luke 19:11–27
41. The Importunate Widow	Luke 18:2–5
42. The Pharisee and Tax Gatherer	Luke 18:10–14
43. The Two Sons	Matt 21:28
44. The Wicked Vine Growers	Matt 21:33–43; Mark 12:1–9; Luke 20:9–15
45. The Fig Tree	Matt 24:32; Mark 13:28; Luke 21:29–30
46. The Watching Slave	Matt 24:43; Luke 12:39
47. The Man on a Journey	Mark 13:34
48. Character of Two Slaves	Matt 24:45–51; Luke 12:42–46
49. The Ten Virgins	Matt 25:1–12
50. The Watching Slaves	Luke 12:36–38
51. The Vine and Branches	John 15:1–6

Prayerful Emphasis

Luke's Gospel puts a good deal of emphasis on prayer, reporting that Jesus prayed eleven times, much more than any other Gospel. Seven of these prayer times are unique to Luke. Jesus prayed at His baptism (3:21); all night before selecting the twelve apostles (6:12); over the fish and loaves before feeding 5,000 (9:16); just before announcing His coming death to the Twelve (9:18); at His transfiguration (9:29); when the Seventy returned from their mission (10:21–22); when the Twelve saw Jesus praying before asking Him to teach them how to pray (11:1); in Gethsemane before His arrest (22:41–42); and on the cross He prayed, "Father, forgive them, because they do not know what they are doing" (23:34), and later He "called out with a loud voice, 'Father, into your hands I entrust my spirit'" (23:46).

In addition to Christ's own prayer life, Luke records three of Jesus's unique parables on prayer: the friend who arrives at midnight (11:5–13), the persistent widow (18:1–8), and the Pharisee and the publican praying in the temple (18:9–14). Furthermore, Jesus exhorts His followers to pray for their enemies (6:28), for workers to be sent into God's harvest field (10:2), for needed things (11:9–13), "always and not give up" (18:1), and to avoid temptation (22:40, 46). W. Graham Scroggie has noted that Jesus taught prayer "by exhortation, illustration, and demonstration."[10]

Worshipful Exaltation

Luke also places special emphasis on the worship of praising, rejoicing, and glorifying God because of His greatness. Only Luke records the great worship hymns expressed by Gabriel, Mary, Zechariah, the angels before the shepherds, and Simeon.[11] Glorifying, praising, and blessing God occur more in Luke than in all the other Synoptics combined. In addition, joy and rejoicing, exulting, and laughter abound in Luke. Luke ends with the disciples returning to Jerusalem "with great joy. And they were continually in the temple praising God" (24:52–53).[12]

A view of the Temple Mount area from the Mount of Olives.

Importance of Women

Luke also stresses the role of women more than the other Gospels. He mentions women forty-three times to Matthew's thirty, and Mark and John's nineteen. Jesus lifts women up socially and spiritually. Mary sat at Jesus's feet, having "made the right choice" (10:42). Women supported Jesus and His disciples "from their possessions" (8:3). Women lingered at the cross and arrived first at Christ's tomb. What matchless pictures we have of Elizabeth, Mary, Anna, Joanna, Susanna, Mary and Martha, the sinful woman in Simon's house, the widow of Nain, and Mary Magdalene. Who can forget Jesus's parables of the woman sweeping to find her coin (15:8–10) and the persistent widow before the unjust judge (18:2–8)? Women were disrespected among the Gentiles but ennobled by Jesus.

REFLECTION

Christianity and Women

One of the unique features of the biblical Gospels is the high priority placed on the contribution of women. From Mary, the mother of Jesus, to Lazarus' sisters, Mary and Martha, to Mary Magdalene, women played an important role in Jesus's life and ministry. In Acts 1:14, Luke emphasizes that there were women among Jesus's disciples in the upper room and on the day of Pentecost when the church began. Later Luke refers to Dorcas (Acts 9:36), Rhoda (Acts 12:13), Lydia (16:14–15), and Priscilla (18:2) by name. The apostle Paul wrote, "There is no ... male or female; since you are all one in Christ Jesus" (Gal 3:28). Although Jews segregated women in both the temple and synagogue, the early church did not (Acts 12:1–17; 1 Cor 11:2–6).

Practical Application

Luke's aim was to ground Theophilus, a Gentile convert, in the true historical account of Christ as Savior. He presents Jesus as the Son of God in His perfect humanity. Luke's Gospel is the most comprehensive, universal, and individualistic of the Gospel records. He emphasizes forgiveness, worship, prayer, Christ's sympathetic nature, and Jesus's respect for women. Luke includes more about the Holy Spirit and Christ's unique parables than the other Gospels.

As we read Luke's account, we see in Jesus the ideals that every one of us would desire in someone else, let alone ourselves. Charles Spurgeon, the nineteenth-century British pastor said, "Never tolerate low thoughts of Him. You may study, look, and meditate. But Jesus is a greater savior than you think Him to be when your thoughts are at their highest."[13] Jesus made no apologies when He called His disciples. He was direct and decisive. He did not beg or plead. "Follow Me!" is all He said, and people dropped everything and followed him (Luke 5:27–28).

For Further Reading

Bock, Darrell L. *Luke*. IVPNTC. Downers Grove, IL: InterVarsity Press, 1994.
Garland, David E. *Luke*. ZEC. Grand Rapids: Zondervan, 2011.
Hendriksen, William. *Luke*. NTC. Grand Rapids: Baker, 2004.
Marshall, I. Howard. *The Gospel of Luke*. NIGTC. Grand Rapids: Eerdmans, 1978.
Morris, Leon. *The Gospel According to Luke: An Introduction and Commentary*. Grand Rapids: Eerdmans, 2002.
Stein, Robert. *Luke*. NAC. Nashville: B&H, 1992.

Study Questions

1. Who was Luke, what can be known about him, and why did he write his Gospel?
2. Explain how Luke can be characterized as comprehensive, universal, historical, and individualistic.
3. How do the following carry out the theme of Luke: forgiveness, sympathy, prayer, worship, and the Holy Spirit?
4. What characterizes the unique parables found in Luke?
5. Why does Luke emphasize details about healing?

Notes

1. Greek Codex D at Acts 11:27 inserts, "And there was great rejoicing; and when we were gathered together one of them named Agabus stood up." The "we" would indicate Luke as an early Hellenist convert at Antioch. See Doremus Almy Hayes, *The Synoptic Gospels and the Book of Acts* (New York: Methodist Book Concern, 1919), 193; and John Dickie, "Christian," *International Standard Bible Encyclopedia*, ed. James Orr (Grand Rapids: Eerdmans, 1939), I, 622.

2. See Irenaeus, *Against Heresies*, 3.1.1, 3.14.1; Clement of Alexandria, *Stromata*, 1.26; Tertullian, *Against Marcion*, 4.5.3.

3. Robert H. Stein, *Luke*, NAC, vol. 24 (Nashville: B&H, 1992), 21–22, summarizes nine points that demonstrate a common author for Luke and Acts.

4. See Andreas J. Köstenberger, L. Scott Kellum, Charles L. Quarles, *The Cradle, the Cross, and the Crown: An Introduction to the New Testament* (Nashville: B&H, 2009), 259–60.

5. William Kirk Hobart, *The Medical Language of St. Luke* (Dublin: Hodges, Figgis, & Co., 1882) claimed the use of medical language in Luke-Acts pointed to Lukan authorship. H. J. Cadbury, *The Style and Literary Method of Luke* (Cambridge: Harvard University Press, 1920) sought to refute those claims, but his arguments are inconclusive.

6. Stein, *Luke*, 24–26, likes a post-AD 70 date; D. Edmond Hiebert, *An Introduction to the New Testament: The Gospels and Acts* (Chicago: Moody, 1975), 135–39, advocates a date of AD 66 or early 67; Henry C. Thiessen, *Introduction to the New Testament* (Grand Rapids: Eerdmans, 1943), 156–58, and Robert G. Gromacki, *New Testament Survey* (Grand Rapids: Baker, 1974), 111, hold to a date around AD 60.

7. Robert H. Gundry, *A Survey of the New Testament*, rev. ed. (Grand Rapids: Zondervan, 1981), 79.

8. Ibid., 91.

9. Mark 16:19 also mentions Christ's ascension.

10. W. Graham Scroggie, *A Guide to the Gospels* (London: Pickering & Inglis, n.d.), 370.

11. These are commonly called Ave Maria, Magnificat, Benedictus, Gloria in Excelsis, and Nunc Dimittis.

12. The majority of manuscripts have both "praising and blessing."

13. Quoted in R. Lee and E. Hindson, *No Greater Savior* (Eugene, OR: Harvest House, 1995), 11.

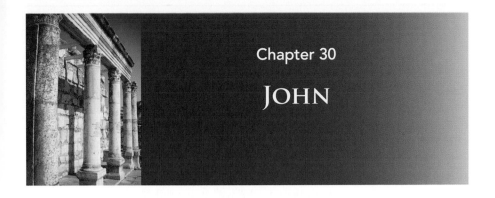

Chapter 30

JOHN

Believe and Live

The Gospel of John is an eyewitness account of Jesus's life and teachings written by someone so close to Jesus that he can confidently call himself "the beloved disciple." Rather than focusing on what was already written, this disciple focuses on events, discourses, and miraculous signs not found in the other Gospels. What emerges is a fresh presentation of Jesus as the Messiah, which fills in the gaps left by the Synoptic writers. It invites its readers to believe that Jesus is the Messiah, the Son of God, and by believing have life in His name.

KEY FACTS

Author:	John, "the beloved disciple"
Recipients:	Greek-Speaking Jews Living Outside of Israel
Where:	Ephesus
Date:	AD 90
Key Word:	Believe (Gk. *pisteuō*)
Key Verse:	"But these are written so that you may believe that Jesus is the Messiah, the Son of God, and that by believing you may have life in his name" (20:31).

Author

The writer of the Gospel identifies himself only as "the disciple Jesus loved" (21:20). Therefore, any argument from internal evidence needs to be established by a process of elimination. Internally it can be determined that the writer was: (1) an apostle (1:14; 2:11; 19:35); (2) one of the Twelve (13:25);[1] and (3) not anyone who is listed with or interacted with the beloved disciple.[2] The fourth Gospel presents the beloved disciple in close relationship with Jesus and Peter (John 20:2; 21:7, 20), so Peter can be ruled out. James, too, can be ruled out because he was martyred by the time the fourth Gospel was written.[3] Therefore, John rises to the top of the list as the most likely candidate for "beloved disciple." Johannine authorship is in line with the external evidence of church tradition that holds that the author of the Fourth Gospel is John, the son of Zebedee,[4] who clearly distinguishes himself from John the Baptist.[5]

Recipients

Unlike Luke, John does not directly identify his audience. However, he seems to assume that his audience has familiarity with Jewish traditions and certain aspects of Jesus's life.[6] At other times he explains things a Hebrew-speaking Jew living in Israel would know.[7] With these facts in view, John's original audience seems to be Greek-speaking Jews who were living outside of Israel. Irenaeus claimed John wrote the Gospel in Ephesus. Several items are unique to John's Gospel: the miracle at the wedding in Cana (2:1–11), Jesus's conversation with Nicodemus (3:1–21), the woman at the well in Samaria (4:5–42), the woman taken in adultery (8:1–11), the resurrection of Lazarus (11:1–44), Jesus's upper room discourse (14–16), His intercessory prayer (17), and Jesus's postresurrection appearance at the Sea of Galilee (21).

Occasion and Date

John was probably written after the Synoptic Gospels and before 1–3 John and Revelation. This dates the Fourth Gospel to sometime after AD 70 and before AD 90.[8] Köstenberger prefers a date of composition during the reign of Domitian (AD 81–96), whose coins were stamped *Dominus et Deus* ("Lord and God"), which is Thomas's affirmation of the risen Christ in John 20:28.[9] John makes his purpose in writing clear: he hopes that by telling his audience about Jesus's signs, which were performed in the presence of His disciples, they might believe that Jesus is the Messiah, the Son of God, and by believing have life in His name (20:30–31).

Outline

I. The Book of Signs (1:1–12:50)
   A. Jesus's Preexistence (1:1–18)
   B. Jesus's Mission to the Jews (1:19–12:50)
II. The Book of Glory (13:1–21:25)
   A. Jesus's Upper Room Message (13:1–17:26)
   B. Jesus's Arrest and Trials (18:1–19:16)
   C. Jesus's Crucifixion, Burial, and Resurrection (19:17–20:29)
   D. Epilogue (21:1–25)

Message

I. The Book of Signs (John 1:1–12:50)

A. Jesus's Preexistence (John 1:1–18)

Referring to creation in the beginning, John says "the Word" existed before creation and was the agent through whom the world was made. John explains that the Word is Jesus, "the one and only Son from the Father, full of grace and truth," who "took on flesh" and "pitched His tent" among us (1:14,

Ruins of the fishing village of Behsaida on the northern end of the Sea of Galilee. Bethsaida was the home of three of Jesus's disciples, Peter, Andrew, and Philip. Peter and Andrew later lived in the nearby village of Capernaum.

author's translation). Ironically, though the world was created by Him, "His own" did not receive Him. But to those who did receive Him by believing on His name, He gave the right to become children of God (1:11–12). This birth as a child of God was a new birth unlike the natural birth of every human; it was not dependent on the will and flesh of mankind but on the will of God (1:13).

B. Jesus's Mission to the Jews (John 1:19–12:50)

In the last half of chapter 1, Jesus's identity is further revealed through the professions of John the Baptist and Jesus's disciples (1:19–51). Collectively the confessions of Jesus's first disciples make clear that they saw Jesus as the Messiah, the Son of God, the Lamb of God, and the King of Israel who was predicted by the law of Moses, the prophets, and by John the Baptist. As such these witnesses identify Jesus as the fulfillment of the prophetic expectations of the Old Testament. Though some of these titles are simply titles concerning Jesus's humanity, others carry heavy messianic overtones. As a prophet the Baptist may have fully understood his profession that Jesus was "the Lamb of God" (cf. 1:29).

Jesus's Mission to the Jews Is Highlighted by Seven Miraculous Signs

1. Turning water into wine (2:1–11)
2. Healing a nobleman's son (4:46–54)
3. Healing a lame man (5:1–9)
4. Feeding the 5,000 (6:1–14)
5. Walking on water (6:15–21)
6. Healing a blind man (9:1–12)
7. Raising Lazarus from the dead (11:1–44)

These "signs" were intended to affirm Jesus's message and confirm His claims. At the end of the Gospel, John adds one final miracle: a miraculous catch of fish (21:1–11) preformed after the resurrection. The Cana cycle is a unified narrative that traces Jesus's early ministry geographically from Cana (2:1) to Cana (4:54). In between, Jesus does His first miracle, turning water into wine, revealing His messianic glory (see Amos 9:13–14). This is followed by Jesus cleansing the temple of the money changers (2:12–23) and meeting Nicodemus, a Jewish ruler in Jerusalem, to whom He explains what it means to be "born again" (3:1–21). In the next section Jesus reveals Himself as the Messiah to a Samaritan woman at a well in Samaria (4:1–42).

When Jesus returned to Cana, He was approached by a royal official who begged Jesus to heal his son (4:46–54). Jesus's response was simply: "Go . . .

your son will live" (4:48–50). At that hour the son was healed (4:53). As a result of this sign, the royal official and his whole household believed (4:53). The Cana Cycle concludes as it began: with a sign that identifies Jesus as the fulfillment of Jewish messianic expectations.

Khirbet Cana in the Asochis Valley. Cana was where Jesus performed His first miraculous sign at the wedding feast.

The Festival Cycle is arranged thematically around Jewish festivals. First Jesus is at an unnamed festival (probably Passover) where He healed a man who had been lame for thirty-eight years (chap. 5). Jesus commanded him, "Pick up your mat and walk" (5:8). Because it was a Sabbath day, the Jewish leaders confronted the man and demanded to know why he was carrying his mat on a Sabbath (5:10). He explained that the One who healed him told him to carry it.

The second stage of the Festival Cycle took place during the Feast of Unleavened Bread (the Passover; 6:4). Jesus fed 5,000 with only five loaves of bread and two small fish. Leaving the multitude, the disciples attempted to cross the Sea of Galilee but encountered a storm. That night Jesus came walking to them on the water and calmed the storm. The following day Jesus rebuked them for their preoccupation with perishable bread and encouraged them to focus on the "spiritual food" (i.e., eternal life) that only He could provide. He tells them, "I am the bread of life" (6:35). Anyone who partakes of the true bread from heaven will have eternal life (6:48–58). Jesus, the True Bread, therefore, supersedes the bread of the Passover.

Jesus makes two claims during the Feast of Tabernacles (chaps. 7–9): first, He is the water of life (7:37–39); and, second, He is "the light of the world" (8:12). By making these claims at the Feast of Tabernacles, Jesus implies that He is the Messiah. Because of His claims, the Jewish leaders attacked Him verbally (8:13). This section climaxes with the Jews picking up stones to stone Jesus because of His claim to be eternal when He said, "Before Abraham was, I am" (8:58). John uses this central "I am" declaration (see Exod 3:14) to affirm the deity of Christ. John uses this to formulate Jesus's seven "I Am" declarations:

1. "I am the bread of life" (6:35).
2. "I am the light of the world" (8:12).
3. "I am the door" (10:9).
4. "I am the good shepherd" (10:11).
5. "I am the resurrection and the life" (11:25).
6. "I am the way, the truth, and the life" (14:6).
7. "I am the vine" (15:5).

These affirmations in the form of descriptive word pictures are reinforced by Jesus's miracles of feeding the 5,000 (chap. 6), healing a blind man (chap. 9), and raising Lazarus from the dead (chap. 11). The message about the "good shepherd" comes during the Feast of Dedication (chap. 10).[10] The Festival Cycle and the "Book of Signs" conclude with Jesus's anointing, His triumphal entry, Mary anointing Jesus's feet, and some God-fearing Greeks coming to inquire about Jesus (12:20–32).

II. The Book of Glory (John 13:1–21:25)

A. Jesus's Upper Room Message (John 13:1–17:26)

The next five chapters directly anticipate the approaching end of Christ's life and focus on His preparation of the disciples for the next stage in salvation history. By the time of Jesus's last supper, Judas's heart was already set on betraying Jesus, and Jesus already knew that "the Father had given everything into His hands, that He had come from God, and that He was going back to God" (13:1–3). Jesus, therefore, got up from supper, laid aside His robe, and began washing the disciples' feet.

The foot washing is, therefore, an action lesson that prepared Jesus's disciples for serving one another in such a way that their love and unity would show the world they were His disciples (13:35; 17:22). After Jesus sent Judas out into the night, Jesus began to teach those who were "His own" (13:1).

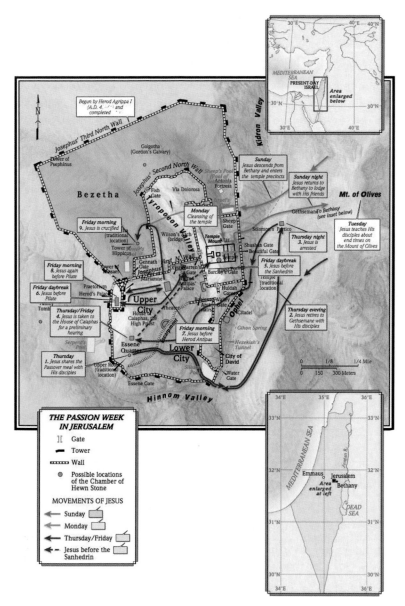

THE PASSION WEEK
IN JERUSALEM

)[Gate
▬ Tower
▭▭▭ Wall
◉ Possible locations
of the Chamber of
Hewn Stone

MOVEMENTS OF JESUS

◄— Sunday
◄— Monday
◄— Thursday/Friday
◄- Jesus before the
Sanhedrin

In this discourse (13:31–16:33) Jesus prepared His disciples for what was to come after He returned to the Father. He comforted them by promising to prepare a place for them and to bring them to Himself (14:2), to send the Holy Spirit to guide and teach them (14:26; 16:12–15), and to continue to abide with them even after His glorification. After His Farewell Discourse, Jesus prays His high priestly prayer for Himself, His disciples, and future believers (chap. 17). Jesus prayed for the Father to glorify Him so that He may, in turn, glorify the Father (17:2).

B. Jesus's Arrest and Trials (John 18:1–19:16)

Having finished His prayer, Jesus entered into the garden where He was met by Judas (His betrayer) and armed soldiers. Peter drew his sword and struck the servant of the high priest. Jesus rejected this intervention and went willingly to be judged by Annas the priest. Then Jesus was taken to Pilate the governor, who attempted to avoid being involved in Jesus's trials, but the Jews insisted that Roman law did not allow them to put anyone to death. Pilate, therefore, questioned Jesus concerning His claims to kingship and His origin (18:33–37). Jesus responded by acknowledging that He came into the world to testify of the truth and that His kingdom is not of this world (18:36–37). In the end Pilate attempted to have Jesus flogged and released, but the Jews insisted they would rather have a thief set free than Jesus and that, if Pilate thought otherwise, he was no friend of Caesar's (19:12). Ultimately Pilate conceded and allowed Jesus to be crucified, even though he found no grounds for charging Him (19:6, 15–16).

"Ecce Homo" ("Behold the Man") by Antonio Ciseri (1821–91).

C. Jesus's Crucifixion, Burial, and Resurrection (John 19:17–20:29)

Jesus was then crucified under a sign that read, "Jesus of Nazareth, King of the Jews." Through the course of His crucifixion, John recorded a series of prophetic fulfillments. First, the soldiers' *division of Jesus's clothes* is viewed as fulfilling Ps 22:18. Second, *Jesus asked for a drink*, thereby fulfilling Ps 22:15. After this Jesus uttered the words "it is finished" and died. After Jesus's death the Jews requested that those being crucified have their legs broken in order to expedite their death so they could be taken down before the Sabbath. However, because Jesus was already dead, they did *not break His legs*. Instead, they *pierced His side* with a spear, and at once blood and water came out. These were the last of the prophetic fulfillments. Third, "Not one of His bones will be broken"; and, fourth, "They will look at the One they pierced" (Exod 12:46; Num 9:12; Ps 34:20; Zech 12:10).

The Garden Tomb. "There was a garden in the place where he was crucified. A new tomb was in the garden; no one had yet been placed in it. They placed Jesus there because of the Jewish day of preparation and since the tomb was nearby" (John 19:41–42).

Jesus was buried in a new tomb by Nicodemus and Joseph of Arimathea (a secret disciple of Jesus, 19:38–42). However, when Mary Magdalene came to visit the tomb, it was empty. Peter and John, upon hearing the news, came and saw for themselves (20:3–10). Jesus then appeared to Mary Magdalene in the garden and His disciples on three separate occasions (20:11–19). During these appearances Jesus comforted Mary, convinced Thomas of His resurrection, and reassured Peter that he was forgiven for denying Him.

Jesus showed Himself to seven disciples who fished all night and caught nothing (21:3). Jesus provided them with an abundant catch, then had breakfast with them on the shore. Jesus asked Peter three times, "Do you love me?" (21:15–17). Upon Peter's positive confession Jesus recommissioned him to service.

D. Epilogue (John 21:1–25)

A two-verse epilogue verifies the authenticity of the Gospel account and observes that while Jesus did many other things, no one could possibly write them all down. If anyone did, even the whole world could not contain all of the books that would have to be written.

Signature of the Sevens

The fourth Gospel is saturated with the thoughts, imagery, and language of the Old Testament. It is also interlaced with a brilliant repetition of sevenfold patterns. Of its 879 verses, 419 contain the words of Jesus. In these passages we hear the Savior's voice and feel His heart.

There are seven public discourses: (1) New Birth (3:1–36); (2) Water of Life (4:1–42); (3) Deity of the Son (5:19–47); (4) Bread of Life (6:22–66); (5) Life of the Spirit (7:1–52); (6) Light of the World (8:12–59); (7) Good Shepherd.[11] These are followed by seven private discourses: (1) New Commandment (13:31–38); (2) Promise of His Return (14:1–14); (3) Another Comforter (14:15–31); (4) True Vine (15:1–11); (5) Love One Another (15:12–27); (6) Spirit of Truth (16:1–33); (7) Intercessory Prayer (17:1–26).

Seven times John refers to Scripture being fulfilled (7:38; 13:18; 15:25; 17:12; 18:9; 19:24; 28, 36). He uses seven Old Testament symbols to convey truth: brazen serpent, manna, lamb, water from the rock, pillar of fire, shepherd, and the vine. John lists seven miracles from Jesus's earthly ministry as signs to the Jews, and he quotes the statements of seven men about Jesus: John the Baptist, Andrew, Philip, Nathaniel, Peter, Nicodemus, and Thomas.

Practical Application

John's Gospel makes clear that its record of Jesus's messages and His miraculous signs was written "that you may believe . . . and that by believing you may have life in his name" (20:31). While all four Gospels are evangelistic, John's Gospel is recognized as the "Gospel of belief" because of its emphasis on knowing (56 times) and believing (98 times) the truth (46 times). In this way the reader is captivated by the dramatic results of believing the truth about Jesus and confessing as did Thomas, "My Lord and my God!" (John 20:28).

The uniqueness of the fourth Gospel has long made it a favorite of Christian readers. It presents a comprehensive picture of Christ that emphasizes His deity and eternality as well as His humanity and compassion. He engages saints and sinners alike. He discusses theology with Nicodemus (ch. 3) and cultural differences with the Samaritan woman (ch. 4). He uses every opportunity of Jewish tradition to point His listeners to divine truth.

Jesus's life is so attractive that even unbelievers are forced to admire His humility, intelligence, and insight. One cannot read John's account of the Savior and not be compelled to admit as did those who heard Him in person, "No one ever spoke like this man." Above all else, John's Gospel calls on us to believe as did he that "Jesus is the Christ, the Son of God" (20:31).

For Further Reading

Blomberg, Craig L. *The Historical Reliability of John's Gospel: Issues & Commentary*. Downers Grove, IL: InterVarsity, 2002.

Carson, D. A. *The Gospel According to John*. Grand Rapids: Eerdmans, 1991.

Köstenberger, Andreas J. *Encountering John: The Gospel in Historical, Literary, and Theological Perspective*. Grand Rapids: Baker, 1999.

Morris, Leon. *The Gospel According to St. John*. NICNT. Grand Rapids: Eerdmans, 1971.

Towns, Elmer. *John: Believe and Live*. TFCBC. Chattanooga: AMG, 2002.

Study Questions

1. How does John's Gospel emphasize the deity of Jesus?
2. How does this Gospel differ from the Synoptic Gospels?
3. How does John divide his story geographically and thematically?
4. Why does John place so much emphasis on believing the gospel?
5. How should this affect how you present the gospel?

Notes

1. John 13 presents the beloved disciple as present at the last supper. Matthew and Mark seem to indicate that only Jesus's twelve disciples were present at the last supper (Matt 26:20; Mark 14:17).

2. Cf. chaps. 13–16; 21:2.

3. Moreover, there would not be enough time for rumors to spread that he would live until Jesus comes (John 21).

4. Irenaeus, Clement of Alexandria, Tertullian, Theophilus of Antioch, Origen, and others ascribe the book to John.

5. John the Baptist appears twenty times in John's Gospel: 1:6, 15, 19, 26, 28, 29, 32, 35, 40; 3:23, 24, 25, 26, 27; 4:1; 5:33, 35, 36; 10:40, 41.

6. For example, John assumes that his audience is already aware of the story of Jesus's anointing (chap. 12). Further, John seems to expect his audience to be familiar with the ceremonies of the Jewish festivals (chaps. 5–12).

7. Such as "Jews have no dealings with Samaritans" (4:9 NASB) and that Mary was the one who washed Jesus's feet (11:12).

8. The Rylands Fragment evidences a first-century date for the Gospel.

9. Andreas Köstenberger, *Encountering John* (Grand Rapids: Baker, 2009), 25–26.

10. Jesus's Good Shepherd claims are fitting in the setting of the Feast of Dedication because the celebration focused on the deliverance of Israel through the Maccabean family. Jesus was the Messiah who, in the spirit of Judas Maccabeus, would shepherd His people to the promises of God at the Feast of Dedication.

11. Leon Morris, *The Gospel According to John*, NICNT (Grand Rapids: Eerdmans, 1971), 65–67.

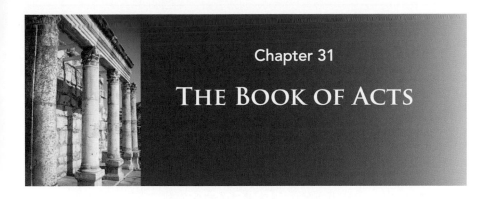

Chapter 31

THE BOOK OF ACTS

Witnessing to the World

The book of Acts is the second volume written by Luke. He addresses the Gospel to Theophilus, which means "lover of God" or "friend of God." "The Acts of the Apostles" isn't a survey of the ministry of all twelve disciples; rather it is about Peter (chaps. 1–12) and Paul (chaps. 13–28). But in another sense it's not really about them; it's about what the Holy Spirit does through them. Thus, this book could be titled, "The Acts of the Holy Spirit."

The key word is "witness," used more than thirty times. After the Holy Spirit was poured out on the believers at Pentecost, "those who were scattered went on their way preaching the word " (Acts 8:4). The early Christians were so totally convinced that Jesus died for their sins and rose from the dead that they literally gave their lives to witness to the world about what He had done.

LUKE	ACTS
1. Christ began to teach the Word.	The Holy Spirit spreads the Word.
2. Christ did miracles to show His deity.	The Spirit miraculously transforms individuals.
3. Christ was crucified and raised again.	Christ is exalted by the Holy Spirit.
4. The Son of Man came to save all.	The Holy Spirit came to bring people to salvation.

In the Old Testament God's glory dwelt in a tabernacle and in the temple, but in the New Testament God's Spirit lives in the lives of believers, and they carry Him into the marketplaces and streets as they witness the power of Christ's resurrection. In the Old Testament the Jews were a separate people from the Gentiles, distinctive by the circumcision in their body, plus their language, religious observances, and dress. In the New Testament believers go to everyone—Jews and Gentiles—witnessing what Jesus Christ can do for them. Their impact on Roman society was so great that it was said of them, "These men who have turned the world upside down have come here too" (17:6). The book of Acts begins with the red-hot enthusiasm of a growing church in its first thirty years, and in these thirty years we see all the strengths and weaknesses that will be characteristic of the body of Christ in the next 2,000 years.

KEY FACTS

Author:	Luke
Recipient:	Theophilus
Where:	Unknown (probably in Rome during Paul's imprisonment, 28:16–31)
Date:	AD 60–62
Key Words:	Witness (Gk. *martus*) and Church (Gk. *ekklesia*)
Key Verse:	"But you will receive power when the Holy Spirit has come on you, and you will be my witnesses in Jerusalem, in all Judea and Samaria, and to the end of the earth" (Acts 1:8).

Author

The similarity of the introductions in the Gospel of Luke and the Acts of the Apostles indicates that the same person wrote both books (see discussion of authorship of the Gospel of Luke). Like the Gospel of Luke, Acts is dedicated to Theophilus (Acts 1:1), and the author begins with a clear reference to the Gospel: "I wrote the first narrative" (1:1). The traditional view throughout most of church history is that Luke was the author of both. D. A. Carson and Douglas Moo write, "Luke's authorship of these two books went virtually unchallenged until the onset of critical approaches to the New Testament at the end of the eighteenth century."[1] However, there is no serious external evidence to support the critical view.

The author of Acts is clearly an eyewitness of much of what he writes (note his use of "we" in Acts 16:10–17; 20:5–15; 21:1–18; 27:1–29; 28:1–16, indicating that he was a traveling companion of Paul on these occasions).

Luke was a medical doctor (Col 4:14), and the book of Acts was written by someone who could do careful research (Luke 1:1–4) and had an interest in miracles of healing (3:6–9; 8:7; 9:18, 38–40; 14:8–10; 16:16–18; 19:11–12; 28:3–6), an approach expected of a doctor. Also the classic Greek style of Acts suggests an author who was well educated. All the evidence points to Luke the physician as the author.

Not much is known about the early life of Luke. Most say he was a Gentile, and some claim he was a Greek; however, others believe he was a Jew. Tradition says Luke was born in Antioch (modern-day Syria), although some say he was from Tarsus (modern-day Turkey). This view claims he studied medicine in the same city as Paul's early education and that in the early days they knew each other. Some claim, although it cannot be proven, that Luke was an indentured slave/servant of Theophilus and that the two books were written for his former benefactor.

Recipient

The primary recipient of the book of Acts was a man named Theophilus (Luke 1:3; Acts 1:1). The introduction to Luke calls Theophilus "most honorable," a term similar to "most excellent," which was used of the Roman officials Felix and Festus (Acts 23:26; 24:3; 26:25). Thus, it is possible that Theophilus was a Roman official or nobleman who became a Christian. Of course all that is actually known is that Theophilus was a believer who needed or wanted credible instruction concerning the life of Jesus (the Gospel of Luke) and the growth of the church (the Acts of the Apostles). The fact that Luke and Acts circulated in the early church with the other Gospel stories indicates that Luke must have intended the recipients of both books to be more than just this one man. The explanation of Jewish terms and culture indicates that these books were intended to help a broader Greek audience who lived in the far corners of the Roman Empire and did not have a firsthand understanding of the life of Christ (in Luke) or an appreciation of how God used Peter, Paul, and other leaders in the growth of the early church (in Acts).

Occasion and Date

The introduction to Luke suggests why the two books were written and how they were to be used, "So that you may know the certainty of the things about which you have been instructed" (Luke 1:4). The books were written to give a credible record of Jesus's life and death, then a documented account of the growth and success of the early church. The phrase "know . . .

about the things you have been instructed" suggests the books were written to those who were believers. They needed to be grounded in the truth. This implies they shouldn't base their faith on exaggerated claims or human theories about what may or may not have happened.

It would seem certain that Acts was written before AD 70 when Titus destroyed the temple in Jerusalem. This event was so decisive in the ongoing controversy between Jews and Christians that it seems inconceivable Luke could have left it out. Following this same line of reasoning, Luke doesn't mention Nero and Rome's burning and the resulting persecution of Christians when Nero blamed them for the destruction of the city (AD 64–65). Also, the book of Acts ends before any mention of the results of Paul's trial (AD 62). Then a likely date for Acts is approximately AD 62. It was probably written in Rome while Paul was a prisoner and "stayed two whole years in his own rented house" (28:30).

Genre and Structure

The book of Acts is written in the style of ancient historical writing, interspersed with personal biographies.[2] It also contains twenty-three speeches, which make up one-third of the book.[3] Acts traces the growth of the church in three concentric circles, "But you will receive power when the Holy Spirit has come on you, and you will be my witnesses in Jerusalem, in all Judea and Samaria, and to the end of the earth" (1:8). The church succeeds in witnessing in the first circle in Jerusalem, for "every day in the temple, and in various homes, they continued teaching and proclaiming the good news" (5:42). The church was successful in the second circle of Judea and Samaria because Luke records that "the church then had peace throughout Judea, Galilee, and Samaria, and it became stronger as the believers lived in the fear of the Lord. And with the encouragement of the Holy Spirit, it also grew in numbers" (9:31 NLT). The gospel went out to the third circle that reached the ends of the earth when it reached Rome, the hub of the empire, and from this vibrant city Christians (including soldiers [Phil 1:13; 4:22]) carried the gospel to the ends of the (known) earth.

Outline

I. **Witnessing in Jerusalem (1:1–8:3)**
  A. Birth of the Church at Pentecost (1:1–2:47)
  B. Expansion of the Church in Jerusalem (3:1–8:3)
II. **Witnessing in Judea and Samaria (8:4–12:25)**
  A. Ministry of Philip (8:4–40)
  B. Conversion of Paul (9:1–31)
  C. Ministry of Peter (9:32–12:25)
III. **Witnessing to the Uttermost Parts of the Earth (13:1–28:31)**
  A. Paul's First Missionary Journey (13:1–14:27)
  B. Jerusalem Council (15:1–35)
  C. Paul's Second Missionary Journey (15:36–18:22)
  D. Paul's Third Missionary Journey (18:23–21:19)
  E. Paul's Arrest, Imprisonment, and Voyage to Rome (21:20–28:31)

Message

The birth and growth of the church in Acts reveals God's plan to take the gospel to the world as an extension of the Jewish messianic hope from its beginning in Jewish Jerusalem (Acts 1) to the heart of the Gentile world

Sections of the eastern wall of the old city of Jerusalem.

in Rome (Acts 28). As Luke traces the story of the birth and growth of Christianity, he records the earliest history of the Christian church.

I. Witnessing in Jerusalem (Acts 1:1–8:3)

A. Birth of the Church at Pentecost (Acts 1:1–2:47)

Following the resurrection, Jesus appeared to the disciples for forty days, commissioning the disciples to be His witnesses from Jerusalem to the ends of the earth (1:1–3). After Christ's ascension the disciples and 120 people received the baptism of the Holy Spirit on the day of Pentecost, a Jewish feast held fifty days after Passover (2:1–13). As a result of Peter's preaching, 3,000 people were saved and baptized, and the New Testament church was launched (2:14–47).

B. Expansion of the Church in Jerusalem (Acts 3:1–8:3)

Once the church was established, Luke records how the Jerusalem church grew. The author meticulously records the numbers of converts, which immediately begin multiplying by the thousands (4:4). At the end of the first major section of the book, Luke emphasized that "the word of God spread [and] the disciples in Jerusalem increased greatly in number" (6:7). Throughout the book of Acts, Luke traced numerical growth as an evidence of God's blessing. Although many Jews became disciples, there was strong opposition by Jewish officials, and Stephen became the first Christian martyred for preaching the gospel (7:1–60).

II. Witnessing in Judea and Samaria (Acts 8:4–12:25)

A. Ministry of Philip (Acts 8:4–40)

After the martyrdom of Stephen, Philip, one of the seven original deacons (7:1–6), went to Samaria preaching the gospel with great power and success (8:4–17). In response to the Samaritans' conversions, Peter and John came from Jerusalem to lay hands on the new believers and imparted the Holy Spirit to them, demonstrating continuity between the Jewish and Samaritan believers. Later Philip was led of the Spirit to witness to the Ethiopian eunuch on the road to Gaza (8:26–39). After Philip explained Jesus to him from Isaiah 53, the eunuch believed and was baptized. His return to Ethiopia is credited with spreading the gospel into Africa at that time.

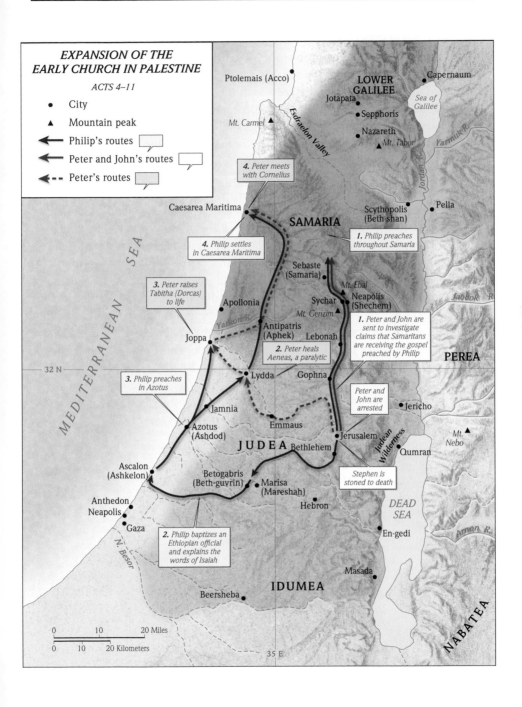

EXPANSION OF THE EARLY CHURCH IN PALESTINE

ACTS 4–11

- ● City
- ▲ Mountain peak
- ← Philip's routes
- ← Peter and John's routes
- ◄-- Peter's routes

Ptolemais (Acco)

LOWER GALILEE

Capernaum

Sea of Galilee

Jotapata

Sepphoris

Mt. Carmel ▲

Esdraelon Valley

Nazareth

▲ Mt. Tabor

Yarmuk R.

Jordan

4. Peter meets with Cornelius

Caesarea Maritima

SAMARIA

Scythopolis (Beth-shan)

Pella

1. Philip preaches throughout Samaria

4. Philip settles in Caesarea Maritima

Sebaste (Samaria)

Mt. Ebal

Jabbok R.

MEDITERRANEAN SEA

3. Peter raises Tabitha (Dorcas) to life

Apollonia

Sychar

Neapolis (Shechem)

Mt. Gerizim ▲

Yarkon R.

Antipatris (Aphek)

Lebonah

1. Peter and John are sent to investigate claims that Samaritans are receiving the gospel preached by Philip

PEREA

Joppa

2. Peter heals Aeneas, a paralytic

32 N

3. Philip preaches in Azotus

Lydda

Gophna

Peter and John are arrested

Jericho

Jamnia

Emmaus

Mt. Nebo ▲

Azotus (Ashdod)

JUDEA

Bethlehem

Jerusalem

Judean Wilderness

Qumran

Ascalon (Ashkelon)

Betogabris (Beth-guvrin)

Marisa (Mareshah)

Stephen is stoned to death

Anthedon Neapolis

Hebron

DEAD SEA

Gaza

En-gedi

Amnon R.

2. Philip baptizes an Ethiopian official and explains the words of Isaiah

N. Besor

Masada

Beersheba

IDUMEA

NABATEA

0   10   20 Miles

0   10   20 Kilometers

35 E

B. Conversion of Paul (Acts 9:1–31)

A decisive event in the history of Christianity took place when Saul (later Paul), a member of the Jewish Sanhedrin, was converted to Christ on the road to Damascus. Blinded by a vision of the risen Christ, Saul was later healed and baptized by a disciple named Ananias. Immediately the converted Saul became a bold proclaimer of the gospel of Jesus, the promised Messiah. Saul would eventually exchange his Jewish name for the Greco-Roman name Paul, as he expanded his ministry to the Gentiles.

C. Ministry of Peter (Acts 9:32–12:25)

The next major events in the history of Christianity included Peter's ministry to the Jews in Syrian Antioch (9:32–43), his vision at Joppa (10:1–8), and his witness to Cornelius, which resulted in the conversion of the first Gentiles (10:9–48). These chapters contain the accounts of Christianity's first break with Jewish dietary laws, social customs, and the inclusion of Gentiles. The salvation and baptism of Gentiles at Caesarea opened the door to the next level of world evangelism. Later the good news spread to Syrian Antioch, and many believed (11:19–30), but Jewish leaders killed James and had Peter thrown in jail (12:1–19). Not long after this God brought Herod's life to an end because he accepted worship (12:20–25).

Ruins of Caesarea Maritima on the Mediterranean Sea. This was the area where Herod died.

III. Witnessing to the Uttermost Parts of the Earth
   (Acts 13:1–28:31)

A. Paul's First Missionary Journey (13:1–14:27)

Next the church advanced to Cyprus and Asia Minor as Paul, Barnabas, and John Mark were sent out as missionaries from the church at Antioch in Syria (13:1–3). While they were ministering on Cyprus, a Jewish magician was struck blind, a Roman proconsul was converted, and Saul's name was changed to Paul (13:4–12). From Cyprus the team moved into Asia Minor (modern Turkey), to Pamphylia, and then into the province of Galatia. At Perga, John Mark left and returned to Jerusalem while Paul and Barnabas went on to Pisidian Antioch, Iconium, Lystra, and Derbe before returning to Antioch in Syria. There was opposition to the gospel in Cyprus (13:6–11), Antioch (13:45), Iconium (14:5), and Lystra (14:19), but later Paul returned to these places to strengthen the saints in each city (14:21–28).

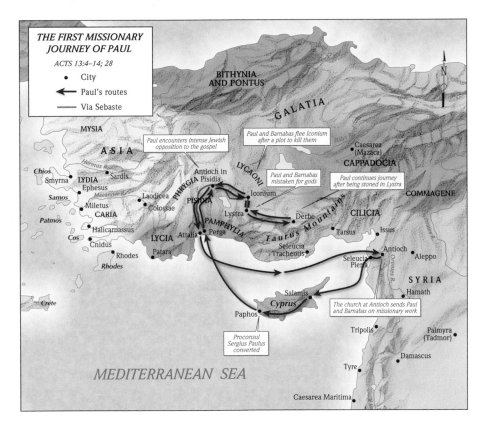

B. Jerusalem Council (Acts 15:1–35)

A serious disagreement arose at Antioch as to whether the new Gentile converts needed to be circumcised. The church sent Paul and Barnabas to Jerusalem to report on their Gentile mission and to settle the issue with the apostles. The Jerusalem Council was held in AD 49, where it was determined that Gentiles were not required to be circumcised (15:10) and that both Jews and Gentiles were saved by grace through faith alone (15:11). James, Jesus's brother, pastor of the Jerusalem church, presided over the council. A letter was then issued declaring their official position and circulated to the churches expressing apostolic authority (15:22–30).

The rocky outcrop known as Mars Hill in Athens seen from the Acropolis.

C. Paul's Second Missionary Journey (Acts 15:36–18:22)

Upon returning from Jerusalem, Paul and Barnabas decided to revisit the converts from their first journey. However, a disagreement arose over taking John Mark along. Ultimately, Barnabas took Mark and retuned to Cyprus. Paul chose Silas and took the overland route through Syria and Cilicia to southern Galatia. At Lystra, Timothy joined them, and they continued west to Troas, where Paul received the "Macedonian call" to take the gospel to Greece (16:9–10). Luke then traces Paul's evangelistic mission to the Greek cities of Philippi (16:11–40), Thessalonica (17:1–9), Berea (17:10–14),

Athens (17:15–34), and Corinth (18:1–17), and then to Ephesus in Asia Minor (18:18–22).

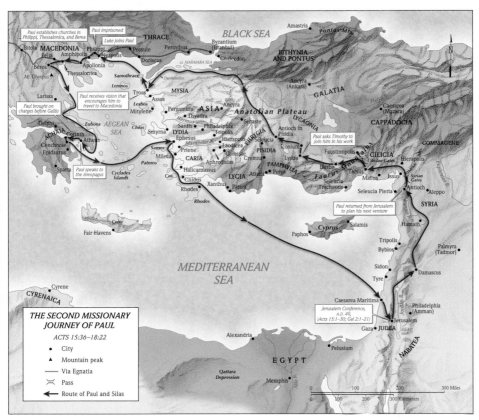

D. Paul's Third Missionary Journey (Acts 18:23–21:19)

Shortly after arriving back in Antioch, Paul began his third missionary journey, retracing the steps of his second journey, until he came again to Ephesus (19:1–19). Paul's evangelistic ministry was so successful among the Gentiles that a public demonstration broke out in the arena led by silver-smith idol makers whose business losses were extensive because of the great number of Christian converts. Leaving Ephesus, Paul ministered to the churches throughout Macedonia and Greece (20:1–2) and backtracked again to Troas (20:3–6) where he raised young Eutychus from the dead (20:6–12). From there Paul sailed to Miletus where he met the Ephesian elders. Following a tearful farewell, Paul sailed to Tyre and traveled on to Caesarea and Jerusalem.

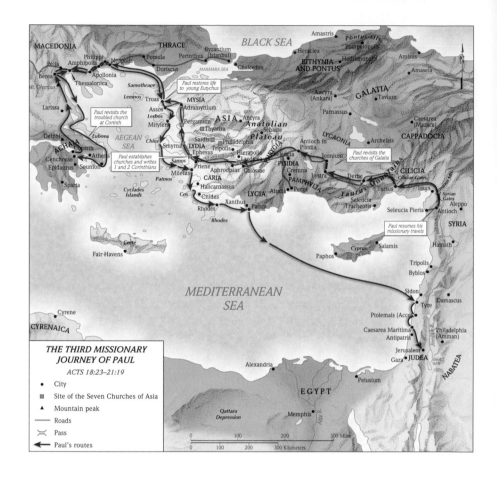

THE THIRD MISSIONARY
JOURNEY OF PAUL
ACTS 18:23–21:19

- City
- Site of the Seven Churches of Asia
- Mountain peak
— Roads
✕ Pass
◀— Paul's routes

E. Paul's Arrest, Imprisonment, and Voyage to Rome (Acts 21:20–28:31)

At Jerusalem, Paul was arrested by Jewish authorities, and he defended himself before the Sanhedrin (22:30–23:10). Tensions were so high the Roman authority transferred Paul to Felix, the governor at Caesarea. During his two years at Caesarea, Paul presented his case before Felix, Festus, and Herod Agrippa. In the meantime, being a Roman citizen, Paul appealed to Caesar and was sent to Rome. However, the voyage ended in a shipwreck off the island of Malta before Paul was finally placed under house arrest in Rome where he continued preaching the gospel of Jesus Christ (28:31).

Practical Application

The book of Acts begins with Peter preaching the gospel in Jerusalem, the metropolitan center of Judaism. It ends with Paul preaching the gospel in Rome, the metropolitan center of the Roman Empire and the Gentile world. Interestingly, there is no conclusion to the Acts of the Apostles. The final verses read, "[Paul] welcomed all who visited him, proclaiming the kingdom of God and teaching about the Lord Jesus Christ with all boldness and without hindrance" (28:30–31). Luke does not conclude with a sermon, nor is there a benediction or signature by Luke. The author simply ends by bringing the reader the latest news in the ongoing ministry of the risen Savior through the Holy Spirit.

There are five key ideas in Acts; four of these are key words: *witnessing* (19 times), *church* (56 times), *Holy Spirit* (41 times) and *prayer* (27 times). The other is that of the growth of the church and the spread of the Christian gospel, which is attested throughout the book (2:41; 4:4; 6:7; 8:25; 10:44–48; 13:12, 43; 16:14–34; 17:6, 12; 18:10). The book of Acts is filled with gospel preaching, including sermons by Peter, Stephen, and Paul. "Believers who were scattered preached the Good News about Jesus wherever they went" (8:4 NLT). They used "saturation evangelism," using every available method at every available time to reach every available person. So they were accused of having "filled Jerusalem with your teaching" (5:28). They went door to door (5:42) and shared Christ at work and in the marketplace. They used many techniques involving witnessing (*martureō*) (1:8); talking (*daleō*) (4:1); evangelizing (*evangelizō*) (8:4); explaining (*dianoigō*) (17:3); teaching (*didaskō*) (6:48); reasoning (*dialegomai*) (18:4); discussing (*suzeteō*) (6:9); announcing (*kerussō*) (8:5); and making disciples (9:22).

The church met in synagogues, by the riverside, on Solomon's porch, in an upper (banquet) room, on mountains, in caves, in various homes of believers (6:42; 10:25; 16:40; 17:7; 18:7), and in lecture halls (19:9), or at any place they could gather. First they met for prayer (1:14) then added evangelism (2:14), teaching (2:42), Communion (2:42) and fellowship (2:42). The church slowly organized itself, first adding a twelfth apostle to take Judas's place (1:15:26), then deacons (6:1–7). Next they ordained elders (11:30; 14:23); and when there was a major doctrinal problem, they called a church council (15:1–12). Then they agreed on a written explanation that was to be circulated among the churches (15:20–35). When faced with persecution, Irenaeus said, "They despised death, and even showed themselves superior to death."[4]

The church is victorious because its witness is empowered by the Holy Spirit. The book of Acts is filled with prayerful intercession and becomes a prayer manual to succeeding generations. The church is praying in the upper room when Acts opens (1:14). After the Holy Spirit was poured out at Pentecost, they continued daily in prayer (2:42–6:4). The apostles went daily to the temple to pray (3:1). When persecution broke out, they prayed (4:24). Paul fasted and prayed three days after meeting Jesus on the Damascus road (9:9–11). Both Cornelius and Peter were praying when God directed an outpouring of the Holy Spirit on the Gentiles (10:2 ff). Prayer delivered Peter from prison (12:5). As the church was praying (13:2–3), the Holy Spirit called Paul and Barnabas to their first missionary tour. Paul met people praying by a river in Philippi, and when arrested and beaten, he sang psalms and prayed in prison (16:25). And Paul healed the sick with prayer (28:8). Spirit-empowered, praying believers were used by God to launch the church, and the same are needed to continue its impact in today's world as well.

For Further Reading

Bock, Darrell L. *Acts*. BECNT. Grand Rapids: Baker, 2007.

Bruce, F. F. *Commentary on the Book of Acts*. NICNT. Grand Rapids: Eerdmans, 1964.

Ger, Stephen. *Acts: Witness to the World*. Chattanooga: AMG Publishers, 2004.

Polhill, John. *Acts*. NAC. Nashville: B&H, 1992.

Stott, John. *The Message of Acts*. The Bible Speaks Today. Downers Grove, IL: IVP, 1990.

Toussaint, Stanley D. "Acts." *BKCNT*. Ed. John F. Walvoord and Roy B. Zuck. Wheaton: Victor, 1983.

CHRONOLOGY OF ACTS[5]		
Event	**Chapter**	**Date**
Christ's Ascension	Acts 1	May, AD 33
Pentecost	Acts 2	May, AD 33
Peter and John Arrested	Acts 3–4	Summer, AD 33
Apostles Arrested	Acts 5	AD 34
Deacons Appointed	Acts 6	Winter, AD 35
Death of Stephen	Acts 7	Spring AD 35
Samaritans Believe	Acts 8	Summer, AD 35
Saul's Commission	Acts 9	Summer, AD 35
Saul's Damascus Ministry	Acts 9	AD 35–37
Saul Returns to Jerusalem, Sent to Tarsus	Acts 9	Fall, AD 37
Peter Meets Cornelius	Acts 10	AD 40
Paul in Antioch	Acts 11	AD 42
Death of James and Herod Agrippa	Acts 12	AD 44
Saul and Barnabas in Jerusalem	Acts 12	Fall, AD 47
First Missionary Journey	Acts 13–14	Spring, AD 48–Fall 49
Jerusalem Council	Acts 15	Late AD 49/Early 50
Second Missionary Journey	Acts 16–18	Spring, AD 50–Fall 52
Third Missionary Journey	Acts 18–21	Spring, AD 53–May 57
Paul Imprisoned	Acts 22	June, AD 57–Summer 59
Voyage to Rome	Acts 27	Summer, AD 59–March 60
Paul's Roman Imprisonment	Acts 28	March, AD 60–Spring 62
Death of James		Spring, AD 62
Death of Peter		Summer, AD 64
Death of Paul		Early AD 68
Jerusalem Destroyed		Summer, AD 70

Study Questions

1. One of Luke's goals was to show the movement of the gospel from Jerusalem to Rome. What were the evidences of that growth?
2. The book of Acts is about prayers and God's answers to them. Where and when did people pray, and what was the outcome?
3. The book of Acts is about witnessing. What are ways this was accomplished?
4. The book of Acts is about the Holy Spirit. How did the Holy Spirit work, and what were His results?
5. What principles can we derive from Acts about evangelism, church planting, and church growth?
6. What personal lessons and challenges have you learned about God's calling on your life from the book of Acts?

Notes

1. D. A. Carson and Douglas J. Moo, *An Introduction to the New Testament*, rev. ed. (Grand Rapids: Zondervan, 2005), 291.

2. Darrell Bock, *Acts*, BECNT (Grand Rapids: Baker, 2007), 15.

3. For a list of the speeches, see Joseph Fitzmyer, *The Acts of the Apostles*, Anchor Bible (Garden City, NY: Doubleday, 1998), 103–5. See also John Polhill, *Acts*, NAC (Nashville: B&H, 1992), 43–47.

4. Francis X. Glimm, Joseph M.-F. Marique, and Gerald G. Wals, *The Apostolic Fathers*, vol. 1 of *The Fathers of the Church* (Washington, DC: Catholic University of America Press, 1947), 119.

5. Steven Ger, *The Book of Acts: Witness to the World* (Chattanooga: AMG, 2004), 9.

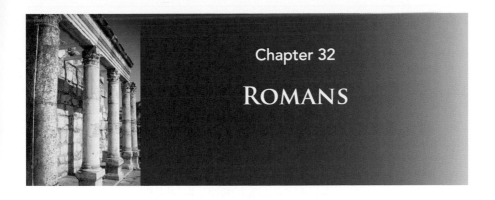

Chapter 32

ROMANS

Power of the Gospel

P eople have called the apostle Paul's great epistle to the Romans "the most profound work in existence" (Samuel Coleridge). Martin Luther called it the "purest gospel." The teaching of Romans is not only crucial for Christian theology, but the greatest revivals and reformations throughout the history of Christianity have resulted from an increased understanding and application of the teaching of this epistle. Mankind is faced with a monstrous problem: How can a person be rightly related to the God who created the universe and will someday righteously judge all people? All are condemned by sin, with no hope of reconciliation with God on their own. Paul says the answer is the gospel of Jesus Christ. The Christian *euangelion* (gospel) is the universal message of God's saving grace through faith in Christ.

KEY FACTS

Author:	Paul
Recipients:	Believers at Rome
Where:	Corinth (Achaia, Greece)
Date:	Winter of AD 56/57
Key Word:	Gospel (Gk. *euangelion*)
Key Verse:	"For I am not ashamed of the gospel, because it is the power of God for salvation to everyone who believes, first to the Jew, and also to the Greek" (1:16).

Author

The epistle to the Romans identifies its author as Paul, a slave of Christ Jesus (1:1). He twice refers to himself as an apostle to the Gentiles (11:13; 15:15–20). Paul's Hebrew name was Saul, and his Roman/Greek name was Paul. He probably had both names from childhood since he was born a Roman citizen (Acts 22:28) of Jewish parents (Acts 23:6; Phil 3:5). In his epistles he always refers to himself as Paul. Luke used the name Saul only in Acts 7–13, and Paul used it in describing his conversion experience (Acts 22:7, 13; 26:14) since he was quoting Jesus in the Hebrew (or Aramaic) language.

Paul's principal achievements were twofold: (1) He wrote thirteen books of the New Testament, which are a primary source of theological information; and (2) he was the principal leader in extending the church into Asia Minor and Greece, becoming known as the premier apostle to the Gentiles. Acts 13–28 focuses mainly on the ministry of Paul. Paul was a unique Christian leader: a fearless champion and exponent of Christianity, a genius of church planting and discipleship, and the most influential missionary, preacher, and teacher of the early church. Dedication and intensity were primary attributes. The book of Acts ends by describing Paul's first imprisonment in Rome. He was apparently released from this incarceration about AD 62 and conducted a vigorous ministry in

Nero, Roman emperor from AD 54 to 68. Nero was emperor when Paul wrote his letter to the Romans.

Crete, Asia (the province), Macedonia, and perhaps Spain. During Nero's persecution (c. AD 64–68), Paul was again arrested and put in a Roman prison. This time there was no hope of release (2 Tim 4:6). According to later church writers he was beheaded (probably AD 66–67).

Recipients

The epistle was written to believers in Rome (1:7, 15). At this time Rome was the largest and most important city of the world. Its population is estimated at one to four million. There was a large percentage of slaves and poor people. About a dozen Jewish synagogues were located throughout the city.

Archaeologists have discovered an inscription on part of a pavement (dating from about AD 50) found near the theater in Corinth mentioning "Erastus," who was the aedile of the city of Corinth. An "aedile" was in charge of the financial matters of the city. Romans 16:23 says, "Erastus, the city treasurer . . . [greets] you." This "Erastus" is probably the same person mentioned in this inscription, which can be translated, "Erastus in return for his aedileship laid [the pavement] at his own expense."

Paul did not start the church at Rome (1:13), and there is no definite record of how the church began. There are three principal suggestions:

1. Jews who were saved in Jerusalem on the day of Pentecost when the church began (Acts 2:10) returned to Rome and founded the church.[1]

2. The Roman Catholic view is that the apostle Peter went to Rome about AD 42 and founded the church. There are four principal objections to this view: (a) there is no evidence that Peter was in Rome before AD 62 at the earliest; (b) in his prison epistles written from Rome (AD 61–62), Paul never mentions Peter; (c) Luke does not mention Peter in his record of Paul's arrival in Rome in Acts 27–28; and (d) Paul states in Romans 15:20 that he didn't build on "someone else's foundation" (that is, he didn't try to establish churches where other apostles had already done so), yet he wanted to go to Rome to establish the brethren (1:11) and preach the gospel (1:15).

3. Paul's converts founded the church. Many of Paul's converts in Greece and Asia Minor later went to Rome. His greetings in Romans 16 reveal that Paul had many personal acquaintances in the Roman church. Priscilla and Aquila were among those who had a church in their home in Rome (16:3–5). This view seems preferable.

The church in Rome probably consisted of at least five household churches rather than one large church. Five assemblies are apparently greeted in Romans 16:5, 10, 11, 14, 15. In addition, at the beginning of the epistle, Paul addresses the believers as "all who are in Rome," rather than "the church at Rome." The Roman church consisted of both Gentiles and Jews, but the majority were Gentiles. Paul emphasizes that he was an apostle to the Gentiles (Rom 1:5; 11:13; 15:16). In 9:3 he speaks of the Jews as "my" brothers, not "our" brothers. And in Romans 16 more than half the names of people greeted by Paul are Latin or Greek.

The Roman Forum with columns of the temple of Saturn in the foreground.

Occasion and Date

The book of Romans was written in Corinth, in the province of Achaia. Paul said that he was leaving for Jerusalem soon (Rom 15:25). Further, in Rom 16:1 Paul mentions Cenchrae as the home of Phoebe, who took the letter to Rome for Paul; Cenchrae was a seaport of Corinth, about four miles away (cf. Acts 18:18).

Paul's letter to the Romans was likely written during the winter of AD 56/57 near the end of Paul's third journey (c. AD 53–57). Priscilla and Aquila, whom he first met in Corinth during his second journey and who accompanied him to Ephesus thereafter, were back in Rome by the time Paul wrote Romans (16:3). And since Paul states that he was about to leave for

Jerusalem (and then to Rome, Rom 15:25), this must have occurred during his third journey, since Paul did not go to Jerusalem at the end of his second journey (Acts 18:22).

The excavations of Corinth showing the shops in the agora.

Genre/Structure

Epistles are the most common literary form in the New Testament. They are "occasional" letters; that is, they were designed to deal with specific situations. Their style was part everyday correspondence (like most personal letters today) and part literary production (with rhetorical strategies intended to advance theological and practical arguments). Paul's epistles typically begin with his name and some designation of his recipients, followed by a greeting, blessing, and thanksgiving to God for what he had recently heard about the recipients, then the body of the letter in which he presents both theological and practical concerns, followed often by a lengthy conclusion in which he summarizes his points and gives final greetings.

Paul's epistle to the Romans is Paul's most extensive theological writing. It stands first among the epistles because it is the longest and because it was considered the most significant apostolic letter. Many theological leaders, including Augustine, Luther, Melanchthon, and John Wesley, have claimed that Romans changed their lives and ministries more than any other part of the Bible.

Outline

Message

I. Introduction (Romans 1:1–17)

Paul introduces himself to the Romans as a slave of Jesus Christ and one who was set apart to preach the gospel, focused on Christ Himself (1:1–6). Paul wants to visit the Roman believers soon and lists some reasons he is longing to see them (1:11–15). Before moving into his doctrinal presentation, Paul states the theme of his letter in two ways: (1) the gospel is the power of God that leads to salvation (1:16), and (2) the righteousness of God by faith is revealed in the gospel (1:17).

II. Doctrine (Romans 1:18–11:36)

The first major portion of the body of Paul's letter to the Romans deals with doctrine (1:18–11:36), moving from condemnation (1:18–3:20) to salvation (3:21–8:39) to vindication (9:1–11:36).

A. Condemnation: The Revelation of God's Wrath (Romans 1:18–3:20)

Paul begins the doctrinal portion of his epistle by describing the revelation of God's wrath on all mankind. He shows first that the pagans (unrighteous, idolatrous people) of the world are under God's wrath because they rejected the knowledge of God available in creation and turned to idolatry instead. God in turn gave them over to a life of immorality and depravity (1:18–32). Second, moralists (those who profess to have a personal moral code—both Gentiles and Jews) are under God's condemnation. Though they think they are righteous by their own standards, they don't match up to God's standards. Third, Jews specifically are under condemnation because, though they have God's law and think they're righteous, they are actually breaking it in many ways (2:17–3:8). Finally, Paul shows that the whole world is under sin and therefore guilty before God. All are accountable, and no one can be justified by his own good works, with or without the law (3:10–20).

B. Justification: The Imputation of God's Righteousness (Romans 3:21–5:21)

The answer to mankind's dilemma is that God's righteousness is revealed to man through the gospel, bringing salvation by faith. Paul describes first the imputation of God's righteousness to man—justification (3:21–5:21), and second, the impartation of God's righteousness in and through man—sanctification (6:1–8:39). Justification includes the imputation of God's righteousness by means of faith in Jesus Christ. This justification was provided by Christ's substitutionary death on the cross as a satisfaction for man's sin for all who come to Christ in faith (3:24–26). Justification by faith makes all equal before God and gives the law its rightful place of condemning sin (3:27–31).

Ancient city wall of Rome.

The story of Abraham demonstrates that salvation and God's righteousness are God's gift through faith (4:1–23). Even though people are still sinners, Christ died for them and made reconciliation to God possible (5:1–11). Adam's sin brought death into the world for everyone, but Christ brought grace, life, and justification (5:12–21).

C. Sanctification: The Impartation of God's Holiness (Romans 6:1–8:39)

This leads Paul into the second aspect of salvation: sanctification, the impartation of God's righteousness in and through the believer to conform him progressively to the image of Jesus Christ. Since Christ was his substitute on the cross, the believer died with Christ and is identified with Him also in His resurrection. The believer should therefore consider himself dead to sin but now alive to God and God's righteousness (6:1–14). He should yield both himself and his body to God in order to live God's righteousness every day (6:12–14). The believer is not free to sin now that he is under the grace of God (6:15). Obedience to a master makes one a slave of that master, so the believer should now yield himself to his new master (God) to fulfill His righteousness (6:16–23). This brings progressive holiness (sanctification) in the present life. The believer's eternal life is a gift from God (6:22–23) and can't be earned. The presence of the indwelling Holy Spirit has set believers free from the law and the rule of sin and death (7:1–11). Although believers live in a sinful, corrupt world, the Spirit gives a believer a new life (7:12–25) and understands every person's weakness, so no matter what problems arise, nothing can separate that person from God's love (8:26–39).

D. Vindication: Israel's Future Redemption (Romans 9:1–11:36)

Now Paul returns to the question of Israel in order to vindicate God's righteousness in His dealings with the Jews. He shows that God's present rejection of Israel for their unbelief is not inconsistent with God's promises to them (9:6–13). God never promised that all the physical descendants of Abraham would be saved. Israel is guilty for rejecting God's righteousness by faith and trying instead to establish their own righteousness (9:30–10:4). They ignored Old Testament teaching on the gospel of grace. Salvation was always available through faith (10:5–10) to both Jews and Gentiles (10:11–13). The Jews simply needed to acknowledge Jesus Christ as Lord and Savior (10:9–10), but most refused to do this. The gospel was preached to Israel; they heard it (10:18) and understood it (10:19–20) but rejected it. They therefore stand under the condemnation of God (10:21).

But God is not finished with Israel. Israel's rejection is neither complete nor final (11:1–10), for God always has a believing remnant among His people, as seen in the case of Paul himself. The rejection is also temporary since God is using the present hardness of Israel to pour out blessings on the Gentiles (11:11–15) and will one day restore the Jews as a nation in God's favor. Israel's future restoration is certain, as one day all Israel will be saved (11:25–27) and God will have mercy on them (11:28–32).

III. Duties (Romans 12:1–15:13)

The third major section of Romans describes the duties of those who are justified. These include duties toward the brothers (12:1–21), toward the government (13:1–14), and toward the weak and the strong (14:1–15:13). The foundation of all of Christian conduct is the consecration of the believer's life to God by presenting his body as an offering for God's service (12:1) and the transformation of the believer's life daily through the continual renewing of his mind and attitude (12:2).

A. Toward the Brothers (Romans 12:1–21)

Believers must live in humility and love toward other brothers and sisters in the assembly. They are to use their spiritual gifts in accordance with the ministry God has assigned to them (12:6–8). They should love others sincerely and zealously, and respond to evil treatment with blessing and humility, without taking vengeance (12:9–21).

B. Toward the Government (Romans 13:1–14)

Believers need to be in subjection to their government because its authority ultimately comes from God and God has designed civil government to punish evil and reward good (13:1–7). The duty that a believer owes to others is to love them since loving one's neighbor fulfills the requirements of the law toward others. The new age is at hand, and Christians must change their conduct to conform to the character of Christ (13:11–14).

C. Toward the Weak and the Strong (14:1–15:13)

Paul ends his discussion of duties with four strong exhortations designed to promote harmony in the church between those who are weak in faith and those who are strong: (1) the weak and the strong must accept each other since both are accepted by God, both belong to God, and both will be judged by God (14:1–12); (2) the strong believer should not cause the weak believer to stumble in his life but rather be concerned for him (14:13–18) and do what leads to peace and edification (14:19–21); (3) the strong believer needs to help the weak believer, just as Christ did not live to please Himself but took upon Himself the sins of the world (15:1–6); (4) both the weak and the strong should accept one another, just as Christ has accepted both Jews and Gentiles in the Church for God's glory (15:7–13).

IV. Conclusion (Romans 15:14–16:27)

Paul revisits his motivation for writing the letter. God has given him the ministry of apostle to the Gentiles, and he has preached the gospel to Gentiles all the way from Jerusalem to Illyricum (northwest of Greece). Everything Paul has accomplished among the Gentiles was done by Christ Himself (15:18). Paul now wants the Romans to pray that he will at last be able to come to them and others further west

The exterior of the Colosseum (Flavian Amphitheater) in Rome. Its construction was begun under the emperor Vespasian in AD 72. Many Christians were martyred here during the early persecutions, which lasted until Emperor Constantine's rule.

in the blessing of God (15:22–33) after a brief detour to Jerusalem.

The final chapter is filled with greetings for those whom Paul knows by name in Rome. He mentions the one who is taking the letter to them—Phoebe (16:1–2) and his old friends Aquila and Priscilla. The final benediction summarizes many of the topics Paul emphasized throughout the epistle (16:25–27).

Practical Application

The epistle to the Romans is Paul's theological and practical magnum opus. He believed God wanted him to take the gospel westward beyond Rome (beginning at Spain), but he needed the support of the Roman church to do this. Therefore, Paul threw everything he had into this letter to convince the believers at the center of the Roman Empire that they could trust him, his goals, and his preaching. Paul said he was not ashamed of the gospel (Rom 1:16). In fact, he eventually gave his life for it. Have you ever been ashamed to admit you are a Christian? Was it because you weren't living right? Because others were treating you wrongly? Or were you embarrassed by the attitudes of other professing Christians and didn't want to be identified with them? We can't always make others do the right thing, but we can certainly decide to live out our own faith in the power of the gospel of God's grace. If He loves you enough to save you, He loves you enough to keep you.

THE SIGNIFICANT EVENTS OF OUR SALVATION[2]	
Foreknown	Previously known in an intimate, personal way.
	Rom 8:29; 11:2; 1 Pet 1:2
Predestined	Beforehand encircled and destined for salvation
	Rom 8:29, 30; Eph 1:5, 11
Called	Specifically called and chosen for salvation
	Rom 8:30; Eph 1:4; 1 Pet 1:1–2; 2:4; 9
Justified	Legally acquitted, to receive imputed righteousness from Christ
	Rom 3:5, 21; 4:3, 5; 8:30, 33; 2 Cor 5:21; Gal 5:5; Eph 4:24
Sanctified	"Set aside," made holy by being joined to Christ
	Rom 1:7; 1 Cor 1:2; 6:11; Eph 1:4, 5:26; 1 Pet 1:2
Glorified	Positionally, already glorified in the mind of God
	Isa 43:7; Rom 8:30

For Further Reading

Kroll, Woodrow. *Romans: Righteousness in Christ*. Chattanooga: AMG, 2002.
McClain, Alva. *Romans: The Gospel of God's Grace*. Winona Lake, IN: BMH Books, 1979.
Moo, Douglas. *Romans*. NICNT. Grand Rapids: Eerdmans, 1996.
Morris, Leon. *The Epistle to the Romans*. Grand Rapids: Eerdmans, 1988.
Mounce, Robert. *Romans*. NAC. Nashville: B&H, 1995.
Murray, John. *The Epistle to the Romans*. Grand Rapids: Eerdmans, 1997.
Schreiner, Thomas. *Romans*. BECNT. Grand Rapids: Baker, 1998.

Study Questions

1. How is righteousness related to faith?
2. What is justification, and how does it relate to God's grace?
3. What are the fruits (results) of justification?
4. What did Paul mean by "grace" in Romans?
5. What is Paul's answer to the problem of sin in Romans 6–7?
6. In what way is the Holy Spirit important to living a Christian life?
7. What does Paul teach in Romans about the Jewish "remnant" and the future of Israel?
8. Who should obey governmental authority, and why?
9. Who are "weaker" believers, and what should the church do about them?
10. What was Paul planning to do after writing this epistle, and why?

Notes

1. Acts 18:2; Suetonius, *Claudius* 25.4; cf. Harry J. Leon, *The Jews of Ancient Rome*, updated ed. (Peabody, MA: Hendrickson Publishers, 1995), 23–27.

2. Woodrow Kroll, *Romans: Righteousness in Christ* (Chattanooga: AMG, 2002), 140.

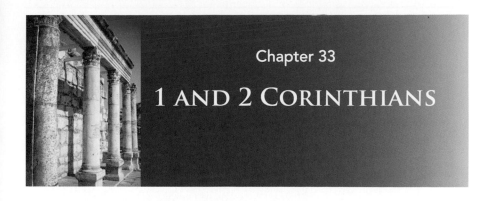

Chapter 33

1 AND 2 CORINTHIANS

Grace Under Siege

P aul's letters to the Corinthians deal with the challenges of Christians living in a hostile culture. The church at Corinth was far from the ideal model of a first-century apostolic church. It was planted in one of the most difficult and challenging cities in the Roman world. To this burgeoning young church, with all its potential and all its problems, Paul wrote these intensely personal letters. Their challenges were not unlike the challenges facing the church today. Living by faith in an unregenerate world is never easy. Thus, Paul reminds us, as well as them, of the gospel—"by which you are being saved" (1 Cor 15:2). And he challenges each generation of believers to be "steadfast, immovable, always excelling in the Lord's work" (1 Cor 15:58).

1 CORINTHIANS

Problems in the Church

First Corinthians is a letter from a missionary pastor who came as a father (4:14–15) to address a local church about local church problems. He wrote with love and a spirit of gentleness, hoping the issues would be resolved so he did not need to come later with discipline (4:21). Some of the problems of the city of Corinth caused problems in the church in Corinth.

KEY FACTS	
Authors:	Paul
Recipients:	The church at Corinth (1:2)
Where:	Ephesus
Date:	AD 56
Key Word:	Love (Gk. *agapē*)
Key Verse:	"Now these three remain: faith, hope, and love—but the greatest of these is love" (13:13)

Author

First Corinthians 1:1 identifies Paul as the author of this letter, a fact that is generally accepted (see also 1:12–17; 3:4–6, 22; 16:21).

> Both 1 and 2 Corinthians are attributed to Paul in their salutations and show every historical and literary evidence of Pauline authorship. Indeed, the Pauline authorship of 1 Corinthians has never been disputed and the letter is already attested in the 90s by Clement of Rome (cf. 1 Clem. 37:5; 47:1–3; 49:5) and in the first decade of the second century by Ignatius (cf. Ignatius Eph. 16:1; 18:1; Rom. 5:1, etc.).[1]

What is more, the contents of this book coincide with what is known of Paul in his travels in Acts.

Recipients

The city of Corinth, a Roman colony, was the capital of the Roman province of Achaia. Situated on the Peloponnesian peninsula, Corinth was located by the isthmus that joined the Ionian and Aegean seas. The area was a center for commerce, bringing many travelers through the region. As a result, Corinth was known for its wealth and for being the center of worship of Aphrodite, goddess of love and immorality. From this city Paul wrote the first chapter of Romans containing the most graphic description of immorality in the New Testament. Some of that climate had infected the church there.

Occasion and Date

First Corinthians was written while Paul was in Ephesus near the end of his third missionary journey, putting the date at AD 56 (16:5–9). Paul planted a church in the city of Corinth on his second missionary journey (Acts 18:1–18), staying with them for a year and a half (Acts 18:11). On his third missionary journey, Paul's main stop was in Ephesus where he remained

The area where the shops and agora of ancient Corinth were located.

and ministered for about two and a half years (AD 53–56; cf. Acts 18:23–19:41). While in Ephesus, Paul heard some negative news about how the Corinthian church was handling an immoral situation. He wrote them a letter, which is now lost to us but is referred to in 1 Corinthians 5:9. Some of Chloe's household (1:11) visited Paul in Ephesus and told him that his earlier letter was misunderstood (5:10–11) and that quarrels were causing divisions in the church.

Genre and Structure

First Corinthians is a pastoral letter to a local church from a father addressing his spiritually erring children (4:14–21). After the introduction (1:1–9), Paul immediately confronted the matter of divisions in the church at Corinth (1:10–4:21). Paul spoke to three moral issues in the church: incest (5:1–13); litigation between believers (6:1–11); and sexual immorality with prostitutes (6:12–20). Finally, Paul gave spiritual answers to various questions passed on to him from the readers (7:1–16:12) and ended the letter with a benediction (16:13–24).

Outline[2]

Message

The problems of the local church of 1 Corinthians were rooted in a sinful self-centeredness. Paul suggests that these issues can be effectively solved by spiritual men who give themselves in sacrificial service to their Lord and walk in imitation of Christ. Paul told the Corinthians to "imitate me, as I also imitate Christ" (11:1; cf. 4:16). The letter demonstrates a spiritual man's response as correct doctrine is applied to life.

I. Introduction
(1 Corinthians 1:1–9)

Paul's introduction began on an encouraging note. He describes the church at Corinth in view of God's sovereign call and sanctification (1:1–3). Even though there were serious problems in this church, the readers belonged to God and were set apart in this evil city to accomplish His purposes.

II. Reproof: "I Urge You"
(1 Corinthians 1:10–4:21)

Paul began the body of his letter with an issue that was at the root of their problems: the need for unity around the gospel message. Their problem (1:10–17) arose when various groups sided with different leaders who best

The archaic temple of Apollo at Corinth.

represented their view of Christianity. This resulted in divisions and quarrels (1:10–17). Paul attempted to correct their worldly thinking by explaining how the wisdom of God differed from the wisdom of the world (1:18–2:21). God's wisdom triumphs over the wisdom of the world (1:18–2:5) because the world looks at the message of the cross and sees foolishness, whereas it is really the power of God to save those who believe.

The unbeliever (*psychikos anthropos*) cannot accept the things of God, but the spiritual person (*pneumatikos*) has the mind of Christ (2:14–16). The Corinthians were operating as immature, baby Christians, still using the wisdom of the world, resulting in divisions among them. They were still fleshly (*sarkikos*), still controlled by the flesh, and living like the unsaved, according to human wisdom (3:1–3). Each of these leaders was used by God in different ways to build up the church, so God would reward each according to his faithfulness and his fruit (3:5–4:5). No one should boast about any one of them. Rather, they should rec-

The Corinth Canal.

ognize that all of these leaders were "fools for Christ," who were willing to suffer for the gospel and to love the Corinthians (4:6–21).

III. Correction: "You Are Inflated with Pride" (1 Corinthians 5:1–6:20)

Paul next wrote to address moral problems in the church. First, he responded to a report that had come to him regarding immorality in the church (5:1–13). Instead of dealing with the problem, the Corinthians permitted it; they were proud of their tolerance. However, Paul instructed them not to fellowship with a brother who willfully and openly sins. Second, in the matter of litigation between believers (6:1–11), Paul was surprised that believers were taking Christian neighbors into civil courts. Paul told the Corinthians that to go before a pagan law court was inconsistent with their standing before God. The third problem area Paul addressed was sexual immorality with prostitutes (6:12–20). He emphasized that the believer's body is a temple of the Holy Spirit, bought with a price. Our responsibility is to serve and glorify God with our body, not to give it over to the fulfillment of its lusts.

IV. Instruction: "Do Not . . . Be Unaware" (1 Corinthians 7:1–14:40)

In the third section of the letter, Paul answered questions posed to him by the Corinthians, as indicated by the repeated introductory phrase "about" (*"peri de"*) in 7:1, 25; 8:1; 12:1; 16:1, 12. To begin with, Paul answered questions regarding marriage (7:1–24). First, marriage, a gift from God, is good. Second, if a person struggles with temptation to immorality, then marriage is God's provision to handle that temptation (7:1–7). Third, inside marriage, sexual relations are expected, and submission of one's body to the mate is the norm (7:5). Next Paul answered questions about divorce and the solidarity of marriage (7:10–11). Husbands and wives should not divorce. Those who do should either remain unmarried or seek to be reconciled to their mates. Fifth, when the marriage involves a believer and a nonbeliever, even then they should not seek to dissolve the marriage (7:10–16). God might use the believer to reach the unbeliever and the children. Next, Paul answered questions regarding whether single people should marry (7:25–40). Paul did not have a command from the Lord but was only giving his opinion as one who had godly wisdom (7:25). The principle is that the highest good results where one is able to give the most undistracted devotion to the work of the Lord.

Paul next answered questions regarding certain aspects of worship (8:1–11:34), specifically food offered to idols and sharing in pagan festivals (8:1–11:1), plus the wearing of a head covering by women (11:2–16). Central to these topics are Paul's admonitions to resist anything that might be seen as idolatry, not to misuse your freedom in Christ, and to submit yourself for the higher good of others.

Paul's instructions for the Lord's Supper (11:23–26) taught that the elements of the Supper reflect Jesus's sacrificial death, and participation in the Supper proclaims that selfless act. Those who eat or drink in an unworthy manner are guilty of the sin of self-centered gratification, the sin that caused Judas to betray Jesus (11:27–34). All should examine their attitudes before partaking in this ordinance of the church.

Finally, Paul answered questions regarding key theological topics (12:1–15:58) beginning with spiritual gifts (12:1–14:40).There may be many kinds of spiritual gifts, but all come from the Holy Spirit, with a common purpose in serving the whole body. All believers have been baptized into the one body of Christ, so all are part of the church. Like the members of the human body, each person has his or her own role, and all the gifts of the Spirit are to be used in coordination not competition.

Next Paul focused on the importance of love (12:31b–13:13). Without love (*agapē*), spiritual gifts have no value. In a brief, poetic section, Paul described love in action (13:4–7). In contrast to the spiritual gifts, love is permanent. The need for gifts will pass away some day, but love will always be present. "When Christ returns, there will be no need for prophecy, tongues, or the limited knowledge the church gains in this world. All these gifts only provide glimpses and foreshadows of the perfection that will come."[3]

Paul's Love Poem: 1 Corinthians 13:4–8

Love is patient, love is kind.
Love does not envy,
is not boastful, is not arrogant,
is not rude,
is not self-seeking, is not irritable,
and does not keep a record of wrongs.
Love finds no joy in unrighteousness
but rejoices in the truth.
It bears all things, believes all things,
hopes all things, endures all things.
Love never ends.

REFLECTION

What Are Your Spiritual Gifts?

God not only gives us the gift of faith, but He also empowers us with other gifts to serve Him. What gifts has He given you, and how are you using them to serve Him? One way to identify your gifts is that they give you a sense of blessing and fulfillment when you use them to God's glory. At the same time they will bless those with whom you share them.

V. Teaching: "I . . . Tell . . . You a Mystery" (1 Corinthians 15:1–16:12)

There was also controversy about the topic of the resurrection (15:1–58). Some of the readers believed in Christ's resurrection but not in the resurrection of believers (15:12–13). To refute that idea Paul presented the importance of Christ's resurrection in the understanding of the gospel message (15:1–11). Numerous resurrection appearances, including one to Paul, testify that Jesus is alive.

But if some argue that there is no resurrection, then Christ was not raised either, and all the benefits of His resurrection are lost (15:12–34). However, since His resurrection is valid, based on eyewitness accounts, then our resurrection is a certainty. Because we shall be raised, believers have a motivation to endure suffering in ministry. Believers will eventually have a new body, suited for heaven, in the image of Christ. Whether we are raptured or die first, all believers will be changed from corruptible mortals to being clothed with incorruptible immortality. Then the final victory over death will be accomplished.

VI. Final Exhortations, Greetings, and a Benediction (1 Corinthians 16:13–24)

In the closing verses Paul encouraged the readers to a theological and spiritual maturity governed by love (16:13–14). He identified other servants of God to whom they needed to be in subjection, a direct counter to the partisan approach he had heard was present among them. After exchanging greetings, Paul gave one last instruction: "If anyone does not love the Lord, a curse be on him" (16:22). The encouragement here was toward devotion to the Lord, attached to a condemnation for those who live differently. It is followed with "*Marana tha*," May the Lord come quickly!

Conclusion

In this first letter to the Corinthians, Paul wrote to a church with many problems and questions. At the bottom of all their problems was a self-serving, indulgent attitude in contrast to the death of Christ as a self-giving sacrifice for the sins of others. Paul addressed their errors, both in theology and in practice, leading them from personal gratification to selfless love of others in the context of service to God.

Practical Application

Today we can measure our spiritual maturity by asking how we deal with key practical issues. Are there divisions among us caused by focusing on certain Christian heroes, or do we strive for unity? Do we value tolerance so highly that we do not confront sinners? Are we more interested in the wisdom of this world than the wisdom that comes from God? Do we follow biblical instruction concerning marriage and sexual relationships? Are we using the spiritual gifts God gave us to serve others or to glorify ourselves? Do we think about how our actions might be a stumbling block to others and thus consider them more highly than ourselves? The spiritual person seeks to have the mind of Christ and follow His instructions.

2 CORINTHIANS

Power in Weakness

Second Corinthians is the most personal of all Paul's letters as he reveals his own heart for this church and his ministry in general. This is a realistic letter about the ministry and the minister. It tells of the highs and lows, the joys and struggles, the privileges and sufferings. The frailty of the minister, however, is more than matched by the power of God.

KEY FACTS

Authors:	Paul
Recipients:	The church at Corinth
Where:	Macedonia
Date:	AD 56
Key Words:	Ministry (Gk. *diakonia*) and Glory (Gk. *doxa*)
Key Verse:	"Now we have this treasure in clay jars, so that this extraordinary power may be from God and not from us" (4:7).

Author

The salutation in 1:1 and a personal reference in 10:1 identify Paul as the author of this letter. Along with 1 Corinthians, the historical connections with Acts and the literary evidence easily fit Paul as the author. Since the second century scholars have considered 2 Corinthians to be Pauline in authorship.[4] Most hold that Paul himself was the original author,[5] although there is scholarly debate regarding the *unity* of the original composition (especially 6:14–7:1).

Recipients

The book is addressed "To the church of God at Corinth" (1:1; see 1 Cor 1:2). Paul adds here, "with all the saints who are throughout Achaia." Paul spent a year and a half in Corinth during his second missionary journey (Acts 18:11) and another three months on his third journey (Acts 20:3). Luke's description of the third journey used the broader area descriptions of Achaia (Acts 18:21) and Greece (Acts 20:2), indicating Paul ministered outside the bounds of Corinth as well. Therefore, Paul intended that this letter should be circulated throughout the area.[6]

Occasion and Date

Paul wrote this letter about six months after he wrote 1 Corinthians while still on his third missionary journey somewhere in Macedonia. The date was in the fall of AD 56. After the visits and letters mentioned in the introduction to 1 Corinthians, Paul continued his contact with the church. The problems in the church were not totally resolved, so Paul made a second visit to Corinth from Ephesus, mentioned in 2 Corinthians 2:1–2 as a visit that caused them sorrow. Paul was challenged by some in the church when he arrived (2:5–8; 7:12).

Genre and Structure

Second Corinthians is a pastoral letter from Paul to the church in Corinth. It is the most personal of all Paul's letters. Following the

Remnants of the Diolkos, the paved road built in ancient times across the Isthmus of Corinth. This was a rudimentary form of a railway over which ships were transported from one side of the isthmus to the other, saving significant navigational time and effort.

introduction (1:1–11), Paul went immediately into a lengthy personal section giving an inside view of the ministry, centered on the anxiety he experienced when Titus did not come (1:12–7:16). He ended on a note of confidence when he finally met up with Titus. Paul demonstrated that he was a true apostle and that God was working through him. He closed with instructions concerning preparation for his coming visit (13:11–14).

Outline

I. Introduction (1:1–11)
II. Personal Defense (1:12–7:16)
    A. Explanation of Paul's Previous Plans (1:12–2:13)
    B. Paul's Inside Perspective on the Gospel Ministry (2:14–6:10)
    C. Paul's Relationship with the Corinthians (6:11–7:16)
III. Practical Needs (8:1–9:15)
IV. Powerful Appeal (10:1–13:10)
V. Conclusion (13:11–14)

Message

The message of 2 Corinthians is that the gospel ministry is carried out by the power of God through frail ministers. Paul related his own great inadequacy because of his physical limitations and God's adequacy and power through Paul's frailty. In a climatic statement Paul wrote, "But He said to me, 'My grace is sufficient for you, for my power is perfected in weakness.' Therefore, I will most gladly boast all the more about my weaknesses, so that Christ's power may reside in me" (12:9).

I. Introduction (2 Corinthians 1:1–11)

Paul introduced himself as an "apostle of Christ Jesus by God's will" (1:1). He was indeed an apostle, but it was by the will of God, not by his own doing. As was his custom, Paul included a thanksgiving: he blessed God as "the God of all comfort" (1:3–11). In light of all the struggles he would talk about in this letter, he told the Corinthians that God is the one who brings comfort out of affliction. To express God's "comfort," Paul uses forms of the Greek *paraklēsis* nine times in verses 3–6.

II. Personal Defense (2 Corinthians 1:12–7:16)

As he began the body of his letter, Paul allowed the readers to see his vulnerability. He told them why some plans were changed, revealing his own anxiety over the delay of Titus with news from them (1:12–2:13). He interrupted that story with a lengthy aside giving an inside perspective on the minister who is God's vessel (2:14–6:10). Finally, he returned to the story, letting them know what happened when Titus came with the news of their response (6:11–7:16).

A. Explanation of Paul's Previous Plans (1:12–2:13)

The first change grew out of Paul's original plan to visit the Corinthians. He gave the details of that plan and assured the Corinthians that his intentions were sincere (1:17–22). The reason he did not come that way was so that he might not come to them in sorrow again. He wanted his next visit to be a joyful one. So instead of traveling to Corinth, Paul wrote to them, sending Titus with the letter to show his love for them (1:23–2:4). The second issue involved a person who had previously offended the church or Paul or both (2:5–11). Initially the church punished the man, but now they should forgive, comfort, and reaffirm their love for him since the man had repented. Paul had forgiven the man and they should also.

The site of ancient Corinth at the foot of the 1,886-foot-high Acrocorinth, on top of which was the temple to Aphrodite. In the foreground are the ruins of the Temple of Apollo.

B. Paul's Inside Perspective on the Gospel Ministry (2:14–6:10)

After mentioning the coming of Titus in 2:12–13, Paul wrote a lengthy, parenthetical digression about the ministry, picking up the story of Titus again in 7:5. In this digression Paul told what it was like to be the vessel (4:7) God uses.

First, the ministry is an opportunity to display the glory of God (2:14–4:6). The word "glory" (Gk. *doxa*) is a key word in this section, occurring fifteen times. The glory of the ministry is compared to a glorious Roman triumphal procession where Christ is the conquering Ruler and his ministers are part of the procession (2:14–17). Part of the glory of the ministry is reflected by those who receive it (3:1–3). Their changed lives demonstrate the impact of the gospel message as they become living letters of commendation, testimonies of God living in them. In a series of contrasts, Paul shows how the glory of the new covenant is greater than the old covenant (3:4–18).

Second, the minister accepts his weakness because of the opportunities it affords (4:7–5:10). The weakness of the minister is seen in contrast to the glory of the new covenant ministry. His weakness is the vehicle for showing off the power of God (4:7–15). In a graphic word picture, Paul compared himself to

The Lechaion road entered Corinth from the north, connecting it with the port on the Gulf of Corinth.

a clay jar, out of which shines the "light of the knowledge of God's glory in the face of Jesus Christ" (4:6).

Paul wanted the Corinthians to understand his motivations of ministry in view of standing one day before the judgment seat (*bema*) of Christ (5:11–13). Knowing the fear of God moves the minister to persuade unsaved people to become Christians. The God who has reconciled us to Himself has given us a ministry as ambassadors of reconciliation, motivating others into that same relationship (5:16–6:2). The minister, in response, endures many hardships in order not to discredit the ministry (6:3–10).

C. Paul's Relationship with the Corinthians (6:11–7:16)

Returning to the story about Titus, Paul explained that he was at one of those low points in the ministry when he came into Macedonia. But God lifted him up by the coming of Titus and the news of the Corinthians' response, giving him joy and comfort (7:2–16). He rejoiced because their grieving according to the will of God produced a godly repentance. He also rejoiced because of a positive impact on Titus. Finally, Paul also rejoiced in his renewed confidence in them (7:16). With this matter now cleared, Paul turned to the mutual ministry in which they were both engaged: the offering for Jerusalem.

III. Practical Needs (2 Corinthians 8:1–9:15)

Paul urged the readers to follow through on their earlier commitment to give (8:1–15). Being in Macedonia, Paul told the Corinthians that the Macedonians were giving a contribution as well (8:1–5). In fact, they had gone beyond their ability to give, making it a truly sacrificial gift. Here were people ministering out of their weakness, an example of what he had just written about in this letter.

Paul's Thorn in the Flesh

A "thorn in the flesh" is an idiom for something painful (e.g., Num 33:55; Ezek 28:24). There are various interpretations of Paul's "thorn in the flesh." Many take this to be a physical ailment Paul experienced (see Gal 4:13–15). Others think it might have been continuing persecution from his enemies (see 2 Cor 12:10). Paul viewed whatever it was as a weakness, designed to keep him humble. He was content because it allowed the power of God to reside in him.

IV. Powerful Appeal (2 Corinthians 10:1–13:10)

Finally, Paul responded to those who criticized his apostleship. Turning to those who had attempted to discredit his ministry and apostleship, Paul emphasized his theme: the human vessel is weak so that the power of God might be seen. First, he laid down a challenge to those who opposed him (10:1–18), warning them against judging outward appearances (10:7–12). Paul used the same technique of boasting the opponents had used (11:1–12:13). He joined his opponents in boasting, but he focused on his own weaknesses, with a goal of showing how the power of God works through a weak vessel. To keep him from exalting himself, God gave him a thorn in the flesh. God refused to take the cause of his suffering away, so Paul accepted this as God's will because it allowed the power of God to reside in him (12:7–10). Paul also made clear that his real reason for writing was not to defend himself but to build up his readers by teaching them the biblical role of the ministry and the minister. Paul challenged the Corinthians to examine their behavior to see if they were living according to the faith (13:5–10).

V. Conclusion (2 Corinthians 13:11–14)

In his brief conclusion (13:11–14), Paul exhorted his readers to respond maturely, giving the promise of God's love and peace. He exchanged greetings and closed with a benediction.

Practical Application

Paul built three main sections around his theme of ministry and the minister. First, affliction is shared by those who minister so that they do not trust in themselves but in God. Second, not wanting the Corinthians to discredit their ministry, Paul urged them to follow through on their previous commitment to give an offering. Third, Paul displayed his own weaknesses in order that the power of God might be seen through him. Paul's hope was that the Corinthians might learn from this letter, reject the false apostles, and correct their error so that when he came he would see them living out the faith they professed.

The Corinthian letters remind us that no church is perfect and that the work of the ministry can be difficult. We are all fallible people attempting to serve the infallible God. Despite our weaknesses and failures, Paul reminds us that genuine love is necessary in order for Christians to get along with one another this side of heaven. Only in the final resurrection will we become all that God has planned for us in the glorification of our eternal state.

For Further Reading

Barrett, C. K. *The First Epistle to the Corinthians*. New York: Harper & Row, 1968.

————. *The Second Epistle to the Corinthians*. New York: Harper & Row, 1973.

Blomberg, Craig. *1 Corinthians*. NIVAC. Grand Rapids: Zondervan, 1995.

Garland, David. *2 Corinthians*. NAC. Nashville: B&H, 1999.

Lowery, David. K. "1 Corinthians." *BKCNT*. Edited by John F. Walvoord and Roy B. Zuck. Wheaton: Victor, 1983.

Mitchell, Dan. *First Corinthians: Christianity in a Hostile Culture*. Chattanooga: AMG Publishers, 2004.

————. *Second Corinthians: Grace Under Siege*. Chattanooga: AMG Publishers, 2008.

Pratt, Richard, Jr. *1 & 2 Corinthians*. HNTC. Nashville: B&H, 2000.

Study Questions

1. What is the emphasis that Paul gave to the use of our bodies in 1 Corinthians? How does that relate to the theme in the book of self-sacrificial service to others?
2. In 1 Cor 8:1–11:34, Paul addresses topics of Christian liberty and the exercise of our rights. How does this compare with our cultural view of exercising our rights and freedoms?
3. What guidelines did Paul suggest regarding the use of spiritual gifts?
4. How does the description of love that Paul gave in 1 Corinthians 13 relate to the theme of the book and the need for self-sacrificing service to others?
5. How does God use our weaknesses to fulfill His purpose in our lives?

Notes

1. S. J. Hafemann, "Corinthians, Letters to the," in *Dictionary of Paul and His Letters*, ed. Gerald F. Hawthorne and Ralph P. Martin (Downers Grove, IL: InterVarsity Press, 1993), 175. Paul also names Sosthenes as a coauthor. This may be the same Sosthenes mentioned in Acts 18:17.

2. Outline based on D. Mitchell, *First Corinthians: Christianity in a Hostile Culture* (Chattanooga: AMG Publishers, 2004), ix–x.

3. Richard L. Pratt Jr., *I & II Corinthians*, HNTC, vol. 7 (Nashville: B&H, 2000), 234.

4. S. J. Hafemann, "Corinthians, Letters to the," in *Dictionary of Paul and His Letters*, ed. Gerald F. Hawthorne and Ralph P Martin (Downers Grove, IL: IVP, 1993), 175.

5. See D. Mitchell, *Second Corinthians: Grace Under Siege* (Chattanooga: AMG Publishers, 2008).

6. See chap. 1, "How We Got the Bible."

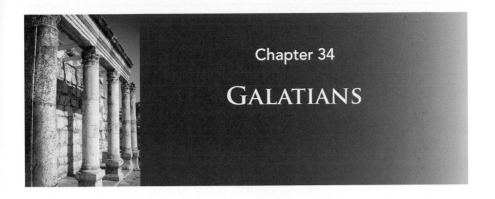

Chapter 34

GALATIANS

Grace Through Faith

P aul writes with holy indignation over the news that the Galatians were being influenced by Judaizers who would have Gentile believers circumcised and live by the law. Because the Judaizers attacked Paul's credentials as an apostle, he defends himself with proof of divine apostolic authority. He answers with sound doctrinal explanations, biblical illustrations, and some practical exhortations for Christian living.

KEY FACTS

Author:	Paul
Recipients:	Churches in the Roman province of Galatia
Where:	Unknown
Date:	Circa AD 49–55
Key Word:	Grace (Gk. *charis*)
Key Verse:	"I have been crucified with Christ and I no longer live, but Christ lives in me" (Gal 2:20).

Author

The apostle Paul can be called the apostle of Christian liberty. He argued strenuously that Gentile believers were free from the law of Moses. During the first missionary journey of Paul and Barnabas, about AD 47–48, they evangelized and planted churches in four cities in the southern territory of

Galatia—Antioch, Iconium, Lystra, and Derbe (Acts 13–14). They preached in Jewish synagogues, then reached out to Gentiles who lived in the region. Paul and Barnabas were driven out of Antioch, Iconium, and Lystra by angry Jews and city officials. In spite of persecution, Paul and Barnabas organized churches and appointed elders in each church on their way back through these four cities (Acts 14:23).

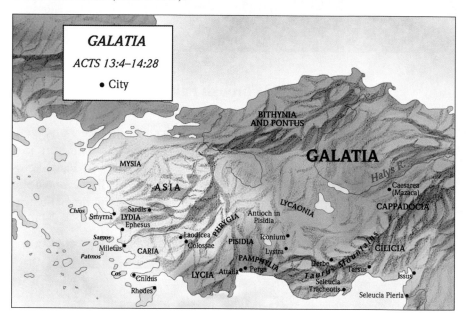

Recipients

Galatians can be termed the Magna Carta of Christian liberty. It states unequivocally that salvation is through faith alone, in Christ alone, by grace alone, without works of any kind. People Paul had evangelized in the Roman province of Galatia on his first missionary journey were in danger of turning from pure faith in Christ to the heresy of a works-based system of salvation. Some were accepting the Jewish rite of circumcision as necessary for salvation.

The central part of Asia Minor, or present-day Turkey, is an agricultural region. In the centuries before Christ, this area was in turmoil with various tribes seeking control through military conquest. The Celts, or Gauls as they were also called, were among these tribal groups. When the Romans invaded the area, these Gaelic peoples had their own kingdom until their leader Amytyas died in battle in 25 BC, just six years after Caesar Augustus became Roman emperor. Rome then managed the territory as an imperial province, adding some land to the southern part of the province. Rome called this province Galatia after the people who lived there.[1]

Occasion and Date

Paul wrote Galatians to counter the Judaizers, a group of converted Jews who infiltrated the church and taught that one must keep the law of Moses in order to be saved. Paul wrote boldly and forcefully to argue for the freedom of the believer in Christ.

The question of when Galatians was written and to whom it was penned revolves around how the word "Galatians" was used in Galatians 3:1. Does "Galatians" refer to the Gaulic tribesmen as an ethnic group, or is

The tell of Derbe in modern Davri, Turkey.

it a reference to those living in the Roman province called Galatia? The ethnic Gauls lived in the northern part of the Roman territory, but the cities Paul and Barnabas visited on their first missionary journey were located in the southern reaches of the province. Those who take the south Galatian view emphasize the fact that Barnabas is mentioned in the epistle to the Galatians. But Barnabas was not on the second journey. The second journey may have taken Paul and Silas into the northern part of the province according to Acts 16:6, which says, "They went through the region of Phrygia and Galatia."

If the south Galatian view is correct, the letter of Galatians was probably written as early as AD 49, making it the first or earliest of Paul's epistles.[2] If the north Galatian view is correct, the letter was probably written after Paul and Silas toured that part of the province on their second missionary journey. The date of writing would then be set around AD 55.[3] However, neither view affects the basic interpretation of the book.

Genre and Structure

The letter divides into three major sections: (1) a *personal* section (chaps. 1–2); (2) a *doctrinal* section (chaps. 3–4); and (3) a *practical* section (chaps. 5–6).

Outline

I. Personal Section (1:1–2:21)
   A. Paul's Greeting and Theme (1:1–9)
   B. Paul's Apostolic Authority (1:10–17)
   C. Paul's First Visit to Jerusalem (1:18–24)
   D. Paul's Second Visit to Jerusalem (2:1–10)
   E. Paul's Rebuke of Peter at Antioch (2:11–21)
II. Doctrinal Section (3:1–4:31)
   A. Paul Rebukes the Galatians (3:1–14)
   B. The Law and Abraham's Covenant (3:15–22)
   C. The Law and Christian Faith (3:23–4:7)
   D. The Folly of Returning to the Law (4:8–20)
   E. The Allegory of Ishmael and Isaac (4:21–31)
III. Practical Section (5:1–6:18)
   A. Maintain Christian Liberty (5:1–12)
   B. Walk by the Spirit (5:13–26)
   C. Bear One Another's Burdens (6:1–10)
   D. Concluding Remarks (6:11–18)

Message

I. Personal Section (Galatians 1:1–2:21)

A. Paul's Greeting and Theme (Galatians 1:1–9)

In Paul's opening words he refers to himself as an apostle of Christ and as such gives the basis for his authority to speak boldly for Christ. He addresses himself to "the churches of Galatia," probably those he and Barnabas founded on their first missionary journey in Acts 13–14. Paul sends these believers grace and peace (1:3). Grace (Gk. *charis*) was a traditional Greek greeting but is heightened by the unmerited favor we have in Christ Jesus. Peace (Heb. *shalom*) was the traditional Hebrew greeting but is also enriched by the perfect peace we have with God through trusting Christ as our Savior.

Paul accuses these Galatians of "so quickly turning away from him" (Christ) to "a different gospel" (1:6). Paul uses two words meaning "another." One is *heteros*, "another" of a different kind; the other is *allos*, "another" of the same kind. Paul says they have gone to a completely different kind of gospel. Paul even warns that if he himself, or an angel from heaven, or anyone were preaching a *different* gospel, he would be under a curse (Gk. *anathema*, 1:8).

B. Paul's Apostolic Authority (Galatians 1:10–17)

Those causing trouble in Galatia were no doubt questioning Paul's apostolic authority, so Paul addressed that issue. Paul's commission came directly from Christ on the Damascus road (Acts 9:1–9), not from some human appointment (1:11–12). From Damascus Paul went into the desert territory of Arabia. There he realized that when he persecuted a believer, he was persecuting Christ because all believers are part of Christ's spiritual body (1:13–17).

The window in the city wall of Damascus that may be the site of Paul's escape in a basket from the city.

The city wall of biblical Damascus.

C. Paul's First Visit to Jerusalem (Galatians 1:18–24)

Next Paul recounts his first visit to Jerusalem (1:18–24). On the road to Damascus, Paul received his call from Christ to be an apostle; he did not receive it from any of the other apostles in Jerusalem. It was three years later when Paul went to Jerusalem for fifteen days that he met Peter for the first time (1:18). Paul also met James, Jesus's earthly brother, who became a leader in the Jerusalem church, but these men did not make him an apostle.

D. Paul's Second Visit to Jerusalem (Galatians 2:1–10)

Paul writes, "Then after fourteen years I went up again to Jerusalem with Barnabas" (2:1). If Paul was saved on the Damascus road in AD 32, fourteen years later would be about AD 46 (sometimes called the "famine visit"). Paul says they went to Jerusalem because of "a revelation" (2:2), possibly a reference to the prophecy of a famine by Agabus in Acts 11:28–30. The Antioch church then organized a relief mission led by Barnabas and Saul, as Paul was then called. A Gentile believer, Titus, was with Barnabas and Paul, and Paul makes the point that Titus was not "compelled to be circumcised"

(2:3). The point of this story is that the Galatian Judaizers were insisting that Gentiles had to keep the Jewish law, which included circumcision. But Paul includes Titus to demonstrate that the leaders of the Jerusalem church, including Peter, James the Lord's brother, and John stood for freedom from the law for Gentile converts. In that same meeting Paul and Peter were recognized as having a mission to both the Gentiles and the Jews (2:7–8).

E. Paul's Rebuke of Peter at Antioch (Galatians 2:11–21)

Paul next relates how Peter came to the Syrian Antioch church and was mingling and eating with Gentile believers until some Jerusalem Jewish believers came. Then Peter stayed aloof from the Gentile Christians (2:11–12), and Barnabas was led astray to follow his example. But Paul says this was "hypocrisy" and was "deviating from the truth of the gospel" (2:13–14). The truth of the gospel is that belief in Christ is all that matters, not separating from supposedly unclean persons, practices, or foods. That led to Paul's statement in Galatians, "We . . . know that a person is not justified by the works of the law but by faith in Jesus Christ" (2:15–16). The grace of God is the all-important issue. Paul adds that "if righteousness comes through the law, then Christ died for nothing" (2:21). When Paul says, "I have been crucified with Christ" and "Christ lives in me" (2:20), he is expressing the truth of our spiritual union with Christ.

II. Doctrinal Section (Galatians 3:1–4:31)

A. Paul's Rebukes of the Galatians (Galatians 3:1–14)

"You foolish Galatians!" is how Paul begins chapter 3. Then he asks six telling questions. "Who has cast a spell on you?" (3:1). "Did you receive the Spirit by the works of the law or by hearing with faith?" (3:2). "Are you so foolish?" (3:3). "After beginning with the Spirit, are you now going to be made complete by the flesh?" (3:3). "Did you experience so much for nothing?" (3:4). "So then, does God give you the Spirit and work miracles among you by your doing the works of the law? Or is it by believing what you heard?" (3:5). The answer to each of these rhetorical questions is that faith, and faith alone, has accomplished their salvation, not the works associated with the law of Moses.

Paul uses Abraham as an example of one justified by faith. Abraham "believed God, and it was credited to him for righteousness" (3:6). Gentiles are saved this same way. In fact, Abraham was an uncircumcised Gentile when God saved him. The law requires perfect obedience, and since no one is perfect, all are condemned by the law. Only faith in Christ's finished work can save anyone. Christ redeemed us by becoming a curse for us when He hung on the cross (3:13).

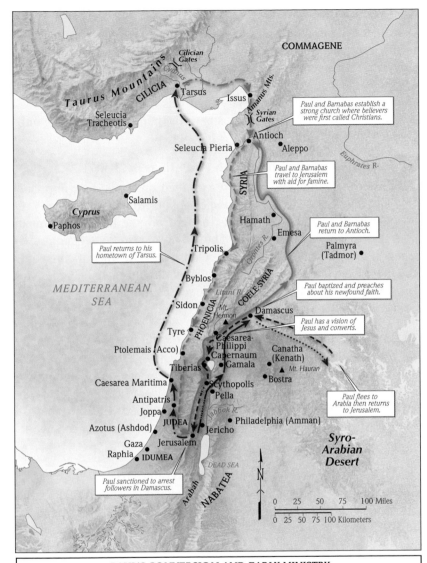

PAUL'S CONVERSION AND EARLY MINISTRY

ACTS 9:1–30; 11:19–30; 12:24–25 GAL. 1:11–24

- • City
- ▲ Mountain peak
- ⨱ Pass
- ← Paul sent to Damascus
- ◄···· Paul spends time in Arabia
- ◄– Paul returns to Jerusalem

- ◄· Paul flees from Hellenists
- ◄· Paul and Barnabas travel to Antioch
- ◄– Paul and Barnabas sent to Jerusalem
- ← Paul and Barnabas return to Antioch
- ▢ Kingdom of Agrippa I

B. The Law and Abraham's Covenant (Galatians 3:15–22)

In the next section of his letter, Paul contrasts law with promise. God's promise to Abraham was in the form of a covenant. The Abrahamic covenant resulted in Christ's coming as the "seed" of Abraham (3:16). The law "came 430 years later" than Abraham's covenant, so it cannot annul God's promises to Abraham (3:17). Paul asks: "Why then was the law given?" (3:19). The law cannot give life (3:21), but it does have the purpose of revealing our sinful character before God.

C. The Law and Christian Faith (Galatians 3:23–4:7)

"Before this faith came, we were confined under the law, imprisoned" (3:23). The law locked us up, so to speak, but provided no remedy. Only faith in Christ can atone for sin and free us from the law's condemnation. "This faith" means faith in Christ. The law was also "our guardian" (Gk. *paidagōgos*) to lead us to Christ (3:24). Consequently, when it comes to salvation, there is no longer a difference between the Jew and the Greek, for all are one in Christ (3:28). All believers are adopted heirs and sons, so everyone can call Him Father (4:5–7).

D. The Folly of Returning to the Law (Galatians 4:8–20)

In this passionate section Paul chides and pleads with his converts because they were ceremonially observing "special days, months, seasons, and years," indicating that the Judaizers were having success among them (4:8–10). When Paul first brought the message of Christ to them, they received Paul and his message, but now it appears that he is an enemy (4:16). Paul asks, "What happened?" (4:15 HCSB).

E. The Allegory of Ishmael and Isaac (Galatians 4:21–31)

Paul now takes up the allegory of Ishmael and Isaac (4:21–31) based on events in the life of Abraham. Abraham had two sons, Ishmael and Isaac. Ishmael came from Hagar, his slave, and stands for a works-based solution to the problem of Sarah's barrenness (4:21–23). Isaac represents God's provision for His unconditional promise to Abraham (4:23). Hagar stands for Mount Sinai, or the law of Moses, and corresponds to the Jerusalem of Paul's day with its emphasis on keeping the law for salvation. Sarah, the mother of Isaac, stands for freedom and Christian liberty (4:26–27). Paul even notes that the slave son, Ishmael, persecuted the freeborn Isaac (4:29). The conclusion to Abraham's dilemma was God's command to listen to Sarah, who begged Abraham to "drive out the slave and her son" (4:30; see Gen 21:8–12). Paul's conclusion was that "we are not children of the slave but of the free" (4:31). Paul calls his readers "brothers," trusting they will respond positively and similarly cast out the Judaizers.

III. Practical Section (Galatians 5:1–6:18)

A. Maintain Christian Liberty (Galatians 5:1–12)

Paul next urges the Galatians to "stand firm" in Christ's liberty (5:1). To fail to do this would mean "you have fallen from grace" (5:4). This is not referring to losing one's salvation, but to "fall from grace" meant falling short of the grace of God by "trying to be justified by the law" (5:4). Paul confidently believes they will not accept these false views of salvation (5:10).

View of the surrounding valley from atop the unexcavated city mound of ancient Lystra in south-central Asia Minor (modern Turkey).

B. Walk by the Spirit (Galatians 5:13–26)

Paul next issues a number of brief positive commands. These practical spiritual exhortations are to "serve one another through love," to "love your neighbor as yourself," and to "walk by the Spirit" (5:13–16). When the Galatians follow these exhortations, Paul says, "You will not carry out the desire of the flesh." Paul then contrasts the works of the flesh with the fruit of the Spirit. The fruit of the Spirit is a ninefold result which includes "love, joy, peace, patience, kindness, goodness, faithfulness, gentleness, and self-control" (5:22–23).

C. Bear One Another's Burdens (Galatians 6:1–10)

In this final practical section Paul exhorts his readers to "carry one another's burdens" (6:2) but at the same time exhorts each to "carry his own load" (6:5). It is our spiritual duty to restore a brother who has fallen into "any wrongdoing" (6:1), while we walk in the Spirit. Paul then mentions sowing and reaping to explain that we reap what we sow and in proportion to what we sow. "The one who sows to his flesh will reap destruction from the flesh, but the one who sows to the Spirit will reap eternal life from the Spirit" (6:8).

D. Concluding Remarks (Galatians 6:11–18)

In his concluding remarks (6:11–18), Paul draws attention to the "large letters" he has written in his "own handwriting" (6:11) to demonstrate the authenticity of his letter.

Practical Application

Paul's letter to the Galatians is still a trustworthy, up-to-date antidote for a works-based attempt to gain heaven. Simple faith in Christ's death, burial, and resurrection as payment for our sin is the only way of salvation. Works of any kind cannot be added to gain salvation. Trust in such works is an indication that one's faith is wrongly placed. Saving faith must be placed in Christ's finished work on the cross—nothing more and nothing less. Salvation is by faith alone in Christ alone by grace alone. That is God's plan, and it is so simple that a child can understand it.

Paul's letter was strong, confrontational, and to the point. But it was also personal and practical. His list of the fruit of the Spirit is one of the finest expressions of Christian character in the entire New Testament. Fausset wrote, "The 'fruit of the Spirit' is singular because, however manifold the results, they form one organic whole springing from the Spirit."[4] They remind us of Jesus's illustration of the vine and the branches (John 15:1–8). He is the root and source of our spiritual life and we are the branches that produce the fruit of the Spirit.

REFLECTION

The fruit of the Spirit is expressed in a ninefold description:

Love: compassion
Peace: cheerfulness
Patience: endurance
Kindness: benevolence
Goodness: moral virtue
Faithfulness: confidence
Gentleness: sensitivity
Self-control: discipline

Which of these qualities are most clearly expressed in your spiritual life? Which need more development? How is God working in your life to grow you into a mature believer?

Paul ends his letter with words of practical application that still resonate with us today. He urges us to walk in the Spirit, carry one another's burdens, and work for the good of others. Ultimately, we, like Paul, must not glory in ourselves but only in the cross of Christ (6:14). It is there alone that we truly die to ourselves and find real life in Christ alone.

For Further Reading

Bruce, F. F. *The Epistle to the Corinthians*. NIGTC. Grand Rapids: Eerdmans, 1982.
George, Timothy. *Galatians*. NAC. Nashville: B&H, 1994.
Hendriksen, William. *Exposition of Galatians*. NTC. Grand Rapids: Baker, 1968.
Kent, Homer A., Jr. *The Freedom of God's Sons: Studies in Galatians*. Grand Rapids: Baker, 1976.
Lightfoot, J. B. *The Epistle of St. Paul's to the Galatians*. Grand Rapids: Zondervan; reprint, 1965.
Schreiner, Thomas R. *Galatians*. ZECNT. Ed. Clinton E. Arnold. Grand Rapids: Zondervan, 2010.

Study Questions

1. What were Paul's personal motivations to write such a blunt letter with negative accusations?
2. What was the main doctrinal problem Paul corrected in this letter?
3. What is the purpose of the law in relationship to the gospel of grace?
4. Why did Paul want his readers to reject the bondage that comes with obeying the law?
5. How did Paul describe freedom in Christ?

Notes

1. See John Saul Howson, "Galatia," in *Smith's Dictionary of the Bible*, vol. 1, ed. H. B. Hackett (Grand Rapids: Baker, reprinted, 1971), 854–55; M. J. Mellink, "Galatia," *The Interpreter's Dictionary of the Bible*, vol. 1, ed. G. A. Buttrick (New York: Abingdon, 1962), 336–38; and E. M. Blaiklock, "Galatia," in *The Zondervan Pictorial Encyclopedia of the Bible*, vol. 2, ed. M. C. Tenney (Grand Rapids: Zondervan, 1975), 624–26.

2. Supporters of the South Galatian View include William M. Ramsay, *A Historical Commentary on St. Paul's Epistle to the Galatians* (Grand Rapids: Baker; reprinted, 1965), 1–234; and such well-known commentators as F. F. Bruce, William Hendriksen, Homer A. Kent Jr., and Timothy George (see bibliography for latter three).

3. The North Galatian View is supported by J. B. Lightfoot, *The Epistle of St. Paul to the Galatians* (Grand Rapids: Zondervan; reprinted, 1966), 18–35, as well as by Theodor Zahn and James Moffatt.

4. A. R. Fausset, *Commentary on the Old and New Testaments*, 6 vols. (Grand Rapids: Eerdmans, 1945), 2:337.

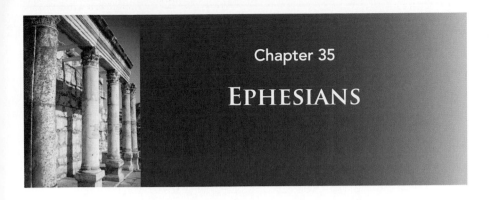

Chapter 35

EPHESIANS

Winning the Battle

P aul's letter to the Ephesians is both personal and pastoral, theological and practical. It opens with a salutation and closes with a benediction. In this amazing letter the imprisoned apostle pours out his heart to the
beloved Ephesians in what Goodspeed called "a great rhapsody of salvation."[1] William Hendriksen said, "It is both a spontaneous utterance of his
heart and a careful composition of his mind."[2] In this letter Paul writes to the
Christian believers in Ephesus and the surrounding region. This is the place
where Priscilla and Aquila assisted Paul during his two-year ministry in the
city, and during that period there was a dramatic confrontation with pagan-
ism, mysticism, and the occult (Acts 19).

Paul's letter to the Ephesians is a comprehensive presentation of the universal church or the body of Christ (1:22–23). Ten times in this letter Paul
reminds the Ephesians that believers are "in Christ." Therefore, the believer
has heavenly privileges ("the riches of his grace") because Jesus lives in
heaven and we are "in Him" (the theme of chaps. 1–3). The second section of
Ephesians (4:1–6:9) exhorts believers to live (walk) on this earth according to
the riches they have in heaven. The final section (6:10–18) tells believers how
to fight (warfare) against evil powers they face on this earth.

In the latter section of Paul's letter to the Ephesians, he describes the
armor of the Christian with analogies from the typical Roman armor of the
time. The believer is urged to put on the "full armor" of God (6:11), which
includes the helmet of salvation, the breastplate of righteousness, the belt
of truth, the shoes of peace, the shield of faith, and the sword of the Spirit
(6:14–17). Only when we are properly covered (Greek, *panoplia*) are we prepared to withstand the schemes (Greek, *methodia*) or "methods" of the Devil.

KEY FACTS

Author:	Paul
Recipients:	The church at Ephesus
Where:	Rome (while Paul was in prison)
Date:	AD 61–62
Key Word:	Heavenlies (Gk. *epoupanioi*)
Key Verses:	"For you are saved by grace through faith, and this is not from yourselves; it is God's gift—not from works, so that no one can boast. For we are his workmanship, created in Christ Jesus for good works, which God prepared ahead of time for us to do" (2:8–10).

Author

Conservative authors believe Paul is the author, based on both internal and external evidence. The internal evidence is seen in the salutation, "Paul, an apostle of Christ Jesus" (1:1). Also, we know Paul was in prison

The exterior of the theater at Ephesus.

so he identifies himself, "I, Paul, the prisoner of Christ Jesus on behalf of you" (3:1). The familiar Pauline vocabulary and theology are additional reasons to believe Paul wrote Ephesians. The external evidence that Paul wrote Ephesians is that the letter was frequently quoted as written by Paul by many early church fathers in the second century, including Irenaeus, Clement of Alexandria, and Tertullian.[3]

Those who deny that Paul wrote the book of Ephesians point to the lack of personal references that are found in most of Paul's other letters. However, some scholars believe the letter was written to be circulated among a number of churches in the region (cf. Revelation 2–3). If so, we would expect fewer specific personal references. Paul clearly states, "Tychicus, our dearly loved brother and faithful servant in the Lord, will tell you all the news about me so that you may be informed. I am sending him to you for this very reason, to let you know how we are and to encourage your hearts" (6:21–22). Therefore, any personal remarks by Paul would be delivered by Tychicus in person. Other objections based on similarities between Ephesians and Colossians are answered extensively with comparative charts by Hendriksen who concludes that the similarities are due to a common author, not different authors.[4]

Recipients

The city of Ephesus was the capital of Asia Minor and the center of Roman authority in the area. Clinton Arnold notes: "Ephesus was the leading city of the richest region of the Roman Empire. With a population of 250,000 people, only Rome and Alexandria were larger."[5] Ephesus was connected to the sea by the Cayster River, which flowed into a large man-made harbor. Today the artificial harbor is clogged with silt draining from the surrounding mountains. The city was built on a major road approximately two miles in length between two gently sloping mountains. The road through the city reached far into the interior of Asia Minor and was connected by highways to all the other chief cities of the province. Ephesus was easily accessible by both land and sea. Its location therefore contributed to its religious, commercial, and political diversity and importance. Because of this, Paul considered Ephesus as crucial for the evangelization of the area. He spent two years in Ephesus, and, as a result of his ministry, "all the residents of Asia, both Jews and Greeks, heard the word of the Lord" (Acts 19:10).

Who Was Diana?

The city of Ephesus was devoted to the fertility goddess Diana, known to the Greeks as Artemis. Pictured as a multibreasted female mother goddess, she was viewed by the Ephesians with great reverence as their patron deity. Her temple housed an encased meteorite, which they believed fell from heaven from Jupiter (Zeus) himself. Her worship included magic, spirit powers, books of spells and incantations, and silver figurines of the goddess. When the Christians at Ephesus forsook these pagan practices, business fell off, leading to a public protest led by Demetrius the silversmith at the theater (Acts 19:21–41).

Artemis (Diana), patron goddess of Ephesus.

Ephesus tolerated numerous Greco-Roman deities, but it was especially known for the goddess Diana (also called Artemis). Olympic games (*Artemisia*) were held in her honor, and one month of the year was named for her. Ephesus was famous for its temple of Diana, considered one of the seven wonders of the ancient world, and its theater (Acts 19:27–29). Religious pilgrims from around the world came to worship and to give their wealth to sacrifice at the temple. Because people also stored their money for safekeeping in the temple, it became the city's bank, and its priests became bankers of the ancient world.[6] Paul's ministry in Ephesus was so effective that many turned away from idolatry—so much so that the artisans employed by the temple rioted in retaliation against Christianity (Acts 19:23–41).

Occasion and Date

Paul speaks of himself as "the prisoner" (3:1; 4:1), and the book of Acts ends with Paul in prison in Rome, which seems to be the obvious place where Paul wrote this letter. Also, the phrase, "I am an ambassador" (6:20) may suggest that Paul is in Rome, the city to which ambassadors were sent from other nations. If written during Paul's Roman imprisonment, the letter dates to approximately AD 61–62. In Rome, Paul was able to rent his own dwelling place, had a reasonable amount of liberty to preach and teach, and was able to write letters (Acts 28:30; Eph 6:19–20; Col 4:3–4). Perhaps he was motivated to write when news came about some problems in the churches at Ephesus and Colossae. Since the letters to the Ephesians and the Colossians are so similar and since the two cities were only about 100 miles apart, both letters were likely written and delivered about the same time.

The south entrance gate to the agora and the Library of Celsus at Ephesus. The library was constructed in the early second century AD (110–135).

Genre and Structure

The absence of personal greetings in this letter suggests to some scholars that perhaps, when Paul wrote, he intended for other churches in the province of Asia to read this letter along with the church at Ephesus. If so, Ephesians is a circular letter. Furthermore, some ancient manuscripts omit the phrase "at Ephesus" (1:1), and some scholars believe a space was left open so the names of other churches could be substituted when the messenger delivered them. However, it should be noted that there are no existing ancient manuscripts of the letter addressed to alternative locations—only Ephesus. In addition, the practice of leaving an open space for different recipient names to be inserted is not a known practice in the ancient world.[7]

There is great similarity between the style of Ephesians and Colossians, which leads many to conjecture that one of the letters is an imitation of the other. Many scholars who deny that Paul wrote Ephesians believe that a follower of Paul had a copy of Colossians and reworked it to produce

Ephesians. However, as Clinton Arnold argues, "A much better explanation is to postulate the same author giving a fresh exposition of a similar theme (with different emphases) a short time later for a different audience."[8]

Outline[9]

I. **Plan of God (1:1–2:22)**
  A. Blessings in Christ (1:1–23)
  B. Body of Christ (2:1–22)
II. **Provision of God (3:1–4:16)**
  A. Mystery of Grace (3:1–21)
  B. Message of Unity (4:1–16)
III. **Power of God (4:17–6:24)**
  A. Believer's Walk (4:17–6:9)
  B. Believer's Warfare (6:10–24)

Message

I. Plan of God (Ephesians 1:1–2:22)

A. Blessings in Christ (Ephesians 1:1–23)

Paul opens his letter with an expression of blessing (Gk. *eulogētos*) to God who has given believers many spiritual blessings in Christ (1:3). Arnold calls it "a poetically crafted explanation of praise for the plan of God brought into effect by Jesus Christ."[10] The passage emphasizes the sovereignty of God's plan, which was brought into effect by Jesus Christ. This remarkable plan includes His spiritual blessings that are ours both on earth and in the heavenly realms.

B. Body of Christ (Ephesians 2:1–22)

Paul uses the figure of a temple to describe the church (2:19–22) as a spiritual building in which all the different elements (people groups) are welded together into a collective unity. Notice that Paul says, "You are also being built together for God's dwelling in the Spirit" (2:22). The church is a society of people: "So then you are no longer foreigners and strangers, but fellow citizens with the saints, and members of God's household" (2:19). The church was built; yet it continues to grow. Every time people are converted, they are added to the church. Once in a church, they can grow in Christ, which builds the strength of the church. While believers are the church and the bride, Christ is the Bridegroom. Just as God compared Israel's relationship to Him to a marriage throughout the Old Testament (e.g., Hos 3:1), so the New Testament presents a union between Christ and the church using the metaphor of marriage. Both Christ and the church are bound by significant self-sacrifice. Christians must sacrifice themselves for Christ, just as Christ made the ultimate sacrifice for them. The purpose of the bride or church is to be free from blemish and sin; it should be spotless.

II. Provision of God (Ephesians 3:1–4:16)

A. Mystery of Grace (Ephesians 3:1–21)

Paul pictures believers as being "in Christ." This is a special relationship with God because they are perfect in Christ. The concept of being "in Christ" is a description of being placed into Christ at salvation with an ongoing experience throughout one's Christian life. The believer enjoys an intimate relationship with Jesus Christ; just as a child is in the mother's womb before birth and is a part of his mother, so the believer retains his individual personality while being "in Christ" and being intimately related to Him.

The concept of being "in Christ" grows out of the promise Jesus made in the upper room the night before He died when He said, "You are in me, and I am in you" (John 14:20). When people receive Christ as Savior, Jesus enters their life ("I

A part of the Roman Harbor baths and gymnasium complex excavated at ancient Ephesus.

in you"). As a result of that initial experience of salvation, the believer is placed into the person or body of Christ who stands at the right hand of God the Father in glory. Being "in Christ" represents the believer's standing in glory. Paul uses the phrase "in Christ" 170 times in his writings to refer to church-age believers to whom the mystery of God's grace was already revealed.

B. Message of Unity (Ephesians 4:1–16)

Paul exhorted the people of Ephesus to be found "making every effort to keep the unity of the Spirit through the bond of peace" (4:3). Seven times in the next verses Paul describes the unity as "one body," "one Spirit," "one hope," "one Lord," "one faith," "one baptism," and "one God." He summarizes the basis of unity: there is "one God and Father of all, who is above all and through all and in all" (4:6). Remember, Jews and Gentiles were initially in constant conflicts over circumcision (Acts 15) and legalism. A Jew was not supposed to enter a Gentile home; at the same time many Gentiles were hardheaded toward the Jewish ceremonial law and its requirements of purity.

The answer to unity is the fact that we are "in Christ" and all of us are members of "the body of Christ." Both Jew and Gentile are reconciled to God the Father; both are reconciled to other believers so that "he might reconcile both to God in one body through the cross by which he put the hostility to death" (Eph 2:16). Notice that Paul never exhorts both factions to "make peace with one another." Instead Paul exhorts them to be reconciled to Jesus Christ who is "our peace" (2:14). Therefore, the key to unity is always Jesus Christ and our relationship to Him.

The odeum (theater) at Ephesus was built in AD 150. It seated 1,400 spectators. This odeum was used as a council chamber as well.

III. Power of God (Ephesians 4:17–6:24)

A. Believer's Walk (Ephesians 4:17–6:9)

Of all the cities where Paul ministered, perhaps the Ephesians had more evidence of satanic activity and demonic oppression than any other place (Acts 19:11–20). Therefore Paul warns "against the rulers, against the authorities, against the cosmic powers of this darkness, against evil, spiritual forces in the heavens" (6:12). Earlier Paul exhorted, "Don't give the devil an opportunity" (4:27). Some scholars even believe Paul includes the evil world when he describes Christ as being set above "every ruler and authority, power and dominion" (1:21).

B. Believer's Warfare (Ephesians 6:10–24)

Spiritual warfare takes place both in heaven and on earth. Because believers have victory in Christ in heaven, they should and can have victory on this earth. So Paul exhorts believers to prepare for spiritual battle on this earth: "Stand, therefore, with truth like a belt around your waist" (6:14). Paul also exhorts believers to take armor to their chests (6:14), sandal their feet with the gospel (6:15), take the shield of faith (6:16) and the helmet of salvation (6:17), and finally use Scripture as "the sword of the Spirit" (6:17). The bottom line of spiritual warfare is Christ's authority over Satan and demons. When Christians are equipped with spiritual armor, they are equipped to stand firm and win a victory for Jesus Christ.

REFLECTION

ARE YOU "IN CHRIST"?

Being "in Christ" means that you totally belong to Him. True believers are in Him, and He is in us. We often express this by saying Jesus lives in our hearts. Does He live in your heart? Have you had a life-changing personal encounter with the living Christ? If not, why not? If He really is who He claims to be, He deserves your faith in response to His grace. Think about it. Maybe it's time you invited Him into your heart by calling on His name and asking Him to come in.

Practical Application

A practical and devotional commentary on Ephesians[11] divides the book into three parts: (1) chapters 1–3: The Wealth of the Christian; (2) 4–6:9: The Walk of the Christian; and (3) 6:10–23: The Warfare of the Christian. The letter to the Ephesians motivates the reader to triumph over the challenges of this life and to experience the abundant life Christ offers. The theme essentially highlights three truths: (1) the believer's exalted *position* in Christ;

(2) the believer's *duty* to walk according to his position in Christ; and (3) that victory is *possible* because of the Word of God and the Holy Spirit.

The book of Ephesians reveals Paul's prayerful desire that believers may know Christ more intimately by (1) having "a spirit of wisdom and revelation in the knowledge of him" (1:17); (2) Paul prays "that the eyes of your heart may be enlightened" (1:18); and (3) that they may understand "the immeasurable greatness of his power to us" (1:19). Because Paul experienced this power in his own life, he wanted believers to experience the same victory. In his second prayer (3:14–21), Paul prays, "Now to him who is able to do above and beyond all that we ask or think according to the power that works in us" (3:20). Paul prays: (1) that the believers would "be strengthened with power . . . through his Spirit" (3:16); (2) that Christ "may dwell in your hearts through faith" (3:17); and (3) that the believers would be rooted and grounded in love to understand the length, width, and height of God's love (3:18). Paul's purpose is that Christ should receive "glory in the church . . . to all generations, forever and ever" (3:21).

Ephesians is a book of grace, truth, and love. In it, the apostle Paul combines each of these elements to describe the believer's walk. We are saved by grace by believing the truth of the gospel and expressing it in our love for God, His people, and His church. In this powerful and positive letter, Christ is exalted and God's plan for the church in this dispensation is revealed.

The letter to the Ephesians contains practical advice about the unity of the body of Christ—the church (4:1–16), personal relationships within that body (4:25–32), genuine worship (5:15–21), and marriage and family living (5:22–6:4). In fact, Paul's advice about the family is one of the most practical statements in all of Scripture regarding husbands, wives, parents, and children. His admonition to husbands to love their wives "as Christ loved the church" (5:25) reveals the heart of God for genuine Christian marriage, in contrast to the pagan practices of the proper treatment of women that changed the role of women in Christian civilization.

The most basic elements of the Christian life are clearly highlighted in Paul's letter to the Ephesians. Salvation is by grace through faith and not of works (2:8–9). Yet, Paul also understood that believers saved by grace were also "created in Christ Jesus for good works" (2:10). Those who have been born again by God's Spirit will reflect God's character in their lives and demonstrate His love and power to the world at large by their good works. In other words, our deeds are the evidence (fruit) of our salvation but not the cause (root) of our salvation.

As you read Paul's description of true spirituality, ask yourself, "Where do I stand with God?" If I am truly seated with Christ in heaven (2:6), I have every reason to experience a winning walk on earth. If God is for us, who can be against us?

HOW BELIEVERS ARE TO WALK[12]	
Walk carefully	Eph 5:15
Walk as wise	Eph 5:15
Walk in "newness of life"	Rom 6:4
Walk not after the flesh	Rom 8:4
Walk honestly	Rom 13:13, "behave properly" (NASB)
Walk by faith	2 Cor 5:7
Walk in the Spirit	Gal 5:16
Walk worthy of the Lord	Col 1:10
Walk "in him"	Col 2:6
Walk in wisdom	Col 4:5
Walk worthy of God	1 Thess 2:12
Walk in the light	1 John 1:7
Walk in truth	3 John 4

The believer's walk is a demonstration of our being "filled with the Spirit" (5:18). Paul's use of the imperative mood literally means "keep on being filled" (or controlled) by the Spirit. Only then can we hope to live as God really intends for us to live. Although Paul was imprisoned in Rome, his thoughts were with the disciples in Ephesus and their daily walk with Christ. His love for them was a reflection of his love for Christ, desire for His presence, and devotion to His service.

For Further Reading

Arnold, Clinton. "Ephesians." *ZIBBC*. Ed. Clinton Arnold. Grand Rapids:
     Zondervan, 2002, 300–341.
————. *Ephesians*. ZECNT. Grand Rapids: Zondervan, 2010.
Hendriksen, William. *Exposition of Ephesians*. Grand Rapids: Baker, 1995.
Hoehner, Harold W. *Ephesians: An Exegetical Commentary*. Grand Rapids:
     Baker, 2003.
Stott, John R. W. *The Message of Ephesians: God's New Society*. Downers
     Grove, IL: IVP, 1979.

Study Questions

1. What spiritual privileges and blessings do we receive in Christ?
2. Why is it important for us to trust the sovereignty of God in our
    lives?
3. Make a list of the various responsibilities mentioned in Ephesians
    that tell the believer how to walk.
4. Why is unity so important for the Christian faith?
5. What principles of spiritual warfare can be drawn from Ephesians
    that will give us victory in our daily struggles?

Notes

1. E. J. Goodspeed, quoted in F. F. Bruce, *The Epistles to the Colossians, Philemon, and the Ephesians*, NICNT (Grand Rapids: Eerdmans, 1984), 229.

2. William Hendriksen, *Exposition of Ephesians*, NTC (Grand Rapids: Baker, 1995), 69.

3. Ibid., 69.

4. Ibid., 55–56.

5. Clinton Arnold, "Ephesians," in *ZIBBC* (Grand Rapids: Zondervan, 2002), 3:301.

6. Ibid., 3:303.

7. Clinton Arnold, *Ephesians*, ZECNT (Grand Rapids: Zondervan, 2010), 26.

8. Ibid., 53.

9. Main points based on J. Witmer and Mal Couch, *Galatians and Ephesians: By Grace Through Faith*, in Ed Hindson, ed., TFCBC (Chattanooga: AMG, 2009), 101ff.

10. Arnold, "Ephesians," in *ZIBBC*, 3:305.

11. Ruth Paxton, *Ephesians: The Wealth, Walk, and Warfare of the Christian* (Grand Rapids: Revell, 1939). A similar outline is found in Watchman Nee, *Sit, Walk, Stand* (Fort Washington, PA: Christian Literature Crusade, 1957).

12. Whitmer and Couch, *Galatians and Ephesians*, 190.

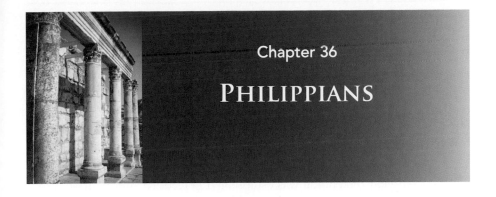

Chapter 36

PHILIPPIANS

The Mind of Christ

I n this brief and intensely practical letter, the apostle Paul speaks to the vital necessity for all believers in Christ to live their Christian faith in a practical and relevant way in order to fulfill the plan of God for their lives and fully glorify God the Father. Thus, Paul conveys his passion for all believers to have the mind of Christ as they function within the body of Christ.

KEY FACTS

Authors:	Paul
Recipients:	The church at Philippi
Where:	Rome
Date:	c. AD 60
Key Word:	To think, to have an attitude (Gk. *phroneō*)
Key Verse:	"Adopt the same attitude as that of Christ Jesus" (2:5). "Let this mind be in you which was also in Christ Jesus" (2:5 NKJV).

Author

The apostle Paul, a close friend of the people of Philippi and founder of the Philippian church, wrote this letter to them from his prison in Rome. The genuineness of Paul's authorship has never been in serious question. Paul claims to be the author (1:1), and early external testimony attributed the letter to him. See also "Author" section of Ephesians, Colossians, and Philemon. Paul originally arrived in Philippi on his second missionary journey (Acts 16:12–40) where a Christian assembly was apparently established in the home of Lydia, a Jewish convert. His time spent in Philippi was marked by dramatic conversions, a public beating, a powerful earthquake, and a public apology.

Recipients

This ten-year-old church was established in Acts 16 after Paul obeyed a vision to leave Asia (Minor) and go to Europe to preach the gospel. Upon arriving in the Gentile-populated city of Philippi in Macedonia, Paul preached the gospel to anyone who would listen. The congregation established at Philippi after this brief trip is best described as meager. The membership included Lydia (a businesswoman) and her household, a Philippian jailor and his household, a former demon-possessed girl, and undoubtedly a handful of others. From these humble beginnings, this church grew into a strong, healthy, mature, and God-honoring congregation (1:1b).

Philippi's acropolis seen from the hill where Cassius's forces camped in 42 BC. The Battle at Philippi was one of the strategic engagements between Julius Caesar's assassins, Brutus and Cassius, and his avengers, Marc Antony and Octavian. The victory of the latter forces was a critical step toward Octavian becoming Caesar Augustus (Luke 2:1).

Occasion and Date

This intimate and personal letter from Paul was written because the Philippians had heard that Paul was not doing well in prison. Maybe they had heard that Epaphroditus, whom they had sent to Paul, was near death after arriving in Rome. Paul drafted this letter and sent it by Epaphroditus to encourage the Philippians that Paul himself was rejoicing in the Lord, that Epaphroditus was doing better, and that their friend Epaphroditus should be honored for his service for God to Paul (2:25–36). The letter was likely written around AD 60 during Paul's Roman imprisonment.[1]

Summary of Correspondences Between Paul and the Philippian Church		
Communication 1:	Acts 16:12–40	Paul's first visit during his second missionary journey.
Communication 2:	Acts 20:1–6	During Paul's third missionary journey, Paul visited with them as he had to go through Philippi once again.
Communication 3:	Acts 21–28	Correspondence during Paul's imprisonment.

Genre and Structure

In this brief letter Paul emphasized that believers can experience true joy by living out the mind of Christ within the body of Christ, adopting the attitude of remembrance (1:1–2), prayer (1:3–11), selflessness (1:12–20), confidence (1:21–30), unity, humility (2:1–11), evangelism (2:12–18), servitude (2:19–30), gratitude (3:1–11), commitment (3:12–21), joy (4:1–9), and support (4:10–23).

Outline

I. Joy of Christ (1:1–30)
II. Humility of Christ (2:1–30)
III. Goal of Christ (3:1–21)
IV. Peace of Christ (4:1–23)

Message

I. Joy of Christ (Philippians 1:1–30)

Paul expresses his deep, heartfelt thanks to God for the Philippians "for every remembrance" of them (v. 3), suggesting he prays for them every time he offers prayers (v. 4). He was rejoicing, but he knew it would be difficult for some believers in Philippi to believe that God was still working mightily in his life while he was in prison. Thus, Paul's hope was to offer practical encouragements to his friends at Philippi[2] so they would not be tempted to doubt God's faithfulness even in dire circumstances. Paul stresses that all of the hardships they had heard about should be viewed through the eyes of faith in a God who is always in control. Paul observes, "What has happened to me has *actually* advanced the gospel" (1:12, emphasis added). Thus, Paul could emphasize the joy of the Lord (18 times in this book), despite his circumstances.

II. Humility of Christ (Philippians 2:1–30)

Philippians 2:1–11 provides a profound example of how to live out the attitude of humility like Christ. Paul says we should live in unity (v. 2), humility (v. 3), and selflessness (v. 4). He then gives Jesus Christ as the supreme example for believers to follow. All believers should respect, revere, and desire to imitate Jesus Christ (v. 5). Paul rightly thought

Northern shops of the Roman Agora (market/civic center) at ancient Philippi in Greece.

that if Jesus, "the head of the body" (Col 1:18), could live by these humble attitudes while He dwelt upon the earth (cf. John 13:15), then certainly the members of the body of Christ should live by them as well.

Paul's passionate desire was that the believers in Philippi remain spiritually effective and strong, so he encouraged them to "hold firm to the message of life" (2:16). "Hold firm" (*epecho*, give heed, or stay the course) emphasizes a firm commitment to the faith necessary to remain as bright "stars" in this dark world (v. 15). The Philippians knew that Paul had exhibited this same level of spiritual commitment in his own life when he sang praises while suffering in the Philippian jail (Acts 16:25) and when he praised God while in confinement in Rome (1:12–18).

III. Goal of Christ (Philippians 3:1–21)

Paul leaned on the righteousness of Christ as payment for his sin (3:9). He wanted to commune with the Lord Jesus who provided salvation for him (3:10). Paul lived with the reality that as a result of his salvation he would someday see the Lord face-to-face (3:11). In sharing his testimony, Paul shows how a sincere testimony of Jesus Christ's life-changing power can both encourage the believer and serve as a powerful witness to an unbeliever. Paul pursued Christ as passionately as a runner would pursue the goal and prize of winning a race (3:12–14). He remembered how esteemed athletes were commended by high officials, and Paul longed to receive his reward for faithfully fulfilling "God's heavenly call" (3:14, 20–21).

The ancient theater at Philippi.

IV. Peace of Christ (Philippians 4:1–23)

True joy and peace are not contingent on circumstances but rather on knowing that an all-powerful and all-loving God is in control (4:6–8). When joy is fully experienced, the evidence of a level of trust and peace can only be produced by God Himself. Paul evidenced this level of peace and joy as he purposed in his heart to praise God, even while he was in prison on his first trip to Philippi (Acts 16:25). Paul testified of God's sovereignty in his current confinement in Rome (1:12–16, 18b) and thus offered himself as an example of a person who was at peace with his circumstances (4:9; also 3:17; 1 Cor 11:1).

Practical Application

In this brief letter Paul provides practical answers to the frequently pondered question, "How can I truly bring glory to God?" *Having the mind of Christ in the body of Christ* is the way every believer can bring glory to God. Paul emphasized that we can experience true joy when we let the mind of Christ control our remembrance (1:1–2), prayers (1:3–11), selflessness (1:12–20), confidence (1:21–30), unity, humility (2:1–11), evangelism (2:12–18), servitude (2:19–30), gratitude (3:1–11), commitment (3:12–21), joy (4:1–9), and support (4:10–23). A mere cursory reading of Philippians shows that Paul had "no sympathy with a cold and dead orthodoxy or formalism that knows nothing of struggle and growth."[3] Paul ends this extremely practical letter with the ultimate purpose for why he strove to have the *mind of Christ in the body of Christ* and why he pleaded with other believers to do the same—for the eternal glory of God the Father (4:20; cf. 2:11).

For Further Reading

Bruce, F. F. *Philippians*. GNC. San Francisco: Harper & Row, 1983.
Gromacki, Robert. *Stand United in Joy: An Exposition of Philippians*. Woodlands, TX: Kress Christian Publications, 2003.
Melick, Richard R., Jr. *Philippians, Colossians, Philemon*. NAC. Nashville: B&H, 1991.
O'Brian, Peter. *Commentary on Philippians*. Grand Rapids: Eerdmans, 1991.
Silva, Moises. *Philippians*. 2nd ed. BECNT. Grand Rapids: Baker, 2005.
Thielman, Frank. "Philippians." In *Romans to Philemon*. Ed. Clifton E. Arnold. Vol. 3 of *ZIBBC (NT)*. Grand Rapids: Zondervan, 2002.

Study Questions

1. What were Paul's conditions when he wrote to the Philippians?
2. What made Paul rejoice?
3. In what ways does Paul liken the Christian life to a race?
4. Why were the Philippian Christians close to Paul?

Notes

1. Richard Melick Jr., *Philippians, Colossians, Philemon*, NAC (Nashville: B&H, 1991), 22.

2. Gleaned from Robert Gromacki, *Stand United in Joy: An Exposition of Philippians* (Woodlands, TX: Kress Christian Publications, 2003).

3. Harold J. Greenlee, *An Exegetical Summary of Philippians* (Dallas: SIL International, 2001), 224.

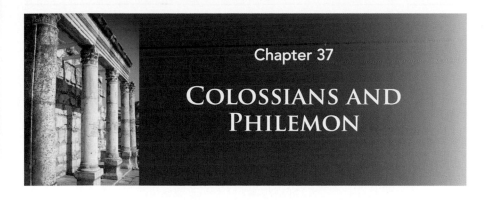

Chapter 37

COLOSSIANS AND PHILEMON

Living for Christ

The ancient city of Colossae remains unexcavated, its buried treasures awaiting discovery.[1] What is known of the city is that it was religiously pluralistic with numerous cults and deities. The local people of the first century AD feared spirits, demons, and departed ancestors. Their forms of worship often included ecstatic self-mutilation and flagellation in order to ward off evil spirits and human curses.[2] Into this environment of religious paranoia, the gospel of salvation by grace was spread in the house churches of Nympha (Col 4:15) and Philemon (Phlm 2). Yet even there new heresies threatened the infant churches, and Paul wrote this marvelous letter (Colossians) to combat error and point his readers to the preeminent Christ, who alone could guarantee their eternal salvation. At the same time Paul wrote a personal letter to Philemon who was living at Colossae.

COLOSSIANS

Preeminence of Christ

Epaphras came to Rome telling Paul of the problems in the church at Colossae. Some believers were insisting on observance of Jewish religious days with strict diets and asceticism of the body. Other believers were following "philosophy," and still others were guilty of praying to angels. Paul wrote the letter to the Colossians, including one of the most complete statements about the true nature of the person of Christ in the New Testament (1:15–26). He described the indwelling Christ as the basis of Christian living (1:26–28; 3:1–3). Christ is the true wisdom (2:2–4), ascetic practices are useless (2:20–23), and the abundant life is found only in Christ (3:1–5). Paul sent this letter to Colossae by Epaphras and also sent one by Onesimus, a runaway slave, to his master who lived in Colossae, suggesting how he should receive back his slave.

KEY FACTS	
Author:	Paul
Recipients:	The church at Colossae
Where:	Rome (from prison)
Date:	AD 60–62
Key Word:	Preeminence (Gk. *prōteuō*)
Key Verse:	"He is the head of the body, the church, who is the beginning, the first-born from the dead, that in all things He may have the preeminence" (1:18 NKJV).

Author

Most biblical scholars agree with the traditional view that Paul was the author of Colossians. External evidence supports Paul's authorship, such as the testimony of early church fathers like Irenaeus, Clement of Alexandria, and Tertullian. An abundance of internal evidence suggests Paul was the author as well (1:1, 23; 4:18). Note that Onesimus is mentioned in both letters (Col 4:9; Phlm 16), suggesting Onesimus was returning with Tychicus as they delivered the two letters (Col 4:7; Phlm 23).

Recently some critical scholars proposed that an unnamed follower of Paul wrote the letter after his death, using Paul's name to give the letter authority. They claim the

A twelfth-century codex showing the first page of the letter to the Colossians.

references to "wisdom," "knowledge," and "basic principles of the world" (Col 2:8, 20 NKJV) are terms used in Gnosticism, a heresy that did not fully invade the church until the second century. However, precisely identifying the source and date of this heresy has proved notoriously difficult for scholars. It is also possible the heresy may include some form of Jewish mysticism.[3]

Critics claim that the cosmic or exalted manner of describing Jesus Christ in Colossians was not used until the second century. Nevertheless, in order to counter false teaching, Paul focuses the reader on the supremacy and preeminence of Jesus Christ (1:15–20), similar to John's statements about Christ in Revelation. In addition, this high Christology is consistent with the exalted statements found in the earlier undisputed letters of Paul (Rom 10:6–13; 1 Cor 8:4–6; Phil 2:6–11).[4]

Recipients

Colossae, Hierapolis, and Laodicea (4:13) form a triangle on the Lycus River in Phrygia (Asia Minor, today called Turkey) about 100 miles from Ephesus. Colossae was a prosperous city, but about the time of this letter, it declined into a smaller town, perhaps due to severe earthquakes in that region.

Apparently Paul never visited Colossae (2:1). The Colossians received the gospel through Epaphras (4:12–13), himself a Colossian. Perhaps when Paul was ministering in Ephesus, the gospel reached Colossae: "And this [ministry in Ephesus] went on for two years, so that all the residents of Asia, both Jews and Greeks, heard the word of the Lord" (Acts 19:10). Perhaps Philemon visited Paul in Ephesus and was converted.

Overviews of the Nymphaeum (public fountain) at Laodicea. The main basin was converted into early Christian use as part of a church.

Occasion and Date

Epaphras, who originally planted the church in Colossae (1:6–7), likely brought a report of the "Colossian heresy" to Paul in Rome (1:8). For some reason Epaphras was detained in Rome as a prisoner for a short while (Phlm 23). Later Paul decided to write to the Colossians; and in order to get the letter into their hands as soon as possible, he sent the letter with Tychicus and Onesimus. Paul probably wrote Colossians in AD 62 while he was a prisoner in Rome (Col 4:10; Phlm 1) and living in his own rented house (Acts 28:16, 30). In these circumstances Paul had the mental freedom to deal with the various issues brought to him about the church in Colossae. He talked to his companions on these issues (Col 4:10–15) and wrote this letter to address several of these problems.

Outline

I. Doctrine: Preeminence of Christ (1:1–2:23)
    A. Exaltation of Christ (1:1–23)
    B. Explanation of Wisdom (1:24–2:3)
    C. Examination of Heresy (2:4–23)
II. Ethics: Identification with Christ (3:1–4:18)
    A. Position in Christ (3:1–4:6)
    B. Commendations and Greetings in Christ (4:7–18)

Message

I. Doctrine: Preeminence of Christ (Colossians 1:1–2:23)

A. Exaltation of Christ (Colossians 1:1–23)

While the sister book, Ephesians, emphasizes the members in the body of Christ (Eph 4:25), Colossians puts emphasis on Christ as the head of the body, citing an early Christian hymn to explain the preeminence of Christ. Although the name *Jesus* or *Christ* is not referenced in this hymn, He is the obvious subject of the hymn. The first part of this hymn praises Christ for His work as Creator God, and the second part deals with His role as Redeemer God. Christ has made the Father knowable, available, and approachable to all believers at all times (1:15–17). Thus, He is the "image of the invisible God" and the Creator of heaven and earth (vv. 15–16), making reconciliation between God and man by His blood (vv. 19–20).

B. Explanation of Wisdom (Colossians 1:24–2:3)

Paul explains that true biblical wisdom was based on Old Testament truth, but now it is even more "fully known" through Christ Himself (1:25). He explains, "The mystery hidden for ages and generations but now revealed to his saints" (1:26) is "Christ in you, the hope of glory" (1:27). Jesus predicted this fact the night before He died: "You are in me, and I am in you" (John 14:20). To be a Christian is to have Jesus Christ living in your life. The essence of God's mystery or wisdom is Jesus Christ. Paul's desire was "that they may have all the riches of complete understanding and have the knowledge of God's mystery—Christ" (Col 2:2). When they have Christ, they have "all the treasures of wisdom and knowledge" (2:3).

Paul's Use of the Word *Mystery*	
The mystery:	"Christ in you, the hope of glory" (Col 1:27)
The mystery:	The gospel to all nations (Rom 16:25)
The mystery:	"We shall not all sleep, but we shall all be changed" (1 Cor 15:51 NKJV)
The mystery:	Gentiles made fellow heirs through the gospel (Eph 3:3–9)
The mystery:	"Of lawlessness" (2 Thess 2:7)
The mystery:	"Of the faith" (1 Tim 3:9)
The mystery:	"Of godliness" (1 Tim 3:16)

C. Examination of Heresy (Colossians 2:4–23)

The foundation of the Colossian heresy was grounded in *gnōsis*, that is, unknowable wisdom and mystery. Technically the cult of Gnosticism did not develop into a full threat to the church for over half a century, though its seeds were manifesting themselves early. Paul seems to sum up this heresy calling it, "philosophy and empty deceit based on human tradition, based on the elements [Gk. *stoichia*] of the world" (2:8). Bruce notes that rabbinical Judaism also included features of mystery initiations, known as "*merkabah* mysticism," which emphasized techniques for experiencing divine visions in which angels served a mediatorial role.[5] Some of the Colossians were emphasizing Jewish rites of circumcision (2:11), kosher food (2:16), Sabbath keeping (2:16), and laws of purification (2:14). Paul answers the circumcision issue by reminding the Colossians that they were baptized with Christ because they were "buried with him in baptism . . . raised with him . . . from the dead" (2:12). No other initiatory rite is needed. Paul answers the food issues by reminding them, "These are a shadow of what was to come" (2:17). Paul said Christ fulfilled the law, thus keeping the obligations of the law is no longer necessary because Christ took "it away by nailing it to the cross" (2:14).

II. Ethics: Identification with Christ (Colossians 3:1–4:18)

A. Position in Christ (Colossians 3:1–4:6)

New Testament believers live in two realms. They live on this earthly realm, and they live in the heavenly realm above, which is similar to the term Paul used in Ephesians, in "the heavens." Paul reminded them how they should live in this earthly life with the encouragement, "As you have received Christ Jesus the Lord, continue to live in him" (Col 2:6). Their earthly life should be "put to death . . . your worldly nature: sexual immorality, impurity, lust, evil desire, and greed" (3:5). The Colossians were to set their minds on what is above, not on what is on the earth (3:2). They should focus on their heavenly standing because "you have been raised with Christ, seek the things above, where Christ is, seated at the right hand of God. Set your minds on things above" (3:1–2). Paul reminds them, "You died, and your life is hidden with Christ in God" (3:3). These statements indicate that people will struggle to live on earth as citizens of heaven, but they also promise that victory comes from "being renewed in knowledge according to the image of your Creator" (3:10).

Paul then turns from negative issues to positive admonitions: "Put on compassion, kindness, humility, gentleness, and patience, bearing with one another and forgiving one another if anyone has a grievance against another. Just as the Lord has forgiven you, so you are also to forgive" (3:12–13). "Put on" (3:12) is an imperative verb, imply-

The top of Tel Colossae, near Honaz, Turkey. Colossae has never been excavated.

ing a sense of urgency. First, they are to remember that they are "chosen ones" (3:12) so they should act accordingly. Second, they must accept other believers (the basis is that all are one in the body of Christ) because they died together and were raised together (3:11). Third, they must forgive as they have been forgiven (3:14). Fourth, they are admonished to let the peace of Christ control their hearts (3:15); and fifth, they must let the words of Christ dwell in their minds (3:16). The sixth exhortation involved actions, namely, "Do everything in the name of the Lord Jesus" (3:17), suggesting that believers are ambassadors for Christ and therefore should live Christ-centered lives in all their words, actions, and attitudes. Finally, Paul adds a section of practical observations addressed to wives, husbands, children, fathers, slaves, and masters (3:18–4:1).

Paul ends this practical section with an emphasis on prayer. They are to give constant attention to prayer with an alert attitude, that is, keep awake or be spiritually watching. Paul applies this truth so "that God may open a door to us for the word" (4:3).

B. Commendations and Greetings in Christ (4:7–18)

Despite the fact that he was in prison, Paul still sought opportunities to minister for Christ by affirming his fellow believers who shared his interest in spreading the gospel. Paul wanted the Colossians to know that all his helpers were faithful servants of God who loved the Colossians. Their desire was for the Colossians to follow the instructions in this letter (4:17).

PHILEMON

Transformed by the Gospel

Onesimus was Philemon's runaway slave from Colossae who encountered Paul in Rome. Onesimus accepted Christ, and Paul sent him back to his owner, Philemon. Because Onesimus could be punished or even put to death, Paul interceded for him, asking Philemon to accept Onesimus as a brother and saying that he, the apostle, would repay anything Onesimus had stolen.

KEY FACTS	
Author:	Paul
Recipient:	Philemon, at Colossae
Where:	Rome (from prison)
Date:	AD 60–62
Key Word:	Brother (Gk. *adelphos*)
Key Verse:	"And if he [Onesimus] has wronged you in any way, or owes you anything, charge that to my account" (v. 18).

Author

Paul introduced himself as "a prisoner of Christ Jesus" (v. 1) while he was also a prisoner in Rome, although he had freedom to live in his own rented house. He was awaiting trial by Emperor Nero because of the charges made against him by the Jews in Jerusalem (see Acts 23–26). Paul was in prison for two years and was able to receive visitors (Acts 28:30). During this time he wrote four letters (Philemon, Ephesians, Philippians, and Colossians) called the Prison Epistles.

Recipient

Philemon, a wealthy businessman who lived in Colossae, owned slaves (at least Onesimus was his slave). Apparently the church met in his house; and according to tradition, his son, Archippus, was its pastor. Philemon is recognized by almost all Pauline scholars as written by Paul. Recent scholars have suggested that Onesimus actually may have run to find Paul in Rome in order to secure

The Lycus River Valley as seen from Colossae.

his help in reconciling him with his owner, Philemon.[6] Whatever circumstance brought them together, Paul's letter gave him an opportunity to express Christian grace in regard to the issue of slavery in the Roman world.

Occasion and Date

The epistle to Philemon is Paul's appeal to Philemon, a wealthy believer in Colossae, to receive back his runaway slave, Onesimus, who was converted through Paul's ministry. The key theological picture is Christ interceding to the Father to forgive our sins, just as Paul interceded to Philemon to forgive Onesimus's sins. Just as Christ took our sins upon Himself, so Paul asks Philemon to place Onesimus's responsibility upon him (v. 18).

Paul sent Onesimus back to Colossae with Epaphras, who delivered these two letters. The letters to the Colossians and to Philemon are identified similarly: (1) both sent by Paul and Timothy (Col 1:1; Phlm 1); (2) both mention Onesimus (Col 4:7; Phlm v. 10); (3) both refer to Epaphras (Col 4:12; Phlm 23); and (4) both mention Paul's companions: Mark, Aristarchus,

Demus, and Luke (Col 4:10, 14; Phlm 24). This would date both letters at the same time (AD 60–62). Because Onesimus and Philemon were both transformed by the gospel of Christ, they should, therefore, receive each other as *brothers* (key word).

Message

Paul takes up a quill to write a personal letter to a close friend about a problem concerning a runaway slave. Paul feels Onesimus should not face his master alone when he returns. Writing with large letters because of his advanced age or nearsightedness (v. 19), Paul is gracious and understanding, asking Philemon to forgive Onesimus because "you owe me over and above your very soul" (v. 19, Moffatt). The problem was intensified because Onesimus probably stole valuables when he ran away to Rome. Some think the slave's money ran out and he sought out Paul (maybe he would have known Paul was a prisoner in Rome). Others think Paul providentially ran across Onesimus in Rome where Paul recognized the slave and led him to Christ. Onesimus's attitude toward life was transformed, and Onesimus willingly (not as a mandated slave) gave devoted service to Paul.

Paul pleads with Philemon to take Onesimus back and forgive him for both the crimes of stealing and running away. Paul makes himself personally responsible for the amount stolen: "Charge that to my account" (v. 18). Paul pleads for Philemon to receive Onesimus back as he would receive Paul (v. 17). Paul reminds Philemon of his obvious Christian responsibility and that he led Philemon to Christ (v. 9). Paul tells Philemon to receive back his runaway slave "on the basis of love" (v. 9). Paul is suggesting Philemon not only forgive his crimes but also give Onesimus his freedom. The Bible does not tell us what Philemon did. Tradition claims Onesimus was forgiven and eventually became bishop over the churches in Berea (Greece).

The story of Philemon and Onesimus is one of grace and compassion based on the principle of Christian love (v. 9). Such compassion comes from the heart (v. 12). It is given freely, not by compulsion (v. 14). Such compassion is based on Christian brotherhood (v. 16) and a willingness to forgive as God has forgiven us (v. 17). This is a letter written from prison on behalf of a slave. It is one of the most personal, loving, and appealing letters in the New Testament. It so powerfully expresses grace that one wonders if this little letter would have been placed in the Bible if Philemon had not taken the appropriate action.[7]

REFLECTION

Christian Opposition to Slavery

Opposition to slavery by evangelical Christians is one of the hallmarks of church history. Paul's instruction to Philemon is indicative of the biblical worldview of the essential equality of humans and the wrongness of oppressing others (Deut 23:15–16; Col 3:22–23). Opposition to the African slave trade was voiced in eighteenth-century England by evangelicals George Whitefield and John Newton. The latter influenced young William Wilberforce to bring the matter before the British parliament in 1787. Wilberforce delivered his first great parliamentary speech for abolition in 1789. Undaunted by resistance, Wilberforce eventually saw the British parliament and the US congress abolish the slave trade in 1807. Still, he pushed further for the emancipation of all slaves in the British Empire. This was finally passed by parliament a few days before his death in 1833. Because of this precedent, African slaves were set free by the Emancipation Proclamation of President Abraham Lincoln in 1863. As the "conscience of England" and the moral leader of British evangelicals, Wilberforce was buried in Westminster Abbey.

Conclusion

Philemon is Paul's shortest epistle. In the past some have called it a "postcard." Today it might be referred to as a "text message." Its message is that the gospel transforms our lives and makes us all brothers and sisters in Christ. Martin Luther is quoted as saying, "We are all the Lord's Onesimi" (using the Latin plural of Onesimus). We cannot pay our debt to God because we have rebelled in sin, stolen what was His, and run away, just as Onesimus did. But Jesus Christ offers us eternal freedom because he paid our debt just as Paul settled the debt with Philemon.

Practical Application

Colossians reminds us of the centrality of Jesus Christ. He is the "image of the invisible God" (1:15), the "head of the body, the church" (1:18). Therefore, Christ is the preeminent person in the universe, who reconciles us to Himself by "his blood, shed on the cross" (1:20). Because of who Jesus is and what He has done for us, we are new creations "in Christ" (3:11). On that basis, Paul instructs us to do whatever we do "from the heart," as something done for the Lord" (3:23).

The book of Philemon gives practical principles about how Christians should deal with the social evils in every era. Today we may face the evils of illegal drugs, pornography, sex predators, etc. Laws by themselves do not completely solve these problems; it takes the transformation of individuals by Jesus Christ, which will enable them to do what is right even without any laws. Paul presented principles that focused on transformed believers, knowing that in time transformed people would transform society. The brotherhood of believers is more than living by new laws; we are brothers and sisters in Christ because we both have a new Master—Jesus Christ. Therefore, this little letter of approximately 500 words was the beginning of the abolition of slavery in the world.

For Further Reading

Bruce, F. F. *The Epistles to the Colossians, to Philemon, and to the Ephesians*. NICNT. Grand Rapids: Eerdmans, 1984.

Gromacki, Robert. *Philippians and Colossians: Joy and Completeness in Christ*. TFCBC. Chattanooga: AMG, 2003.

Harris, Murray J. *Colossians and Philemon*. Exegetical Guide to the Greek New Testament. Grand Rapids: Eerdmans, 1991.

Hendriksen, William. *Colossians and Philemon*. NTC. Grand Rapids: Baker, 1964.

Moo, Douglas J. *The Letters to the Colossians and to Philemon*. PNTC. Grand Rapids: Eerdmans, 2008.

Study Questions

1. What is the theme of Paul's hymn that praises Christ (Col 1:15–20)?
2. What was the possible nature of false teaching at Colossae?
3. Explain the spiritual death, burial, and resurrection of the believer with Christ.
4. How should the heavenly standing of a believer influence his earthly state?
5. What motivated Paul to write to Philemon?
6. How does the letter to Philemon indicate we should deal with repentant sinners?

Notes

1. The archaeological site of Colossae was identified by W. J. Hamilton in 1835.

2. For a detailed discussion of the spiritual climate in Colossae, see Clinton Arnold, "Colossians," in *ZIBBC* (Grand Rapids: Zondervan, 2002), 3:371–76.

3. See the discussion of the "Colossian heresy" in Andreas J. Köstenberger, L. Scott Kellum, and Charles L. Quarles, *The Cradle, the Cross, and the Crown* (Nashville: B&H Academic, 2009), 605–9.

4. Ibid., 602.

5. F. F. Bruce, *The Epistles to the Colossians, to Philemon, and to the Ephesians*, NICNT (Grand Rapids: Eerdmans, 1984), 95–96.

6. For further discussion of the relationship of Paul, Onesimus, and Philemon, see S. M. Baugh, "Philemon," in *ZIBBC* (Grand Rapids: Zondervan, 2002), 3:514.

7. See Charles Ray, *First & Second Timothy, Titus, and Philemon* (Chattanooga: AMG, 2008), 217.

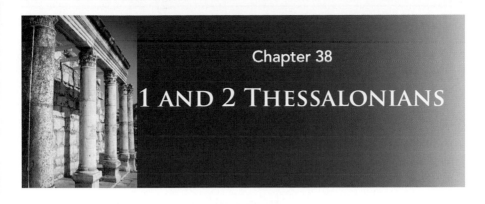

Chapter 38

1 AND 2 THESSALONIANS

The Last Days

The Christians at Thessalonica experienced a miraculous transformation of their lives when they turned from idolatry to Christ. Paul spent only a short time with them, but by the time he wrote to them a few months later, they had come together as a dynamic Christian fellowship. However, they had serious questions about the future and the return of Christ.

1 THESSALONIANS

The Return of Christ

First Thessalonians is one of Paul's most personal letters—an intimate, affectionate, heart-to-heart talk with a young church. With tact and humility the apostle comforts them about concerns they have related to the death of loved ones and Christ's imminent return.

KEY FACTS	
Author:	Paul
Recipients:	The church at Thessalonica (Macedonia)
Where:	Corinth (Achaia, Greece)
Date:	AD 51
Key Word:	Caught up (Gk. *harpadzō*)
Key Verses:	"For the Lord himself will descend from heaven with a shout, with the archangel's voice, and with the trumpet of God, and the dead in Christ will rise first. Then we who are still alive, who are left, will be caught up together with them in the clouds to meet the Lord in the air, and so we will always be with the Lord" (4:16–17).

Author

Paul identifies himself as the author of 1 Thessalonians twice in the epistle (1:1; 2:18), giving internal evidence of his authorship. Paul notes that Silas (Silvanus) and Timothy are with him (1:1). Both accompanied him during the evangelization of Thessalonica and were well known to the readers. External evidence also testifies to Paul's authorship. The early church (Irenaeus, Clement of Alexandria, Tertullian) unanimously affirmed the Pauline authorship and canonicity of the letter.[1]

Recipients

The city of Thessalonica was named about 315 BC by Cassander, one of Alexander the Great's generals, after his wife. It became the capital of Macedonia in 148 BC and a free city in 42 BC. Thessalonica became an important trading center because it was a seaport on the Aegean Sea and because the principal Roman road going east and west between Rome and Asia Minor (the Egnatian Way) went through the city. During Paul's time it had a population of about 200,000, mostly Greeks.

The seafront promenade of Thessaloniki, Greece, on a clear spring day.

The church at Thessalonica was founded by Paul during his second missionary journey (c. AD 50–52). After receiving a vision and call to go to Macedonia while he was at Troas in Asia Minor (Acts 16:9), he went to

Philippi (with Timothy, Silas, and Luke) and planted a church there during intense persecution (Acts 16:12–40). He then (with Timothy and Silas) followed the Egnatian Way west 100 miles to Thessalonica. Acts 17:1–10 describes his ministry there, probably during the winter of AD 50–51. By the time of the writing of 1 Thessalonians, the believers were organized as a church (1 Thess 1:1) and had leaders (5:12) and a congregation that included both Gentile (1:9) and Jewish converts (Acts 17:4) from the working class (1 Thess 4:11).[2]

Occasion and Date

After quickly evangelizing Thessalonica, Paul, Silas, and Timothy went west 50 miles to Berea (Acts 17:10–15). There Paul preached in the Jewish synagogue with a good response. However, he was driven out by jealous Jews from Thessalonica. Paul then went to Athens, where Silas and Timothy joined him (1 Thess 3:1), but Paul sent Timothy back to Macedonia to check on and encourage the new churches at Thessalonica and Philippi (3:1–5).

Paul then went on to Corinth, probably arriving in the spring of AD 51 where he had a successful eighteen-month ministry (c. March 51 to September 52). Silas and Timothy returned to Paul at Corinth from Macedonia about May of AD 51. They brought a good report about the churches there but also mentioned some problems (cf. 1 Thess 3:6–7; Acts 18:5). Paul then wrote his first epistle to the Thessalonians in late spring or early summer of AD 51 (cf. Acts 18:1, 11). Therefore, 1 Thessalonians is one of Paul's earliest epistles (only Galatians may be earlier).

Genre and Structure

First Thessalonians is one of Paul's most intimate and personal epistles. Paul's approach is gentle and loving. There is an air of expectancy concerning the return of Christ. There are no quotations from the Old Testament, and it is not primarily a doctrinal epistle. Paul is concerned to answer some of the questions currently troubling the believers at Thessalonica (cf. 4:9; 5:1).

The epistle divides easily into two major sections. The first is personal and historical, containing a commendation of the readers (for their fruitfulness, their reception of the gospel, and their current proclamation of the gospel; 1:1–10), a recounting of Paul's conduct at Thessalonica during his second missionary journey (his motives, his affection, and his integrity; 2:1–12), and a statement of Paul's concern for the believers (their suffering and persecution, his desire to see them and know how they're doing; 2:13–3:13). In chapter 4, Paul says,

"Finally ..., brothers" (4:1 HCSB) and begins the second major section—practical and hortatory. This section contains exhortations for the believers to be sanctified in their lives (4:1–12), explanations concerning the resurrection and the rapture and how they relate to both dead and living saints (4:13–18), an extended description of the coming Day of the Lord (5:1–11), and some exhortations about the conduct of the church (5:12–22).

Outline

   I. Example of the Believer (1:1–10)
  II. Exhortation of the Believer (2:1–3:13)
 III. Encouragement of the Believer (4:1–5:28)

Message

I. Example of the Believer (1 Thessalonians 1:1–10)

Paul begins his epistle by praising the Thessalonians based on his past relationship to them and the tremendous example they provided to other believers (1:7). He thanks God for their faith, hope, and love (cf. 1 Cor 13:13) and commends them for their fruitfulness (obedience to God), their reception of the gospel, and their proclamation of the gospel to others (1:2–10).

The ancient agora in Thessaloniki.

The theme of the epistle is given in 1:9–10: they turned to God (past) and now wait for Christ to return from heaven (present), who will deliver believers from all wrath to come (future).

II. Exhortation of the Believer (1 Thessalonians 2:1–3:13)

Paul next describes his past conduct among the Thessalonians (2:1–12). When he first ministered among them, he was not deceitful or insincere. In fact, he would have given them his own life, such was his affection for them (2:1–8). Furthermore, he worked hard to make his own living so that they would not have to support him. He was blameless and treated them like his own children. They had received his teaching as the Word of God (2:13). They had even suffered for that Word (2:9–16). Paul is so concerned about them that he sent Timothy to encourage them (3:1–10), and Paul prays that they will love one another and live holy lives (3:11–13).

III. Encouragement of the Believer (1 Thessalonians 4:1–5:28)

The will of God for the Thessalonian believers is that they might be progressively sanctified and have a strong hope for the future. They should abstain from immorality of every sort (4:1–8). They should live a life of love toward others, lead a quiet life, mind their own business, and work with their hands (4:11–12).

Concerning their fellow believers who have died, they should remember that at the rapture they will all be resurrected and translated (glorified) together, to be with Christ forever (4:13–18). The fact that both dead and living believers (those "in Christ") will be "caught up" (Gk. *harpazō*) together points to the promise of a future event.

Because of the promise of the rapture, believers will not suffer the wrath of the Day of the Lord (5:1–11). Therefore, in these last days it is necessary to be watchful so that they will not be found in the same stupor in which unbelievers are living. As they wait and watch, they should edify one another, respect their elders and leaders, and remain blameless toward God and the world (5:12–22).

| The Rapture and the Second Coming Contrasted ||
Rapture	Second Coming
Believers are judged and rewarded (1 Corinthians 3).	Unbelievers and Israel are judged (Matthew 25).

The Rapture and the Second Coming Contrasted (continued)	
Rapture	**Second Coming**
Christ comes to claim his bride, the church (1 Thessalonians 4).	Christ comes with the bride (Revelation 19).
Christ comes in the air (1 Thessalonians 4).	Christ returns to the earth (Matthew 25; Revelation 19).
The focus is comfort (1 Thessalonians 4).	The focus is judgment (Revelation 19).
The church is emphasized (1 Thessalonians 4).	Israel and the world are emphasized (Revelation 12–19).
The rapture is imminent (John 14; 1 Thessalonians 1).	Many signs are predicted (Matthew 24; Revelation 6–18).
The tribulation begins (Revelation 1–6).	The messianic kingdom is established (Revelation 20).

2 THESSALONIANS
The Day of the Lord

Paul's second epistle to the Thessalonians emphasizes a different aspect of future events from the first epistle. Whereas 1 Thessalonians teaches the imminence (any moment possibility) of the Lord's return to "catch up" believers to himself, 2 Thessalonians emphasizes the coming judgment on the enemies of Christ and focuses on Satan, the Antichrist, and the world. The eschatological passage in 2 Thessalonians 2 describes the great tribulation and the destiny of Satan's lawless one.

KEY FACTS

Author:	Paul
Recipients:	The church at Thessalonica (Macedonia)
Where:	Corinth (Achaia, Greece)
Date:	AD 51
Key Word:	Lawlessness (Gk. *anomia*)
Key Verse:	"Brothers, stand firm and hold to the traditions you were taught, either by our message or by our letter" (2:15 HCSB).

Author

Paul identifies himself twice in 2 Thessalonians as the author of the epistle (1:1; 3:17). As in 1 Thessalonians, he notes that Silas and Timothy are with him (1:1). No early church writer questioned the authenticity of Paul's authorship. The style, vocabulary, and teaching of 2 Thessalonians demonstrate that the epistle is Pauline. However, some critics claim the reason 1 and 2 Thessalonians are so similar is because someone other than Paul is trying to imitate Paul in 2 Thessalonians. However, it is likely that the similar words, tone, and attitudes demonstrate that the same author, Paul, wrote both, one letter shortly after the other to the same church.

Recipients

This epistle is addressed "to the church of the Thessalonians" (1 Thess 1:1; 2 Thess 1:1). See discussion under 1 Thessalonians.

Occasion and Date

Paul wrote both epistles to the Thessalonians from Corinth during his eighteen-month stay there. According to Acts, Paul, Silas, and Timothy were present together in Corinth (Acts 18:5). The one who delivered 1 Thessalonians to the church apparently brought back a further report from Thessalonica. Some of the news was good; the brethren were continuing to grow and to remain faithful in spite of persecution. But other news was bad: the persecution was intensifying. There was a false report (pretending to be from Paul himself) that the rapture had already happened and they had missed it and that the Day of the Lord (the predicted tribulation) had already come (2 Thess 2:1–2).

Close-up of the triumphal arch, built in AD 303, of Roman emperor Galerius. It sits astride the Egnatian Way in the center of Thessalonica, Greece. The arch commemorates Galerius's victories over the Persians.

In view of these reports, Paul quickly wrote his second epistle to the church at Thessalonica. It contains both (1) commendation and (2) doctrinal and practical correction. It dealt with the new questions raised among the Thessalonian believers. Paul's answers extend his teaching and exhortations to higher levels. Second Thessalonians apparently followed the first epistle by no more than a few months. The probable date for the writing of the second epistle is therefore the summer or fall of AD 51.

Genre and Structure

Second Thessalonians is a brief but intense letter expressing Paul's concerns for the suffering of the Thessalonian believers and for their apparent confusion about the future. Three major purposes may be discerned: (1) exhortation—to exhort and motivate the Thessalonians to persevere in suffering (chap. 1); (2) doctrine—to clarify the events and order of the Day of the Lord and the tribulation (chap. 2); and (3) practice—to correct those who were refusing to work (chap. 3).

Outline

   I. Revelation of Jesus Christ (1:1–12)
  II. Rebellion of the Antichrist (2:1–17)
III. Responsibility of the Church (3:1–18)

Message

I. Revelation of Jesus Christ (2 Thessalonians 1:1–12)

Paul begins on a positive note, commending the believers for their endurance and faith under severe persecution and thanking God for their faith and love (1:3–4, not hope because they had apparently lost it because of unsettling rumors). In speaking of the coming judgment of God on the world "at the revelation of the Lord Jesus from heaven" (1:7), Paul assures the believers that God will take vengeance on their persecutors and will be glorified over them at the end of the age (1:5–12).

II. Rebellion of the Antichrist (2 Thessalonians 2:1–17)

Paul's second epistle attempts to make clear that the persecutions being suffered by the church should not be confused with judgments that God will pour out on the world of unbelievers on the Day of the Lord. Paul clarifies some things regarding "the coming of our Lord Jesus Christ and our being gathered to him" (v. 1, the rapture). The Day of the Lord will not begin until the "man of lawlessness" (the Antichrist) is revealed (2:3). He will be known by his blasphemous character (2:4–5), by the removal of the restrainer (2:6–7), and by the power of Satan that backs him up (2:8–10). He will be destroyed by God (2:8). He will deceive many (2:9–11), and everyone who falls into his deception will be judged by God (2:12).

Names of the Antichrist	
The little horn	Daniel 7:8; 8:9
The coming prince	Daniel 9:26
The king who will do whatever he wants	Daniel 11:36
The man of lawlessness	2 Thessalonians 2:3
The man doomed to destruction	2 Thessalonians 2:3
The lawless one	2 Thessalonians 2:8
The Antichrist	1 John 2:18
The beast out of the sea	Revelation 13:1; 17:8

Besides the revelation (unveiling) of the man of lawlessness, something else has to occur before the Day of the Lord can begin: the "apostasy" (Greek *apostasia*, 2:3). People have interpreted this in numerous ways, but it probably refers either to the rapture (translated as "departure") or a rebellion (defection) against God by falsely professing believers or the unbelieving world at large. If it refers to the rapture, Paul uses the word to refer back to "our being gathered to him [Christ]" in verse 1. If it means "apostasy" or "rebellion," perhaps Paul is thinking of the warnings he will later give in 1 Timothy 4 ("in later times some will depart from the faith," 4:1) and 2 Timothy 3 ("hard times will come in the last days," 3:1). Thus, Paul teaches that the rapture will precede the removal of the "restrainer," the revealing of the Antichrist, the time of tribulation, and the final Day of the Lord.[3]

III. Responsibility of the Church (2 Thessalonians 3:1–18)

Finally, Paul commands the Thessalonians not to be idle or lazy. They must separate themselves from brethren who live unruly or disobedient lives (3:6). They should follow the example and teaching of Paul, working for their own food and persisting in doing good (3:7–13). People who don't work become meddlers and busybodies. Some believe these people quit working because they were waiting for the rapture. Paul commands them to get to work and not interfere with the work of others (3:11). He tells the church, "Take note of that person; don't associate with him, so that he may be ashamed." However, these kinds of disobedient people should still be admonished as brothers, not treated as enemies (3:14–15).

Paul closes his second letter with an appeal that the "Lord of peace" would grant the church peace in every way and that His grace would be with them all (3:16–18). To be certain they knew for sure the letter was genuine, he personally signed it in his own handwriting.

REFLECTION

If Jesus is coming again, the most important question you can ask yourself is, "Is He coming for me?" Only you can answer that question. Jesus promised to return for His own (John 14:1–3). That promise can be your assurance if you believe it and receive it as God's free gift.

Practical Application

The Christians at Thessalonica were a joy and inspiration to Paul and became devoted followers of Christ. In spite of their troubles, they were being sanctified by the Holy Spirit and could rest assured that Christ was coming one day for His own. Paul was concerned about his infant churches, especially when false teachers were influencing them. The apostle's letters to the Thessalonians tell us how to live in light of the second coming of Christ. We can look forward to this return to rapture the living and resurrect the dead (1 Thess 4:16–17). We do not need to live in fear of His return but can look forward to it in confident expectation. In the meantime we are assured that the lawless one (Antichrist) cannot be revealed until after the restrainer is removed (2 Thess 2:7–8). Because of this assurance we can live for Christ effectively in a fallen world knowing that when He returns we will reign with Him. We can face the future with confidence because we know the one who holds the future in His hands.

Paul only spent three weeks in Thessalonica, preaching the gospel, winning the lost, and establishing the church. Yet, in that short amount of time he laid the theological foundation for their understanding of the major elements of Christian doctrine, including eschatology. For Paul, the doctrine of the second coming of Christ was a message of hopeful anticipation. It gives us confidence that history is progressing toward a God-ordained goal. Prophecy is not about what is coming in the future; it is about who is coming in the future.

Paul's first letter is filled with admonitions for the family of believers in the church. They are to love one another (3:12; 4:9), comfort one another (4:18), encourage one another (5:11), live at peace with one another (5:13), and seek the good of one another (5:15). His second letter reminds us of the importance of living in community with other believers. Throughout the New Testament we find believers assembling together in Christian communities called "churches" or "assemblies." Believers are encouraged to gather together on earth in light of our eventual gathering (Greek, *episunagoges*) in heaven at the Lord's return (2 Thess 2:1).

REFLECTION

As you examine your own spiritual life, ask yourself if your faith is growing in fellowship with other believers or struggling in isolation. If you are struggling, why not open up to another believer? Share your struggles and let God speak to your heart through His people. Those who are real will love you, care for you, and help you. Don't try to go it alone. That's what the church is for.

For Further Reading

Couch, Mal. *The Hope of Christ's Return: A Premillennial Commentary on 1, 2 Thessalonians*. Chattanooga: AMG Publishers, 2002.

Green, Gene L. *The Letters to the Thessalonians*. PNTC. Grand Rapids: Eerdmans, 2002.

Martin, D. Michael. *1, 2 Thessalonians*. NAC. Nashville: B&H, 1995.

Stallard, Mike. *1 & 2 Thessalonians: Living for Christ's Return*. TFCBC. Chattanooga: AMG Publishers, 2009.

Stott, John. *The Gospel & the End of Time*. Downers Grove, IL: IVP, 1991.

Thomas, Robert L. "1 and 2 Thessalonians." In *Ephesians Through Philemon*, vol. 11 of *EBC*. Grand Rapids: Zondervan, 1996.

Walvoord, John F., and Mark Hitchcock. *1 & 2 Thessalonians Commentary*. Chicago: Moody Press, 2012.

Study Questions

1. Why did the Thessalonians think their persecutions might indicate that they were already in the Day of the Lord?
2. What is your view of the rapture, and how does it fit with the details of 1 and 2 Thessalonians?
3. List all the words you can find that refer to God's judgment and state who is being judged or punished in each case.

Notes

1. Andreas J. Köstenberger, L. Scott Kellum, and Charles L. Quarles, *The Cradle, the Cross, and the Crown* (Nashville: B&H Academic, 2009), 433.

2. For a detailed background description of Thessalonica, see Mal Couch, *The Hope of Christ's Return* (Grand Rapids: Kregel, 2001), 31–37.

3. See details in Tim LaHaye, Thomas Ice, and Ed Hindson, *The Popular Handbook on the Rapture* (Eugene, OR: Harvest House, 2012).

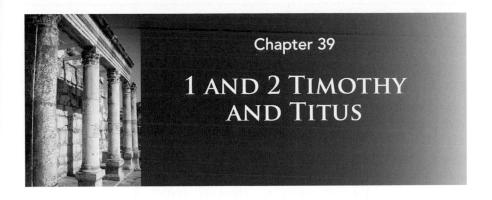

Chapter 39

1 AND 2 TIMOTHY AND TITUS

Pastoral Letters

P aul's letters to Timothy and Titus are collectively known as the Pastoral Epistles. They express Paul's love for the church and his advice to pastors. Together they comprise the heart of Paul's principles for pastoral ministry in the early churches. At the same time they provide guidelines for today's churches as well.

1 TIMOTHY

Pastoral Principles

Paul wrote 1 Timothy to encourage Timothy to live the gospel and fight to defend it (1:18–19). The apostle then gave instructions about the role of women (2:8–15) and men (3:1–16) in the church. Finally, Paul exhorted young Timothy to stand against false doctrine and ungodly practices, to "fight the good fight of the faith" (6:12).

KEY FACTS	
Author:	Paul
Recipient:	Timothy
Where:	Macedonia
Date:	AD 64
Key Words:	Fight (Gk. *agōnizomai*) and warfare (Gk. *strateia*)
Key Verse:	"Fight the good fight of the faith" (6:12).

Author

The internal evidence demonstrates that "Paul, an apostle of Christ Jesus" wrote this letter (1:1). It is hard to imagine how someone other than Paul could have penned the letter, attributed it to Paul, and fabricated an entire set of circumstances surrounding the writing of the letter (e.g., 1 Tim 1:3–7, 18–20). It seems much more plausible to take the ascription of authorship to Paul at face value, especially since there is little evidence for the existence of pseudonymous letters in the first century AD. The early church fathers such as Ignatius, Polycarp, Irenaeus, Tertullian, and Clement of Alexandria say Paul was the author. Modern critics question the advanced church structure and organization reflected in the letter, but there is no sufficient reason that such development did not exist in the early churches. Paul placed Timothy over the church at Ephesus (1 Tim 1:3), though there is no evidence that Paul ever visited Ephesus again after his tearful departure (Acts 20:25; 2 Tim 1:4). Paul left Trophimus sick at Miletus (2 Tim 4:20), then went to Macedonia by way of Troas (2 Tim 4:13). From there Paul wrote his first letter to Timothy.

The Upper Agora of the ancient Asia Minor seaport of Ephesus. This agora was the site of the city's political and judicial institutions. The town hall, the theater, the Roman baths, and the plaza of the agora can all be seen in this photo.

Recipient

Timothy was probably converted to Christianity as a youth when Paul visited his home in Lystra on the first missionary journey with Barnabas (1:2). However, Timothy was reared by his godly mother, Eunice, and influenced by Lois, his godly grandmother (2 Tim 1:5). Apparently, he memorized large sections of the Old Testament (2 Tim 3:15). Many believe Paul and Barnabas stayed in Timothy's home on that first visit, so when Paul was stoned (Acts 14:19), Timothy was either an eyewitness to the stoning, or at least the young lad saw the results. When Paul challenges Timothy to "share in suffering for the gospel" (2 Tim 1:8), Paul is reminding Timothy of his sufferings at Lystra. On his second trip to Lystra, Paul chose Timothy to go with him and assist in ministry. On that trip Paul removed any obstacle Timothy might have had to ministry among Jews by having the young man circumcised (Acts 16:3).

Occasion and Date

Paul wrote this letter after his first imprisonment in Rome (Acts 28, see Introduction to Ephesians, Philippians, Colossians, and Philemon). Paul was released probably in the fall of AD 62 and began revisiting the churches in the spring of AD 63. At that time Paul wrote to Timothy, who was ministering in Ephesus. Paul was probably in Macedonia (1:3), though it is possible he was already in Greece to confront Jews with gnostic tendencies who wanted to be known as "teachers of the law" (1:7). While there he wrote to Timothy in the summer of AD 64.

Genre and Structure

Paul's first letter to Timothy is the earliest of the Pastoral Epistles and opens with an introduction (1:1–3), followed by instructions on how to fight heresy and defend the truth (1:4–20). This is followed by instructions on public prayer (2:1–8), the role of women in the church (2:9–15), standards for church leaders (3:1–16), how to contend against false doctrine (4:1–16), and the ministry of church leaders and the place of widows in the church (5:1–25). The letter closes with a charge to church leadership (6:1–19) and a conclusion (6:20–21).

Outline

I. Church Instructions (1:1–3:16)
   A. Defend the Faith (1:4–20)
   B. Public Worship (2:1–15)
   C. Church Leaders (3:1–16)
II. Personal Instructions (4:1–5:25)
   A. Preach the Truth (4:1–15)
   B. Pastoral Care (5:1–6:2)
   C. Prescription for Leaders (6:3–21)

Message

I. Church Instructions (1 Timothy 1:1–3:16)

A. Defend the Faith (1 Timothy 1:4–20)

Paul was concerned about false teaching that was slipping into the church (1:3–4). Just as right teaching will lead to godliness and right living, so false teaching will lead to perversion in life and the destruction of believers. The key role of the pastor is to provide proper biblical teaching, "This charge I commit to you, son Timothy . . . having faith and a good conscience" (1 Tim 1:18–19 NKJV). False teachers in the church (1:20) were guilty of "paying attention to deceitful spirits and the teachings of demons" (4:1) and discouraging godly living and Christian service. While the New King James Version calls this the "doctrines of demons," it does not mean demons are the subject matter of false teaching but rather they are the source behind false doctrine that was infiltrating the church.

B. Public Worship (1 Timothy 2:1–15)

The early pastors were men of prayer (Acts 6:4), and Paul directs men (*aner*, males) to pray. This does not mean men should only pray in church services; it directs prayer "everywhere" (2:8 NKJV). And it includes all kinds of prayer, (1) intercession (*deēsis*, petition for need); (2) prayers (*proseuchē*, personal devotion to God); (3) intercession (*enteuxis*, confidence the answer will come); and (4) giving thanks (*eucharistia*, offer gratitude). He also advised women to dress modestly and let their good works testify to their faith (2:9–11).

Paul declared there is only one mediator for salvation—not many or one among many—the man Christ Jesus (2:5). Because Jesus came in the flesh, He "gave himself as a ransom for all" (2:6). Paul wants all saved because Jesus died for all. But this is not universalism; each must come to "the knowledge of the truth" (2:4).

C. Church Leaders (1 Timothy 3:1–16)

Paul describes the qualifications of a bishop (another word for a pastor is *elder*, 5:17). He doesn't give a job description but rather explains his inner character, knowing that good character (sensible, highly respected, hospitable, able to teach, gentle, not greedy, a good manager) will guide how the elder functions in the church. His purpose is to make sure believers "know how people ought to conduct themselves in God's household,

A seventeenth-century painting depicting Paul writing his letters.

which is the church of the living God" (3:15). Paul made clear that belief couldn't be separated from behavior. He didn't want church leaders to live like the false teachers, with their conceit, slander, and greed (6:3–5). Paul also instructs Timothy to "pursue righteousness, godliness, faith, love, endurance, and gentleness" (6:11).

II. Personal Instructions (1 Timothy 4:1–5:25)

A. Preach the Truth (1 Timothy 4:1–15)

Paul began this letter (1:3–6) dealing with the false teaching of Judaizers, but now he turns his attention to the early problem of Gnosticism. Paul confronts the "deceitful spirits" that are the subtle influences of demons (4:1). Paul identified two acts of heresy: forbidding marriage and abstinence from food. Paul's answer is that God created them and believers are to receive them with thanksgiving (4:3). Timothy should be a good servant of Christ who uses his spiritual gifts and is trustworthy (4:11–16), not one who speaks about "pointless and silly myths" (4:6–7).

B. Pastoral Care (1 Timothy 5:1–6:2)

Paul explains that the church should care for widows "who are genuinely in need" (5:3). The criteria for "the widow who is truly in need" (5:5) are that she: (1) is a Christian, i.e., trusts God (5:5); (2) has no family to care for her (5:4–5, 8); (3) gives herself to Christian matters (5:5, 10); (4) is at least sixty years old (5:9); and (5) doesn't give herself to pleasure (5:6). Those who do not qualify are: (1) younger women who should marry, (2) idle widows, and (3) gossips and busybodies (5:11–14). In addition, pastors should get paid (5:17–18) but should not be appointed until they have proven they are of godly character (5:22–25).

C. Prescription for Leaders (1 Timothy 6:3–21)

Paul warns about anyone who "teaches false doctrine" (6:3), is conceited, argumentative, envious, a slanderer, and has a depraved mind (6:4–5). Then Paul describes: (1) the life of a godly teacher (6:6–10); (2) the goals of such a teacher (6:11–16); and finally, (3) the duties of a teacher (6:17–19). This letter contains the earliest instructions for church leaders and orderly arrangement of the local church. These instructions were simple embryonic seed explanations and, according to Dean Alford, "are altogether of an ethical, not of a hierarchical kind."[1] The simplistic nature of the early church was that of a spiritual family or community of believers mostly meeting in private houses.

REFLECTION

The Ideal Pastor

On the basis of Paul's instructions to Timothy and Titus, we have the clearest pattern for pastoral ministry anywhere in the New Testament. Based on Paul's biblical guidelines, how would you describe the ideal pastor? How should pastors balance preaching the truth, confronting evil, and loving people? How would you describe your own pastor? If you were a pastor, how would you apply Paul's guidelines to your ministry?

2 TIMOTHY

Perseverance

This tender letter was written by Paul to Timothy his "dearly loved son" (1:2) just before Paul's martyrdom. Apparently Timothy was leading the church in Ephesus, so Paul wrote, "I long to see you so that I may be filled with joy" (1:4). After this letter no further mention is made of Timothy (with the possible exception of Heb 13:23). Tradition claims Timothy was martyred about the end of the century.

The dominant theme is the church's departure from the truth (1:15; 2:18; 3:8; 4:4). Paul recounts, "All those in the province of Asia have deserted me" (1:15). Therefore Paul's theme is "be strong in the grace that is in Christ Jesus" (2:1) and "preach the word" (4:2 KJV) and "what you have heard from me in the presence of many witnesses, commit to faithful men who will be able to teach others also" (2:2). In a moving final appeal, the aged apostle urges Timothy, "Before God and Christ Jesus, who is going to judge the living and the dead, and because of His appearing and his kingdom: Preach the word" (4:1–2).

Key Facts

Author:	Paul
Recipient:	Timothy at Ephesus
Where:	In prison in Rome
Date:	AD 66, just before Paul's execution
Key Word:	Be strong (Gk. *endunamō*)
Key Verse:	"Continue in what you have learned and firmly believed" (3:14).

Author

There is strong internal evidence that Paul wrote 2 Timothy. Paul claims to be the author (1:1). Everything about this letter is Pauline: sentence structure, vocabulary, and thought development. At the outset Paul refers to "the

Snow on some sycamore (platanus) trees near the Tiber, in Rome.

promise of life in Christ Jesus" (1:1), which is his comfort as he faces death. Paul is a prisoner (1:8, 16), and the apostle talks of his confinement as "being bound like a criminal" (2:9), which was much more severe than his first Roman imprisonment. Paul apparently was tried in court during this second imprisonment and was awaiting execution, for he says, "The time for my departure is close" (4:6). Paul was apparently arrested in Troas (4:13) where he had left behind his coat and books. But this second time in prison Paul was isolated from friends (4:11). Apparently only Luke could visit Paul in prison for medical treatment. Tradition suggests Paul died in Nero's persecution after the great fire in Rome (July 19, AD 64). That persecution continued until Nero's death in AD 68, but Paul died during the height of this persecution about AD 66.

Recipient

As Paul was facing many hardships and persecution in prison, he remembered his faithful coworker Timothy (1:3–5). Timothy persevered, in contrast to those like Hymenaeus and Philetus who had "turned away" (1:15 HCSB). Plus Paul urged Timothy to "stir up the gift of God" (1:6 NKJV). The word *anazopureō* is the picture of hot coals without a flame, but when they are stirred up or breath is blown upon them, they burst once more into flames. Paul's strongest command is "preach the word" (4:2). The idea of preaching is to announce boldly as a herald (*kerussō*, to proclaim). Because of this objective, Paul told Timothy, "Study to shew thyself approved unto God" (2:15 KJV).

Occasion and Date

Paul is in prison and knows he will be executed soon. He wants to see Timothy one last time. He asks, "Make every effort to come to me soon" (4:9). The seriousness of Paul's situation is clear, for later in the letter Paul pleads, "Make every effort to come before winter" (4:21). It was not so much that Paul needed encouragement, but the aged apostle wanted to encourage Timothy to carry on the ministry after he was gone. Paul didn't need encouragement; he testified, "The Lord . . . will bring me safely into his heavenly kingdom" (4:18). This letter must have been a terrific blow to Timothy. Whether he arrived before Paul was executed is not known. But Paul looked death confidently in the face and was ready to meet the Lord. He could say, "I have fought the good fight, I have finished the race, I have kept the faith" (4:7). This letter was written shortly before Paul's death in AD 66.

Outline

Message

I. Perseverance (2 Timothy 1:1–18)

Paul was abandoned by many, and others were abandoning Christianity. In the face of rejection and disappointment, Paul remembers Timothy, his faithful coworker, "I constantly remember you" (1:3). Paul uses most of this letter to urge Timothy to persevere. Paul does not give in to Timothy's timid spirit but exhorts him "to stir up the gift of God" (1:6 NKJV). "God has not given us a spirit of fear" (1:7), therefore, "don't be ashamed of the testimony about our Lord" (1:8). The basis of perseverance is that God "has saved us and called us with a holy calling" (1:9). Therefore, Paul could testify, "I am not ashamed, because I know whom I have believed and am persuaded that he is able to guard what has been entrusted to me until that day" (1:12).

II. Propagation (2 Timothy 2:1–26)

Paul wanted Timothy to see four generations of ministry duplication. The first generation was Paul, who preached the gospel. The second generation was Timothy, who received the gospel from Paul. The third generation was the people converted when Timothy preached, i.e., "commit to faithful men" (2:2). The fourth generation includes the "others" who were taught by faithful men from the third generation (2:2). The key to the growth of Christianity is passing the faith to others. Paul gives several illustrations of faithfulness in ministry: a soldier (2:3–5), an athlete (2:5), a farmer (2:6–7), a craftsman (2:15–16), a serving dish (2:20–21), and a servant (2:24–25).

III. Perilous Times (2 Timothy 3:1–9)

The King James Version describes the conditions as "perilous times" (2 Tim 3:1, from *chalepos*, which means hard or difficult times). These conditions apply primarily to the end times. Foreseeing these trends Paul says, people will be "lovers of self" (3:2) and "lovers of money" (3:2). Then Paul describes them as "boastful, proud, demeaning" (3:2). Some will even express rebellion against their own parents (3:2). Paul foresees a time of unrestrained self-centeredness that will characterize the "last days" (3:1).

IV. Perfect Word (2 Timothy 3:10–17)

The foundation for our faith is "the sacred Scriptures" (3:15), i.e., *gramma*, the word meaning "writings." Then Paul told why the Scriptures are absolutely reliable, "All Scripture is inspired" (3:16), i.e., *pasa graphe* (singular), suggesting the whole is inspired as well as the parts. Inspiration, *theopneastos*, means "God breathed." Since God is per-

The Mamertine prison in Rome, Italy, where Paul was imprisoned at one time.

fect and all knowing, when He breathed inspiration on the Scriptures, they were perfect. Also, since God breathed His life or Spirit into Scriptures, those who read and believe will receive the life of God. When the Scriptures are applied (for doctrine, reproof, correction, and instruction in righteousness), then the man of God may be "complete, equipped for every good work" (3:17).

V. Precious Ministry (2 Timothy 4:1–22)

Paul tells Timothy, "I solemnly charge you" (4:1, *diamarturomai*, which carries a moral obligation) to "preach the word" (4:2). This imperative demands that he should give a formal presentation of God's Word with authoritative emphasis. Paul then told Timothy to "rebuke, correct, and encourage" (4:2). It's not Timothy's opinion that he is to preach; it's what God commands, so don't be afraid.

Finally, Paul returned to the theme of the end times because at that time people "will not tolerate sound doctrine" (4:3). Paul told Timothy to "endure hardship" (4:5) and to "do the work of an evangelist" (4:5). Paul knew his ministry was almost over (4:6), yet he was satisfied that he had given everything he could and done everything he could to evangelize the world in his lifetime. Second Timothy is more personal than 1 Timothy. Winter was coming; Paul wanted his coat and books. This letter was written in the face of growing persecution. Paul doesn't promise blue skies over the rainbows but rather suffering and difficulties. Yet in the face of all these problems, "there is reserved for me . . . the crown of righteousness, which the Lord, the righteous Judge, will give me on that day, and not only to me, but to all those who have loved his appearing" (4:8).

TITUS

Blessed Hope

Paul's short letter to Titus is an extremely practical book that is focused primarily on church ministry and, secondarily, on Christian discipleship. Though it contains a classic description of the grace of God in salvation (2:11–14; 3:4–7), there are six references to "good works" on the part of the believer (1:16; 2:7, 14; 3:1, 8, 14). "Sound doctrine" (healthy teaching) must be adorned with good behavior and holy living (2:1 NKJV).Titus is most like 1 Timothy in its content.

KEY FACTS	
Author:	Paul
Recipients:	Titus (and believers in churches at Crete)
Where:	Macedonia (Philippi or Thessalonica)
Date:	About AD 63
Key Words:	Good works (Gr. *kala erga*)
Key Verses:	"For the grace of God has appeared, bringing salvation for all people, instructing us to . . . wait for the blessed hope, the appearing of the glory of our great God and Savior, Jesus Christ . . . a people for his own possession, eager to do good works" (2:11–14).

Author

The author of the epistle to Titus was the apostle Paul (1:1), though this is disputed by most critical scholars. See 1 Timothy for the evidence and arguments for Paul's authorship of the Pastoral Epistles. Titus was quoted by Clement of Rome in his epistle to the Corinthians (AD 95),[2] in the epistle of Barnabas, and the epistle to Diognetus (second century).

Recipient

Paul addresses the epistle to "Titus, my true son in our common faith" (1:4). Both of Titus's parents were Greek (cf. Gal 2:3). Titus was Paul's representative to the church at Corinth during the third journey (2 Corinthians 7–8). He later joined Paul in Macedonia to report on conditions in the Corinthian church and delivered Paul's second epistle to the Corinthians (2 Cor 8:16–17). He also was Paul's representative to the Cretan churches after Paul started or ministered in those churches and moved on (Titus 1:4–5). Later Paul urged Titus to join him at Nicopolis for the winter (3:12), and Titus was with Paul in Rome for part of his last imprisonment, before he moved on to Dalmatia (2 Tim 4:10). Church tradition claims Titus spent his later years as the overseer of the churches on Crete. The Cretan people had a negative reputation in the Mediterranean world. Paul quotes the Cretan poet Epimenides as saying that Cretans were "always liars, evil beasts, lazy gluttons" (1:12). Many classical writers had written of the untruthfulness of the Cretans. The Greek verb *kretizein*, meaning "to act as a Cretan," became synonymous with the idea of "playing the liar."

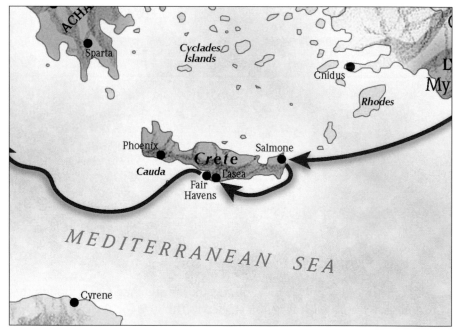

Paul stopped in Crete on his voyage to Rome. Many scholars believe Paul was released from house arrest in Rome. Between this time and the time of his second imprisonment in Rome, he and Titus preached the gospel on Crete.

Occasion and Date

The epistle to Titus was probably written about the same time as 1 Timothy (c. AD 63) and in the same location (Macedonia). It was composed after Paul's release from prison in Rome (c. AD 62) but before Paul's later arrest by Nero (c. AD 64–67).

Genre and Structure

Titus displays the epistolary genre typical of the apostle Paul. Of major significance is its similarity to 1 Timothy. Except for the salutation (1:1–4) and the closing (3:12–15), only two doctrinal passages (2:11–14; 3:4–7) have no resemblance to 1 Timothy. Paul wrote in order to: (1) encourage and strengthen Titus in his mission on Crete; (2) reinforce Titus's authority among the churches on Crete; (3) instruct Titus and the churches in church organization; (4) preach on Christian behavior and good works; and (5) ask Titus to meet him in Nicopolis that winter and to help Zenas and Apollos on their journey.

Outline

I. Task of Titus (1:1–16)
II. Teaching of Titus (2:1–15)
III. Testimony of Titus (3:1–15)

Message

I. Task of Titus (1:1–16)

The body of the letter outlines the task Paul left Titus to accomplish on Crete. First, he needed to appoint elders in every city (1:5–9). Elders were local church leaders that had the responsibility in each church to guide the believers, like a shepherd leads his flock. These elders should be spiritually mature and in subjection to sound teaching. They must be above reproach or publicly blameless (1:6–9), particularly in their family life, self-control, goodness, and faithfulness to the Word of God. Titus must also reprove the rebellious people who are influencing the churches. They practice deceit and need stern reproof (1:10–13). Their deeds are worthless (1:14–16). The Cretans were by nature unruly and ungodly, especially since they were being influenced by Judaizers who continually opposed Paul's gospel of grace.

View of Crete's Psiloritis Mountains.

II. Teaching of Titus (Titus 2:1–15)

Positively, Titus must exhort with sound doctrine (teaching that edifies) in order to produce good Christian behavior (2:1). The old men should be sober (serious and self-disciplined); the old women should be holy in their behavior; the young women should be sober, loving, chaste, and in subjection; and the young men should be serious minded. Titus must be an example to all of them, sound in life and teaching (2:7–8). The reason for living a godly lifestyle is God's grace (2:11–14), which teaches all believers that they should live soberly and righteously because of the blessed hope of Christ's return and the believer's redemption and purification. Paul speaks clearly and candidly of the deity of Jesus Christ as "our great God and Savior" (2:13).[3] Titus should therefore exhort and reprove with authority (2:15).

III. Testimony of Titus (Titus 3:1–15)

Believers must be subject to governmental authority, as people who are "ready for every good work" (3:1). Since these people were saved "not by works of righteousness that we had done, but according to his mercy" (3:5) and justified by God's grace (3:7), they should live a life of good works toward all men. Titus must avoid and reject contentious men, so those who continue to be divisive after two warnings (3:10–11) should be treated as sinners and rejected (presumably kept out of church gatherings and not allowed to teach believers). Paul closes the epistle by asking Titus to meet him at Nicopolis for the winter, as soon as either Artemas or Tychicus, two of Paul's other coworkers, could arrive to take Titus's place on Crete. Titus and Paul had been coworkers for many years, and Paul had come to trust Titus to solve some really tough problems (see 2 Corinthians 7–8). Now, following Paul's release from imprisonment in Rome, they had made a joint spiritual investment in the founding and growth of churches on the Greek-speaking island of Crete.

Practical Application

Paul's pastoral letters emphasize the importance of Christian leadership. They emphasize the centrality of preaching the gospel, defending the faith, and living the life that exalts and exemplifies Jesus Christ. As you read his list of qualifications for church leaders, ask yourself if you measure up to these standards. If not, why not? What should you do to let God use you to spread the gospel, teach His truth, and live the life He can use to display His glory in the world in which you live?

For Further Reading

Guthrie, Donald. *The Pastoral Epistles*. TNTC. Grand Rapids: Eerdmans, 1990.
Kent, Homer. *The Pastoral Epistles: Studies in I and II Timothy and Titus*. Winona Lake, IN: BMH Books, 1995.
Knight, George. *The Pastoral Epistles*. NIGTC. Grand Rapids: Eerdmans, 1992.
Köstenberger, Andreas J. "1–2 Timothy, Titus." *EBC*. Edited by Tremper Longman III and David E. Garland. Grand Rapids: Zondervan, 2005.
Lea, Thomas, and Hayne Griffin. *1, 2 Timothy, Titus*. NAC. Nashville: B&H, 1992.
Towner, Philip H. *The Letters to Timothy and Titus*. NICNT. Grand Rapids: Eerdmans, 2006.

Study Questions

1. What in Timothy's background influenced him to have the meek, retiring personality that appears in this letter?
2. What topics do 1 Timothy and Titus have in common?
3. How are atonement, redemption, and sanctification related to one another?
4. How does the emphasis on good works in Titus relate to the similar emphasis in the epistle of James?
5. What kind of leaders did Paul want in churches?
6. Describe the arrangement Paul suggested for local churches.
7. What do the Pastoral Epistles teach us about church leadership?
8. What were the main differences between Paul's first and second imprisonments?

Notes

1. Dean Alford as quoted in introductory notes in E. W. Bullinger, *The Companion Bible* (Grand Rapids: Kregel Publications, 1999), 1799.

2. *1 Clement* 2.7; 33.1.

3. See Daniel B. Wallace, *Greek Grammar Beyond the Basics: An Exegetical Syntax of the New Testament* (Grand Rapids: Zondervan, 1996), 276.

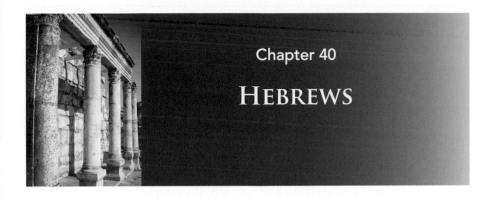

Chapter 40

HEBREWS

Holding on to Grace

During difficult times of hardship and persecution, Christians are often told to trust Jesus and have faith. But often during these times doubt and despair tug at our souls, dragging us away from faith and telling us no one understands our despair. We may even start to wonder if we could lose our faith altogether. Hebrews, unlike any other book of the New Testament, calls its readers to endure in faith and to hold fast to Jesus's message. It reminds us that many people of faith have endured hardship even when God's promises seemed lifetimes away. As the author of Hebrews unfolds these truths, it becomes clear that we are not alone in our sufferings; we are surrounded by a crowd of faithful witnesses, and we too must continue in faith, focusing on Jesus, our Great High Priest, as we run the race toward God's everlasting kingdom.

KEY FACTS

Author:	Unknown
Recipient:	Unknown
Where:	Unknown
Date:	Before AD 70
Key Word:	Better (Gk. *kritton*)
Key Verse:	"Therefore, since we have a great high priest who has passed through the heavens—Jesus the Son of God—let us hold fast to our confession" (4:14).

Author

Many have held Paul as the author of Hebrews. There are several points of contact between the content of this book and the content of Paul's other letters:

1. Jesus's preexistence and creatorship (Heb 1:1–4; Col 1:15–17)
2. The giving of gifts by the Holy Spirit (Heb 2:4; 1 Cor 12:11)
3. The humiliation of Christ (Heb 2:14–17; Phil 2:5–8)
4. The new covenant (Heb 8:6; 2 Cor 3:4–11)

However, even the early church was not in agreement about who wrote it. Though the Eastern Church held that Paul was the author early on, the majority of the Western Church did not hold to Pauline authorship until the late fourth and early fifth centuries. Pauline authorship was then accepted in the West until it was challenged again during the Reformation.

Some obstacles to Pauline authorship are as follows:

1. Hebrews is anonymous, whereas Paul's thirteen letters begin by naming him as the sender.
2. Hebrews contains no greeting or prayer for the people as Paul's letters traditionally do.
3. Hebrews does not use the phrase "Christ Jesus," as Paul's letters do.
4. Stylistically, the Greek of Hebrews seems more polished than that of Paul.
5. The vocabulary and argumentation is different from Paul's letters.
6. The author of Hebrews states that salvation "had its beginning when it was spoken of by the Lord, and it was confirmed to us by those who heard him" (2:3). This seems inconsistent with Paul's claims elsewhere that he did not receive the gospel from any man but through a vision of Jesus Christ (Gal 1:12).

In light of the challenges to Pauline authorship, it is better to admit that the identity of the author of Hebrews is uncertain. A few things are certain: (1) Assuming that the Timothy mentioned in 13:23 was the same one who traveled with Paul on his second and third missionary journeys, the author was someone who knew Timothy and lived in the first century AD. (2) He had a thorough knowledge of the Old Testament. (3) He was an eloquent speaker and/or writer. While some questions are unanswered, the church views Hebrews as an important witness to Jesus's identity and ministry as the Son of God and our Great High Priest.

Recipients

Scholars are equally unsure of the identity of the people who received the book of Hebrews. One clue in 13:24 states, "Those who are from Italy send you greetings." However, this statement can be interpreted in two ways: (1) "Those from Italy" could refer to people from Italy who were away from their home living in a foreign land—meaning this letter was written *to Italy*. (2) It could refer to believers in Italy sending their greetings to an unspecified city—meaning it was written *from Italy*. Therefore, without any explicit mention of the book's audience, it is only possible to speak about the characteristics of the audience rather than their geographic location. The content and argumentation of the letter seem to indicate that the recipients were believers who were tempted to go back to Judaism by observing Old Testament feast days and temple practices, including animal sacrifices.

Occasion and Date

The letter implies that Jewish Christians were considering returning to the sacrificial system of old covenant Judaism.[1] They are urged to hold firm to their confession (3:6, 14; 4:14; 10:23) because Jesus is the Great High Priest of a new covenant; therefore, there is no going back to the old covenant sacrificial system of Judaism. A date sometime before AD 70 seems likely for two reasons. First, the sacrificial ritual is consistently described in the present tense (7:8; 9:6–7, 9, 13; 13:10). This would seem to indicate that the temple is still in use and that the book should be dated sometime before the temple's destruction in AD 70. Further, since the author of Hebrews is showing that Jesus made the greatest and final sacrifice when He offered Himself, it is hard to believe that he would not have explicitly pointed out the relationship between Jesus's ultimate sacrifice and the destruction of the temple.

Genre and Structure

Some view Hebrews as an epistle because it does have an epistolary conclusion, but on the other hand it does not begin with an epistolary greeting or blessing. Others, noting the book contains oral features, have described Hebrews as a sermon or even as a series of sermons. Without knowing for certain if this book is a single letter, a single sermon, or a series of sermons, the book's structure is difficult to identify and outline. However, the book seems to include theological, biblical, and practical matters. The Greek phrase the author uses to describe what he has written—"message of exhortation" (Heb 13:22)—is the same phrase used in Acts 13:15 when the synagogue leaders ask Paul if he has a message he wants to speak to the people.

Outline

I. Theological Declaration: Superiority of Christ (1:1–7:10)
   A. Jesus the Son Is Superior to Angels (1:1–2:18)
   B. Jesus the Son Is Superior to Moses (3:1–19)
   C. Having a Great High Priest: Hold Fast and Draw Near (4:1–16)
   D. The Son as the Great High Priest (5:1–7:10)
II. Biblical Explanation: Priesthood of Christ (7:11–10:39)
   A. Priesthood in the Order of Melchizedek (7:11–28)
   B. Priest of the New Covenant (8:1–13)
   C. Priestly Sacrifice of Christ (9:1–10:18)
   D. Transition: Since We Have a Great High Priest, Draw Near, Hold Fast, and Consider (10:19–39)
III. Practical Application: Living by Faith (11:1–13:25)
   A. Examples of Faith (11:1–40)
   B. Lifestyle of Faith (12:1–13:25)
     1. Fix Your Eyes on Jesus and Endure Discipline (12:1–17)
     2. Mount Sinai Versus Mount Zion (12:18–24)
     3. Practical Exhortations and Benediction (13:1–25)

Message

I. Theological Declaration: Superiority of Christ (Hebrews 1:1–7:10)

A. Jesus the Son Is Superior to Angels (Hebrews 1:1–2:18)

The author of Hebrews sees himself as living at a significant time in history because "long ago" God spoke through the prophets, but now He has spoken through His Son, Jesus (1:1; 2:9). As God's Son, Jesus is superior to the prophets and even the angels. As God's Son, He is the radiance of God's glory and the exact representation of His nature. Though the Son's coming did not occur until "these last days," the Son has worked in the world long before this time. In fact, He is credited as the Creator of the world (1:2–3) who laid the foundation of the earth and made the heavens with His hands (1:10). In addition, He is the One who sustains the world by the power of His word. Since God's children (mankind) were flesh and blood, the Son, too, became flesh like them so He could become a merciful and faithful High Priest in order to give a sacrifice for their sin (2:14–18).

After this was completed, Jesus returned to His position of authority in heaven. While He was for a little while made lower than the angels, He has now been crowned with glory and honor, and all created things are now under

His authority (2:6–8). He is now the Heir of all things and has a more excellent name than even the angels (who would now worship Him). This position of honor will remain His even after the heavens and the earth become worn out like old garments. And as old garments they will be changed, but He will remain the same.

Warning 1: Don't Neglect Salvation (2:1–4)

Because this Son, Jesus, is greater than the prophets and the angels, there is a greater responsibility for those who hear the message to accept it and a greater judgment for those who do not.

B. Jesus the Son Is Superior to Moses (Hebrews 3:1–19)

The author continues to emphasize the unique importance of Jesus's sonship by comparing Him to Moses. Moses is the prophet who wrote the first five books of the Old Testament, liberated the people from slavery in Egypt through miraculous means, and led the people to the Promised Land. The Jews of Jesus's day were expecting a prophet like Moses to come sometime in the future (Deut 18:15–19). With these things in mind, Moses could be viewed as the premier prophet in all of God's salvation history until the coming of the Son. From this comparison the author concludes that while Moses was a faithful servant of God, Jesus's position as a faithful Son is worthy of more glory than Moses' position as a servant.

Warning 2: Don't Harden Your Heart, but Enter God's Rest (3:7–4:13)

Having compared Jesus to Moses, the author now compares the people that followed Moses with those who are following Jesus. He explains that those who followed Moses in the wilderness had unbelieving hearts and sinned against God.

C. Having a Great High Priest: Hold Fast and Draw Near (Hebrews 4:1–16)

In the final three verses of chapter 4, the warnings are buffered with a message of hope: believers should stand firm in their confession because they have something those following Moses did not have, i.e., Jesus, the Son of God, as their Great High Priest. He "sympathize[s] with our weaknesses" and gives people confidence to approach the throne of God to receive mercy and grace in their time of need (4:14–16).

D. The Son as the Great High Priest (Hebrews 5:1–7:10)

Chapter 5 begins by comparing Jesus's priesthood with Aaron's. There are some simi- larities: (1) in both priesthoods God chose men to be the high priest; (2) both offered gifts and sacrifices for the sins of men; and (3) both in their humanity dealt gently with people and were sympa- thetic to any weaknesses. However, key differences set Jesus's priesthood apart from Aaron's: (1) though Jesus was "tempted in every way as we are" (4:15), He did not sin; (2) as a sinless priest, Jesus did not have to offer sac- rifices for Himself as Aaron did; (3) Jesus was not of the Levitical priesthood descended from the Levites but is God's Son, and "a high priest forever according to the order of Melchizedek" (6:20); and (4) Jesus was perfect and became to all those who obey Him the source of eter- nal salvation. Therefore, believers have an anchor for their souls which is secured in heaven (6:19).

High priest.

Warning 3: Don't Fall Away from the Faith (5:11–6:20)
The author of Hebrews expresses concern for his audience. He rebukes them for their lack of maturity and the danger of falling away from the faith. But he buffers this warn- ing with the encouragement that he is convinced of better things for them: they too will inherit God's promises. God cannot lie, and they too will enter into the holy place that Jesus, their High Priest, has entered before them.

II. Biblical Explanation: Priesthood of Christ (Hebrews 7:11–10:39)

A. Priesthood in the Order of Melchizedek (Hebrews 7:11–28)

After the third warning, the author picks up where he left off in 5:10, continuing his discussion on the importance of Melchizedek. He looks to Genesis 14, the passage where Abraham pays Melchizedek a tithe and notes that: (1) Melchizedek was a priest of God; (2) his name means "king of righ- teousness"; and (3) his title "king of Salem" means "king of peace." So it can be said that he is both a priest and a king of peace and righteousness. Beyond this, however, the biblical narrative is silent concerning Melchizedek's identity and origin. The author of Hebrews explains that Abraham's tithe to Melchizedek shows that Abraham and all of his priestly descendants are inferior to Melchizedek. His main point is clear enough: the Melchizedekian priesthood is greater than Abraham and the Levitical priesthood that came out of him.

Reconstruction of Herod's temple (20 BC–AD 70) at Jerusalem as viewed from the southeast. The drawing reflects archeological discoveries made since excavations began in 1967 along the south end of the Temple Mount platform gateway.

B. Priest of the New Covenant (Hebrews 8:1–13)

The author of Hebrews argues that Moses' law appointed priests who were weak and needed to offer sacrifices for their own sins before offering sacrifices for the people (7:27). Because these priests were mortal, there needed to be a whole succession of priests. There was, therefore, a need for a priest who was more permanent. He finds this permanence in Jesus's priesthood because it is not based on the old law but on God's promise, which came after the law. The promise that he's referring to is Psalm 110:4, which states that the messianic King would be "a priest forever according to the pattern of Melchizedek." Since this priesthood is based on this promise, Jesus is not disqualified for being born of the kingly line of Judah rather than the priestly line of Levi. On the contrary, like Melchizedek, he is a priest of a different sort, a holy, innocent, undefiled priest whose office is permanent and heavenly. As such, He has offered Himself as one sacrifice for all and is able to "save completely those who come to God through him, since he always lives to intercede for them" (7:25–27). He should therefore be seen as "the guarantee of a better covenant" than that of Moses and the Levitical priests (7:22).

C. Priestly Sacrifice of Christ (Hebrews 9:1–10:18)

In chapter 8 the author of Hebrews develops what it means for Jesus to be the Mediator of this better covenant. He quotes Jeremiah 31 at length to give scriptural proof for his claim that a new covenant has come which supersedes the old. He concludes: "By saying a new covenant, he has declared that the first is obsolete. And what is obsolete and growing old is about to pass away" (8:13). The author begins by painting a picture for his reader of the earthy sanctuary of the first covenant. He reminds them that the earthly tabernacle allowed limited access to God; plus the continual need for sacrifice

The temple veil is a curtain that separated the most holy place from the holy place. Only the high priest was allowed to pass through the veil and then only on the Day of Atonement.

reveals the old system's limitations. It could not fully restore the worshipper's relationship with God, and the blood of animals could not take away sins (9:8–10; 10:4). The old system was insufficient and needed to be replaced.

With these insufficiencies in view, Jesus's priestly duties were not performed in an earthly sanctuary, a mere copy of the heavenly, but in the heavenly sanctuary itself (9:24). When He did so, He did not offer the blood of animals continually but His own blood once for all (9:12). Because Jesus offered this greater sacrifice in a greater sanctuary, He has removed sin and attained eternal redemption for all of God's people and has enacted the new covenant predicted by Jeremiah (9:11–13; 10:16–17). He has brought forgiveness so there is no longer any need for an offering for sin (10:18).

D. Transition: Since We Have a Great High Priest: Draw Near, Hold Fast, and Consider (Hebrews 10:19–39)

In light of what Jesus has done, the author encourages his audience to: (1) have confidence to enter into the holy place through Jesus's blood; (2) draw near with a sincere heart in full assurance of faith with a clean conscience and pure bodies; (3) hold fast to their confession without wavering; (4) not forsake assembling together with other believers; and (5) encourage one another as they see the day of salvation drawing near (vv. 19–25).

Warning 4: Don't Shrink Back in Your Confession (10:26–39)

Now that Jesus has replaced the sacrificial system, there is no other sacrifice for those who reject Him. Therefore, the author warns them to persevere in their confession because those who shrink back from their confession are: (1) trampling on the Son of God; (2) profaning the blood of the covenant; and (3) insulting the Spirit of grace.

III. Practical Application: Living by Faith (Hebrews 11:1–13:25)

A. Examples of Faith (Hebrews 11:1–40)

In chapter 10, the author of Hebrews encourages his audience to find support and encouragement by assembling together with other believers. Once again he turns his attention to the fellowship of a common faith. He explains that "faith is the reality of what is hoped for, the proof of what is not seen" and that through faith our ancestors were approved (11:1). He mentions Abel, Enoch, Noah, Abraham, and Sarah and then explains that all of these "died in faith, although they had not received the things that were promised. But they saw them from a distance, greeted them, and confessed that they were foreigners and temporary residents on the earth" (11:13). These people sought after a heavenly country which was better than their own, and God prepared a heavenly city for them. His list continues with accounts of the faith of Isaac, Jacob, Joseph, Moses, and Rahab. He laments that he does not have time to talk about Gideon, Barak, Jephthah, David, Samuel, and the prophets.

B. Lifestyle of Faith (Hebrews 12:1–13:25)

1. Fix Your Eyes on Jesus and Endure Discipline (12:1–17). In light of these examples of faith, the author of Hebrews encourages his readers to fix their eyes on Jesus with the same intensity that a runner fixes his gaze on his goal. And like runners they must continue with endurance and rid themselves of any sin that could trip them up in the race of life. Jesus Himself modeled this; by fixing His eyes on the joy ahead, He endured the cross, despised the shame, and sat down at the right hand of the throne of God (12:1–3). By looking to Jesus, it became clear that their sufferings were small compared to His. They had not yet suffered to the point of shedding blood as He did.

2. Mount Sinai Versus Mount Zion (12:18–24). This section emphasizes the blessings of their stage of salvation history by comparing two holy mountains. The first is Mount Sinai where Moses received the law. The author

A training track at Olympia. The author of Hebrews used athletic imagery in exhorting fellow Christians.

reminds his readers that when God made Himself known on this mountain, it was touched with blazing fire, darkness, gloom, and a whirlwind. The people could not even touch the mountain, or they would be put to death. But the present audience had come to Mount Zion and the city of the living God (the heavenly Jerusalem) where the mood is one of celebration and fellowship. Here myriads of angels are gathered, along with the assembly of the firstborn whose names are written in heaven, i.e., God who is the Judge of all, the spirits of righteous people made perfect, and Jesus (the Mediator of the new covenant).

Warning 5: Don't Reject the Words of God (12:25–29)

For the fifth time in the book, the author pauses to warn his audience: "See to it that you do not reject the one who speaks. For if they did not escape when they rejected him who warned them on earth, even less will we if we turn away from him who warns us from heaven" (12:25).

3. Practical Exhortations and Benediction (13:1–25). The end of the book is composed of a long list of practical exhortations encouraging people to be hospitable, moral, prayerful, continually praising God, and holding to the truth, etc. It concludes with a short benediction that: (1) wishes that God would equip them with all that is good to do His will; (2) urges them to receive His word of exhortation; (3) informs them that Timothy was released and may come with him to visit soon; and (4) greets all the leaders and saints.

Practical Application

Hebrews, unlike any other book of the New Testament, calls us back to endure in our faith and to hold fast to Jesus's message. It reminds us that many people of faith have endured hardship and endured even when God's promises seemed lifetimes away. It reminds us that Jesus Himself was no stranger to suffering. As God's Son, He was greater than the prophets and the angels; yet He entered humanity to suffer in unthinkable ways. In all of this, He did not sin. Through His endurance He set an example for us in righteousness and became a greater High Priest than the world has ever known. We are not alone in our sufferings; we are surrounded by a crowd of faithful witnesses; and we too must continue in faith, focusing on Jesus, our Great High Priest, as we run the race toward God's everlasting kingdom.

For Further Reading

Bruce, F. F. *The Epistle to the Hebrews*. NICNT. Grand Rapids: Eerdmans, 1990.

Ellingworth, Paul. *The Epistle to the Hebrews: A Commentary on the Greek Text*. NIGTC. Grand Rapids: Eerdmans, 1993.

Ger, Steven. *Hebrews: Christ Is Greater*. Chattanooga: AMG, 2009.

Guthrie, George H., and Janet Nygren. *Hebrews: Running the Race Before Us*. Grand Rapids: Zondervan, 2009.

Hughes, Philip E. *A Commentary on the Epistle to the Hebrews*. Grand Rapids: Eerdmans, 1997.

Johnson, Luke Timothy. *Hebrews: A Commentary*. Louisville: Westminster John Knox, 2006.

Study Questions

1. Hebrews has a major emphasis on endurance for salvation. How does this fit with other New Testament texts that seem to indicate that salvation is eternally secure?
2. If Jesus is the High Priest and no other sacrifices are needed, what implications does this have for the concept of the priesthood of the believer?
3. Why is this book so helpful for Jewish Christians?
4. If Jesus is our High Priest, whose sacrifice of Himself is sufficient to pay for our sins, do we need anything else to save us?
5. Have you trusted the sacrifice of Christ for your salvation?

Note

1. While this book has practical application for Gentiles, the fact that circumcision is not mentioned is evidence that the book was more concerned with a Jewish return to Judaism than a Gentile conversion to Judaism. See Steven Ger, *Hebrews: Christ Is Greater* (Chattanooga: AMG, 2009), 10. He observes, "Most assuredly, if the author of Hebrews penned his letter subsequent to the Temple's destruction (AD 70), it is inconceivable that this master of rhetorical persuasion would fail to mention or allude to the crowning illustration of the argument."

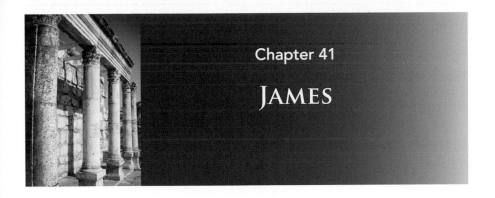

Chapter 41

JAMES

Faith That Works

Perhaps the first New Testament letter written, James provides a balanced picture of good works as evidence of true faith. He had no use for people who only had a religious profession but did not live according to the Word of God (1:23). He also warned of the perils of wealth (5:1–3), while exercising sympathy for the poor (2:5). James uses short, pithy sentences that encapsulate a truth, a style found in the wisdom books of the Old Testament.

KEY FACTS

Author:	James, son of Mary and Joseph, half brother of Jesus
Recipients:	The twelve tribes in the Dispersion
Where:	Unknown
Date:	AD 40–42
Key Word:	Trials (Gk. *peirasmos*)
Key Verse:	"Blessed is the one who endures trials, because when he has stood the test he will receive the crown of life that God has promised to those who love him" (1:12).

Author

Two of Jesus's twelve apostles were named James: James the son of Zebedee (Matt 4:21), who was martyred by Herod early in the book of Acts (Acts 12:2), and James the son Alphaeus (Matt 10:3), who was perhaps James the Younger (Mark 15:40). The martyrdom of James the son of Zebedee in AD 44 likely took place too early for him to have written this letter. Little is known of James the son of Alphaeus, so it is unlikely he was responsible for this letter either.

Many Bible scholars believe that James, the half brother of the Lord (Gal 1:19) and a significant early Christian leader, is the most likely author. He was a witness of the resurrected Lord (1 Cor 15:7), presided over the Jerusalem Council (Acts 15), and was considered one of the pillars in the church at Jerusalem (Gal 2:9). Early church tradition tells of his martyrdom in AD 62.

A model of Jerusalem in the first century AD showing the Roman fortress Antonia with its four massive towers just north of the Temple Mount. To the left of the fortress is the Pool of Bethesda where Jesus performed one of His miracles.

Recipients

James writes "to the twelve tribes dispersed abroad"—that is, Christian Jews living outside the Holy Land. Many of them may have visited Jerusalem for the various feasts and would have sought instruction and direction from a leader of the mother church of Christianity: the Jerusalem church. They would have wanted to know what it meant to be a Christian in their daily lives as messianic believers.

Occasion and Date

While some scholars believe James wrote this letter toward the end of his life (c. AD 62), others think he wrote it in the mid- to late 40s, which seems more likely. James probably wrote to Christians who were still meeting in synagogues (2:2), which was an early practice until the church at Corinth began meeting next door to the synagogue (Acts 18:1–8). Another argument for an early date is that many teachings found elsewhere in New Testament letters are not mentioned in the epistle of James, not even the controversy over circumcision of new Gentile converts that erupted in Acts 15 (AD 49). Since James did not mention this controversy at all, it is often assumed that he wrote early. Therefore, James's letter is one of the earliest (if not the earliest) books of the New Testament.

Genre and Structure

Since James was a half brother of the Lord Jesus, one might expect quotations from Jesus in his epistle. Though James does not quote the Gospels directly, he does quote the things Jesus could have said in His public and private conversations (compare Jas 1:2 with Matt 5:11; Jas 2:5 with Matt 5:3; Jas 3:12 with Matt 7:16–20; Jas 5:12 with Matt 5:34–37; Jas 4:10 with Matt 18:4; and Jas 5:1 with Luke 6:24).

James has some striking *aphorisms* (a concise statement of a principle that also defines its meaning) in his epistle.

- "An indecisive man is unstable in all his ways" (1:8 HCSB).
- "Human anger does not accomplish God's righteousness" (1:20).
- "Don't you know that friendship with the world is hostility toward God?" (4:4).
- "Resist the devil, and he will flee from you" (4:7).
- "The prayer of a righteous person is very powerful" (5:16).

James is also pictorial in his language, using word pictures or similes.

- "For the doubter is like the surging sea, driven and tossed by the wind" (1:6).
- "Now if we put bits into the mouths of horses so that they obey us, we direct their whole bodies" (3:3).
- "And consider ships: Though very large and driven by fierce winds, they are guided by a very small rudder wherever the will of the pilot directs" (3:4).

- "You do not even know what tomorrow will bring—what your life will be! For you are like vapor that appears for a little while, then vanishes" (4:14).

The turbulent waters of the Mediterranean Sea as seen from Caesarea Maritima. James urged his readers to be people of faith and not doubt. "For the doubter is like the surging sea, driven and tossed by the wind" (Jas 1:6).

Outline

I. Faith Tested (1:1–26)
II. Faith Authenticated (2:1–26)
III. Faith Demonstrated (3:1–5:19)

Message

I. Faith Tested (James 1:1–26)

Wherever Jewish people went, they were often shunned, neglected, or persecuted. When Jews took on the faith of Jesus Christ, there was double reason to alienate them or to persecute them. So James begins describing their faith as tried by fire, "Consider it a great joy, my brothers and sisters, whenever you experience various trials, because you know that the testing of your faith produces endurance" (Jas 1:2–3). Therefore, one of the principles of living an effective Christian life in a sinful world is knowing how to respond to all types of trials and testings. He reminds his readers that such trials are inevitable experiences that test our commitment to Christ. For true believers, trials produce endurance and strengthen our faith. Those who pass these tests will receive the crown of life (1:12).

James teaches that God is waiting to give wisdom to anyone who asks for it: "Now if any of you lacks wisdom, he should ask God, who gives to all generously and without criticizing, and it will be given to him" (1:5 HCSB). The phrase "without criticizing" means God will not find fault with those who acknowledge their need of wisdom, nor does God slap the hand of those who ask for it. The person who seeks wisdom must not be "double minded" or "unstable" (1:8 KJV).

REFLECTION

Finding God's Will

Are you struggling with God's calling on your life? Do you really want to know and do His will? Read His Word, live by its principles, seek godly counsel. But most of all, ask Him for wisdom. He will never lead you to contradict His Word but will prompt you by His Spirit to do what is right.

One of the most practical principles of James's wisdom involves being a "doer" and not just a "hearer" of the Word of God (1:22–25). He adds that those who only hear the Word of God deceive themselves (1:22). That man is "looking at his own face in the mirror" whereas the King James Version calls it his "natural face." The original Greek uses the word *genesis* (only here and chap. 3:6 and Matt 1:1), which literally means "looking into the face of his birth." James wants each person to look in the mirror and not "[forget] what kind of person he was" (1:24). The person who "is not a forgetful hearer but a doer who works . . . will be blessed" (1:25). Therefore, James believes the

Ancient bronze mirror.

real Christian is the one who lives by the principles of the Word of God, i.e., a doer of the Word.

II. Faith Authenticated (James 2:1–26)

James is probably best known because of his teaching on faith and works. Some have felt James's view of works is in contrast to Paul's teaching on faith. Paul declares, "We have been declared righteous by faith" (Rom 5:1), whereas James seems to say the opposite: "You see that a person is justified by works and not by faith alone" (Jas 2:24). Others view James as a complement to Paul's teaching because Paul urges his readers to do good works but only as a natural outcome of the fruit of their faith (Romans 12; Gal 5:18, 22–23; Eph 2:10; Titus 2:7). In the same manner James constantly tells a person to live by good works that grow out of a life of faith: "Show me your faith without works, and I will show you faith by my works" (Jas 2:18).

James writes to many Jewish believers who are apparently confused about their new role as Christians. While they lived in the past under the law as Jews, now they were saved by faith (2:14–26). James deals with those who feel they can live by faith but they don't have to "work out" their practical obedience to Scripture. Perhaps they believed they could live as they wanted. But James uses negative motivation: "You believe that God is one. Good! Even the demons believe—and they shudder" (2:19). Another negative illustration is aimed at the rich (a recurring theme in James): "If a brother or sister is without clothes and lacks daily food and one of you says to them, 'Go in peace, stay warm, and be well fed,' but you don't give them what the body needs, what good is it?" (2:15–16). James says that faith is "dead by itself" (2:17).

James uses two Old Testament illustrations to show the works of people who were saved by faith. First, *Abraham* offered his son Isaac to God. James makes the statement, "You see that faith was active together with his [Abraham's] works, and by works, faith was made complete" (2:22). Then James uses the illustration of *Rahab* the prostitute when he said, "Wasn't Rahab the prostitute also justified by works in receiving the messengers and sending them out by a different route?" (2:25). He concludes, "For just as the body without the spirit is dead, so also faith without works is dead" (2:26). He is not teaching salvation by good works but by the kind of faith that transforms lives. Such faith is demonstrated by good works.

III. Faith Demonstrated (James 3:1–5:20)

James gives three pictures to describe the dangers of the tongue. First, it is like a *small bit* put into the mouth of a horse to make the animal obey (3:3). Second, the tongue is like a *small rudder* that can control a large ship through fierce winds. Third, the tongue is like a *small fire* that ignites a large forest fire (3:6). Because the tongue pollutes the whole body (3:6), James says it creates a fire of hell, that is, *Gehenna*. This seems to be a reference to the fires of destruction associated with the judgment of God. Authentic Christians will obey the wisdom of biblical principles by controlling what they say, hence controlling their actions.

James warns about fighting, coveting, and friendship with the world (4:1–5) but encourages submission to God, cleansing your hands, and humility (4:6–12). He also exhorts his readers against being presumptuous about tomorrow, for only God knows the future (4:13–17). James warns the rich not to abuse their workers (5:1–6), and he advises people to be patient, stop complaining, and endure to the end (5:7–11). When James deals with suffering, sickness, and healing, he asks, "Is anyone among you suffering? He should pray" (5:13). Then he assures them, "The prayer of faith will save the sick person, and the Lord will raise him up" (5:15). But before one prays, it is necessary to examine whether sin has made them sick: "If he has committed sins, he will be forgiven. Therefore, confess your sins to one another and pray for one another, so that you may be healed" (5:15–16). The promise of healing is attached to the condition of confessing sin and getting forgiveness.

One should "call for the elders" (5:14) of the church in praying for healing. Why elders and not a traveling evangelist or some other person? Because elders have spiritual oversight of the flock of God, and they probably know of any sin or rebellion in the life of the sick person that may have led to this illness. Because elders have the command to "shepherd God's flock among you" (1 Pet 5:2), they must exercise watch care and pray for those in their flock. Therefore, based on their spiritual relationship to the sick person, they can provide healing for the soul before they provide prayer for the body. James emphasizes that the intense prayers of the righteous are powerful, citing the example of the prayer of Elijah (Jas 5:16–18).

Practical Application

James writes to believers who are suffering trials and temptations because of their faith in Jesus Christ. He uses the style of the wisdom literature of the Old Testament, i.e., a number of pointed truths written in a solitary sentence that are clustered together to make a point. He tells his readers to expect trials and to demonstrate their faith by their works. James is hard on the rich, especially when they exploit the poor. He puts great value on God's wisdom and emphasizes a proper relationship between faith and works. James's letter is a reminder to all of us to live the faith we profess.

For Further Reading

Davids, P. H. *The Epistle of James: A Commentary on the Greek Text*. NIGTC. Grand Rapids: Eerdmans, 1982.

Hiebert, D. E. *The Epistle of James: Tests of a Living Faith*. Chicago: Moody Press, 1979.

Martin, R. P. *James*. WBC. Waco: Word, 1988.

Maynard-Reid, P. V. *Poverty and Wealth in James*. Maryknoll: Orbis, 1987.

Moo, D. J. *The Letter of James*. PNTC. Grand Rapids: Eerdmans, 2000.

Richardson, Kurt. *James*. NAC. Nashville: B&H, 1997

Study Questions

1. How should a believer react when facing trials?
2. What is the genre (style) of James's writing?
3. In what ways do Paul and James agree about faith and works? How do they seem to disagree? How can we reconcile both of their viewpoints?
4. What is the basic contribution of the book of James to the rest of Scripture?
5. In what ways do you need to be more consistent in living what you claim to believe?

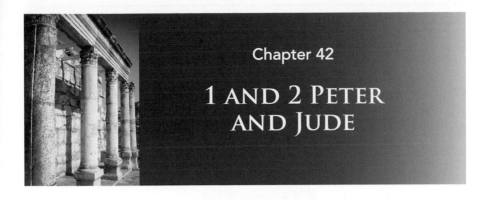

Chapter 42

1 AND 2 PETER AND JUDE

Making a Difference

T he letters of Peter and Jude elucidate the gospel, express genuine piety, and call for the defense of the Christian faith. They emphasize making a difference in an unbelieving world by living right in a world gone wrong. The great Reformer, Martin Luther, called Peter's books, "pure gospel . . . the grandest of the New Testament."[1] Although he questioned whether Jude was merely an abstract of 2 Peter, his fellow Reformer John Calvin viewed it as consistent with "the purity of apostolic doctrine."[2] What is clearly evident in all three letters is the call to endure suffering and defend the faith. Once converted to faith in Jesus Christ, the early Christians stood apart from both Greco-Roman culture and Jewish legalism. They often experienced persecution, punishment, discrimination, imprisonment, and sometimes even death. In light of these challenges, Peter and Jude wrote to encourage the believers to endure suffering and stand firm for the faith.

1 PETER

Endure Suffering

Author

Simon Peter, one of the three people in the inner circle of our Lord's disciples, ascribes his name to his first letter, "Peter, an apostle of Jesus Christ" (1:1). Originally, Peter was a fisherman who lived in Capernaum on the shores of the Sea of Galilee. His brother Andrew brought him to Jesus Christ, and in that first encounter (John 1:40–42) his name was changed from Simon to Cephas (Aramaic meaning "a rock or stone"). In his first letter Peter claims to be a "witness to the sufferings of Christ" (5:1) and that he wrote the letter with the help of Silvanus (Silas) (5:12). The early church universally accepted the letter as being authored by Peter.

Some current scholars raise questions about Peter's authorship, suggesting the excellent style of Greek does not seem to represent a fisherman. However, Peter was probably fluent in Hebrew, Aramaic, and Greek and perhaps had access to good Greek literature at Capernaum, a sophisticated town of wealthy Jewish leaders. Also, Peter dictated the letter to Silvanus (5:12) who was a Roman citizen (Acts 16:37–38) who knew Greek well (Acts 15:22–23, 27).

Peter was the spokesman of the disciples in the upper room, and he preached the powerful sermon on Pentecost where approximately 3,000 believed in Christ (Acts 2:41–42). Afterwards he also preached in Jerusalem, Judea, and Samaria, and worked some miracles. Peter introduced the gospel

Roman aqueduct at Caesarea Maritima (where Peter preached to Cornelius), which transported water to the city from the Carmel Mountains.

to Gentiles in the home of Cornelius in Caesarea (Acts 10). Peter was an energetic disciple: ardent, impulsive, and a man of action as he followed the Lord.

Personality Profile

The name *Silas* (Latin, *Silvanus*) means "person of the woods." He was a prominent member at the Jerusalem Council (Acts 15) and left Jerusalem with the apostle Paul to report to the churches the decision of the Jerusalem Council that Gentile Christians were accepted into the church (Acts 15:22, 27, 32). After Paul and Barnabas went their separate ways, Silas accompanied Paul on the second missionary journey. He was imprisoned with Paul at Philippi (Acts 16:19, 25, 29) and was involved in the riot at Thessalonica (Acts 17:4). Silas went to Berea with Paul but remained with Timothy as Paul went on to Athens to preach (Acts 17). Peter describes the letter of 1 Peter as "through Silvanus, a faithful brother" (1 Pet 5:12) and suggests he was either the amanuenses, i.e., the stenographer who copied the epistle for Peter, or actually contributed to the epistle by adding ideas, words, etc. The time, place, and manner of his death are unknown.

Recipients

This epistle is addressed to the five Roman provinces in northwest Asia Minor: Pontus, Galatia, Cappadocia, Asia, and Bithynia (1:1). Peter calls his readers "temporary residents" (1:1; 2:11), identifying them as part of the Jewish Dispersion (1:1, i.e., sojourners of the scattering), thereby identifying his readers as converted Jews. These titles describe these believers by using a spiritual picture of their task of living for Christ in a non-Christian culture. Peter Davids notes that the letter seems general in nature since it lacks personal greetings and personal details.[3]

At ancient Cappadocia, volcanic eruptions and later erosion resulted in this unique landscape. Digging in the sandstone, dwellers established houses, churches, catacombs, and even entire underground cities.

Occasion and Date

Peter was the apostle to the Jews and ministered predominantly in churches that were Jewish in nature. The Christians in Asia Minor were experiencing serious trials and persecution. Even though Paul also ministered in this area, Peter may have felt compelled to write his letter of encouragement and exhortation as well. If Peter wrote this letter from Rome, the probable date was AD 64, after Paul's release from his first imprisonment and before his execution circa AD 66. Peter's reference to "Babylon" is understood by most commentators as a veiled reference to Rome, which would have been easily understood by Jewish Christians.

KEY FACTS

Author:	The apostle Peter
Recipients:	Believers in Jewish churches in Asia Minor
Where:	From Rome (called Babylon in 5:13)
Date:	AD 64
Key Word:	Suffering (Gk. *pathēma*)
Key Verse:	"Dear friends, don't be surprised when the fiery ordeal comes among you to test you as if something unusual were happening to you" (4:12).

Outline

I. Character of the Believer (1:1–12)
II. Challenge of the Believer (1:13–2:10)
III. Conduct of the Believer (2:11–4:19)
IV. Commitment of the Believer (5:1–14)

Message

I. Character of the Believer (1 Peter 1:1–12)

Peter makes clear that true Christian believers are different from the rest of the world because they were "born again to a living hope" (1:3 NASB). The new birth (Gk. *anagennaō*) assures the believer of "an inheritance that is imperishable . . . kept in heaven" (1:4) and "guarded by God's power" (1:5). Therefore, even the believer's present suffering is nothing more than being "refined by fire" to the "praise, glory, and honor at the revelation of Jesus Christ" (1:7).

II. Challenge of the Believer (1 Peter 1:13–2:10)

Because we have been born again (cf. John 3:3), believers are called to personal holiness. We are to live in such a way that our personal conduct reflects the reality of God's power in our lives. Having been redeemed from our "empty way of life" (1:18) as unbelievers, we are transformed by the "precious blood of Christ" (1:19). Therefore, we are living stones in the temple of God where we serve as the "holy priesthood" of believers (2:5).

III. Conduct of the Believer (1 Peter 2:11–4:19)

Peter challenges his readers to submit to "every human institution" in order to silence the unfounded criticism of unbelievers (2:13–14). By doing good to all people, believers and unbelievers alike, we display the glory of God to a fallen world. Therefore, we are to display the grace of God to human masters (2:18–25) and unbelieving spouses (3:1–7) so that our prayers will be answered. These practical teachings enabled Christians to develop a spiritual and practical lifestyle that challenged the pagan world's understanding of human relationships. Christians viewed themselves "as God's slaves" (2:16) and therefore truly free from the dominion of the world.

IV. Commitment of the Believer (1 Peter 5:1–14)

Peter closes his first letter urging elders to "shepherd God's flock" by "being examples to the flock" because Christ, the chief Shepherd, shall appear to reward His faithful servants (5:2–4). He reminds pastors to be humble (5:6) and to resist the Devil who prowls around "like a roaring lion" (5:8). He closes with the benediction of "peace to all of you who are in Christ" (5:14).

Shepherd leading his sheep.

Practical Application

Peter reminds his readers that they are "strangers and temporary residents" (2:11), thus identifying them as citizens of another country, not primarily of this earth. Therefore, they must expect trials and sufferings, just as their Savior underwent great sufferings in shedding His blood for these sojourners (4:12–19). But while on this earth, Peter says they must subject themselves to "every human authority because of the Lord" (2:13). Their Christian duty included their earthly citizenship.

The interior of the Colosseum (Flavian Amphitheater) in Rome. Seen here are the remains of the complex set of rooms and passageways for wild beasts and other provisions that would have been hidden beneath a wooden floor.

Peter instructs believers to expect suffering, "Dear friends, don't be surprised when the fiery ordeal comes among you to test you as if something unusual were happening to you" (4:12). Being a Christian does not exempt people from suffering. Christians identify with Christ because they are partakers of His sufferings (4:13). Peter probably remembers that Jesus said on the night of His death, "If the world hates you, understand that it hated me before it hated you" (John 15:18), and "If they persecuted me, they will also persecute you" (John 15:20). At the same time he reminds his readers, "Let none of you suffer as a murderer, a thief, an evildoer, or a meddler" (1 Pet 4:15). Believers are to live above our circumstances in order to make a difference in the world in which we live.

2 PETER

Growing in Grace

Although Peter's first letter prepares believers for persecution and suffering, his second letter warns against false teaching and instructs Christians how to deal with heresy.

KEY FACTS

Author:	The apostle Peter
Recipients:	Believers in Asia Minor and elsewhere
Where:	Probably from Rome
Date:	Circa AD 65–67
Key Word:	Knowledge (Gk. *gnōsis*)
Key Verse:	"But grow in the grace and knowledge of our Lord and Savior Jesus Christ" (3:18).

Author

The author identifies himself as "Simeon Peter, a servant" (1:1), which suggests his willingness to do whatever his Master directs. In his first epistle he says, "Peter, an apostle of Jesus Christ" (1:1), suggesting he is writing from a position of authority. There is abundant external evidence that Peter was the author. Many church leaders identify Peter as the author, i.e., Origen (c. 250), Cyril of Jerusalem (386), Athanasius (370), Augustine (430), and

A house of Capernaum venerated by early local Christians as the home of the apostle Peter.

Jerome (420). Even Clement of Rome in his letter to Corinth (95) quoted from 2 Peter as did Irenaeus (200). Eusebius divided Christian literature into "genuine" and "questionable" and put Peter's letters in the "genuine" category.

The author identifies himself as an apostle of Jesus Christ. Also, when he mentions his approaching death (1:14), it is probably a reference back to Jesus's prediction of his martyrdom in John 21:18. The fact that the author claims to be an eyewitness of the transfiguration (1:16–18) again points to Peter's authorship as does his reference to an earlier epistle (3:1), which he wrote to the same readers. The writer even claims to have known Paul (3:15–16). Finally, many words in 2 Peter were found in his speeches in the book of Acts as well as his first epistle.[4]

Occasion and Date

Since Peter refers to a previous letter, the date has to be shortly after 1 Peter was written, i.e., around AD 65–67. It was written shortly before the death of Peter: "I know that I will soon lay aside my tent, as our Lord Jesus Christ has indeed made clear to me" (1:14). If Peter was executed in Rome by Nero, as Christian tradition suggests, this letter would have been written shortly before his death.

Outline

I. Confidence in God's Word (1:1–21)
II. Condemnation of False Teachers (2:1–22)
III. Concerning the Lord's Return (3:1–18)

Message

I. Confidence in God's Word (2 Peter 1:1–21)

Christians are given everything needed for "life and godliness" by the grace of God, by which we become heirs of "great and precious promises" and "share in the divine nature" (1:3–5). All of this is made possible by faith in the prophetic promises of God's Word, which were inspired by the Holy Spirit (1:19–21). Confidence in the divine inspiration of Scripture is the basis of our faith in its promises, prophecies, and principles.

II. Condemnation of False Teachers (2 Peter 2:1–22)

Peter warns his readers that just as there were false prophets (Gk. *pseudo-prophetes*) in Israel, so there will be false teachers in the churches. They will bring in "destructive heresies," even denying the Lord "who bought them" (2:1). This seems to indicate that Christ died for all men and will judge those who reject Him. Peter characterizes false teachers as sensual, sensational, and greedy. He warns of their destruction by the examples of fallen angels, the people of Noah's day, and the cities of Sodom and Gomorrah (2:4–10).

III. Concerning the Lord's Return (2 Peter 3:1–18)

Finally, Peter warns that scoffers will come in the last days ridiculing the idea of the Lord's return, insisting that life will go on as it always has (3:3–4). However, Peter insists that the Lord will return like a thief (Gk. *kleptos*), unexpectedly, and will catch the unbelieving world unprepared even as He did in Noah's day when the flood swept them away (3:5–10). In light of the ultimate judgment of this world, believers are urged to look for "new heavens and a new earth" (3:13).

Day of the Lord Prophecies	
It is a day of reckoning.	Isaiah 2:12
It comes with fury and anger.	Isaiah 13:9
It is destruction from the Almighty.	Joel 3:12–13
The sun and moon will be darkened.	Joel 2:31
Multitudes will come to the valley of decision.	Joel 3:14
It will be a day of wrath.	Zephaniah 1:14–18
All nations will gather against Jerusalem.	Zechariah 14:1–4

Practical Application

Peter is the first to warn the church that the Lord's coming might be delayed, whereas the writings of Paul and others suggest that Jesus could come at any moment (in the rapture). Peter suggests that believers may be called upon to suffer in the interval until the Lord returns. Even so, Peter rebukes those who scoff at the idea of His coming (3:14). He goes on to suggest that "the Lord does not delay his promise, as some understand delay, but is patient with you, not wanting any to perish but all to come to repentance"

(3:9). So, why is the Lord delaying His coming? So He can give extra time for people to repent and receive the Lord.

JUDE

Defend the Faith

As the early church grew in size and moved into its second generation, false teachers found their way into leadership and began teaching "damnable heresies" (2 Pet 2:1 KJV). Therefore God raised up a writer uniquely equipped to address the problems of heresy and warn of its consequences. Jude wanted to write concerning "the salvation we share" (v. 3) but directed his readers to "contend for the faith that was delivered to the saints once for all" (v. 3).

Author

People usually identify Jude with one of the following men. First, Jude was one of the original twelve disciples. The apostle John identifies him as "Judas (not Iscariot)" (John 14:22). He was also called "Lebbaeus, whose surname was Thaddaeus" (Matt 10:3 KJV). The second suggestion is that Jude was the half brother of Jesus mentioned in Matt 13:55. The third view is that Judas was the son of the apostle James, which would make him a grandson of Zebedee (Luke 6:16; Acts 1:13). The name Judas comes from the Hebrew "Judah," which means "praise." Judas is the Hebrew spelling, while Jude is Greco-Roman.

Most evangelical scholars identify Jude as the brother of Jesus. Douglas Moo states, "The author of this letter is almost certainly Judas, the brother of Jesus, for he identifies himself as a 'brother of James.' This must be the famous James who led the Jerusalem church (cf. Acts 15:13–21; 21:18), 'the Lord's brother' (Gal 1:19)."[5] Most Catholic scholars accept the same identification, preferring to view Jude as a "cousin" of Jesus. The only other specific biblical reference to him is in Mark 6:3. Paul's brief allusion to the "Lord's brothers" in 1 Corinthians 9:5 may include him.

If the writer is the half brother of Jesus, it was only natural for him to write about the "salvation we share" (v. 3) because he probably was converted after the resurrection of Jesus Christ. He identified with those who came to faith in Jesus as the promised Messiah. His humble reference as a "servant of Jesus Christ" (v. 1) indicates that all Christian believers, even Jesus's relatives, shared a common salvation and, thus, equal relationship.

KEY FACTS

Author:	Jude (disciple/brother of Jesus)
Recipients:	To those called, sanctified, and pre-served (v. 1)
Date:	Circa AD 66
Key Word:	Contend (Gk. *epagōnizomai*)
Key Verse:	"Contend for the faith that was deliv-ered to the saints once for all" (v. 3).

Recipients

The recipients were well taught in Scriptures because Jude uses four illustrations from the Old Testament to make his point: First, the Jews delivered out of Egypt later rebelled against God (v. 5); second, angels who didn't keep their first estate (v. 6); third, Sodom and Gomorrah as an exam-

Two sides of the Papyrus Bodmer VIII, an early New Testament papyrus that contains all the text of 1 Peter, 2 Peter, and Jude.

ple of those who deserved the punishment of eternal fire (v. 7); and fourth, Michael disputing with the devil over the body of Moses (vv. 8–11). Jude's reference to both Old Testament examples and those of Jewish noncanonical books indicates his readers were Jewish Christians.

Occasion

Jude treats apostasy as though it had already begun to creep into the church. Jude recognizes that heresy was in its first stages and had not spread widely throughout the church. But rather "some men" (v. 4) had crept into the assembly bringing false doctrine. The word *paraisduein* was used to describe a peddler trying to get his wares into a home or an exile who had slipped secretly back into a country to erode the laws of a king he was trying to depose. Although these false teachers apparently professed some degree of faith, Jude describes them as "ungodly" or lacking personal faith in Jesus Christ as personal Savior. Further, they perverted biblical teaching to justify their loose moral lifestyles. They rejected the deity of "Jesus Christ, our only Master and Lord" because false teachers rejected His authority over their lives.

Jude warns against these threats and gives instructions on how to keep these false teachings from spreading. As in 2 Timothy and 2 Peter, Jude deals with the threat of apostasy in both positive and negative ways.

Outline

I. Warnings About False Teachers (1–16)
II. Words of Encouragement for Believers (17–25)

Message

I. Warnings About False Teachers (Jude 1–16)

Jude urges fellow believers to contend for the faith (v. 3). The word "contend" (Gk. *epagōnizomai*) refers to an athletic competition such as a race or wrestling match. It is Jude's way of telling these believers to contend actively and aggressively for the fundamentals of the Christian faith. He reminds his readers that God's judgment fell on the exodus rebels (v. 5), fallen angels (v. 6), and Sodom and Gomorrah (v. 7), and parallels them to the rebellion of Cain, Balaam, and Korah (v. 11). They are described as waterless clouds, fruitless trees, waves of the sea, and wandering stars (vv. 12–13).

II. Words of Encouragement for Believers (Jude 17–25)

Jude concludes by addressing his readers as "dear friends" (v. 17). He encourages them to continue to "build yourselves up in your most holy faith" (v. 20) and to continue evangelizing others as "snatching them from the fire" (v. 23). He concludes his letter with one of the most beautiful and often quoted doxologies in the New Testament, "to the only God our Savior, through Jesus Christ our Lord, be glory, majesty, power, and authority before all time, now and forever. Amen" (v. 25).

Parallel Passages—Jude and 2 Peter		
Jude 4	Godless men who deny the sovereign Lord	2 Peter 2:1
Jude 6	Angels held in darkness for judgment	2 Peter 2:4
Jude 7	Sodom and Gomorrah to ashes	2 Peter 2:6

Parallel Passages—Jude and 2 Peter (continued)		
Jude 8	These men arrogantly slander celestial beings	2 Peter 2:10
Jude 9	Michael did not bring a slanderous accusation	2 Peter 2:11
Jude 10	These blasphemers are like brute beasts	2 Peter 2:12
Jude 11	They have followed the way of Balaam	2 Peter 2:15
Jude 12	Clouds without rain, driven by a storm	2 Peter 2:17
Jude 13	Blackest darkness is reserved for them	2 Peter 2:17
Jude 16	They lust, boast, and flatter	2 Peter 2:18
Jude 17	The apostles of our Lord foretold	2 Peter 3:2
Jude 18	In the last days scoffers will come	2 Peter 3:3

Practical Application

1. Immorality Leads to Heresy

Jude uniquely ties together doctrinal error with the immoral lifestyle of false teachers suggesting immorality leads to heresy. But this question is more urgent than theoretical. Jude indicates that Christians who begin following Jesus Christ but slip into immorality can end up in false doctrine and/or heresy. When believers slip into immorality—sins of the flesh and the heart—they face one of two alternatives: either give up their heresy and return to Jesus Christ or else justify their immorality by false teaching. Therefore to Jude, immorality opens the door to heresy: "Some people, who were designated for this judgment long ago, have come in by stealth; they are ungodly, turning the grace of our God into sensuality and denying Jesus Christ, our only Master and Lord" (v. 4). Here Jude suggests they first turn to immorality and then they deny the Lord. When Christians turn away from the light, they become blinded and live in darkness. And in that blackness they must deny Jesus Christ who is the Light of the world.

2. How to Remain Faithful in the Face of Heresy

Jude suggests to "build yourselves up in your most holy faith" (v. 20), which is being grounded in the Word of God. Second, we protect ourselves when we pray "in the Holy Spirit" (v. 20). Third, believers must establish a meaningful relationship with others; "keep yourselves in the love of God" (v. 21). Fourth, hope, "waiting expectantly for the mercy of our Lord Jesus Christ for eternal life" (v. 21). In the fifth place they must be involved in ministry: "Have mercy on some, who are doubting" (v. 22 NASB). And of course, they must be involved in evangelism: "Save others by snatching them from the fire" (v. 23). Next we must be separate from sin and sinners, "hating even the garment defiled by the flesh" (v. 23). Eighth, assurance in their hearts will deliver them from falling into fleshly sin and/or heresy: God "is able to protect you from stumbling and to make you stand in the presence of his glory, blameless and with great joy" (v. 24).

For Further Reading

Davids, Peter H. *The First Epistle of Peter*. NICNT. Grand Rapids: Eerdmans, 1990.
————. *The Letters of 2 Peter and Jude*. PNTC. Grand Rapids: Eerdmans, 2006.
Green, Gene L. *Jude and 2 Peter*. BECNT. Grand Rapids: Baker, 2008.
Grudem, Wayne. *1 Peter*. TNTC. Grand Rapids: Eerdmans, 1988.
Jobes, Karen H. *1 Peter*. BECNT. Grand Rapids: Baker, 2005.
Moo, Douglas. *2 Peter and Jude*. NIVAC. Grand Rapids: Zondervan, 1996.
Schreiner, Thomas R. *1, 2 Peter, Jude*. NAC. Nashville: B&H, 2003.

Study Questions

1. How do Peter and Jude encourage us to remain faithful to God?
2. How does Peter connect the problem of suffering to the Christian doctrine of suffering?
3. In what way do believers "share in the divine nature" (2 Pet 1:4)?
4. What advice does Peter give about dealing with those who criticize us?
5. What mistakes are made by those who scoff at the idea of the return of Christ?

Notes

1. Martin Luther, *Commentary on Peter and Jude* (Grand Rapids: Kregel, 1990), 10.

2. John Calvin, *Commentary on the Epistle of Jude* (Grand Rapids: Eerdmans, 1978), 427.

3. Peter Davids, "1 Peter," in Clinton Arnold, *ZIBBC* (Grand Rapids: Zondervan, 2002), 4:123.

4. See details in W. Baker, *James and Peter*, ed. M. Couch and E. Hindson, TFCBC (Chattanooga: AMG, 2004), 95–98.

5. Douglas Moo, "Jude," in Clinton Arnold, *ZIBBC* (Grand Rapids: Zondervan, 2002), 4:230.

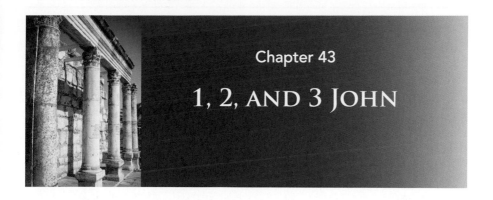

Chapter 43

1, 2, AND 3 JOHN

Fellowship in the Truth

The letters attributed to John are among the most personal, practical, and insightful of all the New Testament letters. By means of personal letters, Christians communicated with fellow believers throughout the Roman Empire. In these particular letters believers are encouraged to love one another, hold to the truth, avoid false teachers, and live in the light of God's salvation.

1 JOHN

Blessed Assurance

KEY FACTS	
Author:	John
Recipients:	Believers
Where:	Unknown (possibly Ephesus)
Date:	AD 85–95
Key Words:	Know (Gk. *oida* and *ginōskō*)
Key Verse:	"I have written these things to you who believe in the name of the Son of God so that you may know that you have eternal life" (1 John 5:13).

Author

This epistle begins without any introductory greeting and without identifying the author by name. Internal evidence shows that the writer is an eyewitness of Jesus (1:1–4) and writes his audience as one in a position of authority (1:6; 2:15, 24, 28; 3:14; 4:1; 5:21). The author uses simple Greek sentences and incorporates themes that contrast opposites such as: (1) light and darkness; (2) life and death; (3) love and hate; (4) truth and lies. People are said to fit into one or the other of these opposites. All of this internal evidence is consistent with Johannine authorship. Likewise, external evidence supports this conclusion.[1] For more about John, the son of Zebedee, see the introduction to John's Gospel.

The traditional site of the tomb of John the apostle near the ancient city of Ephesus, an important religious center of early Christianity.

Recipients

The epistle's lack of formal epistolary introduction limits the scope of how much can be known about the epistle's original audience. The author did not greet a specific church or group because he wanted the letter to be circulated among as many churches as possible. Certainly the epistle is intended for believers (1 John 2:12–14, 19; 3:1; 5:13), and its message is one that has application to all churches.

Occasion and Date

No specific information in 1 John assists in pinpointing an exact date when it was written. However, church tradition suggests John was in the later years of his life and living in Ephesus when he wrote this letter. Many scholars conclude that the epistles were written soon after he completed his Gospel. In addition, these letters do not seem to indicate that the persecution under Domitian (c. AD 95) had yet begun. Therefore an acceptable date range for all of three epistles would be between AD 85 and 95.

Outline

I. Walking in the Light (1:1–2:29)
II. Fellowship in Love (3:1–5:21)

Message

In this letter, just as in the Gospel, John affirms that a person's assurance of eternal life is not something to be experienced only after death, but it begins at the moment of salvation. All true believers, therefore, are not only looking ahead in faith toward something future but can already know their eternal destiny with great assurance. Therefore, John uses the words *oida* and *ginōskō* (both meaning "to know") seventy-seven times in thirty-two verses, many of which are reaffirming what his audience already knows, including: (1) the truth (2:2); (2) that they have a relationship with God (2:3–5, 13–14); (3) that He hears and grants their prayer requests (5:14–15); (4) that Jesus was righteous, did not sin, came to take away sin, and that when He appears they will be like Him (2:29; 3:2); (5) that sin is not characteristic of someone in fellowship with God (3:9; 5:18); and (6) the final hour is at hand (2:18).

I. Walking in the Light (1 John 1:1–2:29)

After establishing his credibility in the prologue, John summarizes the message that he has heard as "God is light, and there is absolutely no darkness in him" (1:5). With this message in view, he reasons that anyone in their assembly who claims to have fellowship with God but continues to walk in darkness (sin) is deceiving himself and others. However, those who walk in the light (righteousness) of Jesus are forgiven, cleansed from their sins, and experience true fellowship (1:6–10).

After this John moves on to speak about believers' assurance of salvation (2:3–15). Those who keep Jesus's commandments can have assurance of salvation when they are in proper relationship with him, and God's love is perfected in them (2:3, 5). When they obey His commandment to love one another, they walk as Jesus walked (2:6). They do not love the world or the things of the world (2:15). However, those who profess to know Jesus yet do not keep His commandments are liars and the truth is not in them (2:4). From this it can be concluded that the way someone treats others is a window into their soul. Those who love one another are walking in the light and have sure footing; those who hate others are walking in darkness and are blinded by the darkness (2:9, 11).

John admonishes believers not to love the sinful world or the things of the world (2:15–16). John's second admonition is that his readers should abide in the truth (2:24–28). In light of Antichristlike false teachers, John reminds his readers that they are equipped to resist the lies of the world. Jesus has anointed them with the Holy Spirit who will guide them away from false teachers and lead them into truth (2:26–27).

II. Fellowship in Love (1 John 3:1–5:21)

Now John focuses on God's love for them. God displays His love by calling them His children (3:1). God has revealed that they will become like Jesus because they will see Him as He is (3:2).

The Church of Saint John near Ephesus. Late in the fourth century a church was built over a grave, supposedly the tomb of John, the beloved disciple. It was originally built in the shape of a cross.

In the meantime all who look forward to the second coming of Jesus purify themselves, just as He is pure (3:3). In fact, John goes as far as saying that "everyone who remains in him does not sin; everyone who sins has not seen him or known him," and "everyone who has been born of God does not sin, because his seed remains in him; he is not able to sin, because he has been born of God" (3:6, 9). Jesus came to destroy the works of the Devil; and, therefore, those who are of Jesus should have no association with sin, which is the work of the Devil (3:8–9). "But if anyone does sin, we have an advocate with the Father—Jesus Christ the righteous one" (2:1).

John's third admonition is for believers not to be surprised by hatred from the world (3:10–15). The Old Testament account of Cain and Abel reveals that Cain hated his brother because of his righteousness so he murdered him. John, therefore, admonishes his readers, "Do not be surprised, brothers and sisters, if the world hates you" (3:13). The children of the Devil will hate the righteous, and he who hates is a murderer and does not have eternal life (3:15).[2] The children of God, on the other hand, love one another and have passed from death to life (3:14).

John's fourth admonition is that believers must not believe every spirit but test the spirits to see whether they are of God (4:1). If a spirit does not confess that Jesus Christ has come in bodily form, then that spirit was not sent from God but is the spirit of the Antichrist (4:2–3).[3]

After this admonition John returns again to his discussion of love. In this section John drives his point home concerning why love is so characteristic of those who have fellowship with God. He explains that love is the nature of God. Therefore, everyone who loves is born of God and knows God; the one who doesn't love as he ought does not know God (4:7–8). Jesus's self-sacrifice for our sins has made this love possible and is the model believers should follow. Therefore, true love is not that we loved God but that he first loved us and sent His Son (4:9–10).

John then reviews what he has told them up to this point concerning love and abiding with an unseen God (4:12–21).

- God is love and he who abides in love abides in God and God in him (4:8, 16).
- We love because He first loved us and sent His Son (4:10, 19).
- Love for one another is evidence of abiding with God; His love is perfected in us (1:9, 11; 3:14; 4:12).
- God's Spirit is evidence that God abides in us (3:24; 4:13).
- Whoever confesses that Jesus is the Son of God abides in Him (2:22; 4:15).

- Whoever claims to love God must love their brother also (2:9–10; 3:17–18; 4:21).

God's Spirit bears witness to Jesus's life and death.[4] This witness is greater than the witness of men because it is from God about His own Son. This witness lives in believers, but those who do not believe God are making Him out to be a liar. This is the testimony that the Spirit brings, "God has given us eternal life, and this life is in his Son. The one who has the Son has life. The one who does not have the Son of God does not have life" (5:11–12). This testimony should give assurance to those who believe in the name of the Son of God, for they have eternal life (5:13–20).

REFLECTION

Can We Really Know for Sure?

John's letters clearly distinguish between believers and nonbelievers. "The one who has the Son has life. The one who doesn't have the Son of God does not have life" (1 John 5:12). It can't be much clearer than that. Either you have Christ or you don't. That's why John adds, "I have written these things to you ... so that you may know that you have eternal life" (1 John 5:13). It's not enough to hope you are going to heaven. You need to know for sure. That's why John wrote this letter. If you're not sure, make sure. Eternity is too long to be wrong.

2 JOHN

Avoid False Teachers

In his Farewell Discourse Jesus taught that His disciples would be known by their love for one another (John 15:12). However, as John showed in his first letter, fellowship with God is not only a matter of love but also of sound doctrine. Followers of Jesus must be careful not to sacrifice truth in the name of love. In this second letter John warns his readers to have nothing to do with false teachers; to show hospitality to them would be to share in their wickedness.

KEY FACTS

Author:	John "the Elder"
Recipients:	The "elect lady and her children"
Where:	Unknown
Date:	AD 85–95
Key Word:	Remain (Gk. *menō*)
Key Verses:	"Anyone who does not remain in Christ's teaching but goes beyond it does not have God. The one who remains in that teaching, this one has both the Father and the Son" (vv. 9–10).

Author

Bust of Roman emperor Traianus (Trajan) who reigned from AD 98 to 117. The bust is on display in Ankara's Museum of Anatolian Civilizations. Irenaeus affirmed that John lived in Asia until the reign of Trajan.

The author of 2 John and 3 John calls himself "the Elder." While scholarship has not come to a consensus concerning who this elder is, similarities between the first two letters attributed to John indicate that both were written by the same person. These similarities are: (1) The historical situations in 1 and 2 John are similar. Both speak of people who "went out" and "who [deny] the Father and the Son" (1 John 2:19–23; 2 John 7). (2) Both books call these false teachers "antichrists" (1 John 2:18; 2 John 7). (3) Both stress the importance of the love command and that it was "received from the beginning" (2 John 4, 6; 1 John 3:11, 23; 4:7); and (4) both rejoice in seeing their children walking in the truth of the gospel.[5]

Recipients

The recipients are identified in the opening verse as the "elect lady and her children." Under debate is whether this should be taken (1) literally—meaning a Christian woman and her children—or (2) figuratively—as a title representing a local church ("elect lady") and its members ("her children"). While no other manuscript uses the title "elect lady" for a church, the New Testament does refer to the church as "the bride of Christ." Given this, a figurative/symbolic usage seems more likely. Regardless, though, the recipients of this letter are followers of Jesus whom John wants to encourage and protect.

Occasion and Date

The occasion and date are similar to 1 John (see notes on 1 John). Second John focuses on making sure churches do not extend hospitality to false teachers and thereby unknowingly support their itinerate ministry. He instructs them not to allow false teachers into their homes (vv. 10–11).

Genre and Structure

Second John is a typical first-century letter consisting of an introduction (vv. 1–3), a body (vv. 4–11), and a conclusion (vv. 12–13). It is personal and pastoral yet poignant and powerful.

Outline

  I. Introduction: Grace, Mercy, and Peace (1–3)
 II. Body: Truth and Deception (4–11)
III. Conclusion: I Hope to Be with You (12–13)

Message

I. Introduction: Grace, Mercy, and Peace (2 John 1–3)

John "the Elder" expresses his love for "the elect lady and her children" and wishes them grace and mercy from God the Father and the Lord Jesus Christ.

II. Body: Truth and Deception (2 John 4–11)

John expresses the joy he felt when he learned that some members of the recipient's church body were following the Father's command to walk in truth (v. 4). However, John still sees a need to admonish them to love one another by walking according to God's commands because many false teachers and antichrists were teaching that Jesus did not come in the flesh (vv. 5–8). Those who taught this heresy were not abiding in a proper understanding of Christ and did not know God (v. 9). Therefore, he cautions them to avoid these false teachers at all costs.

III. Conclusion: I Hope to Be with You (2 John 12–13)

As quickly as this letter begins, it comes to its conclusion. John looks forward to meeting them as he knows it will prove to be a joyous time for everyone. His letter ends by sending greetings from their "elect sister." This could be the church of Ephesus where John pastored.

3 JOHN

Accept True Teachers

Every church should be led by godly leaders whose main concerns are to walk in true fellowship with God and to equip and support the saints. Unfortunately some church leaders are more concerned with their own self-image than with what is best for the church as a whole. Third John provides a window into a church body that was in the midst of a struggle between godly and ungodly leaders.

KEY FACTS	
Author:	John "the Elder"
Recipients:	Gaius
Where:	Unknown
Date:	AD 85–95
Key Word:	Imitate (Gk. *mimeomai*)
Key Verse:	"Dear friend, do not imitate what is evil, but what is good. The one who does good is of God; the one who does evil has not seen God" (11).

Author

Like 2 John, the epistolary introduction identifies the author simply as "the Elder" (see introductions to 2 John and John). Note the many similar characteristics between 2 John and 3 John: (1) Both were written by "the Elder" (2 John 1; 3 John 1). (2) Both describe the letter's recipients as those who are loved "in the truth" (2 John 1; 3 John 4). (3) Both rejoice that "children" are "walking in the truth" (2 John 4; 3 John 4). (4) Both conclude with almost identical statements explaining that the author wants to speak with them "face to face" (2 John 12; 3 John 13–14). These internal similarities are strong indicators that one individual was responsible for writing all three epistles—namely, the apostle John, the son of Zebedee.

Recipient

Little is known concerning Gaius, the man named as the recipient of this epistle. He was probably a member of a church in Asia Minor where John's influence was prominent.

Occasion and Date

Whereas 2 John warns its readers that they should avoid false teachers, the concern of 3 John is that the church should show hospitality to true teachers. While Gaius and Demetrius were doing their part to support these teachers, Diotrophes turned them away. John, therefore, writes to commend Gaius and Demetrius and rebuke Diotrophes. The date is between AD 85 and 95.

Genre and Structure

Third John is a typical first-century letter consisting of an introduction, a body, and a conclusion.

Outline

I. Introduction: My Dear Friend (3 John 1–4)
II. Body: You Are Faithful (3 John 5–12)
III. Conclusion: I Hope to See You Soon (3 John 13–14)

Message

I. Introduction: My Dear Friend (3 John 1–4)

John "the Elder" expresses his love for his "dear friend Gaius" and wishes him prosperity in all things, including spiritual and physical health. John rejoiced to hear that he was walking in the truth (vv. 1–4).

II. Body: You Are Faithful (3 John 5–12)

John commends Gaius for his faithfulness in lovingly helping fellow Christians and strangers who were traveling because he has helped those who "set out for the sake of the Name" (v. 7). Without the support of believers like Gaius, traveling teachers would be hard-pressed because they chose not to accept missionary support from the Gentiles they were teaching (v. 7). Similarly, John commends Demetrius for his good testimony (v. 12) and urges his readers to imitate that which is good and avoid that which is evil. However John has a stern rebuke for Diotrophes, who is turning away traveling teachers because of his desire to be the most highly regarded person in the church. And then Diotrophes goes a step further; he castigates those who accept itinerant teachers. Though John had attempted to correct Diotrophes in the past, he refused to be corrected in this matter. Therefore, John warns that when he comes to visit, he will expose Diotrophes's evil deeds. He encouraged Gaius not to imitate what is evil but to imitate what is good (v. 11).

III. Conclusion: I Hope to See You Soon (3 John 13–14)

John explains that he hopes to come soon and to tell them what he has to say in a face-to-face discussion. He looks forward to this meeting as he knows it will prove to be a joyous time for everyone.

Practical Application

John wrote his letters in order to: (1) equip his readers to discern who was and who was not in proper relationship with God; (2) affirm his readers in their faith; and (3) warn them concerning false teachers. John maintained that those who left the fellowship of believers were not in true fellowship with God in the first place. Those who have fellowship with God will walk in light rather than darkness, love one another, believe in the name of Jesus, affirm that Jesus came in the flesh, and follow God's commandments. As you read these letters, let their timeless truths challenge you about your fellowship with God.

For Further Reading

Akin, Daniel L. *1, 2, 3 John*. NAC. Nashville: B&H, 2001.
Brown, Raymond E. *The Epistles of John*. Anchor Bible. New York: Doubleday, 1982.
Johnson, Thomas. *1, 2, and 3 John*. NIBC. Peabody, MA: Hendrickson, 1993.
Kruse, Colin G. *The Letters of John*. Grand Rapids: Eerdmans, 2000.
Ryrie, Charles. "Epistles of John," in *Wycliffe Bible Commentary*. Chicago: Moody Press, 1992.
Stott, John R. W. *The Letters of John*. TNTC. Grand Rapids: Eerdmans, 1988.

Study Questions

1. What does John mean by "walking in the light"?
2. Why is Christian fellowship important to believers?
3. How can we know for sure that we have eternal life?
4. Is the tile "elect lady" literal or figurative?
5. What kind of hospitality should we extend to missionaries and traveling teachers today?

Notes

1. Church fathers such as Irenaeus (c. 140–203), Clement of Alexandria (c. 155–215), Tertullian (c. 150–222), and Origen (c. 185–253) present John as the author.

2. See John 15:18.

3. These false spirits do not seem to be denying the existence of Christ but were denying that Jesus actually had a physical body. Theologically speaking, this denial undermines the gospel itself; if Jesus didn't have a physical body, then His sacrifice would not be sufficient to atone for the sins of mankind. Beyond this, it undermines many statements in the Gospels that give evidence that Christ had such a body (Luke 24:39, 43; John 19:28, 34; 20:20, 27).

4. John also states that the water and the blood bear witness to Him (5:6). There is no universal agreement concerning how water and blood bear witness to Jesus. Possibilities include: (1) Jesus's own baptism and crucifixion; (2) Jesus's baptizing ministry (baptizing others in the Spirit) and crucifixion; (3) natural birth and crucifixion; (4) Jesus's body was made up of the elements of water and blood; proponents of this view cite ancient Jewish sources that held that the human body is composed of two elements: water and blood; (5) the sacraments of baptism and the Eucharist. See Colin G. Kruse, *The Letters of John* (Grand Rapids: Eerdmans, 2000), 174–78.

5. First John 1:3–4; 2 John 4. The list above was adapted from Kruse, *The Letters of John*, 36–37.

Chapter 44

REVELATION

The King Is Coming

T he book of Revelation is the greatest book of apocalyptic literature ever written. It captivates our attention, stirs our imagination, and points to our glorious future destiny. The reader is swept away as the panorama of the future unfolds in a series of seven visions in lucid detail and symbolic pictures. This final book of the biblical record is the capstone of divine revelation. The biblical title of the book is "The Revelation of Jesus Christ" (1:1) based on the word *apokalypsis*, the Apocalypse, meaning "the unveiling." Accepted as inspired Scripture from the earliest times of the Christian era, the book nevertheless has been vigorously debated in regard to its authorship, date, and proper method of interpretation.[1]

KEY FACTS

Author:	John
Recipients:	Churches of Asia Minor
Date:	AD 95
Key Word:	Witness (Gk. *marturia*)
Key Verse:	"Therefore write what you have seen, what is, and what will take place after this" (1:19).

Author

The traditional view of the Christian church has long held that John the apostle was the author of the Revelation as well as the Gospel and epistles that bear his name.[2] Opposition to the authorship of John began with Marcion, a second-century heretic who rejected all the New Testament authors except Paul. Dionysius of Alexandria in the third century argued that the irregularities in the Greek grammar of the Apocalypse stood in marked contrast to the "elegant diction" of the Gospel and epistles of John. Critical scholars have generally followed this same observation suggesting another John (the elder) wrote the book.[3] On the other hand, irregularities in the Apocalypse may be due to John's feeling compelled not to alter his original vision, which he recorded as he received it.

The internal evidence for the apostle's authorship includes his use of triplets (cf. John 1:1; Rev 2:2), sevenfold arrangements, and the prominent use of terms like "witness," "life," "faith," "light," and "spirit," which appear in his other writings. Only John's Gospel and Revelation refer to Jesus as the "Word" (Gk. *Logos*), the "Lamb," the "water of life," and "he who overcomes." Both books include an invitation to one who is thirsty (John 7:37; Rev 22:17), and both make extensive use of the preposition *ek* ("out of") and *kai* ("and"), reflecting the Semitic background of the author.[4]

The author of the Revelation was certainly familiar with the Old Testament. Bruce Metzger noted: "Of the 404 verses that comprise the 22 chapters of the book of Revelation, 278 verses contain one or more allusions to an Old Testament passage."[5] The author was a Jewish Christian who probably lived in Asia Minor in the first century AD. Metzger concludes, "Certainly from the mid-second century onward the book was widely ascribed to the apostle John, the son of Zebedee."[6]

Recipients

John addresses "the seven churches in Asia" (1:4). These seven literal churches existed in Asia Minor in the first century AD. Ephesus was the largest city in the list and presumably the largest church. All seven were connected by the local Roman highway in a circular pattern going from Ephesus to Smyrna and Pergamum and turning inland to Thyatira, Sardis, Philadelphia, and Laodicea.[7] Revelation 2 and 3 are individual "epistles" written to the seven churches of Asia Minor by Christ Himself. The general condition of these churches is described as wealthy, prosperous, lukewarm, tolerant of heresy, and having lost their first love. This hardly describes the newly founded churches of the 50s and 60s AD. The potential persecution these churches were facing reflects the widespread persecution of Christians under Domitian, the Roman emperor (AD 81–96) at the end of the first century.

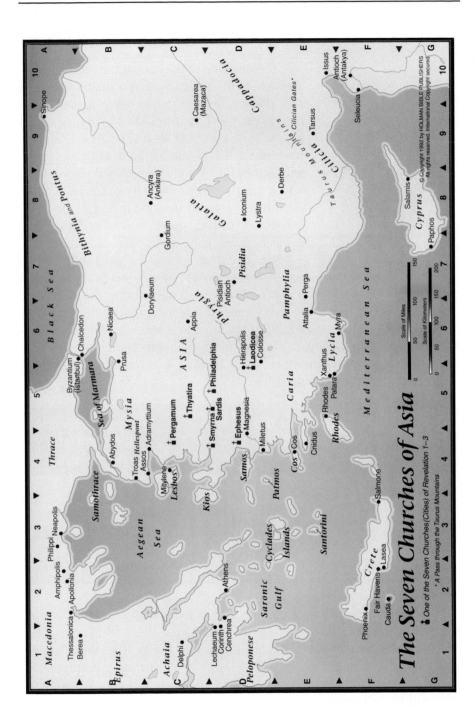

The Seven Churches of Asia

✝ One of the Seven Churches(Cities) of Revelation 1–3

* *A Pass through the Taurus Mountains*

© Copyright 1992 by HOLMAN BIBLE PUBLISHERS
All rights reserved. International Copyright secured.

Occasion and Date

Bust of Domitian, brother and successor to Emperor Titus.

The question of the date of the original composition of the Apocalypse is a matter of extensive debate. Some scholars have argued for a date as early as Claudius (AD 41–54) and others as late as Trajan (AD 98–117). Liberal scholars have attempted to date the book as late as possible because of its highly developed Christology, which clearly affirms the deity of Christ.[8] On the other hand preterists insist on dating it before AD 70 because of their insistence that all or most of it was fulfilled in the destruction of Jerusalem.[9]

Many scholars propose a date either in the time of Nero (AD 64–67) or Domitian (AD 95–96). However, those favoring the early date have no external evidence prior to the sixth century (AD 550) and are forced to attempt to rely on internal evidence to support their view. Ironically, those who lived closest to Nero's time did not believe the book was written then. Mark Hitchcock summarizes the external evidence in the following chart:[10]

Witnesses for the Domitianic Date (AD 95)		Witnesses for the Neronic Date (AD 64–67)
Hegesippus (AD 150)	The Acts of John (c. 650)	
Irenaeus (AD 180)	Primasius (c. 540)	
Victorinus (c. 300)	Orosius (c. 600)	
Eusebius (c. 300)	Andreas (c. 600)	Syriac Version of NT (550)
Jerome (c. 400)	Venerable Bede (c. 700)	Arethas (c. 900)
Sulpicius Severus (c. 400)		Theophylact (d. 1107)

The internal evidence for the late date of Revelation is equally impressive. The condition of the churches of Asia Minor show all the characteristics of second-generation churches that were lapsing from their original zeal and enthusiasm. Polycarp (AD 110) indicates the church at Smyrna did not exist during the time of Paul's missionary journeys in the 50s and 60s. In regard to the church at Laodicea, Paul mentions them three times in his Colossian letter (2:1; 4:13, 16) in a positive light in circa AD 60–62. It hardly seems conceivable that the Laodiceans could grow so lukewarm in their faith (3:16–22) if this letter was written as early as AD 64–67.

All things considered, both internal and external evidence leans strongly in favor of a date of AD 95–96 for the composition of Revelation by John while he was in exile on the island of Patmos in the Aegean Sea, some forty miles off the coast of Ephesus. The fact that Domitian was known for exiling political dissidents, whereas Nero executed them, lends even more support to the later date, as does the fact that Domitian was the first Roman emperor to insist that he be worshipped as deity throughout the entire empire.[11]

Overview of the island of Patmos.

Genre and Structure

John explains what he "heard" and "saw," in descriptive symbolic language. Some of his symbols are drawn from the Old Testament (e.g., Lion of Judah, song of Moses, tree of life, Lamb of God), and some symbols are from the New Testament (e.g., Word of God, Son of Man, bride of Christ), but other symbols have no biblical parallel and are unexplained (e.g., scarlet beast, seven thunders, mark of the beast). A few symbols are specifically identified (e.g., seven lamps are seven churches, and the dragon is Satan) or are self-explanatory (e.g., numbers, seals, songs, trumpets). While the

Apocalypse is symbolic, the symbols depict real people, things, situations, and events.

Several elements make Revelation unique among Bible books. The basic structure of the book is woven around a series of threes and sevens. The overarching triplet (1:19) reveals past, present, and future realities.

Past: "What you have seen" (chap. 1)

Present: "What is" (chaps. 2–3)

Future: "What will take place after this" (chaps. 4–22)

The most significant number in Revelation is seven. There are seven churches, spirits, stars, lampstands, horns, eyes, angels, seals, trumpets, bowls, thunders, crowns, plagues, mountains, kings, songs, and beatitudes. In addition, there is a sevenfold description of Christ (1:14–16), a sevenfold message to each church (2–3), sevenfold praise of the lamb (5:12), sevenfold results of judgment (6:12–14), seven divisions of humanity (6:15), a sevenfold blessing (7:12), a sevenfold triumph (11:19), and seven "new things" (chaps. 21–22).

Other prominent numbers include twelve. There are twelve tribes of Israel, twelve apostles, twelve gates, and twelve foundations of the New Jerusalem, twenty-four elders (a double twelve), and multiples of twelve: each of the twelve tribes contains 12,000 people, making a total of 144,000 (12 x 12,000) and the wall of the New Jerusalem measures 144 cubits (12 x 12). The purpose of the Revelation is to reveal the future. Everything in the book points to the second coming of Christ.

Outline

I. Preface: Vision of the Coming King (1:1–20)

II. Proclamation: Letters to the Seven Churches (2:1–3:22)

    A. Ephesus: Preoccupied Church (2:1–7)

    B. Smyrna: Persecuted Church (2:8–11)

    C. Pergamum: Political Church (2:12–17)

    D. Thyatira: Prosperous Church (2:18–29)

    E. Sardis: Powerless Church (3:1–6)

    F. Philadelphia: Persevering Church (3:7–13)

    G. Laodicea: Putrid Church (3:14–22)

III. Problem: Seven-Sealed Scroll (4:1–5:14)

IV. Process: Seven Seals and Seven Trumpets (6:1–11:19)

V. Players: Seven Key Figures in the Eschatological Drama (12:1–13:18)

VI. Plagues: Seven Bowl Judgments (14:1–19:21)

VII. Postscript: Millennium and Eternal City (20:1–22:21)

Message

I. Preface: Vision of the Coming King (Revelation 1:1–20)[12]

The opening chapter serves as an introduction to the entire book. It is the revelation (Gk. *apokalypsis*, "unveiling") of Jesus Christ through His angel to His servant John (v. 1). John, in turn, is told to record all that he saw in the vision and send it to the seven churches in Asia Minor (vv. 2, 4). Jesus is depicted as "the faithful witness" (v. 5, Gk. *marturia*) who reveals future events that will "soon take place" (1:1), emphasizing the *suddenness* with which they will soon transpire (cf. 2:16; 3:11; 11:14; 22:7, 12, 20).

On a Sunday morning ("the Lord's day"), John heard a voice "like a trumpet" (v. 10) and turning to see who was speaking to him, he saw "One like the Son of Man," dressed like the high priest of heaven (v. 13).

The description of the glorified Savior (vv. 13–16) follows a sevenfold pattern, which is later repeated in the letters to the churches (chaps. 2–3):

1. Hair: "white as snow"
2. Eyes: "a fiery flame"
3. Feet: "fine bronze"
4. Voice: "sound of cascading waters"
5. Right hand: held "seven stars"
6. Mouth: "sharp double-edged sword"
7. Face: "shining like the sun"

The grandeur of this description points to the majesty, purity, and authority of the coming king. The sword coming out of His mouth is His only weapon, in contrast to the bow of the Antichrist (6:2). He who spoke the world into existence at the moment of creation will use the "sword" of His spoken word to conquer the world at His return (19:15). In the meantime the Savior commissions John to record: (1) "what you have seen" (past); (2) "what is" (present); (3) "what will take place after this" (future) (1:19).

II. Proclamation: Letters to the Seven Churches (Revelation 2:1–3:22)

Before the Apocalypse pronounces a message of judgment on the unbelieving world, it first calls the churches to repentance. In these letters the Lord of the church speaks lovingly but firmly to the churches in words of both commendation and condemnation.[13] The message to each church follows the same sevenfold pattern:

1. Commission: "To the angel of the church"
2. Character: "The One who . . . says this"
3. Commendation: "I know your works"
4. Condemnation: "But I have this against you"
5. Correction: "Repent . . . turn . . . change"
6. Call: "He who has an ear, let him hear"
7. Challenge: "To him who overcomes"

A. Ephesus: Preoccupied Church (Revelation 2:1–7)

Ephesus, to which Paul's letter to the Ephesians was written, was one of the outstanding churches of the first century. Paul, Timothy, John, Apollos, and Aquilla and Priscilla were all there in the apostolic era. Yet, as time wore on, they had begun to lose their first priority and became preoccupied with other things. Commended for their good works, they were challenged to regain their "first love" and serve the Lord with renewed passion.

B. Smyrna: Persecuted Church (Revelation 2:8–11)

There were no words of condemnation or correction for the persecuted believers at Smyrna, a city that prided itself on its emperor worship. The name of the city came from the aroma of a perfume made there by crushing the resin of a small thornbush. It was an apt description of the fragrance of the many martyrs who gave their lives there for the cause of Christ, including John's own disciple Polycarp who was burned at the stake in AD 156.

C. Pergamum: Political Church (Revelation 2:12–17)

A massive Roman fortress sat on the acropolis at Pergamum on the Mediterranean coast. This was the site

Roman columns at Smyrna.

of the first temple in the area dedicated to the Caesar cult, erected in honor of Augustus in 29 BC. The Pergamenians worshipped power. The Roman army was headquartered there; and the temple of Zeus, the god of power, dominated the city "where Satan's throne is" (2:13). There was no distinction in Pergamum between religion and politics, and the believers were often caught in the temptation of political correctness that led to spiritual compromise.

Bath-gymnasium complex at Sardis dating from the time of Hadrian, emperor in the second century AD. It was situated in the heart of the city along the main avenue. Measuring about 5.5 acres, the complex was completed in the middle of the second century AD.

D. Thyatira: Prosperous Church (Revelation 2:18–29)

The longest letter was written to the church in the smallest town. Thyatira was known for its clothing industry: weaving, dyeing, and sewing were major sources of income, especially for women. The town was dominated by trade guilds that required religious participation and were dominated by powerful and prosperous women. It is no surprise then that a prosperous woman, symbolically called "Jezebel," functioned as a false teacher in the church and tolerated false doctrine.

E. Sardis: Powerless Church (Revelation 3:1–6)

Sardis was an old city that had formerly been the capital of the region under the Persians. It was later destroyed by the Greeks and rebuilt by the Romans. The church, like the city, was dying, and only a few believers remained (3:14). The Lord challenged them with five staccato imperatives: Wake up! Strengthen! Remember! Obey! Repent!

F. Philadelphia: Persevering Church (Revelation 3:7–13)

Known as the "gateway to the East," Philadelphia sat in a lush valley in the heart of Asia Minor, near the pass into the Timolous Mountains. It was literally the "open door" between East and West. The church persevered with "limited strength" (3:8 HCSB) and was commended for their endurance and promised to be kept "from" (Gk. *ek*) the "hour of testing" (tribulation) that would eventually come on the whole world (3:10).

G. Laodicea: Putrid Church (Revelation 3:14–22)

In contrast to the open door at Philadelphia, Laodicea was the church of the closed door at which the Lord of the church is pictured as knocking (3:20). It is also described as putrid and lukewarm, despite its material prosperity.

In these letters to the seven churches, the Lord gives personal encouragement to keep the faith, endure persecution, remain zealous, and seize the opportunity to spread the gospel. Since each letter urges the reader to heed what the Spirit says to all the churches, we today must also take these admonitions to heart.

Ruins of Roman arches at Laodicea, a city of Asia well known for its wealth. In AD 60, Laodicea experienced a devastating earthquake and was able to rebuild without relying on financial assistance from Rome. Lydia, one of the original members of the church at Philippi, was a businesswoman from Laodicea. The risen Christ knew Laodicea well. He reminded them of their spiritual poverty and called on them to repent (3:14–22).

III. Problem: Seven-Sealed Scroll (Revelation 4:1–5:14)

The scene shifts dramatically at this point. John is summoned into the throne room of heaven and views everything from this point on from a heavenly perspective. The vision of heaven turns the reader's attention from earth to heaven and from time to eternity. It introduces the problem of the seven-sealed scroll and the dramatic solution in the appearance of the Lamb. John's description of the scene emphasizes the inaccessibility of the throne that is separated by lightning bolts, peals of thunder, angelic creatures, and a sea of glass (4:2–7). In addition, John sees twenty-four elders, robed in white, representing the church in heaven.

The problem that emerges is that no one was found "worthy" (Gk. *axios*) to open the seven seals on the scroll in the hand of the Father. The angelic creatures (*seraphim*, Isa 6:2–3) flew about the throne announcing the thrice holiness of the Triune God using the words "worthy" (*axios*) and "holy" (*hagios*). Only one is "holy" and "worthy" to approach the throne of God, take the scroll, open the seals, pronounce its judgments, and bring the kingdom of heaven to earth. Suddenly, the Lamb (Christ) appears seated on the throne coequal with the Father, and the problem is solved. He takes the scroll, and all the elders and angelic creatures fall down in worship, proclaiming to the Lamb, "You are worthy" (5:9–10).

IV. Process: Seven Seals and Seven Trumpets (Revelation 6:1–11:19)

The process of divine judgment is unleashed by the opening of the seven seals. This results in a series of catastrophic events that express the "wrath of the Lamb" (6:16). Pretribulationalists believe the rapture of the church (1 Thess 4:13–17) takes place prior to these judgments since the church, the bride of Christ, is the object of His love and not His wrath (cf. Eph 5:22–32; 1 Thess 5:9).

Then Christ (the Lamb) opens the seven seals and releases their judgments. The first four seals release the four horsemen of the apocalypse and a wave of wars on earth. Seals five and six reveal matters in the heavens (martyrs and cosmic disasters), and the seventh seal results in the sounding of the seven trumpet judgments (chaps. 8–9).

The seven seal judgments are as follows:

1. White horse: war (6:1–20)
2. Red horse: bloodshed (6:3–4)
3. Black horse: famine (6:5–6)
4. Pale horse: death (6:7–8)
5. Martyrs: "How long?" (6:9–11)
6. Heavens shaken: "Great day of . . . wrath" (6:12–17)
7. Seven trumpets: Silence, then disaster (8:1–3)

Galloping across the horizon, the four horsemen appear suddenly, riding forth in silence, successively releasing the human instruments of vengeance to execute their divinely appointed tasks. Though these judgments

are providential, they are executed by human agencies. Armies are marching, men are fighting, and the world is at war. They are led by the rider on the
white horse, the imposter with a bow, not a sword. This is not Christ, as some
suppose, but the Antichrist who plunges the world into chaos in the last days.

Between seals six and seven, the seventh chapter serves as an interlude
revealing a host of people saved "out of the great tribulation" (7:14). They
include the 144,000 from the twelve tribes of Israel (7:4–8) and an innumer-
able host of Gentiles (7:9). Finally, the seventh seal is opened (8:1), followed
by a period of silence, broken by the sending of the seven trumpets of judgment (8:7–21; 11:15–19):

1. Rain of fire: vegetation burned (8:7)
2. Fireball: oceans polluted (8:8–9)
3. Falling star: rivers polluted (8:10–11)
4. Sun darkened: air pollution (8:12–13)
5. Demonic plagues: torment (9:1–12)
6. Great army: 200 million (9:13–21)
7. Divine wrath: heaven opened (11:15–19)

Another interlude occurs in chapters 10–11 with the sounding of the
seven thunders, which John was told not to record (10:4). The appearance
of the two witnesses (Gk. *marturia*) follows, but their preaching mission
ends after three and a half years (42 months or 1,260 days) with their martyrdom, resurrection, and rapture into heaven (11:1–12). These events are
followed by the sounding of the seventh trumpet, the opening of heaven, and
the revealing of the ark of the covenant (11:15–19).

V. Players: Seven Key Figures in the Eschatological Drama (Revelation 12:1–13:18)

Right in the middle of the Apocalypse, chapters 12–13 reveal seven symbolic "signs" that give the reader a sketch of the hidden forces and worldly
powers that are behind the great climax of history. The author defines the
major players of the apocalyptic events as he reveals how the struggle
between God and Satan will come to its ultimate finish in the closing chapters (chaps. 14–20) of Revelation.

The seven symbolic players on the end times' scorecard are as follows:

1. Woman: Israel, mother of the Messiah (12:1–2)
2. Dragon: Satan, the old serpent, the Devil (12:3–4, 9)
3. Male child: Jesus Christ ascended to heaven (12:2, 5)

4. Michael: Archangel who battles Satan (12:7–12)
5. Remnant: Seed of the woman (12:17)
6. Beast of the sea: Antichrist (13:1–10)
7. Beast of the earth: False prophet (12:11–18)

Many mistakenly identify the woman (12:1–2) as the church, but this woman is depicted as the "mother" of Christ, not the "bride" of Christ. Her symbols (sun, moon, stars) are taken from Genesis 37:9, which refers to the family of Jacob (Israel). The beast of the sea is consistently referred to as the "beast" throughout the rest of the book, whereas the beast of the earth is later called the "false prophet" (19:20; 20:10). The "beast" (Antichrist) is pictured as a political ruler, whereas the false prophet is a religious leader who deceives unbelievers into taking the mark of the beast (13:16–18).

Jezreel Valley (Armageddon) and Mount Gilboa.

VI. Plagues: Seven Bowl Judgments (Revelation 14:1–19:21)

Following the typical pattern of the Apocalypse, chapter 14 serves as an overview of the events that follow in chapters 15–19. The chapter opens with the 144,000 on Mount Zion (14:1–5), and proceeds to the proclamation of the three angels (14:6–13), followed by the reaping and harvesting of the earth (14:14–20). Chapter 15 introduces the bowl judgments that are to follow in chapter 16. As each angel pours out his goblet (KJV, "vial") from the great bowl of God's wrath (cf. Isa 51:17), the intensified judgments impact the entire world. The human race has gone beyond the point of no return, and it is too late to turn back.

The seven bowl judgments are basically on the same objects as the trumpet judgments but with greater intensity. Identified as the "seven last plagues" (15:1), the bowls are as follows:

1. On the earth: malignant sores (16:2)
2. Into the sea: oceans polluted (16:3)
3. Into the rivers: rivers polluted (16:4)
4. Upon the sun: scorching heat (16:8–9)
5. Throne of the beast: darkness and pain (16:10–11)
6. River Euphrates: kings of the East (16:12–16)
7. Into the air: "It is done!" (16:17–21)

The judgment of the sixth bowl results in the unsaved nations of the world under the leadership of the beast gathering their armies to the "great day of God" at the battle of Armageddon (16:14–16). The stage would now be set for the final confrontation between Christ and Antichrist. Chapters 17–18 describe the fall of Babylon (called "Mystery, Babylon the Great," KJV), the kingdom of the beast. This is turn, sets the stage for the nineteenth chapter, which opens with four hallelujahs of praise, followed by the marriage of the Lamb in heaven. The fact that the church, the bride, is pictured in heaven with Christ indicates the rapture (1 Thess 4:13–17) happened earlier.

The great climax of the book comes in Revelation 19:11–16 as Jesus Christ, the "Faithful and True" rider on the white horse rides out of heaven with His bride, the church, robed in white from the wedding (19:8). The true King of kings and Lord of lords speaks and with the sword of His mouth slays the rebel army and casts the beast and the false prophet alive into the lake of fire (19:20).

VII. Postscript: Millennium and Eternal City (Revelation 20:1–22:21)

The book of Revelation ends with a dramatic postscript that describes the millennium (1,000 years) in which Satan is bound in the abyss and Christ and His saints rule the world with a "rod of iron" (20:1–6). As ideal as this era will be, it is not heaven but an earthly kingdom. After the thousand years Satan is released and attempts a final revolt of unbelievers who were born during the millennial years (20:7–10). Satan is finally cast into the lake of fire, and the great white throne judgment follows, which results in all the lost of all time being cast into the lake of fire, which is the "second death" (20:11–15).

The final chapters of Revelation (chaps. 21–22) describe the ultimate prophetic vision of the eternal state, which includes seven new things: new heaven (21:1), new earth (21:1), new Jerusalem (21:2), new world order (21:5), new temple (21:22), new light (21:23), and new paradise (22:1–5). This is the picture of the grandeur of the eternal city where all the redeemed of all time will live in peace and harmony forever. Sin, rebellion, sorrow, sickness, pain, and death are eliminated. It is paradise regained, and the tree of life is there (22:2). But even more importantly, God is there and everyone "will see his face" (22:4).

Artist's rendering of the New Jerusalem.

Practical Application

Bible prophecy is not written to scare us. It is written to prepare us. It calls us to faith and personal preparation to be ready when the Lord returns or calls us home. Revelation ends with an invitation as the Spirit and the bride say, "Come!" (22:17), and Jesus assures, "Yes, I am coming soon." John adds the final, "Amen! Come, Lord Jesus!" (22:20). The emphasis of Revelation is to assure us that Jesus is indeed coming again. The ultimate question is: Is He coming for you?

For Further Reading

Hindson, Edward. *Revelation: Unlocking the Future*. Chattanooga: AMG Publishers, 2002.

Morris, Leon. *The Revelation of St. John*. TNTC. Grand Rapids: Eerdmans, 1977.

Mounce, Robert. *The Book of Revelation*. NICNT. Grand Rapids: Eerdmans, 1977.

Patterson, Paige. *Revelation*. NAC. Nashville: B&H, 2012.

Thomas, Robert. *Revelation 1–7: An Exegetical Commentary*. Chicago: Moody Press, 1992.

———. *Revelation 8–22: An Exegetical Commentary*. Chicago: Moody Press, 1992.

Walvoord, John. *The Revelation of Jesus Christ*. Chicago: Moody Press, 1966.

Study Questions

1. In what way does Jesus reveal the future to John in the Revelation?
2. How do the letters to the seven churches speak to us today?
3. What is the significance of the seven seals, trumpets, and bowls?
4. Why does Revelation depict Christ as a Lamb?
5. What actually occurs at Armageddon when Jesus returns?
6. What does the promise of the New Jerusalem (eternal city) mean to you personally?

Notes

1. For details see Donald Guthrie, *New Testament Introduction* (Downers Grove, IL: InterVarsity Press, 1990), 929–62.

2. See Robert Mounce, *The Book of Revelation*, NICNT (Grand Rapids: Eerdmans, 1990), 27–39. He notes the apostolic authorship of John was held by Papias (130), Justin Martyr (135), Irenaeus (180), Clement of Alexandria (200), Tertullian (210), and Origen (250).

3. Cf. C. B. Caird, *A Commentary on the Revelation of St. John* (New York: Harper & Row, 1966), 1–7; R. H. Charles, *A Critical and Exegetical Commentary on the Revelation of St. John* (Edinburgh: T&T Clark, 1920), cxvii–clix.

4. There are more than 1,200 uses of "and" (*kai*) in the book of Revelation, more than any book in the New Testament. They often form a series of *kaimeter* patterns linking lists and numbers.

5. Bruce Metzger, *Breaking the Code: Understanding the Book of Revelation* (Nashville: Abingdon, 1993), 13.

6. Ibid. For alternative theories see Guthrie, *New Testament Introduction*, 945–48.

7. William Ramsay, *The Letters to the Seven Churches of Asia* (New York: Armstrong, 1904), 190–92.

8. See Mounce, *Revelation*, 31.

9. K. Gentry, *Before Jerusalem Fell: Dating of the Book of Revelation* (Tyler, TX: Institute for Christian Economics, 1989).

10. Mark Hitchcock, "Revelation, Date of," in T. LaHaye and E. Hindson, eds., *Popular Encyclopedia of Bible Prophecy* (Eugene, OR: Harvest House, 2004), 336–39.

11. Metzger, *Breaking the Code*, 13–20.

12. Outline based on Edward Hindson, *Revelation: Unlocking the Future* (Chattanooga: AMG Publishers, 2002), xiv.

13. See Edward Meyers, *Letters from the Lord of Heaven* (Joplin, MO: College Press, 1996).

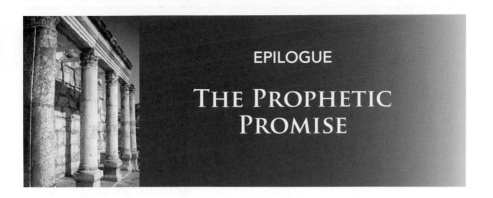

THE PROPHETIC PROMISE

It's All About Him!

The prophetic promise of God unfolds throughout the books of the Bible from one end to the other. Walter Kaiser calls it the single best principle for understanding the biblical revelation. "God's revealed promise," he wrote, "is not that of a fideistic imposition on the text of a later Christian faith . . . It is rather the claim of the canon itself."[1] The Old Testament authors describe the God-like characteristics of a coming Messiah, compelling the reader to see one who is more than a mere man. The Hebrew Bible refers to Him as the seed of Abraham, a descendant of the tribe of Judah (Gen 49:10) through the line of David (2 Sam 7:16). He will come as a king, and every knee will bow before Him (Isa 45:23). But He will also be a suffering servant who will be despised and rejected (Isa 53:1–9).

The Old Testament contains more than a hundred prophecies about a person who is coming in the future to fulfill God's promises to His people. Nonetheless, the Hebrew canon came to a close; and no one came to fulfill the hopes, dreams, pictures, types, and prophecies of the ancient biblical writers. No one came; that is, until He came—Jesus of Nazareth—who dared to say, "Everything written about me in the Law of Moses, the Prophets, and the Psalms must be fulfilled" (Luke 24:44). The entire Old Testament is a record of God's promises, and the New Testament is the record of their fulfillment.

Without Jesus the Old Testament remains silent and unfulfilled. Without Him the messianic predictions are but silent echoes of a long-forgotten past, quickly dismissed by critical scholars as nothing more than the wishful thinking of Jewish mythology. But for the Christian believer, they are "very great and precious promises" from men who "spoke from God as they were moved by the Holy Spirit" (2 Pet 1:4, 21 HCSB).

The Old Testament propels its readers to look beyond its pages for its final answers. It betrays what Philip Yancey calls "a gradual but certain movement toward grace."[2] Without the Old Testament one cannot fully understand the New Testament. Terms such as *law*, *sacrifice*, *lamb*, *priest*, *prophet*, and *king* leap from the pages of the Hebrew Scriptures. So do names such as Abraham, Moses, David, and Isaiah. These lay the foundation for all that follows in the New Testament. It is in its pages that we learn that Jesus of Nazareth is the fulfillment of the hopes and dreams of the prophets, priests, and people of Israel. For all that was promised to the patriarchs, and confirmed by the prophets was fulfilled in "Jesus Christ, the Son of David, the Son of Abraham" (Matt 1:1).

The story of the Bible begins in the Garden of Eden and ends in the eternal city, the New Jerusalem. In between stands the person of Jesus Christ. His cross and the empty tomb make all the difference. After 400 years of silence, a baby's cry marked the greatest turning point in human history. The incarnate God had entered the human race in a box in a barn in Bethlehem. The Messiah in a manger, wrapped in a blanket. Only God could have orchestrated such a thing. The very scenery of that night shouts to us of the love of God. The Light of the World had burst into the darkness of that night. The baby who broke God's silence that night would become our High Priest, who offers up "prayers and appeals with loud cries and tears" (Matt 28:19); His words still shape the Christian faith and ministry today.

Jesus is the executor of the new covenant made in His own blood (Heb 9:22). This is the New Testament story. The Savior died for our sins, taking the wrath of God in our place. He rose from the dead to secure our eternal salvation. And He calls us to trust Him and receive the benefits of salvation as a free gift of His grace (Eph 2:8–9). In the book of Acts, He is the ascended Lord of the Church, who rules in the hearts of believers by His Spirit. In the letters, he is Lord of our lives, and in the Revelation, He is our coming King. The Bible makes some bold claims about Jesus. It even goes so far as to insist that our eternal destiny rests on our faith in Him alone.

Notes

1. Walter Kaiser, *Toward an Old Testament Theology* (Grand Rapids: Zondervan, 1978), 41–42.
2. Philip Yancey, *The Bible Jesus Read* (Grand Rapids: Zondervan, 1999),12.

NAME INDEX

573

SUBJECT INDEX

A

Aaron   *66–67, 74–76, 152, 514*
Aaronic blessing   *74, 80*
Abednego   *263–64*
Abel   *4, 263, 517, 547*
Abraham   *14, 33, 35–37, 40–41, 43, 45, 101, 111, 114, 123, 297, 351, 353, 373, 375, 388, 417–18, 442, 444, 446, 478, 514–15, 517, 526*
Abrahamic covenant   *37, 41, 43, 45, 52, 75, 135, 446, 517*
Absalom   *117, 123*
Achaia   *344, 411, 414, 424, 432, 481, 486*
Achan   *96, 101*
Acrocorinth   *434*
Acropolis   *404*
acrostic   *2, 195, 242*
Adam   *3, 35, 38–39, 45, 140–41, 373, 375, 418*
Aegean Sea   *482, 559*
Africa   *ix, 164, 168, 400*
agora   *415, 425, 455, 484, 494*
Agur   *195–96*
Ahab   *30, 129, 131, 135, 299*
Ahasuerus (Xerxes)   *157, 164, 166–71*
Ai   *93, 96, 101*
Akkadian   *263*
Alexander the Great   *251, 269, 333, 482*
Alexandria   *333, 372, 381, 394, 453, 470, 482, 494, 554, 556, 570*
Amalekites   *107, 121*
amanuenses   *345, 530*
Amarna Tablets   *49*
Amenhotep II   *49–50*
Ammonites   *85, 105, 107, 109*
Amorites   *96*
Amos   *32, 130, 180, 182, 282, 285–89, 299, 303–4, 308, 386*

anathema   *442*
Andrew   *365, 385, 529*
angel   *54, 108, 142, 268, 270, 298, 319, 362, 371, 374, 442, 561–62, 567*
Angel of the Lord   *43, 46, 222, 235*
angels   *178, 186, 190, 266, 379, 469, 473, 512–13, 519, 537, 539–40, 560, 567*
Annas   *376, 390*
anointed   *119, 225*
anointed one   *119, 225*
Antichrist   *240, 259, 268–71, 274, 486, 488–90, 547, 561, 566–68*
Antioch (Pisidia)   *351, 372, 381, 394, 397, 402–5, 440, 442–44*
Antioch (Syria)   *351, 371, 397, 402, 444*
Antiochus III   *334*
Antiochus IV Epiphanes   *153, 261, 269–70, 334*
Antipater   *336*
anti-Semitism   *169*
Aphrodite   *424, 434*
Apocalypse   *6, 346, 555–56, 558*
apocalyptic   *1, 31, 223, 263, 346, 555, 566*
Apocrypha   *11*
Apollo   *426, 434*
Apollos   *505*
apostasy   *88, 103, 107, 116, 128, 133, 140, 289, 311, 327, 489, 539–40*
apostle(s)   *xii, 3, 6, 8–11, 14–15, 18, 39, 79, 111, 181, 186, 190, 284, 289, 339, 341, 343–48, 351–52, 355, 357, 359, 362, 364, 374, 378, 380, 384, 404, 407–8, 411–14, 420, 433, 437, 439, 442–43, 451–52, 463, 475, 481, 486, 490, 493–94, 498–500,*

503, 505, 521, 529–32, 535–36, 538, 541, 544, 552, 555–56, 560
apostolic authority   *340, 404, 439, 443*
apostolicity   *8*
Aqaba   *50, 187*
Aquila   *413–14, 420, 451*
Arabia   *50–51, 60, 222, 267, 443*
Arad letters   *237*
Aramaic   *148, 150, 159, 220, 237, 259, 262, 264, 274, 332, 350–53, 412, 529–30*
archaeology   *25, 50, 93, 262, 293, 480*
Aristobulus II   *335*
Aristotle   *340*
ark, of Noah   *40*
Ark of the Covenant   *56, 66, 88, 117, 120, 123, 135, 141, 143–44, 566*
Armageddon   *223, 568, 570*
armor of God   *459*
Artaxerxes   *149, 153, 157, 162, 166, 270, 332*
Artemis (Diana)   *454*
Asa   *131, 143*
ascension of Christ   *343, 361, 371, 374–75*
Ashurbanipal   *144, 293, 307*
Asia Minor   *346, 403, 405, 412–13, 440, 447, 453, 471, 482, 494, 531–32, 535, 552, 555–56, 558, 561, 564*
Assyria   *137, 144–45, 216–17, 219, 222–24, 236, 275, 281, 287, 306–9, 313, 329*
Assyrian   *26, 31, 132–33, 135, 137, 143, 215, 217, 221, 223, 230, 251, 283, 286, 292–93, 297–99, 306–7, 309, 312–13*
Assyrian captivity   *26, 133, 286*

576

SCRIPTURE INDEX

IMAGE CREDITS

Biblical Illustrator, Nashville, Tennessee: pp. 157, 166, 168 (British Museum, London), 170, 217 (British Museum, London), 224 (British Museum, London), 244, 263, 267 (British Museum, London), 313 (British Museum, London), 316, 323, 334, 414, 524, 533

Biblical Illustrator (Joy Borgan, photographer): p. 336 (National Museum of Roman Art, Merida, Spain)

Biblical Illustrator (Terry Eddinger, photographer): p. 290

Biblical Illustrator (Tom Hook, photographer): p. 452

Biblical Illustrator (G. B. Howell, photographer): pp. 66, 184 (Louvre Museum, Paris), 238, 286, 333 (Acropolis Museum, Athens), 355

Biblical Illustrator (Amy Kellstrand, photographer): p. 310

Biblical Illustrator (Scott Langston, photographer): pp. 94, 415, 425, 544

Biblical Illustrator (Linden Artists, London, England): p. 65

Biblical Illustrator (James McLemore, photographer): pp. 5 (right), 95 (bottom), 278, 325

Biblical Illustrator (Richard Nowitz, photographer): p. 502

Biblical Illustrator (David Rogers, photographer): pp. 25, 120, 250, 253, 276, 282, 295, 306, 447, 454, 457, 471, 494

Biblical Illustrator (Michael Rutherford, photographer): pp. 48, 177, 188

Biblical Illustrator (Bob Schatz, photographer): pp. 7, 30, 40 (top), 47, 50, 75, 95 (top), 105, 109 (top & bottom), 121, 133, 176, 187, 194, 251, 288, 299 (Museum of the Ancient Orient, Istanbul), 300, 320, 363, 366, 373, 376, 387, 399, 402, 416, 420, 441, 455, 458, 467, 474, 534, 562, 563, 564

Biblical Illustrator (Louise Kohl Smith, photographer): pp. 87, 122, 152, 365, 531

Biblical Illustrator (Stephen Smith, photographer): p. 559

Biblical Illustrator (Ken Touchton, photographer): pp. 2, 3, 82, 85, 92, 151, 185, 204, 206, 207, 220, 334 (bottom), 413, 466

Biblical Illustrator (Jerry Vardaman, photographer): p. 113

Biblical Illustrator (Justin Veneman, photographer): pp. 5 (left), 158, 321

Brisco, Thomas V.: pp. 404, 426, 522

Corel Images: p. 379

Cox, Charles: p. 514

HCSB Study Bible: p. 44

Holman QuickSource Guide to the Dead Sea Scrolls: pp. 216, 337, 345

Illustrated World of the Bible Library: pp. 40 (bottom), 49, 71, 164, 218, 236 (bottom), 268, 412

iStock: pp. 226, 434

Latta, Bill, Latta Art Services, Mt. Juliet, Tennessee: pp. 141, 142, 155, 515, 516

Popular Bible Prophecy Commentary: p. 254

Popular Encyclopedia of Bible Prophecy: p. 265

Rose Guide to the Temple: p. 57

Scofield Collection, E. C. Dargan Research Library, LifeWay Christian Resources, Nashville, Tennessee: pp. 24, 174, 198, 209, 368, 443 (left)

Smith, Pat Marvenko, Revelation Illustrated, http://www.revelation illustrated.com: p. 569

Smith, Marsha A. Ellis: p. 535

Staatliche Museen zu Berlin, Germany: p. 287
Stephens, William H.: pp. 269, 279, 327, 332, 350, 375, 518, 525

Tolar, William B.: pp. 108, 294, 487

Trainor, Rev. Dr. Michael, and Rosemary Canavan: p. 476

University of Chicago: p. 260

Wikimedia Commons, http://en.wikipedia.org: pp. 6 (public domain, University of Michigan, Ann Arbor Library, author unknown), 55, 58 (Lancastermerrin88), 74, 84 (Giovanni Dall'Orto), 110 (Golf Bravo), 130 (British Museum, London; Steven G. Johnson), 143 (Wilson44691), 180 (NASA, ESA, M. Robberto [Space Telescope Science Institute/ESA] and the Hubble Space Telescope Orion Treasury Project Team), 212, 234 (public domain, Berachyahu ben Neriah), 236 (top, public domain, reproduction of Rembrandt painting), 248 (public domain, Jasmine N. Walthal, US Army), 249 (Trjames), 340, 342, 351 (Asaf T.), 358 (Almog), 385 (Chmee2), 391 (Berthold Werner), 427 (Frank van Mierlo), 432 (Dan Diffendale), 435 (Jeanhousen), 464 (Marsyas), 470, 482 (Philly boy92), 484 (public domain, Snowdog), 497, 499 (Barbaking), 506 (Jerzy Strzelecki), 539, 546, 549 (Bjorn Christian Torrisen), 558 (Jastrow 2006), 567 (Tal Oz)